EMPIRES APART

EMPIRES APART

A HISTORY OF AMERICAN AND RUSSIAN IMPERIALISM

BRIAN LANDERS

PEGASUS BOOKS
NEW YORK

EMPIRES APART

Pegasus Books LLC
80 Broad Street, 5th Floor
New York, NY 10004

First Pegasus Books cloth edition 2010

ISBN: 978-1-60598-106-2

10 9 8 7 6 5 4 3 2 1

Printed in the United States of America
Distributed by W. W. Norton & Company, Inc.

‘There are now two great nations in the world which, starting from different points, seem to be advancing toward the same goal: the Russians and the Americans. Both have grown in obscurity, and while the world’s attention was occupied elsewhere, they have suddenly taken their place among the leading nations, making the world take note of their birth and of their greatness almost at the same instant. All other peoples seem to have nearly reached their natural limits and to need nothing but to preserve them; but these two are growing. . . . Their point of departure is different and their paths diverse; nevertheless, each seems called by some secret desire of Providence one day to hold in its hands the destinies of half the world.’

Alexis de Tocqueville, De la Démocratie en Amérique *(1835–40)*

‘The one duty we owe to history is to rewrite it’.

Oscar Wilde, Intentions *(1891)*

CONTENTS

ACKNOWLEDGEMENTS

It may seem perverse to start by thanking a rival publisher but this book would never have seen the light of day without the support, advice and practical assistance of my colleagues at Penguin. So many of them have contributed in so many ways that I cannot begin to thank each of them by name - thank you all.

Despite the numerous introductions my colleagues provided I have no agent to thank. With the exception of the one who considered this book 'approaching the wild borders of Chomskystan' all the agents who read my manuscript came out with the same response: love the book but as you're not a celebrity, politician or academic the big bookselling chains won't stock it. I hope they are wrong and feel incredibly lucky to have stumbled across a publisher, Corinne Souza at Picnic Publishing, who responded so eagerly to my manuscript. Corinne has patiently guided me through the intricacies of an industry I quite erroneously thought I knew. My editor Simon Fletcher was equally patient in making me completely rewrite the middle third of the book to produce a far more coherent narrative as well as stripping away the distracting footnotes and obsessive capitalisations with which I had littered my original text. John Schwartz produced a cover I love and Judith Antell and Alex Hippisley-Cox helped ensure that once produced the book hopefully will have an audience.

My greatest debt must be to all those writers whose works I have devoured and regurgitated in forms that they may or may not recognise. I have listed all the sources at the back of the book and comment on some of the most influential texts on the website www.empiresapart.com. I especially appreciate permission to quote from the following verbatim: Niall Ferguson, *Empire* (Penguin Books Limited, copyright © Niall Ferguson, 2003); Samuel Eliot Morison, *The Oxford History of the American People* (Oxford University Press, 1965, by permission of Oxford University Press, Inc.); Peter Neville, *Russia, the USSR, the CIS and the Independent States* (published in the UK by the Windrush Press, a division of the Orion Publishing Group and in the US as *A Traveller's History of Russia* by Interlink Books, an imprint of Interlink Publishing Group, Inc.; text copyright © Peter Neville, 2001); and Richard Pipes, *Russia Under the Old Regime* (Weidenfeld & Nicolson, a division of The Orion Publishing Group).

Finally for far too long my wife and family have put up with me spending weekends and holidays buried in my notes. My thanks to my wife Sarah, son Joseph and daughters Catherine and especially Alex, who obliterated my own feeble attempt at a website and substituted her own creative flair.

Writing is a thoroughly selfish pursuit, I hope that some readers feel as challenged as I have been by the prospect of encountering new ways to interpret the past, understand the present and prepare for the future.

FOREWORD
BY ANDREAS WHITTAM SMITH

Brian Landers has written a piercing account of American history from its colonial beginnings to its present role as an unacknowledged empire that bestrides the world. Concerned as he is to expose the myths that nations create about themselves, he bases his analysis upon a revealing comparison of American and Russian expansion through the centuries. This technique forces the observer to recognise similarities, identify differences and question why both similarities and differences exist. In a sense, then, the reader gets two books for the price of one, Russian history as well as American.

The parallels are striking. In the very same decade, the 1860s, Russia emancipated its serfs and the US freed its slaves. The ideology of corporate capitalism emerged at the same time as Marxism. Both nations marched towards the Pacific from their ancestral lands, from the Thirteen Colonies in the one case and from Muscovy in the other. Both reached the ocean by conquest of nomadic tribes – or as Americans like to say, by 'settlement' or 'colonisation' or, occasionally, by 'annexation'. And finally, to take a question, was there really any difference between the Monroe Doctrine that America used to justify its interventions in Latin America and in the Caribbean and the concept of 'Pan-Slavism' that Russia prayed in aid when exercising its designs on the Balkans?

This approach leads to a major theme of Mr Landers' work, that the US is and always has been an imperialist power. Americans act like imperialists, he writes, but don't talk like imperialists. It isn't even an established 'fact' that there is or ever has been an American Empire. What is a fact, however, is that since the US marines invaded Libya in 1805, American troops on average have intervened somewhere abroad more than once a year.

Mr Landers is not a conventional historian. His skills are derived from a business career as well as from the academy. This unusual combination produces rare insight. He also has a way with aphorisms. 'Russia is an inferiority complex trying to find itself. America is a superiority complex trying to sell itself.' That is what *Empires Apart* seeks to demonstrate.

CHAPTER 1
RURIK'S LAND

History is portrayed as a science. Remains are located through geophysics, their age is determined by radio carbon dating and they are analysed through DNA testing. The results are served up on TV history channels dedicated to revealing the truth about the past. And yet popular history remains as much subject to emotion as to reason. Centuries-old battles are refought in the cities of Northern Ireland or the mountains of Kosovo. Lawyers make money trying to redress the evils of slavery or the Holocaust. Russians deny the crimes of Stalin, and Americans forget that they once owned an empire stretching from the Caribbean to the Philippines.

History may be consciously rewritten; much more often it simply evolves. Each generation reworks the tales handed down to it. The experiences and values of today colour the stories of yesterday. The history of all nations is modified, but the embellishments of Russian history are in a class of their own.

The Influence of Champagne

The English invented champagne in the seventeenth century. Each autumn barrels of sharp white wine were imported from north-eastern France, where the wine would normally have rested in the barrel until fermentation was complete. But in England it was bottled and stored away. In spring the wine warmed up and started to ferment again. Soon the corks started to pop. The world's most famous sparkling wine had arrived, not in the vineyards of rural France but in the vaults of urban London.

Champagne only exists because of a geographical quirk, the absence of vineyards in seventeenth-century England, yet champagne is quintessentially French. No French man or woman asked to identify the originator of champagne would suggest an Englishman. They might pick Dom Perignon, the late seventeenth-century cellar master of the Abbey of Hautvillers who perfected the blends that make champagne what it is today, or perhaps Madame Clicquot, the nineteenth-century businesswoman who introduced mass production to the champagne houses. History disregards the reality that what the English were doing with their wine initially horrified French purists. Dom Perignon spent many years searching in vain for ways of stopping his precious wine being polluted by bubbles. But it doesn't really matter whether the English played an important part in its history or whether the whole tale is an invention. Champagne is a French tradition; the English are not part of the story. The present is the consequence of the past, but the past is an invention of the present.

The trivial example of champagne is mirrored in the story of nations. For if nations are formed by their histories, as they surely are, it is equally true that history is written by nations.

The history of many nations starts in the fields where the champagne grapes now grow. In particular Russia and America owe their character to an event that took place there more than a millennium and a half ago, an event that is almost completely missing from their popular histories. Each year thousands of tourists descend on the region of Epernay, Reims and Châlons, to soak in the heritage of Dom Perignon and Madame Clicquot. What they rarely come to commemorate is another heritage, infinitely more influential, infinitely more savage. Brutal not Brut. Here two great armies faced each other in one of the bloodiest battles ever fought. When the gory hand-to-hand fighting was over it is said that 160,000 lay dead, more lives lost in a single day than the United States lost in Europe in the whole of the Second World War. Had the battle gone the other way America and Russia would not be the societies they are today. It could be said that the battle of Châlons, fought in AD 451, determined the future of western European culture and the values that would be carried to the New World. It certainly determined that the future of eastern Europe would be very different.

By the middle of the fifth century the Roman empire was near its final collapse. The 'barbarians' were not merely at the door but inside. At Châlons Roman legions fought alongside Germanic tribes like the Franks and Burgundians, who not long before they had been fighting against. It is often said that victors write histories, but in this case it is the loser whose name is remembered. The Christian forces were led by the long-forgotten Roman general Aetius Flavius and the Visigoth king Theodoric. Their opponent was Attila the Hun.

The Huns emerged out of the vast central Asian wilderness to storm into Europe in AD 375. The pagan tribes and Roman armies that stood in their way were destroyed. The ferocity and scale of the Hunnish forces carried all before them, and they had soon conquered much of what is now eastern Europe. In 445 Attila sealed his authority by founding a new capital on the Danube, Buda, and murdering the only serious competitor for overlordship of the Huns, his own brother.

It was inevitable that Attila would look further west, to Rome, and not everyone viewed the prospect with terror. Honoria, the sister of the Roman emperor Valentinian III, wanted to share imperial power and wrote to Attila offering herself – and half an imperial throne – in marriage. Valentinian found out and Honoria was thrown into prison. Attila now had an excuse to invade on behalf of his potential bride, but he realised that rushing straight to Rome was not the easiest way to grab the riches of the Roman empire. Instead he crossed the Rhine into Gaul with an army of 700,000 and set about destroying as much of the area that is now France as he could. Like the English centuries later he laid siege to Orleans, but, without the help of a Joan of Arc, the inhabitants held Attila off long enough for Aetius Flavius and Theodoric to march to the rescue. Attila turned to face them, and both armies raced for the summit of a long sloping hill at Châlons; the Romans got there first. Attila launched charge after charge on the hill but Aetius held him off. Meanwhile Theodoric and his Visigoths stormed into the Attila's Ostrogoth allies. Theodoric himself was hit by a javelin, thrown from his horse and trampled to death by his own cavalry, but his son Thorismund grabbed his father's crown and wheeled round to smash into the Huns' flank. Attila, now under attack from all sides, pulled back into his camp. As night fell Attila built a huge pyre in the middle of his camp, including the wooden saddles of his cavalry and the loot he had taken on his campaigns. When the attack came next morning he planned to sit at the top of the pyre and perish in the flames, surrounded by the spoils of war – and those wives unlucky enough not to have been left at home in Buda.

What happened next is open to dispute. When dawn broke the carnage must have been clear to all. The number of dead is impossible to know and may well have been exaggerated. Attila's losses were enormous, but the Christians too must have been stunned by their losses. America lost 47,000 in the war in Vietnam and the nation was traumatised; Aetius and Thorismund may have lost as many in just a few hours. Few will have wanted another day like that. Attila and his forces were allowed to return to the lands we now know as Hungary. Christendom was saved.

The battle of Châlons determined that western Europe would develop with the trappings of Roman Christianity, not Hunnish paganism. Had Attila won, western Europeans would act differently now, they would probably speak different languages, they would even have looked different, as more Asiatic DNA filtered into the gene pool. Châlons has been hailed as the triumph of 'civilisation' over 'barbarism'. It allows the values, creeds and political structures of the western world to be traced back in an unbroken line to ancient Greece and Rome. It was Greco-Roman civilisation that triumphed on the plains of Châlons, it is argued. The values of Greek democracy and Christian charity, from which eastern Europe never benefited, survived to shape the world we now live in.

Some historians have written about the battle in terms little short of racist. The victory of the Christian Visigoths, wrote the Hon. Rev. William Herbert in 1838, 'preserved for centuries of power and glory the Germanic element in the civilisation of modern Europe', giving us two traits unknown to the Slavic nations, 'personal freedom and regard for the rights of men', and 'the respect paid by them to the female sex, and the chastity for which the latter were celebrated among the people of the north. These were the foundations of that probity of character, self-respect, and purity of manners which may be traced among the Germans and the Goths even during pagan times, and which, when their sentiments were enlightened by Christianity, brought out those traits of character which distinguish the age of chivalry and romance.'

The reality is quite different. Neither side had any concept of the 'rights of man' and even less the rights of women. Nobody was fighting to protect (or destroy) the heritage of Aristotle and Justinian. Châlons was a battle between two sets of barbarians, one of which called itself Christian.

Theodoric I, who died on the battlefield, and whose Visigoths determined the outcome of the battle, was no Christian knight. Thirty years earlier he had allied himself with another marauding tribe whose name remains a curse to this day, the Vandals, and launched a surprise attack on the Roman rear. He then invaded Roman Gaul and as late as 439 destroyed a Roman army at Toulouse. His alliance with the Romans at Châlons was no act of solidarity with Roman civilisation. Visigoth ethics were little different from those of the Huns. Two years after Châlons the reign of Theodoric I's eldest son, Thorismund, was cut short when he was assassinated by his brother Theodoric II.

The Romans were no better. The next year Aetius met a similar fate. Châlons was the last great victory for the Roman army. Temporarily it seemed that the empire might survive. Aetius returned to Rome covered in glory, far outshining the emperor. Valentinian's reaction was to stab the commander-in-chief to death. It did not do Valentinian much good. His reign ended the next year when he in turn was murdered by two of Aetius's former bodyguards. At least Aetius outlived Attila who, the previous year, had been found dead in his bed, covered in blood. Legend has it that his latest wife, a young Burgundian princess, had taken a final revenge for his rampage across western Europe.

The defeat of Attila determined the course of history. Whatever the reality in terms of the relative barbarism of Hun, Visigoth and Roman, the battle made possible a western Christian 'civilisation'. Moreover the victory ensured that this Christian west stood confident in its superiority over a barbarian east. The battle ensured that western and eastern Europe would develop along different paths, but it did not determine where those paths would lead.

West and East Divide

The division between 'western Europe' and 'eastern Europe' that so conditioned thinking for much of the twentieth century can be traced back to Châlons. Yet the terms would have been meaningless to those involved. The very concept of Europe is a geographical abstraction meaning different things at different times. Originally it referred just to the central part of Greece; then it was extended to the whole Greek mainland before including the landmass behind it. For centuries it referred to an area ending at the river Don; most of modern Russia was a dark and unknown territory beyond Europe. Today's frontier of Europe and Asia, which extends Europe to the Urals, is just a line drawn on a map by an obscure cartographer named Vasiliy Tatischev. Europeans are not in any meaningful sense an ethnic group.

The line drawn by Tatischev illustrates that not only do the powerful rewrite history but they can rewrite geography as well. Under tsars like Ivan the Terrible, Russia was regarded by the nations further west as decidedly un-European. When a later tsar, Peter the Great, attacked the leading European monarch of his day, Charles XII of Sweden, and captured territory in 'Europe proper', the rest of Europe shuddered. Peter was determined that he would be treated as a civilised, European monarch but that presented a difficulty: Russia was no more part of Europe than Egypt or the newly discovered lands across the Atlantic. Peter overcame this difficulty by simply redefining Europe. His court cartographer, Tatischev, declared that the Ural mountains were the 'natural' border between Europe and Asia. By a stroke of his pen he made most of Peter's subjects Europeans, a proposition grudgingly and gradually accepted by the rest of the continent.

If the victors of Châlons had been asked to which geographical entity their nations belonged they would have replied not 'Europe' but the 'Roman empire'. And the Roman empire had never extended beyond the Elbe.

Within its frontiers the Roman empire continued for centuries after its fall to have an influence on nearly every aspect of life: culture, religion, language, law, architecture, warfare, technology. The list is almost endless. That influence was more long-lasting and more profound in some parts of the empire than others, and in some cases spread well beyond its frontiers. But the one part of Europe on which Rome had virtually no influence at all is what today we call Russia.

If the defeat of Attila is cited by historians as a turning point in western history, its impact on the east was no less important. Attila returned defeated to his base on the Hungarian plains. His power was broken. Although he raided into Italy, attacking Milan and Padua, within two years the man himself was dead. The way lay open for other peoples to emerge on to the stage of history. The group that did so was a tribe that the victors of Châlons may never have heard of, and certainly would not have imagined their descendants would ever fear: the Slavs.

When people in the west talk about 'Europeans' they usually mean peoples like the Germans, French or Italians. Yet by far the most numerous ethnic and linguistic group in Europe is the Slavs. Three great streams surged out of the Carpathian mountains. The western Slavs became the Poles, Czechs and Slovaks of today. The southern Slavs became Serbs, Croats and Macedonians. In time many western and southern Slavs converted to Roman Christianity and took on the Latin script. The third stream, the eastern Slavs, became today's Ukrainians, Belarus and Russians. For them there was to be no exposure to Rome and its ways.

The Russian language, for example, has very few words of Latin origin (oddly one of the few is the one Russian word all westerners know: tsar, like kaiser in German, is a corruption of the Roman Caesar).

The early Slavs took over vast tracts of land, and took it by force, but they seized the land to use not just for plunder. And as settlers they were soon subject to the bane of all inhabitants of that vast region between the Elbe and the Urals: the constant threat of invasion. Hordes periodically swept in from the east or the north. The flat expanse of steppe provided no natural defences. Rather than acting as barriers, the wide rivers provided further routes of access. Before the Huns came the Sarmatians and Goths. After the Huns came the Avars and Khazars. It is easy to see European history as one long succession of Asian barbarians hurling themselves west in a torrent of violence to be eventually smothered by, and subsumed into, the grip of western civilisation. In reality the traffic was not all one way, and the way the picture of history is depicted depends more on the painter than the painted. One particularly destructive barbarian raped and pillaged his way from Europe into Asia in a haze of alcohol and violence, but even today there are children's books glorifying the murderous exploits of Alexander the Great.

After the Khazars the next invading tribe came from the far west: the Vikings, known more correctly as Varangians. (Those Norsemen who settled in Europe west of the Elbe had semi-permanent homes called 'viks', thus Vikings; those who settled to the east had more transient 'vars', thus Varangians.) In 862 Novgorod fell to the Viking leader Rurik. Rus was born. Rurik's successors raided down the Dnieper and across the Black Sea to Byzantium. In 882 they captured Kiev and made this their capital.

Like the Vikings in Normandy, the Varangians merged quickly into local society, much more quickly than the Normans themselves would when they invaded England two centuries later. Rurik's followers changed the head but not the body and soul of Slav society. Within fifty years Varangian princes were giving their children Slavic names, although the process worked both ways. Millions of Russians today bear the names Oleg, Olga and Igor, derived from the Viking gods Helge, Helga and Ingvar. Rurik's descendants also married into the nobility of the Merja, a Finnish tribe living in the area where the Oka river meets the Volga, what is now Moscow, binding Finns into the new nation. Within a century mercenaries from Rus were fighting as far away as Syria, Cyprus and Crete, and a Russian fleet had rampaged along the coast of Asia Minor.

One of Rurik's successors, with the distinctly un-Viking name of Svyatoslav, entrenched the power of Rus. Svyatoslav destroyed two of the most powerful competing states in the region, the khangate of the Khazars and the kingdom of the Bulgars. He was a physically imposing man who shaved his head, except for a single lock of hair signifying his noble birth, and famously wore a huge gold earring bearing a ruby between two pearls. On the way back to Kiev from his victories in the south nomadic tribesmen ambushed him, and his famous skull became a drinking goblet for a Pecheneg warlord.

Russia, however, was established.

The Coming of Christ

Soon after the Vikings came a force that was to have a much more profound influence on the new society: Christianity. One of the earliest converts was Svyatoslav's mother, who seems at the time to have been called by her Norse name Helga or Helgi, but is now more commonly referred to as Olga. Olga was clearly an exceptional woman. Legend has it that her husband died when he was literally torn apart after being captured by an opposing tribe, who bent down two large saplings, tied one to each of his legs, then watched as they sprang back upright. Their chieftain then invited Olga to marry him, to which she responded by inviting him to send emissaries to escort her to him. When they arrived she had them, still in their carriages, buried alive. In 957, with a largely female retinue, she led an expedition of merchants to Constantinople through the very same regions where her son would lose his head. The emperor Constantinus VII has left a detailed description of her visit, which evidently impressed him enormously. He is said to have proposed marriage to her; clearly it was a truth then universally acknowledged that a woman in possession of a large fortune must be in search of a husband. Olga preferred Christianity to remarriage, and asked the emperor to act as her godfather when she was baptised. He could hardly say no, and once christened Olga was able to point out that under the rules of her new religion godparents cannot marry their godchildren.

Although Svyatoslav's mother converted to Christianity, wholesale conversion did not take place until the reign of his grandson Vladimir. 'Conversion' in the tenth century had nothing to do with a sudden realisation that turning the other cheek was more morally responsible than hunting people to sell into the slave markets of Asia Minor. Vladimir, after all, had reached the throne by first murdering his older brother. Conversion was about power. Vladimir sent envoys to investigate not only Christianity (in both the Roman and Byzantine versions) but also Islam and Judaism. Byzantine Christianity won, because of the power of the Byzantine emperors and the majesty of Byzantine churches. According to an early collection of texts known as *The Russian Primary Chronicle*, Islam was rejected because, as Vladimir told the Muslim delegates 'Rusi est' vesele piti, ne mozhet bez nego byti' – Russians are merrier drinking; without it they cannot live. At least that is one version of history. An alternative, more feminist, history of Russian Christianity puts the conversion down firstly to Olga and secondly to an even more remarkable woman. Forty-two years after Olga's perilous journey from Kiev to Byzantium another woman travelled in the opposite direction. The story behind that journey could have come straight from a children's book of adventures. It concerns a little group of orphans who triumphed over all odds and changed the world.

The Byzantine emperor Romanus II died leaving four children under ten to carry on without him. Enemies surrounded the Byzantine empire, and few could have expected great things from the four orphans. And yet the two brothers, Basil II and Constantine VIII, ruled jointly for the next forty-nine years. Their older sister went west, marrying the German king and eventually ruling as regent over the Holy Roman empire. She was by far the most powerful woman in the world at that time. The youngest sister, Anna, who was just two days old when her father died, travelled north and, some would argue, in doing so had greater impact on world history than her three siblings put together.

For a quarter of a century after their father's death the children and their advisors safely steered the course of empire. Then the Rus appeared, this time in a less diplomatic guise than Olga. Her great-grandson Vladimir unexpectedly captured the town of Kherson on the Black Sea coast. From here he posed a real threat to Constantinople. Anna's brothers turned to a favorite Byzantine weapon: marriage. Anna's elder sister Theophano had already been married off to the German king Otto II, whose father threatened Byzantine possessions in the west. Anna proved every bit as resourceful as her sister. The prospect of exchanging life as a twenty-six-year-old Byzantine princess for that of the sixth wife of a barbarian king in some remote northern settlement cannot have been attractive – and Vladimir himself could not have seemed the most desirable of husbands. In a phrase that needs no translation he was described by the contemporary Bishop of Merseburg as a 'fornicatur immensus'. Anna had no desire to go to Kiev as a hostage, whatever the diplomatic niceties implied by marriage. The one fact the conflicting accounts agree on is that she was a seriously reluctant bride. Nevertheless she was dispatched to Kherson by her brothers. According to tradition, when she arrived she found that Vladimir had been struck blind, although blind drunk seems more likely. Anna announced that he would never see daylight again unless he saw the light of Jesus Christ and embraced her religion as ardently as he wished to embrace her body. Vladimir converted on the spot, regaining his sight and gaining his bride.

Once Vladimir and Anna were back in Kiev she set about the mass conversion of the Rus, starting with Vladimir's already numerous children and proceeding to mass baptisms in the Dnieper. The huge statue of a Norse god that had dominated Kiev was torn down, churches were thrown up and Russia was placed firmly on the road to Orthodoxy. The picture of the redoubtable Anna bringing sanctity to the barbarian hordes of Rus is a romantic one. The story of the two sisters Theophano and Anna captured the imagination of the great eighteenth-century historian Edward Gibbon, who wrote movingly of the way these two eastern princesses changed their worlds. In reality virtually nothing is known about Anna's life once she left Kherson to join her husband's newly Christian harem. She probably died childless, but in legend she was the mother of Russia's first two martyred saints, Boris and Gleb. And when, some generations later, the Muscovy princes laid claim to the title tsar, it was in part through Anna that the purple of Caesar was said to have passed from Rome via Byzantium to Kiev.

Vladimir's decision to follow Byzantium rather than Rome ensured that the final access route along which 'western' tradition, the heritage of the Roman empire, might pass had been blocked. Although Byzantium claimed to be the true guardian of that heritage it would itself be effectively snuffed out with the rise of Islam in the region, leaving Russian Christianity, like everything else in Russia, to develop along its own unique path.

Within three centuries small bands of marauding Norsemen had transformed the peasant tribes along the Dnieper river into one of the most sophisticated societies in Europe. Indeed within two centuries of the Vikings' arrival Kiev had blossomed into one of Europe's leading cities. Four hundred churches loomed over the city, among them the famous cathedral modelled on, and named after, St Sophia in Constantinople. Dominating the major trading routes along the Dnieper between Europe and Asia, it was home to numerous rich merchants. There were no fewer than eight major markets, selling everything from the agricultural produce that provided the backbone of the local economy to furs such as sable and beaver.

Rus was far from democratic, as slavery was still the foundation upon which economic life depended, but society was considerably less autocratic than in much of Europe. There were serfs, but unlike their western counterparts they were free to leave their land and move around the country. Local assemblies consisting of all free adult males governed the towns. Most importantly the prince shared power not only with the great nobles but also with an increasingly important class of landed aristocracy. These 'boyars' were to be a crucial feature of Russian life for centuries to come.

The influence of Kievan Rus was felt from the Baltic in the north to the Black Sea and the Byzantine empire in the south. Yaroslav the Wise, who ruled from 1019 to 1054, was one of the leading statesmen of Europe. The traditions of his people had, since the time of Attila, diverged widely from those of the rest of Europe, but he was pointing them back towards the west. Yaroslav married the daughter of the King of Sweden, and his daughters married the kings of France, Hungary and Norway. His daughter Anna caused a particular stir when she arrived at the court of her future husband, Henri I of France. To their amazement the French courtiers discovered that, unlike their king, their new queen could read and write. She signed the nuptial vows in Cyrillic and Latin lettering, while the French king signed an illiterate 'X'.

The story of early Russia, of Vikings, Huns and Byzantium, captures all the characteristics that lie at the centre of the way the west pictures Russia. It is a story at once romantic and brutal, mystical and majestic. And, as so often in Russia, it is also a story that could be totally untrue.

Russian History: True or False?

The outstanding feature of the birth of Russia is that nobody is really sure how it happened. There were no Founding Fathers, no Plymouth Rock. Russia's history is founded not on what we know but on what we want to believe.

On 6 September 1749 Gerhard Mueller, the official imperial Russian historiographer, rose to deliver a speech to the Imperial Academy of Sciences in St Petersburg. His theme was the role of the Vikings in the birth of the nation. The very name Rus, he asserted, came from Scandinavia, although rather than being derived from Rurik Mueller he believed it had first attached to Swedes from the Uppland area of Roslagen. He never finished his speech. Pandemonium ensued, with Russian nationalists outraged at what they regarded as an attack on the Slavic soul of their motherland. For them the mere suggestion that the barbarian west might have contributed anything to the culture of Holy Russia was heresy. Viewed through the prism of their Slavophile philosophy, it was as obvious to them that Russia had never been anything other than Slav as it was to later Americans that their nation had never been anything other than anti-imperialist. After an enquiry the Empress Elizabeth ordered Mueller's records destroyed and his publications banned. He spent the rest of his life researching the history of Siberia.

The debate continued into the twentieth century. Soviet historians continued the anti-Viking line. To accept it, they argued, would imply that Slavs needed the help of foreigners to create an independent state, clearly an untenable position. To bolster their arguments they pointed to a Syrian Christian history from AD 555, which talks about the 'Hros' living in the area south of Kiev, surely the ancestors of Slavic Rus. In fact it seems probable that Hros was not the name of a tribe at all but was a corruption of the Greek word 'heros' meaning just what it suggests, 'heroes'.

Today the role of the Vikings is generally acknowledged, but not universally so. One of the most interesting theories about the origin of the Russians was put forward by Omeljan Pritsak, the Harvard Professor of Ukrainian History, in the 1970s. For him the Rus originate not in Scandinavia or the Caucasus but in the small town of Rodez in south-central France. Pritsak starts his story in the middle of the eighth century, with Arabs controlling the eastern and southern shores of the Mediterranean and the Spanish peninsula. Muslims and Christians faced each other across the Mediterranean in uneasy peace. The problem both sides faced was that peace meant no booty, above all the booty that economic life depended upon: slaves. Neither side was supposed to enslave its co-religionists, and so they needed an external source. This they found in the vast lands between the Elbe and Syr Darya rivers, which became 'Sclavia', the land of the 'sclavas', slaves or slavs. Slave hunting was highly organised. Factories for the production of eunuchs were located in Verdun in the west and Khwarizan in the east. By the end of the ninth century two international networks controlled the slave trade: the Jewish Radhaniya based in Marseilles, and another group based in the city that today is known as Rodez, called in Middle French 'Rusi'. Thus the origin of their name: the Rus.

At first the Radhaniya had the advantage. Being Jews they could travel through the warring Muslim and Christian forces to the Khazar slave markets on the Caspian Sea. Such was their power that the Khazar rulers converted to Judaism; the first Jewish state of the modern era was established in southern Russia. The Muslims and Khazars stood between the merchants of Rusi and the slaving routes along the Volga and Don. But there was an alternative way to reach the Volga, north through the Gulf of Finland and down the Neva. To use this route the Rus needed allies. Just as the Radhaniya allied with the warlike Khazars the Rus allied with the Vikings, thus the appearance of Rurik.

Whatever the true story of the origins of Kievan Rus, the final irony is that very little of it took place in what is now Russia. The westward expansion of the Slavs came up against the forces of Roman Christianity in the form of the Teutonic Knights, a crusader military order that had lost interest in Jerusalem when it realised that the Baltic lands were much easier prey. The knights held the Baltic coastline as far east as today's Lithuania, Latvia and Estonia. The border between the knights and the Rus went right through the middle of these now independent states. Kiev itself is now the capital of an independent Ukraine and much of the original Rus is now Ukraine or Belarus. Of modern Russia only the western edge fell within Rurik's legacy. It's as if the Boston Tea Party had taken place in Mexico.

Like the first Americans, the first Russians were hemmed in and, if they wanted their nation to grow, would have to fight their way out. The Americans faced the British to the north and occasionally effective powers to the south. The Russians faced Teutonic knights to the west and occasionally effective powers to the south. For both, the route to expansion involved taking on the nomadic tribes that stood between them and the Pacific. Success in this endeavour depended on numbers, organisation and above all technology, in particular the technology of death.

The Americans burst out of their initial settlements because they were much better at killing their foes than their foes were at killing them. The gun is mightier than the bow, and it was the tribesmen who were virtually exterminated. In the case of the Russians it was nearly the other way round; before they could expand they first had to face the threat of near extermination. The nomads they faced had the superior technology, and ironically that technology was the bow.

The arrival of the Mongols could have written Kiev and its people out of history. The Rus, however, survived. Almost simultaneously on the other side of the world another mighty city simply disappeared from all but the most specialised of history books. Cahokia was in its own way just as imposing as Kiev. Estimates of historical populations are always difficult but Cahokia at the time perhaps had 20,000 inhabitants, making it smaller than Kiev but larger than London. The United Nations has designated Cahokia's remains as a World Heritage Site, but in fact there is little physical trace of Cahokia today and virtually no memory of it in the people who occupy the lands it once ruled. Russians may argue about the validity of tracing their history to Rurik, but most Americans are happy to trace their history no further than Columbus. Cahokia, dominating an empire from its position on the Mississippi opposite today's St Louis, might as well have existed on the moon.

CHAPTER 2
AMERIGO'S LAND

Russia's early history has become clouded as its Slavic population quite naturally emphasises its own contribution and lets fall into historical oblivion the contributions of others. History is a process of simplifying the past. From the millions of daily events only the essential few are remembered by the next generation, and of those far fewer are handed down any further. A name here and an event there passes on to become 'history'.

The process happens as much in America as Russia. One or two names – Christopher Columbus, Pocahontas – are remembered; one or two stories of heroism are recorded. The unpalatable fades away. The basic truth that the early settlers took what was not theirs is neither affirmed nor denied, it is simply ignored. The ideology it implied is never expressed.

Most nations take their histories back as far as possible. King Arthur is part of British history, even though countless invasions have wiped out most of the gene pool, language and culture of Arthurian Britain. America is almost unique in claiming no such historical continuities. The people who lived in America in King Arthur's time are not part of what made modern America. Other nations recognise that their institutions and values have changed radically over the centuries of their history, but America's values are often assumed to have arrived with the first white settlers and remained constant ever since. Like the chivalrous knights of

King Arthur, the Pilgrim Fathers continue to provide a standard to live up to: the difference is that most people accept that the Round Table is a fairy tale.

Spanish Exploration and Conquest

Sir Walter Scott, Leon Trotsky, Albert Einstein, Thomas Malthus, Sigmund Freud, Marie Curie and Henry Ford have one thing in common – they have all contributed to the *Encyclopaedia Britannica*; although Henry Ford almost certainly paid someone else to write his piece on mass production. Before the advent of the internet the *Encyclopaedia* had a well-deserved reputation for packaging scholarship and academic excellence in bite-sized pieces. Founded in Edinburgh in 1768, it became, despite its name, quintessentially American, ownership having passed across the Atlantic in 1901. For thirty years the *Encyclopaedia* was the personal fiefdom of US senator William Benton, whose life, it was once said, demonstrated that 'in America there still isn't much that money can't buy'. The *Encyclopaedia Britannica* tells Americans all they need to know about the world.

As befits one of the most important cities in the medieval world Cahokia has a reasonable length entry in the twelve volume *Micropaedia*. Oddly, though, the entry starts in 1699, three centuries after the magnificent native city had been deserted, and describes the city as having been founded by French missionaries from Quebec. It goes on to discuss its capture by the United States on 4 July 1778, and such key events as the establishment of the Parks College of Aeronautical Technology, before concluding with a single sentence mentioning that to the north-east is 'the location of a large prehistoric Indian city'.

Only in America could pyramids constructed nearly four thousand years after the pyramids of Egypt and a city that flourished a thousand years *after* the glories of Rome be described as 'prehistoric'. In America history starts with Columbus; before him there was no America.

In one sense it is true that before Columbus and his contemporaries there was no America. The word America itself was a neologism invented by a German cartographer who, when he changed his mind and tried to invent a new name, discovered that it was too late; the term was already established.

The New World was discovered by a man who was born as Christoforo Colombo in Italy, who died as Cristóbal Colón in Spain and is known in the English-speaking world by the anglicised form of his forename and the latinised form of his surname. Christopher Columbus was a seasoned traveller long before he reached the New World. He sailed to Ireland and Iceland with the Portuguese navy and traded along the coast of west Africa. But the event that launched him west was one of those turning points in world history that, like the battle of Châlons, inevitably prompts the question of what might have been. Before Columbus Christianity was the religion of one obscure corner of the globe, a not particularly attractive fringe of the Eurasian landmass sandwiched between the civilisations of the east and the Atlantic Ocean. Islam and the religions of Asia had far more adherents, and in many ways seemed to possess far greater dynamism. A betting man would not have wagered on Christianity becoming the first global religion.

It could be argued that the most 'civilised' part of Europe at the start of the fifteenth century was southern Spain, the only significant non-Christian part of the continent. The Moors had created an empire that fostered intellectual enquiry, artistic near-perfection and unparalleled tolerance. The most creative and productive Jewish community in the contemporary world lived alongside mosques and palaces of a quality unsurpassed in the history of Islamic art, indeed in the history of any art.

The Moors surpassed their Christian neighbours in all the arts but one: warfare. In 1492 Granada, their last stronghold in Europe, fell to the Spanish monarchs Ferdinand and Isabella, who had waged what might today be called a jihad against them. The elegant beauty of palace and mosque was replaced by the heavy angularity of fort and cathedral, Islamic tolerance gave way to the Inquisition and the search for new realms in science and philosophy became voyages of discovery in a far more literal sense.

One of the minor mysteries of history is what Christopher Columbus was doing at the siege of Granada. But present he was, and being there clearly stood him in good stead in his search for sponsors for his voyage west. He was able to persuade Ferdinand and Isabella that their desire to attack Islam around the globe could be helped by an expedition westwards to the spice islands, China and on to India, the back door to the Islamic world.

On 12 October 1492 he landed on an island in the Bahamas, and eventually returned to report that he had reached the Indies. Legend has it that Columbus first learnt of the existence of a new world from Norse sagas heard on his trip to Iceland. Scholars are still arguing about whether Columbus ever travelled that far north, but if he did there could be some truth in the story. The Viking settlements in North America disappeared within a generation or two but the homeland of those early pioneers, the Norse settlements in Greenland, continued right up until the end of the fifteenth century, the very time that Columbus was supposedly visiting the Norse Icelanders.

Every schoolboy knows that Columbus proved the sceptics wrong by demonstrating that the world was round. The Church taught that the world was flat, and in a famous meeting Church leaders accused Columbus of heresy for daring to suggest otherwise. Unfortunately for schoolboys the Church did not teach that the world was flat and the confrontation with Columbus never took place; the whole story was an invention of the American journalist Washington Irving, who in 1828 wrote what purported to be a biography of the legendary explorer. Nevertheless Irving's fictional version of Columbus's intellectual achievement remains embedded in popular mythology. His was a noble triumph of scientific enquiry over brute ignorance, but in fact the ignorance was all on the part of Columbus. The ancient Greeks had long since proved that the world was round and no educated person seriously argued otherwise. Indeed the Greeks had correctly calculated that Asia was well over 10,000 miles west of the then known world, far too far for any sensible mariner to attempt without starving to death before he was halfway there. The great contribution of Columbus was to do the sums again and get them wrong. He estimated that the Indies were barely 3,000 miles away, just about within reach. They were not, but fortunately for him the West Indies were.

After landing in the Bahamas in 1492 Columbus turned south and arrived in the Caribbean, where one of his three ships was wrecked. Columbus left the crew of thirty-nine behind on the island of Hispaniola (modern Haiti and the Dominican Republic) to start the first European settlement in the New World since the Vikings. When he returned a year later he discovered that the Taino natives had killed all the settlers. He responded by killing hundreds of natives and sending 550 back to Spain to be sold as slaves, the first New World exports. To Columbus's dismay the slaves were not a commercial success; all those who did not die on the voyage did so soon after arriving in 'civilisation', falling prey to the sicknesses of the Old World. The fate of the Taino was to be the forerunner of the fate awaiting all the native people of North America. When Columbus arrived in Hispaniola there were at a conservative estimate 300,000 Taino. Sixty years later there were less than five hundred.

Between 1492 and 1504 Columbus made four voyages to the New World, and in 1499 landed on the mainland. That date is important; Amerigo Vespucci, after whom America is named, may have got there first. (As so often even the association of Amerigo and America is disputed; Rodney Broome in his work *Amerike* claims that America is named after the Welshman Richard ap Meryke.)

Columbus's career ended in disgrace as he fell out of favour with the royal court. Even the Spanish crown found his rule over their new possessions unduly brutal, and after his third voyage he was brought back to Spain in chains. He managed one last voyage, and explored the coastline of Central America still convinced that he had reached Asia and was about to encounter the mouth of the Ganges. He died in poverty in Vallodolid, Spain, in 1506 but his voyages did not end there. Nearly forty years later his body was carried across the Atlantic to be buried alongside his son Diego in the cathedral of Santo Domingo, in fulfilment of his dying wish to be buried in the new world he had discovered. Today tourists can see the urn containing his remains, forty-one bone fragments and a bullet from a youthful wound, in the Columbus Lighthouse, an enormous pyramidal monument that dominates the city. Thousands of miles away in Seville tourists visiting the cathedral can also wonder at what are claimed to be his remains. The Spanish government insists that they brought Columbus's remains back after the Spanish-American War drove them from the Caribbean. In death Columbus appears to have perfected the art of being in two places at once.

Columbus was a genuinely intrepid explorer whose name today is dotted across the globe from Colombia to Colombo to British Columbia (none of which he actually visited), but the name attached to the continents of the New World belongs to someone entirely different. Amerigo Vespucci's life may not be as mythical as Rurik's but his relationship with what is now called America is almost as problematic. The two versions of the travels of the dead Columbus are mirrored on a larger scale in the multiple versions of the life of Vespucci.

Amerigo Vespucci was born in Florence in 1451 where, in version one, his family moved in the same circles as Michelangelo and Savanarola, and he himself went to Spain as the representative of the Medici family. He led three (and in some versions four) voyages to the New World. In 1497 he sailed along the coast of South America, two years before Columbus reached the mainland, and realised that this was not the Indies but a new continent. His scholarly letters excited admiration throughout Europe, and when the German professor of cosmography Martin Waldseemuller wanted a name for the 'fourth continent' he naturally chose that of the man who had first realised that such a continent existed. Vespucci went on to be appointed chief pilot of Spain and died burdened with honours in Seville in 1512.

Version two describes a very different man. This Vespucci was a wheeler-dealer, a promoter and entrepreneur rather than a great explorer. The sole voyage to the Americas that historians can be certain he made was as part of an expedition led by Alonso de Hojeda, whose name has passed completely out of history. The other claimed voyages are pure imagination. He claimed to have come within 13° of the south pole and to have reached geographical co-ordinates located in British Columbia on the west coast of Canada, both somewhat improbable. His letters were appreciated more for their description of the sensual proclivities of the natives than for any scholarly value, and naming continents after Vespucci rather than Columbus is a nonsense.

Arguing the merits of the various versions of Vespucci's life is good sport for historians, the majority of whom probably now accept that Vespucci did make a number of voyages and was more than a simple con man. Whether he was the first to reach the American mainland, however, is still doubtful. The strongest candidate for that honour is neither Vespucci nor Columbus but yet another Italian. The Venetian John Cabot, sailing in the service of the English King Henry VII, reached the mainland on 24 June 1497. Like Columbus he was sure he had found the coast of Asia. The following year he sailed west again, confident that he would soon be landing in Japan; he was never seen again.

Although Cabot certainly touched the soil of the New World, even he may not have been the first European since the Vikings to do so. In 1472, twenty years before Columbus, two Scandinavians named Dietrich Pining and Hans Pothorst reached the rich fishing grounds off Newfoundland and may well have stepped ashore on the same coastline that Bjarni Herjolsson the travelling salesman had reached 500 years before. They were searching for a north-west route to Asia, and had they realised what they had stumbled upon, and broadcast their exploits as effectively as Vespucci, the new continent might have been named after the captain of their expedition, a Portuguese mariner named Joäo Vaz Corte Real. At a stroke Americans could have become Realists.

Whatever the truth about Vespucci the name America stuck, and Spanish adventurers followed rapidly in the wake of Columbus and his comrades. With just a few men the early conquistadors destroyed the vast empires of the Incas and Aztecs with amazing speed, slaughtering thousands in their pursuit of gold. As their name implies these conquistadors set out to conquer. Their ideology was no secret: to them the New World offered people to subjugate, gold to loot and land to steal. In 1533, the year Ivan the Terrible came to the throne, Pizarro completed the conquest of the Inca empire. By the time the first Romanov ascended the Russian throne eighty years later permanent Spanish, French and English settlements on the North American mainland were established in Florida, Quebec and Virginia.

The passage west did not, as Columbus had promised, provide a back door through which to strike at Islam, but the Spanish took equal exception to the religious customs of their native opponents. The Inca priests had a particularly nasty way of dealing with those who displeased them. The unfortunates were taken, possibly after being drugged, to altars high above the congregation. There the high priests slashed their chests and pulled out the still beating hearts to appease the Inca gods. The Spanish were shocked by such barbarism. Spanish priests preferred to torture those who displeased them, then tie them to a stake, surround it with logs and set the unfortunates ablaze. This, they believed, would appease the Spanish god. To their victims there was probably little to choose between the two forms of execution, but to history one is human sacrifice, the most unforgivable of abominations, while the other is the Spanish Inquisition, an unfortunate example of religious fundamentalism.

Not only do historical facts look different when viewed through different prisms, but new 'facts' can suddenly appear. As with tracing the origins of Russia to southern France, the discovery of America has been subject to countless bizarre theories. Irish monks almost certainly reached Iceland before the Vikings, but the story of St Brendan sailing his leather boat right across the Atlantic is pure fiction, as is another fable used later to support British claims to North America: the tale of Prince Madoc.

At Fort Morgan on Mobile Bay, Alabama, there is a plaque erected by the Virginia Cavalier Chapter of the Daughters of the American Revolution. It commemorates the landing on the shores of Mobile Bay in 1170 of Madoc ab Owain Gwynedd, a Welsh prince driven from his homeland by the advancing Normans. The story goes that Madoc and his people first travelled inland and built a fort at Lookout Mountain, near DeSoto Falls, Alabama, which, it is claimed, has proved to be virtually identical to Madoc's original home at Dolwyddelan castle in Gwynedd. Over succeeding centuries Madoc's descendants multiplied but were pushed north by various native tribes. Later European explorers reported numerous stories of bearded white Indians speaking a Welsh-like language, and some claimed to have found them. As late as 1841 George Catlin published a learned treatise, *Letters and Notes on the Manners, Customs and Condition of the North American Indians*, which devoted sixteen of its fifty-eight chapters to the Mandans of the Missouri river, whose physical characteristics and language, Catlin claimed, proved them to be the lost tribe of Madoc. Unfortunately, shortly after Catlin left them smallpox arrived, and the Mandans became extinct.

The story of the Welsh prince is almost certainly a sixteenth-century invention designed to bolster the territorial claims of the Welsh Tudors who wore the English crown. Such fables about who discovered America are matched by similarly improbable stories about what they found when they got there.

Before Columbus

When the Europeans arrived there were throughout the Americas a huge variety of peoples and customs. The first Americans crossed over from Siberia and moved south to populate the whole landmass. The question of when this happened has been the subject of much debate. To a layman the question seems fairly academic, but the way answers to this question have changed says much about the ideology of history. Today the debate is grounded in hard scientific fact, but for most of America's history the debate was conducted in a very different way. Rather as Russian historians were determined to prove that their nation's greatness owed nothing to non-Slavs like Rurik, American historians and scientists were determined to prove that nothing of any value predated the arrival of the white man.

Nowadays there are broadly two strands of thought. One is based on differing interpretations of scientific evidence. The other is the large body of American thought usually labelled 'creationism', in some manifestations of which God is thought to have woken up one day in the relatively recent past and populated the Americas with natives ready for the white man to come and civilise. Little more than a century ago a third strand was the most widely accepted in educated circles. It called itself scientific, and the science it espoused was the opposite of creationism: evolutionism.

The guiding principle of the evolutionists was 'survival of the fittest', and it became an article of faith with American scientists and historians that given the 'primitive' nature of the natives that greeted the arrival of the first European settlers they must have been less evolved than the white man. It was argued, therefore, that they could have been there only a few thousand years; this explained why they had developed neither the moral values necessary for a civilised life nor the scientific understanding necessary to properly exploit the resources of nature. Well into the twentieth century the curator of physical anthropology at the Smithsonian Museum was insisting that the antiquity of the 'Indian . . . cannot be very great'.

Then in 1927 a team of archaeologists in New Mexico found a stone spear point embedded in the ribs of an ice age bison. Since then more finds along with improved radiocarbon dating and DNA analysis show that the first nomads trekked down from the Bering Strait at least 23,000 years ago and perhaps as much as 40,000 years ago. It hardly matters exactly when the trek started, the important point is that it was a long time ago; and indeed there may have been various waves of immigrants. Not surprisingly, then, the newcomers had evolved in radically different ways as they moved south. Rather than facing tribes of more or less similar 'Indians', the Europeans were arriving in a land populated by people as different from each other as Romans and Russians. There were at least 375 native languages being spoken in North America when the Europeans arrived. Differences of language, culture, political sophistication, technology and religion were massive. Combined with the enormous distances that separated the various groups, there was one thing of which the European invaders could be certain: there was absolutely no chance of the 'natives' uniting.

The main civilisations in the Americas were in central and South America, but early explorers found massive earthworks covering hundreds of square miles in Ohio; 12 foot high walls enclosed perfect circles, squares and octagons, many of them fifty times the size of a football pitch. They have now largely been destroyed by the advances of 'civilisation', but archaeologists have still managed to find below the earthen structures thousands of amazingly beautiful artefacts: copper head-dresses in the shape of deer antlers, human hands crafted in mica, shells from the Gulf of Mexico and obsidian from the Rocky mountains. They also found evidence that the Hopewell people who lived there had taught themselves to grow crops from seed, something that early Europeans copied from the Middle East. Or had the Hopewell also learnt from the Middle East?

Again, early American scientists were unwilling to believe that the savages their forefathers wiped out could have produced such enormous monuments. Numerous theories were propounded to explain their origins; perhaps visiting Phoenicians or even the lost tribe of Israel. Eventually the Smithsonian assembled a team of experts and, after ten years of study, concluded that all the fanciful theories were false. The Hopewell Mounds had been constructed by the ancestors of the 'Indians' whom the early settlers had encountered when they arrived. While east and west were battling each other at Châlons, the Hopewell people were knapping flint blades, working copper from the shores of Lake Superior and crafting jewellery from bears' teeth.

Seven centuries later another native American people was leaving enormous signatures on the landscape. In the Chaco canyon of New Mexico buildings were going up of a size that would not be matched again in North America until the 1920s. Five-storey buildings, some with more than a thousand rooms, were built of sandstone and clay. Huge wooden beams brought over 40 miles from the nearest forest supported the upper storeys and roofs.

In the middle of the eleventh century, as Kievan Rus was reaching its peak, Cahokia itself flourished on the eastern side of the Mississippi. Experts believe the city was a little smaller than the London that William the Conqueror was about to take, or twice its size, or somewhere in between. Its suburbs stretched across the river into what is St Louis today. Cahokia was the capital of a people known as the Mississippian culture. Their buildings were constructed of wood and earth, so, unlike the stone Mayan cities of the same period, little now remains of their complicated architecture and great plazas other than hundreds of mounds dotting the flood plains of the Mississippi. One pyramid-shaped ruin, now known as Monks Mound, covers 15 acres and stretches 100 feet high in stepped terraces: the largest pre-Columbian construction north of Mexico. Nearby is a grand 40-acre plaza and artificial lakes, the largest covering 17 acres. This was not the work of a few primitive nomads living in wigwams.

It is ironic that Americans in their hundreds of thousands visit the pre-Columbian remains of Mexico, but in their own country such remains are obliterated by freeways and shopping malls.

The more intriguing issue, however, is what happened to the inhabitants of Chaco and Cahokia? There were certainly no mighty empires awaiting the first whites to explore North America. Cahokia seems to have lasted little more than a century. At almost exactly the same time as the Mongols were razing the cities of Russia, many of Cahokia's houses were torn down and huge wooden defences were erected, city walls with bastions every 65 feet. The defences did not work. Thousands of arrowheads testify to a vicious battle, thought to have been a peasant insurrection against the wealthy city-dwellers, after which the city was abandoned.

When in 1539 Hernando de Soto, fresh from helping to destroy the Inca empire in Peru, undertook a barbarous three-year trek through the American south-east, the enormous territory the Spaniards called Florida, he found mound-building tribes whose chiefs lived in relative luxury in homes perched above the surrounding countryside. Undoubtedly these were the remnants of the Mississippians. Ethnographers have also found traces of Mississippian culture in tribes as far away as the Osage and Winnebago on the edge of the Great Plains.

Historians were intent not only on showing that the continent's original inhabitants were primitive savages but also that there were not many of them, and that Europeans had 'settled' rather than 'conquered', rather as Jewish 'settlers' occupy the land from which Palestinians have been evicted in more recent times. Nobody knows how many people were living north of the Rio Grande when the first whites arrived. Until fairly recently the number quoted was usually around a million. As archaeological finds continued to increase it became apparent that there had been far more natives than first thought. Henry Dobyns, a respected anthropologist, suggested 18 million. As the debate continued the numbers came down again, but estimates still range from 2 million up to 10 million.

One factor in particular underlies the earlier view that there were hardly any Native Americans in occupation when the whites arrived: when the settlers started moving west they found a largely 'empty' land. The reason for that, however, is not that there had been no natives but that the native population had already collapsed. European colonisers may have been slow to move beyond their initial settlements; European diseases were not. Almost entirely by accident the first European settlers had perpetrated the world's most successful example of biological warfare.

The Scramble for America

Community after community faced extinction with the coming of the white man. A typical case, chronicled in detail by early French missionaries and explorers, was the Huron in southern Canada. Within twenty years of Samuel de Champlain first setting eyes on the Huron, diseases from the trading posts further east were destroying them. Measles struck in 1634, causing blindness and in some cases death. In 1636 it was the turn of influenza, followed the next year by scarlet fever. Then in 1638 came the worst plague of all, smallpox. In five years between a half and two thirds of the entire Huron population died.

The primary reason that Europeans were able to impose themselves so much more successfully on America than on Africa was the balance of biological power. The natives of America had been completely isolated from the rest of the world for millennia. They had no immunity to western diseases and no diseases of their own to give to their invaders, other than syphilis. Africans had not only been exposed to European and Asian traders but they also had a fearful armoury of tropical diseases with which to retaliate. The result was that Africans retained an overwhelming numerical superiority, which American natives lost within a few years of the arrival of the white man.

Columbus had shown that a promised land existed. All anyone had to do was point their ship west; the New World could not be missed. The Spanish and Portuguese grabbed South and Central America and the larger Caribbean islands. They also sent a few expeditions north in search of gold. Coronado reached as far as Kansas in 1540, murdering any natives who got in his way: on one occasion he had a hundred captured warriors burnt at the stake to strike terror into anyone stupid enough to oppose the onward march of European civilisation. The French went further north, seeking furs and fish in Canada.

The English first came to the Americas not to settle but to steal, not to trade but to terrorise. The early history of England and the New World is a history of organised crime, although rather than using terms like 'mobster' or 'gangster' British historians have preferred the more romantic 'pirate' or 'buccaneer' or even 'privateer', as if to imply that armed robbery is acceptable if cloaked in the mantle of private enterprise. (Another term used in some accounts transforms ruthless killers into cuddly pets, as men like the murderous Hawkins are described charmingly as 'sea dogs'). With the exception of west country fishermen the primary objective of the first English mariners venturing westward was to find someone who had already made money there and to take it away. English pirates raided not just the Spanish galleons heading home with their looted gold but anyone with something worth taking. Pirates like Sir John Perrot, Peter Easton (known as the pirate admiral) and Henry Mainwaring attacked the Portuguese, Basque and French fishing fleets that had descended on the immense shoals of cod off Newfoundland. Pirate expeditions were expensive to organise and needed the support, implicit or explicit, of the crown. Pirate captains were not petty criminals escaping to easier pickings in the sun. Henry Mainwaring, for example, was an Oxford graduate and member of the bar. After succeeding as a Newfoundland pirate he returned to England and became Chancellor of Ireland, before dying as an exile in France having chosen the wrong side in the English Civil War.

When the time came to attempt their own settlements many of these pirates played prominent roles. Hawkins was an early advocate of settlement in Virginia. The pirate David Kirke, who had captured a fleet of eighteen French ships in the Gulf of St Lawrence and even raided Quebec, was a prime mover in the creation of the Scottish colony of Nova Scotia. Piracy was to remain a feature of colonial life for many years to come. English settlements in Newfoundland (of which David Kirke was eventually made governor) and Labrador were subject to pirate raids well into the eighteenth century, with French, Dutch and later American pirates finding easy pickings in even the hardiest outposts.

The most successful mobster of all was the Welshman Henry Morgan, whose gang, protected by the Governor of Jamaica, devastated Spanish ports in the Caribbean and Central America. Morgan became one of the wealthiest men in Jamaica, diversifying into legitimate businesses such as sugar plantations. Much of Morgan's life is shrouded in the myths of time, but one story is certainly true. In 1670, with thirty-six ships and a gang of nearly 2,000 men, he attacked the city of Panama, burning it to the ground. On the way back he deserted his men and absconded with most of the loot. This did not make him universally popular, especially as at the time of the raid England and Spain had just signed a peace agreement. Charles II responded to Spanish protests by recalling the governor and ordering the destruction of the buccaneers. Morgan was arrested and transported to London, but spread so much money around that he returned to Jamaica with a knighthood and was made deputy governor.

Although to the Spanish, and to pirates of all nations, the Americas were seen primarily as an opportunity to get rich quick, to many Europeans the new land offered more than plunder. It offered the opportunity for colonisation, somewhere to dispatch surplus populations who would simultaneously become markets for the products of Europe and supply products the home countries could not economically produce themselves. It also offered the possibility of religious freedom. There is a myth that America was created by doughty puritans whose Protestant work ethic formed the philosophical bedrock upon which the wealth and power of the United States was to be built. Like most myths there is an element of truth here. The first European settlers in North America since the Vikings were religious refugees who were confident that their Protestant commitment to prayer and hard work would enable them to create a promised land in the New World.

In 1620 the Pilgrim Fathers fled the orthodoxy of the Anglican Church to found a new society on the coast of New England. But fifty-five years before them five hundred Protestant men women and children had crossed the Atlantic and landed much further south in Florida. These people were also seeking freedom from religious persecution, not from the Church of England but from the Church of Rome. French Calvinists, known as Huguenots, were under tremendous pressure from the Catholic monarchy, pressure that was to culminate in the attempt in 1572 to exterminate them in the Massacre of St Bartholomew.

The Huguenots who fled to the New World seven years earlier were determined to avoid such a fate. They failed. At dawn on 20 September 1565 their settlement, named Fort Caroline, was attacked and most of the inhabitants were killed. Those that managed to escape gave themselves up over the next few days. Perhaps they thought they would be spared, for their attackers were not savage natives but Christian soldiers in the service of one of Europe's most renowned monarchs, Philip II of Spain.

The Spanish commander appealed to his God for guidance, and decided that there was only one way to serve his Lord in these circumstances. Every one of the Huguenots was murdered. When he heard the news Philip II sent his congratulations.

The story of the Huguenot settlement well illustrates the political realities of sixteenth-century Europe. It also illustrates the political realities of today. On one Florida tourist website the only reference to the putative French colony is a one line comment that it was destroyed by the 'brilliant military skills' of the Spanish commander Pedro de Menendez. It does not mention that Menendez had been released from jail in Spain on Philip II's orders specifically to command this mission of extermination. Another website refers to the colonists only as 'French pirates'.

The reality as always is far more complicated than either the 'Protestant martyrs' or the 'French pirates' school of history pretend. The Huguenots were not dour Puritans who wanted the state to leave them alone. Their leader, Admiral Coligny, was a military advisor to the French king, and was well aware of the strategic implications of creating a colony in what the Spaniards regarded as their territory. Their first settlement was founded by Jean Ribault in what is now South Carolina. He left thirty-eight soldiers there and returned to Europe for reinforcements, but the men he left behind mutinied, built themselves a longboat and headed north. Amazingly they happened upon some English fishermen, who ferried them back across the Atlantic. They were lucky. Ribault had returned to France to find the Huguenots suffering violent repression and had appealed to Protestant England for support. Unfortunately for him Elizabeth I was still in her pro-Spain phase, so she threw him into prison in London and told the Spanish ambassador about the garrison in South Carolina. When the Spanish got there they found the settlement deserted, but in the meantime Admiral Coligny was sending reinforcements.

This was the force that founded Fort Caroline in Florida. Although primarily a Huguenot expedition it included among its 300 members pardoned criminals, men described as 'Moors' and even a few Catholics. The colony did not fare well, and some of the settlers may indeed have turned to piracy against the Spanish. Certainly Fort Caroline was visited by the English privateer John Hawkins, who left food for the settlers and returned to Europe to warn Coligny of the dangers facing his enterprise. By this time Ribault was out of jail in England, and Coligny sent him with 600 settlers, including for the first time children, to restock the colony.

Both the French leader Ribault and the Spanish commander Menendez showed flashes of tactical brilliance but Menendez also had the most essential of military attributes: luck. Ribault set off to attack the Spanish in their new settlement of St Augustine, but a storm wrecked most of his fleet on Daytona beach. While Ribault was struggling back, Menendez attacked and destroyed the largely defenceless French settlement. He then marched south and met Ribault and the survivors from Daytona beach struggling north at a site later known as Massacre Inlet. Menendez sent a boat across the inlet to bring Ribault to him. After the Huguenots' formal surrender had been accepted, Ribault and his men were marched ten by ten into the sand dunes and butchered. Only sixteen were spared: ten French Catholics and six cabin boys.

For the first but certainly not the last time conflicts in Europe had determined the course of history on the other side of the Atlantic. Spanish St Augustine rather than French Fort Caroline thus became the first permanent European settlement in North America.

The English and Civilisation

The monarchs of Europe were determined to control the New World as they controlled the old. They wanted territory and plunder but most of them were racked by debt, caused not least by the conflicts between them. To keep public expenditure low they turned to a supposedly modern economic model to establish their empires: colonisation was privatised. The private sector was called upon to put up the funds and to take the risks.

This was the particular model for the Dutch and British empires. From the middle of the sixteenth century until the beginning of the eighteenth the English empire was created and maintained by private enterprise: groups of merchant adventurers were given royal monopolies over trade with the various regions of the world. The most famous was the East India Company, which eventually used its own army to conquer much of India, but there were others covering trade from Turkey to the Pacific. Among the first to be created was the Muscovy Company, which was established in 1555 and handled commerce with Russia; among the last was the Hudson Bay Company, established in 1670 to control the North American fur trade.

Although operating with different corporate structures, the earlier Spanish empire had been built in a similar way. For many of the Spanish adventurers in South and Central America the profits had been worth the risk. That investing in North America was a riskier business was shown by the fate of the first colonists to settle in Chesapeake Bay in Virginia just a few years after the settlements in Florida. Those who survived a native uprising in 1571 decamped the next year. It is fascinating to speculate on what might have happened had they stayed and thrived, for again they were not English Protestants but Spanish Catholics. Perhaps Hispanic Americans would now be turning a blind eye to the illegal immigration of Anglos, brought in to perform the tasks they themselves considered too menial.

In reality it was of course the English who grabbed the long stretch of unattractive shore lying between the French and their furs to the north and the Spanish with their gold to the south. That the shore was already occupied by various native tribes did not bother them. The English developed a justification for their arrival that was to be a feature of American imperial adventures from Cuba to Vietnam to Iraq. The English would bring the joys of civilisation. Thus the promoters of the Virginia Company, incorporated in London in 1606, assured potential emigrants that they would be welcomed as liberators freeing the native people from the brutality of the evil Spanish empire, just as the natives of Iraq would welcome the American troops liberating them from the evil of Saddam Hussein. Clearly the natives were at a much lower level of economic and social development than their natural superiors in England.

The duty of the English was therefore to provide them with all the skills and tools that they needed to play their proper part in the productive process, allowing them to acquire the basic necessities of a civilised life (clothes, for example) while at the same time producing goods for import by the merchants of London and Bristol. Everyone would benefit, but by far the greatest benefit would go to the company's promoters. From the very start there was an enormous social and economic gap between the organisers of the settlements and the mass of settlers, who were drawn from the bottom rungs of English society.

The first English colony in 1585 demonstrated none of the lofty assertions of its promoters. Expecting to be fed by the natives, the colonists were shocked when the initially hospitable locals declined to give up their last remaining stores. The English response followed the Spanish precedent: the native leaders were murdered in an attempt to terrorise the remaining population, but the plan failed. The natives simply left and the starving colonists soon followed.

The next group, which included the first English women and children to attempt to settle in the New World, was unceremoniously dumped in the same place, Roanoke, two years later. (The plan had been to land further north, but the sailors were anxious to be heading south in search of Spanish gold and had no desire to hang around looking for alternative landing sites.) The group's leader headed back to England seeking more support, and when he returned he discovered that the colonists had, for unknown reasons, left for the nearby island of Croatoan. Once again the English mariners showed where their priorities lay and headed south, leaving the settlers to their fate. That fate was to arrive finally near Chesapeake Bay, where the survivors were given refugee status by the natives. However, refugees are rarely popular and a local chief, Powhatan, eventually had them all killed.

More settlements were launched both on the North American mainland and in the string of West Indian islands known as the Lesser Antilles, away from the Spanish garrisons. An attempt was made to establish a settlement on the island of St Lucia in 1605, but it was immediately destroyed by the native Caribs. A similar fate met a settlement on Grenada four year later. A small but successful colony was established on Bermuda, and in 1616 it issued its own coins, the first British colony to do so. Meantime in 1607 two more attempts were made on the mainland. A settlement on the coast of Maine faced native hostility and, following a miserable winter, the settlers sailed home in the spring. Further south the story was different, and the first permanent English settlement was established in Jamestown. At last the English had the chance to teach the natives the virtues of toiling in the fields to provide food for the white man.

The English were above all commercial colonists. Their policy towards the natives was to mould them into the commercial way of life of England, to turn hunters into farm labourers. For all the later mystique surrounding the piety of the Pilgrim Fathers, the most distinctive feature of the early English colonies was that, unlike those of Catholic Spain and France, there were no missionaries. In other respects the behaviour of the English varied little from the Spanish, from whom they claimed to be liberating the natives. When the natives failed to appreciate the benefits of civilisation, the English settlers soon lost any vestige of civilisation themselves. Alan Taylor quotes numerous examples, and one in particular shows a degree of barbarism of which Ivan the Terrible would have been proud. When, in 1610, locals refused to provide the Jamestown colonists with any more food, Captain George Perry attacked their village, killing many of the inhabitants and kidnapping the chief's wife and children. On the way back down river Perry and his men amused themselves by throwing the children overboard and shooting them as they struggled in the water. On their arrival in Jamestown the governor was shocked to discover that Perry had brought the children's mother back alive. He immediately had her killed. Terror was the only language some people were thought to understand.

Naturally the 'savages' fought back. In 1622 over 300 immigrants were killed, nearly a third of the Virginia colony's population, in an uprising led by Powhatan's brother. The English retaliated by inviting the Indians to a peace conference, and at the feast afterwards poisoning 250 of them.

In fairness the natives really could be savages at times. A century later, for example, a group of Hopi attacked a village whose native inhabitants had converted to Catholicism. They not only massacred nearly eight hundred, but for good measure ate some of them as a warning to others. And colonial leaders were just as brutal to settlers who stepped out of line as they were to natives.

Both natives and settlers lost far more to disease than to each other. The 24,000 Algonquians who lived around Jamestown when it was founded had declined to 2,000 within sixty years. Data from 1616 shows that of the 1,700 settlers sent out by the Virginia Company since the colony was founded in 1607 only 350 were still alive. The health of the colony both literally and metaphorically was in an almost fatal state when, in 1616, a cure was found – tobacco. Despite the attempts of James I to stop the trade, the addictive properties of the new drug made his entreaties ineffective. As with the modern drugs trade, tobacco barons in the Americas were able to find powerful merchants in Europe to push their products, and huge fortunes were made on both sides of the Atlantic.

With the advent of the tobacco trade Virginia took off. Thousands of immigrants were shipped in, and although they continued to perish at an alarming rate the power and wealth of the oligarchy increased dramatically. By 1635, just twenty-eight years after the colony's creation, the Virginia assembly felt strong enough to arrest and ship home a governor appointed by the company in London. From the very start English colonies had a degree of independence quite unknown in their Spanish and French equivalents.

The early days of English colonialism were characterised by two apparently opposing features. The first was the appalling hardship experienced by the settlers, the vast majority of whom died within a few years of arrival. When Thomas Hobbes, in 1651, described life as 'solitary, poor, nasty, brutish and short', he could have been writing specifically about the American colonies. The second was the fact that immigrants kept coming in ever increasing numbers. Between 1625 and 1640 a thousand indentured servants a year arrived in Virginia. In 1624 St Christopher (now St Kitts) was established, in 1627 Barbados and in 1628 Nevis. Barbados was a particularly successful colony, not least because a century earlier the Spanish had raided the island and exterminated the native Arawak population. 1632 was a bumper year with settlements in Antigua, Maryland and Montserrat. Maryland was established as a refuge for Catholics, but was soon home to disenchanted Virginians irked by the antics of the ruling elite in Jamestown: just twenty-five years after the first colony was established disgruntled elements were already looking to the frontier to escape the rules of colonial society. Above all, in 1620 the Pilgrim Fathers landed in Massachusetts, where they were soon to create a society significantly different from that in the other English colonies of the period.

The apparent paradox of increasing numbers of emigrants heading like lemmings towards their probable death is explained by the economics of colonisation. Many of the promoters were making enormous sums of money; they had every reason to keep sending people out. Those going probably had little idea of what they would find on the other side of the Atlantic, as glowing stories of welcoming natives and abundance continued to pour from the promoters' pens. In any event many emigrants had no choice. They were vagrants scoured from the streets of the main cities and shipped out. All that was needed when they arrived was ever more land to exploit.

The colonists soon developed an argument that would sound strangely familiar to Palestinians expelled from their land centuries later. Looking around at the acres of bush and forest used only for hunting and a few fields producing maize and vegetables, the English declared that it was clear the natives were unwilling or unable to exploit the land themselves. In fact scientists have now shown that the natives' agricultural practices, which involved mixing crops in small patches and selective burning of undergrowth, produced larger harvests, a more balanced diet and a more sustainable environment. But the resulting landscape did not resemble England, and to the English settlers this could only mean that the natives were not managing it as God had intended. God could not have meant his resources to be wasted in this way, and therefore it was obvious that He would approve of the newcomers exploiting the land properly.

The natives did not see it that way, and continued to resist attempts to seize their land. The ideological underpinning of colonisation then moved on to its final stage. Having started with a commitment to the introduction of civilisation, English colonialism in Virginia ended with an explicit commitment to ethnic cleansing. A typical proponent was Sir Francis Wyatt, Governor of Virginia from 1621 to 1626 and again from 1639 to 1642. His first priority, he made clear in 1622, was the 'expulsion of the Savages', declaring that 'it is infinitely better to have no heathen among us, who at best were but thornes in our sides, than to be at peace and at league with them'.

Most of the immigrants were desperately poor, and were brought out to backbreaking toil as indentured servants, virtually slaves for the colonial elite. The reward for the minority who survived their period of indenture was to be free to settle their own land. The problem was that the land was already occupied, and the inhabitants fought to keep it. The solution was genocide. Settlers went hunting for natives. Most often the natives killed were women and children, usually from the more settled agricultural tribes, who were easier to catch than the warriors who presented the real threat.

Within half a century the philosophy of colonialism had moved from liberation through exploitation to genocide.

Not everyone supported ethnic cleansing. In particular the oligarchy who ruled the colony came to have a quite different agenda. They had their estates already, with hundreds of indentured servants on whom their fortunes depended. They traded happily with the natives on the frontier, swapping metal tools, weapons and trinkets for valuable beaver and deerskins. The scene was set for class war, and in 1676 it broke out. The leader of the populist revolt, Nathaniel Bacon, was a young demagogue whose father had sent him out from England in an attempt to make him grow up. Bacon led a number of raids on largely peaceable natives and demanded a free hand to wipe out the 'Indian' population. Bacon was actually a cousin by marriage of the governor, William Berkeley, but his rabble-rousing skills put him at the head of a rebel force that forced the governor to flee from Jamestown.

The first American Revolution was not just about ethnic cleansing, although that was Bacon's overwhelming objective, but was also a true class war. Some modern scholars have even held up Bacon as some kind of progressive populist because he offered freedom to any slaves who supported him. Bacon's rebellion is claimed to be the first example of poor whites and blacks joining together to fight an oppressive oligarchy. Bacon himself produced a 'Declaration', which spelt out various grievances against a colonial elite that was undoubtedly thoroughly corrupt. The legislative councillors paid themselves enormous salaries derived largely from taxes on the less well-off. Berkeley, who had been appointed in 1641 and ruled Virginia with his cronies for thirty-five years, paid himself a salary of £1,000 a year. Small planters were lucky to make £5 profit in that time, and indentured servants were charged £6 for their passage from England. The collapse of the tobacco market only made the position of the small planters worse.

Berkeley was unashamedly autocratic, and his philosophy was more in tune with the emerging autocracy in Muscovy than with any later American notions of democracy. As Hobbes also wrote, those who dislike monarchy call it tyranny, those who dislike aristocracy call it oligarchy, and those who suffer under democracy call it anarchy. Just as Bacon railed against oligarchy, Berkeley saw in democracy the end of civilised government. He praised God that in Virginia there were no such tools of the devil as free schools or the printing press. In 1661 he suspended elections (which in any case had a very limited franchise), and managed without them until Bacon's rebellion.

The revolt was short lived. Bacon burnt Jamestown, but died of dysentery, leaving his rabble leaderless. Berkeley counterattacked, recaptured Jamestown and launched a reign of terror on his opponents, hanging twenty-three of them and plundering their property. The government back in London was thoroughly alarmed and sent a fleet with 1,100 soldiers under Sir Herbert Jeffreys to the colony. Jeffreys was more sympathetic to the frontier settlers than to the oligarchs, and in the short time he was in the colony he introduced measures to rein in the elite's power. Along with 900 of the 1,100 soldiers he died of disease, but not before he had sent Governor Berkeley back to England in disgrace.

Steps had to be taken to meld the elite and the frontiersman together, to avoid a repetition of the disastrous class conflict of Bacon's rebellion. Somehow the tobacco and sugar barons and the poor settlers on the frontier had to feel that their interests were the same. In the eighteenth century this was achieved by positing the British as the common enemy, but in the seventeenth century the colonials were themselves British (or at least English until the 1707 union of England and Scotland). The answer arrived by an accident of economics. Black slavery not only provided labour for the plantations but also a common 'enemy', which was to bind rich and poor whites together in a common political cause for centuries to come.

Slavery

Slavery had been introduced to the Americas by the Spanish but, largely thanks to the vigorous anti-slavery campaign of Bartholomew de Las Casas, had been abolished in the Spanish empire in 1542. This was not an example followed by the other colonial nations.

In the early days of the Virginia colony slavery was uncommon: native slaves ran away, and imported slaves tended to die before their masters had earned enough from them to cover their purchase price. African slaves were not objected to for moral reasons, but were simply too expensive; vagrants from England were a much better investment. The earliest African slaves were treated appallingly, although no worse it seems than indentured servants. In 1650 there were just 300 slaves in the colony. There is some documentary evidence that after a period they could obtain their freedom, if they were in the minority that lived more than a very few years. At least one black ex-slave is known to have successfully sued a white man in court, and even owned slaves himself. There are a significant number of known cases of black men marrying white women and, more rarely, black women marrying white men.

By the end of the colony's first century conditions had changed. The land had been 'tamed', diseases were less virulent and therefore life expectancy increased, improving the payback period for investing in slave labour. Slave traders became more numerous, so supply and price stabilised. At the same time conditions in Europe improved, and indentured servants became scarcer and more expensive. Between 1650 and the end of the century the slave population increased more than forty times, and by 1700 slaves made up 13 per cent of the population.

Although the increase in slavery was driven entirely by economic considerations, the political implications of having an alien minority in their midst were not lost on the governing oligarchy. On the one hand, having a significant new working class element with even more reason to rebel was a real threat. On the other hand, this threat could be used to frighten the rest of the lower orders into supporting the establishment. Dividing the working class was achieved by the quite conscious introduction of institutional racism. Laws were passed that took away virtually all rights from blacks. Freed blacks had their property confiscated, and could even face re-enslavement.

In 1669 the Virginia legislature passed 'An Act About the Casual Killing of Slaves', making it legal to kill slaves who resisted punishment, 'since it cannot be presumed that . . . malice should induce any man to destroy his own estate'. It was an argument not dissimilar to that used centuries later to justify the 'casual' killing of Afghans and Iraqis, which was labelled 'collateral damage'.

The issues of racism and slavery were closely entwined but they were not identical. Slavery came to be justified because blacks as a race were deemed 'inferior'. Right up until 1865 states like South Carolina insisted that black British sailors, although free men, be held in prison while ashore.

Racism was leavened with sexism. As in many other societies, sex was a consuming passion clothed in rank hypocrisy. The first law dealing with sexual relations between the races was passed in Maryland in 1664; 'An Act Concerning Negroes & Other Slaves' was designed to stop the increasing number of marriages between black slave men and free white women. As Alan Taylor has pointed out, for a white man to rape a black slave was not a crime but to marry her was. While male slave owners begat hundreds, and later thousands, of mixed race children with black slaves, any free white woman giving birth to a mixed race child was condemned to indentured servitude. Indeed, sleeping with a black man could result in six months' imprisonment.

Slavery rapidly became a dominant feature not only in Virginia and Maryland but in the vibrant new English colonies springing up in the second half of the seventeenth century further to the south. Fortunes were made in the Carolinas and Jamaica on the broken backs of African slaves. During the seventeenth century the English colonies in the West Indies received more migrants than all the mainland colonies put together, but they could hardly be described as the most 'popular' destination. Most of the migrants were from Africa, and by 1700 no less than 78 per cent of the population were slaves.

It is worth emphasising that the most successful English colonies were initially those in the West Indies. The colonies on the Chesapeake Bay and in New England, which today are taken to form the crucible of Anglophone America, were very much a sideshow. By 1650 there were around 80,000 English emigrants in the New World, of whom well over half were in the Caribbean. Barbados alone had two and a half times the population of Virginia, even excluding the slaves. The success of the West Indian colonies was what spurred the development of settlements on the mainland; and later it was to be the slave economies in the Caribbean that provided the export markets upon which the commercial survival of the New England colonies depended.

The West Indian colonists were themselves to be the founders of the colonies that, even more than Virginia and Maryland, came to typify life on the North American mainland. The Carolinas and Georgia became extreme examples of the two main characteristics of early English colonialism: slavery and genocide. They represented the spirit of the West Indies, and this representation was made manifest in the form of their first governor, Sir John Yeamans.

Charles II had appointed eight of his friends as lord proprietors of a vast territory between Virginia and Maryland to the north and Spanish Florida to the south. With his customary lack of modesty the colony was named after himself, and called simply Carolina. Today it forms the states of North and South Carolina and Georgia. The lord proprietors were interested only in profit and had no intention of risking their own lives in crossing the Atlantic, so they looked for an experienced colonial leader. They found him in Sir John.

The Yeamans were a wealthy Bristol merchant family. Sir John's father was a prominent royalist and his brother mayor of Bristol. John himself made his fortune as a planter in Barbados, and in 1665 he arrived on the mainland with a group of emigrants from Barbados where opportunities were fast declining. Immigrants from England and from Holland (including some from the new Dutch colony in New York) soon followed. They were joined by slaves that Sir John shipped in from Barbados.

The tourist version of Sir John's life is a romantic one, and comes complete with imagined dialogue. He went into partnership with one of the richest men in Barbados, Colonel Benjamin Berringer, who lived with his beautiful wife Margaret on an enormous estate two and a half hours' carriage ride from Bridgetown. With only African slaves and a few white ex-convicts for company, poor Margaret was awfully lonely. 'I am a prisoner in paradise,' she thought. That was before Sir John arrived and swept her off her feet.

In such a closed society affairs of the heart could not remain secret for long. 'Some boys done seen them together,' one of the slaves told the Colonel.

'You know what this means, John,' Berringer told Sir John.

'But I love her,' Yeamans replied. 'These things happen. It's not personal, Benjamin.'

Armed with pistols, the two men stood back to back, then marched twenty paces apart, turned and fired. Sir John had no wish to harm his friend but he knew the colonel would be aiming to kill; he had no option but to do the same. His was the more accurate shot, and Colonel Berringer fell dead.

Within six weeks Sir John had married the lovely Margaret and taken over her estate. But Barbados society shunned the newly weds, and Sir John turned his eyes further west to the verdant pastures of Carolina.

It is a charming story with a core of truth: Sir John *did* kill Colonel Berringer, but almost certainly by poisoning him rather than in a face-to-face duel. And his motivation had more to do with the size of Berringer's estate than the beauty of Berringer's wife. Yeamans was one of the nastiest men ever to have been governor of an American colony. His venality shocked even the lord proprietors, who were especially upset that by enriching himself so assiduously he was depriving them of profit. They decided that he was nothing but a 'sordid calculator', and in 1674 removed him from office. He returned to Barbados, where he died two years later. What happened to Margaret is not recorded.

The links between Carolina and the Caribbean colonies remained strong even without Yeamans. Rich West Indians, known as the Goose Creek men, dominated the new colony's politics for years to come. They also developed a novel form of economic interdependence. The Carolina colonists were given enormous land grants (including a grant to slave owners of 150 acres for every slave they imported), but two factors stopped them exploiting the land: firstly the land was already occupied and secondly tilling the soil and harvesting required an abundance of cheap labour. The obvious solution to both problems was to enslave the natives, but, as in Virginia, that was impractical as the slaves ran away. In this respect the Carolina colonists had an advantage over the Virginians: their links with the Caribbean colonies. A formal barter trade was soon in place: two natives shipped as slaves to Barbados and the other islands could be swapped for one black slave shipped the other way to work in the rice and indigo fields of Carolina; natives were worth less than blacks as they tended to die sooner. For this system to work there needed to be a supply of enslaved natives, and slave raiding became a feature of Carolina colonisation. One well-documented raid by a gang led by Captain James Moore Jr against the Tuscarora Iroquois village of Nooherooka in North Carolina netted 392 women and children for sale as slaves. Far more natives were killed in the raid itself or, in the case of the male captives who were considered unsuitable for slavery, executed afterwards.

Particular targets for the English settlers were the natives in the Spanish territory to the south. Unlike the English the Spanish not only forbade slavery but expended much effort in missionary activities among the natives. The 'Mission Indians' were considered more docile than the tribes to the west, and were therefore a tempting prospect for the slave raiders. The tribal nature of the native population made it easy for the English to divide and rule, and they found many tribes willing to raid deep into Spanish territory to maintain their supply of native slaves. James Moore Sr, the Carolina governor, personally organised a huge thousand-strong army of natives with a few white lieutenants to raid the Spanish missions in Florida. It is thought that about 10,000 slaves were brought back to Carolina, and the destruction wrought was almost total. The native population of Florida was cut by 70 or 80 per cent, as those unfit for slavery were butchered. The raiders reserved a particular fate for any Spanish priests they could capture; they died under unspeakable tortures.

The frontiers of Carolina bore less resemblance to the frontiers glorified in the Cowboys and Indians tales of Hollywood than they did to the frontiers of Rus in the age of the Mongols. The difference was that in the case of Rus the barbarians were trying to break in.

CHAPTER 3
LEGACY OF THE MONGOL TERROR

The lust for empire goes back to biblical times and beyond. The lust for land, power, resources, or simply for conquest has consumed tribes and nations for millennia. Imperialism is not a recent invention, nor is it a European one: empires have existed in the Americas, in Africa and on a gigantic scale in Asia.

One empire in particular exceeded any that had gone before, and crossed from Asia into Europe in an orgy of violence and destruction. The Mongols brought terror to Europe on a scale not seen again until the twentieth century. They left a particular mark on Russia, where all traces of nascent democracy, of which there were very few, were obliterated. The murderous methods of the Mongols survived them as the grand dukes of Muscovy took over the reins of power and began themselves to lust after empire. Ivan IV gave himself the new title of tsar and set out to turn that dream into reality; what the world witnessed was not a dream but the nightmare empire of Ivan the Terrible.

When, nearly four centuries after the Mongol invasion, Michael Romanov founded the dynasty that would rule Russia until the revolution, the guiding principles of autocratic imperialism were firmly established. They were principles that the handful of Englishmen by then settled on the coast of Virginia could choose to ignore or follow as they started to build their own empire.

The Mongols

The bows and arrows of the North American natives were powerless before the microbes and muskets of the Europeans, but those of the Mongols rapidly overcame the Rus.

The Rus were not used to being on the receiving end of such aggression. From their earliest days the Slavs were an expansionist people. In this they prefigured the early Americans, but it is dangerous to draw too many parallels. There were two striking differences between the early American and Russian models of colonisation: the new American colonies had local assemblies with varying degrees of power, and the Rus had no policy or practice of ethnic cleansing.

Before the Mongols had a chance to shoot their arrows at them, the Kiev Rus took the opportunity to shoot themselves in the foot. Yaroslav the Wise ruled for thirty-five years of unprecedented glory, but in death showed none of his famed wisdom. In dividing his kingdom among his five sons Yaroslav guaranteed conflict within and disunity without. Principalities fought each other, and barbarian tribes raided with increasing impunity. In one season alone, in 1160, Cuman tribesmen carried off 10,000 slaves from the region of Smolensk in an uncanny parallel with Governor Moore's raids into Florida half a millennium later.

The pre-Mongol inheritance rules, where titles and land could pass to the eldest relative rather than the eldest child, meant that at one point there were estimated to be four or five times as many princes as there were principalities to fill. As a consequence there were always nobles available for war parties or the founding of new settlements. To the north and east of the early Russian state were the Finns, scattered thinly over a large and relatively attractive territory. Being dispersed so widely, they were easy prey for the far more numerous Rus, and were constantly pushed back by the advancing tide of Russian settlement. This was particularly true along Europe's longest river, the Volga. The Kievan Rus state continued an old tradition of the more or less gradual pushing out of its frontiers, down the Volga and to the east and north. Slowly the primacy of the Dnieper, with Kiev guarding its passage down to the Black Sea, gave way to the Volga as the heartland of the Russian people, with the 2,300 mile river linking the far north to the Sea of Azov on the borders of Asia.

The frontier moved through a process of military colonisation. Princes seized parcels of land by force and their armed bands, or drujinas, then protected settlers arriving from further west. The new settlements on the frontier were quite different from the traditional societies of Kiev. The prince was the undisputed autocrat, whose only legitimacy was force. At the same time settlers intermarried with the native Finns and adopted some of their traditions. The result was the creation of two Russias. In time the distinction became so fundamental that the 'Great Russians' on the Volga and the 'Little Russians' around Kiev came to regard themselves as different nations. The division came to a head in 1169, when the Prince of Rostov-Suzdal became Grand Prince, and used his military might to sack Kiev and forcibly move the capital to his own seat on the Volga far to the north-east.

Thirty-five years later the Third Crusade set off from western Europe to liberate the Holy Land from the infidel, but decided that the Byzantine Christians presented a much more tempting target. Constantinople was taken and its trade routes fell into the hands of the Italian city-states, destroying Kiev's economic supremacy for ever. The Rus were pushed back relentlessly from the south-east, from the south-west by the descendants of Attila's Huns and from the west by the Teutonic knights.

Then came the single most important event in Russian history: the Mongols arrived. (The Mongols in Russian histories are often referred to as Tartars, especially in more recent times when Stalin wreaked particular revenge on them. The elision from one term to the other is confusing for foreigners, but no more so than the elision from English to British in American histories. The term Tartar itself is derived from the Chinese name of one of the Mongol tribes; it has nothing to do with tartare sauce or the tartar on teeth, which comes from an Arabic word meaning resin.) The Mongols first emerged not in what is now Mongolia but further north, where the Huns had created the first state in central Asia, Hsiung-nu, in around 200BC, before being pushed and pulled westwards in the murderous stream of conquest ending at Châlons. Culturally the Mongols drew from both the forest traditions of Siberia and the cultures of the Turkic peoples who had replaced the Huns to control the great sweep of the steppes. Their transformation from a collection of loosely linked, nomadic clans into a unified military and political force was entirely thanks to Genghis Khan.

Genghis Khan was born in a tent on the banks of the river Onon, east of Lake Baikal, in 1162. After the murder of his father he was taken under the wing of a Mongol leader whom he soon overpowered. He set about creating a united Mongol nation by first subduing his closest kinsmen and then extending out to other Mongol and Turkic tribes. Among people where clan connections had been all-important, Genghis Khan introduced and enforced a strictly meritocratic regime. When he had compelled the tribes of central Asia to submit he turned on China. Invasions of China had been tried and failed before; that Genghis Khan succeeded is a testament to the skill with which he waged war, and the ferocity of his troops. In 1214, 75,000 Mongols lay siege to the 600,000 defenders of Peking. The next year the city fell. The Mongols were on their way.

The Mongols changed the world in a way unparalleled since the Romans. No individual Roman leader had anything like the impact on world history that Genghis Khan exerted. China, India, Russia and a host of other nations are as they are today because of the influence of that one man. After conquering northern China in 1215 Genghis Khan led his hordes through Persia into southern Russia. (The word 'horde' derives from the Mongol word for camp.) His son sacked Kiev and raided into Poland and Moravia. The Mongols withdrew only when the time came to elect a new khan, an election attended by emissaries from the Pope and the Caliph of Baghdad. If the latter was trying to curry favour he failed. The Mongols soon fell on to the Muslim world. The only favour they bestowed on the caliph was that in respect to superstitions about not shedding a caliph's blood they wrapped him in a carpet and had their horses trample him to death. Islam might have been destroyed but for the Mongols' defeat by Egyptian forces outside Nazareth. Even more than

Châlons this battle changed the course of world history. As it was, Islam survived and the western Mongols themselves soon converted.

The Mongols combined technology, organisation and tactics to produce a force that was almost unstoppable. The core of their technological superiority was the humble bow and arrow. Their enemies' cumbersome bows were designed for hunting, where the need was to maximise the range at which an unsuspecting animal could be brought down by the first arrow fired. A hunter would not get a second chance. The Mongols were more interested in rapid fire: their bows were small, short-range weapons. Mongol archers could dispatch arrow after arrow, using a stone attached to their thumbs to draw back the bowstring. As with modern technologies, the Mongol arrow designers were forever inventing new, more specialist applications. There were arrows for starting fires or piercing armour, whistling arrows for signalling, arrows carrying miniature grenades, arrows tipped with quicklime or naphtha. Above all, Mongol bows could be fired by fighters on horseback while at full gallop. Indeed, they could be fired accurately backwards at a pursuing enemy. The Mongols had combined artillery and light cavalry in one deadly force.

The superiority of their technology was married with the superiority of their logistics, a superiority entirely owing to the Mongol's most prized possessions: his horses. Each Mongol cavalryman had three or four horses, ensuring there was always a fresh mount when battle commenced, and allowing them to travel phenomenal distances at high speed. Riders in the Mongol postal service could cover over 120 miles a day at a time when roads were virtually non-existent. The horse provided both transport and sustenance: milk, blood and meat. Like their riders the horses originated in the frozen tundra of eastern Siberia; they were used to enduring the bitter cold, and foraged for food below layers of snow. The result was a force as mobile in winter as summer.

In 1237 the Mongols reached Russia. Hitler and Napoleon raced to defeat their Russian enemies before they themselves were defeated by the Russian winter. They failed. The Mongols were a different breed; they waited for winter to arrive and then struck with unsurpassed speed and ferocity. They had passed a relaxing summer exterminating the Bulgar kingdom on the Middle Volga, massacring the 50,000 inhabitants of its largest city in the process. After waiting until the Volga froze over, the Mongol army of 120,000 simply rode across the river and melted unseen into the snow-covered forests on the other side.

Their first target was Ryazan in the east of the country. Here they immediately demonstrated not only the superiority of their military technology and strategy but the two 'virtual' weapons that would become a feature of Russian life for centuries to come: secret intelligence and terror.

The Mongol hordes did not just charge out of Asia obliterating whatever they happened to come across. They gathered vast amounts of information on their enemies and planned their attacks in great detail. Long before the Rus realised what was happening the Mongols had identified all their weak points, both military and political. By taking the province of Ryazan the Mongols could split the Rus forces. More importantly, the province itself was ruled by four princes notoriously unable to agree on anything.

Once the city and province of Ryazan were taken the Mongols unleashed their other, not so secret, weapon. The Russians were to learn a lesson that was never to be forgotten: the power of sheer terror. The entire nobility, men, women and children, was butchered. All the city's women were systematically raped. Survivors were flayed alive in the streets.

The Grand Duke Yuri of Suzdal had been the overlord of the Ryazan princes; he became the Mongols' next target. He left his family for safety in the city of Vladimir so the Mongols headed there. When his wife refused to come out of the church where she was hiding her children the Mongols simply torched the building. Yuri himself was killed in battle a month later, along with most of his army. The Mongols then turned their focus to the far north-east and the rich trading city of Novgorod. Here they met their only serious setback.

From Novgorod to Kulikovo

The story of Novgorod could fill a chapter on its own. Until the time of Ivan the Terrible, centuries after the first Mongols appeared, the city developed along its own unique lines, as it had done in the centuries before the Mongols arrived. In some Russian histories it appears as an Athenian-like city state embracing democracy long before the feudal states of western Europe. Many nations have claimed to be the home of democracy. Greece can point to the glories of Athens, where government by the people, the demos, was first a reality – at least for those parts of the population who were not female, were not slaves and lived during those few periods of Athenian history when the demos held real power. France points to the liberty, equality and fraternity of the French Revolution, although the guillotine is an unlikely symbol of true democracy. America points to the promises of the Declaration of Independence and the US Constitution, promises that rang hollow for generations of black slaves. Britain prides itself on being the birthplace of parliamentary democracy, although the parliament of Iceland is far older. And the Russians have Novgorod.

Novgorod, on the Gulf of Finland, was one of the major trading centres of Europe, and by the middle of the twelfth century it was a functioning democracy, governed by the people, the 'veche'. The veche elected the local officials, even the local bishop. The powers of the local prince were severely limited by formal agreements with the veche, which laid down what he was allowed to do and prescribed in detail what taxes he was allowed to collect: all this well before the English barons compelled King John to subscribe to less onerous restrictions in the Magna Carta. The prince was even banned from living within the city walls; he was essentially a military leader hired by the veche to defend the city.

But to see Novgorod as a gleaming example of democracy in a region tumbling into absolutism is a considerable exaggeration. It is tempting to look back on medieval Novgorod through the prism of modern ideologies as a golden period of European proto-democracy, but the facts are somewhat different. Teleologic is no logic. The veche consisted of all male citizens. Women were not empowered and, although slavery had largely disappeared in the city itself, it still survived in the rural areas over which Novgorod exerted its authority. Minority groups, particularly the rich German merchants, had to live in designated areas and had no formal political power. Meetings of the veche, which could be called by anyone ringing the town bell, could be heated. These meetings were open affairs, and were known on occasions to break up into competing gatherings on either side of the Volkhov river. Disputes were then settled by brawls on the bridge; the concept of the secret ballot was unknown. In practice Novgorod was governed by an assembly of some fifty wealthy merchants, boyars (landowners) and officials. Novgorod was a principality run by an oligarchy, dressed like a republic and remembered as a democracy. In addition Novgorod was an imperial power, grabbing territory as far east and north as the Urals, the upper Volga and the White Sea. No form of government that relies on military might to contain its people within an imperial framework can claim to be a true democracy.

Novgorod withstood the Mongol siege, and as a consequence was able to maintain a degree of the early Rus enlightenment through the dark centuries of Mongol rule. In the long run that may not have helped the city. When Mongol rule finally ended Ivan the Terrible inflicted his own terror on the still independently minded citizens.

Having failed to take Novgorod, the Mongols casually mopped up the remaining Rus opposition over the next two years. At the city of Kozelsk they were taken by surprise when the besieged garrison counter-attacked. Their response was to sack the city with a brutality that even they had not known before.

In 1240 Kiev fell. The Mongols realised that the city was a treasure worth preserving and sent envoys to demand submission. The governor had the envoys killed, and the Mongols wreaked a terrible revenge. The cathedral of St Sophia was the only building they left standing in the whole city. They showed their bizarre sense of honour among the carnage by sparing the life of the governor, who had demonstrated his bravery by executing their envoys.

The Mongols ruled Russia for 250 years, but it is difficult to find anything positive to say about any stretch of their reign. They ended the squabbling of warring princes and imposed central control, but other than that they contributed virtually nothing, destroying what went before without creating what came after. They left a tradition of absolutism, a resigned acceptance of arbitrary authority, an abiding fear of invasion and a distrust of all things foreign. The areas of greatest Mongol influence can be seen in the Russian language – with Mongol or Tartar roots found on the one hand in words relating to whips, chains and slavery and on the other in words like treasury, customs duty and money. What they did not leave was any contribution to culture: no magnificent buildings, no art, no music. They had no significant impact on religion. They produced no heroic kings or mythical sagas. During the Mongol period economic development virtually stagnated. Histories of Russia can leap from 1223, when the Mongols arrived, to 1480, when Ivan III formally ended Muscovy's subjection to the Golden Horde. In between lay the Russian Dark Ages, during which the power of the Mongols slowly disintegrated. They were always more interested in extracting tribute than in administering their empire, and over time the Russian nobility assumed more and more of the effective authority. In particular the dukes of Muscovy came to exercise the power that the Mongols in their distant capital of Sarai lacked the desire or ability to exercise themselves. The cultural developments of the period, like the construction of the Kremlin, started 130 years after the Mongol invasion, and a century later the construction of the Dormition Cathedral in Moscow, owed everything to the re-empowering of the Russian nobility and virtually nothing to their Mongol overlords.

On 8 September 1380 there occurred what has often been described as the most important event in the history of medieval Russia. Indeed, in a survey of schoolchildren in one of the former Soviet Asian republics held in the year 2000 it was cited as the most important event in the previous millennium. The battle of Kulikovo saw Russia throw off the Mongol yoke and unite around the banner of Muscovy. About 200,000 died and the Russian dead, it is said, took seven days to bury.

The Muscovite grand duke Dmitri Donskoy whose military prowess determined the course of the battle is one of Russia's most celebrated heroes; the communists named a Typhoon-class nuclear submarine after him. Kulikovo is Yorktown and Gettysburg combined: it both liberated and defined a nation.

If world history is determined in battle, Kulikovo must rank alongside Châlons and the Mongols' earlier defeat at Ayn Jalut outside Nazareth. At Châlons Attila was stopped in his tracks, saving western European civilisation from being consumed by a barbaric east. At Ayn Julut the Mongol general Kitbogha was killed, and the Mongols never again threatened Islamic civilisation. At Kulikovo the forces of Khan Mamai were destroyed, allowing Russian (and by implication European) civilisation to throw off the chains of Asiatic slavery.

There are, however, some important differences between the three battles. The details of the fighting are unimportant, although it is worth noting that Donskoy's victory was largely because the Mongols' Lithuanian allies failed to turn up. It was also helped by internecine conflict within the Mongol Golden Horde; Sarai had fourteen different khans in the space of twenty years.

Châlons changed history because after the battle Attila went back home and was never heard of again. The outcome at Ayn Jalut was if anything even more decisive. After Kulikovo, however, although Mamai, the Mongol leader, went home, he returned with a vengeance the next year, driving all before him and attacking Moscow. As late as 1451, seventy years after Kulikovo, Mongol armies still raided up to the walls of Moscow. In fact it was to be a century after Donskoy's supposedly epic victory before Russia threw off the Mongol yoke, and then not because of a glorious battle but because the Turkic leader Tamurlane turned all eyes elsewhere and Muscovy was able to creep out of the Mongol tent.

The significance of Kulikovo lies not in the historical reality but in today's perceptions. Kulikovo is the crucible in which modern Russia was born, a furnace of fire and steel that reflects the character of the nation. Donskoy is to Russians in many ways the equivalent of Thanksgiving to

Americans. The Pilgrim Fathers are held up as the first religious refugees fleeing to a promised land, which was destined to be built in their image; Kulikovo is held up as the symbol of Holy Russia, surrounded by enemies and surviving only through its own strength and inspired leadership. Historically both stories are largely fiction. The Pilgrim Fathers were not the first Protestant refugees in the New World (French Huguenots had beaten them to it) and America was taken not with the piety of the Pilgrims but by sheer brute force. The bullet, not the bible, was the true symbol of the new nation across the Atlantic, just as intrigue rather than the blood of Kulikovo was the symbol of the nation forming between the Urals and the Baltic. When Russia at last broke free of its Asian overlords it was less thanks to the valour of Dmitri Donskoy than it was to the diplomatic manoeuvring of leaders such as Ivan I, revealingly known to history as Ivan Moneybags.

It was not until the reign of Ivan III, Ivan the Great, that Muscovite Russia was finally established as a truly independent power. Not only did he end formal subservience to the Mongols, but he also defeated the other two forces that could have smothered the infant state: the Lithuanians and the Khazars. Ivan III also started the tradition of deporting troublesome groups, which was to become such a feature of both Russian and American history. After capturing Novgorod and incorporating it into Muscovy he dispossessed most of the landowners and deported them to the east.

At exactly the same time another corner of Europe was also throwing off the shackles of its Islamic conquerors. But if in Russia the shackles were iron and rusted away, in Spain the shackles were gold and were torn asunder. In Iberia the infidels who had brought culture, tolerance and harmony were replaced by a regime bringing aggression, the Inquisition and Christopher Columbus. In Russia the infidels were replaced by something just as bad, indeed worse: the pure evil of Ivan IV, Ivan the Terrible.

Ivan the Terrible

The one tsar most westerners have heard of lived nearly half a millennium ago. Ivan the Terrible ruled for half a century from 1533 to 1584. While the Spanish were destroying the great empires of the Incas and Aztecs, Ivan IV turned a middle-ranking eastern European duchy into the Russia still recognisable today. If any one man can truly be called the father of Russia it is Ivan IV. His greatness is undeniable. Unfortunately for those who lived under him, he was also quite clearly mad.

It has been argued that Ivan's mental problems had roots in genetic and physical illness. His father, although himself the son of Ivan the Great, was a simpleton, his brother a deaf-mute, and most of his legitimate children died in infancy. Almost certainly Ivan the Terrible suffered from encephalitis, a disease with schizophrenia-like symptoms: aggressive behaviour, marked character change and rapid mood swings. On the other hand, for those who blame mental illness on nurture rather than nature Ivan the Terrible is a classic case study. Rarely can a child's upbringing have foreshadowed so clearly the mania to come. His father died when Ivan was three, leaving the throne to Ivan and effective power to his mother, a foreigner with little love for Russia but greater love for various Russian men. His uncle Yuri challenged Ivan's right to the throne and was thrown into a dungeon to starve. Ivan's mother was poisoned five years later, and within a week the eight year old is said to have arranged for her lover to be arrested and beaten to death. After his mother's murder Ivan escaped from the violent intrigues of the court into such hobbies as pulling the wings off birds and poking sticks in their eyes. With his deaf-mute brother, another Yuri, he wandered around his own palace often hungry and dressed in rags. From this he graduated to roaming the streets with a gang of friends, attacking passers-by. His speciality was inventing ever more ingenious ways of murdering young women, always raping them first. He retained his interest in animals, spending hours throwing cats and dogs from the castle walls.

Power was exercised by ever-changing alliances of noble families. Rivalry between the Shuisky and the Belsky families escalated, and murders and beatings became common even inside the palace. When Ivan was nine the Shuiskys raided the palace, rounding up his confidants. They had the loyal Fyodor Mishurin skinned alive and left on display in a Moscow square. Finally at the age of thirteen, over Christmas in 1543, Ivan asserted himself. He ordered the arrest of Prince Andrew Shuisky and set the tone for his reign by having the prince thrown to a pack of ravenous hunting dogs.

In 1547 Ivan was finally crowned Tsar of all the Russians, the first Muscovy grand duke to assume this title. He went about choosing a wife in a typically forthright manner: he held a beauty parade and chose Anastasia Romanovna. Many boyars resented the match because Anastasia's Romanov family was untitled, although not to remain that way for long. Surprisingly the marriage seems to have been a happy one. Ivan called Anastasia his *'little heifer'*, and she bore him six children of whom only two survived infancy. She had a positive influence on him and they apparently enjoyed thirteen years of wedded bliss. During that period Ivan introduced government reforms, reducing the power of the boyars and thus the opportunities for corruption. He also reformed the Church and the army and set out on the first steps to creating a Russian empire. His forces conquered the khanates of Kazan and Astrakhan and the Baltic cities of Narva and Polotsk. The first English traders started to appear in Russian markets.

The birth of Russian imperialism was one of Ivan the Terrible's most lasting contributions to history. The people of Muscovy and its predecessor states had been largely Russian or Russified Finns. For the first time Ivan turned their eyes outwards, and the 'Russia' he left behind had significant non-Russian populations. The way those populations were integrated, or largely not integrated, into the Russian state had ramifications right down to the present day.

In 1553 one of the key events of the reign occurred. Ivan collapsed with what his courtiers imagined was a fatal fever. He demanded that the boyars swear an oath of allegiance to his baby son Dmitri, but most refused. Ivan recovered, but never forgave what he regarded as treachery.

When Anastasia died seven years later Ivan relapsed violently into the ways of his youth. He launched an attack on the German knights to the west, and lost. In a fury he launched a reign of terror on his own people. Like Stalin centuries later he saw conspiracies on all sides. Almost certainly Anastasia died of natural causes, but Ivan was convinced the boyars had poisoned her and he had many tortured and executed. The boyars were demonised in his mind, just as the kulaks would be later in the mind of Joseph Stalin.

Ivan's behaviour became erratic in the extreme, his moods swinging from violence to repentance, blasphemy to prolonged prayer. Around Christmas 1564 he suddenly announced his intention to abdicate and left Moscow. The populace called for his return, which he eventually agreed to, but only after making clear that he expected absolute power. The tool he used to exercise this power was the oprichniki, the forerunner of secret police everywhere; dressed in black and riding black horses, they created a climate of terror across the empire. Ivan founded a pseudo-monastic order with himself as the 'abbot' and the oprichniki as 'monks', and performed black masses that were followed by orgies and torture. He organised rituals in which men's ribs were torn out with red-hot tongs. Afterwards the tsar collapsed prostate on the altar, before rising to preach wild sermons of repentance to the drunken oprichniki. Sadism was routine. Sir Jerome Horsey, Elizabeth I's ambassador to Ivan's court, described how one prince who had displeased the tsar *'was drawn upon a long sharp-made stake, which entered the lower part of his body and came out of his neck; upon which he languished a horrible pain for fifteen hours alive, and spoke to his mother, brought to behold that woeful sight. And she was given to 100 gunners, who defiled her to death, and the Emperor's hungry hounds devoured her flesh and bones.'* Ivan decided that the citizens of Novgorod were insufficiently respectful, and proceeded to sack the city and massacre its citizens in an orgy of torture, rape and burning. The Volkhov river reportedly burst its banks because of the number of corpses, as men, women and children were tied to sleighs and plunged into the icy waters. The city's archbishop was sewn into a bearskin and then hunted to death by a pack of hounds.

Like Stalin, Ivan frequently turned on his closest advisors: his treasurer was boiled alive and a councillor was strung up, while the oprichniki took turns hacking pieces off his body.

Ivan died in 1584, but long before then had clearly become totally insane. In 1572 he dismissed the oprichniki and abdicated in favour of an obscure Mongol general. After a year in which he regularly visited Moscow to bow before the new tsar, Ivan took the throne back. In 1581 he had a row with his son's pregnant wife, beating her because she wasn't dressed appropriately. His son sprang to her defence, whereupon Ivan hit him with his iron-tipped staff; after several days in a coma his son died. Ivan was consumed by grief and remorse, repeatedly smashing his head against his son's coffin, just as he had smashed his head against the floor when his first wife Anastasia had died. Such behaviour did nothing to restore his sanity, which was in any case exacerbated by his addiction to mercury and his almost certain syphilis. It was not surprising that the tsar had succumbed to the deadly new disease that had been brought back to Europe by Columbus's sailors, given Ivan's legendary carnal appetite for both sexes. Ivan boasted of the thousands of virgins he had deflowered and bastards he had fathered. It is therefore ironic that, although at the end he had to be carried everywhere in a litter while his skin peeled, his hair fell out and his body stank, the symptom that history remembers is that 'the Emperor began grievously to swell in his cods'.

Attempts have been made to argue that Ivan's terror was not unusual. One of the nearest comparisons occurred three hundred years earlier on the opposite side of Europe. Edward I of England was brought up a prisoner of over-powerful lords, and when his beloved wife died he went on a frenzy of territorial expansion in Wales and Scotland, unleashing a storm of massacre and terror upon Scottish cities like Berwick every bit as monstrous as Ivan's assault on Novgorod. But Edward was already entwined by the principles of Magna Carta and the nascent stirrings of parliament. Another English example was a contemporary of Ivan's; while Ivan was sewing Novgorod's archbishop into a bearskin, Henry VIII was making the Abbot of Glastonbury ride naked through the streets before his execution. It is true that the violence and terror of Tudor England has largely been written out of history books, with the dissolution of the monasteries usually presented as nothing more than a few land transfers, but Ivan's sadism was on an altogether different scale.

Ivan's lust for blood and land exceeded Henry VIII's, as did his lust for women – although that comparison is closer. After Anastasia, Ivan married another noted beauty but soon tired of her. His third wife died two weeks after the wedding and his fourth he sent to a convent. His fifth marriage was also short lived. His sixth wife was found to have a lover: he was impaled below her window and she was sent to a convent. She was lucky: wife number seven was discovered not to be a virgin, and Ivan immediately had her drowned. His eighth wife managed to survive three years of marriage and thereby outlived him. Ivan cast his net wide when looking for a wife. In 1567, when he was faring badly in the Livonian Wars, Ivan approached the representative of the Muscovy Company, Anthony Jenkinson, to see if the English queen, Elizabeth I, would marry him and provide a refuge if he had to flee the country. She had other ideas.

One area in which a comparison with England, and in particular with Henry VIII, is valid is the degree to which Ivan achieved a redistribution of wealth. Henry took away the wealth of the Church, Ivan the wealth of the boyars.

The short period in which the oprichniki were active had a profound influence on the development of Russia, not only because of its terror but because of the economic transformation it created. Their primary targets were the old boyar families in the Muscovy heartland, whose land was seized; many of those not killed were deported to more remote regions. Many market towns that had previously been owned by boyars and run as their private property now became the tsar's. From then on the great 'landowners' were not landowners at all; they rented their estates from the tsar in return for service and tax, and he could end their lease whenever he wished. The power of the boyars was destroyed, and in their place Ivan placed the dvoriane, the imperial bureaucrats who were sons and grandsons of royal servants and even slaves. The dvoriane were given enormous local power, which they exploited ruthlessly to enrich themselves, but Ivan made sure that the power they exercised never became a threat to him. None of the provincial governors was allowed to stay in post for more than two years, and one was the norm, while governors were never appointed to areas where they themselves held estates.

Ivan IV gave Russia an imperial autocracy controlling every aspect of life. Nobody else had a shred of effective political or economic power. The empire Ivan bequeathed to his genetically challenged son Fyodor became one of the world's most powerful.

Russia after Ivan

The death of Ivan IV released his people from a tyranny of insane terror. His reign might be expected to be held up as a warning. In fact the opposite has often been true. To many, from the ultra nationalist right to the Stalinist left, he has been a symbol of patriotism and devotion to the motherland. Even today a small but vociferous group within the Russian Orthodox Church argue for Ivan's beatification. His Russian nomenclature, they would argue, more properly translates not as Terrible but as Awesome. In the language of the 2003 Iraq War, his proponents would argue that his leadership embodied not the 'terror' of Saddam Hussein but 'the shock and awe' of Bush II.

With hindsight it is tempting to discern continuity in events across the centuries. The history of terror is an example. From the Mongols, through Ivan the Terrible to Lenin and Stalin, terror has been a repeating feature of Russian life. When developing their theories on the use of terror in such works as Lenin's 1918 booklet *Proletarian Revolution and the Renegade K. Kautsky* and Trotsky's 1920 eulogy to mass terror, *Terrorism and Communism*, the Bolsheviks were certainly drawing on the lessons of history. Stalin seems to have pictured himself quite consciously as inheriting the mantle of Ivan the Terrible. But it is wrong to think that governing through terror is characteristically Russian. For long periods after Ivan IV the Russian state continued without his kind of terror, and with less sadistic coercion. Terror may be a tool to which the ruling elite in Russia has repeatedly turned, but it cannot be said that the acceptance of terror is part of the collective Russian psyche. No people welcome the opportunity to live in a state of perpetual fear. What can more persuasively be argued to be particularly Russian is the acceptance of autocracy.

The philosophical catchword of American history, the ideological concept that Americans believe underpins their whole political culture, is 'democracy'. Russian history has a similar core value: 'autocracy'. In many countries individuals yearn for the state to provide order and decisive government; in most countries the political elites yearn for absolute power. There is nothing particularly Russian about that. Indeed Russia has spawned numerous anarchist movements, demonstrating that autocracy was never universally accepted. As a sweeping generalisation, however, it is fair to assert that Russians have a greater desire for 'strong leadership' than, for example, Americans or Britons. Lord Acton's dictum that 'All power corrupts, absolute power corrupts absolutely' would be instinctively accepted by most Americans but would still provoke debate in Moscow or St Petersburg.

The difference between autocracy and democracy is not that they have opposing aspirations but that they attach different priorities to those aspirations. Autocracy puts order above liberty, the nation above the citizen, collective security above individual freedom, responsibilities above rights. Democracy, at least in theory, does the opposite. Democracy is about citizens selecting their government from among themselves. It implies a theoretical equality between governed and governing; the governed are saying 'we are worth the same as you'. In western eyes the concept of autocracy seems to imply a people saying 'we value ourselves less than we value our rulers', but this is a misunderstanding. Autocracy is based on the premise that everyone has rights and obligations but these rights vary according to one's position in society. The autocrat rules as a father ruled the traditional family; it is his role to protect and provide, and in return receive respect and absolute obedience. Autocracy implies that all people are not equal; it does not imply that Russians attached no value to themselves. Ivan's other legacy enhanced that self-valuation. The birth of empire allowed Russians, after centuries of Mongol rule, to once again feel superior to other peoples. And that superiority reinforced the autocracy because it was the autocrat who had made conquest possible.

Russian imperialism was inextricably wedded to autocracy. In general American imperialism has been driven by individuals and corporations seeking land and wealth; the state intervened later to protect and legitimise their conquests. In Russia the state went first, conquering its way to empire. Of course there were exceptions, like the Russian pioneers in Siberia and Alaska and American military campaigns against the 'Indians' on the western frontier. But in general American imperial expansion has been characterised by Americans replacing or seeking to Americanise the natives of the lands they conquered. In contrast Russian imperialism has sought to rule and exploit the natives, but not necessarily to Russify them. As a consequence Russians (with the notable exception of the Bolsheviks) have no vision of themselves as the prototype for a global civilisation.

Russians and Americans, like many if not most nationalities, tend to regard themselves as superior to other peoples. But Russians have never developed the equivalent of the innate American belief that deep down everyone else in the world really wants to be an American or, at least, would want to be so if only they could be educated to understand the virtues of the American way of life. Ivan the Terrible left a model of empire that had to be imposed rather than sold.

Ivan the Terrible so dominated his age, murdering anyone who might pose a threat to his throne, that his death inevitably left a power vacuum. The consequence was a period known simply as the Time of Troubles, with warring factions at court and more importantly the ever-present threat of invasion. Unlike the Mongol invasion the next one was short-lived, but it too left an indelible mark on the Russian psyche. While the Swedes conquered Novgorod another enemy struck at the heart of Muscovy. The Poles tried to take advantage of the divisions within the Russian nobility, and the centuries-long hatred of Catholic Poland was born. The Time of Troubles lasted just fifteen years, but the chaos and strife were burnt deeply into the Russian folk memory, especially when contrasted with the long and 'stable' rule of Ivan the Terrible. The creed of autocracy could have ended with Ivan's death just as the creed of democracy in America could have been snuffed out by the reality of slavery. In neither case was the development of these values automatic; choices were made consciously as well as unconsciously. There were no democracies in the Time of Troubles but there were alternatives to autocracy. Next door, for example, Polish kings were elected; a proto-democracy had existed in Novgorod in living memory; and Kievan Rus itself was far from a pure autocracy. The concept of a hereditary monarchy providing strong and untrammelled leadership was adopted at the very time when it might be thought the hereditary principle was proving of absolutely no value. A mad tsar had ruled for nearly half a century to be followed by his mentally inadequate offspring, whose incapacity produced chaos and violence. And yet it was the near anarchy of the Time of Troubles that established in the collective consciousness the legitimacy, indeed necessity, of strong leadership, of autocracy.

Just listing the key events illustrates the depths to which the newly reinvigorated Russian state rapidly sank:

- Ivan was succeeded by his retarded son Fyodor I, who 'ruled' for fourteen years.
- When Fyodor died the Time of Troubles really started. The throne was seized by Boris Godunov (a Russian Macbeth, one of the many minor characters in Russian history rescued centuries later from justified oblivion by writers, poets or musicians more interested in dramatic licence than historical fact).
- Boris I was followed by his son Fyodor II, who was almost immediately murdered.
- The invading Poles recognised as tsar an obscure minor noble, Grigory, who claimed to be the son of Ivan IV by one of his later wives. Grigory is sometimes known as the first False Dimitry.
- Grigory converted to Catholicism, but that only hastened his demise. After a year he was overthrown and murdered. His ashes were loaded into a cannon and fired in the general direction of Poland.

- The throne was then seized by Vasilly, who first won a civil war against an army led by a former Ottoman slave and then fought off a pretender who had married Grigory's widow (the second False Dimitry).
- The Poles invaded again, and proclaimed Vladislav of Poland tsar.
- Vasilly turned to Sweden for help. The Swedes sent him a force of English and Scottish mercenaries, but he still lost.
- The Poles installed a new ruler, while the Swedes contented themselves with seizing Novgorod again as a consolation prize.
- Finally, in 1612, the Russians rose up against their invaders and pushed them all out.

Casting around for a new tsar, the Russians alighted on the family of Ivan the Terrible's first wife, Anastasia. After years of total chaos few could have expected the sixteen-year-old Michael Romanov to last for long. Not only did he remain on the throne for thirty years, but the Romanovs survived from the time of the Tudors right up to the twentieth century. Ivan's choice of Anastasia not only brought a virgin bride to his bed but brought the Romanov family to the centre stage of Russian history. The Russian monarchy lasted for 333 years after Ivan the Terrible's death, and for all but the first twenty-nine of those years a Romanov held the throne.

Michael Romanov assumed the throne in 1613, six years after the founding of Jamestown and seven years before the sailing of the *Mayflower*. His accession gave Russians a chance to develop along a different path to the barbaric routes of the Mongols and Ivan the Terrible. Similarly in Massachusetts the English had the chance to avoid the barbaric paths of slavery and genocide along which the colonies to the south were soon to be firmly striding. The Romanovs, to some extent at least, succeeded. The Massachusetts colonists, to a large extent, failed.

CHAPTER 4
LEGACY OF THE MYSTIC MASSACRE

Ivan the Terrible threw all the resources he could command into the cause of empire. He was determined that Russian imperialism, like everything else in his realm, would be controlled from the centre. The tsar himself decided when and where the Muscovite state would attempt to push out its borders. By contrast the English crown had a far more casual approach. The slowly developing English colonies in the Caribbean and on the mainland grew at their own speed. In Russia dreams of empire preceded conquest. In America conquest led to dreams of empire.

Those who organised the settlements in Barbados and Virginia may have done so in the name of the English monarch, but they were motivated more by profit than patriotism. They hoped to make themselves rich. One group of English colonists was different, travelling as servants of their Lord, dedicated to creating a kingdom in His name. History remembers them as the Pilgrim Fathers, and for them dreams did precede conquest. Spreading out from Boston, they were determined to bring the love of the Lord to the New World. What they brought instead was a terror as bloody as Ivan the Terrible's, a terror that paved the way for empire.

Frying Natives

In the annals of terrorist atrocities 5/27 should resonate with Americans as much as 9/11. The events of 27 May 1637 changed the American psyche for ever. History has yet to show that 9/11 will have anything like as seismic a long-term impact. In both cases an act of unprecedented carnage was coldly planned and callously inflicted. In both cases the victims were 'civilians' perversely regarded as 'combatants' only in the eyes of men blinded by religious bigotry. In both cases the objective was to terrorise populations who had no comprehension at all of what was happening to them or of what could possibly be motivating their attackers. In both cases surprise was total.

The villagers of Missituck (now Mystic), Connecticut, had gone to bed as usual on 26 May. Many of the menfolk were away but four hundred (in some versions seven hundred) women, children, elderly and infirm remained. They could have had no idea that all but five of them would never see another sunset.

Just before dawn an English militia leader, Captain John Underhill, looked down on the sleeping village with grim satisfaction. As the first rays of the new day's sun tinged the eastern sky he gave the order to attack. The killing began. Seven years after the founding of Boston ethnic cleansing had arrived in New England. 'Down fell men, women and children,' Underhill wrote triumphantly in his journal, *Newes from America*. 'Great and doleful was the bloody sight to the view of young soldiers that had never been in a war, to see so many souls lay gasping on the ground, so thick, in some places, that you could hardly pass along.'

Underhill returned to Boston a hero. William Bradford, the leader of the Pilgrim Fathers, gave praise for the 'sweet sacrifice' of natives 'frying in the fire'. Seven years later, when the Dutch, who had founded a colony on the Hudson, needed to cleanse their own land they called on Underhill's services again. This time he was even more 'successful', killing more than 500 Algonquian in a single raid on a native village. But it was the Mystic Massacre that had the most profound impact on the development of America. From that moment European settlers realised that the continent was theirs for the taking.

The first Puritan settlers in New England were alarmed by the presence of native tribes around them. They knew nothing of the fate of the early Viking immigrants, but they were certainly well aware of the savage native wars that had erupted in Virginia. They set up local militias to defend themselves against marauding natives. These militias were known as 'trayned bands', because the volunteers were usually placed under the command of someone who had received military training before emigrating. The band at Boston was commanded by Underhill, who had come out from England specifically to take charge of the defence of the new settlement. He quickly established that the best form of defence was offence. The area surrounding the colony had to be cleansed of any threats, and the first of these threats were the Pequot.

In 1634 an English pirate named John Stone had kidnapped several natives and demanded ransom. The native response was to fall on Stone and his crew and kill them all. The English authorities decided that the Pequot were responsible, and demanded that they hand over the heads of Stone's killers. Stone may have been a pirate, but he was a white man doing what white men had the right to do. Even as early as 1634 the settlers had realised that making natives pay 'tributes' was an effective way of funding their colonies; Alan Taylor has succinctly characterised the practice as a protection racket. Some settlers took to holding native children hostage to ensure that their parents paid their tributes. When the Pequot refused to co-operate hostilities broke out.

The native tribes throughout North America were frequently at war with each other, but war to them was quite different from war as understood by Europeans. The objective of native wars was not primarily to kill their enemies but to capture them. The captives swelled the size of the tribe and made it more powerful; the number of people in the tribe also determined its wealth. A few warriors would be killed, often with sickening savagery, but women and children were scrupulously protected: they were the prize. Having no concept of property, the natives had no concept of war fought for territory.

Underhill was used to the norms of Europe, to total war. He insisted in his journal that the Scriptures decreed that women and children must perish with their menfolk. Employing the classic British imperial strategy of divide and rule, he recruited Mohegan and Narrangaset natives as allies.

They led him to Mystic and participated in the subsequent massacre, although Underhill in his journal notes that they cried out that the onslaught was 'too furious and slays too many men'.

When the English arrived in New England there had probably been around eight thousand Pequot, but in 1633 smallpox had halved their numbers. In a matter of months the Pequot War (as this cynical exercise in ethnic cleansing was called) virtually wiped out the 3,000 remaining Pequot – who were killed, shipped off to slave plantations in the Caribbean or sold as slaves to other more friendly tribes. Proportionate to their population the Mystic Massacre was equivalent to more than a million New Yorkers being killed in the barbarism of the Twin Towers attack. Like 9/11 the trauma extended far beyond the massacre site itself.

The Pequot War had two important consequences. First it terrorised and transformed the native population already reeling from the impact of European disease. They had no idea what the Mystic Massacre was about: the concepts of owning land and seizing territory were totally alien, as was the shock and awe of European 'total war' waged against civilian populations. The Mystic Massacre sent a message to all the native peoples, friend and foe, that life would never be the same again: 27 May 1637 marked the end of freedom and independence for the Native American.

The second similarly profound impact was on the whites. Until the Pequot War the Puritans had seen themselves as a tiny group of God-fearing souls in permanent danger of being overwhelmed by the mass of heathen savages by whom they were surrounded. As dawn broke over Missituck on that late spring day the balance of power changed for ever. It really is a date as important in US history as 11 September 2001. The Puritans' glorification of their 'victory' had all the resonance of Osama Bin Laden's rhetoric three centuries later. As the American Alfred Cave in his work on the Pequot War puts it, 'Celebration of victory over Indians as the triumph of light over darkness, civilisation over savagery, for many generations our central historical myth, finds its earliest full expression in the contemporary chronicles of this little war.'

Central as the Pequot War may be to understanding the American psyche, it has largely been written out of conventional history; not by state dictat of the kind that tried to write the Vikings out of Russian history, but simply because the facts of the Mystic Massacre do not fit the picture that most Americans have of their past. The myth of noble Puritans overcoming vicious savages is so ingrained that any contrary examples are assumed to be so atypical as not to be worth recording.

Samuel Eliot Morison was for many years the doyenne of US historians. He was convinced that the 'roots of everything we have today' could be traced back to the colonies of the late seventeenth century. But his view of that period was conditioned by his perceptions of modern America. In his monumental *Oxford History of the American People* published in 1965 there is no mention of the Mystic Massacre, and the Pequot War itself is referred to only in reference to a later conflict, when Morison writes, 'Hitherto, New England had suffered but one Indian war, a short, sharp and decisive conflict with the Pequots in 1637, which saved the land from savage warfare for nigh forty years.' (Interestingly he then goes on to describe the later conflict as a 'war of extermination', but rather than implying that the colonists wanted to exterminate the natives he uses the term to mean that the natives wanted to exterminate the colonists – something that was undoubtedly true but not the end result. As Morison records, at the end of the war the native 'women and children were parcelled out to white families as servants, warriors were sold as slaves in the West Indies and on the Barbary Coast of Africa'.)

What differentiated the Mystic Massacre from ethnic cleansing in the southern colonies was the religious fervour of the New Englanders, a fervour that created a whole new moral underpinning for conquest. The religious dimension of colonisation in New England is what made it unique, and what makes later American imperial expansion so difficult for many Europeans to understand.

The first New Englanders were convinced that their interests were God's interests. The terror inflicted on Mystic was God's holy terror; the muskets that poured death on to native women and children were God's guns. Ethnic cleansing may no longer be part of American imperialism, but American presidents still see themselves as firing the guns of God. Speaking of the invasion of Iraq nearly four centuries later, President Bush II expressed the spirit of Mystic when he proclaimed, 'It is not America which wants to free the peoples of the world. It is Jesus Christ who wants to free them.'

Christianity and the American way of life have become so entwined that it is often impossible to determine which one is inspiring which. The religion of Jesus Christ has been rewritten – not for the first time – to reflect the political ideology of its followers, almost as if the man himself has become an American. The story of the US congressman who insisted that he was not interested in foreign languages – 'If English was good enough for Jesus Christ, it's good enough for me' – is probably apocryphal, but during a speech in 1999 US Attorney General John Ashcroft made a remark that no European would dream of making about their own country, when he proclaimed that America's godly and eternal character made it unique among nations.

Russia, on the other hand, did not see itself as unique. On the contrary, for Russia territorial expansion was a natural consequence of its view of the world as a cockpit of competing powers where the choice was invade or be invaded. For America after Mystic there was no competing power; there were no Mongols, Swedes or Poles, no Napoleon or Hitler on its borders awaiting the opportunity to strike. Just like Russia it accumulated territory and power, but there was no need to flaunt its possessions to awe potential invaders with its imperial glory. For Russia the battle was between weak and strong. To the victor went the glory and the ultimate glory was empire. The Russian tsars were emperors and their creed was imperialism. America's has been an empire that never proclaimed its imperialism; instead, in the words used by Alfred Cave to describe the Pequot War, Americans believe that theirs was not the triumph of the strong over the weak but of 'light over darkness'.

Not everyone approved of Underhill's method of shining the light. Back in England many people were appalled, and called on the New English to adopt a more Christian approach. In response some New England Puritans, for the first time, set out to convert the natives remaining after the Pequot War. They established 'praying towns', where natives who gave up their own culture and adopted the English way of life could live in safety. These settlements appealed to some of the smaller tribes as a way of escaping their larger neighbours, but in the next major conflict in the 1670s the settlers themselves turned on these 'praying Indians'; they were shipped off to concentration camps both to protect them from genocide and to ensure that they had no opportunity to go over to the enemy: even a Christian native could not be entirely trusted. (There is a myth that concentration camps were first used by the British in the Boer War, but herding the praying Indians on to Long Island and Deer Island in Boston Harbour was in practice no different from the later camps in South Africa. Most of the inmates died of disease or starvation or were kidnapped by slave traders.)

Thanksgiving

What was particularly significant about the Pequot War and the Mystic Massacre was where it occurred. The atrocities happened not among the slave fields of Virginia, Jamaica or Carolina, where life was always cheap, but among the farms and chapels of pious New England where the riches of this life were supposed to take second place to the virtues that promised eternal riches in the life to come.

Colonies like Virginia and Barbados reflected the standard form of English colonialism; to the north a radically different economic model had sprung up. New England was the glaring exception to the general picture of slave-based colonisation. While by 1700 slaves formed three-quarters of the population in some colonies, in Massachusetts they numbered less than 2 per cent. New England presented a fundamentally different approach to colonisation. Almost the only feature it shared with the colonies further south was its attitude towards the natives, starting with an equal dependence on disease to get rid of the native population. When the Pilgrim Fathers landed in 1620 they found land cleared and ready for them, and no surviving natives to defend it.

The voyage of the Pilgrim Fathers is the abiding foundation myth of US history. Rather than the slave-holding oligarchs of Virginia and the south, the Plymouth colonists of the north are depicted as the moral bedrock of later American development. (The charmingly named settlement of Cupid's Cove preceded the foundation of Plymouth by ten years but as it was located in what became Canada it is no longer considered part of 'American' history.) These hardy New England pioneers, it is said, lived a life of honest labour and devout prayer, at peace with their environment, their native neighbours and their God. Encouraged by their example, an ever-increasing throng of huddled masses followed them from the poverty of Europe to the endless opportunities across the Atlantic.

In reality the colony established at Plymouth in 1620 had virtually no economic or political significance. Life was incredibly hard and, even without the malaria and other perils of Virginia and the Caribbean, colonists died at an alarming rate. Half the settlers died in the first year. The local natives, contrary to later folklore, were not particularly welcoming. Not surprisingly the huddled masses back in Europe did not rush to follow the Plymouth pioneers, although by 1630 the colony had a population of around 1,500.

Nevertheless the mythological and cultural significance of the Pilgrim Fathers is hard to overstate. Every American schoolchild knows how the gallant band of Puritans escaped to religious freedom on the *Mayflower*, endured unimaginable hardships and eventually survived with the help of friendly natives to celebrate the first Thanksgiving in their Promised Land. It is a heartwarming story of faith, endurance, tolerance and above all triumph. Some of it is even true.

In an odd quirk of history the *Mayflower's* first brush with colonialism was not in North America but much closer to home. The English learnt to colonise in their brutal conquest of Ireland at the start of the seventeenth century. The *Mayflower* played an important role in that campaign by ferrying supplies to the English occupying forces in Sligo and Donegal just eighteen years before ferrying the Pilgrim Fathers across the Atlantic.

The *Mayflower* sailed from Plymouth for the New World with a group of fundamentalist Puritans on board. The sect had first moved to Holland, not to escape persecution in England but to escape such mortal sins as alcohol and dance. There they joined forces with French Huguenot refugees worshipping at the Vrouwekerk (Church of Our Lady) in Leiden. They discovered that the Dutch were just as sinful, and decided to move on. Most of those aboard the *Mayflower* (66 of the 110) were not members of the sect and were travelling for a variety of reasons, many of them financial. The Puritans referred to themselves as 'saints' and their fellow travellers as 'strangers'. Once in the New World the divisions between the two groups broke down and the appalling hardships of the first winter bound the settlers together. Less than fifty survived and what happened next has become the stuff of legend.

The traditional story recounts that on 16 March 1621, an Abnaki native strolled into the Plymouth settlement and started chatting in English which he had learnt from English fishermen. He later returned with another native, named Squanto, who claimed to have visited England and Spain.

Squanto was instrumental in helping the Pilgrims to survive. He taught them which plants were poisonous and which had healing powers, how to tap the maples for their sap and above all how to cultivate corn. Their first harvest that October was very successful and the Pilgrims held a three day celebration to which they invited Squanto, the native chieftain Massasoit and nearly a hundred peaceful natives.

The following year the harvest was not as successful but in the third year the harvest was bountiful again and Governor William Bradford ordered a day of celebration on 29 November, thereafter known as Thanksgiving Day.

The facts described in the traditional version of this story are probably correct; even the presence of English-speaking natives at such an early date is quite possible as west country fishermen for long built seasonal camps along the coast. However, the overall impression given in hundreds of school text books is more than a little misleading. What is left out is more important than what is included. The charming story of interracial harmony reflects only one side of the historical coin. The natives soon got tired of making charitable donations to interlopers intent on occupying their land and as a consequence in the second year the Pilgrims ran short of food. What is missing from the conventional myth is that the colonists knew just how to handle uppity 'Indians', not with Christian tolerance but with the tried and tested methods of Spaniard and Virginian. In 1622, just a year after Squanto arrived at their camp, the Pilgrim Fathers invited a larger group of natives to gather for a conciliatory meeting and then attacked them, proving the superiority of muskets over bows and arrows. Seven natives were captured and then ceremonially hanged. Among the seven was the tribal shaman, to whom the Puritans took particular exception. His head was cut off and mounted on top of the fort at Plymouth to demonstrate to the world whose God was the true God. The next year Governor Bradford was able to gather the Pilgrims for the first real Thanksgiving. (This is the same Governor Bradford who described the natives as barbarous, treacherous savages, and fifteen years later was glorying in natives 'frying in the fire' after the Mystic Massacre.)

The Pilgrim Fathers myth is a classic example of selective history, of the way nations use their histories not as photographs with which to capture their pasts but as mirrors in which to see themselves. And if many conventional US histories provide a less than complete picture of the Mayflower colonists' first few years others add an extra dimension: the divine. In these versions Squanto is elevated into 'a special instrument of God' (a description first applied by Plymouth's Governor Bradford). Squanto's story is made to mirror Moses leading the Israelites out of Egypt through plague and famine. What are sometimes described as Squanto's 'visits' to England and Spain are more correctly described as his capture by slave traders and shipment to Europe. There he was bought by monks and converted to Christianity. Returning from captivity, thanks to the generosity of fellow believers in London, Squanto discovered that God had visited the plague on his tribe and their heathen neighbours: 95,000 natives had died, leaving the country almost empty of human habitation. According to one source Squanto realised that his enslavement had been God's way of saving him from a far worse fate. God had chosen him for a divine purpose, and that purpose of course was to show the Pilgrim Fathers the milk and honey of the Promised Land. Truly Squanto was 'God's hand of deliverance'.

It is easy to be cynical about the small and quite atypical group of settlers on the *Mayflower*, but the reality is that they survived appalling hardships that few modern Europeans or Americans would be willing to endure for the sake of their immortal soul. They were characterised not only by the arrogant certainty that they, uniquely, could unlock the gates of heaven but also by the conviction that to do so required effort, both spiritual and physical. They came to America to work. They were not looking for gold to loot or slaves to do their work for them. They positively welcomed the fact that the soil of New England had none of the tropical abundance of colonies further south. Idle hands were the playthings of Satan himself.

The significance of the Pilgrim Fathers legend in American culture is enormous. The story itself and the facts behind it are not important but the underlying messages are. Most, if not all, tribal groups believe they are special, in some way superior to other mortals. They may put this down to something inherent in themselves or to the power of their gods. What the Pilgrim Fathers myth does for Americans is to consolidate both of these beliefs. The Pilgrims, and by extension all Americans, succeeded because they were chosen by God *and* because of honest toil. Americans are the 'chosen people', a model for other nations, and they deserve to be. God chose them not on a capricious whim but in recognition of their own efforts. Many years later the philosophical justification of American imperialism was articulated by John O'Sullivan in the concept of 'manifest destiny': America's god-given destiny was to rule over lesser people. That philosophy can be traced back as far as 1637, and the paradigm shift that occurred in the world view of New England colonists following the Mystic Massacre. But the massacre has been airbrushed from

American history. The sanitised legend of the Pilgrim Fathers provides reassurance that manifest destiny is about the just reward for virtue, not the bloodstained prize of conquest.

Pilgrims and Puritans

Plymouth would have remained an aberration in English colonial history, destined to disappear like other transient colonies springing up from Newfoundland south, but for events in England where king and country were pushing down the road that would end in civil war. Religious fervour was reaching new heights, with Protestant fundamentalists under attack by an increasingly oppressive monarch. The result was a wave of emigration fuelled purely by religion. The arrival of a thousand Puritan settlers in a fleet of seventeen ships to found Boston in 1630, rather than the solitary *Mayflower* reaching the New World in 1620, is the true take-off point in the history of New England.

Technically the term Pilgrim (with a capital P) is reserved for the *Mayflower* colonists. They were separatists, who wanted complete severance from the existing religious orders in England. The later Massachusetts colonists were Puritans, not Pilgrims, who were content to remain within the existing Church but wanted it to be purified. The leader of the Boston settlers, John Winthrop, was particularly concerned that his flock would be corrupted by the pernicious doctrines of the Pilgrim separatists. Purists get very upset when the two groups are confused. President Reagan outraged them by appealing for a return to the values of 'that old Pilgrim John Winthrop'. President Bush I made things worse when, despite claiming to be a descendant of Pilgrims himself, he dedicated a Thanksgiving speech to 'John Winthrop and his fellow pilgrims'. Bush I made his grasp of history even plainer when he went on to refer (in 1992) to the Pilgrims' arrival 'more than a hundred years ago' – nearer four hundred years, actually.

Of the 21,000 migrants who travelled to New England in the seventeenth century, two-thirds arrived in just twelve years between 1630 and the start of the civil war in 1642. During one short period a stream of migrants left England for reasons that had nothing to do with economics, and it is one of the ironies of American history that today their primary legacy is the economic wealth they made possible. These settlers quickly spread out beyond Boston demonstrating a degree of popular energy unknown in the colonies further south. The scale and speed of colonisation was unprecedented. Ten years after the founding of Jamestown Virginia still had an immigrant population of less than four hundred. After forty years Virginia's non-native population was barely more than 13,000. By contrast Winthrop's Massachusetts colony started with a thousand settlers on day one. Thirty years later there were 33,000 settlers living in New England. Within a few years there were vibrant colonies right along the New England coast. Unlike many of the colonies to the south (and the French settlements to the north) these settlements were self-perpetuating. The Puritans arrived as families and bred rapidly. (By 1700 two in five New Englanders were female compared with one in five Virginians.) The colonists relied on their children to help farm the new land rather than constant immigration of indentured servants or slaves.

By the end of the century the New England colonies were clearly the most dynamic of any European colonies anywhere in the world, and the most likely to become a model for developments elsewhere. The reason lies in religion.

Religious fundamentalism is the key to understanding the early history of New England. Most migrants to the south had little or no choice. By contrast the vast majority of those arriving in Boston wanted to be there. Even though they knew that the chances of survival, let alone prospering, were slim, they were prepared to pay significant sums to leave everything that they knew and voyage to a better life. And if God willed that this life would be in heaven rather than on earth so be it. They knew that conditions would be hard, but they were not afraid to join their maker if that is what He ordained. New England was populated by men and women with the religious certainty of today's suicide bombers.

After the initial burst of enthusiasm in the period immediately before the English Civil War there was relatively little further immigration into

New England for the rest of the century. Religion ceased to be a factor in spurring migration from England. Over the next twenty years two-thirds of those migrating from English ports were bound for the West Indies, searching for Mammon not God. Indeed there was reverse migration when the civil war started; some Plymouth colonists returned to important posts in Cromwell's army and government. The Rev. Hugh Peters, the pastor at Salem, Massachusetts, became the chief chaplain in Cromwell's army, and after the restoration of the monarchy under Charles II was executed for his role in the death of King Charles I. (The English Civil War in some ways prefigured the American Civil War, as New England Puritans returned to fight with the Roundheads and Virginia welcomed escaping Cavaliers. In one of the most obscure battles in American history northern Puritans defeated southern Royalists in the battle of the Severn near Annapolis, Maryland, in 1655.)

The sudden wave of immigration between 1630 and 1642 was radically different to anything seen before or after, and it was the nature of this wave that made the new colonies that were to spring up on the north-east coast fundamentally different to all the others. By the end of the century there were two sets of English colonies in the Americas, which, if it were not for their common language, would have been as different from each other as Afghanistan and Zanzibar.

It is only a slight oversimplification to say that there were three very distinct classes of migrants to most of the colonies outside New England: poor whites, slaves and a minority of the rich. The history of these colonies is the history of the relationship of these classes. While to say that New England had only one class really would be an oversimplification it would not be grossly misleading. And the class that dominated New England was none of the above three. New England was colonised by, and for, what today would be called the middle class. The promoters of the Virginia Company were rich London merchants and lawyers who became even richer by staying at home and sending shiploads of 'sturdy beggars' and slaves out to make money for them. The promoters of the Massachusetts Bay Company were certainly wealthy but they wanted more than profits;

they wanted the key to heaven, and they believed that the key could be found on the other side of the Atlantic – so they themselves had to be 'on board', quite literally. Promoters like John Winthrop travelled with the migrants and ran the company from Boston. The promoters and other migrants took the same risks, had the same objectives and shared the same interests. (The Pilgrim Fathers were actually an exception: the *Mayflower* was financed by the London company of Merchant Adventurers to whom its passengers were indentured for their first seven years in the New World. The Plymouth colony was a commercial enterprise more typical of Virginia and the south than the later religious settlements in New England. *Mayflower* colonists socially were also more typical of the other English colonies: Bradford, their leader, was a cloth worker whereas Winthrop, the Governor of Massachusetts, was a lawyer.)

These were not religious liberals seeking freedom of religion. The rigorously enforced laws prohibiting work, play or even travel on the Sabbath were redolent more of today's fundamentalist Islam or Judaism than of mainstream Christianity. The Puritan migrants were Calvinist zealots who made it clear that heretics such as Anglicans or Baptists were not welcome in their colony. Nor were they content to wait until Judgement Day to witness the wrath of God in such cases. Quakers were regarded as a particular threat, being a sect that 'tends to overthrow the whole gospell & the very vitalls of Christianitie'. On 19 October 1659 Mary Dyer, Marmaduke Stephenson and William Robinson were 'convicted for Quakers' in Massachusetts and led to the gallows with ropes around their necks. Stephenson and Robinson were duly hanged, but Mary Dyer was spared after pleas from the governors of Connecticut and Nova Scotia. Dyer, however, refused to be banished. On 1 June 1660 she was led to the gallows once again and this time was dispatched to her maker. (Unlike Europe the scaffold rather than the stake was the preferred method of execution even for heretics and witches, although hanging at that time meant being hung from a gibbet and slowly and painfully strangled; the 'long drop' hanging – in which the victim died quickly as his or her neck was broken – was introduced much later.) Anyone suspected of communing with the devil faced the hangman's rope. In one case, when a piglet was born with a face that seemed to resemble its owner's, the farmer was hanged, and for good measure so was the sow with which he had so obviously enjoyed carnal relations. The Salem witch trials were only the most famous examples of the Puritans' extreme religious beliefs. Their society was closer to the Iran of the Ayatollahs than to America today.

Like socialist dogmatism in Russia two centuries later, the Puritan dogmatism of the New England settlers was beset by sectarianism. Groups fractured along bitter ideological fault lines comprehensible only to themselves. The abundance of 'empty' land populated only by heathen natives made it easy for dissenting groups to strike out on their own and found new settlements. Although Massachusetts remained the heartland, more conservative sects founded colonies in Connecticut while others moved north to assert control over the fishing settlements being set up by less religiously fixated settlers in Maine and New Hampshire.

Only Rhode Island demonstrated any real signs of the religious tolerance for which America was later to pride itself. Its founder, the dissident Roger Williams, was expelled from Massachusetts in the middle of a bitter winter in 1636. His heresy was to proclaim that religion was a matter of personal conscience; that, as he put it, 'forced worship stinks in God's nostrils'. Rhode Island became the one beacon of religious freedom in a sea of competing orthodoxies as the small colony became home for the rejects from its neighbours. Not only did various Protestant sects coexist but the colony's toleration extended to a small Jewish group. (The history of Jews in America is one example, like English Quakers and various continental European sects, where the early immigrants were genuine refugees escaping persecution. The first Jewish migrants to North America came from South America. A small group of Dutch Jews had settled in the Dutch colony in what is now Brazil. When the colony was seized by the Portuguese the Jews felt the full force of Catholic fundamentalism, and to escape burning at the stake they fled north.)

As time went by religious discrimination became less severe but did not disappear. Anglicans tempted to work or travel on the Sabbath were liable to be arrested and fined by their more puritanical neighbours. Religious dissenters might not be burnt at the stake but other ways were found to exclude them from society; one method of suppressing dissent prefigured a tactic much used in Russia. The Rev. James Davenport, a Yale graduate and great-grandson of one of New England's first Puritan clergymen, provoked a furious reaction with his brand of evangelical fundamentalism. He preached against the iniquities of wigs, jewellery and fine clothes, and with his followers organised the burning of books whose contents he deemed offensive. In 1742 he was arrested in Connecticut, tried, declared insane and banished. He promptly moved to Massachusetts only to be rearrested, retried and declared *non compos mentis* again. Two years later Davenport gave up and recanted his 'errors'; he went on to become Moderator of the Synod in New York. A century later Pyotr Chaadayev, the first great radical Russian philosopher, was declared insane after criticising autocracy, serfdom and the Orthodox Church, and under Stalin the 'Davenport' method of suppressing dissent was to be employed on a horrific scale.

Between God and Slave

After the southern and New England colonies were established an eclectic group of four colonies appeared between them: New York, Pennsylvania, Maryland and Delaware.

Catholics were one religious group who found no welcome in New England. At the same time as thousands of Puritans were escaping from what they regarded as the dangerously papist practices of the Anglican Church of Charles I, others fled for exactly the opposite reason. A year after the *Mayflower* the Catholic George Calvert, the first Lord Baltimore, set sail for the New World and founded the colony of Avalon in Newfoundland. The settlement was not a success, and after George's death his son Cecilius, the second Lord Baltimore, decided to try again further south, and dispatched his younger brother Leonard. In 1634 the

Ark and the Dove landed in Maryland. Among the two hundred religious refugees on board were two Jesuit priests, who had been smuggled aboard before leaving England and who on arrival recited on their bended knees the Litanies of the Sacred Cross. The physical climate in Maryland was more hospitable than Newfoundland, but the same could not be said for the religious climate. The two ships contained Catholic and Protestant colonists but the new colony soon developed a Protestant majority, which resented the power wielded by Calvert's Catholic cronies. In 1689, when the Dutch king William seized the English throne in a *coup d'état* (the 'Glorious Revolution'), Maryland's Protestants seized the opportunity to mount an armed coup of their own, and America's first attempt at religious pluralism outside Rhode Island ended as Catholics lost the right to vote and hold office.

The Dutch settlements on the Hudson welcomed European settlers of almost any persuasion, and when they were captured by the British in 1664 added yet another facet to colonial life. New Netherland became the state of New York. New Amsterdam became the city of New York, and its enterprising burghers were soon making their presence felt in the commercial life of British North America.

The Quaker William Penn founded Pennsylvania. The first settlers there, largely English Quakers and Germans escaping from their war-torn homelands, were distinctive for their relatively civilised treatment of the natives. Even here, however, the exigencies of ethnic cleansing won out when a group arrived in the colony with a very different view of life. In the 1690s Scottish Protestants had been 'planted' in Ireland, particularly in Ulster, to help the English tame what was effectively the first English colony. Ireland was not the Promised Land, however, and many 'Scotch-Irish' moved further west, to the frontiers of Pennsylvania. These new settlers had no truck with Penn's pacifism. They had learnt how to deal with unruly natives in Ireland and followed the same tactics in their new home – stealing, intimidating and killing those whose land they were determined to take over. Those who claimed to know better, including Penn's own family, soon joined them. After William Penn's death his son Thomas led a famously audacious land grab. Having agreed with the local natives to buy a piece of land as big as a man could walk around in a day, Penn had a special trail cleared through the forest and then used trained runners to sprint along it. When the natives refused to hand over the enormous territory Penn had thus gained he employed Iroquois mercenaries to enforce the 'agreement'.

The strangest colony to emerge on the eastern seaboard was named after an English lord, founded by Dutch entrepreneurs based in Sweden and populated largely by Finns.

The Finns are one of the oldest races in Europe, so perhaps some background would be helpful here. At the height of their power some 8,000 years ago these Ural-Altaic peoples dominated a vast land from Mongolia to the Baltic and, according to some, introduced hieroglyphic writing to Egypt. Some Ural-Altaic tribes, like the Finns, settled down, while others erupted in streams of conquest (the last of these to pillage their way west only stopped when their leader Attila was defeated at Châlons). Over time their territory was taken by other groups, especially the Slavs, and their people and languages absorbed, so that in Europe today only the Finns, Estonians and Hungarians remain. The Finns were pushed westward by Slavs expanding to form Russia. In one version of the legend surrounding the founding of Russia, Finns and Slavs joined together to invite Rurik to rule over and protect them. In this version the term Rus comes from the Finnish ruotsaa, meaning to row, the means of propulsion used by Vikings on the rivers of their new domain.

In 1157 another Viking king invaded Finland, but by then the Vikings were no longer pagan barbarians. A mysterious Scottish bishop named Henry accompanied King Erik Jedwardson and, by judicious use of his patron's sword, converted the Finns to Christianity. At the same time King Erik brought the Finns firmly into Sweden's orbit, so that when, at the end of the sixteenth century, the Finns found themselves once again under attack from the Slavs, this time Poles, it was natural for many Finns to move west themselves. Between 1600 and 1650 numerous Finnish settlements sprang up in Sweden, but not everyone welcomed the immigrants. While the Swedish king Gustavus Adolphus used Finnish troops in his conquests across Europe, at home their families were being massacred. A way of solving this 'Finnish problem' was suggested by a man named Peter Minuit.

The first American colonies owed their creation to a small number of energetic men, ranging from the godly to the godless. Peter Minuit was not at the godly end of the spectrum, and is perhaps most charitably described as an entrepreneur. He is known today as the man who bought Manhattan from the natives for a handful of shells, a Dutchman who had been appointed Governor of New Netherland but had fallen out with its proprietor, the Dutch West India Company. Minuit persuaded Swedish leaders not only to allow him and a group of Dutch 'promoters' to set up a colony under the Swedish flag but to put up half of the funds as well. This colony was the ideal place to send surplus Finns, and a trading post was established on the Delaware river in 1638. Minuit himself disappeared in the Caribbean, and neither he nor his ship were ever seen again, but his idea had taken hold on the imagination of his Swedish partners. In 1643 New Sweden was established, populated largely by Finns.

The colony prospered, and soon Finns were petitioning the queen to be allowed to emigrate. In 1655 the Dutch seized the colony but were soon replaced by the English (who, always alive to commercial possibilities, sold the Dutch garrison to Virginia planters as cheap labour for their fields). Eventually the English colony of Delaware came into formal existence.

(The role of Finns in the intertwined histories of Russia and America deserves a book of its own. One of the most curious chapters occurred during the Depression of the 1920s. Stalin decided that Finnish-Americans presented a potentially useful pool of talent and sent recruiters to encourage emigration from the promised land of the past to the promised land of the future. They presented such a rosy picture of life in Russian Karelia that some 25,000 are thought to have sailed east, only to discover that conditions were no better on the other side of the Atlantic. Stalin was unimpressed by their complaints and shipped them off to the gulags.)

The colonies to the north of Chesapeake Bay, in a great swathe from Delaware up to Newfoundland, differed significantly one from another, but they differed much more profoundly from the colonies further south. By the middle of the eighteenth century the northern colonies were developing the heterogeneity of cultures – German, Dutch, Scandinavian, as well as British – and the economic dynamism that would become such a feature of later American history. Economic prosperity depended on trade and expanding markets, and that brought with it more toleration of the religion and cultures of others. That tolerance extended to toleration of the intolerable. Slavery still formed the bedrock of life in British North America. New England's economic well-being depended on providing supplies to the Caribbean colonies, and it soon became home to one of the world's largest merchant fleets, benefiting enormously from the British Navigation Acts, which decreed that only British ships could carry cargo to and from its colonies (and British included New English). As well as protecting their commerce from Dutch and other competitors, the American colonies depended on a British army willing to protect it from the French to the north, the Spanish to the south and hostile natives to the west. Safe behind barriers of tariffs and gunpowder, the English colonies started to prosper.

With wealth came power. Whereas in the early days the English colonial heart lay in the West Indies, it now moved to the mainland. Boston assumed a commanding position controlling the mercantile wealth of all the English colonies, but it was later overtaken by the more cosmopolitan New York. Philadelphia too grew in importance as it took over from Boston the role of provisioner to the southern and Caribbean colonies, being both closer to them and to the more fertile farmlands of Pennsylvania.

Ostentatious displays of wealth began to characterise the cities of the north as much as the grand plantations of the south. The elites aped European culture and started to develop their own. Harvard was founded in 1636, but civilisation was a fragile flower. Forty years later, and only a few miles from Harvard, the new colonists showed another side of their character, demonstrating their continuing intolerance for anyone who crossed the line that separated the godly from the godless.

Joshua Tift made the mistake of quite literally going native. He married a native woman and went to live with her family. Furious Puritans raided their village and captured Tift. What happened then is open to dispute. One respected historian has recently described how the settlers tied Tift's limbs to horses and tore him apart. Another version claims that he was hanged, taken down before he died, cut open and forced to watch his entrails and genitals burning before being beheaded. His body was then cut into four parts and his head displayed on a stake. Whatever the precise form of his death, it was an act of savagery Ivan the Terrible would have understood all too well.

Such acts are not what the early colonists are remembered for. The first English settlers are held up not as exemplars of tsarist-style savagery but as the forerunners of modern democracy. In 1893 historian Frederick Turner argued, in his enormously influential work *The Significance of the Frontier in American History*, that a limitless supply of free land occupied only by insignificant natives led almost inevitably to the values of equality and democracy that form the bedrock of the American political culture. It was the westward expansion of the American frontier, he argued, that ensured that Americans developed the individualism that he thought was the hallmark of American democracy. Proponents of the 'Turner Thesis' argue that the ever-present frontier allowed those dissatisfied with their lot to move on, and so those that remained did so only by consent. That consent was achieved through the granting of personal liberty, individual rights and democracy. At the same time those who moved to the frontiers and beyond were demonstrating the spirit of independence and self-reliance that is the natural corollary of democracy. Later American experience may lend support to this thesis, but the history of the first American colonies presents quite a different picture. In the south, the presence of the frontier made more territory available not for the creation of democracy but for the expansion of slavery. In the north, those moving to the frontiers were not yearning for freedom but were as often dedicated to the theocratic suppression of liberty.

A clearer vindication of the Turner Thesis occurred on the other side of the world. On the wilderness frontiers of southern Russia in the fifteenth and sixteenth centuries disgruntled serfs, escaping criminals and soldiers who had ended up on the losing side created their own society beyond the arm of tsarist autocracy. These horsemen of the steppes were the nearest Russia ever produced to the noble frontiersman and gunfighters of American legend. Eventually their descendants were reabsorbed into Russian society, inspiring hero worship among their compatriots while enemies cowered at the very thought of their name. They were the Cossacks. Thanks to them, Russia would expand to the Pacific at a pace that America would never come close to matching.

CHAPTER 5

RUSSIA BETWEEN WEST AND EAST

History is made up of words, and the nuances of history are determined by the words chosen to describe the events of the past. Russians seized and settled the region on the eastern Baltic coast where the city of St Petersburg now stands just as the English seized and settled the region on the western Atlantic coast where Boston now stands. The settlement of St Petersburg was on an altogether larger scale, and history books talk not of the 'settlement' of Livonia but of its 'conquest'. Nobody talks about the conquest of New England. The creation of the American empire was hidden behind other words. America expanded not by conquest but by 'settlement' or 'colonisation' or, occasionally, by 'annexation'. Russia conquered its way to empire; America merely grew.

America advanced slowly to the Pacific, exploiting the rich resources it found by planting its own natives to replace those already there. Russia advanced to the Pacific more rapidly and found a land that was largely inhospitable; to gain other resources it had to look elsewhere – to 'conquests' in the south and west. Whatever the terminology used, the imperatives that drove Russia to conquer territory in its paths to the Baltic and the Black Sea were the same that drove it to seize the barren lands of Siberia. In the same way the imperatives that drove America westward were the same that led it to attack Canada or annexe Florida from the Spanish. Settling New England and Livonia; annexing Texas and

Turkistan; occupying California and Chechnya: all were manifestations of the same desire to push forward the wild frontiers.

Yermak Timofeyevich: King of the Wild Frontier

Children's tastes are fickle. This year's must-have toy is next year's embarrassing antique. Fads are created and, once their full commercial value has been extracted, they are lost in the dark corners of childhood memory, only to be resurrected much later as sepia-tinted nostalgia.

In 1955 the annual craze was manufactured by Walt Disney with a new television show. Some of the episodes were not long enough, so to pad them out the scriptwriter wrote a song. He had never written a song before, but in just twenty minutes he and a colleague produced words and music; in six months 7 million copies were sold. No record had ever sold so fast. It seemed that every child in the English-speaking world was singing endlessly about 'the land of the free' and its hero, Davy Crockett, 'King of the Wild Frontier'.

A relatively obscure nineteenth-century politician had been turned into a national hero. Within weeks parents were buying Davy Crockett watches, guitars, toothbrushes and lunchboxes. The trademark coonskin cap became obligatory for the street cred of every six-year-old boy (the price of raccoon reportedly leapt from 25 cents a pound to $8 a pound). A year later the craze was over. Television's Davy Crockett had died heroically at the Alamo and actor Fess Parker was off to pastures new, eventually becoming one of California's top winemakers. But the folk-memory remained; a genuine national hero had been created. His name became synonymous with a virile patriotism, so that when the US army decided the next year that XM-388 was not the most gripping of names for its new wonder-weapon, a tiny nuclear warhead that could be fired from a recoilless rifle, they chose to call it the Davy Crockett. (As if to illustrate that the American attitude to foreigners had remained unchanged since Davy Crockett's days, critics concerned about nuclear fallout were told not to worry: the Davy Crockett would stop the Russians in their tracks – and so would only ever be used in Europe, well away from America.)

The equivalent figure to Crockett in Russian mythology is Yermak Timofeyevich, a frontiersman and explorer who preceded Crockett to a martyr's death by 250 years. Yermak's name has remained as commercially potent as Crockett's (one of Moscow's leading restaurants is named after him today), and he has the same heroic significance in the folk-memory of his nation. When the Russian navy commissioned the world's first true icebreaker in 1898, Admiral Makarov named it Yermak. Yermak even has his own song, the tune of which is known to millions of Russians, although unlike Davy Crockett's his is a genuine folk song. Yermak symbolises the coming of age of Russia, and in this too he parallels Crockett. America formed as a collection of dissimilar colonies, uniting in conflict with a distant empire, and then cementing themselves together in a massive expansion that eventually reached the Pacific. Crockett represented that post-colonial frontier spirit when for the first time it became meaningful to speak of 'America' as a nation state. Yermak did just the same for Russia, appearing on the stage of history at a critical point when Russia, having shrunk from the glories of Kievan Rus to the Mongol-dependent Duchy of Muscovy, finally became recognisably 'Russia'.

Muscovy had been just one of many principalities into which the kingdom of the Rus fractured before and after the Mongol invasion. In 1300 it covered more than 7,500 square miles. When Ivan III, Ivan the Great, mounted the throne in 1462 he inherited 166,000 square miles. The secret of Muscovy's astonishing growth was sycophancy; when the khan growled Muscovy grovelled. Such obeisance was rewarded with grants of land and authority. Muscovy not only provided the Mongols with taxes and troops raised from its own lands but also collected taxes from neighbouring princes for the khan. When those princes could not pay the Muscovite princes they first lent them money at usurious rates and then foreclosed on the debts. Not for nothing was Ivan I known as Ivan Moneybags.

When the Mongols finally conceded power in Russia they left no state behind them. Their immediate successors were not monarchs in the sense that the Tudors were monarchs on the other side of Europe. They were warlords whose rule extended as far as their military might; their borders moved from year to year with the vicissitudes of battle. Ivan III may have employed Italian architects to remodel Moscow, and Ivan IV, Ivan the Terrible, may have crowned himself Caesar and styled his capital the Third Rome, successor to the glories of Constantinople, but few western visitors would have shared their vision. Indeed at that time Russia was not even part of Europe, as Peter the Great's court cartographer had yet to move the frontier of Europe east to the Urals. To European monarchs Ivan the Terrible was another barbarian despot who threatened from the east, a bothersome but fortunately unsuccessful invader. This view reflected an innate sense of superiority in the west that was not entirely fair; when Ivan came to the throne his realms were already larger than England, France and Spain put together. But the west's condescension seemed justified by their own military strength and by the weakness of Ivan. That Russia was an alien land with a king some way below the standards of western Europe was made very obvious in 1571 when Devlet Giray, the Muslim khan of Crimea, one of the Mongol successor states, sacked Moscow and captured thousands of Slavs to be carried off as slaves.

Ivan the Terrible needed lands to conquer. Warlords by definition live by war. He could wreak continual terror on his duchy and pass his fearsome reputation on to his heirs, but sooner or later someone more warlike would wrest the crown from his family. He needed external success. Yermak Timofeyevich provided that success, although not in the way Ivan had expected.

In looking for territory to conquer, Muscovy was torn between attacking a prosperous 'civilised' Europe to the west or the crumbling remnants of the Mongol empire to the east. Ivan's preference, like most of his successors, was to go for the richer target rather than the easier, but in the long-running Livonian wars he was outclassed by the Poles and Swedes. In frustration he turned to the south and east. He attacked and destroyed the Tartar khanates of Kazan and Astrakhan. In doing so he doubled the size of his kingdom, pushing down the Volga to the Caspian. In terms of land and people, if not in wealth, the conquest of Kazan represented a step change (indeed a steppe change) in the fortunes of the Grand Duchy.

The seeds of empire were planted on the warm shores of the Caspian Sea but their most dramatic growth was in a far colder climate. One of the world's greatest ever imperial adventures started almost by accident. Countermanding his own earlier instructions, Ivan gave his blessing to a military expedition east across the Urals. Leading the way was Yermak Timofoyevich. Like Davy Crockett, Yermak is revered as an intrepid explorer who went where no white man had gone before (or in Crockett's case at least no non-Hispanic); like Crockett he took it for granted that whatever he found was his – even if the natives disagreed; like Crockett he died a heroic death; like Crockett he is commemorated today as a representative of all that is noble in the nation's past.

Other nations have heroic martyrs who died pushing forward the boundaries of nation and empire. But whereas the iconic status of Gordon of Khartoum in Britain, for example, faded as imperialism lost its seal of popular approval, in America and Russia the hero-worship lavished on the champions of expansionism remains undimmed. What most of these heroes have in common is that the reality differed from the legend.

Crockett's tombstone reads 'Davy Crockett, Pioneer, Patriot, Soldier, Trapper, Explorer, State Legislator, Congressman.' The order should perhaps be reversed. Crocket spent much of his adult life as a professional politician. He used ghost-writers to burnish the frontiersman image as a hardy pioneer and bear hunter. That image helped him to progress from the Tennessee Legislature to the US Congress; Crockett was one of the first Americans to appreciate the value of PR and spin. In turn that spin, enormously magnified by the magic of Disney, is what now constitutes popular history. But the crux of the Crockett legend is true. He did survive the perils of a dangerous frontier – his grandparents were killed in a native attack when his father was away fighting the British – and his major claim to fame during his lifetime was as a commander in the Creek Indian War. (For one group, though, Davy Crockett is famous for something entirely different: to etymologists he is the man who invented the word 'blizzard'.) Above all Davy Crockett died at the Alamo trying to push the frontiers of Anglo-Saxon America further still. Recent research suggests that rather than fighting to the end gun in hand, as legend has it, Crockett and his companions were killed after they had surrendered. Whatever the truth Americans are right to believe that he largely embodied the virtues of independence and freedom under the law (at least for adult white males) which they have long cherished.

In that respect Yermak was totally dissimilar.

In the years after his death Yermak was quickly raised to the pantheon of heroes. He was described as a brave, intelligent and humane conqueror who crossed the Urals to subdue the pagan natives for the greater glory of God and Muscovy. Much of this is nonsense. Yermak was a Cossack freebooter who made his living by following his family into a life of crime, leading a gang of river pirates on the Volga. Chased by troops sent to protect the river shipping, he and his men escaped into the Siberian wilderness.

Russian settlement east of the Urals had started in 1517 when the Stroganovs, a leading Boyar family, were granted a royal charter to mine iron and salt. Once in Siberia, Yermak seems to have operated a protection racket offering to protect the Stroganovs from himself and from the natives. History has taken the rough edges of this part of Yermak's life. One American academic source relates prosaically that Yermak 'entered the service of a merchant family, the Stroganovs' who 'sent Yermak on an expedition to protect their lands in Western Siberia from attack by local tribes'. Yermak's idea of 'protecting' the nascent Russian colonies was strikingly similar to Underhill's approach to 'defending' the nascent English and Dutch colonies. The best form of defence is attack.

Yermak faced a more formidable opponent than the unsuspecting natives of Mystic. Although Ivan had conquered two of the khanates into which the Mongol empire had fragmented, two others stood in the way of his further expansion: Crimea, to the south and the east, and what is today called Siberia – and the city of Sibir and its khan, Kuchum. By medieval standards Sibir was relatively civilised: it exacted tribute from the pagan tribes around it and Kuchum himself read Arabic, although with over a hundred wives he may have had little time for reading. He felt powerful enough to refuse to pay tributes to Muscovy, and Ivan agreed with him, nervously ordering the Stroganovs to stop fomenting trouble with the Siberian chieftain and specifically to halt the practice of hiring criminal mercenaries. However, both Ivan and Kuchum had underestimated the military strength of the Cossack freebooters, and in particular their technological superiority. As the native Americans were discovering on the other side of the world the bow and arrow were no match for the musket and cannon.

Yermak paid no more attention to Ivan's desires in Siberia than he had back on the Volga. And when Yermak captured Kuchum's capital of Isker, Ivan promptly forgot his previous misgivings. Yermak found a treasure trove of furs and sent samples to Moscow. Ivan, licking his wounds after the Livonian wars, was overjoyed. Yermak was pardoned for all his former crimes and reinforcements were dispatched eastwards. Unfortunately conditions had changed dramatically by the time they arrived: Yermak was pinned down in Isker and the arrival of new troops only made matters worse. Soon they were reduced to eating human flesh to stay alive. By then Ivan had died a lingering death. Yermak's death came more quickly. Leading a skirmishing party, he had camped on a river island thinking that the water provided ample protection. He was wrong. Kuchum's warriors forded the river and attacked the sleeping invaders. Legend has it that in a cruel twist of fate Ivan himself was responsible for Yermak's death. Among the gifts Ivan had lavished on his new-found hero were two chain-mail coats bearing bronze double-headed eagles. Seeing his men cut down, Yermak fought his way to the water and tried grab a boat in order to escape, but, weighed down by Ivan's two tunics, he drowned.

Only one survivor made it back to Isker, and when he brought news of Yermak's death the remaining Russians abandoned the town and retreated home.

The Eastern Frontier

Yermak died in August 1585. In the same month a group of settlers landed on Roanoke Island in Chesapeake Bay. The hostility of the natives and lack of supplies sent them packing ten months later, but they took back to England tales of Virginia's rich natural resources, not least in the impressively accurate work of a young settler named Tomas Hariot, whose *Briefe and True Report of the New Found Land of Virginia* was published in Frankfurt in 1590. Reports like Hariot's gripped the imagination of western Europe, encouraging further adventures to the west.

Similarly Yermak's exploits seized the imagination of eastern Europe. His initial success had shown not only what wealth lay beyond the Urals but how easy it was for that wealth to be looted. Soon Russians in far greater numbers were heading east. They eventually cornered and decisively defeated Kuchum in a battle on the river Ob. Eighteen of his wives and daughters and five of his sons were captured. Kuchum himself escaped south and sought refuge with his allies, the Nogais, who, sensing how the balance of power was shifting, murdered him.

Isker was reoccupied, and when Kuchum's successor was hawking nearby he and his courtiers were invited in for talks. Their food and drink were drugged and the whole group was massacred. It was a tactic used thirty years later by the English settlers in Virginia (and after them by the Puritans of New England), and for the Russians was stunningly successful. With the destruction of the Sibir khanate there was no organised army anywhere in the vast territory that stretched, in a broad band between the Arctic Ocean and the Mongolian steppe, all the way to the Pacific.

No sooner had the bodies of Yermak and Kuchum been laid to rest than the forces of popular prejudice started rewriting their stories. Reality gave way to myth, parts of which then resurfaced as accepted historical fact. In the folk tales of the victorious Cossacks Yermak acquired magical powers, and seemed to have developed the ability to travel through time: in some stories he appeared as an Arthurian knight in ancient Rus; in others he fought not the Sibir but the Turks who had ravaged Constantinople. On the other side Anna Reid reports that among the native Tartars history was inverted completely, and Yermak appeared in their ballads as Kuchum's sly servant-boy.

As has happened frequently in Russia the selective rewriting of history was led from the top. Tsars recognised the value of the Yermak story and to the Soviets he was the perfect hero; they attached his name to everything from a power station to whole towns. As happened time and again in Russian history the Church occupied the myth-manufacturing role played in America by Disney and Hollywood. Archbishop Kipriyan of Tobolsk, Siberia's first prelate, declared Yermak a saint and commissioned histories that portrayed Yermak receiving divine guidance, conversing with Christ and working miracles. Once established, the myth became fact. Tales of the martyred Yermak and his noble conquests were passed on in the storytelling of illiterate serfs and the nursery games of the nobility. Just before his death Pushkin was planning an epic poem on the theme. Alexander Kasyanov's opera Yermak premiered in 1957 and in 1996 Viktor Stepanov took the title role in the epic film of the same name. The power of Yermak's image as the embodiment of Russian virtue persists. The film-maker Vladimir Menshov has said of his film version of *Yermak*, 'Our intent was to create the image of a strong Russian man who could make decisions. We wanted to offset the sense of humiliation which has characterised the nation since the Soviet Union broke up.' Yermak represents for Russians just the sort of virile patriotism Crockett has represented for Americans.

Although Yermak's raid ended in his death and Ivan's initial conquests beyond the Urals were small their importance was enormous. Ivan the Terrible's greatest legacy was the concept of empire. He turned a Muscovy obsessed with self-preservation into a Russia determined on conquest. It could be said that in Ivan's reign Russians brought the frontier spirit that was to so characterise America to the plains and forests of Asia. Russians raced across Siberia at an amazing speed. In 1639 Ivan Moskvitin reached the Pacific, just fifty-eight years after Yermak had crossed the Urals. Although Russian colonisation of Siberia and English colonisation of North America started at the same time, Moskvitin had traversed the much larger continent 166 years before Lewis and Clark reached the same ocean from the other side. In less than a century Russia had conquered a third of Asia.

The conquest of North America has been commemorated in so many films that it is easy to forget that the scale of the Russian achievement was so much larger. Siberia is vast. The whole of the continental United States could be placed in the middle without touching any of its edges; indeed the whole of western Europe could then be crammed into the margins and still leave space to spare. Not only were the distances travelled by the early pioneers so much longer, but the conditions they encountered were very much more extreme. The white man's arrival in Siberia at the end of the sixteenth century had more in common with the American expeditions of the Spanish conquistadors at the beginning of the same century than with the far less adventurous exploits of the Anglo-Americans in the two centuries that followed. For example, Vasily Poyarkov mounted a 4,000-mile expedition to the mouth of the Amur river. He returned, but most of his men did not; those that did not starve to death were killed by natives. Semyon Dezhnov's expedition suffered a similar fate: only twelve of the ninety who set out returned. Dezhnov became the first European to find the North-East Passage between America and Asia in 1656, but news of the discovery did not reach Moscow.

The first person credited with proving that Asia and America were not linked arrived in Siberia in the next century, and demonstrated both the amazing achievements of the Russian explorers and the scale of the efforts that the Russian tsars, and in particular Peter the Great, who came to the throne in 1689, threw into imperial expansion. Vitus Jonassen Bering was born in Denmark in 1681. In 1703 he emigrated to Russia and enlisted in the new Russian navy. He distinguished himself during Russia's war with Sweden, and in 1725 was chosen by Peter to lead an expedition in search of the North-East Passage. First Bering had to get men and supplies across Siberia to Okhotsk, which they reached two years after leaving St Petersburg; then he built a ship to carry them to the Kamchatka peninsula, and once there constructed another, *Gabriel*, on which, in the summer of 1728, Bering finally sailed north through what we now call the Bering Strait. On 13 August he rounded the north-east corner of Asia. Bering was convinced that he had sailed far enough north to establish that Asia and North America were not connected, proving the existence of the North-East Passage, but when, five years after leaving, he returned to St Petersburg he was criticised for not actually having seen the American coast – which had been shrouded in fog and so invisible to the expedition.

Three years later Bering left his wife and family for the last time. The Great Nordic Expedition may well have been the largest scientific expedition the world knew before the start of space exploration. Bering led 10,000 men, intending not only to chart the coasts of Siberia and America as far south as Mexico but also to establish Russian imperial claims to as much territory as possible. He planned to send ships to America and Japan to promote Russian commercial interests and to carry out a whole range of scientific research. After again spending two years reaching Okhotsk, Bering spent the next six years exploring Siberia before sailing eastward in 1741 and at last sighting the St Elias mountains on the northern Gulf of Alaska coast on 16 July. Conditions were appalling, and on the way back Bering collapsed with scurvy. The decision was made to seek shelter for the winter on an isolated island off the coast of Kamchatka, huddled in huts made from driftwood dug into the sand. A week before Christmas 1741 Bering died. A few survivors reached home the next summer, carrying news of Bering's momentous discovery.

In sheer determination, endurance and courage Bering's expedition far outclassed that of Columbus, but its historical importance was far less. After his death Bering was largely forgotten, although in one way he mirrored Columbus: his body continued to travel. In 1991 the graves of Bering and five of his companions were excavated. The remains were taken to Moscow for examination. Forensic scientists modelled Bering's head before he and his crew returned, to be reburied on what is now called Bering Island.

Bering was a true explorer, but like the Spanish conquistadors the early Cossack adventurers were less explorers than exploiters. They were looking for precious metals, furs and tribute and had no particular interest in exploration for its own sake. Indeed Dezhnev's amazing discovery of the North-East Passage seventy-five years before Bering would have remained unknown had not one of Bering's scientists found his papers in the Siberian city of Yakutsk.

Above all the Cossacks wanted furs. At its peak in the middle of the seventeenth century fur was Russia's second most important industry. Only agriculture created more wealth, and agriculture provided nothing to compare with the get-rich-quick opportunities in the Siberian fur trade. Beaver, wolf, squirrel, marten, bear and above all sable provided enormous wealth to those who could seize it. By the end of the seventeenth century fur-bearing animals were facing extinction in large parts of Siberia, and this, combined with the new competition from the Hudson Bay Company, drove Russian hunters into ever more inaccessible parts of the continent, making the whole of Siberia theirs. As in America at the same time only one thing stood in their way: the native inhabitants. And just as on the other side of the Pacific the battle between the interlopers and the interloped was entirely one-sided. The fate of the Siberian and American natives is uncannily similar. Guns and germs were the cornerstones of conquest. In their violence the Russian colonisers again mirrored the Spanish conquistadors. Pyotr Golovin, who arrived in the Sakha country in 1640, not only terrified the natives but his own Cossack troops, who petitioned the tsar for his removal, claiming that he had tortured them and their wives: impaling, blinding, pulling out veins and putting recalcitrant troops in giant heated frying pans. Forty years later the still rebellious Sakha rose up under their chief Dzhenik, the Russian Geronimo. But whereas Geronimo was eventually captured and shipped off to a reservation, when Dzhenik was captured he was flayed alive and, perhaps not apocryphally, his newborn son was suffocated in his still-warm skin.

Until they reached the borders of China the Russians faced none of the formidable military forces they were to face later as they expanded west, but they did face resistance. For example, the Buryats, a Mongol people living along what are now the borders of Russia and Mongolia, held them up for over thirty years. The first Russian outpost in Buryat territory, built at Bratsk on the Angara river in 1631, survived just three years before its garrison was massacred. The Buryat wars drained Russian resources but an uneasy peace was finally imposed, broken by a serious revolt in the mid-1690s and scattered insurgency well into the next century.

Yermak and his successors fought their way east with amazing brutality, but the main killer was disease, especially smallpox, syphilis and influenza. Anna Reid describes the effect on the tribes she studied: 'The first epidemic – probably of smallpox – of which records survive broke out in 1630 and may have killed as many as half of all Khant, Mansi, Nenets and Ket. In the 1650s smallpox crossed the Yenisey, killing up to 80 per cent of the northern Evenk and Sakha, and nearly half the Yukagir. In the early eighteenth century it reached Kamchatka, cutting a swathe through the Itelmen and Koryak. Syphilis was a slower killer. Widespread among Russian settlers – no true Sibiryak, it was said, possessed a fully intact nose – it quickly spread to the indigenous people.' The plagues continued right through the nineteenth century. Smallpox epidemics in 1884 and 1889 killed almost a third of the population in parts of Siberia, although by now it struck European and native alike. It is an odd coincidence of history that at exactly the same time (the late 1630s) smallpox killed around 50 per cent of the Khant (a western Siberian tribe closely related to modern Finns and Estonians), and around 50 per cent of the Hurons (a native tribe in southern Canada).

Penetrating deep into eastern Siberia, the Russians established Yakutsk in 1632 and soon heard reports about the Amur river basin, a rich grain-producing region to the south. Three years later the first Cossacks started to settle in the area, but Chinese forces seem to have wiped the colonies out by 1658. The Russians tried again fifteen years later, but in 1686 a powerful Chinese force destroyed the Russian base at Albazin, and in the Treaty of Nerchinsk the Manchus forced a Russian withdrawal north into Siberia, away from the Amur. For the time being the limits to Russia's eastern expansion had been drawn.

Life in the Wild East

The Russian approach to colonising Siberia differed markedly from the English practice in America in four significant ways, reflecting differences in geography, economics, religion and politics.

First, the control and ownership of land was not as important. On the one hand there was no shortage of land in Siberia, so there was less need to drive the native populations off it, and on the other hand much of the land was so inhospitable that the natives were welcome to keep it. The newly conquered territories were not as attractive as the plains of North America, largely for reasons of climate, and so immigration was much lower. Consequently the Russians who did settle needed the existing populations to provide extra labour, food and staples.

Second, the Russians wanted furs, but they did not want to pay for them. It is possible to talk about the English and French fur 'trade' in North America in which, at least in theory, both Europeans and natives gained by the exchange of goods. The Russians, with a few exceptions, did not trade: they exacted tribute – furs to send back home and women for more immediate use. This necessarily implied that the Russian fur expeditions were more brutal; there was only one way to enforce tribute and that was through overwhelming force.

Third, Russian Orthodox Christianity had little desire to proselytise. The native populations were in general allowed to continue with their old religions. The fabulous Buddhist monasteries of the Buryats, for example, were left unmolested; later, indeed, a Buddhist temple was even constructed in St Petersburg. Not until the arrival of twentieth-century communism were the native religions systematically eradicated, their priests murdered and their shrines and centuries-old manuscripts destroyed.

Finally, and most fundamentally, colonisation, although pushed forward by powerful merchants and mercenary Cossacks, was ultimately controlled by the tsar. Russia remained an autocracy and colonisation proceeded in the manner that suited the state. Conquered territory belonged to the tsar and was administered by his centralised bureaucracy. The great departments of state included not just functional offices (like the treasury or the state department in the US) but territorial departments. Under the grand dukes of Muscovy these had been created to administer the territories, like Novgorod, that came under Muscovy's control. In the sixteenth century, when the khanate of Kazan was conquered, it was governed by a new department, and in the next century another was created to handle Siberia. At this time Russia had no concept of private property, and the new colonies simply became part of the tsar's personal estate, to be exploited entirely as he or she wished. There are parallels in the early royal colonies in North America, but these were aberrations that had no lasting impact on American history.

These four factors came together to produce a radically different imperial culture. Because the Russians had little desire to dispossess the natives, and indeed needed their support, and because they were relaxed about native customs, the pressures that led to genocide in America were almost entirely absent. This meant that the tsars were able to use the strategy that the British used so successfully in most of their colonies after the loss of America: co-option. Native chieftains were simply enrolled in the imperial civil service. Kuchum's family in Sibir and Buryat leaders on the Mongolian border were given Russian titles. Some 300 Sibir chieftains entered Russian government service. Over time they became Russified and, as Anna Reid points out, their 'families were assimilated into the mainstream Russian nobility, as proven by the long list of famous Russian surnames with Turkic or Mongol roots'.

The Russian dependence on 'tribute' distinguished Russian imperialism from later American trade-based imperialism, but it did closely resemble the colonialism of the first American settlers. Tribute was as central a part of early American expansion as early Russian. The concept is critical to understanding imperialism. In Russia tribute had been fundamental to the Vikings and Mongols, and continued when the Russians themselves pushed east. The essence of imperialism is that wealth is transferred from the colonised to the coloniser. Over time American imperialism replaced tribute with trade, so that today the United States sucks in raw materials, food and manufactured product from the rest of the world to maintain its disproportionately high standard of living without having to resort to force, but in the earliest days of New England tribute was almost as important for the colonies' survival as it was for the sparsely populated Russian colonies in Siberia.

Violence was an integral part of tribute collection. Like the English colonisers Russians were not averse to taking hostages to ensure that the tributes were paid. In 1632 Pyotr Beketov started the conquest of the Sakha people on the Lena river in the traditional way, demanding tributes, and when that initially failed he killed a few warriors and took the son and nephew of one of the chiefs hostage. Another chief refused to be blackmailed in this way, so Beketov and his Cossacks burnt their village to the ground; three women were the only survivors of the inferno, and Beketov happily reported that all three had been captured by his men. Beketov's motivation may have been quite different to Underhill's at the Mystic Massacre, being naked greed uncloaked by religious bigotry, but the end result was exactly the same.

The fact that Russian imperialists had no concept of ethnic cleansing did not make them any less brutal than imperialists in the New World. Indeed, in order to extract tribute they engaged in massive and systematic terror. In the winter of 1763–64 the natives of the Aleutian Islands midway between Siberia and Alaska rose up in rebellion, killing 150 Russian tribute-collectors. The Russian reprisal two years later was horrific; eighteen villages were destroyed and prisoners in their hundreds were slaughtered. After the massacre the Aleuts never rebelled again.

Nor did the lack of a policy of genocide and the co-option of native leaders imply that the Russians were any less racist than the English. Native tribes were almost universally regarded as slovenly, idle and untrustworthy – characteristics routinely ascribed to American natives by white settlers. The native nobility may have entered the Russian mainstream, but the mass of the native population stayed on the fringes. At best a few of the Russians sent east as imperial civil servants acted with the paternalistic colonial instincts that the British like to believe characterised their own empire. Much more typically, Russians took whatever they could and made no attempt to improve the conditions under which the natives lived.

By western standards the Russian civil service has always been fundamentally corrupt, but this is to misunderstand the basis upon which it has operated. The civil service existed primarily to collect taxes, performing exactly the same role for the tsars as the tsars' predecessors had for the Mongol khans. Each year the tsars decided how much they wanted to spend and told the civil service to collect it. How it was collected was not especially important, and crucially the servants themselves were not paid. Instead they were expected to collect something extra for themselves, just as the dukes of Muscovy had in Mongol times. It was considered perfectly natural that once they had passed on the specified sums to the tsar they then 'fed' themselves; this tradition was known by the Muscovite term of kormlenie. Within reason how much the civil servants 'fed' themselves was up to them. There were periodic attempts at reform; Peter the Great abolished the kormlenie and introduced salaries, but there was never enough cash to pay them and the old customs continued. At one point the government even set up checkpoints on the main road from Siberia to Moscow in order to stop and search returning bureaucrats and their families, to ensure that the amount of plunder they were bringing back was not 'exorbitant'. Stories abound of provincial governors creeping back into Moscow along deserted back roads in the dead of night with their wagons full of ill-gotten booty extorted from the natives.

A few native families may have moved into log cabins and settled into the sedentary ways of their new masters, even in a very few cases converting to their masters' religion, but the vast majority stayed in their felt yurts and continued to worship Buddha, Islam or their shamans. The divide between Russian and non-Russian persists to the present day. Under the communists natives were often installed in leading positions, but almost always with Slavs alongside to pull the strings. Although Siberian natives suffered enormously under Stalin it is revealing that they appear so infrequently in recent accounts of the Siberian gulags; even in their desperation Russian political prisoners could still look down on those among whom they were thrust.

Whether by force or fortune, by the middle of the seventeenth century Russia had an empire of enormous size. Its history from that time up to the recent past is one of almost continuous conquest. In seizing Kazan and Astrakhan and launching into Siberia, Ivan the Terrible not only whetted his nation's territorial appetite but also demonstrated its imperial prowess. For centuries under Mongol suzerainty the dukes of Muscovy had been accreting power and land, but they had remained one among many. Now they were no longer dukes or grand dukes or even kings; now they were emperors, and emperors determined to expand their empire.

Empire

It is worth stepping back from a gradual chronological approach to Russian history to consider the grand sweep of imperial expansion that continued through to the twentieth century. Over the next 250 years there were victories and, less often, defeats that each left their particular marks, but none individually changed the current that Ivan the Terrible set in motion.

After the conquests of Yermak and his successors in the east, Russian eyes turned west again towards the kingdoms of Poland and Sweden, then both far larger than the states of the same name today. Sweden surrounded the whole Baltic; Poland encompassed a great swathe of eastern Europe. In the 1650s, helped by Cossack rebels, Russia took north-eastern Ukraine, including Kiev, from Poland. Then Estonia, parts of Latvia and the site of the future St Petersburg were taken from Sweden. This was particularly important as, following the pattern of the Siberian conquests, the Teutonic nobility of these territories were absorbed into the Russian aristocracy and played a major part in political and cultural life. Towards the end of the eighteenth century and into the nineteenth Poland was again the victim of Russian expansion, losing Belorussia, Lithuania and most of what remained of Ukraine. (Poland in particular suffered from Russian imperial ambition in the nineteenth century. Having been on the losing side in the Napoleonic wars, it was taken by Russia in the Vienna Settlement of 1815 and rebellions against the new masters were bloodily suppressed.) At the same time the other frontiers were not forgotten, as Catherine the Great expanded to the Black Sea and seized Crimea from the Turks. Moldavia (also known as Bessarabia) was seized from the Ottomans and Finland from the Swedes.

For a while Russia rested on its western conquests and turned its eyes south-eastwards again. Georgia, Armenia and Azerbaijan were seized from the Turks and Persians between 1803 and 1828. Russian forces then moved east, facing easier targets as they seized the lands of the Turkmen, Uzbek, Kirghiz and Tadzhek. Even farther east territory was taken from the Chinese, including the port of Vladivostok.

With the coming of the Russian Revolution expansion went into reverse for a while (with the odd exception of the Bolshevik conquest of Mongolia), only to spring into action again after the Second World War when the swathe of 'Soviet bloc' territories from eastern Germany through to the Balkans fell into Russian hands.

Purely in quantitative terms the growth of Russia is startling. As previously mentioned, in 1300 the Duchy of Muscovy covered some 7,500 square miles, while in 1462 Ivan III inherited 166,000 square miles. The growth continued. In 1533 Ivan IV inherited almost 1.1m square miles, and by the end of the century the figure had reached 2.1m square miles: Russia was already as large as the rest of Europe put together. In the next fifty years another 3.8m square miles of largely Siberian territory was added. Russia was by far the largest state in the world and indeed the Russian empire is the largest contiguous empire the world has ever known. Between 1550 and 1700 Russia gained an average of 13,500 square miles a year – as Richard Pipes puts it that is equivalent to adding a country the size of Holland to its empire every year for 150 years. (But as Pipes also points out most of this territory was almost empty: even in the most developed areas in the west of its empire the population density stood at only one to three people per square mile in the sixteenth century compared with one to thirty in much of western Europe.)

The details of its imperial expansion form the core of Russian history, but it is easy to get lost in that detail and lose sight of the overall picture. One of the reasons that the scale of the Russian empire has rarely registered in the west is because of the division between western Christendom and barbarian east that first appeared at Châlons. When Yermak first crossed the Urals Europeans knew more about South America than they knew about eastern Siberia. Maps of the period show improbable kingdoms populated by mythical creatures. Even today the geography of Russia remains unfamiliar. Most educated Europeans could locate the Mississippi, but how many even know that the Ob and Lena are two of the world's mightiest rivers? Azerbaijan and Uzbekistan sound so much more alien than the equally un-English Arkansas and Utah.

Not only are Asiatic Russia and its colonies unfamiliar but the Europe that Russia faced to its west seems strangely disconcerting to modern readers. There are few natural frontiers in the world, and especially so in central and eastern Europe. Modern countries like Ukraine and Belarus simply did not exist. Others have changed beyond recognition. The largest country in medieval Europe was not France or Spain but the union of Poland and Lithuania. In the early medieval period the kings of England still ruled over large parts of what is today France (indeed in 1415, two years after the merger of Poland and Lithuania, the English victory at Agincourt seemed to confirm that position). The Iberian peninsula was still divided between Christian and Muslim. Germany as a nation was unheard of. The path of Russian imperialism is difficult to follow precisely because the patchwork of nation states kept changing. Furthermore, although Muscovy emerged from Mongol rule as the leader of a unified Russian state, what Russian histories often overlook is that the Russia that entered the Mongol realm was not the Russia that emerged centuries later. Much of what had been Russia was liberated not by Muscovy but by Lithuania. The all-powerful Grand Duchy of Lithuania, which soon incorporated Poland, ensured that much of Kievan Rus was oriented not eastwards to the relative barbarism of post-Mongol Muscovy but to the self-consciously civilised Catholic west. For centuries afterwards Russia was obsessed by regaining Kiev and the lands we now know as Ukraine and Belarus. Not until the Second World War were the last remnants of these territories 'returned' to Russian rule, by which time their inhabitants felt anything but Russian; and half a century later they were independent again.

Although the motivation behind this imperial expansion may have been largely economic, few have been crude enough to proclaim their imperial ambitions in purely mercenary terms. Just as American imperialism was cloaked in the philosophical robes of John O'Sullivan's 'manifest destiny', so Russia proclaimed a manifest destiny of its own. Ivan III told the Lithuanian Grand Prince that Kiev and other parts of Ukraine then held by the grand prince were 'all the land of Rus' and 'by God's will, since the days of old, are our patrimony inherited from our ancestors'. At least Ivan III had the justification that Ukraine had once been Rus, but Ivan IV used the same manifest destiny argument in the Livonian wars when invading territory that had never been part of Kievan Rus. Later the doctrine of 'Slavophilism' was developed, which proclaimed the right and duty of the Russian people to occupy the various territories they had conquered.

The First Romanovs

Ivan the Terrible and his grandfather Ivan the Great started this gigantic imperial adventure, but it could easily have stalled on Ivan IV's death. In the Times of Troubles Russian imperial ambitions could have been snuffed out by the two regional superpowers, Sweden and Poland, but in the Romanovs Russia stumbled upon a dynasty that would not merely protect the empire but bring it to undreamt-of glories. The reigns of the first two Romanov tsars, Michael and Alexis, were crucial in re-establishing the power and character of Rus and Muscovy.

When sixteen-year-old Michael Romanov ascended the throne Russia's imperial glories must have been the last thing on his mind. His first priority was survival, and his initial position was incredibly weak. He did not even have the power to select his own wife: when he chose the beautiful Maria Khlopfa, members of a rival family had her drugged and dispatched with her family into Siberian exile. Michael did, however, have a loving patron, his father. Filaret had not been considered for tsar himself for two reasons: he was already head of the Russian Orthodox Church, and at the time he was a captive of the Poles. Michael and Filaret were soon powerful enough to dispense with the national assembly (unlike the head of state in England, Charles I, who tried the same thing eight years later and ended up with neither state nor head).

Around them Europe was in flux. In 1683 western civilisation was yet again saved from the barbarous east when the Polish leader Jan Sobieski defeated the Ottoman Turks outside Vienna. Michael, Filaret and Michael's successor Alexis not only flexed Russia's military might but played a skilful diplomatic game, which resulted in Sweden selling back Novgorod and, of immense psychological importance, Poland being forced to give up Kiev. Alexis started a tradition to be followed assiduously later by America and Russia alike: funding opposition groups in exile in the hope that one day they would return home as grateful allies. In the case of Alexis that meant bankrolling Charles II of England in exile in Holland after the execution of his father.

Alexis was followed first by his sickly son Fyodor, who soon died, and then by one of the towering figures in Russian history, Peter the Great. The succession was not a smooth one, illustrating once again the fragile threads of autocracy. Any one of three half-siblings could have come out on top, and the transition was characteristically violent, pitting the family of Alexis's first wife, the Miloslavskys, against the family of his second wife, the Naryshkins. The Miloslavskys wanted Alexis's retarded son Ivan on the throne or, failing that, his sister Sophia, but the ten-year-old Peter was acknowledged tsar by the Moscow mob. His mother Natalya Naryshkin was appointed regent, but the Miloslavskys had Peter's chief advisor hacked to death in the young tsar's presence and had the head of the Naryshkin family tortured and thrown to the mob. Sophia then became regent to Peter and Ivan as joint tsars (Ivan V being unkindly known to history as Ivan the Fool, although being a fool did not stop him fathering two daughters, one of whom would ascend the imperial throne). Sophia effectively ruled as Russia's first empress until Peter, at the age of seventeen, managed to enlist the support of the Scottish mercenary commanding the Moscow guards and had Sophia banished to a monastery. When Ivan died Peter became undisputed autocrat and started to change the face of Russia for ever.

Peter the Great was the first famous Romanov. Many European and American texts suggest that his greatness arose from his willingness to take on the most important task they appear to consider any Russian leader can perform: he 'opened Russia to the west'. Peter was the first great westerniser, the tsar who cast off the blinkers of prejudice and superstition and took Russia into the modern world. He toured the capitals of western Europe and immersed himself in the traditions, culture and values of the west. Whether working as a humble apprentice in the shipyards of Holland or studying the arts of civilisation at Woolwich Arsenal, Peter supposedly typified the hands-on, real world leadership style more characteristic of new world entrepreneurs than old world autocrats.

Peter's famous visit to the west is frequently pictured as one of the great turning points of world history. Certainly he returned home inspired to change the course of Russian history, but not necessarily in the directions his admirers claim. This visit was not a Victorian Grand Tour peregrinating around the wonders of ancient Rome and Greece; Peter's primary objective was not cultural but imperial. He wanted to learn the military secrets of the western powers in order to strengthen his empire, if necessary at their expense. His choice of England was influenced less by an interest in the workings of a nascent constitutional monarchy than in the lessons to be learnt from the brutal English colonisation of Ireland (his visit came just eight years after the battle of the Boyne, where the military power of Irish Catholicism had been annihilated). He was accompanied not by scholars and artists but by two hundred largely boorish and often drunken hangers-on, and he returned to Russia not when he was satisfied that he had learnt all there was to learn but when summoned home by news of a military revolt (news sent to him by the gloriously entitled Minister of Flogging and Torture). His reaction to the revolt showed nothing of western liberalism and everything of Ivan the Terrible. Peter had hundreds of his opponents roasted alive, broken on the wheel or flogged to death, with their bodies left to rot on street corner displays throughout Moscow.

In terms of geographical size Russia's days of breakneck expansion were over by 1700. But much of the vast new empire was sparsely populated Siberian tundra whose rich natural resources could only be exploited with enormous difficulty. Like Ivan the Terrible before him, Peter's covetous eyes turned west.

At the time Sweden was one of the greatest military powers in Europe. Although it had lost its fledgling American colony half a century earlier, it still dominated northern Europe, and its new king Charles XII, just eighteen when war commenced, was to prove himself a military genius. In launching the twenty-two year long Great Northern War against Sweden Peter set himself on a course that would, if successful, change the balance of power for ever. But to reach that point Peter had to defeat a man whose tactical brilliance and personal courage would soon be the talk of the continent.

Peter moved first, seizing Swedish territory on the eastern side of the Baltic and laying siege to the coastal city of Narva. Charles, after defeating Peter's Danish allies in a stunningly swift campaign, landed 150 miles away with a force just a quarter of Peter's. There was no chance that Charles would attack the Russian troops, especially as the weather was ghastly, so Peter left the siege to confer with his other allies, the Poles. While he was away Charles achieved the impossible. He force-marched his troops through raging blizzards and then launched a frontal attack against all the odds. The Swedish king had horses shot from under him and after the battle found a musket ball caught in his clothing. Part of the

Russian army was routed and the rest, itself larger than the total Swedish force, capitulated. The Russians lost 8,000 troops; ten generals, including the commander in chief, were captured.

Narva was a disaster for Peter but he was determined not to make the same mistakes again. The Russian army was rebuilt, re-equipped and drilled in the precepts of modern warfare. Charles, on the other hand, made many of the mistakes Napoleon and Hitler went on to make: he divided his forces, couldn't decide which were his strategic objectives and fell foul of the Russians' scorched earth policies. In 1709 the story of Narva was repeated in reverse. Charles was besieging the militarily insignificant town of Poltava when Peter appeared with an army more than twice the size of the Swedes' and dug in. Charles, although wounded himself, ordered his troops into another full frontal attack, and they were massacred. Swedish military power was smashed for ever.

Charles himself was fortunate to escape to Turkey, from where he encouraged the Ottomans in their own campaigns against the encroaching Russian empire. Those campaigns could have been successful, for in 1711 the Turks almost captured Peter – but he was able to escape using a classic Muscovite weapon; he bribed the Turkish vizier.

Peter then seized the region round Baku on which Soviet Russia would later depend for its oil supplies, but it was in the west that he made his most far-reaching gains.

After Poltava the Swedes were in no position to withstand Russian demands, but the war dragged on; Charles simply refused to give way. Finally the Swedish king took one risk too many: in an obscure engagement with Danish forces in Norway Charles made the classic mistake of putting his head above the parapet, thus presenting a perfect target for an enemy sniper. Peter reportedly wept at the news of his gallant opponent's demise, and then grabbed control of most of the eastern Baltic coastline from the demoralised Swedes in the Treaty of Nystadt. Among the territory seized was a malaria-riven swamp at the mouth of the Neva river, where Peter began the construction of what was to be his most lasting legacy. On 16 May 1703 he ordered the building of a fortress named after St Peter and St Paul on the delta's Hare Island. Because of the swampy ground the construction of the fortress was a massive operation, requiring the movement of millions of tons of earth and the sinking of large wooden piles into the soil. Once the fortress was complete Peter started on the city around it.

St Petersburg could only have been built in a dictatorship; it was the product of the imagination of a single autocrat. Nobody but Peter wanted it. He was obsessed by a desire to escape from a Moscow dominated in his mind by memories of childhood abuse and treason. He had no interest in the luxurious trappings of Moscow life so valued by his courtiers, and he wanted a port, a maritime gateway to the world, when most of his compatriots had no idea what an ocean was and no desire to find out. He had played with toy navies as a child in a country that had no navy. As soon as he gained access to the Baltic he built himself a real navy and pushed it to a series of victories in the Great Northern War.

Peter determined every aspect of the city's design and construction, using the Italian architect Domenico Trezzini to create a city of broad open streets, canals, cathedrals and palaces with art galleries, libraries and even a zoo, but it was only the institutions of tsardom that made the enterprise possible at all. Hundreds of thousands of people were mobilised and compelled to move to the inhospitable marshes. Over 30,000 (perhaps as many as 100,000) conscripts, prisoners and others died of disease, malnutrition and what today might be called industrial injuries, except that such injuries were often deliberately inflicted. Punishments for trying to escape or simply under performing ranged from whipping through mutilation to, in some cases, execution. (This barbaric cruelty was not unique: in the year St Petersburg was founded the settlers of Carolina launched their infamous slave raids on the Spanish missions in Florida, wreaking a hurricane of murder, torture and rape across hundreds of miles.)

Dysentery and malaria were rife. Whole forests were cut down for timber, hills were levelled and lakes filled. Entire communities were uprooted and shipped west. When his builders ran out of stone Peter simply forbade the construction of stone buildings elsewhere in the empire. There were so few tools that workers were often forced to shovel soil with their hands, an example repeated again 230 years later when Stalin's forced labour built the White Sea canal. The way the whole of society was mobilised has no parallel in the west. This was not slave labour of the sort characterising the new colonies across the Atlantic. Those transported to the new capital were not only serfs grabbed from the land but great lords and their families. When Peter wanted a navy he simply commanded some of his generals to become admirals. When he wanted to populate his new capital leading families were ordered to build houses there at their own expense, with each design determined by the tsar and each location specified on Trezzini's plan.

There was no question of Peter needing to win the nobility's support to carry out these grand designs; as supreme autocrat he had only to command. The nature of the Russian class system not only explains how Peter was able to accomplish such a massive piece of civil engineering but also, some would say, exemplifies how Russian society has operated from the Mongols to the present. One of the most misunderstood aspects of Russian history is the role of the nobility. Westerners whose pictures of Imperial Russia are based on the novels and plays of the nineteenth century filter their understanding through the sieve of their preconceptions, preconceptions based on the 'equivalents' at home. Russian nobles are seen lolling in luxury on enormous estates, surrounded by thousands of serfs over whom they have untrammelled authority – lords of all they can see. They resemble nothing as much as the planter aristocracy of Barbados, Virginia and the Carolinas, with serfs replacing slaves and snowy steppe replacing green fields. Going further back, the court of the early tsars is sometimes pictured in terms of medieval England or France, with mighty local lords competing for influence. Such perceptions are totally unreal.

Central to any understanding of Russia is the concept of autocracy. All power was concentrated in the tsar. There were no local fiefdoms immune from the autocrat's control. The function of every Russian was to serve the tsar, and that was especially true of the aristocracy, the dvorianstvo, which started life in the struggles among the Russian princes to inherit the authority of the Mongols. When the grand princes of Muscovy came out on top the other clan leaders became, quite literally, their servants. Richard Pipes emphasises the supreme importance of this development:

> The Muscovite service class, from which in direct line of succession, descend the dvorianstvo of Imperial Russia and the communist apparatus of Soviet Russia, represent a unique phenomenon in the history of social institutions. No term borrowed from western history, such as 'nobility' or 'gentry', satisfactorily defines it. It was a pool of skilled manpower used by the state to perform any and all functions which it required: soldiering, administration, legislation, justice, diplomacy, commerce and manufacture. The fact that its living derived almost exclusively from the exploitation of land and (after the 1590s) bonded labour, was an accident of Russian history, namely the shortage of cash. . . . The roots of this class were not in the land, as was the case with nobilities the world over, but in the royal service. In some respects, the Russian service class was a very modern institution, a kind of proto-meritocracy. Its members enjoyed superior status but by virtue of their usefulness to their employer. Whatever their advantages vis-à-vis the rest of the population, with regard to the crown their position was utterly precarious.

Pipes describes Russia as a 'patrimonial society'. He means that Russia has been governed the way a traditional father governs his family, not only as the supreme autocrat but as owner of the family assets. The concept of private property has never been fully developed in Russia. All land belonged to the tsar, although he might farm some of it out in return for taxes and tribute. There was no concept of individual rights or the rule of law; the tsar was the only authority. Everyone else was not a 'citizen' but a 'servitor'. Peter, and Russian society, took it as axiomatic that he could do with his property as he wished, and if that meant moving the country's centre of gravity from quasi-oriental Moscow to westward-looking St Petersburg so be it.

Although they happened at about the same time the Russian colonisation of the Baltic littoral was very different to the English colonisation of the Atlantic littoral. Peter's designs on the Neva delta can be contrasted with events less than half a century earlier when, in 1670, three ships from Barbados landed at the mouth of the Ashley river to found a city named after their king. Charles Towne, or Charleston as it became, was founded by a group of eight absentee landowners, the lord proprietors. Their project had none of the urgency or scale of Peter the Great's. They had been granted a charter to found a colony in Carolina, after extensive lobbying, and it had then taken seven years before the first colonists set out. The lord proprietors had none of the tsar's powers of coercion. To encourage settlers from England they offered massive land grants (150 acres per head), allowed a considerable degree of self-government and promised religious freedom. Even with this encouragement the city had a population of just 396 after two years, around 1,000 after ten years and thirty years later the city had reached a population of only 6,600, of whom 2,800 were black slaves. Contrast this with St Petersburg, made the nation's capital in 1712 just nine years after the first fortress was started, and which thirty years later had a population of 150,000.

Charleston and St Petersburg also illustrate the way history is written to reflect contemporary values. Colonisation is something Europeans do to others, and even though in colonising Livonia (the region now dominated by greater St Petersburg) Peter was being as imperialist as the British in America, different words are used. Virginia was 'colonised' or 'settled'; Livonia was 'conquered'. Charleston was attacked and partly destroyed in 'raids' led by native 'chiefs'; when the same thing happened to St Petersburg history speaks of a 'campaign' by a Swedish 'colonel'.

Peter the Great is seen as a warrior and statesman in the tradition of the great European monarchs. He has been praised by many western historians, and condemned by many Russian conservatives, as the champion of progress, liberalism and western civilisation. Fundamentally, however, he was a warlord. His reign can be summed up in two numbers: when Peter reached the throne there were around 16 million Russians; after thirty-six years of almost constant conflict and mounting megalomania there were just 13 million. He was a tsar in the mainstream of the Russian autocratic tradition. In the way he reached the throne, in his casual massacring of his opponents and above all in his imperialism, Peter was part of a long line running from the Muscovite princes who preceded Ivan the Terrible to Stalin and perhaps beyond.

When Peter the Great died in 1725 the transfer of power, usually so smooth in America, was particularly fraught. Peter and his son Alexis could have provided an even better study for psychoanalysts than Ivan the Terrible. Peter wanted a red-blooded warrior for a son; he got Alexis, who was anything but. Bullied, belittled and beleaguered by his father, Alexis eventually fled Russia to seek asylum at the Habsburg court in Vienna. Peter was affronted and had his son kidnapped, smuggled back to Russia and thrown into the dungeons of his new fortress in St Petersburg; he was then tried for treason and sentenced to death. Before the sentence could be carried out Alexis died of the injuries he had received in captivity. Peter's other son then died of natural causes, so when the tsar himself died there was no obvious successor. How power vacuums were filled in such circumstances depended not just on the 'legitimacy' of hereditary claims but on the balance of political and military power among the candidates. This was not a particularly Russian phenomenon: in 1714 Britain reached out to an obscure but 'suitable' German prince who happened to be the great-grandson of James I, and made him George I. For Russia's powerbrokers there was no immediate need to look very far. Despite Russia never having had a female monarch the throne was passed to Peter's wife, Catherine I. When she died two years later the throne passed to Peter's fourteen-year-old grandson, who ruled for just three years before succumbing to smallpox.

The throne should then have passed to Peter the Great's daughter Elizabeth, a twenty-one-year-old with a reputed passion for the delights of the bedchamber, but she was thought too difficult to control. Instead the privy council looked abroad to the two daughters of Ivan V (Ivan the Fool), nieces of Peter the Great. Both had married German princes. The eldest, Catherine, was Duchess of Mecklenburg. She was considered too Germanic and suffered the distinct disadvantage that her husband was still alive. The throne was therefore given to the younger, Anna, the widowed Duchess of Kurland. (Kurland was a duchy that existed for two centuries in what is now Latvia. Its main claim to fame was as the most obscure colonial power in the Americas, when a seventeenth-century duke established a colony on the Caribbean island of Tobago.)

Anna proved less easy to control than had been expected and staged a coup of her own, overthrowing the council that had chosen her and replacing it with German advisers imported from Kurland. She followed the imperial traditions of her predecessors who had pushed out the boundaries in the west by grabbing Polish territory in the War of Polish Succession, and in the south she forced the Turks to allow Russian access to the Sea of Azov. When Anna died in 1740 she nominated the grandson of her sister Catherine to become Ivan VI. Ivan came to the throne at the age of two months. Power was supposed to remain with the former empress's German favourites, but this arrangement only lasted for three weeks before a *coup d'état* gave the regency to Ivan's mother. Her regency in turn lasted for twelve months before Peter the Great's daughter Elizabeth, the lustful Grand Duchess passed over in 1730, mounted her own coup d'état. Ivan VI, by now fifteen months old, was thrown into the dungeons and stayed there as the Empress Elizabeth occupied his throne for the next twenty years.

Elizabeth is mainly remembered now for her legendary and bizarre sex life, which included transvestite parties at which the empress in full male attire derided terrified male courtiers cowering in their ball gowns. Despite her indiscriminate carnal appetites (although she opposed France politically she numbered the French ambassador among her lovers), Elizabeth died childless. Much earlier she had chosen as her successor a German prince who in addition to being her cousin was related to the great love of her life, another, and much more dashing, German prince who had died of smallpox. The cousin, who would become Peter III, was found a suitable wife, and the couple was ensconced in St Petersburg to await his turn on the throne. Peter's wife was a minor German princess named Sophia Von Anhalt-Zarbst, a name considered decidedly un-Russian, and so it was changed to Catherine.

Despite her generally pro-German sympathies Elizabeth was a fierce opponent of the mighty Frederick the Great of Prussia – not surprising given Frederick's views on Russia. In his tract Anti-Machiavel, which attacked Machiavelli's theories of autocracy, Frederick disparagingly compared Russia's vast territory populated by miserable people with tiny Holland's economic and cultural pre-eminence. Elizabeth put Frederick right, as her armies for the first time marched westwards beyond the Baltic battlegrounds on which Peter the Great had achieved his victories and beyond the territories gained in the War of Polish Succession. In 1760, as British troops took Montreal, ending French dreams of a North American empire, the Russian army occupied Frederick the Great's capital: Berlin. It was one of those events that could have changed the face of history; it did not, because Elizabeth's dissolute lifestyle caught up with her. At the age of fifty she died, to be succeeded by her pro-Prussian cousin – who promptly ordered his troops to return home.

Peter III ruled for six months, during which time he tried to turn Russia into his beloved Prussia. His reforms varied from designing Prussian uniforms for his troops to issuing a grandly entitled edict *Concerning the Granting of Freedom and Liberty to the entire Russian Dvorianstvo*, which recognised the increasing power of the nobility by abolishing their compulsory state service and allowing them to travel abroad. Peter's retreat from Prussia had been deeply unpopular at the Russian court and his days were numbered when, to the court's dismay, he started to openly flirt with the Lutheran religion and, to his wife's dismay, even more openly flirt with his mistress Elizabeth Vorontsava. His wife Catherine was not herself blameless, and with her current lover

Grigory Orlov she staged a coup in which her husband was murdered, and she mounted the throne herself.

Not everyone was happy with Catherine's assumption of the throne, and there was another claimant near at hand. The infant Ivan VI, deposed and imprisoned by the Empress Elizabeth, was now twenty-three. An attempt was made to rescue him, but once his gaolers realised what was happening they followed the orders given to them by Elizabeth more than twenty years before, orders recently reiterated by Catherine: they killed their charge. The thirty-four year reign of Catherine the Great had begun. The greatest female tsar of all time sat safely on her throne thanks to the murders of her two most recent male predecessors.

CHAPTER 6
AMERICA BETWEEN EAST AND WEST

By the time Catherine the Great came to the throne Russia was a fully fledged empire. The Grand Duchy of Muscovy handed down by Ivan 'Moneybags' to Ivan the Great and Ivan the Terrible had been transformed. Whole new peoples had been conquered and incorporated to the north, west and south and the massive landmass of Siberia made the Russian empire the colossus of its day. The Russia of Catherine and the Russia of the Ivans had virtually nothing in common but their history; what gave them continuity was the incessant desire to grow – the urge to expand the power and prestige of the nation, the lust for resources and riches beyond their borders.

America would grow in exactly the same way. Since the first English settlers arrived on the continent there had been the same urge to expand, the same insatiable demand for power and prestige. America too changed beyond recognition. The thirteen original colonies perched on the edge of the continent had as little in common with the lost pioneers on Roanoke as with the United States of today.

Russia was cemented together by one central institution: the tsar. The ideology of autocracy carried the Russian nation forward into empire. The early American colonies had no such central institution; indeed they were not even a nation. First they had to throw off the cloak of the British empire, and to do that they needed an ideology that would bind together their disparate interests just as autocracy bound together the melting pot of Russia. They needed democracy.

The Rule of Law

There is a theory that the massive differences between the values of Americans and Russians are rooted not in history or religion or political development but in geography. The line that divides them is a very precise one, and it is not a line dividing east from west but the line of latitude running at 45° north. Most of America is south of that line; most of Russia is north. As a consequence most of the United States is blessed with a clement climate and with productive agricultural land; most of Russia is not. It is argued, therefore, that the colonisation of America followed the pattern set by the western Vikings along Europe's Atlantic coast rather than the Varangians of Rus.

The Vikings first came to western Europe as raiders looking for loot, just as the Spanish conquistadors and English pirates later came to the Americas. But, again like the early Europeans in America, they found a land more fertile and a climate more appealing than the one they had left behind. As a consequence they settled down, becoming the great feudal lords of Normandy and later England. In Marxist terms agriculture produced a surplus they were able to expropriate and exploit. The first Vikings travelling eastwards did so with the same desire for booty, but the wealth they discovered came not from agriculture but from trade. The original Viking leaders of Rus were merchant princes determined to control the trade routes with Byzantium and the east. Rather than seeing land that they could exploit they saw in the Slavs merely a source of tribute – fur, wax, honey and, above all, slaves. Unlike the Vikings of Normandy they were never interested in land itself, which was too poor to produce surplus value they could expropriate, and so they never had any shared interest with the peasant farmers.

That the Vikings of east and west developed different political cultures might be nothing more than a vaguely interesting historical footnote were it not for the fact that those differences, founded on a quirk of geography, led directly to the ideological divide that could have pushed the twentieth-century world into nuclear war.

To its champions American democracy is about equality, fairness and justice; autocracy is about the opposite. The west, it is argued, puts justice above order; Russia has put order over justice. And yet it is one of the ironies of history that the two systems arose because their originators believed the precise opposite of what they are now perceived to represent. Western civil liberties arose because order was thought more important than equality. Autocracy arose because equality took precedence over order. The Vikings who exploded out of Scandinavia were organised perfectly for raiding and looting, but their successors found themselves ruling over vast territories that needed very different management styles. The successors of the western Vikings needed a political model that ensured effective management and protection of their landholdings. Their cousins in the east needed to maintain a model suited to war and ever-changing territorial boundaries.

One group in the west developed a model that differed radically both from Viking tradition and from the traditions of Rome. In the twelfth and thirteenth century the Norman rulers of England, particularly Henry III, institutionalised primogeniture, the assertion that justice is served by passing on all of a family's wealth to the first-born son. To the Vikings and their successors in Rus such a philosophy meant injustice. They considered themselves bands of brothers, often quite literally so, and to them the family meant the whole family. On the death of the head of the family the family's wealth belonged to all the survivors (or at least all the males). The English kings understood that power and wealth deriving from land could only be preserved and enhanced if they remained undivided. If that meant disenfranchising the younger siblings so be it. The Rus also understood the dangers of dividing their patrimonies into weak and competing parts, but if that was the price of equity so be it. (Interestingly one of the first laws most American states enacted during or after the American Revolution was to abolish primogeniture.)

Primogeniture slowly spread east from England, reaching Italy for example in the sixteenth century, but never arrived in Russia. The practical consequence in western Europe was that although junior royals could accumulate power and riches it was always under the overlordship of their senior, the first-born. Princes might fight each other for the crown but nobody challenged the need for a state to have a single monarch. A nobility emerged that was determined to grab and hold on to its share of the nation's wealth, but was always vulnerable to the all-powerful monarch with whom they had to reach some sort of arrangement in order to be able to pass their estates on to their heirs. For the nobles it became essential to find ways to limit the power of the king. Thus arose the concept of mutual rights and obligations between king and subject, and with it the whole panoply of law and eventually parliament. Over time this exercise in power politics acquired the trappings of philosophical debate. The English barons displayed their military might at Runnymede to force King John to accede to their crude demands but did so in the language of Magna Carta, confirming their supposedly 'ancient' rights. The foundation stones of western democracy – the primacy of law, the rights of the individual, the concept of private property, the principle of representational government – were put in place to allow the oligarchs to consolidate their power *vis-à-vis* the monarch.

In Russia, on the other hand, thrones were not passed on to the oldest child; they simply ceased to exist. Nobles established their power base not *vis-à-vis* a king but *vis-à-vis* each other. Warlords and princes competed not for a crown but for territory. The winners incorporated land they had bought or conquered into their own. Possession was not just nine-tenths of the law, it *was* the law. Within a territory the prince's power was absolute; there was no competing authority with which power had to be shared. Even during the Mongol period the Russian princes did not unite with each other; unity was achieved when the more powerful, in particular Muscovy, dispossessed the less powerful. As there was no mutuality of interest between king and subject concepts like the rule of law, developed to protect the oligarchs in the west, simply did not exist. The prince owned his territory and its inhabitants by right of conquest; the vanquished had no rights. Each prince had property and that property included people. To talk of those people having rights was as meaningless as suggesting that the prince's horses had rights. The inhabitants of Muscovy were no more citizens than the occupants of a zoo are citizens. When all property belongs to the tsar there is no need for such niceties as contract law.

By the time the first Europeans arrived in America the concepts of the Magna Carta had become enshrined not only in the laws and institutions they brought with them but also in the language and psyche of the immigrants. Yet in some ways the circumstances in which they found themselves were similar to the early Rus, who had developed as a consequence a very different set of values. Among themselves the settlers needed an acceptance of the rights that by now were truly traditional, but with respect to the natives the situation was very different: there was no commonality of interest; the settlers were as determined to dispossess the natives as the princes of Muscovy had been to usurp their neighbours. The response of the immigrants to this novel situation was to become an integral feature of the American character: they maintained the processes and practices they had brought with them even when the underlying realities were fundamentally different. Thus, for example, they drew up elaborate contracts with native tribes that they knew full well were merely legalising theft; nobody was more aware than Peter Minuit that the price he was paying for Manhattan bore no relationship to its real value, but as far as he was concerned his expropriation was perfectly legal. Time after time treaties and contracts were signed that the Europeans knew were being interpreted by the native signatories as meaning something entirely different to the interpretation that the immigrants intended to enforce.

Treaties were always a temporary expedient, which the settlers recognised would be overtaken by events. As they pushed into new territory they knew that the natives would be pushed aside irrespective of any treaty obligations. It is only a slight exaggeration to suggest that the American approach to treaty-making, which started in treaties with the natives and was honed during the American rebellion, when the new nation's first international treaty with France was promptly ignored, would eventually be extended globally. The early approach to treaty-making had three characteristics: agreements with heathen savages were by definition less sacred than agreements between the settlers themselves; by extension such agreements must reflect the balance of power between the parties rather than any concept of 'fairness'; and as the balance of power was changing agreements would always be temporary. Americans were always aware that they represented progress, so circumstances were destined to change, and thus treaties that were appropriate today could be inappropriate tomorrow. For the United States a treaty is almost always something that resolves in its favour an immediate issue without implying any obligation on those who come after.

The 1850 Clayton-Bulwer Treaty was a classic example. It guaranteed that neither Britain nor America would try to exercise exclusive control over any future Panama canal, but by the time the canal was built the United States felt strong enough not to worry about British influence in the region. Just as treaties with the natives were ignored, as soon as circumstances allowed President Grant demanded 'an American canal on American soil', by which he meant not moving the canal north but moving the American border south. In the words of a later US president, the canal should be 'virtually a part of the coastline of the United States'. The Clayton-Bulwer treaty – like countless American treaties before and after – was consigned to the bin.

The apparent contradiction between the principles of justice and fair play espoused by the early settlers and the reality that was enacted was resolved by a developing belief among the immigrants that if just rules were being followed then by definition just outcomes were being achieved. If a contract is properly drawn up and properly executed then by definition it is a just contract. The central question of western European philosophy, 'when is an action just?', became in America, 'when is an action legal?' That difference in emphasis remains to this day. After the Enron financial scandal in 2002, when company executives amassed millions of dollars by creating fictitious 'off balance sheet' entities, British accountants insisted that it could not have happened in the UK because of the fundamental principle of British accounting, 'substance over form'. In Britain all the rules can be complied with but the substance of the transaction can still be deemed illegal. In America an action must comply with all the rules to be legal, and if all the rules are complied with the action is legal.

Ironically the assertion by the early settlers that their treaties were legal and therefore just is used today in ways that would have horrified them. Davy Crockett TV star Fess Parker went into partnership with the Chumash tribe to develop a massive resort in Santa Barbara, California, arguing that the Chumash were a sovereign nation under ancient treaties, and thus not subject to city council zoning regulations – a consequence surely unanticipated when the treaties were signed.

On a more fundamental level, in their dealings with the natives the first settlers established the mental precedent that processes and principles are the same thing. Thus the processes of democracy came to be indistinguishable from democracy itself, so that in modern times America can install the institutions of representative government in Vietnam or Iraq and then assert, with apparent sincerity, that the resultant regimes are by definition democratic. The institutions of representative government appeared in some American colonies almost as soon as the first settlers arrived. In its fullest form, however, American democracy can be said to have originated with the ratification of the US Constitution in 1788. Before that could happen the new nation had to break away from the British empire.

French America

With hindsight the American rebellion against British rule was one of the most profoundly important events in world history. At the time the rest of the world thought of it as a relatively minor piece of theatre in a global conflict. However bitter the fighting in North America, and however momentous the conclusion, the eyes of the rest of the world were not upon it. It is impossible to understand how English colonists were able to transform themselves into the American nation without understanding what was happening across the Atlantic. In Europe the most important events of the period were happening in the centre of the continent. Russia, Austria and Prussia had between them annexed half of Poland. Austria and Prussia were thrown into the War of Bavarian Succession, and Russia turned its eyes south towards the Ottoman empire, effectively annexing the Crimea and gaining ports on the Black Sea for the first time. Russians colonised down the Volga as energetically as Americans wanted to push to the Mississippi.

On the fringes of Europe were nations not yet ready to intervene in the cauldron of Central European politics. England, Holland and France had long since joined Spain and Portugal in the race for empire. At one time even Scotland, then still fiercely independent, had a colony in Central America, the disastrous failure of which financially ruined the Edinburgh establishment and helped create the conditions for union with England. France especially had emerged as a major power and one determined to establish its authority in both the old world and the new.

The French imperial model contained elements of both the Russian and the English. Like Russia, France's imperial expansion was driven by the state, although not necessarily by the monarch: Louis XV's idea of a call to arms was to throw himself into the embrace of Mme de Pompadour or Mme du Barry. It is interesting to speculate what Peter the Great made of the French monarch's predilections during his extravagant state visit to France in 1717.

In the Americas the early French colonists were just like the early English: they much preferred the West Indies to more northern climes. Despite the high mortality rates ten times as many headed for the Caribbean as for Canada, taking with them shiploads of African slaves. Those French emigrants who survived settled into a life of plantations and piracy. Like the English, much smaller numbers went north to the fishing grounds of Acadia and inland along the St Lawrence river. The French explorer Jacques Cartier ventured along the St Lawrence as far as what is now Montreal in the 1530s, but disease and native hostility compelled early settlements to be abandoned. The French founded a series of trading posts along the Canadian coast, but these too usually succumbed to disease, natives or English pirates. In 1608 Samuel de Champlain founded Quebec. Twenty years later the settlement still had a population of less than a hundred, all men.

As in Siberia the prime rationale for colonising Canada was fur, and to obtain that fur the French needed traders rather than settlers. By 1660 the French had 3,500 colonists in Canada (including the fishing settlements of Acadia) compared with 58,000 English colonists on the mainland. Like their Cossack counterparts, the French travelled enormous distances into the unexplored. In 1682 La Salle travelled right down the Mississippi to the Gulf of Mexico.

The prospect of encircling the English colonies, which had just spread south to Carolina, appealed to Louis XIV and La Salle was sent back to the Gulf to plant a colony at the Mississippi's mouth. Incredibly he couldn't find the river again and was murdered by his own men, who were themselves then wiped out by Karankawa natives. His successors did found a number of small settlements in what they called Louisiana (a region much larger than the modern state of the same name), but they never had the numbers of the English. In the eighteenth century France encouraged more colonial settlement, both willing (hard-working German Catholics were particularly important) and unwilling (criminals transported from France and slaves transported from west Africa). Like Carolina, Louisiana soon had a slave majority. At the same time settlers started to farm along the St Lawrence, although always in smaller numbers than in the English colonies to the south. In the vast hinterland the French imperial interests continued to be represented by traders and occasional military garrisons – one on the site of the old native metropolis of Cahokia. In the middle of the century the largest French town in the interior, Detroit, had a population of just 600. In practice the French 'encirclement' of the British colonies advocated by the authorities in Paris and feared by some in London was more apparent than real.

By the end of the seventeenth century the east coast of North America was speckled with very different colonies. In part these differences reflected different national characteristics; the Spanish, for example, were the only imperialists for whom religious conversion of the natives assumed any importance. More important were the different physical conditions the colonists encountered. Although most English colonies followed a policy of ethnic cleansing, in Canada the Hudson's Bay Company wanted furs not farms and followed a native policy more like the Russians in Siberia: exploitation not extinction. By contrast French plantation owners in Louisiana, unlike the French further north, soon developed an explicit policy of genocide to clear the land they seized, committing Mystic-type massacres and glorying in the natives' extinction. As one French priest said of the native population, 'God wishes that they yield their place to new people.'

Although the various colonies were growing, some of them very rapidly, there was plenty of space for them to grow into once the native populations had been cleared. They did not need to fight each other, and at the start of the eighteenth century there was no indication that a single, dramatically different, power would have effective control of most of the continent by the turn of the next century.

The form of government that in Russia would last right up until the twentieth century emerged out of the turbulent period under Ivan the Terrible, the Time of Troubles. The type of government that has persisted in America was formed after a similar period of turmoil. The eighteenth century in North America was marked by almost continuous conflict between immigrants and natives, but – much more important historically – it was also caught up in similarly continuous conflict between the European powers.

In Europe the War of Spanish Succession (1701–14) was followed by a host of other conflicts across the continent: the War of Polish Succession (1733–38), the War of the Austrian Succession (1740–48) and so on. Not all of them spilled over into the colonies of the New World, but most of them did.

The War of Spanish Succession pitted France, Spain and Bavaria against Austria, Holland, England and various German princes in a dispute about whether the king of Spain should be French or Austrian. English colonists in North America were off the mark quickly with an unsuccessful attack on the Spanish in Florida. The French, with their Indian allies, retaliated with attacks on New England, and in 1708 captured St John's, Newfoundland. The English launched counterattacks on Canada, with support from the Royal Navy, but failed to capture anything more significant than Port Royal in Acadia. North America was a militarily irrelevant sideshow, and all the famous battles (like Blenheim and Ramillies) were fought in Europe. In order to maintain its national borders and keep control of the Spanish throne, France gave up Acadia under the Treaty of Utrecht in 1713. The English (or more correctly since the 1707 Act of Union the British) rechristened their new colony Nova Scotia. Despite its potentially strategic position, few American colonists wanted to live there, and after the next war 2,500 immigrants were shipped out from Britain to found the city of Halifax as a counterweight to the French in Quebec and Montréal. In the meantime the French moved to strengthen their position on the continent by building an enormous fortress on Cape Breton Island. Known as the Gibraltar of America, the fortress of Louisburg had walls 40 feet thick, an 80 foot wide moat, the latest artillery and a garrison of 1600 soldiers.

Despite the formal peace French privateers used Louisburg as a base to attack British shipping. Further south British and British-American smugglers continued to flout Spanish colonial regulations. In 1739 Britain and Spain were at war again in the War of Jenkins' Ear. British attacks on Florida and Spanish attacks on Georgia and South Carolina all failed, and in 1744 France intervened. By now the conflict was called the War of Austrian Succession. Again, the French and their native allies attacked all along the frontiers of New England and Nova Scotia. In response a massive colonial force was put together under the command of a wealthy Maine merchant, William Pepperell, with troops from the New England colonies, ships from the West Indies, artillery from New York and provisions from Pennsylvania. Supported by the Royal Navy, Louisburg was taken after a forty-seven day siege in June 1745. The significance of the Louisburg victory lay not in the capture of territory but in what it said about the stage of development reached by Britain's American colonies. The colonial oligarchs had put together an army many thousand strong and defeated a major European power. Admittedly the arrival of a British fleet had proved decisive in cutting off the French garrison but the victory belonged to the colonial army. It was a forewarning of events just thirty-six years later at Yorktown, when another colonial army repeated the same feat but with Britain and France playing on opposite sides.

Louisburg was a startling victory for the colonists, but it went almost unnoticed back in London; all eyes there were looking north. Within days of the news that Louisburg had fallen there began what might have been called the War of British Succession. The Jacobite leader Bonnie Prince Charlie, with French support, landed in Scotland and marched south to reclaim the throne from its German occupant, the Hanoverian George II. He reached Derby and, with a French army preparing to invade as well, the citizens of London were in a state of almost total panic. They had no interest in events across the Atlantic. The Jacobite advance was only stopped when a Hanoverian double agent persuaded the Jacobite leaders that a non-existent army was blocking their way to the capital. The Bonnie Prince turned round and marched back north. The twenty-four-year-old Duke of Cumberland, son of George II, who had been summoned back from his role as commander-in-chief of the allied forces in the War of Austrian Succession, took command of his father's troops and chased after the retreating Jacobites. He caught up with them on the killing fields of Culloden (often wrongly characterised as an English massacre of Scots; in reality Cumberland's army included many Lowland Scots and even some Highlanders). After the battle Cumberland embarked on a sadistic reign of terror across the Gaelic-speaking Highlands, which destroyed a vibrant culture and prompted yet another stream of emigrants to the New World.

Two years later, in the Treaty of Aix-la-Chapelle, Britain gave Louisburg back to France in exchange for the much more attractive prize of Madras in India.

The American colonists were well aware of their low priority in the eyes of the government in London. A congress was held in Albany in 1754 to discuss ways of resisting French attempts to block the expansion of the British colonies. This congress was attended by representatives of New York, Pennsylvania, Maryland and the New England colonies and by representatives of the Six Nations of the Iroquois (who according to Benjamin Franklin often displayed greater diplomatic skills than the colonists).

A few months later a Virginian force under George Washington set out to take a French post on the site of today's Pittsburgh. Washington made his fortune by speculating in frontier land and was determined that the Ohio territory should belong to Britain not France. He surprised a French detachment, killing some and capturing others, including the commander – who was quickly murdered in controversial circumstances: it is claimed that while Washington was talking to him one of the Virginian's native allies unexpectedly sunk his tomahawk into the captive's skull. Washington was himself soon defeated and captured, but was released. He returned with a larger force of British soldiers, only to be defeated, spectacularly, again.

War between France and Britain was formally declared again in 1755, with the start of the Seven Year War. British forces caused havoc in Nova Scotia; Louisburg fell again in 1758 and this time British troops razed it to the ground. Thousands of French settlers in the colony they knew as Arcadia fled south, first to New Orleans, established earlier in the century, and then into the bayous of Louisiana, where 'Arcadian' would be contracted to 'Cajun'. After some initial French successes the British eventually took Quebec and Montréal and a string of French colonies in the Caribbean. In 1762 Spain intervened in support of France, but British forces soon grabbed the key Spanish strongholds of Havana and Manila – so that in negotiating an end to the conflict with the Treaty of Paris in 1763 neither France nor Spain had much bargaining power. France was the biggest loser, giving up all claims to territory in North America. Spain and England swapped cards: Spain gave up Florida, but took over

New Orleans and parts of Louisiana from the French. Spain also retained Cuba, provoking outrage among American colonists who had provided around one in four of the troops that had captured Havana. Britain now controlled the whole of the continent east of the Mississippi. The new king, George III, must have surveyed his empire in North America with satisfaction; only two threats were faintly visible – the Spanish west of the Mississippi and the natives.

Prelude to Revolution

The natives by now came in two varieties: red and white. As is well known the early European navigators sailing west thought they had found the Indies and naturally labelled the natives 'Indians', but less well known is that the term 'Red Indian' had nothing to do with supposed red skins. Many native tribes covered themselves with red ochre at certain times of the year as an insect repellent. The original inhabitants of Newfoundland, the Beothuk, for religious reasons, stained themselves and their clothes with ochre all year round and were called the Red People by neighbouring tribes. The Viking sagas spoke of natives wearing red clothing, and to the first modern Europeans arriving in Newfoundland the Beothuk were 'Red Indians'. The term survived but the Beothuk did not: the last survivor surrendered to the British in the eighteenth century and died in slavery.

The campaigns of the 'white' natives against the 'red' natives continued alongside the wars between the colonial powers. To avoid losses to themselves colonists became adept at using one tribe to suppress another: in 1715 Cherokees were used by English colonists to put down a Yamasee revolt in South Carolina, and in 1729 the French used Choctaws to put down a revolt by the Natchez. The colonists' native allies usually learnt too late that loyalty was not a white man's trait. After the ethnic cleansing of the Yamasee the Carolina colonists put a bounty on all 'Indian' scalps, and a revolt by the Cherokee in 1759 was brutally suppressed by British troops.

The Dutch, soon followed by the English, introduced the practice of offering a reward for scalps delivered to the authorities. The practice was highly popular: in Massachusetts the bounty paid for native scalps rose from £12 in 1703 to £100 by 1723. Prices varied according to 'quality'. The British authorities offered their native allies just £8 for the scalp of a French soldier but £200 for the scalp of the Delaware general Shinngass. The French themselves paid bounty-hunters for scalps when exterminating peaceful natives in Newfoundland.

It is hard to think of a more blatant manifestation of genocide or ethnic cleansing than putting a bounty on the scalps of men, women and children of another ethnic group, and yet the sheer brutality of early colonisation has been largely erased from popular history. One particular episode shows how distorted folk memories can persist into the electronic age, deadening people to the truth about their own history. Most ethnic groups in America have their own websites and the 'Scotch Irish' are no exception. The Scotch Irish were one of the most vociferous groups pressing for ethnic cleansing on the borders of Pennsylvania in the middle of the eighteenth century. In and around the village of Paxtang (or Paxton) in particular there were large numbers of men anxious to apply to the natives the treatment their own Scottish ancestors had applied to the Catholic Irish. They were known as the Paxton Boys, and one version of their story is recounted on www.scotchirish.net. Scotch Irish settlers on the Pennsylvania frontier needed protection against native attack, but the 'pacifist and self-righteous' Quaker authorities in Philadelphia refused to help. The Paxton Boys then led 1,500 settlers in a march on Philadelphia where they presented their 'just complaints'. According to the website, 'This single action is credited as being the first act in the American War of Independence', and the Paxton Boys went on to play their full part in the American Revolution. The website does not mention the events that preceded the march on Philadelphia. There had been a native uprising, known as Pontiac's rebellion, in which numerous frontier settlers had been killed. British troops suppressed the rebellion, but the Paxton Boys used the events as an excuse to demand the eradication of all natives. In December 1763 they attacked a village of the Conestoga natives who had lived peacefully alongside their white neighbours throughout the rebellion. Six natives were killed and fourteen captured; within days all fourteen prisoners had been brutally murdered.

Horrific as the Conestoga massacre was, it is worth remembering that at exactly the same time on the other side of the continent the Russians were massacring far, far greater numbers as they suppressed the Aleut revolt on the islands between Siberia and Alaska; as with so much else this aspect of life on the American frontier was the Russian frontier writ small. In the Aleuts' case there was not even pretence at remorse from those in authority; while the Pennsylvania governor issued warrants for the arrest of those responsible for the Conestoga attack, but met a wall of silence among the Scotch Irish community. The Paxton Boys then moved to attack Christian natives living near the town of Bethlehem. The natives managed to escape and were given protection in the city of Philadelphia. In response the Paxton Boys marched on the city, as described on the Scotch-Irish website. (It may be a sign of the way political values from one epoch continue down the years that when the Ku Klux Klan was established 103 years later, to terrorise freed black slaves, all six of the founders came from the Scotch-Irish community.)

With a belated sense of fair play George III attempted to provide a degree of protection to his 'red' subjects by forbidding all new white settlements west of a 'proclamation line' along the Appalachians, a line that in practice offered no real protection to the red natives and created another grievance to add to the growing list of the white natives. The list lengthened again when the colonial authorities pardoned Pontiac, the chief of the Ottawa tribe who had led the recent rebellion. Although the colonists still thought of themselves as Britons, their interests and values increasingly diverged from those of the Britons back across the Atlantic.

While the threat posed by France and Spain remained, the British colonists were happy to be protected by the British army and navy. Similarly many colonial industries – sugar, tobacco, shipping and indigo, for example – were happy to be protected by laws shielding them from global competition, which could have snuffed them out before they had a chance to establish themselves. The Treaty of Paris, however, seemed to remove the threat of European military intervention, and colonial industrialists and traders were growing strong enough to stand on their own two feet. The British empire was spreading around the globe and within it the North American colonies were starting to loom especially large. In 1775 London remained by far the largest English-speaking city in the world, but three cities were competing for the title of the empire's second city: Edinburgh, the ancient capital of Scotland; Dublin, whose commercial pre-eminence dated back to the Vikings; and Philadelphia, less than a century old.

King and colonists started to survey the same landscape through different ends of the telescope. The crown tired of subsidising the colonies by providing free protection. Realising that the colonists were becoming rich enough to pay for their own defence, British taxpayers wanted them to do so. The colonists, realising that the only protection they now needed was from natives whom they could handle perfectly well themselves, saw no reason to pay for anything. The phrase 'No taxation without representation' came to sum up a position that had originally been advanced in the 1730s to protest at the imposition by the king of a tax on the import into the mainland colonies of molasses from the French and Dutch West Indies. At that time the refrain had failed to resonate, partly because links were still strong between many of the mainland colonies and colonies like Jamaica and Barbados, which the Molasses Act was designed to protect, partly because the very real French threat muted all opposition to the crown and partly because the molasses tax was never very rigorously enforced. Forty years later the position had changed. In 1773 the parliament in London passed the Tea Act and the citizens of Boston reacted with fury, casting shiploads of tea into Boston harbour rather than paying the iniquitous import duties.

The Boston Tea Party is another of those foundation myths, like the story of the Pilgrim Fathers, known to everyone. It was the moment when the patience of the colonists snapped, a tax too far imposed on toiling Americans to pay for the whims of a foreign king. There is, however, a flaw in the conventional story: the Tea Act did not impose a horrendous new tax on the American colonists; it reduced by three-quarters an existing tax.

The American Revolution is often pictured as downtrodden colonists throwing off the weight of an oppressive and suffocating regime. This is simply not the case. It is worth putting at length the conclusions of Harvard professor Niall Ferguson in Empire. *How Britain Made the Modern World:*

> There is good reason to think that, by the 1770s, New Englanders were about the wealthiest people in the world. Per capita income was at least equal to that in the United Kingdom and was more evenly distributed. The New Englanders had bigger farms, bigger families and better education than the Old Englanders back home. And, crucially, they paid far less tax. In 1763 the average Briton paid 26 shillings a year in taxes. The equivalent figure for a Massachusetts taxpayer was just one shilling. To say that being British subjects had been good for these people would be an understatement. And yet it was they, not the indentured labourers of Virginia or the slaves of Jamaica, who first threw off the yoke of Imperial authority.

The key questions become, then, why was New England the tinder-box and what lit the fire? The answers are best provided, perhaps, not in the faculties of history but by using a favourite tool of modern business schools: the case study. An example might read:

> Your corporation has established a dominant global position in its markets with only one major competitor, which you have significantly outgrown by large-scale investment. You have funded this investment by issuing corporate debt and this is now causing cash flow problems. Your traditional markets have become saturated and are starting to come under attack from new entrants so that your production capacity exceeds demand and stock turn is deteriorating. You have a market study on a new territory that shows significant potential demand, weak local competition

(small scale and highly fragmented) and underdeveloped distribution channels. The market is highly protected, but you believe there is an opportunity to use your lobbying power to change government policy. What should you do?

This, in fact, would be a very poor case study because the answer, in business school parlance, is a 'no brainer' – you lobby hard, move into the new market on as large a scale as possible, take over the distribution channels and seize a controlling market share before local firms can consolidate and fight back. The flaw in this answer is that it assumes that everyone plays by the same rules; in the real world, if the stakes are high enough, competition can get very dirty; in 1770s New England it got deadly. Local firms quite literally fought back, and the world was never the same again.

The London oligarchs who had set up the East India Company were having a hard time. They had outgrown their major rival, the Dutch East India Company, but by 1770 were facing the very real prospect of bankruptcy and were desperate to find markets for the tea grown on their Asian plantations. The North American colonies were an attractive market and the Tea Act made it more attractive. This Act was not about raising money for the British crown but about providing state aid to the world's largest multinational company. The East India Company decided to do what today's multinationals would regard as a commonplace – enter the market and use its enormous scale to destroy the local competition. By appointing its own agents in the American colonies and importing not only tea but a host of other essentials, the company planned to take control of the local economy.

Only one group stood to lose from the Tea Act: not the toiling masses of Massachusetts but what American history books usually refer to as Boston 'merchants', in other words the smugglers who controlled an important part of Boston's mercantile trade. Colonial business leaders like John Hancock, one of the richest men in New England and prime mover in the Boston Tea Party, would have been ruined. Just as families like the Kennedys thrived 160 years later when alcohol smuggling oiled Boston's commercial wheels, so political power in mid-eighteenth-century Massachusetts floated on a sea of contraband.

Millionaire entrepreneur turned historian Ted Nace characterises the colonists' action as 'a highly pragmatic economic rebellion against an overbearing corporation, rather than a political rebellion against an oppressive government'. He concludes that one of the basic reasons for the American Revolution was 'colonial opposition to corporate power'.

This, however, is not the popular version of history. Once again it has been rewritten not, like Russia, by dictat from above but by the gradual expunging of what was and its replacement by what should have been. Ferguson points out that 'Contemporaries were well aware of the absurdity of the ostensible reason for the protest', but nevertheless it is this absurdity that has remained in the popular memory.

The American Rebellion did not start with the Boston Tea Party but with another of those events that are now firmly lodged in the annals of received American history: 'the shot that was heard round the world'. British soldiers marching to Concord to seize an illicit arms stash were confronted at Lexington by an armed militia famously aroused by Paul Revere riding through the night. Somebody fired the famous shot and British troops then opened up, killing eight militiamen. To say the shot was heard around the world is somewhat of an exaggeration. As Edmund Burke had complained a few months earlier, as far as the British public were concerned a 'robbery on Hounslow Heath would make more conversation than all the disturbances in America'. (The phrase itself comes from a poem by Ralph Waldo Emerson: 'Here once the embattled farmers stood, And fired the shot heard round the world.' He is probably correct that the first shot was fired at the British troops rather than by them, but to this day nobody can be sure who actually pulled the trigger.)

The British troops carried on to Concord, but on their way back the redcoats were repeatedly ambushed by American guerrillas and only the arrival of reinforcements prevented a complete massacre; 273 British soldiers died. The attack on the British troops had been well prepared.

Revere was only one of the riders who were waiting to summon the militia if the troops left their barracks. (And he certainly did not do this by shouting 'the British are coming' as legend asserts: at the time both sides considered themselves British.)

History is an interpretation of reality; it bears as much relation to the real events on which it is based as *West Side Story* does to *Romeo and Juliet*. Not only do later generations rewrite history to reflect the prejudices of their age, but the participants themselves construct instant history to suit the needs of the moment. Today's history started life as yesterday's public relations. The stories of Lexington and Concord are classic examples. Both sides blamed each other for firing the first shot, and in no time at all reality was being shamelessly embroidered.

The Massachusetts Assembly gathered depositions from alleged eye-witnesses for publication in Britain, which claimed that in the British retreat from Concord 'a great number of the houses on the road were plundered and rendered unfit for use; several were burnt; women in childbed were driven by the soldiery naked into the streets; old men, peaceably in their houses were shot dead; and such scenes exhibited as would disgrace the annals of the most uncivilized nation'. The official British line, contained in the reports sent home by the British commander, was relatively subdued, but the reaction of the loyalist population can be gauged by a letter written by the sister of a government official in Massachusetts. This reported that on their return through Lexington the British troops 'found two or three of their people lying in the agonies of death, scalped and their noses and ears cut off and eyes bored out, which exasperated the soldiers exceedingly'.

As in all wars the two sides, loyalist and rebel, were seeing different realities. In such circumstances a peaceful resolution of their differences became impossible.

The American Rebellion

Once the first shot had been fired at Lexington it quickly became clear that the rebels would not fight a defensive war. Right from the first they were convinced that others would inevitably come to share their dream. In particular they looked at the other British colonies, and their first move was to strike north, capturing Montréal and halting only after being heavily defeated in an assault on Quebec. The Americans were taken aback by the failure of Canadians to accept the invitation of the Continental Congress to join the rebellion and by their vigorous resistance to being invaded – prefiguring perhaps the differing reactions of invader and invaded in twenty-first-century Iraq.

For eight years the conflict dragged on. After their initial success the rebels suffered from British and loyalist counterattacks. Only a curious reluctance on the part of the British commanders to push home their advantages and skilful manoeuvring by the rebels stopped the incipient revolution being crushed. George Washington's army of 11,000 famously spent the winter of 1777 at Valley Forge, Pennsylvania, where nearly a quarter died of starvation and disease and another thousand deserted. Valley Forge marked the low point in the rebels' cause. The next year France and the self-declared United States of America signed a treaty committing each not to make peace with Britain before the other. The following year Spain joined them. Initially the advent of their new allies did little to help the rebels, who suffered more significant defeats and continued harrying from the Iroquois allies of the British. Washington was faced with mutinies in Pennsylvania and New Jersey, and the US navy was forced to recruit from jails and among British prisoners of war. The rebels lost one of their most brilliant commanders when Benedict Arnold went over to the British, determined, in the old quip, to prove himself 'the ablest general on both sides'.

The rebels, by now a genuine American army rather than a collection of local militias, did not give up. They retained real popular support and the conflict took on all the characteristics of a war of liberation. The rebel generals and their troops proved more skilful and more committed than their opponents. Helped by monumental British errors, the war moved to its climax at Yorktown. The scene was set for a repeat of the siege of Louisburg, the Gibraltar of America, albeit on a far larger and more significant scale. Oddly Gibraltar itself played a key part in the final outcome. A Spanish siege of Gibraltar, exacerbated by French attacks in Asia, stretched the Royal Navy to breaking point. British forces proved incapable of fighting a global war, and a much larger French fleet not only overwhelmed the British fleet in Chesapeake Bay but also landed 3,000 French troops to support the Americans besieging Yorktown. On 18 October the British commander, Lord Cornwallis, surrendered.

The loyalist and British forces in New York still held out, and Washington himself did not believe that Yorktown would settle the conflict, but the British parliament, riven by doubts about the war from its inception, decided to capitulate. Within weeks tens of thousands of loyalists were fleeing for their lives, enriching the Caribbean colonies and especially Canada, and leaving behind spoils for the victors. As J.M. Roberts has pointed out, 'There were fewer emigrants from France during the French Revolution than from the American colonies after 1783. A much larger proportion of Americans felt too intimidated or disgusted with their revolution to live in the United States after Independence than the proportion of Frenchmen who could not live in France after the Terror.'

The conflict that began on Lexington Green in April 1775 was at the same time a war of independence, a revolution, a civil war and a tiny fragment of a global struggle. It has even been described by Kevin Phillips as a religious war, pitching Congregationalists, Presbyterians and Low Church Anglicans against High Church Anglicans, repeating the divisions of the English Civil War. Not surprisingly simplistic attempts to describe its origins are doomed to failure. On both sides different groups had different interests. The financial imperatives of the merchant leaders of New England were different to those of their opposite numbers in more cosmopolitan New York; the land hunger driving the ethnic cleansers on the borders of Pennsylvania and South Carolina was no longer shared by the settled farmers of Connecticut and Massachusetts; the lives of the patrician oligarchs of Virginia had no more in common with the fisherfolk of Maine than they did with their own slaves. In Britain the country gentry were pressing for higher taxation on the colonies to avert a threatened rise in land tax at home at the same time as Parliament, in an attempt to defuse the growing crisis, resolved not to tax any colony that would pay for its own administration, defence and judiciary. Underlying these varied sectional interests was a growing psychological gulf between the two sides, a gulf that is inevitable in any empire: the chasm between the coloniser and the colonised. As John Adams later put it, the war itself was a consequence of a 'Revolution in the minds of the people', a revolution that he believed had been developing for more than a decade before the first drop of blood was spilt. The crux of the American rebellion is that less than two hundred years after the first English settlement the settlers had become natives. The days when the colonies had been the property of court favourites and London merchants had long since gone, and with them the essential unity of the Anglo-American political establishment. Although bonds of friendship and blood still stretched across the Atlantic they were increasingly tenuous. More than half the colonial population was of non-British origin – native, African or, the biggest group, German and German-Swiss. Furthermore three-quarters of British immigrants in the eighteenth century were Scottish or Irish, neither of whom had any particular love for what they regarded as the 'English' crown.

To the colonists the British authorities and the British army were no longer their fellow Britons but agents of an occupying power. The colonists may still theoretically have been Britons, but they were second-class Britons. George Washington was horrified to discover in 1754, when he was promoted to lieutenant-colonel in the British army, that he would be paid less than British-born officers of the same rank.

Although the majority of colonists undoubtedly chafed at their second-class status it is important not to over-emphasise the extent of discontent. As Niall Ferguson has written, 'The Hollywood version of the War of Independence is a straightforward fight between heroic Patriots and wicked, Nazi-like Redcoats. The reality was quite different. This was indeed a civil war that divided social classes and even families. And the worst of the violence did not involve regular British troops, but was perpetrated by rebel colonists against their countrymen who remained loyal to the crown.'

Around half of all the British colonies in the Americas did not rebel. One of the first actions of the Continental Congress was to place a trade embargo on the colonies that stayed loyal. Bermuda was particularly hard hit. The colony had been controlled by a group of oligarchs known as the 'forty families' since its establishment 130 years earlier. They had strong commercial links with the rebel leaders and a deal was soon reached. On 14 August 1775 two American ships anchored in Tobacco Bay, Bermuda, under cover of darkness and were loaded with barrels of gunpowder; ransom paid, the blockade was lifted. Thereafter Bermudian sloops regularly flouted the Royal Navy's blockade to carry salt to Washington's army. The far more populous and important Caribbean colonies, which were to be in the forefront of the fighting as the French captured island after island, stayed loyal, and Jamaica became a key base for the British navy. The rebels did capture and briefly hold the Bahamas.

The bulk of the colonial population was on the mainland and here the call of the rebels was much more strongly heeded. Of the eighteen mainland colonies only five did not join the rebellion, although in New York loyalists were probably in a majority when the war started. Of the thirteen most developed colonies only Quebec stayed loyal. In the less developed colonies Georgia went with the rebels and Newfoundland, Nova Scotia, East and West Florida stayed loyal, but with such tiny populations they made no difference to the balance of power.

Despite their widely different, indeed conflicting, interests the majority of the colonists rose up in rebellion. Initially they were united in their opposition to the crown but in little else; they needed a stronger glue to bind them together. That glue proved to be the ideology of democracy. The very first Continental Congress held in Philadelphia a year before the rebellion broke out, and including representatives of twelve of the eventual thirteen seceding colonies, adopted a lofty 'Declaration of Rights and Grievances' designed to grab the ethical high ground.

The American War of Independence was the first war to be fought overtly for an ideology. The rebels were not fighting a nationalist war, as the concept of America as a nation did not yet exist, nor were they following charismatic leaders promising them wealth and glory. They were not even fighting for 'freedom' in the sort of practical sense that would have been understood by those fettered by the shackles of slavery; they fought for the ideology of what today is called democracy.

(There is a danger in using the term 'democracy' as its meaning has changed considerably over the last two centuries. Many of the Founding Fathers of what today proudly calls itself the world's leading democracy would have been horrified to be labelled democrats, a term that, especially after the French Revolution, implied an element of mob rule. As one eminent historian, Samuel Eliot Morison, has written, the clergy and political leaders of New England considered democracy to mean 'terror, atheism and free love', and they fought to ensure that America would not become 'too democratic for liberty'.)

The proclamation that above all others captured the spirit of the times, and has echoed through the centuries since, was adopted by the Continental Congress on 4 July 1776. The Declaration of Independence, written primarily by Thomas Jefferson, contains one of the most moving passages written in English, but much of it is tawdry, for example a caricatured attack on George III and a condemnation of the proposed boundary of the colony of Quebec. Congress made revisions to his draft, which upset Jefferson deeply; most famously his denunciation of aspects of the slave trade was deleted entirely at the insistence of South Carolina and Georgia. After all that, however, there remain the few short lines that for millions have come to define the American dream. Jefferson's words have transcended place and time to speak to generations the world over: 'We hold these truths to be self evident, that all men are created equal, that they are endowed by their Creator, with certain inalienable Rights, that among these are Life, Liberty and the pursuit of Happiness. That to secure these rights, governments are instituted among Men, deriving their just powers from the consent of the governed.'

Those two sentences encapsulated the ideology of a people throwing off the chains of old world authority to embrace the freedoms offered by a limitless frontier. Nothing could have been further from the ideology of autocracy so firmly rooted further east, where even as the Congress was debating Jefferson's words Russian colonisers were pushing down the Volga, driven not by a yearning for freedom but by the command of their tsar.

Jefferson's stirring declaration was read out in pulpits, town halls and assemblies throughout the rebel areas and beyond. If ever a piece of paper captured the soul of a people this was it.

The seed of American democracy was planted in the summer of 1776, but the ground had been prepared in the preceding months, largely by one of the most remarkable men of the eighteenth century.

Thomas Paine and Tadeusz Kosciuszko

Thomas Paine was an Englishman who had arrived in the colonies two years earlier at the age of thirty-seven. In a pamphlet entitled *Common Sense* he set forth the case for American independence in blunt and persuasive terms:

> I have heard it asserted by some, that as America hath flourished under her former connection with Great Britain, that the same connection is necessary towards her future happiness, and will always have the same effect. Nothing can be more fallacious than this kind of argument. We may as well assert, that because a child has thrived upon milk, that it is never to have meat. . . . I am not induced by motives of pride, party, or resentment to espouse the doctrine of separation and independence; I am clearly, positively, and conscientiously persuaded that it is the true interest of this continent to be so; that every thing short of that is mere patchwork, that it can afford no lasting felicity, – that it is leaving the sword to our children, and shrinking back at a time, when, a little more, a little farther, would have rendered this continent the glory of the earth.

Much of the pamphlet now seems dated, and some has proved simply wrong. 'Nothing but independence', he wrote, 'can keep the peace of the continent and preserve it inviolate from civil wars.' But at the time *Common Sense* was an instant bestseller; half a million copies were printed, galvanising republican sentiment throughout the colonies and later throughout Europe. Paine inspired a political fervour, providing a ferment of new ideas and a resounding call to arms only matched since by Karl Marx.

At the time the American rebels proclaimed that they were fighting for 'liberty' and 'freedom'. When the term 'democracy' later came to summarise the cause, this was to some extent rewriting history. Men like Thomas Paine were indeed fighting for democracy – for representative government, free speech and personal liberty – but many of the rebels had a much more limited definition of freedom. Their objective was freedom from Britain, national liberation. Particularly in the southern colonies the aspirations for democracy were viewed with deep suspicion; the ruling elites had no intention of sharing power with the common man. The enslavement of blacks, eradication of natives and disenfranchisement of women were simply taken for granted.

(It is another oddity of history that the American Rebellion led to women getting the vote for the first time in history – not in America but in Africa. Many slaves who had fought for the British escaped to Nova Scotia from where they were settled in the new African colony of Sierra Leone and, irrespective of gender, given the vote in 1793.)

Some colonists rebelled precisely because they did not believe that all men are created equal. In June 1772 Lord Mansfield, chief justice of the king's bench in London, made a ruling in the case of James Somersett that sent shudders of apprehension across the southern colonies. Somersett was a slave who had been taken to England and had then run away; he was recaptured, but Mansfield ordered his release because, he declared, slavery was fundamentally 'odious'. The decision outlawed slavery in England. Seven months later the courts in Boston were asked to rule that the Mansfield decision should apply to the

American colonies. They declined to do so, but many in the south had an uneasy premonition of the way British opinion might move.

The issue of slavery divided the northern and southern colonies from the very beginning. It is difficult today to understand how deeply entrenched slavery was in the moral mindset of most of the south. It was not the case that a few greedy slave owners were ignoring the principles enshrined in the Bill of Rights for their own selfish purposes. When it became apparent that an influential part of northern opinion was pushing for slavery to be outlawed in the new nation, petition upon petition circulated in the south expressing indignation in the most graphic terms: emancipation would mean 'The horrors of rapes, murders and outrages' along with 'Want, poverty, distress and ruin to free citizens, neglect, famine and death to the black infant'. Appeals were made to God, as the Old Testament apparently showed that 'slavery was permitted by the Deity himself', and to the Bill of Rights, which southerners held protected the property rights they exercised over their slaves. As one petition asserted, 'We have sealed with our blood title to the full free and absolute enjoyment of every species of our property,' by which the petitioners meant their slaves. Of particular concern were the slaves liberated by the defeated British army, who now had the temerity to demand the rights of free men. The proponents of slavery were every bit as scathing in the denunciation of the abolitionists as their Quaker and Puritan opponents were of them. 'No language can express our Indignation, Contempt and Detestation of the apostate wretches,' said one pro-slavery petition in words that could have easily come from the other side.

Not only were there enormous differences between southern and northern colonies, differences which within a century would erupt in civil war, but even within these groups tensions ran high. A collection of thirty-six towns on the borders of New York and New Hampshire declared themselves an independent country in 1777 under the name New Connecticut. George Washington had to use his personal authority to prevent the armed invasion of the fledgling republic that was urged on him by congressional resolutions. (Once the war was over the independent 'nation', by now renamed, applied for admission to the Union but still met vigorous opposition: only the payment of a $30,000 settlement to the state of New York enabled Vermont to become the fourteenth US state.)

The inhabitants of Vermont might not have wanted to be part of New York or New Hampshire, but they wanted to be free of the British yoke. One of the strengths of the rebel ideology was that terms like liberty could be so inspiring while remaining so nebulous. Under the banner of freedom congregated not only colonists of sharply different political hues but also idealists from all over Europe. The most famous was the French Marquis de Lafayette. First as a volunteer with George Washington's forces and then as a French officer, Lafayette played a key role in the eventual American victory. His efforts were clearly in the French national interest, but he was also fired by a genuine commitment to liberty. (Oddly, the man who supposedly encouraged him to join the American rebels was George III's younger brother, who had left Britain after making an 'inappropriate' marriage.)

The twentieth century saw men from all walks of life abandon their homes to fight as foot soldiers with the international brigades in the Spanish Civil War or the mujahaddin in Afghanistan but the international volunteers in America, although some of them motivated by the same sort of ideological fervour, were very different. Many of them were part of a military elite that moved easily across borders and bonded quickly with the new American officer class. American representatives in France were instructed to hire mercenaries from the French army and navy, especially artillerymen and engineers. Encouraged by their government, dozens of French officers joined the American forces. Mercenary soldiers were a common feature of warfare in the period. Among the French army volunteers was the Bavarian Johan Kalb, who became a major-general and died heroically at the battle of Camden and the Irishman Thomas Conway, who also became a major-general in the revolutionary army but fell out with George Washington and was eventually wounded in a duel with one of Washington's supporters. (Conway returned to France in disgrace but rose to become governor of the French colonies in India.) Such men worked for whoever paid them and were as likely to offer their services in support of oppression as of freedom. As the Marquis de Lafayette returned to France from his successful defence of democracy the Comte de Langéron was leaving France to spend a lifetime successfully defending autocracy. Not only did Langéron fight for the Russian tsar against the Swedes and Turks but he also led his infantry corps all the way to Paris in the war against Napoleon. (He eventually became a count of the Russian empire, military governor of various newly conquered regions in the south and commander-in-chief of an elite Cossack 'host'.)

As an illustration of how value-laden vocabulary can colour historical perceptions, the mercenaries who fought on the rebel side are usually referred to as 'volunteers', the term 'mercenaries' being reserved for the troops George III recruited from his family's native Germany. To picture these foreign 'volunteers' as champions of liberty may be naïve, but some, like Lafayette, undoubtedly were. The Venezuelan professional revolutionary Francisco de Miranda was another.

One idealist even more important than Lafayette in terms of later European history was Tadeusz Kosciuszko, the son of a minor Polish noble who had trained at the military academies in Warsaw and Versailles. Kosciuszko had travelled extensively in western Europe before returning to Poland in 1774, where he became the tutor to the daughter of a Polish general. What happened next is unclear, but it would appear the couple tried to elope; only Kosciuszko got away. Returning to France he was caught up in the same idealistic fervour as Lafayette and set sail for America. There his skills as a military engineer were immediately recognised, and he played a key role in the rebel victory, eventually becoming one of Washington's senior generals. Among other things he organised the siege of Charleston that broke British power in the southern colonies. Thomas Jefferson remarked that 'He was as pure a son of liberty as I have ever known.' It was a judgement many Poles came to share when he returned home to continue the fight against imperialism – this time battling an altogether stronger foe, Catherine the Great of Russia.

Although men like Lafayette and Kosciuszko provided the military skills that the fledgling American army desperately needed, it was the inspirational ideology of Thomas Paine that motivated the rebel forces and provided the political certainties that have endured to this day.

When Paine arrived in the colonies success both for the rebels and for himself must have seemed unlikely. In England Paine had been a failure: failing in marriage (twice), failing as a corset-maker and finally dismissed as a troublemaker from his role as a customs officer. His only success had been to attract the attention of Benjamin Franklin, who helped him make his way in Pennsylvania. Paine produced numerous propaganda pieces during the war and also wrote stirringly in condemnation of slavery and in affirmation of the rights of women. In 1781 he travelled to France and returned with money and weapons for the insurgents. All the profits from his writings he gave to the rebel cause, but when he petitioned Congress for financial assistance after the war he was turned down.

In 1791, by which time he had returned to England, Paine wrote his masterpiece *The Rights of Man*, in support of the French Revolution and denouncing poverty and war. This work attracted so much controversy that he was forced to flee to France. There he was initially welcomed, but when he opposed the execution of Louis XVI he was imprisoned. He eventually returned to America, but discovered that his last great book, *The Age of Reason*, with its plea for religious toleration, had destroyed his reputation there. Americans were not ready to tolerate any religion but their own. Paine, already in poor health, slumped into alcoholism and died in New York in 1809.

With the writing of *Common Sense* Paine crystallised an ideology that would remain permanently ingrained in the psyche of America. Not only was it the ideology of democracy; it was the ideology of an all-encompassing democracy. In the introduction to his pamphlet Paine included a simple sentence that was to be profoundly significant: 'The cause of America is, in a great measure, the cause of all mankind.' He was advocating a new form of government not just for thirteen rebel colonies but as a model for the world. Paine was convinced, as succeeding generations of Americans have been convinced, that American democracy is a fundamentally better form of government than any other, and that because it is better it should be universal.

The American Rebellion was an ideological war, and ideologies are universal. The rebels convinced themselves that they were fighting for a better world in which nothing that needed to be improved could not be improved. They had a totalitarian zeal to transform everything around them – even the language they spoke and wrote. In the middle of the war John Adams, who would become America's second president, took time out to campaign for an academy to 'correct' and 'improve' the English language. (The American Academy of Language and Belles Lettres was finally set up in 1820, presided over by Adams's son, America's sixth president, but had virtually no impact.)

Many of the Founding Fathers spoke of the nascent nation's future status as an 'empire' spreading its values way beyond the existing frontiers of the new United States of America. But first they needed a period of peace. Disregarding their earlier treaty with France, American envoys signed a peace agreement with Britain on 30 November 1782. The next year France and Spain followed suit, Spain regaining Florida and France gaining islands in the Caribbean and Gulf of St Lawrence. The United States gained its independence and, in a sign of things to come, demanded and received unrestricted fishing rights along the Newfoundland coast where New Englanders had previously been banned. The new Treaty of Paris was sent back to Congress to ratify, and on 14 January 1784 the war was officially over. The merchant princes of Boston could turn their eyes to the American hinterland and gather the riches waiting to be exploited there.

Theirs were not the only eyes to glisten with excitement at the opportunities awaiting them in that vast and 'empty' continent. At the very time Congress was debating the treaty that would end America's subservience to the British empire, merchant princes of a very different empire were waiting for the snows of winter to melt. When the ice had cleared their leader Grigori Shelikhov set sail for Kodiak Island, to found the first permanent Russian settlement in Alaska.

CHAPTER 7

THE EMPIRES GET GOING

There are parallels between early America and Russia but they are somewhat forced. Both nations treated the native populations they encountered on their way to the Pacific in remarkably similar, and brutal, ways and both have written much of this out of their popular histories. Both nations relied for their economic well-being on a heavily exploited underclass of slaves or serfs. Both the proud successors to the Kievan Rus crown and the Founding Fathers of the United States of America proclaimed their nations to be empires favoured by the same God. But in most respects the two societies were fundamentally different. The Russian tradition of autocratic government and the English concept of the rule of law were ideologically poles apart. Differences of geography and geopolitics were profound: the might and scale of Catherine the Great's empire dwarfed the new nation clinging to the eastern seaboard of a largely unexplored continent. America and Russia had, in substance, little in common, and the chapters into which their stories can be divided rarely overlapped. During the nineteenth century this changed. The two nations moved along increasingly similar paths and were buffeted by increasingly similar forces. By the end of the century both were great imperial powers and both were coming to terms with the transition from agricultural to industrial societies. Two great historical currents dominated the nineteenth century in both Russia and America: the continual enlargement of the nation and what might be called the struggle for the nation's soul, a struggle concluded in both cases by civil war.

Enlightenment: Russian and American Style

Soviet leaders and historians were fond of describing the Bolshevik victory in the Russian Civil War as the most important event in the history of the world. The Russian Revolution, they insisted, changed the course of human development for ever. They were wrong, but for more than half a century many hoped or feared that they might be right.

Revolutions by definition change their worlds, but some more than others. The English Revolution (usually called the English Civil War) turned the nation upside down: the hereditary monarch Charles I lost his head and was effectively replaced by the military dictatorship of Oliver Cromwell, albeit tempered with the trappings of democracy, but a dozen years later Charles II was back on the throne and English life continued much as before. The American Revolution created a nation that would determine the future of the world, but that was only apparent with hindsight; at the time hardly anyone in the rest of the world considered that the political antics of a few remote colonials had any global significance. Other revolutions throughout Europe made more or less difference to their own histories but had no impact beyond their borders.

In the last 250 years only two revolutions had an instantaneous impact on the history of the western world: the Russian Revolution and before that the French Revolution.

The execution of Louis XVI and the welter of bloodletting that followed terrified the monarchies of Europe and triggered a tidal wave of ideological ferment. Everywhere forms of government that had evolved gradually over centuries, or even millennia, were forced into new directions. New philosophies, new moral certainties and uncertainties, new values rolled across Europe colliding with centuries-old traditions, assumptions and creeds. The result was an intellectual maelstrom in which everything was effectively questioned and nothing was definitively answered. And while this fervour was gripping the 'intelligentsia', itself a concept unknown and unknowable in the centuries before, technology was changing the world all around. Startling advances in science and engineering throughout the nineteenth century delivered the power of steam, the economies of mass production, the benefits of vaccination and the brutality of the machine gun.

At the end of the eighteenth century it was far from obvious that Russia and America would develop as they did. The United States of America did not emerge from the American Revolution a paragon of political purity. John Quincy Adams (President Adams II) called the American Constitution, nowadays held up as a model for the world, a 'morally vicious . . . bargain between freedom and slavery'. (In determining how to allocate representatives in the new Congress the constitution even defined the precise mathematical relationship between free men and slaves: a slave was decreed to be worth three-fifths of a white.) The fine words of Thomas Paine and Thomas Jefferson stirred the spirit and inspired a revolution, but a nation imbued with the ideology of democracy was not the same as a nation able to function as a democracy. Popular will could cast out an unpopular monarchy, but could not be guaranteed to sustain its replacement. Army mutinies and a threatened *coup d'état* forced the new federal government to flee from Philadelphia to Princeton. The merchant oligarchs of Boston who had done so much to stir up opposition to the British set about exploiting their power over the local economy with such greed that farmers in western Massachusetts rose up in armed rebellion, only to be crushed by the Boston militia. For a time it looked as though the new republic would be stillborn; indeed the continuing unity of the United States remained uncertain for the next century. There was talk of a northern breakaway confederacy, and Colonel Aaron Burr attempted to create his own empire west of the Mississippi.

But despite its internal strains the fledgling nation survived and eventually thrived. Its institutions may have wobbled but they did not fall. The Declaration of Independence and the Constitution of the United States, with the Bill of Rights constituting its first ten amendments, were manifestations of the democratic ideal destined to become a model for nations everywhere. Millions of the world's downtrodden masses would heed their noble vision. The phrase 'We hold these truths to be self evident, that all men are created equal' reverberated around the globe.

Two million migrants had voyaged west across the ocean in the course of the eighteenth century, but not all were drawn by dreams of freedom; indeed the vast majority were not. For every free white migrant reaching the western shore three black slaves arrived in chains. The American Revolution changed for ever the political landscape inhabited by the white elite; it changed not at all the economic landscape inhabited by the vast bulk of the population – black, native and white alike.

Had slaves lived as long as whites, the startling reality is that at the time of its birth the United States of America would have been a predominantly black nation. But they did not: a quarter of slaves died in their first year in the land of the free; a third died within three years. Life expectancy varied from colony to colony, as the conditions in which slaves existed varied with the economic superstructure built largely on their backs. In the Caribbean and southern colonies (Carolina and Georgia) small white elites held sway over a black majority. The only way to maintain power in such a society was through sheer brutality; blacks were literally beaten into submission. By contrast, in the colonies from Delaware up to Newfoundland there were 'only' around 30,000 slaves by the middle of the century, and in general they were perceived to be less of a threat to the established order and consequently were usually better treated. Between these two extremes were the 150,000 slaves in Virginia and Maryland. Even in the north there was a world of difference between the lot of a black slave and that of a white servant. When slaves stepped out of line all the savagery the Puritans had demonstrated in their ethnic cleansing of the native population reappeared. In 1712, at a time when Peter the Great was pushing tens of thousands to their deaths building St Petersburg, white Americans responded to a 'rebellion' by just two dozen black slaves in New York with a round of sadistic ritual executions: burning at the stake, hanging in chains to starve to death, slowly breaking on the wheel and plain hanging on the gallows until strangled to death.

The ideology of democracy united the seceding colonies in their successful struggle against British rule but there remained deep divisions between them. The democratic vision of Thomas Paine resonated with the religious fundamentalism of much of New England and instilled in the mass of the population of the northern states an instinctive, almost atavistic, attachment to such concepts as liberty, however defined. Such an attachment was largely absent further south where liberty was a dangerous concept; social hierarchy determined political life and economic life was founded on slavery. There the lesson of the American Revolution was not that righteousness will triumph but simply that America will triumph. The rest of American history reflects the fusing of these two traditions. Political debate in the northern colonies was conducted in the language of moral and religious principle; in the south and the increasingly important west the language was of glory and self-interest. By the end of the nineteenth century a common language had emerged in which America's glory became synonymous with God's will. In a phrase much used at the time, conquering its neighbours became America's manifest destiny.

This was a concept that would have been well understood by Catherine the Great. The belief in a manifest destiny to continually expand the empire had been a part of the vision that had inspired Russian leaders since the first Viking warlords set off looking for spoils; it was part of the fabric of tsardom.

Nobody embodied Russia's struggles for territory and soul more than Catherine. In her reign the Russian empire's frontiers were pushed dramatically outward and, for the first time, notions of liberty gained a tentative foothold in the recesses of autocracy. When she ascended the imperial throne George III was the confident master of his American colonies and George Washington was an officer in the British army. By the time she died thirteen of those colonies had won their independence, and George Washington had become the first president of the United States of America.

Catherine was one of the most important figures of her time, indeed of any time. She steered her nation through a period when the divine right of monarchs was under unprecedented attack. And yet, like her predecessor the Empress Elizabeth, Catherine the Great is now mainly remembered for her sexual exploits, in particular that she was killed while making love to a horse. The story of her equine death seems to have been invented in France very soon after the supposed event, and despite being widely quoted is a complete fantasy. In fact Catherine collapsed on the toilet and was carried to her bed where she passed away peacefully some hours later. Tales of her debauchery were rampant in western courts during her lifetime; British diplomats seemed to be particularly interested in relaying whatever gossip they could uncover or manufacture. When Britain threatened war over Catherine's seizure of an obscure medieval fortress in Ukraine, the British press published cartoons of her that verged on the pornographic. Gaggles of historians have been kept busy researching Catherine's love life. Prodigious numbers of putative lovers have been advanced, although Peter Neville quotes the conclusion of one respected expert, J.T. Alexander, that there were 'only' twelve. Of course had Catherine been male the subject would have warranted very little attention, given her monumental achievements in other areas.

Catherine is another of those Russian leaders credited with opening up the country to the west, in her case particularly to France. Russian aristocrats frequented the salons of Paris and their children were introduced to the literature and music of France by the French tutors they brought back with them. French language and manners came to dominate the imperial court. Catherine herself entered into regular correspondence with Voltaire, quoted Montesquieu and invited Diderot to visit St Petersburg. She bought one of the largest collections of Old Masters in Europe, previously owned by Robert Walpole, Britain's first prime minister. She was, it is said, a child of the Enlightenment, although her liberal reforms tended to be restricted to matters, like the education of girls, that did not threaten the core prerogatives of the regime.

Like that other 'Great' westerniser, Peter the Great, at heart Catherine the Great remained an autocrat of the traditional school. The new philosophies spawned the American Revolution and then, even more alarmingly, the French Revolution, and Catherine took fright. When Diderot published his *Encyclopedie* Catherine banned it, and when the Orthodox Metropolitan Arseny Matseevich questioned her interference in church affairs she had him thrown into prison.

It would have been inconceivable for a foreign-born woman to lead America, as Catherine the Great led Russia, if only because neither women nor the foreign-born could stand as candidates in presidential elections. American presidents were to be white male Protestants. In the early days it looked as though the new nation might develop its own informal aristocracy; four of the first six presidents were slave-holding Virginia oligarchs and the other two were a father and son from one of New England's patrician dynasties. Later presidents were less aristocratic and two forces emerged to shape the political leadership. The first was an institution for whom the term 'force' was particularly apposite – the army, from whose ranks a great many presidential candidates emerged. The second was political parties.

Although not foreseen when the constitution was drafted, parties almost immediately became a fundamental part of American political life. In Russia's imperial court factions jostled for influence, but open opposition to the tsar's policies was pointless; with very few exceptions personal ambitions did not extend as far as replacing the tsar. In America, on the other hand, factions could hope that open opposition would be rewarded at the next election. The Founding Fathers divided into a southern faction known as Republicans and a northern faction, the Federalists.

The Federalists soon showed that Americans could be just as tyrannous as any British king or Russian empress. The 1798 Sedition Act introduced the US version of crimes against the state, making the publication of 'any false, scandalous and malicious writing' a high misdemeanour. Twenty-five Republicans were quickly arrested, most of them editors whose newspapers were simultaneously shut down. Vermont congressman Matthew Lyon was thrown into prison for criticising President Adams's 'ridiculous pomp'. When Jefferson and the Republicans took power in 1800 the Sedition Act was repealed, and all those who had been convicted were pardoned. Not until the 1948 Smith Act was merely advocating a political belief once again made a federal crime.

Thomas Jefferson envisaged a rough egalitarianism in which all white males would be more or less equal. On the other hand Alexander Hamilton and the Federalists regarded the rule of the 'well-born' as both inevitable and desirable (an odd creed for a bastard). Hamilton is sometimes described as a 'typical' New Yorker, but he was born and brought up on the tiny Caribbean island of Nevis, one of the colonial outposts that remained loyal to Britain, and always retained a lingering attachment to the mother country and its aristocratic mores. As secretary of the treasury he set the financial priorities of the new nation, and the main priority was the maintenance of oligarchy. In Morison's words, Hamilton determined that 'The old families, merchant-ship owners, public creditors, and financiers must be made a loyal governing class by a straightforward policy favouring their interests.'

In fighting for independence the state and federal governments had amassed considerable debts, and Hamilton proposed to pay them off by raising taxes; for him this was essential to establish the creditworthiness of the United States in the fledgling international capital markets. But some states, like Virginia, had already repaid their debt and saw no reason they should foot the bill for states like Massachusetts which hadn't. The original loan certificates had been issued to revolutionary soldiers in lieu of pay or represented loans made by patriotic citizens who, in many cases, had given up all hope of having their money returned, and had sold their certificates for virtually nothing. There was outrage that rather than repaying the original holders, £80m of previously worthless paper was now in the hands of speculators – including it is said members of Hamilton's wife's family – who were set to make a fortune. Nevertheless Hamilton went ahead.

In the long run it was Hamilton's proto-capitalism rather than Jefferson's romantic revolutionary purity that proved the more enduring. It was also more influential on the other side of the world. A Russian edition of Hamilton's 1791 *Report on the Usefulness of the Manufactories in Relation to Trade and Agriculture*, sponsored by the minister of finance, was published in St Petersburg in 1807. The two nations were still poles apart but their two ideologies were starting to overlap.

Territorial Aggrandisement

At the same time that ideological currents were changing America and Russia, America and Russia were changing the lands around them. The armies of both nations spent most of the nineteenth century pushing out the frontiers of empire. Indeed the outstanding feature of American and Russian history in the period from the US Declaration of Independence in 1776 up to the fall of the Romanovs in 1917 was what might be called territorial aggrandisement. Both nations were totally committed to their own expansion and both realised their ambitions. Catherine the Great and her successors continued a long tsarist tradition, firmly believing in their divine right to conquer; her American counterparts believed equally firmly that their new nation, representing as it did God's will on earth, was destined to surpass all others.

There are clear historical parallels between the Russian conquest of Siberia and the territorial expansion of the United States, but by the time Catherine came to the throne the campaigns against the Siberian natives were almost over; only a few tribes in the Aleutian Islands on the way to Alaska remained to be 'pacified'. From then on Russian imperialism was primarily focussed on the Christian states to the west and the largely Muslim states to the south. Under her leadership Russia conquered most of Poland and gained access to the Black Sea, grabbing the whole area around the Sea of Azov, the Crimea and the port of Odessa. America, on the other hand, still had a whole continent of natives to displace.

During their war against the British the colonial rebels had been desperate for native allies. In 1775 the new Congress concluded its first treaty with natives living in southern Ohio and Indiana, a treaty that suggested the creation of a fourteenth native state with representatives in the Congress. Once the war was over, however, the victors turned on what the Declaration of Independence had described as 'the merciless Indian Savages'.

Fifteen years after that first treaty was signed it was ripped up. In 1790 and again in 1791 the American army invaded what was called the Northwest Territory, a vast swathe of land between the Ohio and Mississippi stretching from Pennsylvania as far west as the modern states of Michigan and Wisconsin. On both occasions it was soundly defeated by native forces led by the Miami general Michikinikwa or Little Turtle. In 1794 a reorganised army made one final attempt at conquest. British troops moved south from Canada in support of the natives but in the event failed to intervene, although a hundred British volunteers stiffened the resistance in the battle of Fallen Timbers that eventually took place south of Detroit. An enormous force of Shawnee, Ottawa, Chippewa, Miami, Delaware, Pottawatomi and other tribes under Little Turtle and the Shawnee general Blue Jacket faced the American troops of General Anthony Wayne. The American advance guard of Kentucky militia were ambushed, and when they turned and ran the Shawnees made the crucial mistake of leaving their heavily defended positions to set off in hot pursuit, running into the path of the main American force and into range of their artillery. The Americans successfully counter-attacked and by the end of the day native troops were streaming north seeking British protection; those left on the battlefield were scalped and mutilated by the American soldiers. Losses on both sides were heavy, with the casualty rate highest among the British volunteers who had fought to the end. The American army then advanced along the Maumee river, destroying native villages and crops in an orgy of ethnic cleansing.

In the subsequent Treaty of Greenville the natives were forced to give up most of modern Ohio and Indiana and the site of today's city of Chicago. The treaty was a total travesty: the federal government solemnly guaranteed territory to the natives that it had already sold to speculators or promised to revolutionary war soldiers. Any idea of the natives having a state of their own had evaporated. America would expand through further white (or black and white) colonisation, not through the incorporation of native states. And it would expand by force. In 1797 American settlers in Natchez rebelled against the Spanish authorities; US troops marched in and the future state of Mississippi was born. It was a demonstration of what would happen repeatedly in years to come from Florida to Hawaii.

Not everyone agreed that every opportunity to expand the nation should be seized. In 1798 the Venezuelan revolutionary Francisco de Miranda, who had fought for the rebels in the American Revolution and taken part in the French Revolution, approached the American government with a plan for American troops, supported by the British navy, to liberate Latin America from the Spanish empire and in the process grab Florida and Louisiana for themselves. Alexander Hamilton was a fervent enthusiast and put himself forward as commander of the US forces but President Adams I vetoed the project. Seizing land occupied by Europeans was quite different to seizing land occupied only by 'Indians'.

When the Founding Fathers declared it to be self-evident that all men were created equal most of them had taken it for granted that such equality did not extend to the natives. Thomas Paine's irreligious idealism was not shared by most Americans and particularly not by the fundamentalists of New England who so influenced the development of the nation's political ideology.

Looking at early American history though the prism of today's religious ideologies it is easy to misinterpret its religious dimension. The Puritans were not bringing with them the religious conventions of their mother countries; they were fundamentalists escaping from religious convention. There was no inevitability in their own religious certainties becoming the American orthodoxy. The exalted position of religion in America today is due to the outstanding economic success of the New England settlers who were able to translate their economic dominance into political and cultural power, instilling a version of their Puritan values on the rest of society.

Things could have been different. This was the age of the Enlightenment. In Europe Frederick the Great, in his political testament of 1768, famously described Christianity as 'an old metaphysical fiction, stuffed with miracles, contradictions and absurdities, which was spawned in the fevered imaginations of the Orientals and then spread over Europe, where some fanatics espoused it, some intriguers pretended to be convinced by it and some imbeciles actually believed it'. In 1740 Frederick, anxious to find settlers to come into his under-populated domains had made plain that 'if Turks and heathens came and wanted to populate this country, then we would build mosques and temples for them'. Nothing could have been further from the ideology that was developing on the other side of the Atlantic.

A macabre example of the fusion of the democratic spirit and horrific savagery towards the continent's original inhabitants occurred in the spring of 1782. The British had surrendered at Yorktown the previous year but not yet formally conceded defeat when Shawnee natives murdered two settler families in what is now Ohio. The local militia decided that Christian natives from the Moravian townships on the Muskingum river were somehow involved and surrounded a large group of native men, women and children whom they found gathering corn. After herding them into two large huts the militiamen, in the spirit of frontier democracy, had a vote to decide whether to take the prisoners to Fort Pitt or kill them on the spot. The result was another massacre.

Having objected to paying taxes to the British, the inhabitants of the thirteen colonies were none too happy to pay taxes to a central government after Independence. Fortunately the new government had an alternative source of revenue: it would sell off the land to the west of the 1763 proclamation line that the British had tried to reserve for the natives.

The major difference between the agricultural methods of the new 'white' natives and the old 'red' natives was their impact on the environment. In Virginia, for example, tobacco farming ruined the land to such an extent that further tobacco cultivation became prohibitively expensive (as Samuel Eliot Morison notes, the only industry able to replace the wealth previously generated by tobacco was 'slave-breeding'). As agricultural land in the east rapidly became exhausted the federal government, dominated by plutocrats and in particular the southern planter aristocracy, ensured that policy on the sale of 'new' land favoured large-scale purchases. As the original tobacco and cotton plantations declined the plantation owners were able to buy massive new estates to the west, shipping their slaves with them and creating new states based firmly on the institution of slavery. The first two were the tobacco states of Kentucky and Tennessee. Later, when they had been cleansed of their native populations, came cotton states like Louisiana and Alabama.

The westward expansion of the slave states mirrored the experience of territorial expansion in early Russia. There, colonisation had been driven by a desire for new agricultural land, although not as a means of generating wealth; the Rus and their Russian successors needed to find new land, however poor, simply to provide food for their population. Often Russian colonisation had been to replace land that had already been worked to exhaustion, just as was happening in early nineteenth-century America. Russian colonisation was also driven by the slave trade. Slaves were the principal export commodity for early Russia; but with the fall of Byzantium this export market suddenly disappeared and a use had to be found for slaves at home. The answer was colonising new land. Similarly in America the success of slave breeders, the decline in death rates among slaves as malaria and other diseases were brought under control and the continuing (if lessening) inflow of new slaves from Africa, the Caribbean and Florida prompted the search for new territory suitable for slave labour. Colonisation of this territory brought further wealth to an already dominant planter aristocracy.

The economic imperatives of the slave trade were absent further north but here too those who were already wealthy, or who had access to wealth to fund their speculative investments, were the ones to benefit from westward expansion. In colonial times many of the revolutionary leaders including Thomas Jefferson and Benjamin Franklin had speculated in land, particularly in the Ohio Valley – territory claimed by France and occupied by natives. George Washington started buying land as a teenager and amassed a fortune as land prices soared. After Independence Congress provided that land in the Northwest Territory would be sold in plots no smaller than a square mile (640 acres), and in practice most of the land was taken by speculators like the Ohio Company of General Knox, which acquired 1.5m acres at $1 an acre. In 1796 the Land Act doubled the price of public lands to $2 an acre, making speculators even more likely to be the prime beneficiaries.

Typical of the period was the Yazoo Land Fraud. In 1795 a corrupt Georgia legislature sold 35m acres of land along the Yazoo river to speculators for 1½ cents per acre. The next year a new legislature rescinded the sale but the speculators pursued their claim for compensation through the courts, and eventually in 1810 the US Supreme Court ruled that however corrupt the motives of the legislators the original deal had been valid. In 1814 Congress provided $4.2m to compensate the disgruntled speculators. The case yet again demonstrated the precedence of legality over justice.

In the same year as the sale of the land on the Yazoo and a year after the battle of Fallen Timbers, Spain conceded the US navigation rights on the full length of the Mississippi: the gateway to future expansion was open. In Russia colonisation continued along the Volga, albeit more slowly than in contemporary North America. The rigid social structures in Russia meant that there was little room for individual initiative when it came to colonisation. The social pressures that kept the American frontier expanding westward were almost entirely missing. Nor was there a pool of 'sturdy vagabonds' of the type England had dispatched across the Atlantic in the previous century. The economic imperative to colonise new land and thereby maintain or increase agricultural production remained and Catherine resorted to immigration to settle the new lands. Both America and Russia benefited from the desire of land-hungry German farmers to escape their warring princes. The ethnic German communities along the lower Volga that two centuries later excited the paranoia of Joseph Stalin had their roots in the incentives Catherine had offered their forebears.

Controlling the Volga gave Russia access to the Caspian Sea, but what Catherine wanted, like Peter the Great before her, was access via the Black Sea to the Mediterranean. Unlike Peter she got it, pushing the Ottoman Turks aside in a series of battles that saw Russian armies storming through what today are the states of Moldova and Romania. A British naval captain, John Elphinston, was made an admiral in the imperial navy; sailing from Kronstadt in the Baltic around Europe to the Aegean, he destroyed the Turkish fleet at Chesme Bay, forcing Turkey into granting independence to the Crimea. That independence lasted less than a decade before Russia formally annexed the whole of Crimea, gaining a Black Sea coastline stretching from Odessa in the west to the Sea of Azov and beyond in the east. In 1783 a treaty with Georgia extended the Russian zone of influence even further.

The incorporation of Georgia is a classic example of Russian imperial expansion. Threatened by the Islamic forces of Turkey and Persia the Georgian king Irakli agreed to Russian suzerainty over eastern Georgia. Once established there Russia annexed the remainder of his kingdom eighteen years later. Annexation in this case was very different from the American annexations of Spanish possessions like Florida, Texas and New Mexico that started in the very same year, 1801. Florida was annexed to gain territory to be settled by Americans and their imported slaves; the existing natives and their leaders were an impediment to be removed. Russia on the other hand was as keen to gain population as land. The Georgian leaders were courted and recruited into Russian service, and the nobility were given Russian imperial titles of higher rank. The vast mass of Georgians continued life as before; only in the last days of the Romanovs in the 1890s was there any attempt to Russify the annexed people by making Russian the language of instruction in schools.

Catherine's southern conquests provided Russia with outlets to the Black Sea and, vitally, a granary. The Russian heartland had poor soil and often atrocious weather but the newly conquered territories provided rich agricultural land, which, along with the subtropical produce of

Georgia, sustained a 300 per cent growth in the Russian population in the nineteenth century.

That Russia and America had much in common was demonstrated by the life of one of the most unusual characters in late eighteenth-century history. Elphinston was not the only mercenary Catherine recruited to the Russian navy. A far more famous figure was a Scottish slave trader, freemason and pirate with an assumed Welsh name who, after leaving Catherine's service, died in Paris where he was buried in an unmarked grave, only to be exhumed more than a century later and carried across the Atlantic in what may well have been the most impressive naval cortege in history. His story is a bizarre example of the increasingly intertwined histories of America and Russia.

John Paul was born in Kirkcudbright in 1747 and went to sea at the age of thirteen. Four years later he went into the slave trade, but reputedly left in disgust. Known for his fiery temper, Paul was arrested in Tobago for 'excessively' flogging his ship's carpenter and sent home to Kirkcudbright, where the charges were dismissed. He returned to the Caribbean but had to move on again after killing a sailor in a dispute over wages. He fled to Virginia, where his brother had settled, and changed his name, first to John Jones and later to John Paul Jones.

When war broke out between the colonists and Britain, John Paul Jones joined the rebels and depending on who is telling the story either became the most heroic figure in the infant US navy, famed especially for his defeat of HMS *Serapis* off Flamborough Head in Yorkshire, or became the leader of a gang of American and French pirates who preyed on British merchantmen, raided the town of Whitehaven in Cumbria and returned to Kirkcudbright to steal the Countess of Selkirk's family silver. Posters distributed throughout the rebel colonies and signed by John Hancock on behalf of the infant Congress suggest that both versions of history are true. They encouraged sailors to join John Paul Jones Esq. 'for the Glorious Cause of their country' and, perhaps more importantly, to 'make their fortune'.

Jones became a hero not just in America but in France, and it was here after the war that Thomas Jefferson, the new American ambassador to France, arranged for him to become Admiral Pavel Dzhones in the Russian navy. According to legend, at the battle of Liman he carried out a night-time reconnaissance of the Turkish fleet in a rowing boat before destroying fifteen of their ships, killing 3,000 of their men and taking 1,600 prisoners at a cost of one ship lost and just eighteen Russians killed. On settling in St Petersburg he was charged with molesting the ten-year-old daughter of a German immigrant and, although the charge was dropped, returned to Paris, where he died at the age of forty-five. He was buried in an unmarked grave.

Like Columbus, his body was not to remain at peace. The story of John Paul Jones had assumed mythic proportions in America and, despite the objections of his family in Scotland, plans were made to transport his remains across the Atlantic, providing they could be found. In 1905 his grave was at last identified. The American government sent four cruisers, escorted on the final leg by seven battleships, to bring the 'Father of the American Navy' back 'home'. In 1913 his body was finally laid to rest in a marble sarcophagus, modelled on the tomb of Napoleon, at the Annapolis Naval Academy. It is another of the ironies of history that the father of the US navy achieved a higher rank in the Russian navy than he ever did in the American.

Tadeusz Kosciuszko and The Polish Question

John Paul Jones was not the only veteran of the American Revolution to make his mark on the history of Russian imperialism. The Polish army engineer Tadeusz Kosciuszko, who played a key part in the siege of Charleston, had returned home and was to prove as formidable an opponent to Catherine as he had to the British. Although Catherine's conquests in the south had given Russia what she desperately needed economically, agricultural wealth and access to warm water ports, it was to her campaigns in the west that Catherine devoted most of her energies. Poland blocked the westward expansion of her empire and Catherine was determined to crush the old enemy once and for all. Standing in her way were two men: Tadeusz Kosciuszko and, before him, an even more remarkable figure, Stanislas Poniatowski.

Most of Catherine's lovers played no role in history and have been long forgotten. Grigory Orlov, who helped kill her husband, is an exception, as is Grigory Potemkin – although the latter's fame owes less to his naval victories than to a later tsar naming a battleship after him and Eisenstein's monumental film of the crew's mutiny. None of her other lovers, however, rose as high, or fell so low, as Stanislas Augustus Poniatowski.

Poniatowski's story reflects the turbulent and confused nature of the region on which Catherine had set her sights. His father was the Palatine of Krakow and had been the close companion of the Swedish king Charles XII in his campaigns against the Russian army of Peter the Great; Stanislas himself became an officer in the Russian imperial army before becoming the Polish plenipotentiary ambassador at the imperial court in St Petersburg. There the British ambassador introduced him to the Grand Duchess Catherine Alexievna and the two became lovers. In 1758 he was suddenly recalled home, when the Polish authorities realised he was conspiring to deprive Catherine's husband of the throne. Catherine quickly replaced him with Grigory Orlov, who then helped her seize power.

Two years later the Polish throne became vacant. Poland was ruled by an elected monarch and this apparently democratic mechanism led to constant power struggles among the nobles who formed the electorate. Catherine sent in her Cossacks to 'persuade' the voters to elect her former lover as King Stanislas II. His was to be the first of a long series of puppet regimes that Russia imposed on eastern Europe, but this puppet promptly cut his strings. Stanislas instituted a series of dramatic reforms reducing the power of the aristocracy and strengthening the authority of the state. Civil war broke out between Stanislas and reactionary nobles supported by Catherine, and in 1772 she used the resultant instability as an excuse to engineer with Austria and Prussia the First Partition of

Poland, in which Russia grabbed 36,000 square miles and nearly 2 million inhabitants, mainly 'White Russians'. Just as the Americans were to do in their western conquests, Russia followed a policy of biting off parts of its victims, signing treaties promising to respect the new frontier, regrouping and then invading again.

Russia was still treated as a second-class nation by the western European imperial powers, but this was starting to change.

Britain, France and Spain, who were constantly at war with each other, had no respect for neutrals in general and neutral shipping in particular. The rules of the game were changed on 28 February 1780 when Catherine II signed the Declaration of Armed Neutrality. This asserted that neutral ships should be able to travel freely anywhere, including along the coastlines of nations at war, and that cargo in neutral ships (with the exception of munitions) could not be seized even if it belonged to enemy citizens. What made the declaration more than just a pious aspiration is that Catherine backed it up by force. She dispatched three powerful naval squadrons to the Atlantic, Mediterranean and North Sea. Furthermore she declared that other neutral nations were free to join her for collective security: Denmark, Sweden and Holland were among the first to do so. The Declaration of Armed Neutrality lasted just three years, but Catherine had not only established the reputation of the Russian imperial navy but established significant new principles of international law – principles that were to be followed a quarter of a century later by another, and much newer, imperial power when the US navy intervened decisively in the Mediterranean.

Catherine was determined to humiliate her former lover, Stanislas Poniatowski, and in 1782 compelled him to accompany her and her latest lover, Potemkin, on their triumphal progress through the newly conquered Crimea. Stanislas, however, continued with his reforms, encouraged by the revolutions in America and France, giving new rights to both the peasants and the increasingly important urban population. Catherine and the Polish aristocracy were appalled, and in 1792 the Russian army poured across the border with the support of Prussia and of reactionary Polish aristocrats. They were met by the hero of the American revolutionary war Tadeusz Kosciuszko.

Kosciuszko had returned to Poland in 1784, and at first was unable to get a commission in the Polish army because of his liberal views. He settled on his family estate, where in a startling gesture he freed many of his serfs. As Poland under Stanislas became more liberal Kosciuszko returned to favour, helped by the woman with whom he had tried to elope fourteen years earlier (who was by now married to a Polish prince). When Catherine invaded, Kosciuszko took command of 5,000 Polish troops confronting 20,000 Russians at Dubienka near the Austrian border. When the Russians crossed through Austrian territory in an attempt to encircle the Poles, Kosciuszko fought his way out inflicting massive casualties. The battle of Dubienka was Poland's only 'victory' and Stanislas was forced to abandon his reforms. In the Second Partition of Poland Catherine grabbed most of the former Grand Duchy of Lithuania. Kosciuszko escaped to France, where the revolutionary government made him an honorary French citizen.

Under the Second Partition Prussia and Russia grabbed two-fifths of Poland and Russian troops occupied the rest. Even the Polish nobles who had initially welcomed the invasion objected and, as in America twenty years earlier, the spirit of rebellion stirred. Kosciuszko, returning to Poland, was given command of the rebel forces and led them to victory at Raclawice. However, the forces ranged against him were enormous. As in America the rebels turned to France for support, but this time in vain (even though by distracting Prussia and Austria the Poles enabled the French republic to survive). Kosciuszko lost Krakow and retreated to Warsaw, where he was besieged by Prussian and Russian forces for nearly two months before uprisings elsewhere brought him relief.

Eventually at the battle of Maciejowice Kosciuszko was wounded and taken prisoner – allegedly proclaiming 'Poland is not dead while we live', words now incorporated into the Polish national anthem. The Russian army then completed the destruction of the Polish forces in the traditional manner, attacking the Warsaw suburb of Praga and massacring the entire population. The remaining rebels surrendered, and hundreds were executed or deported to Siberia. King Stanislas was forced to abdicate and eventually died in exile in St Petersburg. Kosciuszko was imprisoned.

The battles of Fallen Timbers and Maciejowice occurred within two months of each other, and illustrate both the similarities in fact between the two empires and the differences in perception. Maciejowice is still remembered as one of the key events in eastern European history; no serious history of the region can fail to dwell on its significance. Fallen Timbers on the other hand, when it is remembered at all, is just one more of the many minor skirmishes that marked the westward march of civilisation. In reality Fallen Timbers was one of the most important battles ever fought on the North American continent.

Both battles, Fallen Timbers and Maciejowice, resulted in devastation for the losers. In the Treaty of Greenville the natives were forced to give up much of the Midwest from Ohio to Michigan. In the Third Partition of Poland, Poland-Lithuania was removed from the map of Europe in the words of the treaty 'now and for ever'. Austria, Prussia and Russia carved up the territory between them. Russia took the old Grand Duchy of Kurland from where the Empress Anna had come exactly seventy years before.

The difference between the two conflicts was not in the fighting or the subsequent peace settlement but in the differing population dynamics. The Shawnee and other tribes, not particularly numerous before Fallen Timbers, were simply swamped afterwards. Native villages were replaced by cities like Chicago, Cleveland, Toledo and Detroit. Had the natives been victorious at Fallen Timbers it is possible that the history of the world would have been very different. If the British forces stationed just a few miles away at Fort Miamis had come to the aid of their native allies the Americans could have been denied a victory. Almost certainly the United States would have agreed to the creation of a native buffer state north of the Ohio between them and the British pushing south from Canada. Such a state would probably have been short lived, but rather than being conquered by America it might well have chosen to be annexed by the British; thousands of migrants to the New World may have settled in the

Canadian provinces of Illinois and Michigan and in the great Canadian cities of Chicago, Detroit and, in succeeding decades, Seattle and even San Francisco. However, the natives lost and the resultant demographics made it impossible to ever conceive of their reversing the tide of history. In Poland on the other hand the Poles remained, and the tide was free to flow back and forth again and again as history unrolled.

The eradication of Poland was Catherine the Great's final triumph, and the next year she died. The daughter of a minor German noble had changed the face of Russia for ever. Having destroyed Poland, as she thought, it is another of history's ironies that her Prussian birthplace, Stettin, is now the Polish city of Szczecin.

The nature of any society is often illustrated by the way power is transferred from one leader to the next: simple inheritance or bloody coup, peaceful election or violent revolution, dynasty or democracy. Between the death of Catherine the Great in 1796 and the murder of the last tsar in 1917 there were six Russian tsars and twenty-eight US presidents. The American system by and large provided a means of ensuring the peaceful transfer of power from one leader to the next and the peaceful transition from one political creed to another (with the glaring exception of the civil war). Three of the twenty-eight presidents were assassinated, but in each case by deranged fanatics rather than as part of a calculated seizure of power. In contrast three of the six tsars met violent ends, the first being Catherine's successor – murdered in 1801 in a palace power struggle.

Catherine's murdered husband, Peter III, had not been the most intelligent of men, but her son and successor, Tsar Paul, was worse. (This does not imply a genetic link: Catherine's husband was almost certainly not her son's father.) Catherine herself recognised her son's unsuitability. She wanted her grandson Alexander to succeed but had not got around to formalising the arrangement when she died. Paul's five-year reign started bizarrely (he had his father's skeleton exhumed and laid alongside his mother's body) and ended violently when he was assassinated by a group of guards officers. Alexander succeeded him as Catherine would have wished.

The dawning of the nineteenth century saw the arrival of the last batch of Romanov tsars, the Alexanders and Nicholases (Alexander I, Nicholas I, Alexander II, Alexander III and finally Nicholas II). It would be simplistic to say that the Romanov line deteriorated as the century went by, but it certainly started with one of the towering figures of world history (Alexander I was the only great tsar not to be labelled Great, perhaps because the sobriquet Alexander the Great had already been taken) and ended with the vacillating Nicholas II's abdication and murder.

Each of the five tsars was different, but through the whole century a consistent picture emerges: an ebb and flow of timid reform and draconian but ineffective reaction at home, and abroad the constant expansion of empire. The pattern of reform and repression can be summarised very simply:

- Alexander I (1801–25): reformer; became religious reactionary
- Nicholas I (1825–55): thorough reactionary
- Alexander II (1855–81): emancipated the serfs but became reactionary
- Alexander III (1881–94): thorough reactionary
- Nicholas II (1894–1917): forced into reform and abdication.

If imperialism is one element of continuity in Russian history, over the final century of the Romanov regime this pattern of creeping reform and panicked reaction is another.

One of the first actions of Catherine's successor, the short-lived Tsar Paul, was to release Tadeusz Kosciuszko. Still recovering from his wounds, Kosciuszko travelled to the United States where he was welcomed as a returning hero and given a stipend by Congress, but he remained at heart a European and moved back to France. Kosciuszko's fame literally towers over others – Australia's highest mountain is named after him – but the two figures who were truly to tower over the early nineteenth century were now striding on to the European stage. One, Napoleon, everyone has heard of; the other, Tsar Alexander I, is much less well known, but in the end it was Alexander who brought down Napoleon.

Napoleon and Alexander

Napoleon left his mark on nearly everything he touched, from the principles of European law to the minutiae of weights and measures, and he reinforced French delusions of grandeur and Russian paranoia. But in some ways his most lasting legacy was to double the size of the United States of America.

Americans were outraged when waning Spain ceded Louisiana to powerful France, but Napoleon was more interested in suppressing a slave rebellion in the wealthy French West Indies than in trying to enforce claims over 828m square miles of what was largely wilderness. Although France now laid claim to an enormous territory encompassing all or part of modern Montana, North and South Dakota, Wyoming, Colorado, Nebraska, Minnesota, Iowa, Missouri, Kansas, Oklahoma and Arkansas, Napoleon soon abandoned his initial dreams of mightily extending the French empire in North America. President Jefferson was able to purchase the whole of French Louisiana for just $15m in cash and cancelled debt. The American envoys who negotiated the Louisiana Purchase had been intending to buy a much smaller area, indeed they had no authority to make the deal they eventually agreed, but Napoleon needed money to finance his campaigns in the east. After much debate the US Congress gave their retrospective approval. The United States assured its generally unhappy new citizens that they were fortunate that it preferred 'justice to conquest' – preferred purchase to conquest might have been more apposite.

There remained one problem for the US negotiators – how to raise the cash. The problem was solved by the British banker Alexander Baring, who arranged a loan of $11.25m in the form of twenty year bonds paying 6 per cent interest; Alexander Hamilton's insistence twenty years earlier on honouring the revolutionary war debt paid off, as the credit rating of United States was now rock solid. Napoleon accepted the bonds and promptly sold them to raise cash; ironically the largest purchaser was the Russian tsar. The wealth of the Romanovs ultimately made possible not only Napoleon's assault on their empire but also the massive expansion of the empire that in the next century would surpass theirs to dominate the world.

When Napoleon staged his *coup d'état* in November 1798, Alexander's father Paul was still tsar. It would be difficult to think of two societies further apart than tsarist Russia and revolutionary France, but Tsar Paul believed he sensed a kindred spirit in Napoleon. France was disintegrating into chaos as the terror of the guillotine was followed by virtual civil war. Tsar Paul was not alone in seeing the need for a voice of authority to lift France out of chaos; as so often, a military strongman seemed to be the answer. Tsar Paul's admiration for Napoleon was one of the factors that divided the Russian emperor from his people, and eventually led to his assassination. Alexander came to the throne determined to reverse his father's pro-French policy. The stage was set for conflict on a massive scale.

As so many times before and after, Poland was central to Russia's priorities. The overwhelming characteristic of Russia's attitude to the outside world was fear of invasion – dating right back to the first Slav tribes, through the Mongol period and more recently invasion from Poland. Catherine had determined to remove the Polish threat by dismembering the Polish commonwealth and dividing it between Prussia, Austria and herself. Alexander had a different agenda. He wanted to build on Catherine's imperial legacy by reuniting Poland as part of an expanded Russian empire. Napoleon also had his sights set on Poland, and his war chest was swollen by selling France's North American possessions. The clash between the two men produced the catastrophic French invasion, which confirmed all the worst fears Russia had about the rest of the world.

The two opponents could not have been more different physically: Napoleon short and stout, Alexander tall and handsome. Compared with the sixty-five-year-old Catherine the Great and the near-insane Paul, the new tsar, just twenty-eight, was the Princess Diana of his day – and he knew it. Ignoring more experienced and cautious voices he decided to personally lead his armies into battle at Austerlitz in Bohemia. Napoleon won a stunning victory. (The battle is usually described as being between

French and 'Austro-Russian' forces; the reality is that most of the Austrian army had already been smashed at Ulm and Russian losses outnumbered Austrian by three to one.) Napoleon's armies went on to occupy Berlin and Warsaw. After the disaster at Austerlitz Alexander decided to let his generals take command, but they did no better; following a winter campaign in Poland, Russia suffered an even greater defeat at Friedland and Alexander was forced to make peace. Napoleon and Alexander met on a raft in the middle of the river Niemen to sign the Treaty of Tilsit in 1807.

In an uncanny prefiguring of the Hitler-Stalin pact 132 years later the treaty contained a secret annexe allowing Alexander to occupy Finland, which he invaded the next year. Finland became a grand duchy within the Russian empire, with Alexander himself the grand duke. Alexander was also expanding on other fronts, taking territory from Persia and annexing Bessarabia after a six year war with Turkey. Important as these gains were for Alexander, it was the competition with Napoleon that presented both the greatest threat and the greatest opportunity, and the place where both threat and opportunity were most apparent was once again Poland.

Under the Treaty of Tilsit Russia had agreed to the creation of a French puppet state, the Grand Duchy of Warsaw, which included those parts of Poland not controlled by Russia. Napoleon immediately started recruiting a Polish army that could have only one objective: moving east. Napoleon turned to the hero of the American Revolution and Poland's battles with Russia, Tadeusz Kosciuszko, who was now living in exile in France, and offered him command of the Polish Legion. Kosciuszko demanded a commitment to Polish sovereignty, something the French emperor had no intention of giving, and the two men went their separate ways.

Napoleon well understood the difficulties of campaigning across the Russian steppes, and at first tried to tame Alexander by marrying the tsar's favourite sister (despite not yet having divorced the childless Josephine). When Alexander refused the offer Napoleon lost no time moping; within three days he had proposed to the daughter of the defeated emperor of Austria, and war between the French and Russian empires became inevitable. Although Napoleon had lost a few battles in Spain to the British and been driven out of Portugal by Lord Wellington at the beginning of 1812, he still looked invincible. Allied with Austria and Prussia, and holding the Pope captive at Fontainebleau, Napoleon crossed the Niemen in June with half a million men, the majority drawn not from France but from Spain, Italy, Germany and above all Poland. This was his *Grande Armée*. Six months later just five thousand of them managed to retreat back to Vilnius; it was one of the most significant military disasters of all time. Alexander had defeated the mightiest European army since the Romans.

There has long been a debate about whether Alexander actually knew what he was doing when he destroyed the *Grande Armée*: did he have a cunning plan or did a sequence of tactical decisions by chance cohere into a winning strategy? His military commanders were divided into a majority Russian faction and a minority German faction. The Russian faction, largely Russian aristocrats, many with origins in the warrior tribes of Asia, wanted to fight a head-on offensive campaign against the invader. The German faction, which included many Prussian officers who had emigrated to Russia after Napoleon destroyed the Prussian army in 1806, favoured a more cautious approach. Alexander seemed to oscillate between the two – retreating as the German faction advised, then letting the Russian faction persuade him to make a stand at Borodino and then, when that failed, retreating again.

Whatever the truth about Alexander's strategy, Napoleon certainly had a plan: to defeat the Russian army in battle, take Moscow and force Alexander's capitulation. At first the French plan gave every sign of working. The Russians were defeated in the bloodbath of Borodino and Napoleon's army entered Moscow. As in earlier campaigns in Italy, Spain, Prussia and Austria, Napoleon found himself with his invincible army in control of the enemy's capital; it was now just a question of negotiating the terms of surrender. But Alexander refused to negotiate. The Governor of Moscow had the city torched and Napoleon was left with the most pyrrhic of victories. He could not stay where he was, as his army had no food; he could not destroy Alexander in battle, as after Borodino the tsar avoided any full-scale engagement; he could not advance, as Alexander would just retreat all the way to the Pacific. Napoleon's only option was to turn round and march back the way he had come. But the Russians had by now destroyed everything in their path that the *Grande Armée* itself had not destroyed on its march to Moscow. With winter closing in Napoleon's soldiers starved to death, froze to death or were picked off by Alexander's Cossacks or local militias. If the British thought the retreat from Lexington was bloody, this was ten thousand times worse.

Just as the American War of Independence signalled the triumph of democracy, the destruction of the *Grande Armée* showed the power of autocracy. Any other monarch, in the desperate circumstances Alexander faced after Borodino, would have had to consider the wishes of his nobles, if not the feelings of the citizens of Moscow as their homes were brought down around them. Alexander had none of these constraints. For good or ill the ideology of autocracy had placed total power in the hands of one man. The consequence was the salvation of Russia and the further glorification of the Russian empire. It was a lesson not lost on the Russian people; as in America the triumphs of war were taken as god-given sanction of their view of the world. The same God was apparently endorsing two totally opposed ideologies.

After the disastrous retreat from Moscow Napoleon raised new forces and tried to fight on, but Austria and Prussia swapped sides again and the allies fought their way to the French frontier. The Austrian emperor wanted to make peace but Alexander, who was now the strongest monarch in Europe, refused. Inside France Napoleon fought a brilliant rearguard action, and after a string of minor defeats the Austrian and Prussian leaders again pressed Alexander to negotiate. Instead Alexander sent 10,000 cavalry in a diversionary move that completely fooled the French emperor and directed the bulk of his forces in an attack on Paris. Napoleon had left his capital in the hands of his elder brother Joseph, whom he had made King of Spain, but on 31 March 1814 Paris capitulated (King Joseph fleeing to America with a stash of jewels that financed a luxurious New Jersey exile).

Napoleon was exiled to the Tuscan island of Elba. He was allowed to take his own guards, among whom he chose 120 volunteer Polish lancers. Ten months later he was back in France raising a new army. Knowing that he had to strike before Alexander and the Austrian emperor had time to re-mobilise their forces, Napoleon attacked the Prussian, British and Dutch forces close to home. Heavily outnumbered, he suffered his final defeat at Waterloo (although contrary to Abba's version of history he did not surrender there; retreating to Paris, he found himself without support and eventually surrendered to a British warship).

In British eyes Napoleon was destroyed by Wellington at Waterloo but the reality is that Napoleon's power was gone long before that. Napoleon's enemies had already made their triumphant entry into Paris, where the grand procession was led not by Wellington or his Austrian or Prussian equivalents but, by common consent, by Alexander, the last great Russian tsar. The Russian empire had moved from eastern barbarism to the centre of the European stage. Alexander was greeted with rapturous applause wherever he went; in England mobs surrounded him like a modern pop star and Oxford University granted him an honorary degree.

Not only had Alexander personally emerged as the most powerful monarch in Europe but the Romanov autocracy appeared to be the most successful regime in the world. Few could have predicted that a century later that regime would collapse with the murder of the last Romanov tsar and his family. Whether through skill, luck or sheer bloody-minded endurance Alexander I had destroyed the greatest army Europe had witnessed since the Mongols. (No Frenchman would of course liken the *Grande Armée* to the Mongols; Napoleon's troops are still pictured as the standard bearers of French civilisation, spreading French culture and virtue across the continent. They certainly spread something: scientists examining the mass graves in Vilnius of Napoleonic soldiers who perished in the retreat from Moscow discovered that no less than 80 per cent showed signs of venereal disease.)

One of the great what ifs of history is what would have happened if instead of invading Russia Napoleon had done what many Americans feared he would do – invade America. Napoleon posed the most immediate foreign threat to the new American republic and his navy relentlessly harassed American shipping (the newly independent America had to turn to Britain, which sold or donated munitions, gave naval protection to American ships and provided Caribbean bases for the fledgling US navy.) If, rather than sell his North American empire, Napoleon had used it as a springboard and sent his *Grande Armée* across the Atlantic to seize the wealth that Britain had lost just a few short decades before, the history of the world might have been very different. But that is not what happened.

At the Congress of Vienna held to resolve the territorial and dynastic issues that followed Napoleon's defeat, Alexander gained most, although not all, of the territory he wanted. He made liberal promises about limited self-government in his new Polish colony. Tadeusz Kosciuszko was invited to the congress and offered a leading role, but the Polish hero well understood Alexander's intentions and gave him the same reply he had earlier given Napoleon. He was right to be suspicious: Alexander simply absorbed most of the old Poland into Russia and the new 'self-governing' remnant was placed firmly under Russian control, with Alexander's brother Constantine commanding the Polish army. (Kosciuszko retired to Switzerland, where he died in 1817.) Russia had gained much but not as much as America.

The Louisiana Purchase was almost universally welcomed in the American south but caused consternation in the north, where the prospect of more slave states was met with moral outrage and, more importantly, a recognition that the balance of power would tip away from them. The nineteenth century in America was characterised by the same two themes seen in Russia: continual territorial expansion and ideological conflicts leading to civil war. The views of north and south were starkly opposed on both of these topics. Slavery is the issue normally associated with the political chasm between the two halves of the country, but in the early years it was America's role as a quasi-imperial power that most seriously divided the nation.

Following the conclusion of the Louisiana Purchase the north-south divide came to dominate politics. There was talk of secession, particularly in Massachusetts and Connecticut, and Aaron Burr, dumped as vice-presidential candidate by President Jefferson, tried to get himself elected Governor of New York as the first stage on the road to becoming president of an independent northern confederacy.

Colonel Aaron Burr is one of the characters who had no real historical impact but whose story illustrates the swirls and eddies of the period in which they lived. Burr was at one time talked of as a future president, not least by himself, but is now best remembered for killing Alexander Hamilton in a duel. In 1804, when his plans for a northern confederacy failed, Burr turned his eyes south and west. He gathered round him a motley collection of adventurers committed to grabbing power in the western states and then invading Mexico, where Burr would be proclaimed emperor of a new realm stretching west from the Mississippi. For two years Burr travelled the frontier weaving his plot. Andrew Jackson, later to become US president, helped provide boats and men that were intended to sail down the Mississippi and seize New Orleans (it is ironic that Jackson's later rise to power was based on his reputation as the defender of New Orleans). Burr promised Britain the prospect of a vast new export market stretching from Canada to New Orleans in return for naval support. Eventually Burr was betrayed by one of his co-conspirators and arrested near Natchez, where a grand jury found him innocent of any crime. He disappeared into the Alabama wilderness but was eventually recaptured and sent back east for trial.

The government of Thomas Jefferson argued that as Burr intended to seize New Orleans, recently purchased from France, he was guilty of treason; his defenders argued that he had only ever been interested in seizing territory from Mexico. The case developed into a trial of strength between President Jefferson and Chief Justice Marshall; Marshall subpoenaed letters held by the president but Jefferson simply refused to obey; when Marshall ruled that there was no case to answer, Jefferson threatened to have Marshall impeached, and contemplated amending the constitution to limit the powers of the judiciary. Once released, Burr sailed to Europe where he failed to find anyone to support his plans for revolution in Mexico. He eventually settled into relative obscurity as a lawyer and land speculator in New York, where he lived to see the Texan Revolution of 1835 achieve much of what he had attempted. His last act, a year before his death, was to marry a rich widow who left him after just four months when she discovered he was plundering her accounts.

The antics of imperialists in the south spurred northerners to look westwards themselves, where nothing stood in their way but a few natives. The victory of Fallen Timbers cleared the way for new settlements on a massive scale. The natives were not completely destroyed and in the early nineteenth century another dangerous confederation of Midwestern tribes, led by one of the great native generals, Tecumseh, started to reassert native power before being decisively smashed at the battle of Tippecanoe in 1811. Tecumseh escaped to Canada, where his presence was used by the advocates of a more aggressive foreign policy to bolster their case for a pre-emptive attack on the remaining British settlements in North America.

Although they were keen to cleanse the native tribes from their borders, the northern states were much less gung-ho about attacking the European imperial powers. However, almost all of the early presidents were drawn from the Virginian ruling class, plantation owners with southern values. None illustrated the southern mind-set more clearly than James Madison, elected president in 1808. Facing the prospect of a tough re-election campaign, Madison lighted on the perfect issue to appeal to the southern electorate.

In 1810 American settlers who had moved into part of Spanish Florida staged a revolt. Using a tactic later used on a much larger scale in Texas, the Americans declared their independence. (American history of the period, just like Russian history, is confused by ever-changing boundaries – although then part of Florida the disputed area, centring on the city of Baton Rouge, is today in the modern state of Louisiana – despite not being part of the Louisiana Purchase.) The independent nation of West

Florida existed from 23 September to 6 December 1810, at which point President Madison annexed the whole area below the thirty-first parallel between the Mississippi and Pearl rivers. The popularity of this land grab ensured his successful re-election in 1812.

Encouraged by his success in Florida, Madison and a congressional group known as the War Hawks looked for further conquest. Britain, preoccupied with the Napoleonic wars in Europe, tried to stop American ships trading with the enemy. Using this as an excuse, Madison declared war and launched an invasion of Canada. The British blockade had actually been lifted by the time war was declared but the news had not crossed the Atlantic; by the time it arrived Washington was gripped by war fever, and Madison had no more intention of admitting his mistake than Bush II had when events proved the non-existence of the weapons of mass destruction used to justify invading Iraq.

The War Hawks had their eyes on the fertile territory west of Quebec, modern Ontario, and expected it to fall into their hands. The 1810 census had just revealed the US population to be 7.25 million, while there were fewer than 500,000 whites in the whole of British North America – and that included Americans who had already moved in to settle on the Canadian side of the border. Henry Clay, a War Hawk leader from Kentucky, boasted that his state's militia on their own could deliver Montreal and Upper Canada. But in 1812 the fusion of northern moral crusade and southern imperial ambition had not yet occurred, and the northern states wanted no part of Madison's imperial war. The congressional vote on the declaration of war was 79–49; the representatives of every state from Massachusetts to Delaware voted against, while the southern and western delegations were almost unanimously in favour.

Tempers ran high. When a leading newspaper in Baltimore advocated peace its editor and his supporters were forced to seek sanctuary in the local jail. They were dragged out and beaten by an angry mob who took particular exception to the presence of two army generals. General Henry Lee, known as 'Light Horse Harry', a hero of the American Revolution and close friend of George Washington, was left maimed for life. The other, General James Lingan, who had been wounded during the revolution and spent more than three years as a prisoner of the British, was murdered. When Lingan's killers were brought to trial they were acquitted, after the district attorney expressed regret that Lingan had been the only traitor to die.

When the 'War of 1812' started, the New England and New York militias refused to join the invasion force and the British successfully counter-attacked, seizing Detroit. Contrary to expectations the Canadian militias fought hard, as the region's settlers spurned the invitation to opt for 'liberty' under the Stars and Stripes. The Kentucky militia, on the other hand, rapidly became mutinous, and a council of officers demanded they be allowed to retreat. America and Britain then slogged it out in one of history's most pointless wars. American forces again invaded Canada, burning down the city of York (modern Toronto), and the British retaliated by attacking Washington and burning down the Capitol and the White House. But as Napoleon had found out less than two years earlier, seizing the enemy's capital was no guarantee of ultimate victory; the new colossuses of Russia and America were changing the rules of war. The puny states of western Europe would one day be relegated to the military second division.

In 1813 an attempt at mediation by the Russian tsar, Alexander I, fresh from his success crushing Napoleon, failed and the war finally ended in stalemate. Under the terms of the Treaty of Ghent both parties Returned to Go; Madison had not gained an inch of new territory. Although northern manufacturers prospered as imports were disrupted, opposition to the war there had continued; a vote of thanks for one naval hero was defeated in the Massachusetts legislature as 'not becoming a moral and religious people'.

Ironically the most famous battle of the war (or at least famous to those exposed to 1950s pop music) was fought after the war was officially over. Just as the slow pace of transatlantic communication allowed the war to start, so it also allowed one final pointless slaughter in the battle of New Orleans. The British commander committed one of the biggest blunders in British military history when, rather than exploiting a breakthrough on the American flank, he launched a full-frontal assault on the most heavily fortified enemy positions. 'The Battle of New Orleans', which won the Grammy Award for the Best Song of 1959, described what happened next as the British fled 'down the Mississippi to the Gulf of Mexico' (although in a rare example of cultural sensitivity the version released in Britain meaninglessly substituted 'rebels' for 'British').

The War of 1812 may have been a draw, but to much of the American population the battle of New Orleans reinforced their pride in the nation's military prowess. The fact that many of the British troops came from the Caribbean and were black reinforced Americans' sense of superiority, and their dreams of further conquests.

The 1812 Overtures

Russia had defeated the might of the French empire, and America had defeated the might of the British empire. The two nations emerged from the turmoil of 1812 confident in their own imperial destinies. It was inevitable that these two empires of the future would soon collide. The seeds of the superpower conflict that dominated the second half of the twentieth century were planted long before the advent of communism.

On the surface Russia under Alexander seemed to have become the world's only superpower. The reality was somewhat different. The Russian empire was geographically enormous but economically weak. The tsar's willingness to let his people and his army accept privations on a colossal scale made his military might seem greater than it really was. Russia's agriculture was primitive, its industry basic and its rigid class structure stifling. All that, however, was irrelevant; what mattered was what other people believed about Russia's power and above all what Alexander believed. And what Alexander increasingly believed was that he and Russia had been chosen by God to show the rest of the world the true path to salvation. The Russian empire's role was global, and global included the Americas.

Throughout the reigns of Catherine, Paul and Alexander Russians continued to push east, hunting almost to extinction the fur-bearing animals of Siberia and the Aleutians. Alaska's first man-made environmental disaster arose from the free market competition between American and Russian fur traders as Aleut fur-hunters drove the sea otter to virtual extinction, causing the population of the otters' favourite food, sea urchins, to explode and destroy the underwater forests of kelp on which much of the area's sea life depended.

Tsar Paul chartered the Russian-American Company in 1799, fifteen years after the first permanent settlement in Alaska. At first healthy profits flowed back to the shareholders, including the Romanov family, but, as the French had found on the other side of the continent, a colony could not survive on the fur trade alone: it was time to do more.

In the spring of 1812 Napoleon was massing his troops in Poland ready to strike east, General Andrew Jackson was calling for volunteers for 'the conquest of all the British dominions upon the continent of North America' and in Russia most eyes were turning fearfully west; most but not all. The Russian pioneers in Alaska were looking south – to California.

California offered not only an abundance of sea otters but also fertile agricultural land. In March 1812 the first Russian settlement in California was founded at Fort Ross (from Rossiya, the Russian for Russia). Reminiscent of Peter Minuit in Manhattan, the land all around was bought from the native inhabitants for three blankets, three pairs of breeches, two axes, three hoes and some beads. The settlement initially prospered and farms were established inland. Again like the French, but unlike the English, the Russians intermarried with the Californian natives and the Alaskans they brought with them.

Meanwhile the golden boy of Europe, the young Tsar Alexander I, was becoming ever less attractive as he grew older. He developed an almost messianic conviction that autocracy was God's plan for the entire world. His constant lecturing left other European rulers bemused; when he extended his musings to life across the Atlantic the consequences were more serious. First he tried to extend the frontiers of Russian Alaska further south. In 1821 he decreed that all lands along North America's Pacific coast as far south as Latitude 51° N belonged to Russia. If implemented, a significant part of the Oregon Territory, already claimed by both America and Britain, would have become Russian. Even though the United States only really occupied territory east of the Mississippi, American leaders were convinced that the whole of North America should rightfully be theirs. In 1805 Lewis and Clark had reached the Pacific reinforcing this view. (Some American texts write as if they were the first to cross the North American continent, but they were only sent because it had been done before. In 1801 the Scottish explorer Alexander Mackenzie, who had already twice crossed Canada to the Pacific, published his book *Voyages from Montreal*, directly inspiring US president Thomas Jefferson to send Lewis and Clark to repeat Mackenzie's feat.)

The Russian tsar could pass whatever decrees he liked, but the reality was that he had no way of enforcing them. The settlers at Fort Ross reached agreement with the Spanish to the south but the British in Oregon outmanoeuvred them. In 1839 the Hudson Bay Company agreed a trade deal with the Russian colonies in Alaska, and two years later Fort Ross was sold to American settlers; the Romanov flag was hoisted for the last time over Russian California a few months short of the colony's thirtieth birthday. Fort Ross had been far more successful than the first English settlement on Roanoke Island, but the Russians were too late. North America was no longer 'available'; the world had moved on.

Eventually Russia agreed to site no settlements south of latitude 54° 40° N and America agreed not to settle north of that latitude. In a strange twist of historical fate the territory the treaty gave to Russia – Alaska – is now part of America, and the territory it gave to the United States is not part of America, the British ensuring that it became part of the Canadian province of British Columbia.

Not satisfied with claiming a chunk of North America for himself, Alexander also turned his mind further south. Having inspired the so-called Holy Alliance of Russia, Austria, Prussia and France to crush stirrings of liberalism in Spain and force the restoration of a more autocratic monarchy, Alexander started musing on the desirability of recovering Spain's former Latin American colonies.

Spurred on by the British who were excluded from the Holy Alliance, President Monroe reacted angrily to Alexander's proposals for both the Pacific North-West and Latin America. He told the tsar, and all the other European powers, that the United States would not intervene in European wars and in return they would not be allowed to establish any new colonies anywhere in the Americas. In effect Monroe declared the rest of the western hemisphere a US protectorate.

Alexander had inadvertently caused a doctrine to be accepted that would underlie American imperialism throughout the western hemisphere, and would help inculcate into the American psyche the conviction that their imperialism was somehow qualitatively different to the European imperialisms that it sought to prevent. In proclaiming America's right to deploy military force anywhere in the Americas in order to stop the European powers doing the same thing, Monroe formulated the moral basis for his country's imperial expansion. He was, he insisted, not proclaiming an imperial intent but preventing one. In classic Orwellian newspeak America's fight 'for' empire became a fight 'against' empire; imperialism became anti-imperialism.

The full implications of the Monroe Doctrine were not made explicit until much later. In 1895 the 'Olney Corollary' was added by the American secretary of state, Richard Olney, when he insisted that America had the right to arbitrate in an obscure border dispute between Venezuela and the British colony of Guyana. 'The United States is practically sovereign on this continent,' declared Olney, 'and its fiat is law upon the subjects to which it confines its interposition.'

Since the Mystic Massacre American settlers had believed in their god-given right to exert hegemony over the natives on their frontiers, but now that right was extended to the whole hemisphere. Moreover that right was to be asserted not just over 'merciless Indian savages' but Christian elites, whose Spanish and Portuguese ancestors had crossed the Atlantic Ocean long before the Pilgrim Fathers.

Just as Americans saw their geographic growth as manifesting God's will, so Alexander saw himself as divinely inspired. To an extent rarely seen in tsars before or after, Alexander imputed an almost messianic dimension to his nation's imperialism. His bizarre plan for returning the former colonies of Latin America to their 'rightful' owners was in his mind a logical consequence of God's will that earthly power should rest in the hands of his chosen monarchs, Alexander himself prime among them. Hereditary monarchy was God's preferred form of government, and this formed the moral justification for imperial expansion. Other empires such as the Roman and British convinced themselves that their rule was beneficial for the peoples they subdued, but Alexander believed that the form of his government – autocracy – was in itself beneficial even to nations that remained outside his own empire. This conviction that he had a divine duty to ensure that the world enjoyed the benefits of autocracy was to find echoes in the beliefs of American presidents who were determined that everyone should enjoy the benefits of democracy. Alexander nudged forward the development of an American view of empire that was a mirror image of his own. It too was fundamentally messianic, but the American God had chosen not monarchy but democracy. Both Tsar Alexander and President Monroe believed that their imperial ambitions were not about conquering territory but, in the phrase used to describe the Pequot War, about 'bringing light into darkness'.

Therefore both nations were toying with the prospect that their destinies were not regional but global. Russia already possessed territory in Europe, Asia and North America; America now turned its eyes to the whole of the western hemisphere and less obviously to Africa.

One of the beneficiaries of the war against Britain was the infant US navy. Although many of its ships remained bottled up in port it secured a number of psychologically important victories. Indeed, it was still attacking British vessels off the coast of Africa months after the war was over. This development of naval power helped to make a practical reality not just of Monroe's assertion of the American right to police the western hemisphere but also of the wider flexing of American imperial power across the globe. Within three months of the end of the war that power was being demonstrated in the Mediterranean.

The north African coast was a dangerous place for American ships, which had previously enjoyed the protection of the British navy. Depending on which version is believed, a horde of savage Barbary pirates terrorised peaceful merchantmen or arrogant Christian sailors refused to pay the tributes due to local Muslim rulers. As ships were liable to attack when they were nowhere near the north African coast, the former may be somewhat closer to the truth. In 1804 US navy captain Stephen Decatur had led a night-time raid to rescue a captured American ship and its crew; the raid failed, and the crew languished in jail for two more years until the US Senate agreed to ransom them, but even Admiral Nelson was moved to applaud Decatur's daring. A year later a contingent of US sailors, marines and mercenaries marched 600 miles across the Libyan desert to capture an obscure fort near Tripoli on the north African coast – an event of no historical significance and one that by now would be totally forgotten but for its celebration in the opening line of the US marines' official hymn, 'From the halls of Montezuma, to the shores of Tripoli'.

With their confidence invigorated in the war against Britain, the US navy sailed into the lions' dens again. The first American bombardment of Tripoli took place in 1815, 131 years before President Reagan repeated the exercise. Within months the navy, under Decatur, by now a commodore, had imposed treaties on Algiers, Tunis and Tripoli. Decatur returned to a hero's welcome and at the state banquet in his honour famously proposed the toast 'Our country right or wrong'. Shortly afterwards he was killed duelling with a fellow officer.

It is sometimes imagined that in the early days of the United States the nation's focus was entirely on establishing itself on the North American continent, but the reality is that the US saw itself as a world power almost from its inception. It was also seen as such by others. Denmark and Sweden were among the nations that funded the US navy's operations on the Barbary coast, presaging a pattern to be repeated right up to the first Iraq War. Catherine the Great had developed the concept of nations banding together to enforce 'armed neutrality', but thirty years later it was America rather than Russia that was acting as the world's policeman.

The US navy was soon demonstrating America's new role again, this time in the South Atlantic. The Malvinas/Falkland Islands were claimed by Britain but occupied by an Argentine cattle baron, whose animals were tempting targets for the crews of American whaling ships. Eventually tiring of these depredations, the Argentines burnt two of the rustlers' ships. The US navy responded immediately, not by policing the activities of American whalers but by clearing all Argentines from the islands. In so doing America almost accidentally paved the way for Britain to take possession of the vacant islands, creating a permanent sense of injustice in Argentina that more than a century and a half later would lead to war.

Although the US navy remained small when compared with European counterparts, at least until the 1880s, it proved a highly effective extension to US diplomacy. Japan, for example, had the temerity to declare itself closed to foreigners; the closure lasted for two centuries until the US navy sailed into Tokyo Bay in 1853 and made the emperor an offer he could not refuse. Eighteen years later a US naval task force was sent to Korea, the 'Hermit Kingdom', and when the Koreans made the mistake of opening fire it attacked the defenders' forts, killing everyone inside. Korea realised it stood no chance against the 'barbarians' and opened up its markets.

Closer to home, the War of 1812 had left the Canadian border unchanged, but the US had taken advantage of the conflict to strike at the native tribes on its frontiers. The native leader Tecumseh was finally killed fighting alongside the British and Andrew Jackson, on his way to routing the British at New Orleans, put down a native uprising with exemplary ferocity. When the war was over Jackson led a punitive campaign against the Seminoles in Florida. The fact that the Seminole villages were on Spanish not American soil did not stop Jackson burning them down. The Florida natives were not the only ones to suffer. A small community of former slaves had established itself on the Apalachicola river inside Spanish Florida. The very existence of such a settlement was regarded as a threat to the United States, and in 1816 American troops supported by a naval gunboat and native mercenaries attacked and destroyed it. Prefiguring the attack on tiny Grenada 167 years later, the US responded to international outrage by insisting it was acting in 'self-defence'.

Florida remained Spanish, but Spain was no longer a power to be reckoned with. Jackson marched into northern Florida in what became known as the First Seminole War. He used the same savage tactics against the native Seminoles as he had used against the natives of Alabama, tactics Mongol-like in their terror and devastation. An attempt was made to subject him to congressional censure for his behaviour during the campaign, which included the summary execution of prisoners (among them two Britons seized when Jackson took the Spanish port of St Marks). Most of the cabinet were in favour of censure, as Jackson's actions threatened to precipitate war with both Britain and Spain, but the motion failed. The only cabinet member to support Jackson was John Quincy Adams, who had learnt as ambassador to the Russian court the value of decisive military action in expanding the frontiers of empire.

Spain was powerless to protect its native subjects, and in 1821 bowed to the inevitable and sold the state for $5m. Jackson became Florida's first governor and settlers poured in, preceded by southern slave catchers who rounded up runaway slaves, free blacks and natives for shipping to the new plantations in Louisiana, Alabama and Mississippi. Jackson himself was soon on the move again – his target this time being the White House. In 1824 he was defeated; four years later he made it. In the meantime, in 1825, Alexander I, the last great Russian tsar, had died.

CHAPTER 8

DETERMINED OPPORTUNISM AND CONQUEST

As the nineteenth century progressed the imperial ambitions of Russia and America began to move in parallel, but their ideologies of empire remained very different.

The Russian approach to their empire was simple: it was theirs by right of conquest; no more needed to be said. For Americans pushing to the Mississippi and beyond the position was not as simple. The ideology that underpinned America's existence as a nation was based on a commitment to the rights of man, rights that did not include the right of conquest. Those in their way, whether French, Spanish or native, might represent inferior civilisations or even no civilisation at all, but they were still men. Conquest smacked of theft; to take what had belonged to others there needed to be agreement. But how to make an agreement with natives who had no concept of property? And more fundamentally, how to make an agreement with natives who had no incentive to give up their land? The answer was provided in Britain in the ideas of men like John Locke and Adam Smith, ideas that eventually coalesced into the principles of capitalism. Fundamental to the efficient working of society, they argued, was private property, which the Almighty had bestowed not for its own sake but so that it could be used to benefit all. The natives might regard land as just another part of nature like air or water, which enabled them to hunt and gather all they needed, but that was not what God intended. Land was there to be tilled in order to produce crops that could be traded. It was the concept of commerce that was fundamental to the ethical justification of American territorial aggrandisement. The purpose of land was to grow food for the townspeople back east, to produce crops to export in return for European imports, to offer up gold and silver to further oil the wheels of commerce. The natives were not 'using' their land in the way that God and 'civilisation' demanded, and therefore they should let somebody else take over. Similarly Latin American and Caribbean republics were not governing themselves properly, and so the US had a duty to intervene. As Robert Kagan has pointed out, the same rationale for imposing American values on other cultures would be heard again as American corporations justified their quest for 'globalisation'.

America's imperial ambitions emerged erratically from its ideology rather than being part of some grand imperial design. Kagan, writing about the American purchase of Louisiana, violent conquest of Florida and opportunistic acquisition of Pacific coastline in the first two decades of the nineteenth century, noted the paradox that 'American leaders had a clear vision of a continental empire' but 'had no specific plans to obtain it'. Imperial expansion in the period he characterised as 'determined opportunism'. Russia's imperial strategies were much more straightforward.

Although the two nations had imperial ambition in common they had little else. The way that power was transferred in St Petersburg and Washington in the 1820s showed how fundamentally different the two nations remained. Nevertheless the accession of Alexander I's successor, Nicholas I, and the election of Andrew Jackson started to push both nations along a common path. In the struggle that would emerge for the soul of each empire the innate absolutism of the two men helped create an environment in which compromise became impossible, and eventually led both nations into civil war.

King Andrew

As Alexander grew older his behaviour became increasingly bizarre as he fell under the influence of a Rasputin-like figure, Count Alexander Arakcheyev.

Arakcheyev was not, like Rasputin, a semi-literate peasant, but his antics were equally grotesque. He ordered women to be flogged for washing clothes on the wrong day and had a forest cleared of nightingales when they kept him awake. Arakcheyev was made minister of war after Napoleon's defeat and created military colonies in the newly conquered territories. Hundreds of thousands of serfs were made into soldiers for life and transported to military encampments where they both farmed the land and formed local militias. Alexander and Arakcheyev were trying to do by imperial dictat what in America was happening naturally, just as Peter the Great had done when he colonised the western marshes to build St Petersburg. The spontaneous pressure to colonise and settle ever more land that arose in America could not develop in Russia, because the practices of autocracy allowed no spontaneous actions of any kind.

The serfs of the Arakcheyev colonies were subject to military discipline, with savage penalties for dereliction of duties or desertion, which increased the pressures from below for radical change. These colonies left a profound impression on Russian attitudes to both colonisation and the institution of serfdom. A hundred years later the Bolsheviks introduced the concept of 'labour armies' and Trotsky felt compelled to write of the need for an 'Ideological struggle against petit-bourgeois intellectual and trade-unionist prejudices which see the militarisation of labour or the widespread use of military units for labour as an Arakcheyev system'.

Unlike Russian autocracy American democracy allowed society to evolve as new interests and new philosophies became part of the political process. Andrew Jackson's 1824 presidential campaign demonstrated that new political forces were emerging in America and one day would have to be heard. When, a year later, Alexander I died the familiar problems of transferring power in an autocracy illustrated dramatically the absence of outlets for such new forces in Russia.

The choice of potential candidates was between the eldest of Alexander's brothers, Constantine, and the next eldest, Nicholas. Constantine had married a Polish Catholic, thus disqualifying himself, but as commander of the Polish army he had widespread military support. In St Petersburg Nicholas acclaimed Constantine as tsar. Meanwhile in Warsaw Constantine acknowledged Nicholas. Into this confusion erupted in December 1825 an unprecedented new force: a clandestine network of radical army officers, some opposed to the very idea of monarchical government and all committed to the emancipation of the serfs (although disagreeing on what emancipation actually meant). Whereas American democracy provided a ready channel for army officers to gain political power, in Russia there was only one alternative: attempt a coup. Nicholas reacted promptly; most of the army stayed loyal and the mutinous officers were quickly arrested and their leaders executed. (Among those on the sentencing panel was the French soldier of fortune Comte de Langéron, showing that the contemporaries of Lafayette were not all drawn to visions of liberty and democracy.)

The 'Decembrist' conspirators had no realistic hope of success, but the very fact that such a conspiracy could exist, with members across Russia, was a startling revelation to the Romanovs. Tsar Nicholas I spent the thirty years of his reign trying to ensure that nothing similar could ever happen again. The tool he created was the Imperial Chancellery's Third Directorate which, under his successors, became better known as the Okhrana, the tsarist state's secret police.

The concept of a police state is often associated with the rise to power of the twentieth century's dictators, especially Stalin and Hitler, but in Russia the institutions of the police state were codified by Nicholas I in 1845. He first made explicit the notion of 'crimes against the state', which were defined so widely that they included not just actions but 'intent'. Any action or thought designed to bring the state into disrepute or weaken its authority became illegal. Pipes comments that 'Chapters 3 and 4 of the Russian Criminal Code of 1845 are to totalitarianism what the Magna Carta is to liberty.'

In Russia there has never been a tradition of liberty as understood by Americans. Absolute power belonged to the tsar not because of some aberration in which the rights of citizens were denied but because autocracy was seen by virtually everyone as the natural state of affairs. Citizenship in Russian terms is about duties not rights. If power is the rightful preserve of the tsar it follows that trying to usurp or even share that power is not rightful, is indeed criminal. Thus the tsar is perfectly justified in acting against anyone who questions his authority. The concept of 'crimes against the state' may have been codified in 1845 but it really goes back to Mongol times or even earlier. Since the days of the Mongols power had resided at the top and only at the top. The Bolshevik police state was to continue not just the institutions of Nicholas I but a much older tradition of unfettered central power.

If the succession of Nicholas I to the throne in 1825 indicated merely a slight reinterpretation of centuries-old political traditions, Andrew Jackson's election three years later was thought at the time to demonstrate a radical change in the direction and tone of American political life. Politics dumbed down. Ludicrous rumours circulated, such as the claim that the Pope intended to send millions of immigrants to take over the country, and would then relocate the Vatican to the Mississippi Valley. Whereas Thomas Paine's *Common Sense* had been a bestseller at the time of the American Rebellion, the bestseller sixty years later was Maria Monk's virulently anti-Catholic *Awful Disclosures of the Hotel Dieu Nunnery in Montreal*, which detailed the alleged sexual practices of monks and nuns. (Monk claimed to have been a nun herself but was actually a former prostitute; that did not reduce her popularity on the lecture circuit.)

Intellectual debates among members of the political elite had given way to mob violence in New York and Baltimore in the run-up to the 1812 War. These were not totally new apparitions; after all, the American Revolution had started with mob violence in Boston and Lexington. What had changed is that the old aristocratic structures could no longer contain and manipulate the popular forces the revolution had unleashed.

The best ways to illustrate these developments is to consider the two central characters of the period: John Quincy Adams and Andrew Jackson.

John Quincy Adams, sixth president of the United States, son of John Adams, second president, was an intellectual and diplomat. Part of the New England elite that abhorred slavery but mixed easily with the Virginia aristocracy, Adams II moved as effortlessly in the palaces of Europe as in the salons of Washington and Boston. In 1808 Adams was made the first United States minister to Russia and arrived in St Petersburg just as Tsar Alexander broke off his alliance with Napoleon. He was therefore received as a welcome new ally and set to work enhancing America's position with such success that the United States soon surpassed Britain as Russia's leading trading partner. Adams's imperial vision was of a commercial empire far more sophisticated than the crude territorial ambitions of Jackson. Nevertheless he set out a grand strategy for conquering the continent and in particular was a passionate supporter of Jackson's conquest of Florida, which he insisted was undertaken not to gain territory but to protect the security of the United States (using arguments uncannily similar to those later used to justify invading Iraq). Adams displayed a dedication to public service typical of the earliest leaders, as ambassador to Paris and then St Petersburg, as secretary of state, as president and finally, after his term in the White House, as a simple member of the House of Representatives for the last twenty years of his life. His conscience and his conviction of the moral superiority of his new nation drove all that he did. He was no naïve dreamer, but his realpolitik had at its core a belief that he and his class were destined to rule by virtue of their virtue. His world disappeared for ever with the election of his successor, Andrew Jackson.

In 1824 Jackson gained the most votes but lost the presidential election when a third party candidate swung behind Adams. In 1828 the two men competed again. Yet again the north voted solidly for Adams, but this time the south and west were unanimously behind Jackson and he swept to power. The outstanding feature of Jackson's campaign was its dishonesty. As Samuel Eliot Morison points out, Jackson gained power because of his campaign's 'persistent lying about the "extravagance and corruption" of the honest, efficient and economical Adams administration'. Peddling this nonsense gave him, once in power, an excuse for firing around 40 per cent of the existing senior government officials and replacing them with his cronies.

Jackson is a man whose life is well documented, and yet it is almost impossible to separate man from myth. He is held up as the champion of the common man, the Scotch-Irish frontiersman who overturned for ever the rule of Virginian aristocrats and New England patricians. School textbooks typically portray him as born in poverty – often recording that he was 'the first president to be born in a log cabin'. That is true, but in fact Jackson's father died before he was born and he was brought up surrounded by slaves on the South Carolina plantation of his uncle. At fourteen Jackson was fighting in the American rebellion, and was captured by the British. After the war he is reputed to have gambled away a family inheritance and moved west, where he married his landlady's daughter, despite the lady concerned already being married. (Jackson married her again three years later when she had divorced her first husband. It seems to have been a true love match; Jackson was later to challenge and kill a man who made unkind remarks about her.)

In Tennessee he prospered, becoming the state's first member of the US House of Representatives and serving briefly in the Senate. When war with the British erupted in 1812 Jackson, as a major-general in the state militia, threw himself into the fray (once he had recovered from a pistol wound incurred in a street brawl with future US senator Thomas Benton). Jackson's first contribution to the war effort was to lead a savage campaign against the native Creeks of Alabama and Georgia. He then imposed a punitive 'peace', stripping land and rights from native enemies and allies alike, before gaining even greater glory at the battle of New Orleans.

Jackson was self-consciously the opposite of Adams II, rough and self-made, soldier not diplomat and above all, as he saw it, democrat not elitist. His cabinet was the first to include nobody from New England or Virginia. The crux of what came to be known as 'Jacksonian democracy' was a determination to wrest power and wealth from the eastern ruling class and pass it to the people. In some ways Jackson was the Lenin of America. He cut through the fragile checks and balances created by the Founding Fathers, vetoing legislation and ignoring court rulings. Known to his friends as Old Hickory because of his fabled toughness, he was known to opponents as King Andrew and was censured by Congress in 1834 for his autocratic behaviour; the censure was expunged from the record two years later in a vote moved by Senator Benton from Missouri, the same man who had been engaged in the street brawl with Jackson twenty years earlier. Jackson remained a brawler with little commitment to the precepts of free speech and open debate; he even tried to make it illegal to send anti-slavery literature through the post. One of his lasting legacies was the 'spoils system' – distributing offices and largesse to friends and supporters, the American equivalent of *kormenlie* – the Russian system in which public servants helped themselves to a share of taxation. In the same way that Russia's autocrats needed a massive bureaucracy to manage their empire and gather what they needed above all, taxes, America's democratic rulers needed a similar bureaucracy to manage the affairs of state and to gather in what they needed above all: votes. The principal features of the spoils system were established within fifty years of the revolution, when the original Founding Fathers died off and were replaced by a new breed of professional politicians, most vividly personified by a group known as the Regents who ruled the state of New York. The political elite of New York had been bitterly opposed to the 1812 invasion of Canada and war with Britain, but the American victory in the battle of New Orleans had made these sentiments deeply unpopular. Labelling the old elite as traitors, the Regents, led by Martin van Buren, stormed to power and set about ensuring that they stayed there. (The Regents enriched themselves and the English language; their meetings with sponsors in the lobby of the state capitol in Albany inspired the verb 'to lobby'.) Like kormlenie in Russia the spoils system, although branded by some as corruption, was regarded by others as perfectly natural. Its most famous justification was given by US senator and three-term New York governor William Learned Marcy, when nominating Van Buren to serve as ambassador to Great Britain. New York politicians, he explained, did not pretend to be anything but what they were: 'When they are contending for victory, they avow their intention of enjoying the fruits of it. If they are defeated, they expect to retire from office. If they are successful, they claim, as a matter of right, the advantages of success. They see nothing wrong in the rule that to the victor belongs the spoils of the enemy.' Macy went on to put the same principle into practice internationally: as secretary for war from 1845 to 1849 he helped launch the US invasion of Mexico.

The spoils system spread far beyond New York. In 1820 Congress passed the Tenure of Office Act, which laid down that a host of government appointments should be for four years only, allowing each new administration to reward its supporters when it came to power. In return the office holders were expected to make regular 'donations' to party funds from their government salaries, and to work tirelessly to get out the vote at election time. As Hugh Brogan puts it, politics in America in the nineteenth century was 'as thoroughly, recklessly, unscrupulously and joyously corrupt as the politics of wicked old eighteenth-century Britain'. As long as voting was public voters could be coerced or bribed. Secret voting, known as the 'Australian ballot' following its introduction there in 1856, was not prevalent in America until the end of the nineteenth century. The spoils system continued well into the next century in southern states like Louisiana and northern cities like Chicago. Its underlying principles remain part of the American political culture to this day. Thousands of jobs remain in the gift of politicians, and it is accepted that political patronage will extend from appointments of minor local officials right up to membership of the Supreme Court.

The most infamous beneficiary of the spoils system was Samuel Swartwout. As a twenty-three year old Swartwout was arrested for his part in Aaron Burr's conspiracy to create a western empire. When Burr's trial collapsed Swartwout threw himself into a host of dubious schemes in Europe and the United States, eventually becoming an accomplished land speculator.

As one of the key fundraisers for Jackson's presidential campaign, Swartwout was awarded the most attractive of presidential sinecures – customs collector in his native New York. After serving two four-year terms he left for Europe, whereupon Jackson's successor had the accounts audited and discovered a $1.2m hole. Swartwout eventually returned to New York, and reached a compromise with the authorities under which he avoided prosecution by returning some of the missing funds.

Despite episodes like this, Jackson is still remembered as the great democrat who replaced corrupt aristocracy with frontier egalitarianism. That egalitarianism did not extend to anyone with a black skin. John Quincy Adams spent his final years vigorously denouncing slavery, while Jackson in equally passionate terms denounced the opponents of slavery, accusing them of attacking the very concept of property. Jackson's views were mirrored by Russians desperately trying to stop any move towards emancipating the serfs.

Slavery and serfdom were the foundations on which the agricultural economies of Russia and the southern United States were built. But as the technology of conquest and colonisation moved from musket and horse to mass-produced rifle and steam train the primacy of agriculture disappeared, particularly in the United States.

A Time for Guns

The engine of American territorial expansion was its economy. In the early days the fertility of the land stimulated agricultural production both for internal consumption and for export, primarily to the other British colonies in the Caribbean, and the export trade in turn fostered shipping and commerce. But to generate the wealth needed to take the vast tracts of land acquired by the US government in a great arc from Florida through eventually to Alaska, and then to invest in the infrastructure needed to exploit these new territories, the new nation needed its own industrial revolution. As long as it relied on imports of European manufactured goods the profits at the top of the value chain remained outside its control.

At the end of the eighteenth century those profits were being made by the British, who were starting to overtake France in the economic leadership of Europe (although a fact often forgotten is that Europe still lagged far behind Asia in terms of manufacturing output). The industrial revolution in Britain had started in the textile industry, where the invention of the spinning jenny had revolutionised cotton spinning and allowed Richard Arkwright to create textile factories, whose mass-produced products swept away traditional cottage industries and allowed the formation of the first truly global businesses – buying cotton from Asia and America for the mills of England, and then selling the finished product to the four corners of the earth.

Britain's prosperity came to depend overwhelmingly on its industrial and commercial base, and the superiority of its manufacturing attracted envy from all over the world – as much from the fledgling democrats of America, who had so recently cast off the British yoke, as from tentative westernisers peering out through the fluttering curtains of Russian absolutism. In 1753 two Englishmen, William Chamberlain and Richard Cozzens, set up Russia's first large-scale cotton printing and dye works with the help of subsidies from the Empress Elizabeth, but as with most such schemes it did not last long. Manufacturing took much stronger root in the entrepreneurial climate of the new empire across the Atlantic.

Like Russia, America started on the road to industrialisation by borrowing from Britain, and it is not surprising that the man known as the Father of the American industrial revolution was an Englishman. Samuel Slater was the son of a landowner and speculator in Derbyshire and used his family contacts to become what today would be called a management trainee in one of England's leading textile mills. In 1789 Slater crossed the Atlantic after the Pennsylvania legislature advertised in his local newspaper offering a bounty for skilled migrants. The British government was anxious to maintain its industrial secrets, fearing, quite rightly, that British patents were unlikely to be respected abroad, and had prohibited the emigration of men with Slater's specialist knowledge. He therefore disguised himself as an agricultural labourer and slipped out of the country. Soon he was appointed manager of a struggling textile mill in Rhode Island. Using his knowledge of Arkwright's processes, Slater turned the factory's fortunes round and recognisably modern industrial production in the United States had started. (Slater brought with him not only the technology of early English capitalism but also its values: his first nine employees were all children aged seven to eleven.)

In other industries the transfer of technology was less controversial. The pottery towns of England, for example, sent scores of entrepreneurs and thousands of potters to set up near suitable clay deposits in America to manufacture domestic crockery.

Not all of the building blocks of America's early industrial successes were pirated or imported from Europe. The cotton industry that fed Slater's mills was itself transformed in 1794 when Eli Whitney patented his 'cotton gin'. In India machines had long been used to separate the seeds and fibre of Asian 'long staple' cotton but they didn't work on American 'short staple' cotton, which had to be laboriously cleaned by slave labour. Whitney's machine overcame this problem and American cotton production was revolutionised. Although Whitney patented his 'gin' (a corruption of engine) he was unable to enforce his patent, and his attempt to franchise his invention at what many planters considered to be exorbitant rates (he demanded 40 per cent of their profits) led to years of legal disputes. These were resolved not by the forces of the free market or the courts of justice but by the legislatures of South and North Carolina and Tennessee, who bought out his patent rights. Having failed to make his fortune with his cotton gin, Whitney turned his inventive mind elsewhere and successfully pioneered the mass production of another staple of colonial life: guns. Guns were an essential part of American life. Without the superiority of their firepower the conquest of the native tribes to the west and south would have been far more difficult, and American expansion would have been significantly slower.

In Florida the natives had fiercely resisted the American conquest but were pushed ever further south, where in 1823 they were 'granted' 5 million acres. That arrangement was short lived. By 1830 Andrew

Jackson was president and Congress passed the Indian Removal Act, allowing the government to 'exchange' tribal lands in the east with territory west of the Mississippi – territory already inhabited not only by its traditional occupants but by tribes fleeing from the advancing whites.

The Indian Removal Act created a supposedly permanent frontier at the 95th meridian. Native tribes east of that line were bribed, tricked or forced into migrating west, leaving behind their rich hereditary lands to be settled in Kansas, Iowa or Oklahoma. In 1834 the Indian Intercourse Act prohibited encroachment on the new native reservations, but to little avail. Until 1831 native tribes were treated as foreign nations, but in that year the Supreme Court ruled, in the case of The Cherokee Nation v. Georgia, that they were not foreign states and their land therefore fell under the jurisdiction of the state governments. The court partly reversed itself next year in Worcester v. Georgia, but Jackson simply ignored the court decision, declaring that the chief justice had made his decision and 'now let him enforce it'. In 1838, in one of the most shameful episodes in American history, General Winfield Scott rounded up the Cherokees and put them into concentration camps before forcing them to walk west towards Oklahoma, in what became known as the Trail of Tears. One in four died along the way.

In Florida the remaining Seminoles were coerced into moving to Oklahoma. Around 4,000 natives went, but in 1835 the Second Seminole War broke out when the rest refused to go. The Seminole forces were led by another of the great native leaders, Osceola, who made the fatal mistake of agreeing to negotiate under a flag of truce. He was seized and died in captivity. After seven years of bloody conflict an uneasy peace was agreed, which lasted until the Third Seminole War in 1855. By now the march of 'progress' was unstoppable. As Alexander II, the Tsar Liberator, mounted the Russian throne and moved to emancipate the serfs, Florida bounty hunters were being offered rewards of $500 for native men, $250 for women and $100 for children. By 1858 the Florida wars were officially declared over; one way or another all but a handful of Seminoles had been cleansed from the state.

American treatment of natives in conquered Florida was mirrored in Russian treatment of natives in its newly conquered territory. Revolts in Finland and Poland were put down by force. Poland in particular suffered appallingly. In November 1830 Polish troops in Warsaw rose in revolt and the leaders of the self-governing Polish rump-state proclaimed solidarity with the rebels. The Russian response was overwhelming: rebel forces were crushed, hundreds of rebels were executed, 180,000 were banished to Siberian exile and another 6,000 fled into exile in France. At the same time the rump-state lost the remnants of its independence and its army. (One of those who fled into exile was Count Pawel Strzelecki, who became one of the most famous explorers of his time. Among his achievements was surveying Australia's highest mountain and naming it after the great Polish hero Kosciuszko.)

After completing the ethnic cleansing of Florida the next target of the southern imperialists was Texas. The 1819 Adams-Onís Treaty, under which Spain ceded Florida to the United States also established America's western frontier with the Spanish colony of Mexico, but American adventurers had never accepted the sanctity of their country's borders. In common American parlance the term 'frontier' was not a demarcation line on a map but a vast expanse waiting to be exploited. When Davy Crockett is celebrated as the King of the Wild Frontier, it does not mean that he stood guard on the frontier but that he ignored the legal frontier and pushed on to create his own; and like many others he pushed on to Texas.

The first Americans to invade Texas were known as filibusters. In modern times the term filibuster has come to mean using endless speechifying to stop legislation being approved, but originally it was not legislatures held to ransom but ships; the word originated in the Dutch for pirate or freebooter, *vrijbuiter*, particularly in the Caribbean whence, via Spanish, it passed into English to describe the mercenary gangs operating primarily from the city of Natchez, Mississippi. They were to America what Yermak's Cossack freebooters had been to Russia: lawless ruffians expanding empire by going where presidents and tsars feared to tread.

Under a Mississippi doctor and merchant named James Long, filibusters invaded Texas just months after the US had formally given up claim to the territory under the Adams-Onís Treaty. Spanish troops drove the filibusters out but, with revolution spreading throughout Latin America, Spain was no more able to protect its interests in Mexico than in Florida, and in 1821, the same year that Andrew Jackson was made Governor of Florida, Mexican rebels secured their independence. Long moved in again, but the native Mexicans were no more receptive than the Spanish. Long was captured and six months later, in disputed circumstances, shot by one of his guards.

More peaceful settlement had been welcomed, however, by both Spanish and Mexican authorities. Moses Austin was invited to settle 300 families in northern Texas by the Spanish authorities, later confirmed by the new Mexican government, and in 1821 his son Stephen led the first settlers and their slaves across the border. The Mexicans naïvely believed that the presence of the Americans would help suppress any native uprisings and dissuade any US invasion. Thousands more immigrants soon poured over the border. By 1835 eastern and central Texas was dominated by nearly 30,000 American settlers, who made up over 80 per cent of the population. The Mexican authorities became alarmed, and when they declared slavery illegal the Anglo immigrants also became alarmed. Just fifteen years after being invited in the immigrants proclaimed their independence, and called on the US government to annexe their new nation, just as West Florida had been annexed a quarter of a century earlier, and thereby protect their 'right' to own slaves. (Texas was an important entrepôt for the slave trade. The United States had banned the importation of slaves in 1808 but the potential profits were so large that slavers were willing to run the gauntlet of the Royal Navy to transport captives from Africa via Cuba to Texas, for smuggling across the border to the slave markets in New Orleans.)

The annexation proposal met stiff resistance not only from the Mexican government but also from many Americans. The balance of power within the US was swinging to the rapidly industrialising north.

The addition of yet another slave state in Texas, to be followed no doubt by others as more of Mexico was gobbled up, was not welcomed.

The reaction of the Mexican president Santa Anna to news of the impending revolt was more direct. He marched on the American rebels and besieged nearly 200 Anglo immigrants at the Alamo, a fortified mission at San Antonio. (Anglo is a more appropriate term than American as many of the Alamo's defenders were European immigrants, mainly British.) About 2,000 Mexicans and all but one of the Anglos died. The cry 'Remember the Alamo' became a rallying call, although more appropriate would have been 'Remember Goliad', where, three weeks later, Santa Ana massacred 371 American prisoners of war. Less than a month after the Goliad massacre an American force under Samuel Houston defeated and captured Santa Ana, and forced him to sign a treaty recognising the independence of Texas, a treaty the Mexican Congress not surprisingly repudiated. Houston wanted Texas annexed by the United States, but although President Jackson recognised the independent Republic of Texas even he initially balked at annexation.

Annexation was finally approved by the US Congress in 1845, and the Texas legislature was presented with a choice between accepting annexation or continued independence and a peace treaty with Mexico brokered by Britain. The legislators unanimously chose annexation. Acquiring Texas was important in terms of US economic strategy. The main globally traded resource at that time, and one on which Britain was heavily dependent, was cotton. Blocking British access to Texan cotton helped consolidate US economic power. President Tyler observed that by obtaining a 'virtual monopoly' the US was able to gain 'a greater influence over the affairs of the world than would be found in armies however strong, or navies however numerous'. As he bluntly summarised, 'It places all other nations at our feet.'

The Texan Revolution was fundamentally different to the American Revolution of the previous century. The American Revolution was fought by men who believed they were protecting a heritage of civilisation handed down by their fathers and grandfathers – great cities like Boston, New

York and Philadelphia, fertile plantations and farms, fisheries and ports. The Texan Revolution was fought by men who had only just arrived. The American Revolution was a war of liberation, the Texan a war of conquest. The American Revolution was fought against men who were not that different: they spoke the same language, shared much of the same history, and indeed were often members of the same family. The Texan struggle was a racial war fought not only to maintain the superiority of white over black but to protect whites against government by Hispanics with whom there was no shared culture, no shared values and with whom quite literally there would be no common language.

Former President Adams II declared that the decision to annexe Texas was the 'heaviest calamity that ever befell myself and my country'. The US could have occupied Texas long before it did; Spain would have conceded it in 1819, but Adams II turned it down because he was worried that it would tilt the balance of power towards the slaveholding states. For men like him, to whom slavery was totally repugnant, the admission of Texas represented the end of the Puritan ethic. It also marked the start of war with Mexico.

Manifest Destiny: Chechnya to Cuba

James Polk was elected president on a platform of 're-annexing' Texas, and in 1845 ordered General Zachary Taylor to cross the Nueces river and invade Mexico. The Americans initially staged a three-pronged attack, with Taylor advancing across northern Mexico, Colonel Stephen Kearny occupying New Mexico and then moving into California, and the Pacific fleet landing on the California coast where American settlers had yet again proclaimed an independent republic. Zachary Taylor's military successes made him a public hero, greatly alarming the White House. President Polk sent a naval expedition under General Winfield Scott, the organiser of the genocidal Trail of Tears, to land at Vera Cruz and march inland. Scott overwhelmed the Mexican forces and occupied Mexico City. In the words of their hymn the US marines, having reached the 'shores of Tripoli' forty years earlier, now entered 'the halls of Montezuma'. In the subsequent treaty of Guadalupe Hidalgo, Mexico gave up all claims to California, New Mexico and Texas in return for $18.25m. Polk decided not to try to gain re-election, and Zachary Taylor became one of a long line of generals to move from battlefield to White House. (Oddly, a man whose opposition to this imperial war cost him his congressional seat also went on to the White House: Abraham Lincoln.)

Russian and American troops marched west at the same time. Just after Winfield Scott captured Mexico City the Russians entered Hungary: Nicholas I had dutifully inherited the role of 'gendarme of Europe' from Alexander I, and used his army to suppress revolutionary elements beyond the borders of his empire. Both halves of the Austro-Hungarian empire were in turmoil. In the Hungarian half (which was far larger than Hungary today and extended down into the Balkans) the parliament pushed for more autonomy and demanded major reforms. Hungary was to be a constitutional monarchy, with a powerful parliament including an elected lower house, and its own army. Serfdom was to be abolished and civil rights guaranteed. The parliament made Hungarian the official language of administration, justice and education in all the areas it controlled. Depending upon your point of view this was the proud foundation stone of Hungarian independence, reflecting the throwing off of Germanic cultural, economic and military imperialism, or the descendants of Attila the Hun intent on doing to their own minorities (Croats, Serbs, Germans, Gypsies, Vlachs, Ruthenians and Slovaks) just what they accused the Austrians of doing to them. Many of these minority groups were Slavs, and a Pan-Slav congress in Prague condemned the Hungarians as oppressors, describing them in terms remarkably similar to those used to describe the British at a different congress in Philadelphia seventy-four years earlier. (Pan-Slavism was the Russian equivalent of the Monroe Doctrine, but justified in the name of ethnic solidarity rather than the racial superiority that America increasingly used to justify its interventions in Latin America and the Caribbean.)

Nicholas wanted no revolutionary changes on his borders, and in the guise of Pan-Slavism felt able to justify intervention. Russian troops marched west and occupied Slovakia and Ruthenia. The putative Hungarian revolution was crushed. Lajos Kossuth, who had declared himself leader of an independent Hungary, was forced to flee to Turkey where he was imprisoned. The Turks did not want him in their country; his presence was just the sort of excuse that could be used to justify further Russian aggression (just as the presence of the native leader Tecumseh had been used to justify the American invasion of Canada). On the other hand they were not keen to hand him over to their Russian enemy – but by then there was another imperial power on the horizon. Following American intervention Kossuth was freed and travelled to America, where he received an enthusiastic reception. Abraham Lincoln tabled a Senate resolution, lamenting that the United States had not actively intervened to support the Hungarian revolution. Kossuth joined a group of Hungarian political refugees who had established the community of New Buda in Iowa. Like the Polish hero Tadeusz Kosciuszko he became another of the 'democratic' victims of Russian autocracy to be feted in the United States; and like Kosciuszko he eventually tired of the American way of life and returned to Europe.

Like America Russia was keen to expand – annexing territory to the south and eventually starting a full-scale war with Turkey. The Turkish fleet was totally destroyed at Sinope Bay in 1853, and it looked as though the victory of Nicholas I would be as complete as Zachary Taylor's in Mexico, but there was a fundamental difference in the geopolitics of the two nations: America was the only imperial power on its continent. Russia's invasion of the Turkish-controlled provinces of Walachia (modern Romania) and Moldavia propelled Britain and France into the war on Turkey's side.

The west's fear of the barbarian east flared into outright war in the Crimea. It was a fear that went back to Châlons and would continue into the future. During the cold war the spectre of Red Army troops parachuting into the English countryside or Soviet missiles raining down on New York seemed quite real. With hindsight the threat was plainly hollow and Russia's empire was rotten at the core, but that is not how it seemed at the time. Exactly the same happened in the nineteenth century. Alexander I's military machine overcame Napoleon and rolled on. By the middle of the century the west was shuddering each time the Russian Bear moved. Nowhere was safe. An emplacement built during the Crimean War for a battery of five 8-inch muzzle-loading guns still looks out over Sydney Harbour from Kirribilli Point. It is difficult now to believe that anyone seriously thought that Russia was about to invade Australia, but the alarms of the cold war proved just as far fetched.

At this point the weaknesses in the mighty military machine that Alexander I had thrust into the centre of European political life became evident. Without having to worry about public opinion, or even the opinion of the nobility, the Russian autocracy was able to treat its population as cannon fodder – but it still needed to manufacture the cannon. Russia lacked the economic and organisational resources to turn brute force into lasting success. The death of 300,000 Russians in Nicholas's adventures on the Turkish front and military defeat, along with Austrian pressure, forced his successor, Alexander II, to withdraw.

The Crimean War in Britain is remembered for the blinding incompetence of the British general, Lord Raglan, at the Charge of the Light Brigade, but the Russian general, Prince Menshikov, surpassed him in aristocratic stupidity. Russia's defeat showed plainly to the world that the days when Russia had been the continent's superpower were long gone. Moldavia and Walachia returned to Turkish control, and as so often Russia's attention swung back to the west. In 1863 another Polish revolt was brutally suppressed. Not only were rebels executed or exiled to Siberia as before but Alexander II introduced a deliberate policy of cultural cleansing aimed at expunging Polish culture, language and Catholicism. As in the earlier partitions of Poland, and as Stalin and Hitler would do seventy-five years later, the Russian and German leaders co-operated in destroying any chance of an independent Poland; the Prussian leader Bismarck forcibly repatriated Polish rebels who tried to flee west.

Under Alexander II one particular long-running colonial conflict on the southern frontier was finally 'settled': the Chechens were pacified. Some of the native tribes encountered by the Russians as they expanded their empire were less easily quelled than others, and nowhere was the resistance fiercer than in the Caucasus. Since the time of Ivan the Terrible Russians had been pushing into the region, and in the eighteenth century serious attempts were made to control the Muslim mountain tribes. In the latter half of the century the Chechen Sheikh Mansur declared holy war on the advancing Russians, uniting clans and mobilising resistance until his capture in 1791. In 1817 the leadership of the resistance forces passed to a twenty-year-old Dagestani mullah, Imam Shamil, who fought a bitter guerrilla war for more than forty years. Russia eventually deployed an enormous number of troops, one source says half a million, until Shamil was captured in 1859. His captors wary of the dangers of creating martyrs, he was jailed and later allowed to go into exile in Mecca. Following age-old Russian practice his two sons became officers in the Russian army.

Today the name of Imam Shamil is venerated by Dagestanis and Chechens as much as Kossuth by Hungarians or Kosciuszko by Poles. If in the west the histories of Hungary and Poland are largely ignored, the history of the Caucasus wars is entirely forgotten. Only after the break-up of the Soviet empire did the west suddenly take note of the bitterness still bubbling in the region; bitterness that exploded in the atrocities of the Chechen War. That bitterness has existed since at least the time of Alexander II. Leo Tolstoy, in his novella *Hadji Murat*, set in 1852, wrote, 'The feeling experienced by all the Chechens from the youngest to the oldest was stronger than hate. It was not hatred, for they did not regard those Russian dogs as human beings, but it was such repulsion, disgust and perplexity at the senseless cruelty of these creatures that the desire to exterminate them – like the desire to exterminate rats, poisonous spiders or wolves – was as natural an instinct as that of self-preservation.'

Alexander II was known as the Tsar Liberator for his role in emancipating the serfs. To the Chechens and other conquered people it must have seemed a particularly inappropriate title.

Although the conquest of Chechnya took so many years and so much blood it was not a particularly momentous event in Russian history. The expansion of empire was a given, one of those inexorable tides in the affairs of man that almost all Russians expected to continue more or less without end. Similarly Americans considered their nation-empire was virtually limitless. Having dealt with the Mexicans to the south, attention once more turned north and west.

The British had long settled in what was then called Oregon (the modern US states of Idaho, Washington and Oregon, and the Canadian province of British Columbia). Their main settlement was the great Hudson's Bay Company trading post of Fort Vancouver on the Columbia river, opposite the site of modern Portland, Oregon. Over time the beaver on which the trading post depended were hunted to the brink of extinction and the fertile terrain of the Oregon region started to attract pioneers more committed to farming than to hunting. Most of these pioneers came overland in covered wagons, and for most of them the starting point was Independence, Missouri. The result was that by the 1840s Canadian settlers in Oregon were greatly outnumbered by American. In 1845 the Hudson's Bay Company abandoned Fort Vancouver and retreated north to Vancouver Island.

In an early example of political spin Polk had been elected in 1844 on a platform of both 're-annexing Texas' and 're-occupying Oregon', although in neither case was it obvious that 're-' had any historical justification. In an attempt to stop Canada extending to the Pacific Ocean he demanded that the northern boundary of Oregon be set at 54° 40', the latitude Tsar Alexander I and President Monroe had agreed would be the frontier between Russia and America. As Canadian explorers had crossed the continent before Lewis and Clark, Britain was never going to agree, and Polk eventually settled for 49°, outraging northern imperialists who wanted a massive new Oregon to balance slave-holding Texas.

A wave of anti-English hysteria again swept America. In New York passions ran particularly high when an English actor, William Macready, was given a starring role in a play at the Astor Place Opera House. Despite the play itself being English (Shakespeare's *Macbeth*), demonstrators outside the theatre demanded that Macready (quite probably one of the greatest Shakespearean actors of all time), be replaced by an American. In the subsequent riots more than twenty people died and over a hundred were injured.

Stymied in the north-west, potential opportunities beckoned again in the south. American empire building had always involved a mixture of free enterprise and conventional military force. After the Treaty of Guadalupe Hidalgo sealed the successful outcome of its attack on Mexico, the emphasis moved away from open aggression to the surreptitious activities of the private sector.

American filibusters were still anxious to add more slave states. William Walker and his private army invaded Baja California in 1853, but Mexican troops easily defeated his 300 mercenaries. Escaping back to the United States he was arrested for contravening laws supposedly guaranteeing American neutrality, but was acquitted. He then started a tradition of American intervention in Central America by offering his men to one of the factions competing for power in Nicaragua (just as the US government did repeatedly in the twentieth century). Once in Nicaragua his forces quickly seized power. Walker declared himself president, legalised slavery and started manoeuvring for annexation by the United States. He also started building up the Nicaraguan army in preparation for further conquests, but he was pre-empted by neighbouring Costa Rica (supplied with arms by a British government fearful of America's imperial intentions). Costa Rican troops forced Walker to flee back to the United States, where he attracted enormous crowds wherever he spoke. In 1857 he tried to regain power in Nicaragua but was captured and sent back to the US, where once again he was arrested and then acquitted. In 1860 he made one final attempt to fulfil his dream, this time by attempting a *coup d'état* in Honduras. He was captured by the British, who knew better than to return him to the US; they passed him to the Honduran authorities, who promptly executed him.

Walker and the other filibusters were essentially independent freebooters but they were not acting alone. Just as Yermak and his Cossacks were employed by the Stroganoff family to protect and extend their interests, so Walker had a patron who kept himself well away from the dirty work on the frontier. Cornelius Vanderbilt had become one of the leading plutocrats of his day by exercising a near monopoly over steamships plying on the Hudson river. He also controlled other key routes, one of which was by river and mule across the isthmus of Panama via Lake Nicaragua, and he was anxious that his interest be protected against the twin threats of Latin American nationalism and British imperialism. (Britain had three fledgling colonies in Central America at that time: modern Belize, the Bay Islands off Honduras and Mosquitia with the port of Greytown on the Nicaraguan coast.) The US navy helped Vanderbilt by bombarding Greytown in 1854, safe in the knowledge that the Russian tsar was keeping Britain occupied with war in the Crimea. Vanderbilt then funded Walker's first Nicaraguan *coup d'état*. Later the two men, both with gigantic egos, fell out, and Walker paid the price when Vanderbilt withdrew his support.

The important point about the filibusters is that although they operated outside the law their actions were largely supported by the American public, especially in the south, and their leaders moved effortlessly at the highest levels of American society. A classic example was John Quitman, indicted by the federal government for organising a filibuster expedition to Cuba. Quitman served as governor of Mississippi, as brigadier-general in the Mexican War and as governor of Mexico City during the American occupation. He was governor of Mississippi for the second time when he was indicted, and even after that he continued as a member of the US House of Representatives until his death in 1855. His views were by no means unique. The two US senators from Mississippi (one of whom, Jefferson Davis, went on to become President of the Confederate States in the civil war) openly advocated the conquest of Cuba and the Mexican states of San Luis Potosi, Tamaulipas and Yucatan.

Right up to the civil war there was constant pressure on Mexico to cede more territory so that it could be absorbed 'piece by piece', as Jefferson had advocated for Florida. Under the Gadsden Treaty in 1853 Mexico was compelled to sell what would become the southern parts of Arizona and New Mexico; the price paid was the highest in US history: 19m acres at 53 cents an acre.

Mexico was attractive, especially as its mines were considered eminently suitable for slave labour, but the prospective jewel in the southern imperialists' crown was Cuba, for which Spain was offered \$130m. American colonists had helped Britain capture Havana in 1762, and were outraged when the island was handed back to Spain. Jefferson and Adams II were among the early American leaders who confidently predicted its early annexation. It became an article of faith in the south in the years leading up to the civil war that Cuba had to be taken. Havana, it was predicted, would become the south's New York – the commercial hub for a tropical empire based entirely on slavery.

Cuba was both an opportunity and a threat for the south. As another slave territory it would tilt the balance of power in their favour. If, on the other hand, Cuban slaves ever gained their freedom it would be another nail in the coffin of slave-holding in the United States. In 1791 a slave revolt had erupted in the French colony of Haiti. Initially many Americans had sympathised with the rebel cause, but when a black republic was declared southern slaveholders were horrified, and the United States imposed an economic embargo (similar to that imposed in the twentieth century on revolutionary Cuba). The thought of another black republic in Cuba was terrifying.

When Colombia and Mexico revealed plans to invade and liberate Cuba the United States was bitterly opposed, and in 1848 the US offered to buy the island. Spain would not sell. Many Cuban Creoles favoured US annexation to head off the gathering pressures for emancipation, and Quitman sponsored four filibuster expeditions under the Cuban Creole Narcisco Lopez, but they all failed. Lopez himself was eventually captured and executed by the Spanish.

When, under pressure from British abolitionists, the Spanish authorities on the island started emancipating the slaves war clouds gathered. If they had not rolled north into the conflagration of the civil war there is little doubt that somewhere along the Cuban coast, perhaps even at the Bay of Pigs, US troops would soon have been wading ashore.

The filibusters were motivated by personal greed and their fears for the future of slavery but in as much as they and the rest of the country had any imperial ideology it was a philosophy that came to be known as manifest destiny. This term was first used by newspaper editor John O'Sullivan in 1845. He was writing specifically about the inevitability of the whole of California becoming part of the United States because, he wrote, 'the advance guard of Anglo-Saxon emigration has begun to pour down upon it, armed with the plough and the rifle'. What he called 'imbecile' Mexico would be unable to hold on to its territory. The philosophy soon came to be applied to more than California; indeed, in the same article O'Sullivan celebrated the future annexation of Canada.

Ever since the Pilgrim Fathers a fundamental conviction of many Americans had been that their actions embodied God's will. After the Mystic Massacre that conviction turned from a simple belief that God willed them to settle and prosper among the savages of the New World to a belief that God expected them to displace those savages. This, combined with the more mercenary motives of men like the filibusters, produced an ideology that not only justified territorial aggrandisement but proclaimed its inevitability. God wanted Americans to use the special gifts he had given them to spread their wings over the globe. As Albert Beveridge, senator from Indiana, told his Senate colleagues, God had decreed that Americans were the 'master organisers of the world' and should rule over the 'savage and the senile'.

Right from the nation's birth America's leaders were determined on conquest. Jefferson spoke of the United States covering 'the whole northern if not the southern continent' and more immediately of taking Florida from Spain 'piece by piece'. John Quincy Adams declared that 'the whole continent of North America' was 'destined by Divine Providence to be peopled by one nation'. Both men expressed the commonly held view that it was a matter of time before the Spanish colonies of Cuba and Puerto Rico fell into their hands.

In Britain in the eighteenth and into the nineteenth centuries the notion of 'to the victor belongs the spoils' underpinned not only political life at home but imperial expansion abroad. Greed motivated both. Only with the advent of the Victorians did this give way to something more high-minded. The ending of parliamentary corruption and the creation of a politically independent judiciary at home, and the development of paternalistic notions of 'the white man's burden' and imperial citizenship overseas, were two sides of the same coin – a belief in public service for its own sake and for the sake of others. Whatever the objective reality, the British believed that in their empire justice and fair play took precedence over self-interest. Such a belief has never existed in Russia. Russian imperialism has always been about glory, about tribute, about spoils. 'Greed is good' might be a slogan ascribed to modern Wall Street but it would not be out of place as a description of the Russian imperial ideology. In America high-mindedness and greed co-existed from the earliest days of the New England colonies. After the revolution high-mindedness seemed to have come out on top, but the spoils system and the imperial antics of the filibusters showed that greed had not disappeared. This juxtaposition of idealism and greed continued into modern times. After the First World War Woodrow Wilson was determined to ensure a 'just peace', and joined Britain in opposing French demands for German reparations. After the second invasion of Iraq Bush II rushed to ensure that American corporations (rather than, for example, British) grabbed the spoils of victory.

Whereas Britain claimed to put justice before self-interest, and Russia had no trouble putting self-interest first, America convinced itself that justice and self-interest were the same thing. The essence of empire remained constant – lands that had belonged to someone else were taken away – but America's new ideology fused southern dreams of imperial glory with the northern conviction that God's will informed their every action.

The Road to Civil War

Throughout the nineteenth century and into the twentieth two great questions hung over the Russian and American empires: where would their territorial ambitions carry them and what sort of society would their nations become?

The territorial aggrandisements of Russia and America proceeded in parallel. The two mid-century imperial wars, against Mexico and Turkey, set the tone for the next century. America would feel free to intervene anywhere it wanted in the western hemisphere confident that there would be no opposition. Its overwhelming military power ensured that the United States could achieve its imperial ambitions without having to fire a shot (except when Spain tried to flex its withered muscles later in the century). Russia, on the other hand, was once again surrounded by enemies, its every move circumscribed by the ambitions of competing imperial powers. Nevertheless both nations would expand their borders further. In Russia imperial growth was a continuation of a centuries-old pattern, while in America it reflected the innate dynamism of the newly born nation. In both cases the nation's leaders were convinced that their realms were manifestly destined to grow.

The other great historical theme – the struggle for their nations' souls – was altogether different. There was nothing inexorable about the path along which the two powers developed, and parallels between them, while they existed, were far more tenuous. As the emphasis of history moved from the external to the internal the time had come to put an end to slavery and serfdom.

Although Russian serfdom and American slavery were not the same, campaigners were not slow to draw parallels. Alexander Radischev chronicled the appalling suffering of the Russian peasantry and made explicit comparisons with slavery in the Americas. Catherine's reaction was to sentence him to ten years' Siberian exile (a punishment she considered generous, as he had originally been sentenced to death). American abolitionists pointed to the emancipation of the serfs to bolster their own case.

In *Common Sense* Thomas Paine had claimed that one of the evils of the British was that they 'hath stirred up the Indians and Negroes to destroy us'. Events soon showed that Americans were quite capable of stirring up such trouble themselves, and although the 'Indians' soon lost the power to influence events, the 'Negroes' would nearly wreck the union. From the earliest days slavery divided the country, arousing moral outrage on one side and indignant defence on the other. Men like Thomas Jefferson and Thomas Paine were impassioned in their condemnation of the institution and determined to see its abolition, but their opponents countered with visions of slaves toiling happily in their fields. George Washington, himself a slave owner, complained peevishly about Quakers trying to liberate slaves brought to Philadelphia by southern visitors: 'When slaves who are happy and contented with their present masters, are tampered with and seduced to leave,' he wrote, 'it begets discontent on one side and resentment on the other.' He could have been writing about the 'benefits' of Russian serfdom.

The arguments in favour of slavery and of serfdom were very similar: that their abolition would destroy the American/Russian way of life. But in America the argument was a sectional one; it was not really the American way of life that was threatened by abolition but the southern way of life. There slaves were being bred as a 'cash crop' to be traded at will, and although the importation of new slaves was banned in 1808 the practice continued, as the new nation refused to join in combined operations with the British to eradicate the trade; 300,000 slaves were imported after such commerce was declared illegal. If it had not been for the puritan settlement of Massachusetts there might have been just one set of American values in which slave-holding was considered as naturally beneficial as motherhood and apple pie. But there were by the time of the American Rebellion two sets of values. In the century that followed the tensions between them were papered over but not resolved. Eventually the nation and its institutions simply split apart.

Today's perception of the civil war period owes more to Hollywood than to history: cowboys and Indians roam an untamed landscape and dusty streets echo to the sounds of stampeding cattle or noisy gunfights. The reality of American life was very different. Eli Whitney's success as a gun-maker, for example, says as much about the progress of industrialisation in the north-east as about the need for weapons on the western frontier, but it is the God-fearing, gun-toting men of the frontier that have come to symbolise the spirit of the age. In the final reel right triumphs over wrong, as in a democracy it must surely do, but does so in a hail of bullets rather than a rustle of ballots.

The idea of America as a gun-owning democracy that depended for its liberty on the constitutional right of all free Americans to bear arms is a myth. The vision of sturdy citizens defending their rights and their property in a long line from the militias of the American Revolution through the craggy heroes of the old west to the massed ranks of the National Rifle Association misses the point that the majority of Americans who bore arms in the nineteenth century did so not to defend themselves against the forces of evil but to kill each other in a fratricidal civil war.

Guns were certainly an essential part of American life, but not as a means of defending liberty. Without the superiority of their firepower the conquest of the natives would have been far more difficult (one of the reasons for the success of the Sioux at the Little Bighorn is said to have been that for once they had more modern weapons than Custer's cavalry). The one technology in which America soon led the world was the technology of death epitomised by Samuel Colt, who in 1836 patented the revolver and was one of the first American capitalists to expand overseas. In 1853 Colt leased a government-owned factory in Pimlico and started manufacturing revolvers in London. Britain and Russia were soon at war in the Crimea and Colt's factory was inundated with orders from the British army and navy, but after the war demand dried up and Colt's London operation was closed down. The Colt revolver would for ever be associated not with the Royal Navy but with the cowboys who have come to represent the modern image of nineteenth-century America.

Life on the frontier is often represented as the place and the era that determined the American character. The 'frontier spirit' typified the rugged independence, innate decency and dogged determination to which succeeding generations of Americans have aspired. However unfair it may have been to America's native population, the territorial expansion of the United States not only established the geographical boundaries of the new nation but also, it is claimed, established its unique character.

Growth in the first half of the nineteenth century, although not on the scale of its earlier Russian equivalent, was phenomenal. At Independence nine out of ten Americans lived within 50 miles of the Atlantic; sixty years later the United States stretched to the Pacific. Despite that, in demographic terms the main feature of the period was not westward expansion but urbanisation, and it was the cities that moulded the nascent American character. In 1800 fewer than one in twelve Americans lived in a town of more than 25,000, but as the century wore on urban living became the norm. In the 1840s, for example, although the total population increased by an amazing 36 per cent, the population of cities (defined as towns with more than 8,000 inhabitants) increased by 90 per cent. By 1850 the United States extended across the continent, covering the whole area of today's forty-eight contiguous states, but one in seven of the population lived in the state of New York alone. By 1860 the population of New York was well over a million. It is impossible to understand why the American Civil War happened without understanding the fundamental changes in American society that had occurred since Independence.

Russia was very different. Serfs formed the bedrock of society, as agriculture was by far the most important sector of the economy. There was industrialisation and urbanisation but on a smaller scale. In the latter half of the nineteenth century Łódź in Poland, the second largest city in the Russian empire, was one of Central Europe's largest textile manufacturing locations, but such industrial centres were rare.

It would be unfair to say that at the time of the civil war America was an industrial nation – more than three times as many Americans worked on farms and plantations as worked in manufacturing industry, and it was not until 1921 that census data showed for the first time that more than half the population lived in towns – but the trend towards industrialisation was rapidly accelerating. In the last three decades of the century the number of farm workers would grow by 60 per cent, the number of industrial workers by 135 per cent.

The typical American of the period is sometimes pictured perched on a Conestoga wagon heading off into the Wild West. In fact he or she was much more likely to be sitting in a twelve-seat stagecoach on the way to work in New York City (Abraham Brower had established New York City's first public transport running along Broadway in 1827). Hardy pioneers in their covered wagons braving the dangers of the Oregon Trail have featured in countless cowboy films, but even in the Great Migration of 1843 the number of wagons was less than a thousand. By contrast, just ten years later thousands of city dwellers were travelling between the urban centres of New York and Chicago on the newly opened railway. As tens of thousands of Texans celebrated becoming part of America in 1845, hundreds of thousands of New Yorkers were celebrating the opening of the city's first department store.

Stephanie Williams's account of life in Siberia just before the revolution, with its fur trappers, gold miners and China traders all out to make a quick buck, reads like a story of the Wild West or the California Gold Rush. Although undoubtedly an accurate picture of life on the Siberian frontier, nobody would base a description of the Russian character on it, but that is effectively what many observers have done with America.

The 1997 film *True Women* set out to portray the crucial and under-recognised role of women in the development of nineteenth-century America. It followed the stories of three women caught up in the Texan Revolution of 1835, and made enormous efforts to reflect the reality of frontier life. As a film about women in Texas it was a success, but it was also a parable about the American dream and as such was deeply flawed. In the early 1830s there were at most 10,000 American women in Texas; it may suit modern American sensibilities to believe that the character and values of modern America are derived from women such as these, but in reality they were about as representative of the period as the 10,000 women that an 1832 survey estimated were working New York City as prostitutes.

It is the myth of the frontier that has influenced American values not the reality; Americans are a largely urban people, even if they often behave as if they were beleaguered pioneers living in a world of hostile natives.

That urbanisation could race ahead at the same time that men and women were leaving the cities to head west was down to phenomenal population growth. By 1850 there were nearly six times as many Americans as there had been when the nation was born. Early stage abortion, which had been an accepted form of contraception for America's early colonists, was curbed in Connecticut in 1821 and New York in 1828, and by the end of the nineteenth century abortion had been outlawed throughout the country except in very limited circumstances. More significant was immigration, which shot up from 129,000 in the 1820s to 540,000 in the 1830s, 1.5 million in the 1840s and 2.8 million in the 1850s. Around one in five potential immigrants arriving from Europe were refused entry when they landed, and of those accepted up to one in three subsequently returned home.

Territorial aggrandisement was facilitated by immigrants but not caused by them. Homesteading immigrants often established lives that were immeasurably better than they could have expected in famine-struck Ireland or war-torn Germany, but the real wealth of the west went to those who were already at the top of the ladder. The impetus for further colonisation came not from those who wanted to make their fortunes but from those who wanted to keep the fortunes they already possessed.

Nearly half of the immigrants were Irish, which significantly changed the cultural make-up of the nation. Such changes were not always peaceful. Immigration became a major political issue. Naturalisation regulations were a political football, the residency qualifications being driven by whether the party in power was likely to benefit or suffer from an increase in immigrant voters. A requirement for five years' residence was changed to fourteen years and then back to five. Anti-immigrant groups campaigned to increase the qualifying period to twenty-one years.

In Philadelphia anti-Irish riots led to several deaths, and brawls between Irish and American were commonplace in many cities. On one hand immigration was encouraged by promising liberty under the law and on the other the president was given the power to deport aliens without needing to give a reason. Just as today there was a decidedly racist tinge to the immigration debate. Once the railway construction boom was over Chinese immigration was banned (the 1882 Chinese Exclusion Act suspended Chinese immigration for ten years, but it was extended in 1892 and made permanent in 1902). Simon Schama's recent history highlights not only the appalling treatment meted out to Irish immigrants in the 1850s attacked by the xenophobic 'Know Nothing Party' but also the Chinese railway builders expelled or murdered in the 1870s. By contrast, the first serious restrictions on white immigration were not introduced until 1921.

Immigration, along with the technological developments of the period, changed the character of the whole country. By no means all immigrants remained in the cities of the eastern seaboard. German immigrants in particular streamed into the new states of the Midwest; Milwaukee became a virtually German city. Canals criss-crossed the north-east and then railways linked the country together. The cotton gin changed the face of the southern cotton industry, but it was in the north that the industrial revolution had its real impact. In the first half of the nineteenth century life in the north-eastern states changed at a pace not seen again for another century. By 1850 the US produced around 0.5m tons of pig iron, a tenfold increase in forty years (but still a fraction of the 3m tons produced in Britain). Manufacturing on an enormous scale, cheap and effective transportation, unprecedented standards of public education and massive immigration combined to make the contrasts of north and south, present from the earliest colonial days, overwhelming. In the words of Samuel Eliot Morison, 'By 1850 two distinct civilisations had been evolved.' United in their imperial ambition, Christian religion and republican institutions, they were divided by fundamental economic and moral differences.

It is the great moral divide over slavery that is conventionally posited as the critical fracture that led to the civil war, but to some historians the war was not a clash of moral principles but the continuation of economic conflict by other means: the thrusting entrepreneurial north taking on the economically stagnant south. New economic forces had been unleashed in which unfree labour had no place. What the American economy needed, and what the Russian economy would come to need, were not slaves in the traditional sense but 'wage slaves' who would move around as the market demanded. These historians argue that the irrelevance of the moral arguments against slavery was demonstrated after the civil war, when freed slaves soon discovered that 'freedom' for them would not mean the same as the 'freedom' whites espoused for themselves.

There was a vociferous abolitionist movement in America for whom slavery in any part of the country was abhorrent, but the real political debate was not about the abolition of slavery where it already existed but about whether it should be allowed in the newly acquired territories. Strictly speaking the war between north and south was not about slavery but about territorial expansion and the nature of the American empire. The cause of the conflict was the insistence by both north and south that the way they organised themselves economically – one with slaves and one without – should be replicated in the new states being carved out of the old French and Spanish possessions. If either side had been content to let the other have political domination over the new territories there would have been no war. The south could have continued with slavery if it had been content not to export its culture. If the southern states had not insisted that some of the newly conquered territories had to be open to slavery then the civil war might not have happened, and slavery might have been a feature of American life to this day. Indeed, even once the war had started slavery might still have survived. In the summer of 1864, as the war bogged down in the siege of Atlanta, the Democratic Convention in Chicago – representing a still significant part of northern society – called for an immediate end to the war, with states left free to choose whether or not to permit slavery within their own jurisdiction.

In the words of the old dictum, in politics compromise is less an expedient than a principle. Politicians repeatedly managed to produce compromises on the issue of slavery even when these were met with popular disdain on both sides. American leaders, with some notable exceptions, were concerned primarily not to rock the boat. Slavery was an evil in the north, so ban it in the north; slave-owning was a fundamental right in the south, so maintain it in the south. The Fugitive Slave Act was a typical manifestation of the politicians' skill in reconciling the apparently irreconcilable. Although slavery was illegal in the north, the Act laid down that if southern slaves escaped north they remained legally owned in the south, and therefore should be returned to their legal owner. Over 300 fugitive slaves were shipped back south, often under the guard of armed US troops, to stop abolitionists rescuing them and smuggling them further north to freedom in the British colonies. The Fugitive Slave Act caused popular outrage in much of the north, which in turn enflamed popular opinion in the south where pro-slavery campaigners could point to the abolitionists' flagrant disregard for the rule of law.

The Supreme Court went even further in the Dred Scott case, ruling that Congress could not deprive citizens of their property – and that included depriving slave-owners of their slaves, theoretically making any attempt anywhere to ban slavery illegal.

The causes of the American Civil War were far more diverse than one side's rejection of slavery. The complexities and nuances of the period have largely been written out of popular history, but at the time they were well understood by both sides. Moses Ezekiel, a Confederate soldier who moved to Rome after the war and became one of the most famous sculptors of his day, insisted, 'We were not fighting for the perpetuation of slavery but for the principles of States' Rights and Free Trade.' The man who has become for ever associated with the emancipation of the slaves, Abraham Lincoln, repeatedly made clear that despite his own moral repugnance he was not trying to end the right of existing slave states to continue their peculiar institution. The slave states, however, realised that this position was increasingly untenable. They had seen what had happened in Britain, where moral indignation had led to slavery being banned throughout the empire thirty years before. Many southerners retained contact with Barbados where slavery was abolished in 1838, and, although none of the dire consequences predicted by the pro-slavery lobby had happened, they did not want to repeat the experiment themselves.

Many, perhaps most, northerners regarded slavery as an affront to their moral consciences, but the north was far from united. Many of the newer immigrants, who were themselves often subject to bitter discrimination, were keen to ensure that those on an even lower rung stayed there. First generation Irish Catholics were an important political force by the time of the civil war (they formed 34 per cent of the electorate of New York City, for example), and not only were they not offended by slavery but in Morison's words 'their hostility to abolitionists and hatred of free Negroes became proverbial'.

There were also those in the north who argued that, like serfdom in Russia, slavery would eventually disappear of its own accord because it was inherently inefficient. They pointed out that slavery was declining in Virginia and Maryland and that New York and Pennsylvania had been slave states, but as capitalism expanded slaves there were sold south and the remainder eventually freed. In fact these northern appeasers misunderstood the economics of slavery. In 1958 two Harvard economists, Alfred Conrad and John Meyer, overturned conventional wisdom by asking whether it was economically rational to buy and breed slaves. By looking at the discounted value of expected future income over the life of the 'asset', they were able to demonstrate that slavery was immensely profitable to the whole south in the period immediately before the civil war.

If public opinion in the north was not demanding war to free the slaves, and politicians on all sides were keen to compromise, why then did the war begin? The answer has to be because the 'two distinct civilisations' identified by Samuel Eliot Morison were talking such radically different languages that compromise was impossible. Those languages were determined above all by economics. Very simplistically the southern oligarchs could make their plantations and businesses pay whether or not their states were part of a union, as they relied on markets outside the United States. For them the natural compromise was to let each state do as it wished; they wanted a union in which slavery would be guaranteed for ever, but if that was impossible secession was their compromise position. The northern oligarchs, on the other hand, had few significant export markets, but what they did have is what economists call 'economies of scale' – bigger factories produced proportionately bigger profits – and so they would inevitably fight to protect their existing market from European competition. In the north preserving the union became the overwhelming commercial priority. The northern interest was not what happened to slavery but what happened to the union – their compromise position was to fudge the issue of slavery. Secession, proposed by the south as a compromise, was no compromise at all for the north.

CHAPTER 9
MORE CONQUEST

The moral and political arguments over slavery and serfdom split not just nation but communities and even families. In the United States the civil war forced everyone to take sides. Even the largest remaining native group, the Cherokee nation, divided. Many of its leaders were significant slave owners and it tore itself apart providing troops to both sides. In Britain the non-conformist churches had been at the forefront of the campaigns against the slave trade but in America even they divided, amid much recrimination, into warring southern and northern factions before the civil war, and stayed that way thereafter.

Americans derived conflicting values from a common religion. In Virginia the House of Burgesses passed a law in 1632 requiring 'uniformitie throughout this colony both in substance and in circumstance to the cannons and constitution of the Church of England', but uniformity was something that never happened. The Virginia Company's instructions to its governors made conversion of the natives one of their objectives, and in some parts of the country the churches were still the only institutions offering support to natives and slaves, but in most of the south the Church had become part of the white establishment. There it occupied a role similar to that in Russia, where the Church had never been a force for social change. The Holy Synod created by Peter the Great acted like a government ministry, and was headed by a chief procurator who often had a military rather than clerical background. If any priest discovered evidence of treason, or even treasonous intent, during confession, by law he had to report it. Pipes points out that 'In the nineteenth century, a denunciation of political dissidents was considered a regular part of a priest's obligations', and concludes, 'No branch of Christianity has shown such callous indifference to social and political injustice.' Many churches in the American south came close.

Although calls for justice might not themselves drive reform when added to other economic and political pressures, the demand for change became unstoppable. In 1861 the dam gave way and gave way first in Russia: Alexander II ended serfdom. Twenty million serfs were emancipated, arousing much enthusiasm among abolitionists in America and enormous opposition from landowners closer to home. They argued that any concession to the serfs would fatally weaken the fabric of Russian society, which depended more than most on everyone knowing their place and staying there. They were probably right, but as Alexander himself said it was better to abolish serfdom from above than to wait for serfdom to abolish itself from below. Being an autocrat, Alexander II could do this simply by issuing an edict, in the process earning himself the sobriquet of the Tsar Liberator.

In April 1861 (barely two months after the tsar had acted) the first shots of the American Civil War were fired. Southern forces attacked Fort Sumner in Charleston, South Carolina. America had stumbled into war as if in a trance.

The War Between The States

South Carolina seceded in 1860, and was soon joined by the new slave states that had been carved out of the former French and Spanish realms from Florida to Texas. Most of those seceding had little expectation of war. To them the United States, still less than a century old, had always been a federation of like-minded states; now that the states were not like-minded it was time for southerners to go their separate way. Similarly most northerners were genuinely surprised that southerners were prepared to fight to preserve slavery. Central to 'Yankee' ideology, as with American ideology today, was the concept of progress: they were at the forefront of history; others would inevitably follow in their wake. Northerners believed that the spirit of progress would eventually lead the south to abandon its primitive ways and travel peacefully along the path they had already marked out.

Of those who still believed they could avoid war one man in particular thought he could negotiate a peaceful solution. The Russian ambassador, Edouard de Stoeckl, who had been in America for twenty years volunteered to act as a mediator between Confederate and Federal representatives. Stoeckl was known to have a low opinion of Lincoln and a high opinion of the Confederate leader Jefferson Davis. Unsurprisingly Secretary of State William Seward declined Stoeckl's offer, which had the Confederates' wholehearted support.

Thereafter Russia aligned itself with the north, because Britain and France tended to support the Confederacy and because a reunited United States could be a powerful ally, an ally that Russia desperately needed after losing the Crimean War. In one bizarre episode Tsar Alexander II ordered the Russian Atlantic and Pacific fleets to winter in US ports so that they would not become ice-bound in Russia. The Atlantic fleet sailed into New York and received a rapturous welcome, as the city's inhabitants assumed it was there as protection against the Confederate navy.

The southern states might have peacefully seceded but for the determination of one man to maintain the unity of the nation. Just as modern Russia would not have existed without Peter the Great, so modern America would not have existed but for Abraham Lincoln.

Abraham Lincoln is a classic American icon, the self-made man, born in a log cabin and carried to the highest office in the land by his own abilities. If anything shows the dangers of using the similarities between the emancipation of Russian serfs and American slaves to imply more fundamental similarities between the two societies, it is the contrast between the two emancipators: Abraham Lincoln and the Tsar Liberator Alexander II. Lincoln arrived in the White House because American democracy provided the framework within which his outstanding skills and the persuasiveness of his ideals could take him there. Alexander on the other hand had nothing outstanding about him; his arrival in the Imperial Palace was literally an accident of birth – he had been born there – and his persuasiveness did not help make him tsar – being tsar is what made him persuasive.

One of the clearest expositions of the political issues surrounding slavery was given in a long speech that Lincoln gave in Peoria, Illinois, on 16 October 1854. It is a classic example of the American practice of promoting arguments about legality above arguments about justice. Right from the outset Lincoln made clear that he was not arguing about the 'existing institution' of slavery but about its 'extension'. This, he argued, was essentially a legal matter to be settled by reference to the legal frameworks that had governed America's various imperial aggrandisements. He made an impassioned condemnation of the immorality of slavery, but the great bulk of his speech was devoted not to moral arguments but to legal precedents in French Louisiana and the former Spanish territories, and the legal implications of the Founding Fathers' claims to the Northwest Territory. This speech is a fascinating insight into the mindset of the day. Lincoln made a casual reference to the possibility of annexing Cuba, and emphasised that he was not arguing for the total equality of whites and blacks. Freeing southern slaves, he added, was impractical because there were not enough ships to carry them all back to Africa.

In 1858 Lincoln contested one of the most famous Senate elections in American history, opposing the incumbent Democratic senator Stephen Douglas. The two men took part in a series of debates that articulated more clearly than any modern political confrontation the moral issues dividing the American nation. The Lincoln-Douglas campaign was a throwback to the pre-Jackson era of political debate. Lincoln's speeches in particular are closely argued discourses from an age when sound arguments were more important than sound bites. Douglas was quite clear that the American nation was created by the white man, and that blacks and natives could never have any role in its government; Lincoln was equally clear that when the Declaration of Independence said that all men are created equal it really meant 'all' men without exception. Although Lincoln made his famous remark that 'a house divided against itself cannot stand', insisting that the United States could not continue for ever half slave and half free, he also made it plain that, whatever he personally thought about slavery, he would not attempt to remove it in the southern states.

Nevertheless after Fort Sumner it was clear that the time for peace-making was over and the remaining slave states would have to choose sides. Most, starting with Virginia, went with the south. Despite calls by the rioting Baltimore mob, Maryland stayed with the north. Dramatic displays of force by the Union army also persuaded Kentucky and Missouri to stay loyal, although thousands of men from both states joined the rebel cause. States and individuals had to choose between two entrenched and irreconcilable moral positions.

The Marxist view that the civil war was merely the inevitable victory of industrial capitalism over agrarian feudalism would be more plausible if the south was the impoverished backwater the phrase 'Deep South' sometimes conjures up. But in reality southerners were on average wealthier than northerners; even when the slaves are included *per capita* income was higher in the south than the north. Southerners were fond of comparing the supposedly blissful lives of their slaves with the horrors of life as a northern factory worker. The south was poorer than the north not because its people were poorer but simply because there were fewer of them. The civil war pitted the Confederacy's 9 million population against the Union's 22 million. Added to their numerical weakness was the south's economic dependence on the export trade, particularly cotton, which the northern navy quickly blockaded virtually out of existence. On paper the Confederacy should have stood virtually no chance of success, but at times it looked as if they might win. Strategically they had the easier task: their objective was to make the north leave them alone by causing the enemy enough pain to persuade them to give up the fight and go home. The Union, on the other hand, had to destroy their opponents and occupy their territory. In the early stages the Confederates also had the better generals. The early Union generals did little but add to the English vocabulary: bewhiskered General Burnside provided the word sideburns, and a more common word was derived from the services offered to the troops of General Hooker.

Had the Union army been able to crush the rebels quickly the south might well have been able to negotiate a peace settlement that allowed them to re-enter the Union while keeping slavery. As the war wore on, however, this became less and less likely. Blacks recruited into the Union army became a significant military factor, and it was largely for military reasons that Lincoln issued the famous Emancipation Proclamation eighteen months after the war had started. Just as in the American Revolution people needed an ideological goal to inspire their sacrifice, and in the north that goal became emancipation.

In the civil war white America did to itself what it had been doing to the native population for nearly two centuries, inflicting the full horror of total war but on an altogether more horrific scale. More Americans, well over 600,000, died in the civil war than in all the other wars in American history put together. On a single day at the battle of Antietam nearly half as many Americans died as in the whole of the Vietnam War. Of the 360,000 northern soldiers and 260,000 southern who died, around 110,000 Union and 94,000 Confederate men died of wounds received in battle. Far more died not on the battlefield but in the squalor of disease and hunger that, as Napoleon had discovered, was the inevitable accompaniment of nineteenth-century warfare. The civilian casualties were proportionately lower than in the conquest of the natives, but the conflict still had a profound, if temporary, impact on the structure of American society. The south in particular lost a quarter of its white males of child-siring age.

The legacy of the dreadful death toll was seared into the American psyche: never again would America's boys be treated as mere cannon fodder. Russian autocrats were famous for their disregard for the lives of their own troops, but Russia lost fewer soldiers in all the imperial wars of

Catherine the Great's long reign than America lost in the few short years of the civil war. When it came to future foreign wars the lesson for America was simple: the objective would not just be to win but to win with the minimum of American casualties. That in turn meant whenever possible fighting only when American troops were able to exercise overwhelming military force. It was to be a philosophy that contributed enormously to later US military triumphs but caused repeated consternation to allies; it underlay, for example, the bitter divisions between Eisenhower and Montgomery in the Second World War – and when it failed, as in Vietnam, left many Americans deeply troubled. To Russian leaders in particular the philosophy was totally incomprehensible, and much of Stalin's paranoia about US military intentions during and after the Second World War could be traced to the contrast with his own ruthless willingness to sacrifice millions of his own countrymen.

The civil war both exemplified and exaggerated the impact of military values on the American ideology of democracy. In a frontier society in almost continuous conflict it was inevitable that settling issues by force would become commonplace. Like the War of Independence and the imperial wars that culminated in the invasion of Mexico the civil war reinforced the view, common to most societies at that time, that war was a natural way to solve problems. The civil war had 'cleansed' American society of the stain of slavery and solidified the notion that there were circumstances in which war could be the ethically preferable option. It was a philosophy that led a later advocate of American imperialism, Senator Albert Beveridge, to insist that 'Our Indian wars would have been shortened, the lives of soldiers and settlers saved and the Indians themselves benefited had we made continuous and decisive war.'

America has never been a 'militaristic' nation like the fascist regimes of the twentieth century to whom democracy was a weakness to be eradicated; in the United States, by contrast, military values were sewn into the fabric of democracy.

In moving from the officers' mess to the presidential suite, George Washington, the nation's first president, set the pattern for a surprising number of nineteenth-century presidents who embodied both the popular will of a democracy and the supposed strongman virtues of autocracy. American generals gained their political credibility in fighting the British, the natives or each other. In other cultures military strongmen have used the armed force at their disposal to take power. In America the process was far more subtle. The popularity of conquest and military adventure allowed American generals from George Washington to Dwight Eisenhower to move smoothly into the political arena. Five nineteenth-century presidents were military leaders (Jackson, Harrison, Taylor, Grant and Hayes). A sixth, McKinley, first gained his reputation as a soldier and Abraham Lincoln was not averse to exploiting his role in the militia that put down the native uprising known as the Black Hawk War. Another veteran of that campaign, Jefferson Davies, became President of the Confederate States. (Mexican War veteran Franklin Pierce was one soldier president remembered not for his war exploits but rather for his bar exploits, being, as one contemporary wag remarked, 'the hero of many well-fought bottles'.) Davy Crockett gained his celebrity status and political credibility fighting alongside Andrew Jackson against the Creeks. The victor of the crucially important battle of Tippecanoe, William Harrison, was one of those who went on from the battlefield to the White House, campaigning with his vice-presidential running mate John Tyler on the slogan 'Tippecanoe and Tyler Too'. Those who imagine a golden age of political debate before the advent of public relations and spin should remember the man who claimed to have killed the great native leader Tecumseh: Richard Johnson eventually became vice-president of the United States using what must be one of the most infantile campaign slogans of all time – 'Rumpsey dumpsey, rumpsey dumpsey, Colonel Johnson killed Tecumseh.' ('Tippecanoe and Tyler Too' may have been slogan enough to carry Harrison to the White House, but the slogan of his opponent Martin Van Buren has proved far more enduring – known by the nickname Old Kinderhook after his hometown, Van Buren campaigned with the now ubiquitous incantation 'OK!')

How the values of bullet and ballot were brought together can be illustrated by looking at the lives of those who embodied that nexus, men like Ulysses S. Grant and Robert E. Lee. The northern general William T. Sherman perhaps best personified the contradictions that have come to characterise the American approach to war – the ruthlessly brutal application of overwhelming military force and a near-total disregard of what is now euphemistically termed collateral damage, combined with a passionate commitment to the ideological banner of 'liberty' with repeated public affirmations of the sanctity of the rule of law and the rights of the individual. Even his name, William Tecumseh Sherman, seemed to embody the contradiction. The man who after the war led the US army in some of their most vicious campaigns against the natives was named after Tecumseh, the native chieftain who had defied that same army half a century earlier.

Like many of the civil war generals Sherman first saw service in the imperial wars in Florida and later commanded the San Francisco militia, which played a controversial role in the California *coup d'état* now remembered as the War of Rebellion. But it was in the civil war that Sherman's national reputation was established, first at the battle of Shiloh, where he was wounded and had two horses shot from under him, and above all in Georgia.

Sherman's Georgia campaign, for good or ill, determined how history would remember him. After Atlanta was captured the city was torched and Sherman set out on his twenty-four day 'March to the Sea', destroying everything in his path – not just the infrastructure of fortifications, bridges and railway tracks but homes, crops and livestock. His troops lacked the sadistic cruelty of the Mongols but their aim was the same: to deprive the enemy of all sources of food and other supplies, and to terrorise the civilian population into withdrawing support from the Confederate cause.

In popular memory the civil war ended with the surrender of the gallant rebel general Robert E. Lee to soon-to-be-president Ulysses S. Grant at Appomattox Court House on 9 April 1865. This was the effective end of the rebellion, but much of the rebel army under Joseph E. Johnston remained until it surrendered to Sherman on 26 April 1865. It was typical that Sherman, who is still reviled in the south for his March to the Sea, should offer Johnston such generous surrender terms that the politicians back in Washington immediately repudiated them. It also says much about the peculiar mixture of brutality and chivalry in the civil war that Johnston was one of the pallbearers at Sherman's funeral many years later.

William Tecumseh Sherman is a symbolic figure, but what he symbolises says as much about the political climate of today as about the historical reality of his own period. Westerners are frequently amazed that while many Russians today glory in their new-found freedom others worship the memory of Joseph Stalin, one of the most murderous despots in the whole of human history. And yet the mirror image of this situation exists with regard to Sherman in America. Sherman is one of the great American heroes. He was the man who won the civil war and then pacified the west. He was a man of integrity who ended the 'Indian' menace (although sometimes by imposing absurdly one-sided treaties) and then rooted out corruption among government officials supposedly employed to protect the natives. His sense of honour led him to refuse all attempts to persuade him to stand as president, famously proclaiming 'If nominated I will not accept, if elected I will not serve.' He even had the Second World War's most famous tank named after him. There are, however, historians who would cogently argue that Sherman was one of the greatest war criminals and bigots of all time. His campaigns in the south were characterised by pillaging, plundering and gang rape; long before Hitler Sherman used the phrase 'final solution' to refer to his plans to solve the 'Indian problem' through a campaign of 'extermination', and he explicitly authorised his troops to kill women and children in their campaigns against the natives of the western plains (campaigns designed to further the interests of the railroads in which Sherman was an investor).

The moral complexity of men like Sherman is now largely forgotten; what is remembered is the unambiguous moral virtue of Abraham Lincoln. At his second inaugural Lincoln used another of the phrases which to some have marked him out as the Nelson Mandela of his age when he committed to rebuilding his nation 'with malice towards none and charity for all'. Not everyone felt that way, and when Lincoln was assassinated normal politics resumed.

After the civil war the votes of Florida Democrats were discarded, along with those in South Carolina and Louisiana, in one of the most cynically manipulated presidential elections ever. Southern Democrat politicians connived at Republican vote rigging in return for a commitment not to enforce the fifteenth amendment guaranteeing civil rights for former slaves. Politicians who had been unable to find a compromise that would allow slavery to continue found a way to ensure that its abolition had minimal effect. 124 years later during the presidential campaign of Bush II the judiciary upheld the result in Florida, finding no corruption or malpractice, despite a media furore reflecting political claim and counterclaim over supposed irregularities in the system and allegations of lost votes.

Slaves and Serfs

The emancipations of serfs and slaves happened at roughly the same time, but it is worth stepping back to consider how the two events meshed with the ideologies of the two empires. The forces at work were fundamentally different, not least because American slavery and Russian serfdom were not the same thing.

American slaves had absolutely no rights. Russian serfs in practice, if not in law, had their own strips of land and what they produced was their own. They lived in their own homes, not in slave quarters, and their work was organised largely by their community leaders rather than by overseers employed by the slave owner. Because serfs were attached to the land, landlords could not trade serfs the way that American landlords traded slaves. In the final analysis serfs belonged not to the landlords but, like everyone else, to the tsar. When Catherine the Great gave 600 'souls' to one of her lovers, Grigory Potemkin, he would have known that she could just as easily take them away again. Furthermore, by Catherine's time many serfs, perhaps as many as half, were paying money rents to the landholders and could to some extent move around as they wished and take up whatever occupation they wanted – something quite impossible for most American slaves.

Russian historians insisted that even in ancient times, when slaves were a key part of economic and social life, serfs were not slaves. From the point of view of the serf or slave, however, the difference was almost meaningless. The distinction was only really important to the state: serfs paid taxes, slaves did not. Serfdom was a relic of the Mongol system of taxation where landowners were expected to deliver up dues based on the number of people in each area. The old Muscovite princes had outlawed the practice of the poor pledging themselves as slaves precisely because it reduced tax revenues.

The important point when comparing slavery and serfdom is not their legal status or their relative degrees of immorality, or even the differing levels of protest they engendered in the two societies, but the political frameworks in which those protests were made. Under American democracy the opponents of slavery had a voice that could be manifested as political power. Abolitionists won elections, controlled legislatures and eventually wielded legitimate military force. Under Russian autocracy none of this was possible; no matter how much popular support there was for the abolition of serfdom (and 'popular support' was a totally meaningless phrase in eighteenth- and nineteenth-century Russia) only if the tsar willed it would it happen. In terms of the parallel moral imperatives of abolishing slavery and abolishing serfdom autocracy eventually proved itself superior to democracy. Despite fierce opposition from the landowning class on 19 February 1861 Alexander II issued an edict emancipating the serfs; just nine days later the US House and Senate, in a last desperate attempt to avert civil war, passed a Thirteenth Amendment to the Constitution forbidding Congress ever to abolish slavery. (The outbreak of war stopped the amendment being ratified and twenty months later, after the battle of Antietam, Lincoln issued his Emancipation Proclamation arguing that freeing the Negroes was now a 'military necessity'.)

The American Civil War may have had its origins in economics, but the abolition of slavery was driven almost entirely by ideology. There were economic reasons for ending the institution of slavery and when it came to the crunch in the middle of a civil war there were political and military reasons, but the main motivation of the abolitionists was moral indignation. Slavery was simply incompatible with the official ideology of democracy. That same moral indignation also existed in the struggle against Russian serfdom, but it was not the driving force behind emancipation; equally important was the belief that serfdom was economically inefficient. The modernisers in Russia simply saw serfdom as a backward way to organise production. Emancipation of the serfs was intended to make Russian agriculture more efficient, and as a by-product facilitate the development of modern manufacturing industries. It would allow Russia to take the first real steps down the path of industrialisation, a path already well trodden in America. By cutting the links that tied peasants to the land it made it possible to assemble the huge workforces needed for the newly emerging industrial sector, but this in turn created social pressures that autocracy could not contain.

Serfdom was not considered incompatible with the ideology of autocracy, but it was considered incompatible with a modern, westernised way of living. What only became apparent over time was that in attacking serfdom the philosophical underpinning of autocracy itself was bound to come under attack. Once it was conceded that serfs were not an inferior breed of animal qualitatively different from the rest of society, it became less easy to argue that the nobility were qualitatively superior. If God had not created the serfs to serve had he really created the Romanovs to rule?

Not only was the balance of moral, economic and philosophical argument in America and Russia not the same but the class dynamics were very different. It is no exaggeration to say that in America abolitionists in the north freed the slaves in the south; the slaves themselves played very little part in their liberation. Although a significant number of freed slaves eventually fought for the Union army (and a much smaller number fought with the Confederacy) they were not militarily critical. There had been slave revolts, such as those in New York in 1712, Carolina in 1739 and 1822 and Virginia in 1831, but these were suppressed, often with sickening brutality, and their historical impact was insignificant. By contrast, in Russia peasant revolts, and the fear of such revolts, were potent factors in driving change (just as in Britain the eventual abolition of slavery was driven as much by the impact of the Jamaican slave rebellion as by the decades of moralising by abolitionists).

In the 1770s an illiterate Russian peasant called Emilian Pugachev claimed to be the murdered Tsar Peter III and stirred up a revolt against Peter's widow, Catherine the Great. Pugachev's was not the first such rebellion but the scale of his uprising was dramatic. Initially his support was limited, and he was quickly captured, but when he managed to escape his fame grew and he attracted tens of thousands of Cossacks, native tribesmen and serfs. He defeated the imperial forces sent against him, sacked Kazan and ravaged the towns and villages of the Volga basin, offered bounties for dead aristocrats and tied up a major part of Catherine's army. Eventually Pugachev was defeated near Volgograd and dispatched to Moscow, where his head, hands and feet were ceremoniously chopped off. The Pugachev rebellion terrified the Russian aristocracy by its sheer scale and brutality, but smaller peasant revolts became almost everyday events. In the reign of Nicholas I there were said to have been 556 separate peasant uprisings, prompting his successor Alexander II to try to eliminate peasant unrest by emancipating the serfs. But this proved merely to be a milestone on the way to far more radical change.

In the United States, on the other hand, the abolition of slavery was long regarded as the end of the road; the issue of real civil rights for the descendants of the freed black slaves only became a serious political issue a century later. Today the American Civil War is remembered almost exclusively in terms of the abolition of slavery. It is portrayed as yet another vindication of the values of democracy and the triumph of human rights over manifest evil. The south may have had elements of chivalry and elegance but fundamentally, it is claimed, the war ensured that the core American values of equality and dignity triumphed over racism and discrimination. The problem is that concepts like racism and discrimination are constructs of a much later age. The Union soldiers may have been determined to destroy the monstrous evil of human beings buying and selling other human beings, but they were not fighting to end racism.

The idea of a racially enlightened north fighting a bigoted south is very far from the truth. General William T. Sherman's writings are full of attacks on natives and Jews, and just eight days before Christmas in 1862 General Ulysses S. Grant issued General Order No. 11, expelling all Jews 'as a class' from the newly conquered areas of Kentucky, western Tennessee and northern Mississippi. Men, women and children were given just twenty-four hours to evacuate their homes and leave the region.

The Jewish experience of the civil war casts an interesting sidelight on the values of the two sides. Jews played an important part in southern life. By the end of the eighteenth century there were a number of important Jewish communities in America; the largest, founded in 1695, was in Charleston, South Carolina. At the time of the civil war the majority of America's Jews lived in the south and had absorbed southern values. Abraham Myers, a graduate of the US military academy at West Point, played an important role in the ethnic cleansing of Florida (the city of Fort Myers is named after him). As many as 10,000 Jews, for example Myers and the sculptor Moses Ezekiel, are thought to have fought for the Confederacy.

The most famous Jewish American of his day was probably Judah Benjamin, the US Senate's first Jewish member. What seems extraordinary today is that Benjamin did not represent cosmopolitan New York or liberal New England but Louisiana in the deep south. Born in the West Indies, Benjamin became a lawyer and plantation owner before entering politics. When war arrived he became secretary of war and later secretary of state in the Confederate government. Despite achieving such high office Benjamin was subject to anti-semitic attacks throughout his career. He was falsely accused by other southern politicians of transferring Confederate funds to his personal bank accounts in Europe, and when the war was over had to flee to Britain to escape unfounded accusations by northerners that he had plotted Lincoln's assassination.

One of the dangers of any historical study is the temptation to assume that modern paradigms and values can be applied historically. Views that today may be lumped together and labelled left wing or right wing, liberal or conservative, may in earlier days have been regarded as wildly inconsistent. Conversely historical figures may have sincerely held views that at the time seemed readily compatible but today would seem diametrically opposed. One of the men most active in trying to ensure that freedom really meant something practical to newly emancipated slaves was the genocidal militarist and anti-semite General Sherman. In his mind there was nothing incompatible between his conviction that non-whites were inherently inferior and his determination to ensure that freed slaves could live in dignity and relative prosperity. In his Field Order No. 15 Sherman decreed that a great swathe of territory on the Atlantic coast should be appropriated and given to freed slaves, more than 40,000 of whom took advantage of his offer. They did not keep the land for long.

That the war had not been a fight for racial equality became apparent as soon as the war was over. Slavery could never be reimposed, but other gains that had been made by black people were soon reversed.

The desire of many northerners to ensure that blacks received their full civil rights after the war was undoubtedly genuine. The thirteenth amendment proposed before the civil war had sought effectively to enshrine slavery in the constitution for ever; what actually became the thirteenth amendment after the war banned slavery. A Civil Rights Act was embodied in the fourteenth amendment; interestingly it excepted natives and immigrants. Just three days before his assassination Lincoln pledged to give votes to literate blacks and black civil war veterans, and immediately after the war black candidates were victorious in a number of local elections. The fifteenth amendment made it illegal to prohibit anyone from voting on the basis of their colour, and in 1868 General Ulysses S. Grant was elected president thanks in part to support from

700,000 newly enfranchised black voters. However, intimidation soon made a mockery of declarations of equality.

Lincoln's successors moved quickly to heal the divisions of war, and that meant healing the wounds of southern whites by reversing the gains made by blacks. Slavery was replaced by what on another continent would be called apartheid. In one notorious case a man named Plessy, who had seven white great-grandparents and one black, was jailed in Louisiana for travelling in a whites-only carriage. The case was heard right up to the Supreme Court, who in Plessy v. Ferguson in 1896 upheld the conviction, ruling that the Fourteenth Amendment's guarantee of equal protection for blacks did not mean that states could not treat the races differently. The apartheid doctrine of separate but nominally equal was sanctified by the United States Supreme Court more than sixty years before its application in South Africa. The right of former slaves to vote was effectively removed soon after the civil war, and laws were put in place throughout the south that obliged blacks to enter long term labour contracts and stopped them from leaving their plantations to seek work. Many of the former slaves who had claimed land were forcibly removed as the old southern power structures reappeared. Slavery had been abolished and with it the gross inhumanities associated with the breeding and trading of human beings as if they were cattle, but the day-to-day lives of most of the freed slaves changed very little.

The same was basically true on the other side of the world. Emancipation of the serfs achieved less in reality than many of those fighting for reform had hoped. With their freedom the serfs also received land (something that critically did not happen when US slavery was abolished), but the land was not free. The peasants were expected to pay for it over an extended period, and as a consequence many were soon deep in debt.

The emancipations of serfs and slaves have long been held up as key events in the histories of both Russia and America, and yet the reality is that in both cases emancipation proved largely illusory. Peter Neville concludes that 'There is an uncanny historical parallel between the emancipation of the serfs in Russia and Abraham Lincoln's freeing of the black slaves in the USA in 1863. Lincoln (like Alexander) recognised the evil nature of slavery, and that in addition no democracy could exist "half slave and half free". He too compromised in the Gettysburg address by only freeing the slaves in the Confederate-held states (a fact that is often forgotten). The black slaves received no land, but their freedom also proved to be an illusion in the bitter aftermath of the American Civil War in the southern states. Their disappointment therefore was as great as that of their counterparts in Russia.'

The main difference between the twin emancipations of serf and slave was one of perception. The emancipation of American slaves was perceived to have resolved the burning moral and political issue of the day, whereas the emancipation of the serfs was quickly perceived to have solved nothing. Slaves were legally free and, with the American predisposition to equate legality with justice, this satisfied the abolitionists in their largely black-free states. Theirs had never been a class struggle in the Russian sense; they had not been trying to narrow the enormous gap between rich and poor in American society. They were fighting for the rights of slaves as individuals, not as a class. The Russian peasants, however, had been struggling to change their place in society and to share in the wealth of their 'betters'; they were not going to be bought off by a few legal niceties. For them substance was always more important than form.

To the Little Bighorn and Anadyrsk

The struggle for the soul of America during the civil war had minimal impact on the other great theme of American history, the quest for empire. The latter half of the nineteenth century is often painted as the high point of European imperialism in which the tentacles of the European powers spread out over Africa and Asia. The imperialists of St Petersburg and Washington were no less active.

For Russia, defeat in the Crimean War had merely redirected the imperial urge. Just as America conquered territory in the south-west piece by piece the gradual extension of the Russian empire's boundaries to the south continued slowly but steadily. All the land between the Caspian and Black seas was annexed. Tashkent was taken and made the capital of the governor-generalship of Turkestan. What is today Uzbekistan was seized step by step: the emirate of Bukhara and the khanate of Samarkand in 1868, the khanate of Khiva in 1873 and of Kokand in 1876. America expanded its imperial power directly by outright annexation, as in Florida or Texas, and indirectly through controlling the local ruling elite, as in much of Central America and the Caribbean. Russia did the same: Kokand was annexed outright, while Khiva and Bukhara remained as vassal states under their native rulers.

In America in the decade before the civil war the Sioux were forced out of Iowa and Minnesota and southern plutocrats, anxious to pre-empt their northern counterparts and ensure that the first rail link to the Pacific coast took a southern route, pushed through the Gadsden Purchase from Mexico. Northerners were as ardent imperialists as southerners. New York governor William Seward congratulated Canadians on 'building states to be hereafter admitted to the American union' and opposed the annexation of Cuba only as long as slavery persisted on the island. As secretary of state after the civil war he bought Alaska from the Russians for just $7.2m. (The price was a record low for the territorial purchases made by the United States: 375m acres at just 2 cents an acre.) Seward's ambitions did not stop there. America would become, he declared, 'in a very few years the controlling influence in the world'. This, he correctly predicted, would not be through military conquest but by dominating global commerce, what he described as achieving 'the empire of the world'. He advocated raising tariffs to protect the home market while forcing open in whatever way necessary markets overseas. He was particularly keen to control the trade in the Pacific, and one of his achievements was to gain US possession of the Midway Islands.

After the war the US army waged overtly genocidal campaigns against the Plains Indians and the natives of the south-west; American filibusters were caught and executed while supporting rebels in Cuba; the government of Hawaii was overthrown and the islands annexed;

above all, the United States declared war on Spain in 1898 and, in a tactic followed by Japan forty-three years later at Pearl Harbor, launched a pre-emptive attack on Spain's Pacific fleet. At the end of the Spanish-American War the United States held Cuba, the Philippines, Puerto Rico and Guam. Nobody could be in any doubt that America had now joined Russia as a truly imperial power.

The religious commentator and historian John Robert Seely was not alone in warning of the dangers to the established European order: 'If the United States and Russia hold together for another half-century, they will at the end of that time completely dwarf such old European states as France and Germany.' Seely's response was to call for the strengthening of the British empire, a call that made his book *The Expansion of England* into a bestseller.

Nowadays Britain's imperial past has become the subject of ridicule. The work of the most famous literary exponent of imperialism, Rudyard Kipling, is held up as an example of the racist claptrap that disappeared with the sahibs and memsahibs of the British India Kipling inhabited and extolled. And yet when Kipling wrote his most famous stories, the two Jungle Books, he was living not in the imperial grandeur of Delhi or Bombay but in republican Vermont with his American wife. His most infamous poem, 'The White Man's Burden', was not a panegyric for the British empire, even though the classrooms of British public schools rang out with heartfelt renditions of the opening verse:

> Take up the White Man's burden–
> Send forth the best ye breed–
> Go bind your sons to exile
> To serve your captives' need

Kipling wrote the poem not to glorify a British empire on which the sun was yet to set but as an appeal to the empire he saw rising in its place. 'The White Man's Burden' was Kipling's call to the United States government to take on the role of colonial stewardship of the Philippines, recently conquered in the Spanish-American War.

Americans, however, were not keen to take on the white man's burden. Their concept of conquest was derived from the frontier, where the natives once defeated could be forgotten. The peculiar circumstances of the western frontier have formed the American imperial character that continues to this day: the objective is to conquer; once the battles are over the peace will look after itself, and liberty will prevail just as it did west of the Mississippi. Of course the American way of life prevailed west of the Mississippi because American settlers took it there, something that was clearly not going to happen when America conquered the Philippines in the nineteenth century or Iraq in the twenty-first.

The civil war changed the dynamics of American imperialism. The southern pressure to create new slave states, and so maintain the balance of power in the Senate, was replaced by northern commercial pressures. As America's foreign policy became more interventionist southerners, fearful of enhancing the status of the federal government and the power of northern corporations, campaigned against territorial aggrandisement in Latin America and the annexation of Hawaii. Domestic politics may have changed but to the outside world US imperial policy continued as before.

The island of Hispaniola had had a particularly bloody history ever since Columbus discovered it, and after the civil war the US government sent General Babcock to investigate a proposal to annexe the eastern Spanish-speaking part. He successfully negotiated a treaty under which the Dominican Republic would become a part of the United States, but the Senate rejected it (not least because of fears about increasing America's black population). A presidential commission was set up and again recommended annexation, but again it was blocked. US imperialism was struggling to find a new form that would achieve a new consensus.

Flush with their success in the civil war and still in possession of an enormous army, American eyes turned northwards. The Confederate navy had been greatly strengthened by a steam-powered raider, the CSS *Alabama*, which had been built in Britain, and the victorious Union government demanded compensation; it was suggested that Britain should hand over all her North American colonies. The colonists themselves, however, were bitterly opposed to the idea, and in 1867 Ontario, Quebec, New Brunswick and Nova Scotia formed the Dominion of Canada. The US Congress responded with a resolution condemning the new arrangements and hinting that they were in contravention of the Monroe Doctrine (in fact they were not, as Monroe had explicitly committed the United States to a policy of non-intervention in existing European colonies, and in any case the doctrine was a unilateral proclamation with no standing in international law).

Benjamin Franklin had famously described the division of North America between Britain and the US as 'unnatural' and therefore doomed one day to disappear, and many if not most Americans still agreed. Fearing this, two of Britain's other colonies, British Columbia and Prince Edward Island, joined the new dominion, which also took over the territory controlled by the Hudson's Bay Company. Only Newfoundland remained as a crown colony, and the United States found its northern ambitions stymied. As late as 1910 a free trade treaty between Canada and the United States was scuppered by Canadian opposition, which was incensed in part by the demand of an obscure US congressman that President Taft open negotiations with the British government for the annexation of Canada. (The British colonists had solid economic as well as political reasons for their decision: per capita GDP grew more rapidly in Canada than in the US in the ninety years up to the First World War.)

The first priority of the American government after the civil war was not further annexation but the cleansing and integration of the territory it already had. The emblem of this integration was the completion of the transcontinental railway on 10 May 1869, when the famous golden spike was knocked into the ground by California governor Leland Sanford at Promontory Summit, Utah. The Central Pacific, in which Sanford was one of the five original investors, laid 690 miles of track from Sacramento, California, and the Union Pacific 1086 miles from Omaha, Nebraska. The project knitted the nation together and symbolised the grandeur of the American dream: the definitive study of this first transcontinental railway is appropriately titled *Empire Express*. The creation of the railway has been described as a triumph of American capitalism, with the two railroad companies competing with each other to bring the project to early fruition. In fact the railway owed its existence to extensive professional lobbying in Washington, which eventually resulted in the passage in 1862 of the Pacific Railroad Act. This ensured that as well as generous land grants along the right of way the two companies were subsidised $16,000 for each mile built over an easy grade, $32,000 in the high plains and $48,000 for each mile in the mountains. For the two companies money was the prime objective, and when the two lines neared their meeting point they changed paths to be nearly parallel, so that each company could claim extra subsidies from the government. A disgruntled Congress finally intervened to lay down when and where the railways would meet.

Business and politics were intimately entwined. Not only was Leland Stanford president of the Central Pacific and governor of California at the same time, pushing through state legislation favouring his company in the process, but one of the most passionate advocates of the railroad scheme in the US House of Representatives was the Massachusetts oligarch Oakes Ames, who had invested heavily in the Union Pacific Company – which was headed by his brother, Oliver.

The railroad workers on the other hand were not so well represented, and working conditions were not good, especially in the Sierra Nevada mountains. The two companies made extensive use of immigrant labour – Chinese on the Pacific end and Irish on the other. Although conditions were far easier than on the Trans-Siberian railway (which was also more than three times longer), fatalities were high, especially when the Central Pacific began to use the newly invented and very unstable nitro-glycerine explosive for tunnelling; eventually its use had to be abandoned owing to the death rate among the Chinese workers. The mortality rate was not only high among those working on the railways. The Union Pacific hired marksmen to kill the herds of buffalo, which posed a risk to the trains and more importantly were the main source of food for the natives who needed to be 'cleansed' from the region.

In 1871 the US Congress passed the Indian Appropriation Act, forbidding any future treaties with the natives and declaring that no 'Indian tribe' should ever again be regarded as an independent authority with whom treaty negotiations could be conducted. Once the civil war was over the US army looked west again and started mopping up the remaining native tribes. Compared with the full-scale battles of the civil war the engagements were tiny and usually very one-sided (the most famous exception being the battle of the Little Bighorn). As the whites pushed further and further west in ever-greater numbers, the threat to the natives' way of life became overwhelming. The natives' desperate military responses inevitably failed and were often followed by vicious retribution. A Sioux uprising in Minnesota in 1862 left a thousand settlers dead, but the US army overwhelmed the native forces and, like the tsars in Poland, emphasised their power in a round of public executions. After the Navajo War in New Mexico and Arizona the native survivors were marched 300 miles to a barren reservation to endure four years of near starvation. One of the worst massacres since Mystic occurred when the Third Colorado Cavalry surprised a group of Cheyenne and Arapaho at Sand Creek, and mutilated and murdered hundreds of mainly women and children (the number of dead is variously quoted from 200 to more than twice that number). The purpose of the Sand Creek Massacre was to cleanse the region to make it safe for miners. One remarkable aspect of the massacre, and of the deportations in the south-west, is that they were carried out right in the middle of the civil war; for the US army's imperial mission it was business as usual.

The two most famous encounters between the US army and the natives in the second half of the nineteenth century were at the Little Bighorn and Wounded Knee. At the battle of the Little Bighorn in 1876 General Custer immediately became one of US history's great martyrs, who, like Davy Crockett, had given his life as a sacrifice to America's manifest destiny – pushing onwards the frontiers of civilisation. The US army quite consciously exploited the story, turning the battlefield into a national cemetery. In reality, however, Custer was an unlikely army hero.

George Armstrong Custer graduated from West Point at the bottom of his class and went on to be court-martialled for deserting his troops to visit his wife (while ordering other deserters to be shot). In 1868 he was part of the attack on a native encampment on the Washita river in Oklahoma that came close to being a repetition of the Mystic Massacre, except that Custer seems to have gone out of his way to minimise casualties among the women and children (although many of the women prisoners were subsequently raped by cavalry officers, and Custer himself 'acquired' a young Cheyenne woman to warm his bed until his wife joined him the following year). At the Little Bighorn Custer rushed in where wiser men would have feared to tread, gaining martyrdom for himself and over two hundred men of the US Seventh Cavalry.

The Russian equivalent of George Custer lived and died 130 years earlier. Dmitri Pavlutsky commanded campaigns in Russia's remotest colonial war against the Chukchi in the extreme north-east, just across the Bering Straights from Alaska. In 1731 Pavlutsky lead a force of 700 sleds 900 miles to the Arctic Ocean. His Cossack troops and their native allies claimed to have killed a thousand Chukchi warriors in battle and captured hundreds of women and tens of thousands of reindeer. The Chukchi learnt from their disastrous experience, and when Pavlutsky mounted more expeditions they avoided him and raided, guerrilla-style, the Russian outposts. In March 1747, 500 Chukchi rustlers raided the town of Anadyrsk, driving away seven herds of deer. Pavlutsky set off in pursuit with 131 men. They caught up with the Chukchi on a hill near today's town of Markovo and, without waiting for reinforcements, attacked. The Chukchi were ready, and Pavlutsky and all but a handful of his men died as the native warriors came storming down the hill to meet the advancing Russians in hand to hand combat.

The contrast with Custer could hardly be more marked. Custer's idealised portrait, golden locks flowing, is one of the iconic images of the old west, and the American army was quick to revenge his death. By contrast there are no surviving images of Pavlutsky, no memorials, no heroic stories passed on to generations of Russian schoolchildren.

The Russian response to Pavlutsky's last stand was a few half-hearted raids before Anadyrsk was abandoned and its eight church bells carried mournfully west by its Cossack inhabitants. In 1778 the Chukchi – uniquely among Siberian natives – signed a formal treaty under which Russia allowed them limited self-government, a situation that continued right up to the Bolshevik revolution in 1917. Indeed the Chukchi acted as a bridge between Russians pressing from the west and Americans from the east; the Chukchi traded with American whalers and sometimes travelled as far south as San Francisco.

By contrast there were to be no treaties with the natives who had defeated Custer a century later. Following the Lakota Sioux victory at the Little Bighorn some of the native leaders, most famously Sitting Bull, sought sanctuary in Canada. The remainder, under Crazy Horse, were relentlessly pursued, and after their inevitable surrender packed off to a reservation. Crazy Horse remained on the reservation for just four months before trying to leave to take his sick wife to her parents; he was seized and, with his arms pinioned, bayoneted to death.

As well as the battle of the Little Bighorn, the only other clash between natives and whites to have achieved any great fame occurred nearly a quarter of a century later, in 1890 at Wounded Knee, where the Seventh Cavalry massacred more than 200 hundred men, women and children of the Miniconjou Sioux. Unlike the Little Bighorn, Wounded Knee has not been one of those events permanently seared into the public imagination; in fact it was almost entirely forgotten until the book and later the film *Bury My Heart at Wounded Knee* appeared in 1970. What is most remarkable about the massacre at Wounded Knee is not that it happened but the date at which it happened.

Empire Marches On

By 1890 the era of hardy pioneers pushing into the unknown was long gone. New York and Chicago were competing to prove that the skyscraper had been invented there (New York was earlier, 1868, but Chicago claimed their 1885 effort to be the first to truly scrape the sky).

The authorities in New Orleans were investigating the murder of a city policeman by a shadowy Sicilian gang that they had labelled 'mafia'. In the wider world a German engineer called Gottlieb Daimler had produced the world's first four-wheel petrol-engined car four years earlier, and Queen Victoria had already celebrated her golden jubilee. In Russia the execution of an insignificant revolutionary named Alexander Ulyanov drove his younger brother to devote his life to the revolutionary cause, using the *nom de guerre* of Lenin.

It can be argued that Wounded Knee was part of a chain of events going back to Mystic and beyond; it could equally be argued to be part of a chain going forward to My Lai and beyond. In any event it signalled the end of the line for Native Americans. The poorest county in America today is not in an inner city ghetto nor in a deep south backwater but in the Badlands of South Dakota. Pine Ridge is the home of the Lakota Sioux. Around the site of the Wounded Knee massacre native Americans are sunk in a slough of alcoholism and poverty; and, with an unemployment level of 65 per cent, most can see no way out.

By 1890 the campaigns against the natives were not only over but had already passed from the realms of history into the realms of entertainment. Sitting Bull became a star in the touring Wild West show of Buffalo Bill Cody. Twenty years later Geronimo, who had led one of the last Apache campaigns along the Mexican border and had been shipped off to a Florida reservation, joined other celebrities in Washington for the inauguration of President Theodore Roosevelt. And Roosevelt himself was helped on his way to the White House by his military prowess not in conflict with the natives but in America's first global imperial struggle, for in 1898 America had declared war on Spain.

Before the Spanish-American War there was one last imperial annexation of native land to be consummated. During the civil war the north had been deprived of one essential southern product: sugar. The response was to look elsewhere, and American eyes settled on the islands of Hawaii, 2,000 miles from the mainland. Hawaii had long been an important stopover for American whaling ships, and in 1842 Secretary of State Daniel Webster spelt out American opposition to annexation by any of the imperial powers, a position re-emphasised in 1849 when the United States and Hawaii signed a treaty of friendship. The civil war changed the situation dramatically, and sugar plantation owners from the United States came to dominate the economic and political life of the islands under the so-called Bayonet Constitution of 1887. This was represented as a triumph of democracy over autocracy as King Kalakaua was forced to cede power to an elected assembly, but this assembly was elected not by the people of Hawaii but by property owners, many of whom happened to be American. Pearl Harbor was promptly ceded to the United States. The American oligarchs now in control carried on the traditions of the American pre-civil war filibusters, and had considerable support from influential parts of the US establishment. When Kalakaua's successor Queen Lili'uokalani tried to regain control a group of oligarchs, mainly American sugar planters and led by Samuel Dole, were able to call upon US marines from the USS *Boston*, who landed in Honolulu and surrounded the royal palace with howitzers. The queen was deposed and the plotters declared themselves a provisional government. In a pattern repeated elsewhere throughout the twentieth century the administration of outgoing president Benjamin Harrison encouraged the takeover, with the US minister to Hawaii, John L. Stevens, deeply involved in the planning of the coup. The coup leaders declared Hawaii a republic on 4 July 1894. The next step was annexation by the United States, following the path already trodden in Florida, Texas and California.

In one important respect Hawaii differed from the earlier annexations, and it marked a distinct evolution in American imperial expansion. Spain and Mexico's territories on the North American mainland had been conquered to obtain space for settlement, and American settlers had been the prime movers in the annexation process. In Hawaii the Americans came not as settlers looking for cheap land but as entrepreneurs looking for cheap labour; the muscle for annexation came not from an army of settlers but from US marines. The pressures for annexation arose not from a desire to colonise in the way the original thirteen states and the rest of the mainland had been colonised but from two quite different desires: the desire of a small group of oligarchs to exploit the people and resources of the islands, and the strategic desire of the United States government to protect its military position in the region. These imperial ambitions were not universally popular in the United States. The takeover outraged the new occupant of the White House, Grover Cleveland, who fired Stevens and demanded that the monarchy be reinstated. On 18 December 1893 Cleveland sent an impassioned message to Congress fulminating against the coup and the annexation proposals. The American people, he declared, had never believed that 'a desire for territorial extension, or dissatisfaction with a form of government not our own, ought to regulate our conduct'. He was in absolutely no doubt what had happened:

> The provisional government owes its existence to an armed invasion by the United States. . . . The lawful Government of Hawaii was overthrown without the drawing of a sword or the firing of a shot by a process every step of which, it may be safely asserted, is directly traceable to and dependent for its success upon the agency of the United States acting through its diplomatic and naval representatives. . . . By an act of war, committed with the participation of a diplomatic representative of the United States and without authority of Congress, the Government of a feeble but friendly and confiding people has been overthrown. A substantial wrong has thus been done which a due regard for our national character as well as the rights of the injured people requires we should endeavor to repair. The provisional government has not assumed a republican or other constitutional form, but has remained a mere executive council or oligarchy, set up without the assent of the people. It has not sought to find a permanent basis of popular support and has given no evidence of an intention to do so. Indeed, the representatives of that government assert that the people of Hawaii are unfit for popular government and frankly avow that they can be best ruled by arbitrary or despotic power. . . . I mistake the American people if they favor the odious doctrine that there is no such thing as international morality, that

> there is one law for a strong nation and another for a weak one, and that even by indirection a strong power may with impunity despoil a weak one of its territory.

The irony is that Cleveland had indeed mistaken the American people, for that is precisely what they believed – as the history of the previous century clearly showed.

Cleveland ordered the new American minister in Hawaii to work to restore the queen to power, but the coup leaders simply defied him. Passions rose, particularly in the United States, where in 1898 the Anti-Imperialist League was set up. At its national convention in Chicago in October 1899 it issued impassioned declarations, proclaiming that any attempt to exercise sovereignty over an unwilling people was contrary to the American ideal; but within another two years the league had disappeared.

Four years after the coup in Hawaii conditions were very different. Republican president William McKinley was in charge, the United States was at war with Spain and control of the Pacific was high on America's list of priorities. Hawaii had the best deep-water port in the region, and in August 1898 the islands were formally annexed to the United States. Two years later Dole was appointed its first governor, and for the next half century Hawaii was effectively the private fiefdom of what were known as the Five Companies, the best known being Dole Pineapple.

The ambivalence of America's imperialism was demonstrated again in the remote Pacific islands of Samoa. Almost by accident the United States obtained a naval station at Pago Pago in 1878 through a treaty with the natives. Samoa had limited strategic and virtually no commercial importance. Nevertheless, when Germany tried to annexe the islands American public opinion was outraged; European imperialists were taking away the freedom of poor downtrodden natives. American and German ships confronted each other, and war was only averted when a typhoon destroyed both fleets. Five years later the US did in Hawaii just what the Germans had tried to do in Samoa. Eventually in 1899 there was a classic imperial carve-up, under which Germany got Western Samoa and America got the rest; Britain got the German Solomon Islands. For Germany and Britain their new possessions were minor jewels added to their imperial crowns, but for America this was not imperialism but altruism. Americans were bringing civilisation to distant shores in the way their ancestors had brought civilisation across the Atlantic. The classic example of this, in their own minds, was the war that had only just ended.

The Spanish-American War is one of the most important episodes in American history and one of the most misunderstood. To the vast majority of Americans it was what one commentator has called a 'humanitarian war'. The American Civil War is remembered as a noble war to free the slaves, but that is not what the north set out to do. The Second World War is remembered as a noble war to save the world from the horrors of the concentration camps, but that again is not why the war was fought. The Spanish-American War was the exact opposite: it really was fought to save Cuba from its own holocaust, but that is not how most of the world understood it. Even though Cuba had long been the object of America's imperial desires, Americans maintained that in destroying the last vestiges of the Spanish empire the United States was proving its anti-imperial credentials. For others, American interference in another nation's internal affairs could only be a sign of imperial intent.

The war was a turning point not just in American history but in world history, and set a pattern for what would later be called liberation struggles. The conflict started in 1895. At first America was not directly involved, although war with Spain had been looming for decades. The Spanish empire was on its last legs, and national liberation struggles broke out in Cuba and the Philippines. Spain responded with military force, just as European colonial powers would do in various parts of the world after the Second World War, and the struggles developed into full-scale guerrilla wars. The uprising in Cuba was particularly barbaric: the rebels murdered anyone who did not share their views, destroyed property on a massive scale and executed the emissary Spain sent to negotiate. The Spanish reaction far surpassed the atrocities of the rebels: starving civilians were herded into concentration camps, leading to hundreds of thousands of deaths. An anarchist bomb killed the reactionary Spanish prime minister, and his successor offered autonomy to Cuba and Puerto Rico. This was rejected by the Cuban insurgents, who by now had considerable American support because of the natural identification of many Americans with the rebels' desire to throw off colonial rule, the prospect of profitable opportunities for American corporations and the presence in the United States of a powerful group of Cuban exiles.

The Spanish monarchy regarded Cuba as part of the nation. For Spain rebellion on the island was an attempt at secession that was no different from the rebellion within the United States, which, within living memory, had become one of the bloodiest civil wars in history. How would the US have responded if other nations had intervened in that conflict? Queen Victoria objected that the American insistence on Cuban independence was as absurd as proposing that she give independence to Ireland. To Americans the war was about basic humanity; to nearly everyone else it was about seizing territory. The irony is that however noble the original motives the war became an imperial war, and the American demands soon expanded from Cuban independence to annexation by the US of Puerto Rico and eventually to the conquest of the Philippines.

Although opposed to direct military intervention President McKinley sent the battleship *Maine* to Havana where it mysteriously blew up, killing 266 US sailors. The explosion is now generally agreed to have been an accident, but at the time interventionists like the assistant secretary of the navy Theodore Roosevelt convinced most Americans (and probably convinced themselves) that this was a terrorist attack on American citizens. Public opinion pushed McKinley into a war he did not want and would always regret.

The American army and navy had been preparing for war with Spain long before the *Maine* exploded. The US Navy War College had prepared a number of plans for surprise attacks on Spanish naval forces, and Roosevelt had outmanoeuvred his boss, the secretary of the navy John Long, to ensure that the hawkish Commodore George Dewey was given command of the navy's Asiatic squadron, based in Japan.

The Pope and the major European powers intervened in a last desperate attempt to avert war, but America was unstoppable. McKinley later insisted that if he had been allowed more time by Congress he could have avoided war. He described America's declaration of war as 'the greatest grief of my life'.

Dewey moved the fleet to Hong Kong and then set sail for Manila. On 25 April 1898 America declared war (this declaration was backdated to 21 April to cover a military blockade of Havana that had already been set in place). On 30 April the US fleet of modern warships arrived in the Philippines. Their arrival was not a complete surprise and the Spanish admiral Patricio Montojo had no illusions about the likely outcome of the battle. For fear that the Americans would shell the city he moved his ships away from Manila and into shallow waters, so that when his ships were hit they would settle on to the bottom of the bay leaving enough of the vessels above water to enable his sailors to escape and scramble ashore. The next day, 1 May, Dewey easily destroyed the wooden vessels of the unfortunate Spanish admiral. As an American soldier was to say eighty-five years later, when the United States invaded the tiny Caribbean island of Grenada, it was 'like Star Wars fighting cavemen'. There were no casualties on the American side; 381 Spanish sailors were killed or wounded.

On 3 June McKinley sent Spain his formal demands: annexation to the United States of Puerto Rico, part of the Pacific Marianas islands, a port in the Philippines and independence for Cuba. The Spanish response was to send military reinforcements to the Caribbean, but American forces proved themselves superior. During the battle for Havana Theodore Roosevelt, who had resigned from the department of the navy to get closer to the action, led the famous charge of the US volunteer cavalry against Spanish outposts at San Juan Hill. Detractors would later point out that the hill had been virtually cleansed of defenders by American Gatling guns before the famous charge, and that Roosevelt's cavalry attacking from the right arrived after those attacking from the left had already seized control of the summit, but such carping did not detract from the reckless bravery the future president demonstrated on the day, nor from the mountains of priceless publicity his exploits garnered.

The US navy went on to destroy a Spanish naval squadron off Cuba, and the Spanish forces on the island capitulated. An American invasion of the Caribbean island of Puerto Rico was successful, leaving the Philippines still to fight over.

The war for the Philippines would be a model for many later conflicts. Dewey brought the guerrilla leader Emilio Aguinaldo back from exile in Hong Kong to lead the insurrection. However, following the victories in Cuba and Puerto Rico, it became obvious that Spain would be forced into conceding defeat. Dewey started secret negotiations with the Spanish governor in Manila and the Spanish garrison surrendered to American troops, who in turn stopped the guerrillas entering the city. The result was inevitable: the guerrillas' struggle for liberation from Spain became a struggle for liberation from America.

Emilio Aguinaldo y Famy played a role in Philippine struggles for independence as long and mythic as Tadeusz Kosciuszko's in Poland. Both men initially fought in struggles for national liberation and then went on to see their nations sucked into alien empires, inspiring them to arms yet again. But the two were very different, and although Aguinaldo today is revered by many as the father of Philippine independence, his reputation does not have the unsullied aura of Kosciuzsko. He was already a prominent member of the local elite when he joined a secret society dedicated to driving the Spanish from the Philippines, the Katipunan, in 1895. Guerrilla war broke out the next year, and Aguinaldo grabbed command of the rebel forces after murdering the Katipunan's political leader. When the Spanish offered rebel leaders bribes to go into exile Aguinaldo took the money and left for Hong Kong. After Dewey brought him back Aguinaldo resumed military command of the rebels, and claimed credit for the Spanish army's eventual defeat.

Just as Napoleon's seizure of Poland from Russia had done little to improve the life of ordinary Poles, so the seizure by America of the Philippines gave nothing to the guerrillas who had started the conflict.

Aguinaldo fought on and declared the country's independence on 12 June 1898, but in 1901 he was captured by American troops. He was offered his life if he would pledge allegiance to the United States, which he did. Aguinaldo continued to campaign for independence for over forty years, but before that could be achieved his country was bloodily transferred from one empire to another when Japan seized the islands in the Second World War. Aguinaldo spoke out in support of the Japanese occupation, but in his post-war trial successfully pleaded that he had done so only because the Japanese had threatened to murder his whole family. Finally in 1946 America granted the Philippines independence, insisting that Independence Day be 4 July. Sixteen years later Independence Day was changed to 12 June, in recognition of the day sixty-four years earlier on which Emilio Aguinaldo had first declared independence; Aguinaldo himself rose from his sickbed to attend the celebrations.

At the time of that first declaration of independence the United States was basking in the glory of its victory over Spain. Under the Treaty of Paris Puerto Rico, the Pacific island of Guam and the Philippines were ceded to the United States. It was agreed that Cuba would be granted independence, although under the 1902 Platt Amendment this independence was severely limited: the United States reserved the right to control Cuba's foreign policy, the right to intervene whenever required to protect Cuba from foreign intervention (a wonderfully Orwellian concept) and the right to occupy the island's best port at Guantanamo Bay. (Like its earlier 'purchase' of land from American natives, the United States insists that its 'lease' of the 45 square miles around Guantanamo Bay is entirely legal. Each year it ritually sends a cheque for $4,000, which the Cuban government ritually declines to cash.)

Rudyard Kipling reflected popular sentiments when he gloried in America's reinvigorated imperial ambitions, but one group had been firmly behind President McKinley in his attempts to avert war: corporate America. With the exception of those who stood to gain directly from the conflict, the business elite regarded war as a threat to their expanding commercial interests. Wall Street and the robber barons wanted an empire based on trade, in which they could expand in overseas markets and be protected by tariff walls at home. War would disrupt trade and so should be avoided at all costs, while at the same time as much as possible should be spent on defence as a way of promoting the manufacturing sector. After the war they were equally committed to avoiding the burdens of empire.

One of the leading opponents of US imperialism was steel magnate Andrew Carnegie. In an article entitled 'Americanism versus Imperialism' he described his own vision of America's future in which 'Industrial supremacy of the world lies at our feet'. The United States, he claimed, had been 'permitted' to grab the Philippine islands by Britain, whose overwhelming naval power had stopped Russia, France and Germany grabbing a share. The US had then been required to allow Britain an 'open door' trading relationship with the Philippines. Only if Britain continued to provide protection could the US continue to expand its empire, which, said Carnegie, was quite impractical as it would mean Britain controlling US foreign policy. The US should continue along the path it had long followed of avoiding overseas entanglements. In one passage Carnegie explains how a proper empire works, and why the United States could not follow suit. The example he quotes is Russia:

> Take Russia for instance. Only last year leading statesmen were pushing Britain into a crusade against that country. They proposed to prevent its legitimate expansion toward the Pacific – legitimate, because it is over coterminous territory, which Russia can absorb and Russianize, keeping her empire solid. She knows better than to have outlying possessions open to attack. Russia has always been the friend of the United States. When Lord Palmerston, Prime Minister of Great Britain, proposed to recognize the South, Russia sent her fleet to New York. Russia sold us Alaska; we have no opposing interests to those of Russia; the two nations are the only two great nations in the world, solid, compact, impregnable, because each has developed only coterminous territory, upon which its own race could grow. Even in the matter of trade with

> Russia, our exports are increasing with wonderful rapidity. Shiploads of American locomotives, American steel bridges and American electrical machinery for her leave our shores. Everything in which our country is either supreme or becoming supreme goes to Russia. Suppose Britain and Russia clash in the Far East and we have an alliance with Britain, we are at war against one of our best friends.

Carnegie's admiration for Russia's imperial policies was not perhaps surprising as he shared another passion with Russia's tsar – a determination to eradicate the cancers of radical politics and organised labour, which both men believed were in danger of destroying all that they stood for.

The struggle for the souls of the two empires, which continued in parallel with the development of empire, unfolded in two phases. First there were the dilemmas that emerged from their agricultural pasts – the issues of slavery and serfdom. Then came the dilemmas associated with their industrial futures – the issues of capital and labour. In the first stage the two nations confronted the moral, economic and political issues that arose from the way Russia and the American south had been built on the backs of serfs and slaves toiling in the fields of what were largely agricultural societies. In the second stage the dynamics of manufacturing industry came to the fore. New radical forces emerged after the issues of slavery and serfdom were 'solved'. In America the institutions of democracy would ensure that voices of dissent were either conscripted into the mainstream or left to wither on the fringes; in Russia the repressive apparatus of autocracy pushed dissent into ever more violent confrontation. The result was that a small group of very rich men, personified by Carnegie, would come to determine the course of American history, while in Russia a similarly small group would topple the Romanov dynasty in the name of a nascent industrial proletariat.

CHAPTER 10
SOUL SEARCHING

History is not what is taught in the classroom or buried in academic journals. History is the random collection of pictures and phrases, stories and prejudices that accretes drop by drop in the mind. The images that make up the history of nineteenth-century America and Russia are more likely to be drawn from *Gone with the Wind* or *The Cherry Orchard* than from any school textbook. John Wayne and Leo Tolstoy are more authoritative than any teacher. Countless westerns and the countless pages of *War and Peace* have shaped the prisms through which we view the past, determining what passes on and what is left behind. The unrecorded becomes the unremembered and the invented becomes real.

What passes into history is rarely what seems at the time to be of most consequence. Contemporary fame is no guide to historical longevity. In 1881 Mikhail Dmitrievich Skobelev defeated the Turkomans at the siege of Geok Tepe, bringing Turkmenistan into the Russian empire, and James Abram Garfield became the second US president to be assassinated – but who remembers Skobelev or Garfield today? Certainly far fewer than could name the participants in an obscure Arizona encounter in the same year which immortalised Wyatt Earp in the Gunfight at the OK Corral.

Just as recollections of yesteryear's actions mutate over time so recollections of yesteryear's thoughts and values change almost beyond recognition. Motives are ascribed, values are assumed and opinions are attributed that often say more about the motives, values and opinions of today than of yesterday. The prism of ideology distorts all of history but distorts nothing more than the history of ideology itself. Proponents of 'democracy' see George Washington and George Bush bearing the same, unchanging banner; proponents of 'free' markets equate their cause with the 'freedom' snatched from George III. Opponents of racism imagine their struggle underlying the American Civil War; opponents of imperialism deny that it underlay American invasions of Canada and Mexico. They are all wrong, but not entirely wrong.

There are ideological continuities in history, but not all ideologies demonstrate continuity. Some of the values that make up a nation's soul pass down virtually unchanged from generation to generation; others move on just as history moves on. History reveals a grand enigma: the soul of a nation can change from decade to decade while remaining constant from century to century.

Throughout the latter part of the eighteenth and the whole of the nineteenth century new interests clamoured for political power, new values demanded political recognition, new pressures forced political change. For eighty years 'democracy' provided America with a way of dealing with these changes and transitioning peacefully from one leader to another, but then the new nation collapsed into civil war. Democracy could not reconcile fundamentally different interests and values. Hereditary autocracy in Russia did not so much reconcile differences as suppress them. For centuries this suppression was highly effective, but in the end the same storm of competing interests and values exploded into civil war and in the Russian Revolution the Romanovs were swept away. History was to demonstrate that the Russian Revolution merely replaced one autocracy with another, but no revolution since the French would have a greater impact on the wider world. The currents of controversy and conflict stirred up by the French Revolution would climax in the Russian before reforming, magnified and distorted, to surge through the twentieth century.

Dissidents

'Indifference is the revenge the world takes on mediocrities' epigrams a character in Oscar Wilde's first play. There must have been some who thought the words particularly apposite: because of the indifference of the ticket-buying public the play closed just a week after it premiered. It had the antiquely punctuated title *Vera; or, the Nihilists* and concerned a Russian peasant girl, Vera, who joins the nihilist revolutionaries determined to assassinate the Russian tsar. However, the tsar proves to be not only young and handsome but at heart a nihilist himself. The couple fall in love and in the end Vera kills herself to protect her love and her ideals.

Wilde thought that his play would be seen as a fable about the contemporary struggle for Irish Home Rule, but he had picked the wrong year to produce a play about political assassination. Just a few months before the play was due to open in London both the Russian tsar, Alexander II, and the US president, James Garfield, were assassinated. The play's production was called off and when it was staged in New York the next year, 1882, it flopped.

The inspiration for *Vera; or, the Nihilists* was an event that had occurred just four years before the ill-fated premiere: the attempt by a Russian revolutionary, Vera Zasulich, to assassinate the Governor General of St Petersburg. The life of Vera Zasulich exemplifies the way the currents of opposition eddied to and fro in the last days of Romanov rule, and how those currents have been portrayed in such contrasting ways in the years since. Details of her life have been regularly rewritten. In much the same way that Andrew Jackson's plantation upbringing has been relegated from history to make way for his log cabin birth, so her supporters have concentrated on her poverty-stricken parents without mentioning that her father died when she was three years old, whereupon she went to live with wealthy relatives and received a bourgeois education. What is indisputable is that she joined the radical group Land and Liberty, and in 1876 shot St Petersburg's governor general. The story goes that a revolutionary named Alexei Bogoliubov refused to doff his cap to the governor general, who then had him beaten so badly that Bogoliubov went insane. Vera Zasulich was outraged, although – again depending on which version of history is to believed – this outrage was prompted either by revolutionary solidarity with a man she hardly knew or romantic loyalty to a man whose bed she shared. Zasulich was arrested and charged with attempted murder. The trial became a *cause célèbre*, with the defence producing evidence of massive police abuse. Zasulich became a heroine and she was acquitted by the jury (jury trials having been introduced to Russia just a few years before, during Alexander's early flirtation with liberal reform). When the police tried to re-arrest her the crowd outside the court prevented them, and she went into hiding. Her fame did not last, any more than the fame of many modern celebrities lasts, and she was soon all but forgotten outside the arcane circles of the revolutionary left and the secret police who kept watch over them.

Zasulich remained active in politics as a 'moderate' revolutionary who oppposed the terror tactics of the People's Will and eventually became one of Russia's first Marxists. After going into exile in Switzerland she emerged as a leading propagandist for the illegal SDLP, the Social Democratic Labour party, and translated Marx's works into Russian. At the party congress in London in 1903 Lenin split the SDLP between the 'moderate' Mensheviks and 'extreme' Bolsheviks. Zasulich stayed with the Mensheviks but became increasingly disillusioned with the political squabbles that beset the revolutionary cause. She returned to Russia in 1905 and eventually dropped out of left-wing politics, supporting the tsar's call to arms in the First World War and opposing the Bolshevik revolution. After she died in 1919 the victorious Bolsheviks wrote her out of history; to Soviet historians Vera Zasulich was merely a 'social chauvinist' – one of those meaningless expressions of disdain that the extreme left loved to fire at their fellow travellers. Stalin was characteristically blunter, describing Zasulich as 'an old bitch'.

The pressures for change in Russian society, exemplified by Zasulich's attempt at assassination, came initially from a section of society that had hardly existed not long before. Alexander II may have bought off the peasantry, at least temporarily, but protests by another and much more modern political force challenged the Russian autocracy.

In 1960s America and Europe there was much talk of a new political force: 'student power'. Long haired, dirty, dissolute, free-loving, radical, anarchic, irreligious student rebels were for the first time cleaving society not along lines determined by class or religion or tribe but by age. A whole new generation seemed intent on sweeping away traditional values. Their protests were not as novel as many thought them to be. A century earlier there had also been sixties rebels. Russians were observing exactly the same phenomenon in the 1860s and describing it in exactly the same way – even down to complaints about boys wearing their hair as long as girls. Alexander II had introduced liberal reforms in tertiary education: student uniforms were abolished and students were allowed to travel abroad. The result was that students nibbling the first crumbs of freedom wanted more. Student demonstrators paralysed the University of St Petersburg. 'Nihilists', consisting primarily of students and intellectuals, propounded such dangerous dogmas as social equality. In the west they would have been labelled democrats; in Russia they became communists. Then in 1866 a mentally unstable student tried to assassinate the tsar. Alexander abandoned his liberalism and clamped down on all manifestations of dissent, even circumscribing the teaching of history in case it gave rise to treasonous theories. In 1874 the student protests culminated in a grand demonstration known as the 'Going to the People'. Thousands of students and intellectuals streamed out of the cities into the countryside, determined to help the peasant masses in their struggle for liberation. Not surprisingly the average peasant did not welcome being patronised and their response to this unexpected visitation tended to be curt. At best students and serfs were left mutually bemused. In Going to the People the intelligentsia had gone nowhere, other than the eighty leaders of the demonstration whom Alexander exiled to Siberia.

The various groups of earnest nihilists and populists achieved virtually nothing, just as many would argue their American counterparts a century later achieved little, and again like their successors their very impotence spawned fringe groups calling for more direct action. To some of those demanding dramatic change the message of the failed attempt at Going to the People was that if the peasants would not rise up and save themselves the intelligentsia should do it for them. A revolutionary vanguard would topple the imperial autocracy by destroying the imperial autocrat. There then began a macabre game of 'Hunt the Tsar' or 'Pin the Bomb on the Emperor'. A group calling itself the People's Will set out to assassinate Tsar Alexander. They tried to blow up the imperial train, but derailed another train by mistake. They smuggled a bomb into the kitchens of the Winter Palace, directly below the imperial dining room, but the tsar was late for dinner and missed the massive explosion.

The assassins were not crazed anarchists recklessly hurling bombs around in an attempt to turn order into chaos. Part of the reason for the eventual success of the extreme left in Russia and the failure of even the moderate left in America lay in the nature of democracy and autocracy. Russian tsars were far more powerful than individual political leaders in America, so shooting a tsar would potentially achieve far more than shooting a president. In America power was diffuse. Not only were there powerful local leaders in the individual states but many of the centres of power were outside the political process altogether. Oligarchs like J.D. Rockefeller and J.P. Morgan controlled vast sections of the economy and often exercised effective police power, calling on their private security forces and the forces of the state to suppress opposition. More importantly the people – or at least at that time white males – could make themselves heard: having the ballot Americans had no need of the bullet.

The People's Will may have had a coherent strategy based on a realistic analysis of the tsarist power structure, into which most of the revolutionaries had been born, but they had a totally unrealistic assessment of the power structure of the peasantry. In particular the People's Will failed to understand that the peasants were incapable of spontaneously organising themselves to seize power. Not only had the numerous peasant rebellions shown that their protests were inevitably fragmented and localised, but the Going to the People demonstrations had shown that the Russian peasantry were deeply conservative.

The spirit of the swinging 1860s had virtually no impact on the downtrodden masses. Only within the elite were there any real changes in social attitudes, and then only within a small radical splinter. One example of such a change concerned the status of women. The previous century had witnessed symbolic change: before 1725 no woman had sat on the imperial throne; in the 'Empress Era' from 1725 to 1796 there were no fewer than four tsaritsas – Catherine I, Anna, Elizabeth and Catherine the Great. This female phalanx, however, did not mean there were any fundamental changes in the sexism of Russian society; the tsar was regarded as above gender rather than a gender role model. And after Catherine II no woman ever mounted the throne again.

It was to be half a century after the death of Catherine that real change came, and that among those most bitterly opposed to the Romanovs. A few women joined the revolution: just as rebellious boys let their hair grow long, rebellious girls cut theirs short. Typical among them was Sophia Perovskaya, the daughter of a governor-general of St Petersburg. Born in 1854, she celebrated her twentieth birthday by being thrown into jail in the clamp-down that followed the Going to the People campaign. From then on she spent much of her life in jail or on the run, until on 1 March 1881 she stood on a street corner near the Catherine canal in St Petersburg and gave the signal to two People's Will comrades to throw their bombs at the tsar's carriage. They missed the carriage but the tsar got out to inspect the damage, whereupon another revolutionary threw his bomb and Alexander II was killed instantly. Sophia Perovskaya was arrested and, along with the other conspirators, hanged a few weeks later. At the age of twenty-seven she became the first woman in modern Russia to be executed for crimes against the state.

The period from the assassination of Alexander II in 1881 to the Russian Revolution in 1917 was one of the most critical in Russian history. Conservatives and liberals, socialists and anarchists, reactionaries and progressives were jumbled together in a volatile brew of hopes and fears. The

Romanov autocracy stumbled to its end assailed on all sides by the forces of dissent. And yet for most of the period political activity was mere froth on the stagnant waters of Russian economic life. It is easy to imagine that as the twentieth century approached Russia was a seething mass of discontent, but just as cowboys and Wild West gunfights were totally unrepresentative of contemporary America so revolutionaries and anarchist bombs were no reflection of what was happening in Russian society as a whole. Political activists formed a tiny minority of the population. The left fractured into a multiplicity of nihilists, anarchists, Bolsheviks, social revolutionaries, Mensheviks and so on, and the very act of fracturing made their numbers seem greater than they really were. The proponents of gentle change – those advocating constitutional monarchy, parliamentary democracy and often some form of capitalism – were an equally small minority.

The history of Russia is largely the history of the tsars. Their core beliefs were the nation's beliefs. The nature of the nation depended on them. Quite literally they determined what Russia was; the nation's very frontiers moved in line with their aspirations and fears, their successes and failures. Ivan the Great, Ivan the Terrible, Peter the Great and Catherine the Great all redrew the shape of the Russian empire. In America too individual leaders made their impact on history, but inevitably on a smaller scale. American history is as much the history of parties and movements as it is of great men (unlike Russia, in America there have, as yet, been no great women at the helm). As the nineteenth century progressed parties became more important in Russia, but as long as autocracy survived they remained peripheral. Russian political movements and parties in any case were very different from American parties.

American party political dynamics were transformed by the civil war. The Democrats stood for the defeated, segregationist south and Republicans for the pious, rural mid-west and the aggressive, successful, industrial north-east. In particular the Republicans stood for the aggressive, successful industrialists of the north-east, and so the Democrats became the champions of the urban underclass and of the immigrants pouring into cities like New York, Boston and Chicago.

Although the divisions between the parties were frequently bitter, in the main they lacked the profoundly ideological character of Russian political parties. American parties have, almost from the first, been groupings of interests rather than ideas. Political power became something used not to change society but to protect or promote particular sectional interests. Political affiliations were badges that distinguished one group from another but had no particular intrinsic meaning. Thus it is possible to describe as 'political' the long running Lincoln County War in New Mexico (which included the killing of the pro-Democrat Billy the Kid by Republican sheriff Pat Garrett in 1881), but the events were not party political as would be conventionally understood. Similarly, in the same year Republican mine-owners in Arizona appointed a marshal to take on the supporters of the Democrat county sheriff, but there was virtually no difference ideologically between the two groups: the fact that in the Gunfight at the OK Corral Wyatt Earp and his brothers represented Republican interests and their gunfighter opponents Democrat is incidental.

This is not to say that there were no ideological divisions between American parties, but in general these divisions reflected sectional interests or were secondary to them. In 1888, for example, the presidential election was fought on straightforward issues of economic policy. The Democratic candidate President Grover Cleveland wanted to reduce the tariffs levied on imports and the Republican Benjamin Harrison did not. Those policies reflected the interests of their backers: Republican industrialists did not want to face competition; Democratic voters wanted cheaper goods. In the event the two candidates effectively tied (Cleveland had the most votes but Harrison had a majority in the electoral college). The election was then decided not on the basis of ideology or party platforms; instead New York City Democrats were simply bribed to change sides.

The development of political movements in Russia did not imply a move toward American-style political parties. Russian history is sometimes imagined as a gradual transition from the eastern barbarism of the Mongols and Ivan the Terrible, through the flirtations with the west of Peter the Great and Catherine the Great, to arrive at a nascent parliamentary democracy at the beginning of the twentieth century, a democracy snuffed out by Lenin and, especially, Stalin. It is an attractive picture implying a natural progression towards western values, interrupted during the Soviet era but now free to continue towards its final fulfilment. Unfortunately the picture is just not true. The nineteenth century in Russia saw a flowering of culture – most people asked to name a Russian composer, novelist or playwright would choose a figure from that period – but politically there was no similar blossoming. To flourish democracy's seed must fall on fertile ground and put down roots over decades or even centuries. The seeds of democracy were present in Russia, but they fell on stony ground and never truly rooted. Going into the twentieth century Russia was no more prepared for popular government than it had been a century earlier. After the assassination of Alexander II in 1881 his son, Alexander III, imposed a repression openly dedicated to destroying any signs of progress towards parliamentary democracy. Censorship was rigorously enforced. Education at all levels felt the full weight of the state's authority

Autocracy was not an ideology slowly disintegrating in the face of the advance of western civilisation. After all, the emancipation of American slaves had just been accompanied by the horrific slaughter of the civil war, whereas Russian serfs were emancipated by nothing more violent than the stroke of a pen. To the proponents of autocracy the difference showed the wisdom of entrusting government to a man chosen by God to guide his nation along the paths of righteousness.

The most articulate advocate of autocracy wrote not in the seventeenth or eighteenth century but towards the end of the nineteenth. Konstantin Pobedonostsev was a law professor who became director general of the Russian Orthodox Church and tutor to the tsar's children. He exercised a massive influence over the thinking of the last two tsars, Alexander III and Nicholas II, and that influence was by modern western standards monstrously reactionary. Society, he argued, had been ordered by God from the highest to the lowest because that is the most effective way to organise human existence. Everyone should know his or her place.

Education was largely a waste of time. Educating children beyond the level they needed to fulfil their role in society not only wasted resources but created aspirations that could not be satisfied. The children of miners, he wrote, should spend time down the mines getting accustomed to their future workplace rather than learning physics, which they would never use. To western minds such ideas seem bizarre or even barbaric, but Pobedonostsev was not an ignorant reactionary ranting in the darkness. He quoted Socrates and Antoninus. His writings were peppered with references to John Stuart Mill, Immanuel Kant, George Eliot and Herbert Spencer. He published a detailed critique of the religious views of the British historian John Robert Seeley (although Seeley's famous advocacy of imperialism must have been closer to Pobedonostsev's heart). Pobedonostsev's views on politics are alarming but coherent: the best form of government is the government of a wise and supreme autocrat; democracy is a sham. Individual votes in a democracy are valueless; they only acquire value in the aggregate; and thus the essence of democracy is the manipulation of groups of voters by those who wish to obtain or retain power. This constant manipulation of public opinion, Pobedonostsev argued, led to demagoguery and the debasement of political ideals. This demagoguery was fostered by the press. Journalists and newspaper proprietors had the power to defame, with no right of appeal allowed to those they defamed. Freedom of the press thus became another sham.

Concepts that Americans in particular often regard as divinely ordained – universal suffrage, the rule of law, free speech – were denied not because a megalomaniac tsar was determined to cling on to power but because an important part of society firmly believed that he should be exercising that power. The whole point of society was not to protect the rights of individuals but to promote the collective welfare. Right up to the fall of tsardom there was no common agreement that the law was even intended to produce justice in the western sense. As late as 1909 a distinguished professor of constitutional law was teaching that the proper function of law in Russia was not to ensure justice but to maintain order.

But the maintenance of order was something the Romanov regime was increasingly unable to deliver. For centuries tsarist control had relied on two factors – its monopoly of military force and the lack of any coherent counterforce. As long as the Russian population was thinly scattered over the enormous expanse of the Russian empire any internal threat could be isolated and dispatched. Towards the end of the nineteenth century that changed. Enormous factories in and around St Petersburg and Moscow provided breeding grounds for organised dissent, and when the contagion spread to the army and navy the end of the Romanovs was nigh. The factor that changed the face of Russia for ever was the force that had already determined the soul of America: industrialisation.

The Soul of Industry

One of the key messages of modern American imperialism is that America became the world's most advanced industrial nation because of its free market economy, and that to achieve similar riches other nations must open themselves up to the same free market. However, as Stiglitz clearly shows in his bestseller *Globalization and Its Discontents*, in the nineteenth century it was the US federal government that created economic growth, not the free market. Furthermore the term 'free' when applied to the economy does not mean now what it meant when America was establishing its economic predominance. Today the term means free trade, vigorous competition, minimum state intervention and an absence of corruption – conditions which (except perhaps for the absence of corruption) almost inevitably favour US multinationals. The nineteenth-century free market in America was very different. Shielded behind protective tariffs, supported by state subsidies (often dispensed in highly dubious circumstances), robber barons were left free to wield monopoly power to build enormous private empires.

After Independence one of the first acts of the new Congress had been to impose customs tariffs. It also gave preferential treatment to American traders by setting the tariffs at lower levels for imports arriving aboard American ships. One of the southern complaints before the civil war was that high import tariffs protected northern manufacturers but meant southerners could not buy cheaper goods from overseas. Alexander Hamilton had wanted high tariffs to protect infant industries 'in order to increase national wealth, induce artisans to immigrate, cause machinery to be invented and employ women and children'. Hamilton's proposals were not adopted in their entirety at the time, but the fact is that the US economy developed with exactly the sort of selective protection that it now stops other countries enjoying.

Russian industry was also protected from international competition by the state. One of the first industries to benefit from large-scale mechanisation in both countries was cotton weaving, which grew rapidly in Russia after a high tariff was imposed on cotton imports in 1822. By 1913 Russia ranked fourth in the world for textile production after Britain, the United States and Germany. The ability of America and Russia to gain such a high market share in an industry that Britain had once so comprehensively dominated was largely thanks to protective tariffs. In 1913 average tariff rates on imported manufactures were zero in Britain, 13 per cent in Germany, over 20 per cent in France, 44 per cent in the US and 84 per cent in Russia.

That Russia should have been following policies so contrary to the spirit of modern free markets is not surprising, but what is often forgotten is that the American industrial economy was born in conditions more like today's Russia than today's America. In the last decades of the nineteenth century corruption in America was legendary. A whisky scam in St Louis defrauded the government of millions of dollars in taxes with the connivance of senior officials, including President Grant's private secretary (who like most of those involved managed to escape punishment). In 1872 it was discovered that nearly half of the federal government's subsidy of $50m for constructing the Union Pacific railway had gone missing. One of those implicated was James Garfield, but that did not stop him being elected president (although four months into his term he was assassinated by someone who had been unable to bribe his way into government service). Grant's secretary of war was found to have received kickbacks from men given monopolies to trade on the native reservations, and in the notoriously corrupt naval dockyards a million feet of lumber purchased for the Boston yard simply disappeared.

Many of the most notorious nineteenth-century plutocrats – like John Rockefeller, who in a series of secret deals gained control of the US oil industry, and Andrew Carnegie, the Scottish immigrant who dominated the US steel industry after introducing the radical new manufacturing processes invented in Britain by Sir Henry Bessemer – are remembered today for the charitable foundations that bear their names. But charity for Rockefeller and Carnegie was very much an afterthought, and just as representative were unreconstructed oligarchs like William Vanderbilt, who controlled much of America's transportation and sponsored imperial adventures in Central America, and Jay Gould, a railway speculator who manipulated, bribed and stole his way to a $25m fortune. Gould's exploits included cornering the market in gold to force the price up, and then using inside knowledge to sell out before the federal authorities responded. The business practices of the robber barons make modern American financial scandals seem tame. Rockefeller at one time exercised so much power that he was able to make the railway companies pay him a levy based on the amount of oil they carried on behalf of his competitors – equivalent to Coca-Cola taxing supermarkets for every Pepsi sold.

One of the most infamous plutocrats controlled a sector that produced nothing at all: John Pierpoint Morgan was the robber barons' banker. Morgan, born into the New England plutocracy and educated in Britain, Switzerland and Germany, made his first fortune during the civil war, having avoided enlistment by paying somebody to take his place, a common practice among his class. Morgan became the robber barons' chief financial fixer, putting together cartels that controlled key industries like railroads, shipping and utilities. In partnership with Rockefeller and Carnegie he created United States Steel, the world's first billion-dollar company.

For much of the period between the civil war and the arrival of Theodore Roosevelt it was men like J.P. Morgan and John D. Rockefeller who determined the course of American history rather than the ever-changing occupants of the White House. Most political leaders did what they were told. US senators at that time were selected by state legislatures rather than by direct election, and very few reached the Senate without 'support' from local industrialists or left the senate poorer than when they had entered.

Particularly powerful were the railway oligarchs. It is worth quoting at length the words of one of America's most eminent historians Samuel Eliot Morison:

> The power of an American transcontinental railway over its exclusive territory approached the absolute. A railroad could make an industry or ruin a community merely by jiggling freight rates. The funds at their disposal, often created by financial manipulation and stock watering, were so colossal as to overshadow the budgets of state governments. Railway builders and owners had the point of view of a feudal chieftain. Members of state legislatures were their vassals, to be coerced or bribed into voting 'right' if persuasion would not serve. In their opinion, railroading was a private business, no more a fit subject for government regulation than a tailor's shop. They were unable to recognise any public interest distinct from their own. In many instances the despotism was benevolent; and if a few men became multimillionaires, their subjects also prospered. But others were indifferent to all save considerations of private gain. By distributing free passes to state representatives, paying their campaign expenses and giving 'presents' to their wives, they evaded taxation as well as regulation. By discriminating freight charges between localities and individuals, they terrorised merchants, farmers and communities. Through the press and professions they wielded a power over public opinion comparable to slave-owners over the old South.

Morison's description of post-civil war society as feudal is accurate, but in a sense American society had always been feudal. The original southern colonies had been feudal estates and the plantation owners and New England merchants who instigated the American Revolution exercised quasi-feudal powers in their communities. The essence of Hamilton's view of democracy was government by an elite on behalf of the people. What was new in the period after the civil war was that the oligarchs made little pretence to be governing on behalf of the people; indeed they made great pretence of not governing at all. For perhaps the first time in history the most powerful men in society remained outside the formal structures of government. Their objectives were entirely mercenary, and in the new doctrines of *laissez-faire* capitalism they found an ideology sanctifying their creed of greed: the wealth of nations derived from their efforts, and the role of government was to do nothing more than to ensure that they were not interfered with. The institutions of democracy were not torn down by the new feudal lords but simply bypassed.

The contrast with Russia was stark. There too nascent capitalists were at work but in a far less attractive environment. How do you bribe a tsar who has everything? The relative performance of the railways showed the inherent differences between autocracy and American democracy. For the tsars railways were a strategic not merely economic imperative. The Trans-Siberian railway was the world's longest, built not just to facilitate the exploitation of Siberia's mineral riches but to tie the empire together and allow rapid movement of troops to the eastern provinces. Great efforts were put into developing extensions into China and Manchuria, but within the Russian heartland railway connections were minimal. In America railways criss-crossed the nation in a tangled web that would have horrified a rational planner, but at least they existed. Despite the magnificent achievement of the Trans-Siberian, Russia remained in the era of the horse and cart when America was moving from steam trains to the automobile.

Although most of Russian industry was less developed than its American counterparts this did not imply that Russian civilisation was somehow more backward. The United States was beginning to excel in what might be called practical learning, but in the more intellectual pursuits like literature and science it often lagged behind – despite being free of the heavy hand of autocracy. In Russia the Academy of Sciences, brainchild of Peter the Great, was founded in 1725, and had an enormous impact on scientific development. By contrast the US Congress did not set up the National Academy of Science until 1863. Some tsarist scientists became world famous. Ivan Pavlov's animal experiments gave English the word 'pavlovian' and Pavlov himself a Nobel prize, Nikolai Lobachevski was the first person to develop non-Euclidean geometry, Dmitri Mendelev created the periodic table of chemical elements and the Baltic German Friedrich Struve founded the Pulkovo observatory outside St Petersburg. Russian women were among the first in the world to receive doctorates in scientific disciplines ranging from pure mathematics to zoology. The mathematician Sophie Kowalevski was the first woman in Europe to become a full professor, although she had to go to Sweden to do so.

Tsarism was both a spur to scientific advance, by actively sponsoring research, and a hindrance when scientists reached the 'wrong' conclusions. The works of physiologist Ivan Sechenov were suppressed for their supposed atheism – a problem still encountered by scientists of evolution in America today. Many Russian scientists became political dissidents, for example the biologist and leading anarchist Prince Peter Kropotkin. Police broke up the last lecture given by the great chemist Dmitri Mendelev because they thought he might use it to incite a student uprising. In America too science and politics were never completely segregated; Benjamin Franklin achieved fame in both fields.

The difference between science in the two nations is less in what was achieved than in what is now remembered. Although in the eighteenth and much of the nineteenth centuries both Russian and American scientists were outside the mainstream of scientific development, at that time centred on western Europe, American history has since been incorporated into 'western' experience. Thus Benjamin Franklin is widely remembered as one of the most important figures in the history of science, while his contemporary Prince Mikhail Lomonosov who played an almost identical role, and even did research in many of the same subjects, for example electricity, is now largely forgotten.

Whatever the intellectual attainments of Russian scientists, the practical application of science was far more limited in Russia than in America. The world's first oilwell was drilled by Russian engineers near Baku in the late 1840s, a decade before America's first oilwell in Pennsylvania in 1849, but it was in America that oil corporations quickly achieved pre-eminence. Economic and industrial development across the Atlantic was on an altogether grander scale. One consequence of this was that the political power of the robber barons who controlled that development was far more pervasive. In Russia a powerful group of oligarchs emerged but they never exercised the influence over government of their American counterparts, and the industrial sector itself formed a much smaller part of the overall economy. Nevertheless, by the end of the nineteenth century the manufacturing and mining industries in Russia were becoming far more important than they had been.

After the Crimean War it was obvious to everyone that if Russia was to fulfil its imperial pretensions it needed to industrialise, but industrialisation brought its own problems. First it needed investment, and to a large degree that meant foreign investment. One of the most critical events in the collapse of the tsarist autocracy occurred not on the battlefield or on the barricades of the revolution but in the corridors of power, where diplomats and bankers collide and collude. In 1888 Russia was in desperate need of foreign investment to kick-start its industrialisation, and it turned for help to what was by then the dominant continental power: Germany. For reasons that are still argued over, the German chancellor Bismarck refused all requests for credit, forcing the Russian regime to turn elsewhere, in particular to France. Thus was born the Franco-Russian alliance that pulled the Romanov regime to its destruction on the rocks of the First World War.

As with early American industrialisation foreign entrepreneurs played a key role in kick-starting industrial growth. The modern city of Donetsk, with a population of 1.2 million and one of the largest cities in Ukraine, was founded in 1870 and originally named Yuzovka after a Welsh industrialist, John Hughes, whose factory dominated the local economy. (Donetsk may lack the historical interest of Yuzovka, but it has to be better than the name the city bore from 1924 to 1961 – Stalino.) A crucial difference between American industry and Russian was that in Russia foreign entrepreneurs and companies remained key players long after they had been displaced in America. There were a number of reasons for this, but none had much to do with the supposed virtues of America's 'free' markets.

Some of the reasons were industry-specific. For example, Whitney's cotton gin, which had revolutionised the American cotton industry, worked with short staple cotton; when the American Civil War devastated world cotton markets Russia turned to the new provinces of central Asia as a source of raw cotton, but this meant spinning long staple cotton, which was not only labour intensive but relatively highly skilled and for large scale production required machinery Russia could not produce. Britain dominated the global cotton industry by the end of the eighteenth century and produced most of the world's textile machinery. In 1842 a British ban on machinery exports was lifted and machinery was soon exported to both America and Russia. By copying British technology and then imposing high tariffs on machinery imports, American manufacturers were able to see off British competition. Russia, on the other hand, lacked the ability to create its own machinery, and as late as 1910 nearly 90 per cent of all cotton spinning machinery in Russia was British. Cotton weaving and dyeing also required technologically advanced machinery, and when Britain did not provide it other western nations did. Giant German- and Swiss-owned textile mills imported machinery from their homelands. Not only was machinery imported; even as late as the First World War nearly all Russian-owned textile mills had British technical managers and engineers.

However, the principal reason that so much of Russian industry before the revolution was dominated by foreigners was not specific to the cotton industry but was a consequence of history: unlike America, Russia had never been part of the British empire. In colonial America the local oligarchs, protected from global competition by British trade barriers, built up substantial capital assets. This accumulated wealth was able to fund the development of an industrial economy that was not only far more dynamic than Russia's but balanced local with foreign ownership. In the Russian empire, on the other hand, wealth was sucked into the imperial treasury and most of it spent by the tsar. Therefore for budding entrepreneurs the only source of capital for industrial investment was what remained in the tsar's vaults or what could be borrowed from foreign banks. Not surprisingly foreign banks, at least initially, were more inclined to lend to people they knew, their own nationals wanting to invest in Russia, rather than to the new class of Russian oligarchs. Furthermore, to buy foreign machinery required gold or foreign exchange. America's first industrialists had ready access to the foreign exchange receipts from southern cotton and tobacco exports (which permeated north to merchants, manufacturers and – not to be forgotten – slave traders). Russia's agricultural exports were too small to serve the same purpose.

Both America and Russia were heavily dependent for their economic development on foreign investment, almost all of it from western Europe; by 1914 they were by far the world's largest net debtors. Right up to the First World War the US was the world's largest importer of capital. In 1914 its foreign debt was $7.1bn compared with the next largest debtor nation, Russia, with $3.8bn. The crucial difference between the two countries was that the US was also a significant lender; by 1914 it had overseas investment of $3.5bn (although dwarfed by Britain with $18bn, France with $9bn and Germany with $7.3bn). In terms of net borrowing Russia and America were in virtually the same position, but the US was an integral part of the global economy: in 1897 US foreign investment had amounted to $700m; by 1914 this had almost quintupled.

The reliance of the US on foreign investment caused considerable anguish to the native oligarchs. The January 1884 issue of the New York *Bankers Magazine* commented, 'It will be a happy day for us when not a single good American security is owned abroad and when the United States shall cease to be an exploiting ground for European bankers and money lenders.'

It went on to describe the interest and dividends earned by European bankers as 'tribute paid to foreigners' and as such totally 'odious'.

Russian entrepreneurs were also well aware of their disadvantageous position. As Professor Alfred Rieber has written, many were convinced that 'reliance on foreign skills and capital could turn Russia into a dependency of the west without a single shot being fired'. But there was little they could do about it as long as the tsar, increasingly dominated by his reactionary wife and her spiritual advisor Rasputin, remained committed to a vision of divinely ordained autocracy, which made him nearly as unsympathetic to the arguments of the new capitalist class as he was to those of the socialists and anarchists.

In contrast, across the Atlantic the US economy was entering a period of rapid 'consolidation'. The mechanism for this consolidation was the 'trust', which could bring together all the firms in a particular industry – not just in the new sectors like oil, steel and railways but in older ones such as sugar and tobacco. These trusts were enormous, dominating their domestic market and in some cases controlling production worldwide. No trust was bigger than Standard Oil, owned by John D. Rockefeller, whose personal wealth was equal to nearly 2.5 per cent of the whole US economy (the equivalent of around $250bn today, more than twice as much as Bill Gates). Standard Oil was formed in 1867 but it took a lawyer, Samuel Dodd, to come up with the idea of a trust, and on 2 January 1882 the Standard Oil Trust was formed. A board of trustees was set up and all the Standard properties were placed in its hands. The nine trustees elected the directors and officers of all the component companies, allowing Standard Oil to effectively function as a monopoly. Later Standard Oil pioneered the holding company, which had the same effect.

Public disquiet about trusts increased, and politicians like Theodore Roosevelt, secure in his inherited wealth, recognised not only a political bandwagon they could climb on but, in many cases, a genuine affront to their concept of democracy. If men like Rockefeller and Carnegie represented the new dawn of big business and corporate empire, Theodore Roosevelt represented an altogether older vision of economic and political life. He was born into a wealthy New York family with powerful southern connections on his mother's side. He personified the way America's imperial aspirations had moved on from the Wild West to encompass the whole world, but at the same time he retained the rugged frontier values that had prompted his cowboy heroes to stand up to the cattle barons and outlaws of yesteryear. After the death on the same day of his mother and his first wife Roosevelt bought a ranch in the Bad Lands of Dakota, determined to play cowboys for real. He was appointed deputy sheriff and claimed to have hunted down a gang of desperados, but he soon discovered that the frontier at the end of the nineteenth century was neither as exciting nor as profitable as he had hoped and his gaze turned elsewhere – to glory in warfare overseas and politics at home.

Few American presidents have been able personally to shape their country's history in the way that tsars defined the history of Russia but two or three have come near. Andrew Jackson was one, and two others fired the popular imaginations of their day: Abraham Lincoln, who took his nation into war with itself, and Theodore Roosevelt, who became a symbol of America's imperial wars overseas. Lincoln is probably the only American president between George Washington and modern times that most people can name. Abraham Lincoln's cause, freedom and civil rights for all, has become part of how Americans see themselves today, and that is why he is remembered – despite the fact that Lincoln was actually committed to maintaining slavery in the south and eventually freed the slaves only in the extraordinary conditions of the civil war. Roosevelt's cause, empire and military glory, is no longer a core part of America's self image and Theodore Roosevelt has become an embarrassing footnote to American history – despite the fact that he won the Nobel peace prize for resolving war between Russia and Japan.

Theodore Roosevelt was from the same brave, impetuous and demagogic mould as Winston Churchill. Just as Churchill flung himself into Britain's imperial war against the Boers, Roosevelt threw himself into battle in the Spanish American War, leading what became one of the most famous episodes in American military history – the charge up San Juan Hill in Cuba. Like Churchill, Roosevelt was given political command of the navy despite having no naval experience, although Roosevelt achieved greater success in the Philippines than Churchill achieved in the Dardanelles. Both leaders spent much of their spare time writing: Churchill penned his famous history of the Second World War, Roosevelt his less famous naval history of the 1812 War. The parallels continued in the political world. Churchill was shunned by many in his party (indeed both men changed parties) and was a political maverick who only achieved power owing to the exigencies of war; Roosevelt only became President McKinley's vice-presidential running mate after the incumbent died, and then became president following McKinley's assassination.

Roosevelt's career was dominated by the twin themes of empire and soul. Although most famous internationally for his pursuit of America's manifest destiny, he first achieved political notice at home through his attacks on corporate America and the scandalous behaviour of the robber baron Jay Gould. He launched a series of initiatives against the trusts, and in doing so he deflected much of the popular anger that arose from glaring inequalities of wealth and power. The contrast with Russia was marked. Roosevelt's Russian counterpart, Tsar Nicholas II, also had to grapple with the issues of empire and soul, but not only were there no mechanisms available to him to capture the spirit of dissent, as Roosevelt had done in America, but fundamentally there was no desire to do so. Nicholas, as the supreme autocrat, simply did not believe that his role was to 'represent' the concerns of the people in the way Roosevelt would have understood the term. The tsar was not the voice of the people but its emblem. He represented Russia as parents might represent children, not as elected officials represent their constituents.

Roosevelt, on the other hand, fulfilled another role for his nation's children. On a hunting trip in Mississippi aides presented him with a captured bear cub to shoot, but Roosevelt considered this unsporting. His act of mercy was caricatured in the *Washington Post* and a New York shopkeeper put the cartoon in his window alongside a toy bear made by his wife: the teddy bear was born. (Teddy Roosevelt's generosity to the toy industry was not matched by generosity to the original cub: when the president declined to kill it another member of the party did so.)

New Model Empires

The two most important developments in American history between the civil war and the First World War were the globalisation of American imperial ambitions manifested in the Spanish-American War and the birth and rapid growth of the corporation: the commercial structure that would come to dominate the economy of the world.

Initially the major corporations were the playthings of the new class of oligarchs, the robber barons, who were deeply unpopular with those at the bottom of society who created the wealth so ostentatiously displayed by those at the top. (In another very tenuous link between Roosevelt and Churchill, an explosive book entitled *Coniston* stirred up public anger over the links between the oligarchs and corrupt officials. Its author was Winston Churchill, cousin and namesake of the British politician.)

The unadulterated greed of the oligarchs eventually antagonised just about everyone, from the workers and customers they exploited right up to the most exalted in the land. Supreme Court Justice John Marshall Harlan, a conservative Republican, proclaimed that the country was in real danger from another form of slavery in which a few mighty capitalists controlled, exclusively for their own profit and advantage, the entire business of the country. In England the 1624 Statute of Monopolies had taken away the power of the crown to grant monopolies, but in the United States nothing stopped their development, which often took place – as with the railways – with the active encouragement of the government. State legislatures, especially in the west and south, passed laws to regulate business, but the trusts simply re-established themselves in friendly states like Delaware and New Jersey.

By 1888 public discontent was so strong that both political parties put anti-trust planks into their presidential platforms. In the same year President Rutherford B. Hayes famously recorded in his diary, 'This is a government of the people, by the people and for the people no longer. It is a government of corporations, by corporations, for corporations.' Two years later Congress overwhelmingly passed the first federal trust-busting legislation, with just one vote against in the Senate and none at all in the House of Representatives. The Sherman Antitrust Act, named after Senator John Sherman, brother of the civil war general, declared illegal any contract, combination or conspiracy in restraint of interstate and foreign trade and authorised the federal government to institute proceedings against trusts in order to dissolve them. However, to get through Congress the Act had been made deliberately vague and the Supreme Court initially prevented federal authorities from using the act against their intended targets. Instead the American propensity for legality over justice was seen once again as an Act supposedly designed to curb the oligarchs was instead used to enhance their power. In 1894, in the case of US v. Debs, the Supreme Court ruled that the Act could be used to stop trade unions from interfering with commerce, and in the first ten years of the law's existence many more actions were brought against trade unions than big business. Businesses like the Pullman Railcar Company argued that unions were conspiracies in restraint of trade, and gained legal authority to use state and federal militia to support their union-busting activities.

But by 1904 public pressure became such that the court upheld, by five votes to four, Theodore Roosevelt's dissolution of one of the huge railway monopolies, the Northern Securities Company, and trust-busting became a practical possibility. There were vehement expressions of outrage from the business community at the court's overruling of its earlier decisions, but in 1911 President Taft used the Act against the American Tobacco Company and, most symbolically, against the Standard Oil Trust. Rockefeller's company was broken into parts, including Standard Oil of New Jersey (later renamed Exxon), Standard Oil of New York (Mobil), Standard Oil of Ohio, Standard Oil of Indiana (Amoco) and Standard Oil of California (Chevron). (The companies started rebuilding Rockefeller's old empire in the 1990s, when Exxon merged with Mobil and BP bought Amoco and Standard Oil of Ohio.)

Despite the highly publicised actions taken against a few of the trusts, the character of the American economy had fundamentally changed. The critical point about the robber barons is that they were not aberrations. The transition from family enterprises with family values to modern corporations with modern values was not a seamless reinterpretation of traditional American values but a complete break with the past and an invention of something altogether new. For two generations American business worked in ways that today would be regarded as totally corrupt, and the morality that was re-established afterwards was very different from that which had gone before. For decades it seemed as if the values of Paine and Jefferson had simply vanished. Private greed was not surreptitiously substituted for the public good but actively promoted as the way to achieve the public good, in a proto-Thatcherite ideology which proclaimed that the unbridled forces of free enterprise would amass not just riches for those at the top but wealth for the whole of society. Monopolies and cartels were proclaimed as ways of serving the public by promoting the scaling-up of American industry, which in turn would generate the efficiencies of mass production. When the president of the Reading railroad appeared before the Pennsylvania legislature in 1875 to justify the collective decision of the large coal companies to reduce supply in order to drive up prices, he produced a list of fifty other industries where such practices were openly applied. Producers of schoolbooks, wallpaper and lumber, insurance companies, slaughterhouse owners – they all met in industry associations to fix prices. Large coal companies and railroads combined to ensure that when small mine owners tried to undercut their larger competitors they found it impossible to transport their coal from their mines. Retailers were 'fined' if they sold at prices lower than those fixed by their corporate suppliers.

The interesting question is whether the rapacious capitalism that preceded Theodore Roosevelt helped or hindered the nation's economic development. In the last quarter of the nineteenth century over 700 rail corporations responsible for more than half of the American rail network went bankrupt. Fortunes were made by corrupting government officials, destroying competition at home and preventing competition from overseas, emasculating the state and mercilessly exploiting those at the bottom of society, but the result was a transportation network that was the envy of the world, gas and electricity in municipalities across the country and modern factories with the economies of scale that gave the largest American corporations enormous competitive advantage against their global rivals.

By 1909, 1 per cent of industrial firms produced 44 per cent of US manufactured goods. Between the civil war and the First World War the conditions were established that would enable America to create a commercial empire that, for much of the twentieth century, would dominate the world. It was not entrepreneurial zeal or technological know-how but the ruthless pursuit of profit, and above all sheer scale, that would crush foreign competition. The all-pervading goal of the American business model became size; increased profits came not from improving the business but from increasing its size. Mergers and acquisitions served the dual purpose of eliminating competition and enhancing economies of scale.

The concept of 'scale' is crucial to understanding the American economic model, which would come to dominate the world. In classical economics the term 'economies of scale' meant that as businesses became larger they became more efficient: they could afford bigger and better machines, could employ workers in shifts to get the most out of those machines, could move their goods in larger wagons and so on. But what American monopolists realised after the civil war is that scale above all gave them power: they could pay their suppliers less because the suppliers had nowhere else to go, they could charge their customers more, they could drive smaller competitors out of business. They turned classical theory on its head: rather than growing in order to become more efficient, they realised that by growing they could thrive without having to become more efficient. As long as there were opportunities for growth efficiency was nice to have rather than essential – a philosophy that served US industry well until the rude awakening delivered by Japanese corporations over a century later.

Corporate America was coming of age, and for its leaders the world appeared as a mass of new markets waiting to be conquered. Many Americans, however, still had an older concept of conquest. For them America's territorial ambitions were still undimmed.As the older European empires stumbled,America's imperial destiny became ever more manifest. The Spanish-American War marked a watershed in American imperial history: before that time conquests and purchases had been intended to gain territory to populate; in winning possessions like Cuba and the Philippines, and in annexing Hawaii, America gained territory that was already populated, and populated to such an extent that ethnic cleansing was inconceivable. In any event the ending of slavery had changed both the politics and the economics of expansion.There was no imperative to find more states suitable for slavery to balance the northern expansion. To the victorious northerners the civil war had purified the nation not only from the stain of slavery but from the crude lust for other people's land that had characterised southern imperialism.The value of the new colonies was not in their cheap land but in their cheap labour. There emerged the blend of imperial ambition and ideological sanctity that has since characterised American foreign policy. Now seeking to conquer new markets rather than new territories, it became necessary to cultivate friendly relations with other countries; but how could a nation dedicated to spreading universal democracy be 'friends' with regimes dedicated to the suppression of those very democratic ideals? One way was to consciously separate ideological theory from political reality, most clearly demonstrated in the twentieth century by Nixon-Kissinger realpolitik. Another way, more in tune with the global aspirations of American ideology, was to impute ideological purity to their allies and impurity to their foes. After the civil war it became routine for the United States to attribute their own ideology to whichever side they were supporting in any situation.The civil war was firmly believed, with the benefit of hindsight, to have been a struggle to impose liberal democracy on the despots of slavery. Now that idealism was transferred elsewhere. Even the smallest signs of democratic intent in potential allies were seized upon as indicators of ideological purity. Heavily influenced by its large German-American population, the US backed Prussia in its invasion of France, hailing Bismarck for purportedly implementing the American model of democracy. (The US minister in Berlin, an eminent historian, showed the dangers of historians trying to extrapolate into the future when he declared that Germany would soon be 'the most liberal government in the continent of Europe'.)

The ability to 'see' ideological purity in virulently anti-democratic regimes was to become an outstanding feature of American imperial policy in the next century. America's focus on ideology meant that the actions of regimes around the world would be judged not on their inherent substance but on their political context. Thus when the United States transferred nuclear technology to Iran, Secretary of State Henry Kissinger declared that 'introduction of nuclear power will both provide for the growing needs of Iran's economy and free remaining oil reserves for export or conversion to petrochemicals'. When the shah fell and his Islamic successors continued the nuclear power programme, Kissinger complained that 'for an oil producer such as Iran, nuclear energy is a wasteful use of resources'.

At the same time that Bismarck's Prussia was being upheld as a beacon of democracy, another nascent imperial power was also flexing its muscles across the world. Japan was lauded in the United States for its supposedly liberal and progressive government as it plunged into murderous wars with China and Russia. American support for Japan in its war with Russia reflected two aspects of American politics: the political power of the Jewish lobby and, at that time more important, the innate idealism of the American people. Russian despotism became a political issue in America long before the advent of communism. The anti-semitism of Alexanders II and III provoked massive anger in the United States, where the existing Jewish population, largely of German origin, already wielded considerable political power and was now swelled by hundreds of thousands of Russian Jews. In addition newspaper reports of the barbaric regime in Siberian prison camps caused outrage. Russia responded by condemning the racist treatment of former slaves in the United States. In the 1868 presidential campaign Ulysses Grant vehemently attacked Russian anti-semitism to overcome attacks on his own record of anti-semitism in the civil war. The American Society of Friends of Russian Freedom enjoyed celebrity support across the political spectrum from Mark Twain to Theodore Roosevelt. Russia's obscure imperial adventures in Manchuria made headlines in America, and in an early demonstration of America's bipolar approach to foreign policy despotic Japan's attack on the Russian fleet in 1904 was widely supported. Just forty years after the citizens of New York had given a rapturous welcome to the Russian navy during the civil war they now enthusiastically cheered its destruction. In those forty years both nations had changed: Russia was growing in its traditional manner but America was starting to follow a different path.

The seizure of the Philippines and Hawaii not only marked a turning point in American imperialism but also made the United States for the first time a significant player in the imperial politics of the Pacific. The carving up of Samoa with Germany had been of little interest to the rest of the world, but the occupation of the Philippines was different; it clearly demonstrated that the United States intended to take an active part in Asian affairs. For Japan, rapidly industrialising and modernising its military machine, this was a potential concern – a concern that just forty years later exploded into the attack on Pearl Harbor – but a far more pressing issue in Tokyo was the other imperial power advancing into the region: Russia. Russia's last tsar, Nicholas II, had turned his eyes towards Asia in the perpetual Russian quest for new territories to conquer. The Trans-Siberian railway pushed on into Manchuria. When completed in 1905 it would be the world's longest railway (5,772 miles), travelling a quarter of the way round the earth, across eight time zones and with nearly a thousand stations. It was built to carry Siberia's mineral wealth to Moscow and the west, but it also allowed the rapid deployment of troops. There was still a gap around Lake Baikal, but when that was plugged Russian forces would be able to intervene quickly in regions that Japan perceived as being in its sphere of influence.

In the middle of the nineteenth century Russia had started pushing south from Siberia, exploring the length of the Amur river which China had successfully protected against the first Cossack invaders two centuries before. Conditions in China were now very different, and Russian explorers found the Amur undefended. Nikolay Muravyev, the governor of eastern Siberia, led his troops into the Amur basin and, after repelling British and French attacks on the river's mouth, forced the Chinese to sign the Treaty of Aigun, settling the border between Russian Siberia and Chinese Manchuria on the Amur. In 1860 the city of Vladivostok, destined to become the terminus of the Trans-Siberian railway and Russia's major Pacific port, was founded on the Amur Bay.

In the same year that America attacked the Philippines, Russia obtained its first warm water port on the Pacific by making China an offer it could not refuse for Port Arthur. This increased the tension with Japan, which had itself annexed Port Arthur four years earlier during the Sino-Japanese War. Germany's seizure of nearby Shantung prompted a bizarre Russian demand for 'compensation', on the grounds that it should have been allowed to seize it first.

Russia expanded to the border with Korea. The Hermit Kingdom had been 'opened up' by the US navy in 1871 and was now a free-for-all. Japanese forces there overwhelmed Chinese troops before being forced to withdraw by a 'Triple Intervention' of Russia, Germany and France. Apparently acting on his own authority, the Japanese minister to Korea launched a coup in which the Korean queen was murdered (just two years after the American minister in Hawaii had ousted the Hawaiian queen). The Korean king fled to the Russian legation before having his pro-Japanese ministers executed.

Russia used the covert imperial tactics being pursued elsewhere by the United States, and by 1897 was in effective control of much of Korea: training Korean troops, controlling Korean Customs and establishing the Russo-Korean Bank. At precisely the same time on the other side of the world the United States was doing the same thing in the Dominican Republic. In both cases the control proved precarious. In 1898, under the

Rosen-Nissi Convention, Russia had to yield its dominant position in Korea to Japan, and the next year the American company responsible for the Dominican Republic's Customs was expelled.

Russia then followed another American model. At the time Hawaii was being annexed, as the culmination of secret plans drawn up largely by the former American minister to Hawaii, the Russian minister to Korea proposed something similar. An East Asiatic Company would be set up ostensibly to acquire commercial timber concessions along the Tumen and Yalu rivers, but really to act as the first step in a plan to annexe Korea to Russia. Whereas in Hawaii commercial pressures drove territorial aggrandisement, in Yalu the territorial imperative was driving commerce. The tsar supported the idea and put up the initial funds. Active consideration was given to attracting American investors into the project to deflect international concerns, but it was decided that Americans would be too impatient for profit. Russian timber concessions were obtained on the Manchurian side of the Yalu and soon extended into Korea, but these operations were fronts; most of the Russian workers were in fact soldiers, and the main objective of the Russian 'businessmen' was to survey the region and establish an infrastructure that could be used in future military campaigns. In 1903 Russian soldiers in civilian clothes entered the harbour at Yongampo and began to construct barracks and port facilities.

Korea, and more importantly China, seemed ripe for foreign exploitation. America, in the throes of fighting a guerrilla war in the Philippines, had no wish to annexe territory on the Asian mainland, but it was determined to protect its own commercial interests. US Secretary of State Hay therefore announced an 'open door policy', under which the Chinese economy was to be open for grabs but further annexation of Chinese territory was forbidden. America's growing military power in the region gave weight to Hay's declaration, and when the anti-foreigner Boxer Rebellion erupted in China in 1900 US marines played a key role in ensuring the victory of the Eight Nation Alliance of Britain, America, Russia, Germany, France, Austria-Hungary, Japan and Italy. Under cover of the rebellion Germany, quickly followed by Britain and France, moved to seize Chinese territory and Russia occupied all of Manchuria. Nicholas, however, faced bitter opposition from America, Britain and, especially, Japan, and was eventually forced to recognise Chinese sovereignty over Manchuria and agree to a phased troop withdrawal, which soon stalled.

In 1902 Russia started to reinforce its far eastern fleet, and at the same time Japan completed a programme of naval expansion, helped by Britain. The next year Russia made clear it would not honour its commitment to withdraw from Manchuria, and started strengthening its forces there. If there had been a real willingness to arrive at a peaceful settlement one might have been achieved, but Japan was in expansionist mode and Nicholas was convinced his army could defeat any forces Japan could muster (a conviction expressed in what today would be regarded as amazingly racist terms). Nicholas was wrong.

In February 1904, six years after America's attack on Spain's Pacific fleet, the Japanese without formally declaring war launched a devastating surprise attack on the Russian fleet in Port Arthur, sinking the battleship *Tsarevich* and cruiser *Pallada*. When Japan later attacked Pearl Harbor America was able to regroup and harness its overwhelming economic superiority to reverse the initial Japanese gains. The tsar was unable to do the same. His dismay was compounded the following year when the Russian Baltic fleet arrived in the Pacific, having travelled halfway round the globe (Japan's British allies had refused to let it pass through the Suez canal), only to be annihilated by the Japanese. By then Port Arthur itself had fallen. Russia's forces were as appallingly commanded as they had been in the Crimea. In sailing to the far east, the Russian Baltic fleet managed to create a diplomatic incident by firing on British trawlers in the North Sea – apparently mistaking them for a Japanese fleet!

The war was only concluded by the intervention of Theodore Roosevelt. Less than a century earlier it had been the Russian tsar, Alexander I, who had tried to use his superpower status to end the 1812 War between America and Britain; now it was the American president who brought Russia and Japan together in Portsmouth, New Hampshire, to hammer out a peace treaty. Russia had to give up all claims to Port Arthur, Korea and Manchuria. A secret agreement between America and Japan guaranteed Japan a free hand in Korea in return for Japanese acquiescence in the American occupation of the Philippines. Russia was by now in the military second division of imperial powers, relegated not just by Japan but by the United States and its president.

Territory Belonging to the United States

From the first Muscovite princes, through to Stalin and beyond, the Russian empire expanded sometimes at a gallop, sometimes more hesitantly, sometimes even pulling back a little but throughout using its military might to push out the frontiers. American imperialism demonstrated the same continuity of military expansion from the nation's inception up to the twentieth century, but then it changed: 'imperialism' became a bad word and military conquest ceased to be the cornerstone of imperial policy. It is difficult now to remember how fundamental the ideology of empire used to be to the psyche of the American people. Well into the twentieth century a significant body of American opinion was not only openly imperialist but used that term to mean territorial aggrandisement in exactly the form that had characterised American expansion since Independence. Men like the ideologue of empire Senator Albert Beveridge argued that conquests beyond America's existing boundaries should be treated in the same way that Texas or Florida had been treated. 'The Philippines are ours forever, "territory belonging to the United States", as the Constitution calls them,' he declared. In quoting that phrase the senator adduced in the Founding Fathers an imperialist motivation that has now been largely forgotten. He continued:

> The founders of the nation were not provincial. Theirs was the geography of the world. They were soldiers as well as landsmen, and they knew that where our ships should go our flag might follow. They had the logic

> of progress, and they knew that the republic they were planting must, in obedience to the laws of our expanding race, necessarily develop into the greater republic which the world beholds today, and into the still mightier republic which the world will finally acknowledge as the arbiter, under God, of the destinies of mankind. And so our fathers wrote into the Constitution these words of growth, of expansion, of empire, if you will, unlimited by geography or climate or by anything but the vitality and possibilities of the American people.

In Beveridge's view America was unique. 'Almighty God', he said, 'has marked us as His chosen people, henceforth to lead in the regeneration of the world', adding 'We will not renounce our part in the mission of our race, trustee, under God, of the civilization of the world.' For him the question of America's role in the world was not a political one but something far more fundamental. In one congressional speech he declaimed:

> Mr President, this question is deeper than any question of party politics; deeper than any question of the isolated policy of our country even; deeper even than any question of constitutional power. It is elemental. It is racial. God has not been preparing the English-speaking and Teutonic peoples for a thousand years for nothing but vain and idle self-contemplation and self-admiration. No! He has made us the master organisers of the world to establish system where chaos reigns. He has given us the spirit of progress to overwhelm the forces of reaction throughout the earth. He has made us adepts in government that we may administer government among savage and senile peoples. Were it not for such a force as this the world would relapse into barbarism and night. And of all our race He has marked the American people as His chosen nation to finally lead in the regeneration of the world. This is the divine mission of America, and it holds for us all the profit, all the glory, all the happiness possible to man. We are trustees of the world's progress, guardians of its righteous peace. The judgment of the Master is upon us: 'Ye have been faithful over a few things; I will make you ruler over many things.'

It should not be thought that such views were the rantings of a few on the reactionary right. Beveridge himself eventually left the Republican party and unsuccessfully ran for Senate again as a 'progressive'. His views on the conquest of the Philippines were shared by millions of Americans, from Theodore Roosevelt down. He believed that the occupation of the Philippines 'was one of the noblest examples of patriotic devotion to duty in the history of the world' and laid out a detailed blueprint for the American government of the islands. His only concession to democracy was the suggestion that there might 'possibly' be 'an advisory council with no power except that of discussing measures with the governor-general'. The governor-general, along with the heads of all provincial and district authorities, would of course be American. 'Self-government and internal development have been the dominant notes of our first century,' noted Beveridge; 'administration and the development of other lands will be the dominant notes of our second century.' Only in the very long term would the people of the Philippines be ready for statehood alongside his own Indiana. A more immediate element of Beveridge's plan was 'the establishment of import duties on a revenue basis, with such discrimination in favour of American imports as will prevent the cheaper goods of other nations from destroying American trade'. The empire was to be more about protecting American corporations than spreading democracy.

The ideology of democracy was not replaced by the ideology of imperialism but fused with it. It was precisely because of its democracy that America was justified in imposing its empire on others. Again Beveridge spelt out the ideological justification for imposing servitude in the name of freedom in words that could have been applied to Iraq a century later. There was no contradiction, in his view, in the Founding Fathers espousing self-government for America while denying it to others:

> Let men beware how they employ the term 'self-government'. It is a sacred term. It is the watchword at the door of the inner temple of liberty, for liberty does not always mean self-government. Self-government is a method of liberty – the highest, simplest, best – and it is acquired only

> after centuries of study and struggle and experiment and instruction and all the elements of the progress of man. Self-government is no base and common thing to be bestowed on the merely audacious. It is the degree which crowns the graduate of liberty, not the name of liberty's infant class, who have not yet mastered the alphabet of freedom.

The inherent contradictions in this argument may not have been apparent to Beveridge but they became increasingly obvious to others. For many Americans their nation's conquests during the Spanish-American War seemed more to resemble the actions of the British empire that the Founding Fathers had fought against than the society they had fought to create. The corporations who were becoming the nation's economic driving force did not need military conquests to gain global market share, and the mass of the American population did not need new territories to settle. The American empire had come of age and from now on would develop rapidly in new directions. What could not be transformed so quickly was the ideology that underlay the old imperialism. Beveridge's traditional vision of empire, in which the United States simply kept expanding, disappeared, but the popular belief that America has a unique global destiny remained.

The distinguishing characteristic of American imperialism has been its extreme flexibility. America's democratic ideology always had a global dimension, but how that universal vision manifested itself depended on the circumstances of the time. Kagan's phrase 'determined opportunism' was particularly apposite as American imperialism moved from the continental to the global and adjusted to the age of corporate capitalism. The United States had none of the problems Nicholas encountered in his drive to expand his empire. As Japan and Russia were engaged in full-scale war in the far east the United States was flexing its imperial muscle on the other side of the world. US marines were called in to protect America's imperial business interests by invading the Dominican Republic and re-establishing the control the US business community was in danger of losing. The invasion gave rise to America's most explicit statement yet of its imperial 'rights' in the western hemisphere: Theodore Roosevelt's development of the Monroe Doctrine known as the Roosevelt Corollary. The government of the Dominican Republic was bankrupt and Roosevelt feared that foreign nations, especially Germany, might intervene forcibly to collect their debts. In his annual message to Congress in December 1904 he declared that 'chronic wrongdoing' anywhere in what today would be called the Third World would 'ultimately require intervention by some civilized nation'. From this he concluded that 'in the Western Hemisphere the adherence of the United States to the Monroe Doctrine may force the United States, however reluctantly, in flagrant cases of such wrongdoing or impotence, to the exercise of an international police power'.

What Roosevelt meant by chronic wrongdoing had been illustrated the previous year. The United States wanted to build a canal linking the Atlantic and Pacific through northern Colombia. The Colombian Senate demanded what Roosevelt considered to be an unreasonable rent for the proposed 100-year lease, so a US navy gunboat was dispatched to support a secessionist revolt. The newly formed nation of Panama promptly leased the land to the United States in perpetuity for a 'reasonable' rent.

US marines were soon in action again, in Nicaragua in 1912, and then, having already occupied Cuba, American eyes turned to the other large Caribbean island, Hispaniola. In 1915 the French-speaking half of the island, Haiti, descended into chaos. After a mob hacked the president and the head of the Haitian army to pieces a French naval lieutenant and nine French marines landed to protect the French legation. Claiming that this violated the Monroe Declaration, the United States sent in its own marines who, acting on instructions from Washington, immediately seized $500,000 in gold from the Haitian National Bank. The US occupation lasted nineteen years and provoked bitter resistance; 3,250 Haitians were killed for the loss of just thirteen US troops. The occupation mirrored the brutality witnessed at Abu Ghraib in Iraq less than ninety years later. On one occasion US troops were ordered to shoot all prisoners, and a marine general later testified that many of the Haitian deaths were 'indiscriminate killings' designed to discourage resistance. Despite a presidential commission of enquiry, the only person to be found guilty of any crime was a marine lieutenant, who was convicted of torture and committed to an asylum.

The year after invading Haiti, US marines yet again invaded the Spanish-speaking half of the island, the Dominican Republic, and again the main concern was to gain control of the nation's financial affairs. The paradoxes inherent in the American belief that it was possible to impose liberty were plainly demonstrated, as for eight years the local press was subject to rigorous censorship in the name of freedom.

America's continuing military interventions in the Caribbean and the proclamation of the Roosevelt Corollary were further signs that a mighty new empire had emerged, while at the same time, the end of the nineteenth century, two once-great empires were approaching collapse. The Spanish empire was hastened on its way by American military might, and Russia determined to do the same with the Turkish empire. Turkey had been subject to repeated Russian attacks but still held on to much of the Balkans, and Nicholas II turned his attention in that direction. Once more, however, the crucial difference between the geopolitical circumstances of America and Russia became apparent: while nobody else was likely to intervene if America seized Cuba or the Philippines, the Balkans were a fulcrum of European imperial intrigue and in particular were the back door of another soon-to-be-defunct empire, the Austro-Hungarian.

The end of the nineteenth and early twentieth centuries was an age when the imperial powers played board games with much of the globe. Diplomats, politicians, bankers and monarchs seized and ceded, deposed and disposed without any thought for the occupants of the territories concerned. Great chunks of Asia and Africa in particular were passed around between the great powers. In a typical example Russia mediated in a dispute between France and Germany about whether territory seized by Belgium in the centre of Africa might be taken over by Germany in return for France being given a free hand in Morocco. The European protagonists eventually settled into two camps: Russia, France and Britain in the Triple Entente and Germany, Austria-Hungary and Italy in the

Triple Alliance. America and Japan watched from the sidelines, happy to take advantage of whatever developed.

The various Balkan wars that preceded the First World War saw Turkey losing most of its European empire and Slavs and non-Slavs slugging it out to see who would gain most of the spoils. Russia cheered on the Serbs, Germany cheered on the Bulgarians, and the heir to the Habsburg throne made the mistake of leaving Vienna for Sarajevo and a fatal encounter with an anarchist's bomb. Germany blamed Russia's Slavic ally Serbia for the Archduke Franz Ferdinand's assassination, and the stage was set for the cataclysmic First World War.

Looking back on the nineteenth century it is clear that America and Russia had started to develop increasing similarities. Particular events invite simple comparison: the emancipation of the Russian serfs and of the American slaves; the assassinations by anarchists of Tsar Alexander II and President McKinley; the violent labour unrest in both countries; pogroms of Jews and blacks. These superficial similarities reflect in part the reality that below the surface many of the same forces were at work, in particular those arising from increasing industrialisation, but the outcomes were fundamentally different. In America democracy proved unable to reconcile diametrically opposed positions on the issue of slavery and the nation collapsed into civil war – but its political institutions emerged from that war largely unchanged. In Russia on the other hand the autocracy was able, on the issue of serfdom, to simply impose its own view, but that postponed civil war rather than avoided it, and when war came centuries of tsarist dictatorship were swept away. By bringing very large groups of workers together for the first time, industrialisation and the factory system, often introduced like everything else in Russia on a massive scale, created breeding grounds for radical dissent. The only other place where the downtrodden could associate in such explosive numbers was within the armed forces, and when revolutionary groups gained footholds in the navy and army the days of Romanov rule were numbered.

Although dramatic change in Russia became inevitable, the form that such change would take was totally unpredictable. It is now clear that Lenin and his followers were as amazed as anyone else when the Bolsheviks emerged on top. There were after all similar anarchist and revolutionary socialist groups elsewhere who achieved very little. The world seemed to be in turmoil. Not only did anarchist groups assassinate the tsar and other Russian leaders but their attacks spread across Europe. The King of Italy, the President of France, the Empress of Austria and the prime minister of Spain were killed. An anarchist tried to shoot the Prince and Princess of Wales as their train passed through Brussels, and in the United States President McKinley became the third president to be assassinated when he was struck down by the anarchist Leon Czolgosz. (Czolgosz was a loner regarded by his own family as crazy and refused admission by various anarchist groups who thought he was a spy; he hatched his assassination plan after reading newspaper accounts of the assassination of the Italian king.) Nicholas II had himself been subject to an anarchist assassination attempt when, as crown prince, he had visited Japan. He was saved by the quick action of his cousin, Prince George of Greece, and was left with a scar on his forehead and a bitter hatred of all things Japanese.

Mounting discontent in Russia over wages and living conditions in the new industrial suburbs of St Petersburg coincided with the news of the loss of Port Arthur to the Japanese, and protesters took to the streets. In January 1905 soldiers fired on demonstrators in St Petersburg, an event that came to be known as Bloody Sunday. Reports of an enormous massacre swept across the Russian empire, and conspiracy theories abounded. It now seems certain that the protest leader, a priest named Georgi Gapon, had received funds from the tsar's secret police, the Okhranka (in the same way that front organisations were funded by both the KGB and CIA later in the twentieth century). Gapon fled abroad, and when he returned was murdered by socialists convinced he was an Okhrana *agent provocateur.*

It is quite possible that Nicholas II hoped that a short sharp shock would quell the developing unrest. If this was the case he had miscalculated. Spontaneous demonstrations broke out throughout the empire, particularly in the more recently conquered territories like Poland and Finland. Closer to home the first workers' councils or soviets appeared in St Petersburg and called the whole city out on strike, thrusting to the fore the deputy chairman of the St Petersburg soviet, Leon Trotsky. Sailors on the battleship *Potemkin* famously mutinied, and unions were formed not only among the factory workers and peasants but also among groups as diverse as doctors and ballet dancers. Nicholas had undammed a torrent that looked as though it would sweep him away. Two million people were on strike by the end of the year. The tsar's first reaction to Bloody Sunday was to panic and then to issue a defiant declaration of the absolute primacy of autocracy. As the protests mounted, however, he was forced to issue what became known as the October Manifesto, agreeing to transform Russia into a constitutional monarchy with free elections. This won over the doctors and dancers, and further militancy by the St Petersburg and Moscow soviets fizzled out or was brutally crushed. But Nicholas at heart remained an autocrat, and when the protests had subsided he reiterated his commitment to the supremacy of the autocracy and reined back the reforms promised in the October Manifesto.

The tsar's prime minister, Peter Stolypin, tried to head off rural unrest by giving more land to the peasants and encouraging further settlement of Siberia. In stark contrast with American colonisation of the west, Siberia's bleak climate dissuaded mass migration even after the discovery of rich mineral reserves. The vast territory was only slowly populated, partly through voluntary migration, partly through convict labour but mainly through forced migration: between 1824 and 1899 around 720,000 settlers were simply told to uproot themselves and move to Siberia, many accompanied by their families. Slightly less draconian measures were introduced when the Siberian Resettlement Bureau was set up in 1896 and three-quarters of a million people settled along the route of the Trans-Siberian railway in the next four years. Stolypin's reforms were too little too late, and in 1911 he was assassinated at the opera in the presence of the tsar. His murder well illustrated the chaotic state of political life in the last days of the Romanov regime. His assassin was a revolutionary socialist who doubled as an agent of the Okhrana secret police. At his trial before a military court it was alleged that his objective had been to incite a revolution against the monarchy, although had that been the case he would surely have shot the tsar. Rumours soon started to circulate that the murder had been arranged by Stolypin's rival at court – Rasputin (who was himself murdered by court opponents soon after). As Stolypin's assassin was promptly executed and Nicholas II personally ordered any further investigation to be stopped, the truth may never be known.

Nicholas had underestimated the forces ranged against him, but so had most people. Around the world dissidents were embracing the ideas of the socialist left and labour turmoil was rampant. As industrialisation had progressed so much faster in the west Russia was the last place most revolutionary socialists expected their revolution to start. On paper the conditions looked far more propitious in America. The United States had a revolutionary tradition, and within living memory had torn itself apart in the name of the downtrodden masses on the southern plantations. Socialist principles of equality and justice were inherently compatible with the prevailing ideology of democracy. The capitalist bosses were as rapacious as any in the world, and the working conditions in factories and mines as bad as anywhere else. In the Pennsylvania coalfields children as young as six were employed as 'coal breakers' in conditions as bad or worse than anything endured by southern slaves or Russian peasants. Throughout America there were groups espousing anarchist or socialist ideologies remarkably similar to their Russian contemporaries, much of their literature confidently proclaiming that a socialist millennium was not far away. Violent confrontations between the authorities and striking workers were as common on the streets of Pittsburgh as St Petersburg.

Numerically the left at the turn of the century was probably stronger in America than in Russia. Political activity of all kinds was far more prevalent in the United States, and socialist and anarchist groups of varying hues sprang up and disappeared again. The Socialist party had members all over the country and not just in the big cities; it has been claimed, somewhat improbably, that at one time nearly a third of the adult population of Oklahoma belonged to the party. A socialist textbook called *The Life and Deeds of Uncle Sam: A Little History for Big Children* sold half a million copies. In 1911 thirty-three American cities had socialist mayors. Milwaukee was notorious for its corruption until the socialists swept to power in 1910 and remained there for more than a quarter of a century.

In the 1900 presidential election the Social Democrat Eugene Debs received 0.6 per cent of the popular vote and the Socialist Labour candidate Joseph Maloney 0.3 per cent. Small votes to be sure (even added together they won far fewer votes than John Woolley the Prohibition candidate), but the social democratic parties in Europe were also small in their early days. Just two years earlier the grandly named First Congress of the Russian Social Democratic Labour party, the party that would eventually drive the Bolshevik revolution, had just nine delegates. As the First World War loomed many on the American left were convinced that revolution was on its way and victory over the oligarchs was within their grasp.

To the majority of Americans such expectations were pure fantasy. And it was not only their opponents that regarded American socialism as a lost cause. In early 1917 one dedicated revolutionary, sitting in his rented apartment on New York's 164th Street, despaired of the American socialist movement. Its leaders, he complained, resembled less a working-class vanguard than an assembly of 'successful dentists' who considered President Woodrow Wilson more authoritative than Karl Marx. When news arrived of the uprising in Petrograd that heralded the Bolshevik revolution he quickly gathered his family, rushed to the docks and bade farewell to America without regret. Like Lenin – himself hurriedly returning from exile – the other mastermind of the Russian Revolution, Leon Trotsky, was on his way home.

CHAPTER 11
COMMUNISM AND CORPORATISM

Until the beginning of the twentieth century the values of America and Russia could be easily described: democracy or autocracy at home and imperialism abroad. For centuries Russian autocrats had imposed their will on an ever-expanding empire and, although much younger, America too had ever-expanded its frontiers. The imperial values of both nations were remarkably similar but their domestic values could hardly be more different.

Autocracy was an uncomplicated concept: rule by an omnipotent autocrat. But what was democracy? Rule by the people, the demos, was easy to proclaim but not so easy to define. Democracy was less a philosophical framework than a language that provided slogans – liberty, freedom, the pursuit of happiness, malice towards none – without prescribing substance. In the name of government by the people slaves were bought and sold, native tribes were eradicated, brother fought brother in a bloody civil war and colossal fortunes were amassed with startling amorality.

Where autocracy was constant democracy seemed infinitely malleable. The last tsar Nicholas II lacked the bloodthirsty sadism of Ivan the Terrible or the messianic vision of Peter the Great, but he was equally convinced of his divine right to rule. The prescriptions of Konstantin Pobedonostsev, the great theorist of autocracy, would have sounded eminently reasonable to Catherine the Great generations earlier. By contrast the democracy of John D. Rockefeller bore very little resemblance to the democracy of Thomas Jefferson. The values of democracy mutated, and as they did so they refined the imperial values that underlay America's relations with the rest of the world – the overt imperialism of Andrew Jackson marching into Florida or of Winfield Scott in the halls of Montezuma gave way to the 'banana republics' of the United Fruit Company and the global intriguing of Standard Oil.

As the nineteenth century drew to an end the autocracy of the Romanovs and the democracy of the robber barons faced new challenges as industrialisation sparked massive intellectual ferment. Socialists and anarchists in all their varied hues snapped at the heels of established authority and threatened to bring it down. In the event the malleability of democracy carried it through; the rigidity of tsarist autocracy caused its collapse. A new force appeared on the world's stage threatening to destroy capitalism and promising to end the era of empires. The promises of communism soon rang hollow, but the threat of communism – equally hollow – shaped the century to come. The dogmas of communists and anti-communists would tint the ideological prism through which all modern history is viewed.

Bolshevism Arrives

Lenin and Trotsky returned to Russia to find a situation of near total chaos. Not only had the centuries-old political institutions collapsed but the old ideological certainties had disappeared overnight. Throughout the western world into which Peter the Great had pushed Russia, new political forces of burgeoning industry and organised labour were stirring, each adopting, or having thrust upon them, novel and still developing doctrines and dogmas.

The American oligarchs known as the robber barons and their less powerful Russian equivalents were beginning to espouse theories of economic and social life centring on 'free markets' which inevitably had political implications. Heavily influenced by the survival-of-the-fittest determinism prevalent in the science of the age, they evolved an ideology in which corporate capitalism was not just a way to make a few individuals extraordinarily rich but a blueprint for organising society and ensuring its ever-increasing collective prosperity. In the United States the well-being of its citizens and the well-being of its corporations became two sides of the same coin. As President Coolidge was to say, 'The business of America is business,' or more bluntly, as Alfred P. Sloan, the president of General Motors, is claimed (perhaps erroneously) to have said, 'What's good for General Motors is good for America.' In America this developing ideology of 'corporatism' became over time inextricably interwoven with the ideology of democracy, so freedom and free markets became almost synonymous. In Russia full-blooded corporatism of this type never developed, partly because Russian industrialists never achieved the political power of their American counterparts but more importantly because the ideology of autocracy was far less amenable to infiltration by a corporatist philosophy whose very essence was the dispersal of power among competing corporate entities. Ideological developments in America occurred on the 'right', to use a convenient if sometimes ambiguous term; in Russia they occurred on the 'left'.

The various left-wing groups in Europe and North America were united in their opposition to raw capitalism but in little else. They brought together men and women with an enormous variety of beliefs, and as a consequence left-wing history was a long succession of splits, disputes, faction-fights, regroupings, alliances and internecine warfare. Almost by definition the one attribute they lacked was self-discipline. Lenin changed all that. At the second congress of the Russian Social-Democratic Labour party held in London in 1903 he split the party by his insistence on the professionalisation of revolution, and created the Bolsheviks for whom party discipline was supremely important. In the name of a socialist revolution he had in effect bolted the ideology of autocracy on to the inchoate stirrings of organised labour. The Communist party became the means of driving Russian history forward, just as the corporation would drive the development of America. It was a giant philosophical leap, but one that until the autumn of 1917 remained an aberration on the fringes of radical thinking.

Very little of the turmoil that Lenin and the other émigrés discovered when they returned to Russia was due to the activities of the party. Contrary to the Soviet version of history the Bolsheviks did not bring tsarism down; in the events leading up to the tsar's abdication they played a very marginal role. Indeed, even on the left there were far more influential factions, for example the anarchists and the Social Revolutionaries (who unlike the various Marxist groups believed that the peasantry could be the backbone of the revolution). Nor did tsarist autocracy collapse under the impact of the First World War: comparatively speaking Britain and France were facing greater losses. There were food riots immediately before the tsar abdicated and there was mounting disquiet over the progress of the war, but most of those pressing the tsar to abdicate wanted the war fought more assiduously not less. The reality is that three hundred years of Romanov history just crumbled away. The inept stream of Alexanders and Nicholases who had sat on the imperial throne since Alexander I's triumph over Napoleon dwindled into nothingness. To put it crudely the tsar, Nicholas II, was useless and his German-born wife even more so, and those around him simply got fed up. Right up to his murder in 1916 the mad monk Rasputin had more influence with the royal family than many of the tsar's own ministers. The Russian Revolution owed more to the degeneracy of the Romanov autocracy than to the potency of competing ideologies.

Nicholas is sometimes pictured as a well-meaning if somewhat remote figure; a monarch with the same high intent as his wife's grandmother Queen Victoria, but unable to deal with the currents of revolution around him. The truth is more complicated, for Nicholas was above all an autocrat dedicated to maintaining a form of government that had long disappeared in Britain and which new social pressures and the Romanovs' increasing feebleness made impossible to maintain in the Russian empire. He believed that he could and should control events, but in truth events controlled him.

Industrial and technological change had set in motion a train of events that could not be reversed. Similar developments had occurred or were occurring in the United States, but there they provoked very different reactions. It is only a little too simplistic to say that the Romanov regime instinctively tried to turn the clock back, whereas the instinctive reaction of Americans was to speed the clock forward. There were reactionary forces in both countries determined to return to a simpler, better world, but in Russia that reactionary sentiment – almost entirely absent in Washington – was central to government thinking. All would be well if the nation could be returned to the values of Mother Russia – autocracy, empire and the Orthodox Church. In its increasingly desperate attempts to avert unrest the Russian regime turned to ever more reactionary means. It is worth examining one of these in some detail and to reflect on the sharp contrasts with superficially similar events in America.

On Easter Day in 1903 an orgy of violence was unleashed against Jews in Bessarabia and later in other parts of the empire, all with the tacit approval of the tsar. Nicholas was anxious to distract attention from problems elsewhere and the Jews were a welcome scapegoat. Jewish families were butchered and thousands fled the country, the overwhelming majority to the United States. Small-scale pogroms had occurred in Europe for centuries. One of the most infamous occurred at York in England in 1190. They were particularly common in rural Poland and Russia, and their frequency increased when Alexander III came to the throne in 1881 but it was under his successor, the last tsar, Nicholas II, that the full terror of mass pogroms was launched. Not only were Nicholas II and Alexander III rabid anti-semites themselves but they were convinced that stirring up anti-semitism would deflect criticism of their increasingly ineffective rule. In fact what it did was provide a reservoir of disillusioned Jews in which radical groups could trawl. Leon Trotsky, Rosa Luxemburg, Grigory Zinoviev, Emma Goldman and a host of others were drawn into revolutionary struggle. One secret police report from 1905 showed that of 5,246 dissidents under surveillance in their region 1,676 were Jewish.

Although pogroms in Russia were not new, those that began at Kishinev on Easter Day were notable not just for the numbers of men, women and children massacred and driven into exile but for the more or less open support given by the government. Ludicrous fabrications about the ritual murder of Christian children were printed in the heavily controlled newspapers. The interior minister, Vyacheslav Plehve, claimed that in parts of Russia up to 90 per cent of the revolutionaries were Jewish, and on his specific orders the police stood idly by as the bloodbaths commenced. (At least this is the commonly accepted version of events. Some recent studies have suggested that, despite the tsar's personal anti-semitism, the role of the state in instigating the pogroms has been greatly exaggerated. Evidence of Plehve's involvement, for example, has been exposed as 'bogus' according to Niall Ferguson, who adduces Plehve's cordial meeting with Zionist leader Theodore Herzl as evidence.) Whatever the truth, some Jewish activists were no admirers of the interior minister, and in July 1904 one of them, a leader of the Social Revolutionaries named Evno Azef, took his revenge by ordering Plehve's assassination.

The word pogrom is usually thought of in its original context of attacks on Jews in eastern Europe and Russia (pogrom is Russian for devastation), but it can be used for any violent attack on a minority community. Blacks in America were repeatedly subject to pogroms. The Tulsa pogrom of 1921 was one example but by no means the only one. Another took place on the site of the 'prehistoric' city of Cahokia, now East St Louis, Illinois, in July 1917. Local employers had been importing southern blacks to take on the most menial jobs, paying wages that no white man would accept. In the East St Louis Massacre white mobs rampaged through black areas torching homes and dragging men, women and children on to the street where they were shot, stoned, beaten and lynched. Local newspapers reported 200 deaths, although the true number is probably around half of that. Afterwards 7,000 blacks fled across the Mississippi, most never returning to the remains of their homes.

When Roosevelt I denounced the 1903 Russian pogroms his secretary of state urged caution, pointing out the record number of lynching in the United States in the same year. The pogroms against Jews in Russia were very different to the American pogroms that occurred at around the same time; their scale was usually much larger and in Russia they were sanctioned and even encouraged by the state. More fundamentally pogroms in America conflicted with the official ideology of democracy; by contrast in Russia they reinforced the ideology of autocracy by stressing the purity of Mother Russia. American pogroms have been largely written out of American history because they contradict modern perceptions of what America ought to have been. It is also true that they really were genuine, albeit not infrequent, aberrations. When Ulysses S. Grant issued his General Order No. 11 expelling Jews from Kentucky, Tennessee and Mississippi it was revoked within weeks by Abraham Lincoln. Grant himself explained away his order as an exigency of war, and when the issue was raised in his 1868 presidential campaign he went on the offensive by assailing the contemporary anti-semitism of Tsar Alexander II. Although pogroms and lynchings received local support, and even the tacit support of individual members of Congress, they were never part of the ideology of democracy. To turn anti-semitism into holocaust needs not just the apparatus of autocracy but the ideology of autocracy.

By 1905 the worst of the Russian pogroms were over, but a series of other events in that year were a portent of what was to come. The disastrous Russo-Japanese War, Bloody Sunday, mutiny on the battleship *Potemkin*, widespread peasant uprisings, strikes in St Petersburg organised by Trotsky's workers' soviet, the assassinations of a grand duke and of the Moscow governor, and violent demonstrations throughout Russia's western empire all showed the pressures tsarism was under. The reaction of Nicholas was to give way one minute and then dogmatically reassert his autocratic rights the next. He agreed to set up a parliament, the Duma, with what was for Russia a fairly extensive male electorate, but then declared that his 'supreme autocratic power' included the power to dissolve any Duma that did not agree with him. The first lasted just seventy-three days before Nicholas declared that proposals like universal suffrage and parliamentary responsibility for ministers were just too absurd to be worth discussing.

All the time Nicholas continued with his imperial ambitions, sending thousands of peasants to continue the colonisation of Siberia and sending thousands of troops to suppress a large-scale Muslim uprising in central Asia in 1916. More crucially he started playing politics in the Balkans in pursuit of the centuries-old Russian dream of restoring Constantinople to Christendom. The result was the First World War.

When Russia stumbled into the First World War Nicholas II was still the master of an enormous empire, while scattered across the world were a few fanatical misfits of interest to nobody other than the secret police – men like Lenin, Trotsky and Stalin.

The Russian army marched into Prussia, defeating the German army at the battle of Gumbinnen and forcing the Germans to withdraw troops from the western front at a time when a quick victory there seemed to be within their grasp. From then on, however, Russia was on the defensive, and as the war muddled on Russian casualties mounted alarmingly; they may have exceeded 5 million before the war ended. Disillusion with the war combined with severe food shortages in urban areas came to a head in St Petersburg – recently renamed Petrograd to sound less German (just as German shepherds were renamed alsatians in Britain and the royal family became Windsors). In February 1917 a mutiny in the very guards regiments that had inflicted Bloody Sunday on the workers just a few years earlier signalled the end of the Romanov regime. Nicholas found himself completely isolated as his ministers were arrested by the Duma. In March 1917 he abdicated and was arrested the next day. Little more than a year later he was dead.

When the sixteen-year-old Michael Romanov had been given the throne 304 years earlier hardly anyone had expected him to keep it for long, let alone pass it on to generation after generation, but by the time Nicholas II abdicated in favour of his brother the Grand Duke

Michael the credibility of the Romanov autocracy had completely gone. Michael declined the honour thrust upon him. A provisional government under Prince Lvov took over, and as it promised to fight the war more vigorously it was welcomed by the western allies who prepared to carry on as if nothing had changed. But the end of the Romanovs had in reality changed everything, because they were the state; they personified the ideology of autocracy, and there was no substitute ideology ready to take its place.

The problem that now became apparent was that centuries of autocracy had left a nation with no means of changing to anything else. The result was turmoil. Aristocratic and what might be called 'bourgeois' factions scrambled for parliamentary or extra-parliamentary power, while on the streets and in the factories workers' soviets seized control more or less spontaneously. In some parts of the country peasants turned on their landlords, and in others they continued as if nothing had changed; while the army and navy were racked with intrigue, both in the upper echelons and among the conscripts at the bottom.

Nobody was more surprised by the speed with which events unravelled than the Bolsheviks. As late as January 1917 Lenin was publicly admitting that his generation might not 'see the decisive battles of the coming revolution'. Just a month later the tsar was overthrown. Most of the Bolshevik leaders were in exile – Lenin in Geneva, Trotsky in New York, Stalin and many others in Siberia. Although they all wanted to return immediately the general confusion often made this difficult. The Okhrana had been monitoring Trotsky's activities in New York, and persuaded the British authorities to detain him for a month when his ship stopped off in Halifax, Nova Scotia. The degree of confusion was illustrated when, on their way back from Siberia, Stalin's comrades stopped to send a telegram of congratulations to the man they thought had become the new tsar, the Grand Duke Michael. Heaven knows what the grand duke would have thought on receiving such a message from an obscure bunch of revolutionaries who were supposedly dedicated to the complete destruction of everything he had ever stood for.

Stalin arrived in Petrograd before many of the other Bolshevik leaders. He was soon busy making alliances among the many jostling left-wing factions, trying to find ways of exercising influence on and within the new constitutional institutions. Stalin was conscious that the Bolsheviks had only limited support among the numerous socialist and anarchist groups. The Social Revolutionaries were already edging their way into the corridors of power, and Stalin wanted to get in on the act. When Lenin arrived (courtesy of transport arranged by the German Kaiser, who was anxious to sow further discord), he soon put a stop to any suggestion of the Bolsheviks engaging in constitutional politics.

The chaos continued through the spring and summer of 1917. Peasant uprisings and industrial strikes disrupted production. The provisional government tried to appease the left by appointing a former Social Revolutionary leader, Alexander Kerensky, as prime minister in Lvov's place. (Lvov, in a move that exemplified the massive differences that still existed between political life in Russia and the west, was moved sideways to become the head or procurator of the Russian Orthodox Church.) Another Social Revolutionary was appointed minister of agriculture in an ineffective attempt to stop the increasingly bloody peasant unrest. The Bolsheviks tried to organise a coup and failed, Lenin escaping back into exile; then the right under General Kornilov tried to do the same, and also failed. Finally, after suffering further defeats in the war against Germany, the army turned against the provisional government, and when in October Trotsky stormed the Winter Palace, supported by sailors from the Kronstadt naval base, the government's only support was a regiment of women soldiers. In a sign of how the twentieth century would develop Kerensky was spirited away by American government agents: he spent the rest of his life lecturing in America on what might have been.

The October Revolution gave Lenin power but, like Michael Romanov three centuries earlier, it was by no means clear that he could keep it, let alone pass it on to his successors. In December elections were held in which the Bolsheviks gained just one in seven of the Constitutional Assembly seats. Lenin's response was in the grand tradition of Russian autocracy: he closed down the assembly and made sure there would be no more free elections. He justified his actions by reference to the concept of the 'dictatorship of the proletariat', which was fundamental to Bolshevik thinking. The Bolsheviks were convinced that the 'science' of history, as revealed by Marx, put their cause beyond debate. To oppose them was akin to blasphemy; indeed the self-righteousness certainty of men like Lenin and Trotsky was remarkably similar to that of the early American puritans, albeit deriving from a different gospel.

According to Lenin, 'The scientific concept of dictatorship means nothing else but this: power without limit, resting directly upon force, restrained by no laws, absolutely unrestricted by rules.' The tsars could have said just the same about autocracy. For the Bolsheviks the dictatorship belonged not to a single autocrat but, at least in theory, to a class; in practice the dictatorship of the proletariat meant the dictatorship of the Bolshevik party. As Rosa Luxemburg put it, Lenin's communism was simply tsarist autocracy turned upside down. Trotsky insisted on the right of the party to overrule the decisions of elected representatives because the mission that history had given the party could not be subject to 'the passing moods of worker democracy'. The population at large simply could not be trusted to make the right decisions. It was exactly the same argument that Senator Beveridge was making about the inhabitants of the Philippines at the same time.

In August of the next year the Social Revolutionary Dora Kaplan tried to assassinate Lenin, and the Red Terror was launched; thousands were arrested, some were released or, like the former prime minister Prince Lvov, escaped into exile, but hundreds simply 'disappeared' as the Bolsheviks strengthened their hold.

The most significant internal threats to the new regime were the various armies put together by the supporters of the old regime. The White Armies (so named to distinguish them from Trotsky's Red Army) fought a vicious civil war, and managed to outdo the Reds in terms of sheer terror. Slowly the Bolshevik forces gained the upper hand, helped by the errors of their enemies, by the unpopularity of the *ancien régime* among the peasants, industrial workers and conscript soldiers, and by the Whites' insistence that Russia's old imperial frontiers had to be re-established, which alienated many of the subject peoples of the empire who were starting to dream of freedom.

The Bolsheviks also faced important external threats. France moved its navy to the Black Sea (where it was joined by ships of the US navy) and pumped in cash subsidies to the White Army leaders. Japan invaded in the east, hoping to grab territory in Siberia. British troops landed in Murmansk and Archangel with Canadian and Italian support. The two biggest threats came from America and Germany; by far the most immediate was Germany, with whom Russia was still theoretically at war.

The new regime had a novel approach to international relations. Trotsky, as commissar of foreign affairs, published all the secret correspondence of the tsarist regime, made a few proclamations and then announced he was shutting up shop and everyone else should just leave Russia alone. Life was not that easy, however. The Germans had a massive army on Russia's western frontier, which the Red Army had no hope of defeating. In the Treaty of Brest-Litovsk the Bolsheviks were forced to give up a vast amount of territory that contained around a third of the empire's people and of its industrial capacity.

American intervention was of less immediate impact than German but in the long term was more important. What distinguished the US position from that of most other governments was its motivation. Germany and Japan wanted territory. France wanted its money back: the French had invested heavily in Russia under Nicholas II. Britain did not really know what it wanted but as the premier imperial power of the day knew it ought to want something. The American secretary of state, Robert Lansing, knew exactly what he wanted: Russia under the Bolsheviks was a cesspit of anarchy and revolution from which America was determined to save not just the rest of the world but the Russian people themselves. The American response to the October Revolution was overwhelmingly ideological, more so than that of many other nations, and reflected the bitter ideological battles that had been and were being fought within the United States.

Come the Revolution

The Russian Revolution is often portrayed as the event that determined the ideological battle lines for the twentieth century. In reality the roots of the cold war can be found much earlier – in the period of soul-searching and ideological turmoil that ran from the American Civil War to the First World War. No single event made it inevitable that the world would divide into 'capitalist' and 'communist' spheres. That it did divide was as much owing to developments in America as to those in Russia.

Through much of the world labour unrest and socialist agitation accompanied industrialisation. With hindsight it may seem obvious that revolution was most likely in an autocracy like Russia, where there were no representative institutions to channel protests, rather than in countries where socialist groups could enter the electoral process and disgruntled workers could join legitimate trade unions. At the time, however, it was thought that revolution was far more likely in the advanced industrial nations, which lacked the conservative peasant masses and police state apparatus of tsarist Russia. In particular it seemed to many Americans that their country was ripe for revolution.

There were Marxists in America but the labour movement was never as ideological as Russia's – as evidenced by one of the first trade unions, an Irish secret society with the distinctly un-Marxist name of the Molly Maguires. The Molly Maguires organised a series of strikes in the Pennsylvania coalfields that turned violent, and in 1877 nineteen members were hanged for the murder of a mine owner. The next year twenty-five people were killed in the same state by troops trying to crush a national railway strike. Railway workers continued to be in the vanguard of the workers' struggles, and the quaintly named Knights of Labor organised a series of strikes against the railroad interests of Jay Gould.

As the power of the robber barons in America grew so did protests against them by their workers. Strikes at Carnegie's steelworks and Gould's Missouri-Pacific railroad erupted into violence, leaving many dead and suggesting parallels with the later events in St Petersburg. But again with hindsight it is clear that there was never any real prospect of the oligarchs being overthrown in a Bolshevik-style revolution. Economic, political and social conditions were all very different, and the American left threw up no leaders as unscrupulous in their pursuit of power as Lenin.

In 1883 an event occurred in America that created ripples of anger similar to Bloody Sunday in Russia. Police shot dead four striking workers in Chicago and the next day, when police tried to break up an anarchist meeting in the city, a bomb exploded in the Haymarket killing six policemen. The police opened fire in return. The Haymarket Affair became notorious not just for the deaths on both sides but for the subsequent court case. A number of anarchists were convicted and hanged for the bombing, despite the prosecution conceding that some had been nowhere near the protest. The judge made plain that their real crime was ideological; they were tried for being anarchists.

The Haymarket Affair grabbed the headlines and entered into the demonology of both left and right – as evidence of the vicious anti-worker prejudice of the ruling class and as evidence of the murderous fanaticism of anarchists and socialists. It was just one example of the violence of the period. Another took place in 1891, when Henry Frick, boss of the Carnegie Steel Company, broke a Pennsylvania strike of coke oven workers who were demanding an eight-hour day. Buoyed by his success, the next year he ordered pay cuts ranging from 18 to 26 per cent, and the subsequent strike developed into full-scale gun battles between workers and 300 armed Pinkerton detectives hired by the employers and supported by the state militia. Seven strikers and three strike-breakers were killed, but it was not the dead strikers who hit the headlines – rather the failed attempt by anarchists to assassinate Frick. In the wake of the adverse press coverage the strike rapidly collapsed.

A fundamental difference between social unrest in Russia and America was that because the American population was largely literate the press played a crucial role in political life; controlling the press meant one controlled events. In Russia on the other hand, where the population was largely illiterate and the press insignificant, news spread by word of mouth and was far harder for the authorities to control. American labour protests often had significant local support but, largely through their control of the media, the oligarchs were usually able to contain that support by picturing union activists as terrorists: anarchist aliens posing a threat to the very fabric of American life. Press barons like William Randolph Hearst exercised the sort of power without responsibility that the proponents of autocracy like Konstantin Pobedonostsev were warning against on the other side of the world.

The next big confrontation was in 1894, the year that the last tsar, Nicholas II, mounted the Russian throne. It started with a strike at the Pullman railway company's manufacturing plant near Chicago. The American Railroad Union, led by the socialist Eugene Debs, called for a boycott of Pullman's sleeping cars on the nation's railroads, and within a week 125,000 railroad workers downed tools in sympathy. The government swore in 3,400 special deputies and then, at the railway owners' request, President Cleveland overruled the Illinois governor to draft in federal troops to break the strike. The employers also gained a federal court injunction that ended the sympathy strike. Eventually the Pullman strikers were starved into submission and many railway workers were blacklisted.

The Pullman strike was far from being the last major labour dispute of the era but it signalled that ultimate victory in the battle between organised labour and corporate power would belong to the corporations, which were coming to dominate American economic life. The picture was very different in Russia where industrialisation and its concomitant industrial relations issues were far behind America. Although there had been industrial unrest in the mid-1880s, most famously at the Morozov cotton mills, the first real industrial strike in Russia was the year after the Pullman boycott. The textile workers of St Petersburg were incited to strike when a three day unpaid holiday was imposed upon them. The strike rapidly assumed a political nature, with one of the main organisers being Lenin, who the previous year had returned from a gathering of Russian revolutionaries in Switzerland to set up the Union of Struggle for the Liberation of the Working Class (not for him such quaint names as the Knights of Labor or the Molly Maguires). The St Petersburg strike was quickly crushed, with hundreds of arrests (including Lenin), but it was the germ from which the Russian Revolution would grow.

The St Petersburg strike showed the tsarist regime hitting out in its old-established ways – Lenin, for example, was dispatched into temporary exile – but faced with a new breed of opponent that it simply did not understand. The gulf between tsar and industrial worker was more than unbridgeable; they lived almost literally in two different worlds. By contrast, in America oligarchs and workers lived if not side by side at least in close proximity, and the Pullman strike demonstrated that the American establishment had a much clearer idea of what it was facing and how to overcome dissent. The strike illustrated the increasing tendency of the US government to offer employers moral support and military force, and the willingness of the judiciary to issue injunctions – which became a prime weapon against American unions. Because the ideology of democracy was so widely accepted, the injunctions were usually obeyed even when not enforced by police or military power.

The key difference between the left in Russia and America was that the left in Russia was fighting against the prevailing ideology, while the left in America thought it was fighting for it. The Russian left was determined to overthrow the existing system and introduce something totally new: the apparatus of the state – tsar, governors, judiciary, oligarchs – was rotten and had to be totally destroyed. The idea that the workers' struggle might be restrained by a judicial injunction would have been laughable. The American left, on the other hand, was fighting to cleanse the existing system and restore what it believed had been there before. Corporate power was recognised as something new, and the left believed that fighting against it was to follow in the footsteps of those who had fought to establish America as the bastion of freedom and democracy.

A left-wing commentator wrote a revealing description of the socialists who made Milwaukee for a time one of the most efficiently run cities in America: 'They lived and believed the great American ideals, enriching them with work, labor, and sacrifice, and practical accomplishment. They aren't in the history books we give our children, but it is barely possible that they are a nobler monument to democracy as well as socialism than all the plutocrats we have found it so fatally easy to admire.'

If the institutions of democracy made it easier for the left to organise in America than in Russia, it also made it easier for their opponents to control them. There was no need for an Okhrana secret police to uncover the names of dissidents. In 1909 an American soldier named William Buwalda was court-martialled and sentenced to five years in Alcatraz (later commuted to ten months). His offence was to have attended, along with 5,000 members of the general public, a public meeting in San Francisco addressed by the anarchist Emma Goldman, and to have been seen to applaud her speech. Crimes such as this did not require myriads of secret policemen to uncover.

That is not to say that there was no secret police in America but, characteristically, the American Okhrana was a private corporation. Where the Okhrana owed its loyalty to the Russian autocracy, the Pinkertons owed theirs to the emerging corporate plutocracy. Allan Pinkerton arrived in the United States as a political refugee, having hurriedly left Scotland the day after his marriage to escape arrest for his activities in the populist Chartist movement. Settling in Chicago, he set up the US Secret Service during the civil war and after the war put his expertise at the service of the new oligarchs. An early success for Pinkerton was to infiltrate the Irish trade union movement, the Molly Maguires. Working for the Philadelphia and Reading railroad, Pinkerton's detectives produced evidence that apparently proved that leaders of the movement had been responsible for murdering the owners of a number of small mining companies, coincidentally competitors of Pinkerton's employer. In a somewhat dubious trial the Molly Maguires' leader John Kehoe was one of those found guilty and sentenced to death (although receiving a posthumous pardon from the governor of Pennsylvania more than a century later). When Allan Pinkerton died in 1884 his two sons carried on the company. The presence of Pinkerton undercover agents and armed militia became a feature of industrial unrest well into the next century.

Labour unrest continued on a significant scale, but the response of the political establishment was far more subtle that that of the tsars. As the robber barons and their corporate successors became more firmly embedded into mainstream American society, their worst excesses caused increasing embarrassment. In 1902 a massive strike by anthracite miners was ended when President Roosevelt turned on the mine-owners and threatened to send in troops to take over their mines. Roosevelt's actions illustrate why socialist revolution was never likely in America. Although the robber barons controlled great swathes of the economy and pulled the strings of many political puppets, they never had a monopoly of power. Four-yearly presidential elections and the fragmented nature of power in the federal system ensured that there were always areas they could not control, and there always existed the possibility that the oligarchs' candidates would not achieve the highest office. Vast sections of the American population had no sympathy with striking industrial workers, but equally had little sympathy for their bosses.

Communism Arrives

The same was true in Russia, where the mass of the population may have been fed up with the Romanovs but there was no widespread yearning for a Marxist revolution. The Bolsheviks emerged victorious from the scrum of political factions and sects that were left to scramble for power after the abdication of the tsar thanks to two factors above all: luck and Lenin. Most of the other groups believed that someone else would carry them to power. Anarchists and socialists thought that if they created the right conditions a peasant revolution would erupt more or less spontaneously and reshape society. Many on the far right thought that the soldiers and sailors of the imperial army and navy would allow themselves to be used to impose the will of their nominal commanders. The liberals had an awesome faith in the electorate – however limited in size – and the magical power of the ballot box. What Lenin almost uniquely grasped was that power belonged to whichever group could seize it and hold it while remaining beholden to no one else. What was needed for the Bolsheviks to come out on top was iron discipline within the party and a total disregard for everyone outside.

In 1903 Lenin had split his party by insisting that the only way to achieve their objectives was to create a core of professional revolutionaries inside Russia. The distinctive feature of what came to be called Leninism was the belief that the workers would never mount a revolution on their own; they needed a 'vanguard' to show them the way. And once the revolutionary situation arrived the vanguard would need to assume political control in order to ensure that the workers achieved true socialist awareness.

Although the Bolsheviks described themselves as the vanguard of the proletariat, other groups were often first to the barricades. The Kronstadt sailors were led by an anarchist, Yarchuck, and anarchists were often in the thick of the fighting. What the Bolsheviks had (and what the anarchists lacked almost by definition) was discipline. Lenin was single-mindedly obsessed with gaining and keeping power. Anyone in his way had to be destroyed, whether tsarist reactionary or anarchist revolutionary. Emma Goldman, the American anarchist leader, who met Lenin after he had established himself in power, was appalled at his persecution of the anarchists who had spearheaded the original revolution. She travelled to Russia in 1919 after being deported from the United States, expecting to find a hero. After meeting him she wrote, 'Free speech, free Press, the spiritual achievements of centuries, what were they to this man? A Puritan, he was sure his scheme alone could redeem Russia. Those who served his plans were right, the others could not be tolerated.' Goldman was right to describe Lenin as a 'Puritan': he had the same certainty of purpose and disdain for human weakness as the American Puritans who had been equally determined to create a promised land. She found a man whose morality had more in common with the Machiavellian princes of Muscovy than she had expected. The difference between Lenin and his tsarist predecessors was not what he did but why he thought he was doing it: his ideology.

Lenin represented an ideology as different from his predecessors as the ideology of the early Puritans was from modern corporate America, but America's ideology changed by evolution not revolution. America had been able to collapse into civil war with both sides claiming to be fighting for their democratic rights. The ideology of democracy was so widely accepted that ideology itself played an almost insignificant part in political debate; in Russia ideology was fundamentally important. The difference between the two societies is vividly illustrated in the books that drove them to action.

Karl Marx and Friedrich Engels published the Communist Manifesto in 1848, four years before Marx became a foreign correspondent of the *New York Tribune* and Harriet Beecher Stowe published *Uncle Tom's Cabin*, the book Abraham Lincoln claimed had 'made' the American Civil War. It would be hard to find two works more different. Stowe's graphic depiction of the horrors of slavery struck an instant chord around the world, and within ten years 2 million copies had been sold. Largely devoid of analysis, the novel left its readers rocked with tears and anger, determined to abolish a vile stain on the surface of their society, but content once the aberration of slavery had been swept away to leave the underlying economic and racial structures untouched. The impact of the Communist Manifesto was far less immediate but, its partisans would argue, far more profound. Where Harriet Beecher Stowe gave the world tears, Karl Marx gave it theories.

The core of Marxist theory was the view that history was a sequence of economic stages – slavery, feudalism, capitalism, communism – each leading inevitably on to the next. Capitalism, with its concentration of power and wealth in the hands of the few and increasing exploitation of the many, was destined to be destroyed by a revolution of the industrial proletariat, which in turn would lead to a dictatorship of the working class ushering in a socialist society of genuine equality and dignity for all. Once the workers had developed a state of true 'socialist awareness' the state would wither away, and society would need to evolve no more.

Marx outlines his theory in his most important work, *Das Kapital*, published in 1867. Again its initial impact was far from dramatic. It was two years before a Russian translation appeared, and Marxist ideology seemed so ludicrous that the tsarist regime did not bother censoring it. Twenty years later Marx was being widely read by students and the new intelligentsia but by hardly anyone else, and the Okhrana still regarded the various Marxist groups as light relief compared with the bomb-hurling anarchists. Not until 1896 was there any real indication of what the future might hold; in that year textile workers in St Petersburg went on strike, and among the strike's organisers was the twenty-six-year-old Marxist Vladimir Ilyich Ulyanov: Lenin.

Lenin was one of several pseudonyms used by one of the twentieth century's most remarkable men. It derived from the mighty Lena river, which had captured Lenin's imagination in one of his exiles. He was the son of a schoolteacher father and social worker mother. The family member who most influenced the young Lenin was his brother, who tried to assassinate the tsar in 1887; he failed and was executed. Lenin was soon following in his brother's footsteps with far greater success – a professional revolutionary travelling throughout Europe to spread the message of Marx. In 1890 at the age of just twenty he translated the Communist Manifesto into Russian.

Following the publication of works like the Communist Manifesto and *Das Kapital*, Social Democratic parties imbued with the ideology of Marxism sprang up across Europe and North America. Over time most of these parties gradually changed their objectives, and by 1914 when the First World War started they were more concerned with the reform of capitalism than its overthrow. There were exceptions to this trend, the most important being the Russian Social Democratic and Labour party dominated by Lenin. To emphasise its difference from the reformist parties elsewhere it adopted a new name – the Communist party.

Russia now had two competing ideologies: autocracy and communism. After the revolution these two ideologies merged to create a form of society radically different from anything that had gone before, and yet one that on closer inspection had characteristics that had been there for centuries: a single all-powerful autocrat, a disdain for private property and an imperialism that was to be uncannily similar to its predecessor's. America after the civil war had also witnessed the fusion of two ideologies – its century-old democracy and the new corporate capitalism – but the process was much less dramatic. The society of the robber barons was as different (and as similar) to the society of the Pilgrim Fathers as Stalin's Russia was to Ivan the Terrible's but the changes went almost unremarked. The Bolsheviks claimed to have changed everything and yet much stayed the same; the new American oligarchs claimed to have changed nothing and yet a new way of life had emerged. The souls of both nations continued ever changing and ever constant.

The Bolsheviks set out to destroy not just the Romanov regime but also the whole apparatus of autocracy: they believed that the working class, with the Communist party in the vanguard, would transform every aspect of Russian society, eventually creating the world's first genuine democracy. But Lenin recognised that the socialist nirvana could not be created overnight and that to gain and keep control the Bolsheviks would need many of the same tools as their predecessors: a strong army, an all-seeing secret police and an absence of free elections. He also grasped the importance of the tools of the future: one of the key events of the Russian Revolution was Lenin's radio broadcast to the nation on 12 November 1917, which set the stage for the mass propaganda campaigns that would follow under Stalin.

Lenin realised that even if he crushed all internal opposition his regime would be under constant attack from outside, so he needed to spread his message of revolution. By its very nature Marxism was global. Whereas the Romanovs believed God had entrusted them with a mission to forever expand their empire, Lenin believed that history itself had ordained that the society he was creating would expand to cover the whole world; all societies would pass through feudalism and capitalism to arrive at his doors. Right from the beginning the Bolsheviks were committed to spreading their authority far beyond the borders of Russia, a commitment fulfilled by Stalin's Red Army at the end of the Second World War. It is open to debate whether the train of history set in motion by Lenin, Trotsky and the other Bolshevik founding fathers was bound to follow the track that ended in Stalinism or whether it might, with different drivers, have turned off, but the fact is that Stalinism is where it ended up. The ideologies of communism and autocracy merged to become a new force, and a new force that was inherently imperialist.

Exactly the same sort of merging of ideologies – in this case democracy and corporate capitalism – happened in the United States, but with one massive difference. Unlike communism the new ideology across the Atlantic had never proclaimed its intention to destroy the old; indeed it had never proclaimed itself at all. In the half-century or so after the American Civil War an ideology arose that was to shape the world, and yet did so in such an apparently organic way that few recognised what was happening. Even today the ideology has no commonly recognised name.

The evolution of the ideology of democracy was the most important philosophical development in American history. The evolution of the concept of the corporation was almost as fundamental. The emergence of the corporation as a legal entity with unlimited scope and limited liability made possible a form of imperialism that would change the face of the world.

Corporatism: A Digression

It is possible to understand the history of Russian imperialism without understanding the ideology of communism in any depth. Although communist imperialism was not the same as tsarist imperialism, the fundamentals were not dissimilar: they both relied primarily on crude military force, they both served to magnify the authority of the autocrat, they were both opportunistic in scope but particularly fixated on Poland and the west, they both appropriated territory and property in the name of the state. In the end communist imperialism proved to be a transitory phenomenon with little lasting impact, just one more vagary in the history of the Russian empire. By contrast American imperialism in the century between the Spanish-American War and the invasions of Iraq changed almost beyond recognition, and it is impossible to understand this evolution without understanding the ideology of what might be called, for want of a better term, corporatism.

The period of the robber barons after the American Civil War resembled the Russia of today, with the collapse of old certainties, corrupt government and accelerating technological change making possible the sudden emergence of fantastically wealthy individuals dominating economic and political life. The difference is that today's Russia has jettisoned the ideology of communism without yet developing a universally accepted alternative. In America the ideology and institutions of democracy, although they had failed to prevent a murderous civil war, survived. The institutions continued almost unchanged to the present day, but the ideology underlying them was about to develop in a radical new direction.

European historians have generally regarded the First World War as the great watershed that changed world history for ever. Equally plausible is the claim that the American Civil War marked the beginning of the new age. In May 1863, 3,000 Confederate cavalrymen destroyed a key northern 'asset' near Parkersburg, West Virginia. As flames from the appropriately named Burning Springs flared into the sky, the world witnessed for the first time oilwells and oil supplies on the front line of war. Not only was it a sign of technological change but of political and economic change, for with oil came the corporation.

Before the civil war America had been a land of local lords – southern planters, New England factory owners, New York merchants. Fifty years later the lords were not local but national, and after a further fifty years they were international. The social convulsions brought on by war, the construction of railways knitting the nation together and the economic potential of mass production set the stage for men to wield commercial power on an altogether larger scale – if the right tool could be found. That tool was the corporation.

In modern Russia that tool has arrived ready-made. Everyone knows what an oil company is, and so it was easy for unscrupulous men to carve oil companies out of the old communist structures. Earlier American oligarchs had to make it up as they went along.

Corporations had existed long before Rockefeller and Carnegie, but the robber barons married them to the ideology of democracy in a way unimaginable to the Founding Fathers. When limited liability companies were first proposed in England centuries before, the idea met enormous opposition. Until then all rights had been human rights and all rights implied corresponding responsibilities. The idea that a man could pass some of his rights to a legal abstraction, a corporation, and in doing so limit his own responsibilities, was totally alien. Only in the most exceptional circumstances would the monarch agree to a charter of incorporation, and then it was surrounded by a mass of conditions and was likely to be revoked at any moment. One such corporation, the East India Company, seemed to illustrate exactly the dangers that such charters were supposed to prevent, as it gobbled up territory in southern Asia in just the same way that the tsars were doing further north. It was the prospect of the company starting to throw its commercial weight around in the American colonies that tipped the colonists into revolt, as well as the company's tea into Boston Harbour.

The first stage on the road to the modern corporation was a minor legal development in medieval Europe that embodied a huge philosophical leap – the acceptance that a virtual object, a corporation, could have rights. It is difficult now to imagine a time when this was inconceivable, a time when all rights were human rights. Before the invention of the corporation people were fully responsible in law for their actions, whether they were acting as individuals or in a group. They could of course act in concert, but if someone else felt aggrieved about a group's actions their legal remedy was to sue the group's members. Treating the collective as a legal entity that could sue and be sued in its own right was an enormous leap forward, and one that immediately raised the question of what the entity's legal rights and responsibilities would be.

This question was answered in the next development: the concept of limited liability – the doctrine that a corporation's responsibilities could be more limited than its owners'. If I owe you £100 but only have £50 in the bank you can make me sell my belongings to give you your

£100. But if I create a corporation with limited liability and put £50 in its bank account then that is all you can get back; if my corporation owes you £100 then tough – you still only get £50 and I get to keep my belongings, because my liability is limited to the £50 I invested. The English parliament realised that giving corporations limited liability was a massive step, which created great danger for members of the public who might end up being owed money they could not collect. Parliament therefore made sure that these corporations were only created where there was a specific public benefit that could not be achieved in any other way; charters of incorporation severely limited what the corporations were allowed to do. At first the same philosophy was applied in America. It was a commonplace at the time of the American Rebellion that business should be the domain of entrepreneurs – men who were both owners and managers and who would take full responsibility for their actions. Only in very rare cases was it permissible for an activity to justify the creation of some other form of organisation in which individuals could limit their responsibilities behind the veil of incorporation.

Ted Nace, who saw the American Revolution primarily as an attack on the corporate power of the East India Company, has researched the fundamental changes in US political values since that time. The changes started soon after the United States was born and greatly alarmed many of the Founding Fathers. Nace quotes Thomas Jefferson, who spoke out towards the end of his life against the perils facing the new nation: 'I hope we shall crush in its birth the aristocracy of our monied corporations which dare already to challenge our government to a trial of strength.'

Up until the civil war charters of incorporation were still relatively rare and were granted by state legislators for very specific purposes, such as building a railway, and were always circumscribed by numerous conditions. Corporations were prohibited from doing anything not specifically allowed in their charter, and the charter itself was usually granted for a limited period. Corporations could only operate within the state where they were incorporated, and often the state legislature retained considerable powers to veto activities. In the half-century after the civil war these restrictions were swept away, and today's multipurpose corporations transformed commercial and political life.

The robber barons who came to dominate American industry realised that if the bothersome public benefit requirements could be stripped away the institution of the corporation would both shroud their activities from public view and allow them to raise large sums of money from investors, who were now freed from all responsibility for the consequences of their investment. The federal system of government proved ideally suited to implementing the oligarchs' agenda. Malleable legislators, particularly in New Jersey and Delaware, were persuaded to charter perpetual multipurpose corporations that allowed the oligarchs to do whatever they wanted for as long as they wanted. When other states refused to follow suit the oligarchs simply used their tame legislators in states like New Jersey to set up corporations there, with the power to take over corporations domiciled elsewhere.

The age of the robber barons only lasted thirty or forty years but it changed the face not just of America but of the world. History until the end of the civil war reflected social and economic currents ridden and occasionally diverted by powerful individuals. History was played out at the macro level or the micro: the story of Russia and America in the 1860s could be portrayed in macro terms as the forces of industrialisation undermining slavery and serfdom, or in micro terms as Abraham Lincoln and the Tsar Liberator 'making history'. The robber barons appeared on the stage as one more set of micro-characters 'making history', but they left behind them something altogether new – the corporation. From then on history was driven not just by great social forces and great historical figures but by inanimate legal abstractions that seemed to have acquired the ability to live for ever. Between macro and micro appeared something altogether new.

Quite distinct from the macro-historical forces of ideology, economics and technology and the micro-history of presidents and tsars, there sprang up a murky midi-history in which micro-characters, hidden away in the boardrooms of Standard Oil and US Steel, made decisions which collectively had macro-impacts. Not only did their businesses directly have an impact upon the way people lived but they often exercised real political power; at the turn of the century one wag commented that Standard Oil could do anything with the Pennsylvania state legislature except refine it.

Nowhere was the transition from micro to midi clearer than in the case of one of the most powerful but least known of the robber barons. Minor Cooper Keith's corporation was to wield political power more directly, and for longer, than almost any other. Like so many of his contemporaries Keith made his first fortune building railways; what was unusual is where he built them – south of the border in Central America. He and his brothers set out from New York to make their fortune in Costa Rica. Minor was the only one to survive the appalling conditions in which 4,000 men died building a railway from the capital San José to the Caribbean. The Costa Rican government defaulted on the loans made by British banks to build the railway, and Cooper managed to gain control not only of the railroad itself but 80,000 acres of adjacent land on which to establish banana plantations. He quickly realised that the real money was to be made by controlling the whole supply chain. After establishing the first steamship service carrying fruit from Central America to the United States, he bought out plantations in Panama and Colombia. In 1899 he merged his interests with the Boston Fruit Company, which dominated the fruit plantations of the West Indies, to form the United Fruit Company – the world's largest banana company, with plantations in Colombia, Costa Rica, Cuba, the Dominican Republic, Jamaica, Nicaragua and Panama. Soon the company controlled 75 per cent of banana sales in the United States and effectively controlled the governments of most of the 'banana republics' of Central America. Following the traditions of European royalty, he entered into the local aristocracy by marrying the daughter of the Costa Rican president.

In 1901 Cooper moved into the nation that was to become UFC's base and the archetypal banana republic: Guatemala. As in Costa Rica, Keith built a railway line from the capital to the coast and was given land alongside at ultra-low prices by the Guatemalan dictator, who also granted United Fruit the exclusive right to transport mail between Guatemala and the US and the contract to build telegraph lines alongside the railway. UFC gained control of virtually all means of transport and communications and charged a tariff on everything moving into and out of the country through its ports, including Guatemala's famous coffee.

Cooper Keith died in 1929 but his corporation carried on, becoming a symbol of American corporate imperialism at its crudest.

For the first time ever the pattern of human life ceased to be determined by human beings. Until then history had been a long succession of religious prophets and marauding warlords, of great thinkers and heroic martyrs, of generals and politicians. History had been made by kings and presidents, revolutionaries and despots. Underneath existed great substrata to be mined by myriads of specialists – economic historians, social historians, anthropologists, environmental historians, and so on – but when most people think about history they think about Julius Caesar or Napoleon, Abraham Lincoln or Catherine the Great. And they are right to do so: those are the figures who shaped the way people lived and died and whose legacies endured for centuries afterwards. Ask who in the first half of the nineteenth century had the greatest impact on life in the modern world and there could be interesting debates about the claims of, say, the warlord Napoleon Bonaparte or the inventor of the steam train George Stephenson. Ask the same question about the second half-century and the names of many of the contenders would be hidden behind the veils of corporations. American history books might still concentrate on Congress and the White House, but the reality is that most politicians have had far less impact on the way people live today than a host of forgotten figures whose names are recognised by virtually nobody, figures like morphine addict John Stith Pemberton.

Pemberton was just one of numerous small entrepreneurs who made a living after the civil war producing wine-based stimulants and headache remedies. In today's jargon the market leader was a man named Angelo Mariani, but Pemberton produced an adequate 'me-too' product that enjoyed limited success until, in 1886, Pemberton's home state of Georgia introduced prohibition, and he was forced to modify his formula. Pemberton's accountant suggested a new name for the new concoction based on the main ingredients: coca leaves and kola nuts. Pemberton's French Wine Coca became Coca-Cola. Almost certainly more people today can distinguish Coca-Cola from Pepsi-Cola than can distinguish Theodore Roosevelt from Franklin Roosevelt. Not only is Coca-Cola known to millions of people around the world who have never heard of either Roosevelt, but the impact of the Coca-Cola Corporation as a vector of American pervasiveness has been far stronger and longer lasting than that achieved by any single American president. Coca-Cola could not be further from the first corporate imperialists in Hawaii and the banana republics of Central America. It supports cultural and sporting events wherever it operates, has a rigorously enforced code of corporate ethics and is welcomed around the world. Nevertheless its ubiquitous brown mixture has displaced indigenous beverages, its operations across the globe have helped inculcate American corporate values and millions of dollars of profit have passed back to Atlanta, Georgia. Coca Cola might be said to represent the acceptable face of American imperialism, the face that to many demonstrates that 'corporate imperialism' is a myth.

The Coca-Cola Corporation of today would not have been possible if the lawyers employed by the robber barons had not invented the legal construct we know as the corporation; nor would it have been possible if the robber barons had remained predators perceived by the rest of society to be feasting on the wealth created by others: sooner or later populist politicians would have found a way of bringing them under public control. But wealth buys respectability. By the beginning of the twentieth century the robber barons were being transformed into captains of industry – perceived as serving the public rather than robbing it. Once more the railroads were in the forefront of this transformation. In 1906 Congress gave the Interstate Commerce Commission sweeping powers to inspect the railway corporations' accounts and fix prices. The measures were introduced to assuage popular anger over high fares and the preferential tariffs given to the most powerful corporate customers. It might be thought that the railroad magnates would have reacted in fury to proposals that today would be regarded as old-fashioned socialism, but by the time the measures came in the railway industry itself had changed. In 1883 railroad oligarch William Vanderbilt had famously declared that 'the public be damned!' Twenty years later the public pronouncements of the captains of the railway industry were very different. Now they too favoured reform, at least in public; in the corridors of Washington they were fighting to build in as many loopholes as possible. The new corporate captains had no desire to be forced into giving massive rebates to quasi-monopolists like Standard Oil nor to engage in cut-throat competition with each other; having established their place in society they much preferred the comforting support of the state to the unbridled brutality of the free market. The main beneficiaries of railroad regulation were the railroads – a debt they were to repay twelve years later when the government called upon them to help keep the world's greatest railway, the Trans-Siberian, out of the hands of Russian revolutionaries.

The First World War was a critical time in the evolution of corporatism, as the power of big business reached into the centre of government. The state took on enormous powers, with the War Industries Board introducing central planning on a massive, if hardly Bolshevik, scale. Woodrow Wilson's administration showed how corporatism had moved on from the crude corruption of the robber barons to something more recognisably modern. His most trusted advisor, and head of the War Industries Board, was not the creator of some great industrial monopoly but a Wall Street speculator, Bernard Baruch, who was to go on advising presidents for half a century. Baruch's board rammed through measures that dramatically increased US production, although its decision to regulate wholesale but not retail prices was a speculator's delight.

In almost every society the rich, like Baruch, find it easier to grasp the levers of power than the poor, but what was new in America is that increasingly it was not rich individuals that wielded power but corporations. At the beginning of the twentieth century, for example, the Southern

Pacific railroad, in the words of Hugh Brogan, 'ruled California as its private fief'. And because for corporations, unlike individuals, life can seem infinite, political power can persist for generations: Montana was run as a virtual colony of the Anaconda Copper Company for nearly a century.

Having established themselves in America after the civil war, it was a small step for the corporations to move on to the international stage and assume the role of the earlier filibusters. The individuals who went out to expand the empire now did so with the power of corporations behind them. Whereas Texas had been colonised by bands of settlers seeking a new life for themselves and their slaves, Hawaii was colonised by a small band of corporations seeking profits for their shareholders back home, much as India had been colonised by the East India Company. Minor Keith's operations in Central America provided an extreme example of the new model. In 1910 a group of armed filibusters sailed from New Orleans to Honduras and installed a new president. What differentiated this group from its predecessors was that it was organised by the United Fruit Company, which acted when the incumbent president refused to provide the corporation with tax breaks; the newly installed president gave the company a waiver from paying any taxes for twenty-five years.

More representative was the natural and perfectly legitimate expansion of corporations in search of new markets and cheaper resources, following the example of the gun-maker Samuel Colt. The oil corporations took the lead; by 1885, 70 per cent of Standard Oil's business was outside the US, and it even had its own intelligence service, but the company usually credited as the world's first multinational corporation was far more humble in its aspirations. In 1867, a decade after Colt's failed experiment in London, the sewing machine manufacturer Isaac Singer opened a factory in Scotland, just sixteen years after starting his operations in New York. The Singer Corporation established the model for swallowing up competitors and aggressively expanding overseas; in 1905 it absorbed its leading US rival and opened a second overseas plant in Russia. By the Second World War it had plants in France and Italy and had been joined by a host of well-known American firms. The car industry was one of the first to be dominated by US corporations, like Ford, which opened its first foreign factory in England in 1911, and General Motors, whose cars started rolling off its Danish assembly line in 1924. It is estimated that in 1916, 55 per cent of the world's cars were Model T Fords. After the First World War the historic pattern of foreigners investing more in America than Americans invested abroad was reversed as US corporations expanded into overseas markets.

By achieving a commanding position in foreign markets, American firms established the basis for a new type of imperialism, but an imperialism rooted firmly in the imperialism of earlier centuries. Spanish Louisiana in the quarter century after the American Revolution provides striking parallels to modern corporate imperialism: American settlers moved in and took over much of the commerce of the colony producing and exporting such staples as tobacco, wheat, corn, whiskey and beef. Once in command of the economy the colony would almost inevitably become part of the formal American empire. The same happened time after time until, after the annexation of Hawaii, corporatism entered into the nation's ideological mix.

As corporations like Ford and GM became an established part of global commerce, the ideology of corporatism continued to evolve. The next philosophical development came in the form of a long series of stealthy steps that with hindsight appear as the most gigantic leap of all: the assertion that corporations not only have rights but have the same rights as human beings. Corporations, having been set up precisely to avoid the responsibilities attached to real people, and therefore being given only very limited rights to match their limited liabilities, have in America today assumed the whole panoply of rights guaranteed in the American constitution.

Again the seeds for this development first sprouted in the era of booming railroads. When they were created the railway companies were frequently given massive state support, including grants of public land or the right to compulsorily purchase private land. The quid pro quo was often that the rail corporations had to pay a special tax on that land. In a series of cases before the notoriously biased California courts in the 1870s the companies successfully argued that their 'rights' were being infringed by having to pay a higher rate of tax on their land than human beings. From this small beginning, known as the Santa Clara case, American business over the next century grew a whole array of quasi-human rights, many of which, to Europeans, appear quite bizarre.

To take just one example: on the afternoon of 25 March 1911 fire broke out in a shirt factory on Greene Street, New York; 275 young female workers, most of them recent immigrants, some just thirteen years old, were trapped inside. Passers-by were horrified to see girls leaping to their deaths from ninth-floor windows on to the street below; 146 charred and smashed bodies were eventually taken away. The fire precautions had been virtually non-existent, but in the subsequent trial the factory owners were found to have done nothing illegal. The enormous public outrage that followed led to the first serious attempts to impose safety regulations on American business. The policing of such regulations became increasingly effective over the decades, until sixty-seven years later the doctrine of corporatism halted the trend. In 1978 the Supreme Court held that raids on factories by health and safety inspectors contravened the US Constitution, and in particular the Fourth Amendment, which protected citizens from having their homes searched without a judicial warrant. The Supreme Court held that the health and safety of human beings had to take second place to the constitutional 'rights' of abstract corporate entities.

The fusion of the ideologies of democracy and corporatism is most clearly seen in the way corporations have been able to acquire political rights. One of the most startling features of US politics to Europeans is the vast amount of money that corporate America devotes to political campaigning. There is nothing new in this. In the 1880s and 1890s manufacturers' associations and individual oligarchs spent enormous sums lobbying to maintain and increase tariffs. Woodrow Wilson complained that 'The masters of the government of the United States are the combined capitalists and manufacturers of the United States.' Dwight Eisenhower warned in his farewell address, in January 1961, against the influence wielded by the 'military-industrial complex'. Today there are 60,000 professional corporate lobbyists in Washington DC, outnumbering the elected representatives a hundredfold. In campaigns on social issues, such as the environment and health, as well as on imperial political issues, including tariffs and protectionism, corporations have massively outspent opponents who rely on individual donors. Some states have tried to redress the balance by enacting laws regulating campaign finance, only to see their legislation struck down by the US Supreme Court on the grounds that corporations are merely exercising their 'right' to free speech under the First Amendment – an assertion that would have had the nation's Founding Fathers writhing in their graves.

In the topsy-turvy world of American jurisprudence the First Amendment right of free speech, designed to ensure that the voice of every citizen could be heard, had been turned on its head through what Nace calls a process of 'judicial yoga', to allow corporations to drown out the voices of their opponents in a sea of echoing dollars. Attempts to redress the balance have been repeatedly thwarted. When the Pacific Gas & Electricity Corporation included pamphlets with its monthly bills promoting the political views of its senior management, the state regulator instructed it to be more balanced by once a quarter also including pamphlets from consumer or environmental groups; the Supreme Court ruled that this violated the corporation's 'right' to free speech. In reality it was ruling not only that it was possible for a legal construct like a corporation to have human rights but that senior management had the exclusive authority to determine how those rights were exercised.

Just as the substance of tsarist autocracy re-emerged in the reigns of Lenin and Stalin, so the substance of early colonial feudalism re-emerged in the corporation. People often speak about 'corporations' or 'multinationals' as if the legal fiction that they are independent persons was real, but of course they are not; it is not legal constructs that wield corporate power but a very small number of people at the very top – feudal lords closer in spirit to Russian autocrats than American democrats, and who, at best, treat their serfs with the benevolent paternalism of the Tsar Liberator, Alexander II.

The ideology of corporatism is now so firmly embedded that people can say 'IBM believes' or 'Exxon's position is' without a second thought. But as Supreme Court conservative William Rehnquist said when dissenting from the Pacific Gas & Electricity decision, 'Extension of the individual's freedom of conscience decisions to business corporations strains the rationale of those cases beyond the breaking point. To ascribe to such artificial entities an "intellect" or "mind" for freedom of conscience purposes is to confuse metaphor with reality.' In reality IBM cannot 'believe' anything – its chief executive believes. Exxon cannot have a 'position' on any issue – but its head of public relations can. To say that a corporation holds a view gives that opinion a stamp of authority that endorsement by a faceless chief executive would never achieve. And yet for the chief executive of Exxon to say that his corporation has a 'view' on energy policy because it processes oil is as meaningless as saying that his car has a 'view' for the same reason.

Only humans can express opinions, and yet the US Supreme Court clearly thinks otherwise; so in practice do most people. It is taken for granted that corporate executives lobby not on behalf of their own selfish personal interests but on behalf of a wider constituency, their corporation, of which they for the time being are the unelected autocrats.

By the end of the twentieth century the power of oligarchs in Russia and America was not dissimilar, but in America this power was wielded with far more subtlety from behind the corporate burkha. The original robber barons had wielded their power with little finesse, grabbing riches for themselves like the oligarchs who plundered Russia when communism collapsed, but by the time the Soviet Union vanished in an explosion of greed American corporations had become good corporate citizens.

The rhetoric of class struggle, which was such a feature of political debate when the twentieth century began, had vanished by the time the century drew to a close. The fusion of corporatism and democracy had created a society where capitalism and freedom were seen as two sides of the same coin. For that fusion to occur it was necessary not only for the opposing view – that freedom and capitalism were incompatible – to be vanquished in America, but for it to be prevented from becoming the orthodoxy elsewhere. The contagion of socialism needed to be eradicated, if not by argument then by the Polar Bear expedition.

Ideologies in Transition

Those Russians struggling to overthrow the institutions of autocracy were ranged across an enormous political spectrum, from mild liberals to violent anarchists, but nearly all of them were closer to the ideals of the American Revolution than any of the tsars ever were. When the last tsar fell from power it might be supposed that the western world would therefore have joined in celebration. However, by the summer of 1918 new ideological battle lines were being drawn. As Nicholas and his family faced death in a remote town in Siberia they could have had no way of knowing that on the other side of the globe the curiously named Polar Bear expedition, 5,000 troops of the US 85th Division, 339th Infantry, were preparing to leave their base at Fort Custer, Michigan, bound for Archangel on Russia's Arctic coast. Four hundred of them would be killed as Russian militiamen, in revolution against tyrannical monarchy, battled soldiers of a nation that had been formed in revolution against tyrannical monarchy.

The Polar Bear expedition is one of those odd best-forgotten episodes more typical of British imperial history than American. The US troops tried to fight their way south in the middle of not just a Russian winter but a Russian Arctic winter, in pursuit of an objective nobody really understood. On Armistice Day 1918, when American forces elsewhere were celebrating the end of the First World War, the Polar Bear expedition was battling Bolshevik troops 200 miles south of Archangel. They fought on for another 40 miles until a Russian victory at Ust Padenga signalled the start of the US retreat. The oligarchs at home might have been keen on fighting Bolshevism, but a near mutiny in March 1919 prompted the expedition's withdrawal from Russia in June.

This was not the first western expedition to the region to end in disaster. In the spring of 1554 Russian fishermen encountered a ghostly ship far larger than any they had seen before. It was the *Bona Esparanza*, which had left England a year earlier to search for the Northeast Passage to China. On board were the frozen corpses of Sir Hugh Willoughby, a founder of the Muscovy Company, and his whole crew.

The Polar Bear expedition simply reinforced the ancient Russian fear of invasion. In the contest between Russian and American imperialism, which was to dominate the history of much of the twentieth century, round one had gone to Russia.

If the episode has any historical significance it is as a sign of the muddled thinking that characterised the period. The old-style US imperialism, which had been about grabbing territory for the nation's expansion, had ended with the conquest of the Philippines and Puerto Rico, but America's foreign policy had yet to evolve anything to replace it. Mexico was racked by civil war, which fifty years earlier would have been seen as an opportunity to annexe more territory, but despite pressure from American business interests, especially American mine owners, there was no appetite in Washington for intervention. The government's only action was to send General Pershing racing south in pursuit of the Mexican guerrilla leader, Pancho Villa, who had had the audacity to launch an attack across the border. The Polar Bear expedition was the same sort of raid, which gave the impression of action but had no realistic strategic objective.

A more significant, but in the event just as pointless, incursion occurred at the other end of the Russian empire, and here the influence of corporatism was crucial. Soon after the Polar Bear expedition was dispatched from Michigan a similar force of 5,000 US soldiers, commanded by the macabrely named General Graves, sailed from San Francisco for the Russian Pacific port of Vladivostok. There they joined 3,000 more troops drawn from the US army of occupation in the Philippines. Their objective was far clearer than the Polar Bear expedition's: they were to control the Trans-Siberian railway. After the United States entered the

First World War this railway had gained enormous strategic importance as the most effective way to get American military materiel to the Russian troops in Europe, and in the chaotic weeks before the Bolshevik revolution Kerensky's provisional government asked for US help to keep the Trans-Siberian railway open.

America's railroad magnates, who had pushed forward both the ideological frontiers of corporatism and the physical frontiers of their country, were running out of opportunities within the United States. In looking overseas their eyes had first turned south to Latin America, but they were well aware that the world's greatest prize was in Russia. The scale of the Trans-Siberian far eclipsed anything in North America, and by American standards the Russian technology was primitive; opportunity beckoned. Fired by the happy coincidence of patriotism and profit, the railroad bosses quickly arranged for 285 railway managers and engineers to be commissioned into the US army and sent to Siberia. However, by the time these men could make any contribution to the war effort the Bolsheviks had seized power in Petrograd, and the war was over. The last thing that the outside powers wanted now was for the Trans-Siberian to fall into communist hands, and so in April 1919 the United States, Japan and China carved up the eastern end of the railway between them. The US military contingent was far smaller than the Japanese, who had a much more direct interest in the region and took overall command. American troops found themselves not only fighting alongside the Japanese but under the direct command of Japanese officers as the two great imperial powers fought to crush the avowedly anti-imperialist Bolsheviks.

It would be wrong to paint a picture of a uniformly imperialist America launching the Polar Bear expedition and attacks on the Trans-Siberian railway in an all-out attempt to bring Russia into its own political sphere and destroy the spectre of communism at birth. Americans responded to the Russian Revolution in many different ways. Corporate bosses might have feared a society so clearly dedicated to their elimination, but feelings were equally strong on the other side. When the government chartered ships to carry arms and munitions to the White Army in Siberia, dockers in Seattle and San Francisco refused to load them, and in Seattle they beat up the non-unionised labour brought in to replace them. The innate decency of the American people led to widespread support for a programme of food aid organised by future president Herbert Hoover, and the lives of millions of starving Russians were saved in what Conquest has described as 'perhaps the most effective humanitarian effort ever launched'. (The programme succeeded despite Bolshevik obstruction; when it was over, Stalin – whom Lenin had instructed to keep an eye on the Americans – had all those Russians who had helped organise the programme arrested.)

To Lenin and his supporters around the world, the American military action in Siberia proved the inherently imperialist nature of the capitalist system in general and the American government in particular. But the picture was far more complicated than that. Despite calls for US troops to intervene more vigorously in what was effectively a Russian civil war, General Graves insisted that his troops were there solely to protect the railway. In resisting calls for an anti-communist crusade from US politicians and businessmen, supported by US diplomats in the field, and from other allied powers, especially Japan and Britain, Graves had one very powerful ally: President Woodrow Wilson.

Wilson epitomised the way in which the currents of democracy, corporatism and imperialism were swirling together to create new patterns in the politics of the day. A former president of Princeton University, he is now remembered as the architect of the League of Nations, predecessor of the UN, and a passionate anti-imperialist; but one of his first actions on taking power was to dispatch US marines to seize the Mexican port of Veracruz. During his presidency women obtained the vote, but apartheid in the south reached its high water mark. He was notoriously partial to the interests of bankers and corporate financiers, but created the Federal Trade Commission to regulate corporations engaging in interstate commerce.

The 1912 presidential election, in which Wilson came to power, was one of the most confused in US history. Former Republican president Theodore Roosevelt had fallen out with the incumbent Republican president William Howard Taft, when the latter refused to send American troops to intervene in the civil war in progress in Mexico. (Not that Taft was opposed in principle to foreign adventures; just before the election he sent US marines to invade Nicaragua, where they were to stay for eleven years.) Roosevelt stood as a candidate of his own 'Bull Moose' party, gaining more votes than Taft but letting in the Democratic candidate Woodrow Wilson.

The Democratic party was also split. A populist faction headed by a former presidential candidate demanded legislation to destroy the financial oligarchies of New York and Boston, punitive taxes on corporations and effective action to smash the monopolistic power of the trusts. Wilson had been governor of New Jersey, a state notorious for its corporatist sentiments, and wanted nothing to do with such dangerously anti-American sentiments. Similarly he had no time for those demanding justice for blacks. Brought up in the south during the civil war (his father had been a clergyman with the Confederate army), and owing his electoral success to southern support, he repaid his electoral debt by enforcing apartheid-like measures in large parts of the federal government. Hundreds of black functionaries were fired throughout the south. As Wilson's collector of internal revenue in Georgia explained, 'A Negro's place is in the cornfield.'

Wilson had far more sympathy with women than with the descendants of slaves whose emancipation his family had firmly resisted. In an early demonstration of corporate political power, women's suffrage had been blocked largely by a business lobby of the brewers and distillers, who feared female support for Prohibition, and corporations in industries like textiles, mining and railways who feared that women would throw their weight behind campaigns for greater social benefits. Under Wilson this opposition was overcome, and women in the United States received the right to vote in 1920, two years after women's suffrage was achieved, at least in theory, in Russia.

In 1916 Wilson was re-elected by the last all-male presidential electorate. He campaigned as the man who had kept America out of the First World War, despite pro-war sentiments voiced by the likes of Theodore Roosevelt, but made clear that he was no pacifist. Just as Taft had invaded Nicaragua and installed a puppet regime immediately before the previous election, Wilson invaded the Dominican Republic just before this one.

Because the United States had remained neutral through most of the war, American corporations were able to trade with both sides. By 1917 US trade with the allies had grown sevenfold and with Germany somewhat less. Increasing quantities of military equipment and civilian supplies were bought by the British government and its allies, much of it on credit. American banks and corporations made enormous profits from the conflict, but the cost of the war effort and the disruption of the war itself were making it increasingly difficult for the combatants to fund their purchases. There comes a point where even the largest banks want to see their loans repaid. At the same time Germany's attempts to win the war became ever more extreme, and German submarine attacks claimed more and more American lives. With Russia in turmoil following the tsar's abdication, on 6 April 1917 Wilson signed the declaration of war against the Central Powers. To bring America round to supporting the war he set up a massive propaganda ministry: the US Committee for Public Information. The CPI determined that public opinion was something to be 'manufactured not reasoned with' and recruited thousands of volunteers to spread its message. Americans were told that their nation would become an alien land named New Prussia if Germany won. Hollywood was instructed to ensure that all foreign showings of its movies were accompanied by suitable US propaganda films. It was the first application of modern PR and marketing for foreign policy objectives, and would have enormous implications for the way subsequent generations of American policy-makers sought to guide the democratic process at home and abroad. Wilson thought the war was almost over, and his main objective was to be in a position to influence the peace settlement. He was wrong, and eventually more than 4 million American troops sailed to face the enemy from Flanders to Siberia.

The war changed the balance of power in the world for ever. The role of the United States as effectively the allies' banker fundamentally changed the rules of the game. Three years after the war ended the British ambassador in Washington wrote in despair to his superiors in London that the US intended 'to treat us as a vassal state so long as our debt remains unpaid'. Wilson was determined to use this power to change the world and make it reflect his own vision of a global family of nations working together in a League of Nations. He believed that the empires of the nineteenth century would eventually wither away, much as Lenin expected the state itself to eventually disappear, when people everywhere had reached the right level of development. To this end Wilson supported the determination of General Graves not to get involved in an imperial carve-up in Siberia. But it would be wrong to say that Wilson was anti-imperialist; rather he represented the new corporate imperialism that saw the future in terms of marketing, not marines.

In 1907, in a lecture at Columbia University, Wilson had said: 'Concessions obtained by financiers must be safeguarded by ministers of state, even if the sovereignty of unwilling nations be outraged in the process . . . the doors of the nations which are closed must be battered down.' And after he became president, Wilson continued to advocate 'the righteous conquest of foreign markets'. US interests would be best satisfied, he believed, by creating the sort of conditions under which US corporations could trade profitably with the rest of the world. The dangers for the rest of the world were often obvious. F.A. Mackenzie's *The American Invaders*, published in 1902, is an impassioned attack on the activities of American corporations in Britain; it had absolutely no lasting impact. (One of Mackenzie's complaints was that Americans bought up British government bonds so that British tax revenues had to be sent abroad in the form of interest payments, nowadays more of a problem for American taxpayers.)

Wilson became the first sitting American president to visit Europe when he attended the peace conference at the end of the war to present his famous Fourteen Points, which formed the basis for the Treaty of

Versailles. (As the French leader Clemenceau is reported to have cried in exasperation, 'Even almighty God only had ten'.) Two of the points were harmless generalities about openly arrived at treaties and freedom of the seas, and one tackled the thorny issue of disarmament; nine related to various territorial issues; the remaining two were the most significant. Point XIV set up the League of Nations. The far less famous Point III embodied the crux of Wilson's vision of the twentieth-century world: the abolition of economic barriers. Through his sheer obstinacy Wilson moulded the treaty as he wished and then sailed home to sell it to the American Congress. The only major allied power not to sign the treaty was Russia, for the simple reason that the Bolsheviks were not invited, although Wilson and the British prime minister, Lloyd George, put out secret feelers to Lenin in March 1919. A ragbag of monarchist and socialist émigrés floated around the conference, purporting to represent the real Russia.

When he got home Woodrow Wilson discovered that lofty ideals did not translate into votes in Congress. He had met his match in Senator Henry Cabot Lodge, a representative of a dynasty that has represented the evolving values of American imperialism for centuries. The Cabots arrived in Massachusetts from the Channel Island of Jersey in 1700 and acquired enormous wealth first from the slave trade and smuggling, then in the nineteenth century from cotton mills and later still from heavy industry. They were staunch federalists in the early days of the republic; George Cabot was the first secretary of the navy and sat in the US Senate from 1791 to 1796. Like many New England merchants whose livelihoods depended on trade with Britain, he bitterly opposed the War of 1812; grabbing the Canadian colonies seemed far less important to him than maintaining the sinews of commerce. In 1814 he was named president of the convention held in Hartford, Connecticut, which might, had the war not ended when it did, have led to the dissolution of the Union and the creation of an independent New England.

A hundred years later America's place in the world was far more secure. In the Spanish-American War the United States could grab territory without worrying about the impact on their commercial empire. George's great-grandson, Henry Cabot Lodge, occupied the same Senate seat and was a passionate supporter of the annexation of the Philippines and Puerto Rico. (In the 1916 election he had defeated the head of a very different Massachusetts dynasty, John Fitzgerald, grandfather of future president John Fitzgerald Kennedy.) Henry Cabot Lodge actively supported the war with Spain, spoke out vehemently against the despotic imperialism of tsarist Russia, campaigned for high protective tariffs and led the fight against the Treaty of Versailles. He was an ardent imperialist, who proclaimed that American imperialism was altogether more pure than what he called the 'sordid' imperialism of Britain and Russia. One fellow senator compared his acerbic character to the countryside of his native New England – naturally barren but highly cultivated. He epitomised the imperial values of his age as his grandson, also named Henry Cabot Lodge, was to do half a century later.

In one of the dirtiest political campaigns since Andrew Jackson, the younger Cabot Lodge lost the family Senate seat in 1952 to John F. Kennedy, who eight years later became president – defeating a Republican ticket that included Henry Cabot Lodge as vice-presidential candidate. Despite their history of opposition the two Massachusetts dynasties were close enough for Kennedy to make his former opponent ambassador to the United Nations. Later, as ambassador to South Vietnam, Cabot Lodge was a principal architect of the Vietnam War and helped organise Operation Bravo Two, the military coup that led to the overthrow and murder of the Vietnamese dictator Ngo Dinh Diem (Cabot Lodge always insisted that he had instructed the conspirators to allow Diem to go into exile).

The irony of a Cabot Lodge becoming ambassador to the UN was that his grandfather had prevented America joining its predecessor organisation, the League of Nations. When Wilson returned from Versailles the Republicans, led by Cabot Lodge the elder, saw the chance to gain electoral advantage and whipped up opposition from every quarter: Italian-Americans were told the treaty unfairly rejected Italian claims to parts of the old Austro-Hungarian empire, German-Americans that it demanded unjust reparations from Germany, Irish-Americans that it represented an evil alliance with the British who were fighting to maintain their colony in Ireland. The opposition was almost entirely without principle. Cabot Lodge himself had argued for a League to Enforce Peace while the war was still on, and insisted that he supported the principles of the treaty; his virulent opposition was merely to the details.

There were those who did object in principle. They refused to accept that the United States could ever be bound in any way by a higher international forum. This was to become a common refrain in American foreign policy debate, and it is interesting that Wilson's response was not to argue for the primacy of international law but to plead that the treaty would not involve any diminution of America's traditional prerogatives. He assured his detractors that the Monroe Doctrine, which guaranteed the United States exclusive rights to intervene in the affairs of the other nations of the western hemisphere, would still be honoured. He was fighting the wrong cause: it was not to be the swirling currents of foreign policy debate that sank the treaty but the immediate pressures of electoral politics. The Senate refused to ratify the treaty, and the League of Nations went ahead without its architect.

The stage was now set for a new international order. Just about every part of the globe that could be colonised had been, and the nations of the world sat down to enjoy the fruits of peace. The First World War had been 'the war to end all wars', and from now on conflicts were to be settled around the table through debate and negotiation. Unfortunately such rosy sentiments did not anticipate the likes of Mussolini and Hitler; and missing from the table altogether were the two great imperial powers of the twentieth century, America and Russia.

CHAPTER 12

EMPIRES OLD AND NEW

For centuries Russia and America pushed out their frontiers, and pride in their increasing greatness bound together the myriad peoples of the two nations. By the time of the First World War the spirit of empire helped define what it was to be American or Russian. After the war the architects of the League of Nations promised a new international order in which all nations would be equal, and the Bolsheviks vehemently denounced the old imperial order, but the values that had determined nations' actions for centuries do not change overnight. An end to imperialism could be proclaimed but empires crumble because they lack the power to withstand external foes or to suppress internal ones, not because the cause of empire has become politically incorrect. A belief in imperial destiny – whether acknowledged, as had been the case in Russia, or largely unacknowledged, as in America – infused the souls of both nations.

As far as its neighbours were concerned Russia emerged from the First World War with its mix of autocracy and imperialism painted a new colour – red – but fundamentally unchanged. America's neighbours, on the other hand, who had suffered numerous invasions during the nineteenth century, found that in the twentieth century their frontiers were finally protected. The imperial passions of neither country had gone away, but their souls had evolved, and in so doing they had found radically new ways of channelling the yearning for empire.

The peoples of both nations yearned to make their nations greater, and previously that had always meant making the nation physically greater. In the first half of the twentieth century that physical expansion came to an abrupt halt. In America the dominant ideology was changing: in 1894 Hawaii was annexed in a spirit of blatant imperialism; twenty-five years later an American president was championing a League of Nations designed to ensure that such things never happened again. In Russia the ideology moved on more dramatically. Cataclysmic change consumed the Russian empire and the new autocrats in Moscow were unable to maintain their borders, let alone expand them. The bloody transition from the divine right of the Romanov tsars to the historical inevitability of the Communist party left little energy for imperial adventures.

For half a century it seemed that Russian and American imperialism had died and a new golden age had arrived. Both nations proclaimed their support for the world's poor and oppressed. Both ridiculed the creaking empires of western Europeans still locked in the past. Both turned their eyes inwards. And as both downplayed the imperial yearnings of their own people they underestimated the imperial yearnings of others. The passions that had driven Russians and Americans to the Pacific now fired imaginations in Rome, Berlin and Tokyo. The coming of the Second World War would rouse both nations to fury and the war's aftermath showed that their imperial pretensions, which had seemed to vanish with the First World War, had been not dead but dormant.

The New Tsars: Lenin and Stalin the Terrible

The civil war in Russia was won because the Reds were more popular than the Whites. However tiny the Bolshevik faction may have been when they seized power by the end of the civil war, they had made themselves into a genuinely popular force; not least by their control of the media. In that respect the parallels with the American Revolution are striking, but the Bolsheviks' popularity was not to last. While the Red Army was retaking the Trans-Siberian railway and chasing to and fro in Poland the economy collapsed. The resultant famine claimed 5 million lives. Protests against the Bolsheviks increased in the very places where support had once been strongest, particularly in the great naval base at Kronstadt. The Bolshevik reaction showed dramatically the road Russia was destined to follow.

The Kronstadt mutineers and their anarchist leaders had been at the forefront of the revolution, and thought that this loyalty would protect them. They were wrong; the Red Army, under orders from Trotsky, launched a ferocious attack across the ice and the mutineers who survived were rounded up and shot. The crushing of the Kronstadt soviet not only demonstrated that Russian autocracy had lost none of its steel in the transfer from tsar to commissar but also illustrated for the first time another feature that would become a commonplace of Russian life: the deliberate fabrication of 'history'. Lenin and Trotsky immediately announced that the Kronstadt protesters had been part of a White plot, something they knew to be absolute nonsense. American presidents have lied, and occasionally, as with the Watergate coterie around Richard Nixon, mendacity has been central to the governing culture, but never has an American regime set out with a conscious intent to achieve its ends by the deliberate and massive rewriting of events. The Bolsheviks could never concede that any other revolutionary group might legitimately represent the workers and peasants, and so by definition all dissent must be fomented from outside. Even when everyone involved knew this not to be the case, truth had to be subverted in the interests of the party and its historic destiny.

What many left-wingers outside Russia found hard to accept was that the Bolshevik leaders reserve their bitterest contempt for those on the left who refused to toe the party line. The case of Ukraine is a classic example. Anarchists under Nestor Mhakno fought pitched battles with both Ukrainian nationalists and Russian White Army troops, and in doing so they might have expected active support from their fellow revolutionaries in Russia; indeed the anarchist regime signed a series of co-operation treaties with the Bolsheviks. However, the promised Red Army support never materialised; Trotsky was determined that only his party would have the final victory. Eventually the Bolsheviks arranged a joint military commission at which the Makhnovist delegates were seized and murdered. It was a pattern to be followed by Stalin's followers again eighteen years later, during the Spanish Civil War.

Lenin died in January 1924 after a long illness and the struggle for succession had all the bitterness, confusion and intrigue that had characterised the successions of so many tsars. Lenin's courtiers manoeuvred for power while publicly proclaiming the virtues of collective leadership. In June seven men, including Stalin, were elected full members of the politburo: only Stalin would survive.

A year before his death Lenin, already largely confined to bed, had written a 'Testament' that was to become infamous. In it he warned the party of the dangers in the feud between Trotsky and Stalin, and in a devastating postscript urged that Stalin be removed from his post as secretary general of the Communist party. Only Lenin's illness allowed Stalin to retain any sort of powerbase, and yet six years later Stalin's position was unassailable. Painting a picture of the great Lenin reduced to incoherent ramblings, Stalin persuaded the party to ignore the Testament and then, by playing one faction against another, succeeded in removing everyone who had ever touched the levers of power. In this Stalin was totally ruthless: he eventually had all the other six politburo members killed (although one may have committed suicide). First Trotsky was forced into exile. Then Stalin and the 'right' purged the 'left', and when that was complete Stalin and his own followers purged the right. Finally Trotsky was hunted down and murdered in Mexico.

The ruthless application of terror, the treachery to allies and the total disregard for truth that characterised the Bolshevik regime sprang from the ideology that Marx and Lenin had evolved under which the ends justified any means. They were all attributes totally incompatible with the ideologies prevalent in the west, but all were mere shadows of what was to come under Lenin's successor. There were limits to Lenin's fanaticism: for example, however rancorous the internal party struggles no Communist party member was ever executed under Lenin. That soon changed. Under Stalin the Bolsheviks turned terror on themselves.

Significantly the first communist to be sentenced to death was not one of Stalin's rivals but the Tartar leader, Mir Said Sultan-Galiev, who was charged with the classic imperial crime of demanding an autonomous Tartar republic in the Urals. In supporting Stalin in this case the rest of the politburo seemed not to see that they were creating a precedent that would soon be used against them. (As a footnote, when Soviet archives were opened up under Gorbachev it was discovered that Sultan-Galiev had not in fact been executed in 1928 but imprisoned and then quietly released, only to rounded up in a later purge and shot in 1940.)

Stalin achieved what the tsarist secret police had only dreamed of: he annihilated a whole generation of Russian revolutionaries, men and a few women, who had been part of an international, intellectual, revolutionary ferment, replacing them with men, and even fewer women, who had joined the cause after the revolution, who had no interest in theory or debate, who had virtually no experience of the wider world (and indeed whose contact with that wider world was limited to the foreign forces who had tried to stop their revolution) and whose whole mindset was conditioned by their experience of the chaos of civil war. Unsurprisingly, just as they had after the Time of Troubles, the Russian people, and especially the new communist establishment, responded to a form of government they believed would save them from a repetition of such chaos: autocracy.

It is almost impossible to convey the depth of horror that Joseph Stalin embodied. However many similarities there are between Russian and American histories, there is nothing to compare for sheer scale with the evils of Stalinism; he probably killed in a few decades more human beings than died in centuries of trans-Atlantic slave trading. Parallels with Ivan the Terrible, and in the twentieth century with Hitler, are obvious but recent research shows that Stalin exceeded both in the sheer number of human beings sent to their deaths. In addition to all those executed or consigned to the camps millions died in famines that Stalin quite deliberately inflicted. According to Rayfield, 'The number of excess deaths between 1930 and 1933 attributable to collectivisation lies between a conservative 7.2 and a plausible 10.8 million.' The statistics are too horrendous to comprehend.

Stalin is said to have personally signed 383 printed lists containing around 230,000 names of those to be executed, with the names carefully divided into four categories: military, secret police, general and 'wives of enemies of the people'. And these were just the most senior victims. The terror reached into every corner of Soviet life. An NKVD circular in 1938 detailed how 'socially dangerous children exhibiting anti-Soviet attitudes' were to be sent to the Gulags. Petya Yakir was arrested and tortured for forming an 'anarchist mounted band': he was just fourteen.

Half the membership of the Communist party was arrested and a million party members were executed or died in the camps. The Great Terror unleashed in the mid-1930s was, according to Robert Conquest, the 'defining event' in Stalin's reign. In it Stalin 'finally crushed not merely opposition but any trace of overt independent thought'. Seventy per cent of the Communist party central committee was killed. The great majority of the Union of Writers was executed or sent to the gulags. Quotas were given to death squads throughout the country, and closer at hand Stalin turned on those closest to him, even on those who had carried out his executions. In a series of show trials men who had once been among the most powerful in Russia confessed to the most absurd 'crimes' like 'oppositionism' and 'Social Democratic Deviation' in return for promises that their lives would be saved; promises that were almost never honoured. Torture was meted out to high and low alike. Leading politicians like Kalinin, the Soviet head of state, and Molotov, one time foreign minister, were made to continue as normal while their wives languished in the gulags (remarkably Polina Molotov, a Jew who had made the mistake of suggesting the creation of a Jewish homeland in the Crimea, outlived Stalin and returned from six years in the camps to remarry her husband).

Between 1929 and Stalin's death in 1953, 18 million people were sent to the gulags. There were thousands of prison camps organised into nearly five hundred distinct complexes and producing a third of the country's gold, vast amounts of coal and timber and manufactured goods as varied as artillery shells and office furniture. Men and women were arrested simply because the prison industries needed people with particular types of expertise. Not only were the conditions in the camps unimaginable but many died before even getting there. One report showed that for every eight prisoners dispatched on the three-month train and boat trip to camps in the goldfields of Kolyma in the far north-east of Russia only five reached the port of Magadan alive. After enduring backbreaking labour in temperatures more than 45°C below freezing even fewer returned.

On top of the millions of prisoners dispatched to the gulags 6 million people were exiled to the wastes of Siberia and the Kazakh deserts, and all this with utmost cruelty. During the Second World War Stalin deported more than 2 million ethnic minority men, women and children to Siberia, supposedly for their collaboration with the Nazi invaders. Germans, Crimean Tartars, Chechens, Ingushi, Kalmyks, Karachai and Balkars were loaded into thousands of trucks supplied by the United States government, carted to railway depots and then shipped east. At least a third died en route or soon after arrival. Like so much else in Russian history the deportations mirrored what had happened in America, but did so on a scale whose horror dwarfed the ethnic cleansing of the American natives. Scale is also the main difference between Stalin's actions and those of earlier Russian leaders. During the First World War the tsarist regime deported 250,000 Germans, Gypsies, Hungarians, Jews and Turks from the Russian empire's western provinces for fear they would collaborate with the enemy. Yet again Stalin showed himself to be an old-style autocrat rather than a new-style communist.

In other areas too Stalin acted like the most reactionary of his tsarist predecessors. Genuine scientific enquiry that produced the 'wrong' answer was suppressed; lunatic ideas that provided the 'right' ideas were glorified. Trofim Lysenko promised Stalin that he would produce vast amounts of food by a succession of mad schemes such as freezing wheat seeds to shock them into super growth and making all offices and factories keep rabbits. Lysenko became the most powerful scientist in Russia and sent thousands of his critics to the gulags. The nearest American equivalent operated on a far, far smaller scale. Ewen Cameron, one time president of the American Psychiatric Association, expounded mad theories about 'depatterning' the human mind by giving his victims massive electrical shocks and cocktails of hallucinogenic drugs in order to reorder their 'psychic driving'. His grotesque experiments at McGill University in Canada were funded by the CIA in the hope that he could help improve their interrogation techniques. Cameron's experiments eventually became public, and following a class-action lawsuit the CIA paid massive compensation to his victims (albeit not until 1988, nearly thirty years later). The victims of Lysenko were never compensated.

Like Ivan the Terrible by the end of his reign Stalin was clearly mad. He began to believe his own paranoid fantasies. During the Second World War he spent hours carefully annotating reports on suspects, like the Russian journalist purportedly recruited into French Intelligence by the novelist André Malraux, despite the fact that any sane person could see that the reports were entirely fictitious.

Stalin was a monster with few parallels in human history, who spouted a radically new ideology, and yet what stands out above all is the continuity of the Stalinist period with the preceding centuries of tsarist autocracy. Stalin, like Lenin before him, was a tsar in all but name. On one occasion in 1920 Lenin calmly ordered the execution of the wife and four young daughters of a man who refused to join the Red Army; such callous and casual terror sprang not from intellectual theorising about the inevitability of the proletarian revolution but from the Russian tradition of the unfettered use and abuse of power. Stalin merely carried that tradition to extremes – extremes seen already in the days of rulers like Ivan the Terrible and Peter the Great.

Lenin and Stalin may have started out along a radically new path but they arrived at the same destination as their tsarist predecessors. Nowhere is this seen more clearly than in the evolution of the Russian empire.

The Bolshevik Empire

When they seized power in October 1917 the Bolsheviks proclaimed the end of empire. They needed as much support as they could get, and exploiting unrest among the minority groups within the Russian empire was one way of getting it. One of their very first decrees was entitled 'The Rights of the Peoples of Russia to Self-Determination'. This decree, signed by both Lenin and Stalin, guaranteed, among other things, 'the free development of national minorities and ethnic groups' – including their right to secede. Stalin, who had been given the least important of the fifteen ministries that made up Lenin's government, the People's Commissariat of Nationalities, travelled to Helsinki within weeks of the revolution to promise Finnish independence.

Lenin modified Marxism by stressing the importance of imperialism as the highest form of capitalism. History may yet show him to have been right. The Bolsheviks' anti-imperial declarations were not just cynical tactical ploys but reflected their conviction that the proletariat everywhere would – eventually – choose to follow the communist vanguard. There was no need to forcibly replace a tsarist empire with a Bolshevik empire: the unstoppable forces of Marxist dialectic would propel the workers of the world into a commonwealth of proletarian communist utopias.

Whatever the motivation of the Bolsheviks' espousal of self-determination for Russia's minorities, the policy became academic when the Treaty of Brest-Litovsk dismantled the Russian empire. The Ukraine, the Baltic states and the Caucasus were all stripped away not by the Bolsheviks but by the German and Austro-Hungarian armies. In consolidating its hold on power the new Russian regime soon determined to restore the old frontiers of the Russian empire. A Ukrainian republic had been established for the first time following the German collapse, but the Bolsheviks soon crushed any aspirations for independence. Ancient enmities then surfaced yet again on the Polish frontier. Sensing weakness in their old enemy, Polish troops surged across the border into Ukraine in May 1920 and captured Kiev, birthplace of the Rus. Not for the first time they discovered they had underestimated their foe. Trotsky counterattacked with such vigour that the Red Army was soon on the outskirts of Warsaw. Contrary to Bolshevik theory the Polish working class did not rise up to welcome them. Supported by French troops the Poles successfully counterattacked in one of the most argued-about battles of the twentieth century.

To some the 'Miracle on the Vistula' was one of the most important events in world history, in which the Red Army was stopped from rampaging across Europe and creating Soviet republics in Poland, Germany and beyond. It was the Châlons of the twentieth century. To others the battle of Warsaw was one more minor skirmish in the civil war raging across the former Russian empire – no more significant that the battles going on at the same time in the Baltic states, in Persia (where Britain was supporting anti-Bolshevik Cossacks) and the far east (where the Japanese were clinging on to Vladivostok).

Whatever its true significance, the Russo-Polish War of 1920 throws an interesting light on western perceptions of right and wrong. The avowed aim of the Polish invaders was to make Russia return to the frontier that had existed before Catherine the Great engineered the First Partition of Poland in 1772. Western opinion was overwhelmingly on the side of the Poles, and yet anyone who might have suggested that America should similarly return to its 1772 pre-Independence frontier would have been considered mad. Of course there were enormous differences – not least the absence of any realistic alternative claimant in North America – but through Russian eyes double standards could be clearly discerned.

Double standards were far more obvious in the case of the Bolsheviks themselves who, despite their protestations to the contrary, remained instinctive imperialists. When a Muslim revolt broke out in central Asia in 1916 Lenin reacted in the same oppressive way as Nicholas II: hundreds of thousands of rebels are said to have perished before the insurrection finally crumbled in the mid-1920s. Just as many Americans were claiming that their occupation of Hawaii and the Philippines was not imperialism, so the Red Army's occupation of non-Russian territories was proclaimed to be totally unlike the tsarist occupation that had gone before. Rayfield quotes the Bolshevik leader Zinoviev proclaiming in 1919, 'We cannot do without

Azerbaijan's oil or Turkestan's cotton. We take these things which we need, but not in the way the old exploiters took them, but as elder brothers who are carrying the torch of civilisation.' Samuel Dole could have spoken virtually the same words when he deposed the native regime in Hawaii.

Events in the Caucasus soon showed that new 'anti-imperialists' in Moscow had not given up Russia's imperial dreams. Once the White Armies had been defeated the Red Army was free to turn on the three independent republics that had appeared in the region. Azerbaijan and Armenia were quickly over-run but Georgia was more difficult. Georgia was controlled by the Mensheviks, but politics in the Caucasus had always been more ethnic than ideological. Thousands of minority Ossetians were accused of Bolshevism by the Mensheviks and killed, or died of hunger or disease, leaving a legacy of bitterness that would spill over into war again in the twenty-first century.

In May 1920 Lenin signed a treaty with the Menshevik regime that unambiguously renounced all Russian sovereign rights and recognised the independence of the Georgian state. Nine months later the Red Army invaded, and after ten days of bitter fighting the Georgians capitulated. Stalin returned to the country for the first time in nine years and, despite his title of commissar of nationalities, launched a vitriolic attack on the 'hydra of nationalism'. In a comment that should have served as a warning of what would lay in store if he succeeded to the communist throne, Stalin urged that his opponents be destroyed in the manner of Shah Abbas. Shah Abbas, who ruled Persia in the late sixteenth and early seventeenth centuries, is remembered in Iran for his fairness and wisdom but in Georgia for the orgy of death and destruction that his army inflicted on their country (a reputation perhaps with its basis in the training the Persian army received from British mercenaries, just a few decades before another British mercenary wreaked similar destruction on the natives of Mystic, Connecticut).

In 1922, with Ukraine, Belarus and the three states of the Caucasus back under Russian control, the Bolsheviks debated how the empire should be run. Lenin wanted a union of soviet republics of which Russia would be just one. Stalin attacked this as 'national liberalism' – whatever that might mean – and demanded that the reconquered territories be simply merged into a unitary Greater Russia. Lenin, of course, had his way. When Stalin took power he maintained the form of Lenin's USSR while making it operate as he had wanted. From then on the legal structures of the empire bore very little resemblance to political reality. Stalin was Georgian, not Russian, and throughout his life purists commented on his tussles with the Russian language. But like his foreign-born predecessor Catherine the Great he cloaked himself in the imperial mantle and pushed the boundaries of the Russian empire beyond anything achieved before.

Early efforts to expand the Soviet empire were clumsy and half-hearted, as Stalin was primarily concerned with his enemies at home. The one new conquest achieved by the Bolsheviks happened more by accident than through the application of a grand imperial strategy. In 1920 a gang of anti-Bolshevik Russian renegades known as the Asiatic Cavalry Division rode into Mongolia. Their leader, Baron Roman Fedorovich von Ungern-Sternberg, was a cross between the murderous Yermak Timofeyevich and American filibusters. The Austrian-born Estonian aristocrat, who claimed to be a descendant of Attila the Hun, set about creating his own kingdom in what had been Chinese Mongolia. His brutality was such that even his Mongolian bodyguards were sickened, and eventually they tied him up and left him on the steppe where a Red Army patrol found him. After a cursory appearance before a Siberian court the baron was shot. Recognising the power vacuum this left, the Red Army then marched in to create the first and longest-lasting Soviet colony: Outer Mongolia.

Attempts to foment a communist revolution in China failed when the Chinese communists were routed in April 1927, and this, along with earlier failures in Hungary and Germany, showed that the prospects for global communism were gloomy. This was a major problem for communist theorists, as a key element of Lenin's interpretation of Marx was the notion that the survival of the Russian Revolution depended on the competing capitalist empires being overthrown.

The core of Marxism, as explained earlier, is the belief that history consists of a series of ruling classes replacing each other as the economic organisation of society changes. Eventually capitalism drives out other forms of economic life and the capitalist bourgeoisie takes power. This in turn leads to the creation of an industrial working class, the proletariat, which will in the final struggle of human history overthrow the bourgeoisie in a socialist revolution leading to the creation of a truly classless society – communism. The problem, as Lenin saw it, was that Russia was still a pre-capitalist society; the industrial proletariat needed to maintain the Bolshevik revolution was simply too small to resist the might of global capitalism. Therefore his revolution could only succeed if it was quickly followed by proletarian revolution in countries that had already reached capitalism. As a consequence it was a fundamental tenet of Lenin's version of Marxism that the Bolshevik government in Russia had to use every means at its disposal to spread the revolution. Like many American leaders, Lenin was convinced of the imperative need to export his way of life. The imperial adventures of the communist Russian state would always have the ethical imprimatur of Marxist ideology.

Stalin's only genuinely original contribution to revolutionary theory was to overturn this dogma. Stalin's concept of 'socialism in one country' refuted what virtually all Russian Marxists before him considered fundamental: the imperative need for universal revolution. Stalin argued that socialism could be achieved in Russia even when surrounded by the forces of global capitalism. This novel theory not only enraged Trotsky and his purist supporters; it also involved Stalin removing chunks of his own book *The Foundations of Leninism*, which contradicted his new line. (*The Foundations of Leninism*, a justification of communist autocracy published shortly after Lenin's death, was Stalin's attempt to prove that he was a genuine theoretician. It is now clear that, like Henry Ford's *Encyclopaedia Britannica* article, Stalin's work was ghost-written for him; unlike Ford, Stalin was able to protect his secret by later having his ghost-writer shot.) Of course Stalin interpreted his new position as being fully compatible with Marxism-Leninism, quoting odd bits of Lenin in its support just as the proponents of slavery quoted chunks of the Bill of Rights to support their case.

The new line did not stop Stalin trying to export revolution but it did mean that when the time came to ally himself with Hitler or Churchill there was no ideological barrier stopping him. It also meant that Stalin had no difficulty with the idea of imposing communism on other countries. Lenin and most of his contemporaries had believed that the industrial proletariat would be the engine of revolution wherever it occurred; there was something counter-intuitive about the very idea of using imperial military might to impose a form of government that was supposed to represent the ultimate manifestation of popular will. Stalin simply did not recognise this as an issue, any more than American presidents saw any conflict in using their imperial military might to impose democracy.

Although the ideological contortion of 'socialism in one country' represented Stalin's recognition that spreading communist revolution across the globe was not an immediately realistic objective, it did not stop him trying; more importantly it did not stop many in the west believing that they were in imminent danger of being overwhelmed by the Red Peril. This fear was particularly prevalent in America, and it was not as ludicrous as hindsight makes it appear – as the citizens of Seattle were to discover when a workers' soviet tried to take over their milk deliveries.

The Red Menace

After Woodrow Wilson presidential politics in the United States relapsed into the slough of sleaze in which many of the nation's major cities had long wallowed. When Wilson's successor died unexpectedly in 1923 a stream of scandals suddenly surfaced: the secretary of the interior had accepted loans from a man trying to gain control of government-owned oilfields at Teapot Dome, Wyoming; the head of the Veterans' Administration was embroiled in all sorts of corrupt activities; and even the attorney general had been selling his political services for hard cash. One of the few honest men in government turned out to be the vice-president, Calvin Coolidge, an old fashioned Massachusetts Puritan who set about restoring integrity to political life. He had a hard task as, in the wake of the First World War, America was yet again experiencing Russian history writ small.

The country was racked by social and political turmoil. In 1919, the year after the war ended, more Americans went on strike than in any year in American history other than 1946, the year after the Second World War. Race riots flared up and a revived Ku Klux Klan rampaged in the south. There were a series of anarchist bombings, including an attack on Wall Street. Widespread industrial unrest spread to those supposed to suppress it when the Boston police went on strike. Two anarchists – Nicola Sacco and Bartolomeo Vanzetti – were convicted of murder and executed in Massachusetts on the thinnest of evidence in America's own miniature show trial. Most traumatic of all for the average American, the Chicago White Sox baseball team were discovered to have accepted bribes to lose the world series.

In America the establishment was far more firmly entrenched than the Romanovs. The attorney general led a witch-hunt against the left, with hundreds of anarchists, socialists and communists being rounded up; many were exiled to Russia. Five elected members of the New York legislature were expelled for the grave offence of being socialists.

The pre-war world had gone for ever, and the war itself was just one indication that, like it or not, the United States could not stand aside from the rest of the world.

The American Revolution was part of an international ideological ferment that drew in men like Thomas Paine, Tadeusz Kosciuszko, Johan de Kalb and the Marquis de Lafayette from all over Europe. Even so the principles of American democracy were distinctively British, and it would be misleading to imagine some sort of international revolutionary movement dedicated to the ideology of democracy. By the time of the Russian Revolution this had changed. Socialist and anarchist ideologies were sweeping across borders as freely as Islamic militancy travels today. And as if that was not enough, what some conservatives found particularly perplexing was that the peripatetic revolutionaries were not exclusively male. Women like Rosa Luxemburg became infamous as much for their gender as for their politics. The Russian revolutionaries were overwhelmingly male, but by the standards of their time the fact that women like Vera Zasulich and Sophia Perovskaya played such active roles was itself revolutionary. One woman in particular emerged on to the international stage not only in the vanguard of political change but as a champion of a feminism that was to lie largely dormant for most of the twentieth century. Her story encapsulates the political turbulence that swept back and forth across the Atlantic, just as the story of Tadeusz Kosciuszko exemplified an earlier era of revolution.

Emma Goldman was born in 1869 in a Jewish ghetto in Russia. At fifteen she refused an arranged marriage and was packed off to America, where she was almost immediately caught up in the outcry that followed the Haymarket case. Four anarchists were convicted on the flimsiest evidence of throwing a bomb at the police during a workers' rally in Chicago's Haymarket Square. Emma Goldman later declared that she became a revolutionary on the day they were hanged. She divorced the husband she had just married and threw herself into anarchist campaigning, proving herself to be a formidable orator. She developed her own brand of anarchist ideology, moving away from demands for the immediate and total overthrow of capitalism to championing individual freedom and personal dignity. Goldman took part in the conspiracy to assassinate one of the most rapacious of the robber barons, Henry Clay Frick, who had violently suppressed strikes in the Homestead factory in Pennsylvania, and the next year she was jailed for allegedly urging the unemployed to take bread 'by force', the first of a number of prison sentences for such crimes as distributing birth control literature and campaigning against the First World War. (It was part of much left-wing dogma that the First World War was a capitalist plot designed to increase corporate profits, a view not unique to the left; after the war a US Senate investigation – the Nye Committee – 'proved' that Wall Street had dragged the US into the conflict.)

Goldman was sentenced to two years' imprisonment in 1917 for conspiring to obstruct the draft and, after more than thirty years in the United States, was stripped of her citizenship and deported. J. Edgar Hoover, who managed her deportation, described Goldman as one of the most dangerous women in America. She arrived back in Russia an ardent advocate of the revolution but, like Vera Zasulich, became totally disillusioned by the Bolsheviks. As previously mentioned she met Lenin, and pleaded for free speech and toleration of dissent to no avail. After the anarchist-inclined Kronstadt sailors and soldiers sided with striking workers and were crushed by Trotsky and the Red Army, Goldman left Russia for Britain, describing her feelings of betrayal in two works with the uncompromising titles *My Disillusionment in Russia* and *My Further Disillusionment in Russia*. Her anarchism became less violent, and her virulent opposition to the Russian Revolution left her virtually isolated on the left.

Goldman had unsuccessfully tried prostitution as a way of raising the money needed to finance the assassination attempt on Frick, and her sexual politics were way ahead of her time. She argued that the unequal and exploitative relationship between the sexes was not just a political issue but required wholesale change in personal values, not least among women themselves. Eventually she married a Welsh miner, and ironically her anti-communism and new British passport made her welcome in America, where she gave a lecture tour in 1934. Her old fervour remained. At the age of sixty-seven she went to Spain to support the anarchists, simultaneously facing Franco's fascists and protecting their backs against Stalin's communists before returning once again to her adopted homeland. She died in Chicago in 1940.

The wandering Jewish radical who had treasured such hopes for the Russian Revolution and harboured such fear of American corporatism lived to see the world sliding into a war in which Stalin and Hitler were conspiring to destroy the freedoms she had championed all her life, freedoms that now depended on the might of American industry for protection. The twists and turns of her life had mirrored the times she lived through in both Russia and America: the idealism of late nineteenth-century radicals, the internationalisation of political struggle, the suppression of dissent, the hesitant beginnings of what would much later flower into feminism, and finally the triumph of traditional autocracy in the land of her birth and corporatism in the land of her death.

As corporatism became the dominant ideology in mainstream America, the arrival on the political scene of women and men like Emma Goldman illustrated how opposition to the ruling establishment had become more ideological. The quixotic Molly Maguires and Knights of Labor gave way to the American Federation of Labor and the revolutionary Industrial Workers of The World. The IWW, known as the Wobblies, were totally opposed to capitalism and advocated public ownership, factories managed through what they called 'industrial democracy' and opposition to all forms of nationalism. At its height in 1923 the IWW had a membership of around 40,000, and was a powerful force in places like the south-western oilfields and among the Philadelphia dockworkers.

In 1919, 120,000 workers went on strike in the New England and New Jersey textile industries and perhaps three times as many steelworkers took part in strikes in Pennsylvania. Employers responded by importing tens of thousands of un-unionised blacks from the south. Labour disputes in the coalfields degenerated into pitched battles, which continued on and off for years. Left-wing groups were also particularly strong in the shipyards of the north-west.

In 1889 US naval policy had officially moved away from coastal defence, with the decision to create two huge battle fleets to patrol the Atlantic and Pacific oceans in a determined effort to establish the largest navy in the hemisphere (a position held until then by Chile). The move was seen by others as a clear sign of imperial intent but, just as Adams II portrayed the conquest of Florida as self-defence, senators argued that a strong navy was needed to stop Spain trying to regain Florida or Chile attacking California. In reality neither power had the slightest intention of doing anything so suicidal; Spain was barely holding on to Cuba and American 'fear' of Chile was less influenced by any aggressive intent on Chile's part than the uncomfortable fact that Chile was the only serious regional rival to the United States. (Despite the pretensions of the Monroe Doctrine in the 1867 war between Spain and Chile, the US had stood aside as the Spanish destroyed Valparaiso.)

The US naval build-up established definitively who was top dog in the western hemisphere. In 1891 a popular revolution overthrew the pro-American regime in Chile, and the US sent a battleship to overawe the new government. When American sailors went ashore two were killed in a brawl with locals, who were incensed by US intervention in their affairs. US public opinion ignored its own government's meddling, and popular outrage was such that only an abject Chilean apology prevented war. Three years later, when rebel troops threatened the pro-American government in Brazil, the US navy blockaded their ports to emphasise who was now in charge of the hemisphere.

The naval build-up funnelled government funds into shipyards owned by supporters of the governing party. That party changed four times between 1884 and 1896, causing major disruptions to American shipbuilders – who had thrived in the age of wooden ships but had not kept up with the emerging technologies of steel and steam because of the high prices charged by the American steel cartel. By the First World War most American exports were transported in foreign ships, which suffered at the hands of German submarine attacks and the Royal Navy's blockade of German shipping. Corporate pressure for government funding led to the creation of the Emergency Fleet Corporation, which promoted the construction of new shipyards and purchased the ships they made. In the following few years 647 ships were built and $2.9bn of federal funds was given to the shipbuilding and shipping industries. Although the government owned the ships and bore most of the economic risks, private corporations made huge profits.

The state of Washington on America's Pacific coast was a prime beneficiary. In 1914 there was only one shipyard in Seattle manufacturing steel-hulled vessels; by the end of 1918 there were five. Subsidies were also available for new wooden ships, and owing to the ready availability of timber in the region by 1918 the city boasted twelve yards producing wooden ships. Conflict between the newly powerful bosses and the streams of new workers, many immigrants from northern Europe, was sharp and the bosses had powerful supporters. In one well-documented case in

June 1917 hundreds of men on leave from the navy base in Bremerton, Washington, wrecked the IWW hall in Seattle (the local paper reporting in advance that the sailors would be given special leave in order to expel the IWW from the city).

The federal government had imposed strict wage controls during the war, and when it refused to make up for that in 1919, 35,000 workers in the Seattle shipyards went on strike; contemporary anarchist accounts claimed that the government and employers locked the workers out. Most of the city's 110 unions soon joined the strike and by 6 February 1919, 100,000 workers were reportedly out in a general strike that paralysed Seattle for five days. A workers' soviet, in the form of a 300 member General Strike Committee with a fifteen-member executive, claimed to be running key services from hospital laundries to refuse collection. The strikers consciously modelled themselves on what they – and naïve idealists like Emma Goldman – thought was happening in Russia. One of the strikers' leaflets even bore the slogan 'Russia Did It'. And yet the reality is that conditions were totally different.

The ideology of democracy had taken root in America in a way that had no parallel in Russia. In both countries militant strikers held mass meetings and passed motions demanding that mines and factories be turned over to the workers, but whereas in Russia this was accompanied by calls for violent revolution, in America strikers called upon Congress to amend the Constitution. The leaders of the Seattle soviet may have wanted revolution, but the vast mass of strikers just wanted a pay rise. There was not even the slightest possibility of an armed uprising, and within days the strike fizzled out under a barrage of abuse from most of the local and national press. The one daily newspaper to support the strike was closed by federal agents and key staff were arrested. Faced with armed police and the threat of martial law enforced by federal troops, most of the strikers capitulated within a couple of days. Police and vigilantes rounded up dangerous 'Reds' and the local mayor (who had been elected with the support of organised labour) proclaimed the victory of 'Americanism' over 'Bolshevism'. A few days earlier Lenin had probably been proclaiming just the opposite, as Bolshevik troops defeated US infantry from the Polar Bear expedition at the battle of Ust Padenga.

Corporatism v. Communism

In Russia a tiny radical minority had seized power in the October Revolution and created an apparatus that managed to hold on to that power for most of the twentieth century. In America there was also a tiny radical minority dedicated to socialist revolution, and it might not seem unreasonable for their opponents to have feared that the Russian experience would be repeated. But ideologically conditions were fundamentally different in the two empires. By definition autocracy placed all power in Russia in one set of hands: chop off those hands and power would fall to whoever could catch and hold it. By contrast, in America power was shared and dispersed; even a successful soviet revolution in Seattle (and in reality it never came anywhere near that) or a putsch in Washington DC would have left most of the country's formal political institutions intact. Add to that the entrenched authority of the nation's informal corporate power structures, and the overwhelming appeal that the traditional ideology of democracy had to most Americans, and it is plain that whatever its opponents may have feared and its proponents may have wanted, socialist revolution in America was never a realistic possibility.

Nor was there any chance that the US would repeat the Polar Bear episode. Despite much ideological posturing the country had no real desire to intervene in Russian affairs, just as Russia had no ability to intervene in America. The two imperial giants turned inwards: Stalin to deal with imagined threats and America to deal with mass unemployment. Russian imperial dreams were put on hold and American imperial ambitions were manifest only in the growing internationalisation of corporate power. American industry recognised sooner than American governments not only that the Bolsheviks were here to stay but that they presented opportunities for profit. The Russian oil industry, for example, had been devastated during the civil war (by 1922 most of the wells were either completely idle or operating at much reduced levels), and Stalin turned to American business for help. Enormous quantities of equipment employing new rotary drilling methods were imported, allowing production to become far more efficient than in tsarist times. The Bolsheviks also granted foreign companies concessions to develop oilfields. Of nineteen large oil refineries constructed in Russia between 1917 and 1930 eighteen used imported plant.

Stalin liked to boast of how in 1902 he had been arrested after organising strikes in the oil town of Batum in Georgia. At that time the Baku oilfield produced more than a half of the total world output of crude oil, and Stalin depicted himself as the leader of strikes across the region that crippled the plants of foreign capitalists like the Rothschilds (in reality he had played only a minor role). Twenty-five years later the situation had changed dramatically, and Stalin invited Standard Oil of New York to build a kerosene factory at Batum. The American corporation jumped at the opportunity and was soon exporting to Standard Oil subsidiaries outside the Russian empire. Stalin was then able to generate funds to make enormous industrial purchases from companies like the US giant General Electric.

According to Averell Harriman, American ambassador to the Soviet Union during the Second World War, Stalin had told him that around two-thirds of all the large industrial enterprises in the Soviet Union had been built with United States help or technical assistance.

Lenin himself had been a wholehearted advocate of some aspects of capitalism, especially what was called Taylorism, a supposedly scientific American theory of industrial organisation based on detailed time and motion studies, which the Bolsheviks imposed with no regard for anarchist or socialist principles of workplace democracy.

Whatever the economic links between Russia and America, the world had divided into the two ideological camps that would battle each other for the rest of the century – capitalist democracy to the west, communist dictatorship to the east. Some saw Bolshevism as a beacon of light illuminating the path to a promised land of equality and social justice for all; others perceived it as a godless monster threatening to destroy the very fundamentals of Christian civilisation. Political tracts of the 1920s and '30s seemed to be describing two different nations called Russia: in one a satanic despot sat plotting world domination, unleashing agents of the dreaded Comintern to foment discord across the globe; in the other a kindly Uncle Joe swept away the trappings of privilege to bring the benefits of modern life to peasants and workers alike. What is startling with hindsight is how little resemblance either picture had to reality. The right was correct to paint a terrifying picture of what was happening within Russia, but to extrapolate this into a global conspiracy in which lurking communists were about to overturn western democracy was nonsense. Even more absurd was the belief on the left that Stalin's Russia had anything in common with their own visions of socialist utopia.

The Socialist party in America fractured, with two groups spinning off to sing the praises of Bolshevism; both called themselves communists, and illustrated vividly the fault lines in American society: immigrants formed the Communist party of America and a native-born group became the Communist Labor party. On Moscow's orders the two eventually merged to form CPUSA, but a congressional committee investigating communist activities estimated that there were only 12,000 paying members across the whole of America in 1930. (The CPUSA itself fractured after the Second World War, and its leader Earl Browder was expelled on Stalin's orders for declaring that communism and capitalism could co-exist. In a sign of the times, after the collapse of the Soviet empire Browder's grandson became a multimillionaire by setting up a hedge fund that became the largest foreign investor in Russian equities.)

The presence of vociferous if ineffectual communists in America allowed the advocates of corporatism to use the Bolshevik menace as a way of advancing their own cause. Disputes between labour and capital in America became a life-or-death struggle between 'Americanism' and 'Bolshevism', whereas the reality was that such conflicts existed long before anyone in America had even imagined that Lenin might seize power on the other side of the world. Measures taken after the Russian Revolution to combat 'communism' merely continued earlier attempts by the political establishment to suppress dissent. In March 1917, months before the October Revolution, the Idaho and Minnesota legislatures had already passed the first criminal syndicalism laws used to prosecute left-wing troublemakers. Such laws were one reason why the right succeeded so comprehensively in destroying the American left after the First World War. Just eight years after the abortive Seattle soviet the local branch of the American Civil Liberties Union reported that 'The reason for the decrease in repression is that there is little to repress. Militancy in the labor movement has declined; the radical movements do not arouse fear. Insurgence of any sort is at a minimum. . . . No new repressive laws have been passed, probably for the simple reason that it would be difficult to suggest any.'

At least those on the American right were consistent in their opposition to the communist regime in Moscow. The story on the left was much less clear cut, partly because the facts themselves were not clear cut. Stalin's supporters in the west could point to real achievements. The collapse of the old order in Russia had, as with so much else in Russian history, been on a cataclysmic scale unparalleled in the west. Between 1914 and 1926 around 14 million civilians had died from unnatural causes, including 5 million in the 1921–22 famine. Those who survived were in a pitiful state; 7 million orphans were left largely to fend for themselves as law and order collapsed in large parts of the Russian empire. And yet fifteen years later, while the west was slumped in the Great Depression, Russia's industry was leaping forward, every Russian was in work and new infrastructural projects were being completed almost daily. Superficially it might seem that communism was working and capitalism collapsing.

There were those, like Emma Goldman, who soon came to understand the reality of Bolshevik autocracy and the terror that followed, but many others accepted Stalin's lies with no apparent hesitation. Such credulity reflected not the sophistication of Stalin's propaganda machine or the nefarious actions of his agents in the west but the wishful thinking of thousands of men and women there who needed to believe that the inhumanities, inequalities and exploitation that they saw in their own societies could be abolished. When Stalin pointed to the triumphs of socialism they wanted to believe that those triumphs were real, and that they justified the price being paid in human lives.

It seems incredible now that anyone could have believed that men and women who had dedicated themselves to the cause of revolution really could become the agents of western capitalists, as Stalin claimed at the great show trials – but at the time there were those in the west who believed precisely that. In their determination to see no evil they wrapped themselves in ever more fanciful contortions. In 1935, when Stalin reduced the minimum age at which those found guilty of crimes against the state could be sentenced to death to twelve, some western communists actually argued publicly that this was perfectly sensible as children matured earlier under Bolshevism.

Some people continued to believe in a communist revolution in America long after the ascendance of corporatism had made such a prospect totally unrealistic. Trotsky, back in American exile once again in the mid-1930s, foresaw the revolutionary tradition that had given America its independence continuing to its natural conclusion as American workers, ravaged by the Depression, joined with sections of the middle classes to throw off what he called 'the corporal's guard of billionaires and multimillionaires'. He even envisaged a communist American empire as the rest of the Americas followed the example of the United States. 'I am ready to bet', he wrote, 'that the first anniversary of the American soviets would find the Western Hemisphere transformed into the Soviet United States of North, Central and South America, with its capital at Panama.'

The Invisibilisation of Empire

In fact it was capitalist America that expanded its empire, but in almost entirely new ways. Overt colonisation and annexation ceased to be central features of American imperialism in the twentieth century. There were only minor exceptions; for example, in 1916 the US approached Denmark with an offer it could not refuse: $25m for the Danish West

Indies. Although Denmark remained neutral throughout the First World War the US was worried that German submarines might use the islands, and Denmark was worried that if the US entered the war it would seize the islands anyway. (Not such an unlikely risk: Woodrow Wilson used the German 'threat' to justify invading the Dominican Republic and Haiti, although the real reason for invading Haiti and dissolving the National Assembly was Haitians' refusal to endorse an American-designed constitution that gave US corporations additional rights.) On 31 March 1917 the US took over the Danish colonies and renamed them the US Virgin Islands. Ten years later the inhabitants were made US citizens, in a sign that any possibility of independence had gone for ever.

Stalin set up Comintern to work with idealistic socialists abroad to foment revolutions and thereby expand his empire. American influence overseas required nothing as deliberate. The natural forces of corporate economics pushed domestic corporations into international expansion. Occasionally they ran into opposition and military force was needed. Augusto Sandino tried to organise a revolution in Nicaragua against what he labelled 'Yankee Imperialism', and, as if to prove his point, US marines invaded the country in 1926 and stayed until 1933, when Sandino was executed and the more compliant Anastacio Somoza installed in power. In 1927 just the threat of American intervention was enough to persuade Mexico to end its attempt to nationalise American-owned oil reserves.

During the eighteenth and nineteenth centuries America and Russia had grown in almost identical ways – pushing to the Pacific and mopping up neighbouring states along the way. It would be perverse to describe one as 'imperial' and not the other, but does continuing to talk about American imperialism in the twentieth century make any sense? There was no more territorial aggrandisement (except for a few Caribbean islands), no more conquered colonies, no more annexations of Mexican territory. When at the end of the twentieth century advocates of American imperialism spoke up once again, the empire they trumpeted appeared to be a new phenomenon arising as the world moved from the cold war to the 'war on terror'.

It is true that American corporations in some parts of the world – the United Fruit Company in Central America, oil corporations in the Middle East – exercised effective political power on a quasi-colonial basis, but these were exceptions. They continued the filibuster tradition, but they lacked the ultimate filibuster objective of annexing territory.

American corporations became the vectors for spreading US economic power around the globe, but of itself this no more constituted imperialism than the presence of European and Asian corporations in America demonstrates that the US has become the victim of imperialism. There is no doubt that American corporations were acting within the law and the business ethics of the time; however there are a number of factors that make the term 'corporate imperialism' a useful way of describing events in the twentieth century. First is the sheer scale of American corporate activity. From the moment they woke up and reached for the breakfast cereal supplied by Kellogg's of Battle Creek, Michigan, the daily lives of millions of people around the world were enacted under the shadow of the American business empire. By the end of the century this corporate omnipresence was resulting in massive, unparalleled capital flows back to the mother country – flows that in any other century would be labelled 'tributes'. American business culture became omnipresent, from McDonalds on the Champs Elysée to Coca-Cola cans littering shanty towns across the world. From the carrots of McDonalds (a somewhat unlikely image) to the sticks of the marines America's presence was felt across the globe.

If the period between the two world wars is examined in isolation, talking about an American 'empire' might seem odd, but the use of such an emotive word emphasises the essential continuity of American historical development, just as its use in the Russian context emphasises the continuity between tsar and commissar. The underlying ideology of American imperialism did not go away at the end of the Spanish American War. Democracy, corporatism and imperialism simmered gently together to produce what the mayor of Seattle had called 'Americanism': essentially the old Puritan belief that American society was nearer to perfection than any other, and the rest of the world would one day follow suit. The vision was the mirror image of the global pretensions of Marx and Lenin.

Corporations came to play an increasing role in fulfilling America's imperial dreams, but the value that has remained at the core of the American soul since the War of Independence is not capitalism but nationalism, just as nationalism not communism remained the core value in Russia. Even as corporations acquired ever-increasing power the forces of the free market have always taken second place to the national well-being of the United States. The factors that helped the United States achieve its initial industrial dominance had less to do with free markets than with protective tariffs and state subsidies. When necessary the market was simply swept away. During the First World War the railways were temporarily nationalised and the War Industries Board, headed by Bernard Baruch, was given massive power to regulate business life. The board's quasi-communist central planning led to dramatic increases in production.

In peacetime American corporations used 'market forces' to achieve the scale that allowed them to compete in foreign markets, but they had no intention of allowing foreigners to do the same in their market. The 1922 Fordney-McCumber tariffs were the highest since Independence, but even these rates were exceeded in 1930 when the Smoot-Hawley tariff originally intended to protect farmers became subject to massive corporate lobbying and ended up as a tariff on almost everything. (The curious names attached to many pieces of American legislation derive from their congressional sponsors – in this case Representative Willis Hawley and the improbably named Mormon apostle and US senator Reed Smoot.) In 1932, while the world was wallowing in depression, import duties incredibly reached almost 60 per cent of the value of imports.

US corporations were driven on to the world stage not just by their lust for scale and the impersonal forces of global economics but also by the spirit that had pushed earlier generations to settle beyond America's frontiers in Florida, Texas or California. In expanding abroad American business embodied the aspirations of the American people. Corporations did not need to manipulate US government policy to suit their own ends – it was simply accepted that overseas, as well as at home, what was good for General Motors was good for America. Nowhere was this clearer than in the nexus between the giant oil companies and the guardians of American foreign policy. Charles Hughes, the US secretary of state from 1921 to 1925, was known as the secretary for oil. The state department threatened to prohibit foreign companies from owning oil assets in the US or to designate the existing British- and Dutch-owned oilfields as 'naval reserves', thus stopping their exploitation. Britain reluctantly granted oil concessions it controlled in Iraq to Standard Oil of New Jersey and Standard Oil of New York, and the Netherlands granted concessions in the Dutch East Indies to Standard Oil of New Jersey. The United States supported a particularly vicious dictator in Venezuela, then the world's largest oil exporter, in return for his barring British access to Venezuelan oil. American oil corporations led by Gulf Oil, owned by the family of Treasury Secretary Andrew Mellon, negotiated hugely favourable deals with the rulers of Kuwait, Bahrain and Saudi Arabia with the encouragement of the state department. (As an odd footnote, the man who was instrumental in ensuring that American rather than British oil companies won the oil rights in Saudi Arabia was an upper-class but fiercely anti-establishment British expatriate named Philby, whose son would provide even greater services to the Russian empire as a KGB spy.)

Closer to home the changing nature of the US empire could be seen most clearly in the Dominican Republic, which, with Haiti, occupies Columbus's island of Hispaniola. Agriculturally the country was one of the best endowed in the Caribbean. It had been a prime target for the filibusters before the civil war, and just after that war a proposal to annexe it had been narrowly defeated. Instead the United States relied on its economic muscle, and only intervened directly when the local oligarchy seemed to be losing control or failing to act in America's best interests. The US dollar was adopted as the standard of value in 1897, and towards the end of the nineteenth century an American company was responsible for collecting customs duties and taxes (although in 1899 the company was thrown out when it defaulted on its interest obligations). Military occupations in 1903–05, 1916–24 and 1965–66 were supplemented from 1905 to 1941 by a period as a US protectorate, an arrangement 'negotiated' by Theodore Roosevelt that gave the US control over such key financial levers as the level of foreign debt and the collection of customs duties. In this way the US was able to control events without needing to invest directly in transport infrastructure, education and health services on the Hawaiian model; more importantly such indirect imperial control avoided the necessity to grant the local population the rights expected by US citizens, such as the right to be represented in the imperial governmental institutions in Washington.

This new model imperialism chimed well with the evolving ideology of democracy. Where 'spreading democracy' had once meant annexing territory to allow America itself to spread, it now meant ensuring that other nations played by the democratic rules that would allow American corporations to spread. America's existing colonies became an increasing anachronism, and in 1934 the US Congress in the Tydings-McDuffie Act committed itself to granting independence to its largest colony, the Philippines, in ten years' time (a commitment made impossible by the Second World War but honoured in 1946).

Between the two world wars Russia was unable to expand its empire and America had no need to. Territorial aggrandisement in the United States had been driven by the desire for land to settle and resources to exploit, primarily gold. As America became less tolerant of immigrants the need for new land disappeared, and as the country became self-sufficient in nearly everything there was less pressure to seize the resources of others. In Russia territorial aggrandisement was militarily impossible, but Russia was able to grow in a more traditional manner, a manner that had largely disappeared in America with the taming of the western frontier.

It is easy to forget that at the beginning of the twentieth century one of the world's last great unexplored habitable regions was not in the jungles of central Africa or the Amazon rainforests or the wilds of Borneo but in Europe. What is now the Komi Republic was until the 1920s a vast, frozen and virtually unknown wilderness stretching across the top of European Russia. Its exploration and exploitation are almost entirely thanks to one man, Joseph Stalin, and were accomplished almost entirely with the methods of a man that Stalin consciously emulated, Peter the Great. In 1722 Peter the Great exiled prisoners and their families to the silver mines of Dauriya in eastern Siberia. Stalin did the same sort of thing on a massive scale. Thousands, later hundreds of thousands, of prisoners slaved and died to open up Komi. A typical example of the early exploration was the founding of the city of Vorkuta. The twenty-three men who set off by boat from the prison camp at Ukhta in 1931 could not have been more different from the pioneers in America. Led by secret policemen, most of the party were prisoners, and included geologists specially arrested for their expertise. After paddling through mosquito-infested swamps for hundreds of miles they managed to build a camp and survive through the Arctic winter. In spring they started digging for coal with shovels and picks. Just seven years later 15,000 prisoners were employed in a chain of mines that spread out from the new city of Vorkuta.

As an aside, the sheer scale of unexplored Russia was demonstrated when, as the western world rocked to the Beatles and Rolling Stones, the crew of a KGB helicopter stumbled across a community that could not have been more divorced from the cultural currents of both west and east. Flying over virgin forests in the Urals they were shocked to see signs of human habitation; by chance they had discovered a group of religious dissidents, Old Believers, trying to escape the atheistic tentacles of the Soviet regime. What was amazing was that the community had fled to their forest refuge in 1919 and for half a century had succeeded in remaining undiscovered by one of the world's most omnipotent police states. (The KGB, of course, was not impressed by this feat, and the group's leaders soon found themselves isolated again, this time in the punishment cells of the Potma camp for political prisoners.)

Pushing into uncharted wilderness and pushing into the well-charted territory of others were two sides of the same coin, capturing the same heady mixture of adventure, patriotism and greed.

After the Second World War conditions changed: Russia found itself with sufficient military strength to expand beyond its frontiers once again and America discovered it needed resources from overseas, and once more started to flex its military muscles, but in historical terms the first half of the twentieth century was a period of consolidation and transition for both the Russian and American empires. The Bolsheviks consolidated themselves in power and the world came to terms with an empire moving from an autocracy predicated on the divine right to rule of the Romanov dynasty to one based on the quasi-divine right to rule of the Communist party. In America corporations consolidated their position at the heart of American society, and the imperialism of the Spanish-American War moved to something very different, something that in some ways was not imperialism at all.

The debate about the existence or otherwise of 'corporate imperialism' is essentially a debate about definitions: the growth and influence of American corporations is a fact, but whether it constitutes imperialism is a matter for debate. Another feature that some claim to see in twentieth-century American imperialism is far more controversial because there is no agreement on the underlying facts. It is something that strikes to the very soul of American society, a characteristic that was certainly present before the twentieth century but many would argue has since disappeared: racism. The lines between racism, racial pride and patriotic fervour are blurred and move over time. What was taken for granted in one century may seem totally abhorrent in another. Men whose views would today be described as racist gave their lives to end slavery. Apartheid in America reached its height at the very moment that black and white Americans were together dying for their country in the trenches of Flanders. It is easy to assume that values we treasure like democracy and liberty remain unchanging through the centuries; that the ideology of democracy that Thomas Paine proclaimed is what we believe today. But the reality is that values change dramatically. Until the middle of the nineteenth century there were many church leaders who endorsed slavery and serfdom; today such convictions have simply vanished.

Another belief once widely held that has also disappeared or at least become invisible is the doctrine of eugenics. Named after the Greek for good breeding, this is the belief that the quality of individuals is determined by their genes, and the quality of society by its gene pool. Now considered a Nazi aberration, eugenics was once widely supported. The First International Eugenics Congress in London in 1912 was attended by leading political figures, such as Winston Churchill, and such distinguished scientists as Alexander Graham Bell. Bell presided over the Second Congress, hosted by the American Museum of Natural History in New York in 1921, which again was supported by leading politicians, for example future president Herbert Hoover. The congresses heard learned papers on such themes as the dangerous consequences for Sweden of allowing interbreeding with Finns, and political diatribes on the 'rising tide of color' in America. The ideology of compulsory genetic improvement was certainly not restricted to Germany. The Russian Eugenics Society proposed that the communist state's first five year plan should include the artificial insemination of suitable women with the sperm of suitable men to improve the genetic quality of the Soviet population. It was widely believed that supermen and super-races could be created by proper breeding. After Lenin's death his brain was rushed to the Moscow Institute of Brain Research to see what could be learnt that might help to make others in his image.

The pseudo-science of eugenics was started in Britain, but its most active non-Nazi proponents were in America. The forced sterilisation of 'undesirables' in the US was far from being a central feature of American life but it happened; at least 20,000 were forcibly sterilised in California alone between the early 1900s and late 1960s. The programme was supported by campaigning groups like the Human Betterment Foundation, sanctioned by the Supreme Court and, it is claimed, providing a blueprint for Adolf Hitler's Third Reich, which borrowed heavily from American laws when introducing forced sterilisation for its own 'undesirables'. A typical advocate of ethnic cleansing was Charles Goethe, founder of the Eugenics Society of Northern California, who proclaimed in 1929 that the Mexican was 'eugenically as low-powered as the Negro. He not only does not understand health rules: being a superstitious savage, he resists them.' Today Goethe has a public park named after him in Sacramento, California's capital.

Eugenics was the polite face of racism; underneath it was a far more virulent strain. In 2005 the US Senate passed a motion apologising to 4,743 people lynched between 1882 and 1968. Specifically it was apologising that Congress had three times thrown out a bill, first introduced in 1900, that would have made lynching a federal offence. Most states refused to prosecute whites for lynching blacks, and by refusing to intervene Congress had effectively sanctioned the practice. Not all the victims were black. Immigrants were also targeted, and a century before the Senate apology the US government had paid nearly $500,000 as compensation for the lynching of their citizens to the governments of Italy, Mexico and China. Lynchings are often portrayed as small-scale aberrations carried out by a handful of drunken white males in the middle of the night. In fact, as two researchers put it, 'Mob killings were often carnival-like events. Refreshments were sold, trains made special trips to lynching sites, schools and businesses closed to let people attend. Newspapers ran adverts for them. Corpses were displayed for days. Victims' ears, fingers and toes became souvenirs.' Some victims had their eyes gouged out or their teeth pulled with pliers; others were beaten, burned at the stake, dismembered or castrated.

The Senate acted after the publication of a book of souvenir postcards depicting photos of lynchings – a typical example, showing the burnt corpse of the victim of a 1915 Texan lynching, is inscribed on the back, 'This is the barbecue we had last night . . . Your son Joe.' The senators who in 2005 found such barbarism appalling would probably have denied that there were any real parallels between events in America and the Holocaust in Europe, but racism and anti-semitism were not restricted to Russia and Nazi Germany. American campaigns against 'communists' often highlighted their genuine or imagined Jewish backgrounds, and Henry Ford used the media interests he controlled to whip up anti-Jewish sentiment. Ford, the archetypal corporate magnate of the 1920s, wrote, or had written for him, a book entitled *The International Jew*, which blamed the First World War and nearly everything else on the Jewish race. When Jews escaping Germany after the horror of Kristallnacht tried to settle in Haiti, the United States government used its quasi-imperial authority to 'persuade' the Haitian regime to stop them doing so.

If Trotsky could see hope for his cause in America so too could his most rabid right-wing opponents see hope for theirs. What Trotsky and Ford both misjudged was the degree to which the ideology of democracy was ingrained in the American soul. Demagogues might come to power in Europe, but in America the power of democracy would, it seemed, inevitably triumph – especially as the presidential aspirations of America's very own demagogue were ended in September 1935 by an assassin's bullet.

CHAPTER 13
HOT AND COLD RUNNING WAR

The writing and rewriting of history is no less powerful for being largely unconscious. There have been examples, especially in Russia, of history being deliberately rewritten to present whatever message is politically correct at the time, but more often rewriting merely reflects a change of emphasis. The choice of one word over another fundamentally alters historical perceptions. Empires usually expand through military might. Texas, Tibet and Turkestan have all been absorbed into imperial neighbours, but American sources would say that Texas was 'united with' the rest of America whereas Tibet was 'seized by' China. Official communist histories still reported that the tsars had 'united' Turkestan with the rest of the Russian empire.

'Communism' and 'capitalism', like 'right' and 'left', are similarly terms that mean very different things to those who wave them as banners or hurl them as epithets. Communism melded the slogans of the left on to the traditions of totalitarian autocracy to produce a new ideology that served only the interests of its leadership. Communism came to signify no more than the supremacy of the Communist party – first in the person of Stalin, then in the more diffuse form of the party nomenklatura; a collective leadership with all the classic attributes of oligarchy. Similarly corporatism borrowed the slogans of the right to disguise an ideology that in practice gives enormous power to corporate leaders, another oligarchy.

The competing empires of the twentieth century were often described as capitalist and communist, but this is misleading. Capitalism is a way of describing economic and commercial processes; communism is a theory of how society has, does, will and should function. Capitalism can be observed; communism must be believed. When societies describing themselves as communist have been observed, the startling fact is that they bear virtually no resemblance to communist doctrine. Communism is more religion than science. The ideological opposite number is not capitalism but 'corporatism', a belief system that like communism purports not just to explain the world but to define the values that are ordained to bring about the perfect society.

To identify the 'left' with communism and the 'right' with corporatism is also misleading. Many on the left were deceived by Stalin's slogans, but others provided some of the new ideology's fiercest critics. Men like George Orwell saw exactly what Stalin had done to the ideals of the Russian Revolution, whereas President Truman insisted that Stalin was 'honest' and 'straightforward' and compared him admiringly with his colleagues in Missouri politics. On the other hand some of the most articulate critics of corporatism – from Thomas Jefferson through President Eisenhower to Chief Justice Rehnquist – have not come from the sloganising left.

What communism and corporatism really show is that using terms like left wing and right wing to describe historical forces obscures more than it clarifies. The philosophies of both left and right originated in an ideal of individual liberty from which the two great new ideologies of the twentieth century effectively turned aside.

Allies Apart

Throughout the eighteenth and nineteenth centuries Russia and America annexed territory and seized resources from supposedly savage natives and Christian states alike. By the beginning of the twentieth century the boundaries of the continental United States were fixed and a ragbag of dependencies, territories and colonies speckled the Pacific from Alaska to Manila, with a couple of Caribbean left-overs from the Spanish American War – Puerto Rico and Cuba – thrown in. The borders of the Russian empire had never been fixed, and as the twentieth century erupted into war and revolution it looked as though the empire of the tsars might vanish with the Romanovs; in fact it shrank but was far from disappearing. Between the First and Second World Wars the new Russian leader Joseph Stalin consolidated his tsar-like hold on his people, and American corporations continued their gradual globalisation in search of resources and scale.

The Second World War was to change everything and nothing. The Red Army emerged from the war by far the largest military force in the world, and used its overwhelming superiority to seize half of Europe; the United States emerged from the war by far the largest economy in the world, and used this financial might (rather than its nuclear superiority) to expand and consolidate its informal commercial empire. It seemed that the prediction made by Alexis de Tocqueville more than a century earlier had come true: one day America and Russia would each be 'called by some secret desire of Providence to hold in its hands the destinies of half the world'. The Second World War increased the size of the two empires and destroyed or weakened competing empires, but the basic character of each superpower remained unchanged. Russia had an empire when the war began – stretching from Mongolia in the east to the Caucasus in the south and Ukraine in the west – and it had an empire when it ended, albeit a larger one. America had switched from formal empire to informal empire after the Spanish-American War, and despite ending the war with its army occupying Japan and a large part of Germany continued with this policy.

In some ways the decade after the Second World War was as critical in shaping the two empires as the war itself. It was then that the United States developed ways of ensuring that less powerful governments around the world would support, not hinder, its commercial empire, and Russia showed the first signs that its empire had reached its zenith and was destined to fail.

Initially it seemed that old-fashioned military imperialism survived, and would continue to thrive, in the Russian empire, but that elsewhere it had been replaced by the benign ministrations of dollar diplomacy. Yet paradoxically in the half century that followed it was not to be Russia that most frequently resorted to gunboat diplomacy. The Red Army was in action outside its borders only a handful of times, whereas the US averaged around eight overseas military 'interventions' a year (albeit some on a very small scale).

If in some ways the Second World War created a whole new world, with Russia brutally repressing half of Europe and US troops waging war from south-east Asia to the Middle East, the motivations of the two nations remained constant. Russia wanted two things: a security cordon between itself and its enemies, and to pursue its age-old quest for territory. America wanted two things: the scale that its corporatist economic model demanded, and to pursue its age-old quest for resources (including, from 1941, oil). What both nations had in common was that these objectives – unsurprisingly in both cases naked self-interest – were rarely acknowledged. Instead for the rest of the twentieth century both nations would once again ride to battle under the banner of ideology. From Prague to Kabul the Red Army crushed any signs of independence in the name of universal brotherhood, while US marines fought to impose liberty on unwilling Vietnamese peasants and Caribbean islanders. The ideology of communism crossed swords with that of a newly rampant democracy, a force that before the war had been written off by many on both the left and the right.

In the 1920s and '30s, as the world tumbled into depression, democracies had failed. Men like Mussolini, Hitler and Franco stormed to power promising salvation to their nations and replacing free elections with trains that ran on time. Little men fighting for the 'little man', they delivered short-term gain and long-term pain. Their appeal was not confined to Europe; in America a travelling salesman named Huey 'Kingfish' Long did for Louisiana what Mussolini did for Italy: providing new roads, new schools and corruption on a monumental scale. In 1934 he set his sights on the White House by doing what was then revolutionary: buying time on the radio to spread his message across the nation. Under the slogan 'Every Man A King' he built a movement that soon had 7 million members, nearly three times the size of the Nazi party that had carried Hitler to power the year before. Long promised to give every American family $2,500 and to provide free old age pensions, pledges to be funded by a 100 per cent tax on incomes over $1m and a 100 per cent tax on personal fortunes over $3m. His campaign against corporations and oligarchs struck a chord with large parts of the American population and President Roosevelt is said to have told friends that he feared that he might be the last constitutional president. Huey Long's assassination ended that threat. American democracy had been saved by an assassin's bullet, and Americans sat back to watch the demagogues of Europe lurch into war.

Although fascism and communism were ideologically at opposite ends of the political spectrum, the new generation of European dictators had much in common. Left and right launched bitter attacks on each other, both verbal and, in the Spanish Civil War, on the battlefield, and yet in August 1939 the two supreme autocrats Stalin and Hitler signed a non-aggression pact that paved the way for war. In secret annexes they carved up eastern Europe. The following month Hitler launched the blitzkrieg on Poland that signalled the beginning of the Second World War, and the Red Army rolled west to grab eastern Poland and end the short-lived independence of Finland, Latvia, Estonia and Lithuania. Stalin had recreated the boundaries of the Romanov empire, but he wanted more. In November 1940 he sent his foreign minister to Berlin to negotiate an alliance with Germany, Italy and Japan, but the negotiations foundered on Stalin's insistence on gaining Iran and western India. Instead Hitler turned on Russia, something Stalin had refused to believe could happen; even after the German attack had started, Stalin insisted that the assault must have been launched by renegade generals without Hitler's authorisation. Hitler, of course, did not share his opposite number's sense of solidarity with a fellow autocrat, and Germany and Russia plunged into one of the bloodiest struggles of all time.

America's involvement in the Second World War was far more gradual. In November 1939 the United States agreed to sell arms to the British and French, but strictly on a 'cash and carry' basis. After the fall of France Churchill's pleas for assistance became ever more desperate. Britain was running out of money, a situation exacerbated by losing much of what it had bought from America in German submarine attacks. Roosevelt finally agreed in September 1940 to give Britain and Canada fifty obsolete destroyers in return for rent-free bases in Bermuda, British Guiana and – achieving an ambition that had been there since the nation's founding – Newfoundland. This was not enough to sustain the British war effort and, as Britain had by now largely exhausted its reserves, in March 1941 Congress approved the Lend-Lease programme. Nine months later came the Japanese attack on Hawaii.

One of the myths about the Second World War is that the Japanese attack on Pearl Harbor caused the US to join the allied cause. In fact the US response was to declare war only on Japan. It was three days later, when Hitler declared war on America, that Russia and the United States suddenly discovered they were allies, albeit with very different objectives. How different those objectives were was illustrated by negotiations going on at the very same time on the other side of the world.

In December 1941, as the Japanese bombed Hawaii and prepared to attack the American colony in the Philippines, German troops were poised outside Moscow. Inside the city the British foreign secretary Anthony Eden held discussions with Stalin. With Russian prospects in the war looking as bleak as the Russian winter, Eden was amazed when Stalin declared that the 'main question' for him was British recognition of the territorial gains Russia had made under the terms of the Hitler-Stalin pact (the conquest of Finland, the Baltic states, Romania and part of Poland). As if to illustrate his imperial mindset, Stalin proposed that Britain should take permanent military bases in France, Belgium and the Netherlands. There was no doubt in British minds that Russian imperialism was on the roll once more. Much of Britain's wartime strategy was predicated on containing Stalin's imperial ambitions, but when Churchill, Roosevelt and Stalin met in Tehran in 1943 it appeared to the British that Roosevelt regarded Britain's undoubted imperial past as a bigger threat to the post-war world than Russia's potential imperial future. In the debate about opening a new front against Hitler, in which Stalin wanted the British and Americans to invade France and Churchill wanted to strike at the Balkans to forestall possible Russian intervention, America sided with Russia, effectively consigning the peoples of central and south-eastern Europe to half a century of servitude as part of the Soviet empire. As American men, and more importantly materiel, turned the tide of war against the Axis powers, Russia moved on to the offensive. When Hitler's short-lived empire collapsed, Stalin was able to achieve what earlier tsars had only dreamt of.

Debate still rages over Stalin's intent: was he seeking world domination or merely a security cordon on his frontier? Those with a more limited view of Stalin's intentions point to his actions in places like Greece, where after the war a communist guerrilla army fought a bloody civil war with very little support from Stalin. The Russian leader seems to have regarded his agreements with Roosevelt at Yalta as a division of spoils between their two empires. It is not clear that Roosevelt saw it that way, but the position of the western allies was not always clear. Churchill in particular combined cynical realpolitik with a sincere commitment to protecting other nations from slipping into Russia's maw. In the last days of the war he flung British troops north to the German coast, to stop the Red Army seizing Denmark and fulfilling Peter the Great's ambition of making the Baltic a Russian sea; but the previous October he had met Stalin in Moscow and carved up much of eastern Europe so that, for example, Russia was given a free hand in Romania in return for leaving Greece to Britain.

Whatever the real motives of the various allied leaders, it is clear that having at one stage of the war looked as if it was on the path to destruction the Russian empire ended the conflict stronger than ever. The Red Army was the most powerful land force in the world and Russian troops controlled a broad band of territory from Estonia through Central

Europe to the Balkans. Never had the empire of the tsars stretched so far or held so many.

The Second World War also re-ignited America's global ambitions, which had been in abeyance for a quarter of a century. In economic terms the war had been a tremendous success: the American GDP doubled in under four years because of war spending, while the economies of most of its competitors were smashed. The United States emerged as the undisputed economic powerhouse of the planet. The other allied powers had all fallen definitively into the second division, something the Lend-Lease Program had made abundantly clear.

Under the Lend-Lease arrangements the US sent nearly $50bn of material to its allies, particularly Russia and the largest recipient Britain. To show how totally the international tables had been turned, when the US Congress passed the Lend-Lease Bill they gave it the number 1776, the year of their independence from Britain. (Ironically one of the reasons the young American republic had survived is the lend-lease program Britain had instituted to protect the infant United States from Napoleon's depredations.) US officials were stationed in Britain to police the Lend-Lease regulations. Britain was banned from exporting not just the goods it received but anything similar, even if home made. At the end of the war any materiel that had not been consumed in the conflict had to be paid for. Britain paid the final instalment on its Lend-Lease debt (or more accurately the debt and the interest that had accrued on it) on 31 December 2006.

Historian and Conservative peer Robert Skidelsky has argued that 'the way Washington managed the flow of lend-lease supplies had the effect, and possibly the intention, of leaving Britain dependent on US help after the war on whatever terms America chose to impose'. The terms in the 1946 Anglo-American Loan Agreement were devastating, producing a catastrophic financial crisis in Britain in 1947 that destroyed (or at least emasculated) the competitiveness of British manufacturing industry and ensured that rationing would continue long after the war had ended.

Nevertheless, without this aid Britain would have found it almost impossible to pursue the war against fascism. Theoretically the programme was reciprocal but the United States received only about $8bn in aid, ranging from wool provided by New Zealand to British supplies for US troops stationed in the UK. Lend-Lease was about the new economic superpower keeping the old one afloat. It was also about keeping the communist regime in Russia afloat.

The inherent weakness of the Russian economy was made plain during the war. Clearly the destruction in the west had an enormous impact, but given that most of Russia was not occupied by the Germans and that Stalin had moved much of his industrial plant east of the Urals, the scale of American aid needed to keep the Red Army fighting was surprisingly large. Transport was almost entirely dependent on US aid: practically all aviation fuel, 99 per cent of new railway locomotives, over 400,000 jeeps and trucks, even 15½ million pairs of army boots.

Six years of fighting left the economies of Europe shattered. Providing materiel to fight the war left the US economy resplendent.

The main impact of the war on the United States was psychological rather than economic. Whatever left-wing conspiracy theorists may say, America did not enter the war so that its corporations could make enormous profits, although many did, but to protect itself and its Asian colonies from Japanese attack (at that time the legal status of Hawaii was still somewhere between colony and state). As the US became caught up in the conflict in Europe, America's rationale for war moved from protecting 'the nation' to protecting 'democracy'. Once the war was over it was then a small step for Americans to conclude that as America had been fighting to save democracy, and democracy had been saved, it must follow that America had saved democracy.

American economic muscle had indeed been critical, and without it it is hard to see how the allies could have destroyed the German Reich; but to assert that America saved the world from Hitler is a gross exaggeration. In June 1944, when allied forces stormed ashore on the D-Day beaches of Normandy, the 58,000 Americans were easily outnumbered by the

76,000 troops drawn from the British Empire. The number of Americans killed in the war (less than 300,000) was significantly less than the number of British (357,000), but both were dwarfed by the 27 million Soviet losses. Just as Tsar Alexander had saved the rest of Europe from Napoleon, Stalin had saved it from Hitler.

As the war ended many in Europe, especially on the political left, felt an enormous debt of gratitude to the Russian people, but the overwhelming perception in America was that – as in the First World War – it was the United States that had rescued Europe from the grip of tyranny. Just as British history ascribes Napoleon's defeat to the Duke of Wellington rather than to the Russian tsar, so modern American history ignores the overarching role of Russia's communist dictator. Seen through the prism of ideology it would have been perverse to suggest that democracy had been saved by autocracy. The importance of this ideological perception of the war is hard to overstate; it conditioned American public opinion for decades after, and informed public debate on the wars in Korea, Vietnam, Iraq and a host of minor military interventions. Americans saw themselves as conquering heroes delivering freedom and civilisation, reinforcing a self-portrait that had been part of the American psyche since the first Englishman landed, musket in hand, on the Virginia coast, and the first Puritan brought God to New England.

The importance of ideology in American thinking was illustrated in a post-war exchange between Stalin and Truman, Roosevelt's successor. Truman was incensed that the Russian autocrat had ignored the Yalta commitment to democracy by installing a Communist party dictatorship in Poland. Stalin simply found this incomprehensible. Truman, he said, should mind his own business, pointing out that Russia did not claim the right to interfere in Belgium or Greece. That for America there was a fundamental ideological difference between the two situations was something that the Russian dictator, who always put self-interest before ideology, could not accept. Truman, however, was genuinely motivated by his ideological commitment to democracy as much as by any considerations of the electoral muscle wielded by Polish-Americans, and could not understand how Stalin could apparently be so perfidious.

On one level Americans were sincerely committed to defending democracy in faraway lands and repeatedly demonstrated their innate decency through acts of great generosity. After the First World War the American public helped rescue Russia from famine, and similarly after the Second World War billions of dollars were sent across the Atlantic to rebuild shattered economies. The desire of millions of Americans was not just to help the hungry recover their strength but also to help the oppressed recover their freedom. The ideological component was every bit as important as the humanitarian. US policy was driven by an ideology that saw economic well-being and democracy as two sides of the same god-given coin.

And yet on another level the United States was as determined as the Soviet Union that its own interests should take absolute priority over everything else. Although its proclaimed mission during the war was to save the world for democracy, the underlying mission was always far more parochial: to defend the homeland from attack and recover whatever had been taken from it.

One trivial event illustrated the American mindset. Just as Hitler's declaration of war on the United States made America, Russia and Britain allies, his defeat brought the rationale of their alliance to an end. America's military strategists assumed that once the European war was concluded US troops could be withdrawn from the continent almost immediately: the devastated continent would sort itself out by spontaneously embracing democracy and free markets (an assumption later repeated in Iraq). Based on this assumption, they calculated that with US troops in Europe freed up America could now win the war in Asia unaided. On VE Day, as the victory bells rang out in Europe, President Truman signed an executive order not only cancelling Lend-Lease but embargoing all shipments to Russia and other European nations. Ships already at sea were ordered back to port, and their cargoes were unloaded. Neither Britain nor Russia had any prior warning of Truman's intention, and both were furious: British troops were still engaged in bloody conflict with Japanese forces in Burma, and Stalin was still considering an earlier American request to declare war on Japan. Such was the fury, in particular of Stalin, that a message was eventually sent explaining that the episode had been an awful mistake and the order was rescinded. (But when the war in Asia was over Lend-Lease was again peremptorily closed down.)

However complex the events and motivations of the Second World War really were, it was the perceptions of events that had the most impact on subsequent behaviour. The perception of most Russians was that they had suffered far more than anyone else in a war started by others, and that any gains they had made were no more than their due. The perception of most Americans was that the United States had mounted both a moral and military crusade, and it was this that rescued Europe from tyranny. After the war these perceptions were reinforced on both sides. Countless cinematic epics have reinforced the contrasting versions of events, both of which after all have more than an element of truth. The American film *U-571*, for example, was based on the true story of the capture by British sailors of a German U-boat carrying the famous Enigma code machine – except that Hollywood replaced the Royal Navy with the US navy to produce another 'Americans save the world' adventure. Soviet film-makers did what Stalin and his immediate successors told them to do. Hollywood's role was less clear-cut; it both moulded and reflected an underlying tilt in the balance of American public opinion. Before the war the majority wanted to ignore the rest of the world; during and after the war they were willing to fight to save it.

Empires Re-emerge

Two key events at the end of 1941 determined that the international quiescence of the United States between the world wars would be an aberration. Just as throughout the nineteenth century the US was engaged in almost permanent foreign wars as it pushed its frontiers outwards, so after the Second World War military force would once again become a key element in expanding America's influence in the world.

The first event was history repeating itself, but it had a shattering impact on the American psyche. The Japanese attack on Pearl Harbor mirrored their attack on Port Arthur that had started the Russo-Japanese War and the American attack on the Philippines that had started the Spanish-American War.

Tension between the US and Japan had been growing for some time. After the fall of France Japan, already fighting a brutal war in China, occupied French Indo-China and cast covetous eyes at the oilwells of the Dutch East Indies, perilously close to the American colony of the Philippines. The US imposed an oil embargo, and in November 1940 Secretary of State Cordell Hull approved a contingency plan to drop incendiary bombs on Tokyo, described as a 'city of rice-paper and wood'. By the middle of the next year half of all America's heavy bombers had been transferred to the region, away from the Atlantic sea lanes where German submarines were wreaking havoc. Just weeks before the Japanese attack the *New York Times* reported plans for American bombing raids against Japan from bases in Russia and the Philippines.

Although the Japanese perceived the United States as having been actively hostile, that is not how the American people saw it. Just as after 9/11 Americans were shocked to discover that the lofty sentiments they believed determined their foreign policy could engender bitter hatred in others, so after Pearl Harbor America awoke to the realisation that there were political forces in the far corners of the globe that they could not ignore.

The second event was nearly as significant, but that significance was apparent only to a few in the political and corporate establishment. In 1919 a gloomy report on domestic oil supplies from the US Geological Survey provided ammunition for those demanding that America receive a share in the carving up of the Ottoman Empire after the First World War. In November 1941 an obscure American state department official named William Ferris produced a similar report that caused almost as much consternation in some circles as the attack on Pearl Harbor the following month. The subject matter of the Ferris report was oil. The United States was thought at that time to have 20 billion barrels of oil reserves; as it was using 4 million barrels a day or 1.45 billion a year, within thirteen years all of its domestic reserves would be exhausted. For a nation that was already wedded to the automobile the prospect of running out of oil was unthinkable. It was even more alarming to the oil companies, which were coming to dominate corporate America: at the end of the First World War four of the top sixteen US corporations were oil companies; by the end of the Second World War eight were. The report's conclusion was unequivocal: the United States should pursue a 'more aggressive foreign oil policy aimed at assuring access to petroleum overseas'. As the war progressed the United States found itself supplying not just its own oil requirements but those of its allies, and the expectation of even thirteen years of oil reserves started to look optimistic; securing overseas supplies moved to the top of the foreign policy agenda.

The most obvious place to look for overseas reserves was Saudi Arabia. If the US could control the Saudi oilfields the US navy estimated that American reserves would effectively be doubled. Seizing them by force was no longer the American way and Roosevelt set out to buy control. He signed a declaration that 'the defense of Saudi Arabia is vital to the defense of the United States', and on that basis extended Lend-Lease aid to the oil-rich kingdom (not what Congress had in mind when it approved the Lend-Lease legislation). Soon he went further and proposed that the US government buy the Saudi oil concession, but Congress refused; corporate lobbyists were happy for the government to protect their oil interests overseas, but they had no desire to see the government entering the oil business itself – war or no war.

In 1945 Roosevelt travelled to the Crimea to meet Stalin and Churchill at Yalta. The meeting was monumentally important. The formal declaration spelt out the principles of the United Nations and committed the three leaders to peace and democracy. Informally Stalin seems to have believed that the conference effectively carved up much of the world into Russian and American spheres; he returned home well satisfied. Roosevelt did not return home; instead he flew south to one of the most bizarre diplomatic encounters of the twentieth century.

Fresh from signing a conference declaration that among other things committed the signatories to ending slavery, the American president boarded an American warship, the USS *Quincy*, to meet a man who arrived with a royal astrologer and a retinue of personal slaves. Roosevelt and the King of Saudi Arabia Abdul Aziz ibn Saud spent more than five hours in friendly discussion accompanied only by their interpreters. They had much to discuss – the shape of the post-war world, the future of Palestine and oil. There is no record that they touched on the commitment to eradicate slavery that Roosevelt had signed a few days earlier. They agreed that Saudi Arabia would guarantee to supply the US with oil and the US would guarantee to protect the Saudi despot from external and internal threats. To help the United States to extend this protection the king agreed to the construction of a US airbase in his country. The base was built not on the Red Sea coast, where it could have protected traffic through the Suez canal, or in the north, near the bubbling cauldron of Palestine, but in the east, near the oilfields of Iran, Iraq and the Gulf states. It was a sign that the end of the Second World War was the beginning of a new chapter for the American empire, just as it evidently was for the Russian.

On their side of the 'iron curtain' that now descended across Europe, the Red Army was an army of occupation in exactly the sense that would have been understood not just by the tsars but by the Mongols, Romans and conquering armies since history began. The Baltic states were simply annexed and became parts of the Soviet Union; somewhat more subtle approaches were followed elsewhere. The detailed mechanics of occupation might differ – hymns of imperial glory might be replaced by slogans of worker solidarity and tame local commissars might occupy presidential palaces from Warsaw to Sofia – but in terms of power all roads led to Moscow.

With a few very minor exceptions in the Caribbean and Pacific, America had abandoned the traditional forms of imperialism favoured by Russia. In 1946 the last large American colony, the Philippines, received its political independence, although American troops maintained a presence there and in numerous places around the world. In Germany and Japan US forces were formally an 'army of occupation'. Theoretically their position was similar to that of the Red Army in eastern Germany and in an earlier age that might have led to eventual annexation. By the 1940s, however, the interlinked ideologies of democracy and imperialism in America had evolved so much since the Spanish-American War that it was inconceivable that either Germany or Japan would ever become an American colony in the way that the Philippines had become, or as was happening in Russian-controlled territories.

Roosevelt's negotiations with the Saudi monarch illustrated the fundamental differences between the way that America and Russia were to use their newfound status as the world's superpowers. America would buy what it wanted; Russia would seize it. America's economy had benefited enormously from the war, and Roosevelt and his successors were determined to use that wealth to consolidate their position in the world. The Russian economy, by contrast, had been devastated (although it is worth remembering that Russia as we know it today was not as badly damaged as the western part of its empire: with the exception of the battles in and around Stalingrad most of the fighting and destruction in the Soviet Union took place in what are now the independent nations of Ukraine and Belarus). Stalin's priority was reconstruction, and he used the Red Army to take what he needed. The Russians dismantled two-thirds of the industrial capacity in their zone of Germany and shipped it back to the USSR. Similarly Soviet forces that occupied Manchuria from July 1945 to May 1946 dismantled and removed over half of the Manchurian industrial plant. It was not just machinery that Russia grabbed. Thousands of the fittest and most skilled German prisoners of war were charged with ludicrous crimes like 'aiding the world bourgeoisie' and sentenced to further imprisonment. By 1950 they had 'donated' a billion days of forced labour, and it is estimated that in the immediate post-war period 8 per cent of the Soviet Union's GDP was produced by POWs.

The styles of the two powers were so different that using the term 'empire' to describe both is equivocal. The Soviet bloc was clearly an empire in the sense in which the term had been used for centuries. The United States preferred to see itself as the leader of the free world, but it exerted in practice a degree of control over the economic, political and cultural lives of millions of people beyond its borders that in earlier times had only been achieved by imperial might. For want of a better term, 'empire' remained an easier way to describe America's overseas interests than the academically more precise term hegemony.

After the war the two imperial powers quickly moved to establish their zones of influence. Having failed in his attempt to accomplish Peter the Great's ambition of controlling the Baltic, Stalin demanded parts of Turkey and military bases that would allow him to dominate the Bosporus, thus realising Catherine the Great's ambition of controlling the Black Sea. He went further, demanding naval bases in North Africa and ignoring a previously agreed deadline to remove his troops from Iran. Unlike Central Europe these were all areas that were dangerously close to the oilwells of the Middle East. The United States refused any compromise in the region; after three months of tense sabre-rattling by the US navy the Russians withdrew from Iran and gave up their other demands. (Russia finally pulled out of Iran after Stalin was promised access to Iranian oil and the creation of a joint Russo-Iranian oil company – a promise the Iranian parliament, encouraged by the United States, later reneged on.)

Both Russia and America acted to ensure that their supporters would take power in the areas they controlled. Stalin had signed up to democratic principles at Yalta but had absolutely no intention of observing them – as events in Czechoslovakia soon made clear. The Americans, on the other hand, were genuinely committed to the principles of democracy, but democracy defined in a way that suited them – as events in Italy soon proved.

A Czechoslovak government in exile had been established in Britain in 1940. It included the charismatic Jan Masaryk, son of Czechoslovakia's first president, as foreign minister. Masaryk retained this post in the coalition government that was set up following the country's liberation. Following elections in 1946 the Communist party, which had won

38 per cent of the vote, took an increasingly prominent role in the government and vetoed Masaryk's attempt to join the Marshall Plan, America's proposal for post-war reconstruction. By then American and Russian occupying troops had left, but Russian forces remained poised on the border. In February 1948 a Russian mission flew to Prague demanding further concessions, and the majority of the non-communist cabinet members resigned hoping to force new elections. Instead Stalin installed a communist government with Masaryk as a token independent, continuing as foreign minister. He was not to do so for long. On 10 March, two weeks after the Communist party coup, Jan Masaryk's body was discovered below the window of his second-storey apartment at the foreign ministry. Whether suicide or murder, Masaryk's death closed a chapter in eastern European history; for the next forty years the hammer and sickle flew over Russia's European colonies.

America adopted a somewhat different approach. Where Russia used force and fear to 'enhance' the results of a democratic election, the United States used money. Immediately after the war Communist parties throughout Europe were making impressive gains: one of their next targets after Czechoslovakia in 1946 was Italy. The Italian Communist party had led the fight against fascism and did well in the first post-war elections, so many expected an alliance of communists and socialists to sweep to power in the 1948 elections. It did not because the infant Central Intelligence Agency of the United States channelled millions of dollars to the right-wing Christian Democrats and helped mount a massive media campaign in their favour. Much of the campaign was organised out of the offices of two remarkable brothers at the Sullivan & Cromwell law firm in New York, Allen and John Foster Dulles. Their grandfather had been the archetypal American hero: a millionaire lawyer born in a log cabin and a brigadier general in the civil war before serving as United States minister to Mexico and Russia and as secretary of state, a position his grandson John Foster would occupy under President Eisenhower. Allen Dulles had in many ways an even more powerful position than John Foster as founder and director of the CIA. Together the two men would establish the framework within which US interventions overseas would be managed into the twenty-first century. Nearly sixty years later British newspaper stories about Saddam Hussein's biological and chemical warfare programmes by such reputable authors as Marie Colvin in the *Sunday Times* and Christopher Hitchens in the *Evening Standard* and the *Guardian* were found to be totally bogus: many in the media had been taken in by what appeared to be genuine and well-founded reports. They had been based on 'information' provided by the Iraqi National Congress, which had been paid millions of dollars by the US government to influence world opinion.

Both the Russian and American regimes were well satisfied with their respective strategies in Czechoslovakia and Italy and continued in the same vein. The United States continued to distribute dollars funding a wide range of 'anti-Communist' factions within such supposedly revolutionary groups as the National Union of Students in Britain. The Russians continued their own manipulations.

In Hungary the communists rigged the 1947 elections, purged the socialist opposition and solidified Soviet control. The almost random purges that were a central characteristic of Stalin's rule were quickly extended to the new colonies in the west. In 1952 Rudolf Slansky, former secretary of the Czechoslovakian Communist party, and ten other prominent party members (most of whom were Jewish) were convicted of high treason in a Prague show trial, and hanged. Similar judicial and extra-judicial murders continued throughout the empire. Russian oppression became ever more brutal: Russian tanks were rolling again to suppress revolts in East Germany in 1953, Hungary in 1956 and Czechoslovakia in 1968. But there were limits to what could be achieved by Stalin's crude bullying. In Yugoslavia Tito, the wartime leader of the communist partisans, not only refused to implement Stalin's whims but organised his own purge of Stalin's adherents, safe in the knowledge that while the Red Army's tanks might be omnipotent on the streets of Berlin they would have a much harder time in the mountains, where he had so recently resisted the German Reich.

The relationship between the Russian and Chinese empires deserves a book on its own. Although Mao Tse-tung eulogised Stalin and it suited many in the west to imagine a monolithic Sino-Soviet bloc, the reality is that China never formed part of Stalin's empire, and long before the two nations started firing shots at each other in 1969 China's communists were following an independent path determined entirely by their own self-interest.

While Russia was consolidating power on its borders the US was reaching out more widely. Once the atomic bomb had been dropped the US moved quickly to seize control of Japan. Earlier plans for a joint occupation commission with British, Chinese and Russian representatives were abandoned. During the war America had agreed to restore the territory and naval bases that Russia had lost to Japan in the 1905 Russo-Japanese War, but this pledge too was abandoned. The US occupation forces enforced an economic policy drawn up by an American banker Joseph Dodge. His objective was to stimulate the Japanese economy to reduce the country's dependence on US aid, to help pay for the costs of occupation and above all to create a bastion of American influence in the face of the communist wave that had already swept over China. Claims for reparations by a string of countries (Australia, Britain and China, for example) were dismissed. Dodge's policy was highly interventionist, with little space for the free flow of market forces: import controls ensured that limited resources were directed at those sectors approved by the US authorities, price controls stopped the unfettered oscillations of supply and demand, and wage controls kept the workers in their place. The policies were the exact opposite of the free market nostrums later imposed on third world countries at America's insistence by the World Bank and IMF, but they worked: by pushing Japanese industry to produce for export rather than for domestic consumption, the basis was laid for the Japanese miracle that eventually allowed Japanese firms to rival their US competitors. It was simultaneously a glowing example that other nations would try to repeat and an alarming mistake that US corporations were determined should not happen again.

In Europe America's post-war policy was similarly driven by the need to contain communism. Where Stalin was rebuilding his economy by looting his new imperial possessions, Truman was determined to strengthen the economies in his half of Europe.

In the Marshall Plan, named after the American general who as President Truman's secretary of state devised and pushed the proposal through, $28bn of US aid was pumped into Europe. The sum was gigantic, and dwarfed the copycat Molotov Plan that Stalin belatedly trumpeted for eastern Europe. Like Lend-Lease before it, the Marshall Plan had strategic objectives, to prevent the conditions that might give rise to communist revolution, and economic objectives, to create demand in Europe that would provide profitable opportunities for American corporations; but underlying both was a remarkable degree of generosity on behalf of the American people. Pictures of war-torn cities and starving children were every bit as powerful as the cold calculations of military and corporate strategists. Nevertheless the Marshall Plan was not adopted without debate, and that debate echoed divisions that had been present since the nation's founding.

From their earliest days the imperialism of the north-eastern states was largely commercial. Much of their wealth came from trade, particularly in the early days from the slave trade, and their merchants wanted above all to have easy access to foreign markets and to stop foreigners having access to theirs. The southern states were primarily concerned with direct conquest, in order to gain more land for cultivation. The two imperialisms fused – especially in the march west – but the two strands could still be distinguished: in the debates on the League of Nations after the First World War and most clearly in the debates about the Marshall Plan after the Second. The Marshall Plan was very much the work of the north-eastern establishment, whose bankers occupied key positions in its administration and made huge profits from its implementation. A major beneficiary of the scheme was the investment bank Brown Brothers, Harriman, one of whose partners, Averell Harriman, was sent to Europe to run the plan. By and large southern and western states would have much preferred the funds to be spent at home or devoted to projects in Latin America and Asia, where US corporations would find it easier to exert quasi-colonial control.

Cynics have also pointed out that a large part of the Marshall Plan aid did not end up in Europe. $2bn went to American oil companies, and much of the rest was spent with other US corporations. The aid to France, for example, roughly covered the cost of France reconquering Indo-China, something achieved largely with weapons bought from the US. Similarly the Netherlands was funded to reconquer Indonesia.

In Russia there was no debate about foreign policy, not just because under Stalin there was no fundamental debate about anything but because the over-riding policy objective was clear. At the end of the Second World War Russia had expanded its empire, established a security cordon around the motherland and had the largest and most powerful army in the world. The Russian autocrat had a degree of personal power equal to any tsar and exercised it through an elaborate apparatus of secret police and concentration camps, torture and intimidation, judicial murder and perpetual propagandising. Stalin's primary objective now was consolidation – to extend the fearsome level of control he exercised at the centre over his new colonies in eastern Europe. Guerrilla attacks against the Russian occupiers continued in the Baltic states and Ukraine into the 1950s. Endless streams of propaganda photographs and films of happy throngs in various eastern European nations welcoming their Red Army liberators could not disguise the reality that only a handful of Communist party stalwarts had looked forward to their countries being absorbed into the Soviet empire. Further territorial expansion was a prize Stalin would grab if the opportunity arose but for the time being he could rest on his laurels; isolating his empire from western contamination was more important than enlarging it.

For Truman, returning to the isolationism of the interwar years was not an option, however much vocal sections of the American population might disagree. Two forces were keeping America engaged with the rest of the world: the insatiable lust of US corporations for 'scale' and the nation's need for oil. Both forces have continued until today. The discovery of oil beneath the Gulf of Mexico and in Alaska falsified the dire war-time predictions that America's domestic oil supplies would run out at some point in the 1950s, but the new discoveries merely extended the timelines: US domestic oil production excluding Alaska peaked in the early 1970s, and including Alaska it peaked in 1988. From then on the United States has become increasingly dependent on foreign oil producers, and since 1998 the majority of the oil consumed in America has been imported. Before the Second World War America was the world's largest oil producer; now it is the world's largest oil importer. As more American historical documents become available the impact of oil on US imperial designs has become more apparent. One instance that is now in the public domain is the plan presented to the US cabinet, in response to the global oil crisis in the early 1970s, for US airborne forces to seize the oilfields of Saudi Arabia, Kuwait and Abu Dhabi.

Initially the need to keep foreign markets open for American corporations and protect Middle Eastern oil supplies did not seem much of a problem. America emerged from the war as the world's only true superpower. Not only was this because of its economic might but also because the United States, and the United States alone, possessed the atomic bomb. Russia, the only other conceivable claimant to superpower status now that British empire was in terminal decline, might have the legions of the Red Army, but Stalin would never dare unleash them when faced with certain nuclear annihilation. Then in August 1949 a project involving hundreds of thousands of gulag prisoners digging deep into the earth, and controlled personally by Stalin's secret police chief Lavrenti Beria, came to fruition; in a remote corner of Kazakhstan uranium from the gulag mines exploded: Russia had its own atomic bomb. The world had changed for ever: it had divided into two armed camps whose only threats against each other seemed to be literally mad – Mutually Assured Destruction. It was time to step back and find another way forward.

Bipolarity

In the Second World War Britain and America had fought to make the world safe for democracy, but democracy remained the prerogative of just a small part of the world's population. Throughout the old colonial empires national liberation movements of one form or another had sprung into prominence, and in Asia it became clear that the end was in sight for British rule in India, Dutch rule in Indonesia and French rule in Indo-China. America, in particular, had made its antipathy to traditional forms of imperialism plain, and led the way with the granting of independence to the Philippines – although the impact was somewhat reduced six years later when after a local referendum another left-over from the Spanish American War, Puerto Rico, became incorporated within the United States as a 'commonwealth'.

Not only was change coming to the colonies but the rhetoric of liberation was having its effect in western Europe, where many on the left championed the cause of those like Gandhi and Nehru who campaigned for the right to self-determination. The left had gained a new authority, in part reflecting the sacrifices made by the Red Army and the communist resistance movements in the war against fascism. The communist parties of western Europe gloried in bringing down fascism, while ignoring the fact that in their name Stalin was exerting control over Russia's new imperial possessions in eastern Europe with the same crude application of power that had characterised Russian imperialism for centuries. Practising imperialism at home, communists were eager to further anti-imperialism abroad. (Even so, it could be argued that Stalin's own contribution to the national liberation movements in the third world was wholly negative: scores of potential leaders had gone to Russia for training in the 1930s and never returned, murdered to appease the Soviet leader's increasing paranoia. Men like Jomo Kenyatta and Ho Chi Minh were the exceptions who managed to return home to lead their nations to freedom.)

Russian imperialism might be unchanging, but America's was evolving yet again. During the interwar years isolationism had been a powerful feature of American public opinion, and America's imperial power increased not by seizing new territories but through the increasing dominance of its corporations, occasionally supported in the western hemisphere by direct but temporary military intervention. After the Second World War the picture changed. The Russian empire and 'international communism' emerged as a serious potential threat, and at the same time the operations of American corporations became more extensive so that parts of the worlds that had been of little or no strategic interest to the United States started to impinge on the consciousness of policy-makers in Washington. The difficulty faced by these policy-makers was that despite their involvement in the war the American public had never wholly lost its innate isolationism. Having defeated Japan and Germany, most Americans had no great desire to charge around the world defending other people from the threat of communism or American corporations from threats to their profits.

How then could the US thwart communism, promote corporatism and protect its oil supplies while not appearing to rush into foreign entanglements? Russia could use its military power and secret police apparatus to protect its imperial interests in Poland, Czechoslovakia and the other nations of eastern Europe. What weapons could the US use in its sphere of influence? Up to the Second World War US influence on the rest of the world was primarily economic and cultural. Where Stalin tried consciously to promote communist values through crude propaganda, American values spread around the world by simple osmosis. Accounts of American life in the press and on the radio demonstrated the benefits of living in the land of the free; Hollywood films exemplified the frontier values that seemed to have made America great; and the ever-growing presence of American companies demonstrated the vitality of corporatist democracy. Western Europeans might moan lightheartedly that Americans were 'overpaid, oversexed and over here', but the plight of the citizens in the other half of the continent was immeasurably worse. Seduction by GIs bearing nylons and real coffee was infinitely preferable to the organised mass rape the Red Army inflicted on women in the territories they conquered.

But if the United States wanted to ensure that governments on its side of the iron curtain followed its lead it would need something more than a few Hollywood films. That something more was first demonstrated in Italy: ideology, money and the CIA.

The end of the war signalled the end of the road for the old European empires and the old European style of imperialism. No longer would governors' mansions throughout the world house white-skinned bureaucrats sent out from London, Paris, Brussels, The Hague, Madrid, Rome or Lisbon. Moscow might rule Ukraine or Lithuania in the old tsarist manner, but in its new colonial capitals like Prague and Sofia local apparatchiks were imposed and the puppet-master's strings were carefully hidden from view. The strings emanating from Washington were even less visible. The essence of both American and Russian imperial policy was to exercise power indirectly through local regimes. The policy worked as long as the local regimes acted as expected. When they didn't, Moscow and Washington needed a rationale for changing the regimes; in both cases that rationale was to be found in ideology. The ideology of democracy had glued the American revolutionaries together in the crucible of their nation's birth; now its universality was intended to inspire men and women all over the world.

In the interwar years communism had been a spectre raised at home by those fighting to smash organised labour or obstruct civil rights for blacks, but America's isolationism left it with little interest in communist imperialism abroad. The naïve view of Stalin held by men like Roosevelt disappeared after the war when the reality of Russian imperialism became apparent. The turning point was the communist coup in Czechoslovakia. Up to that point the US Congress had been refusing to authorise full funding for the Marshall Plan, had opposed Truman's military plans and was nervous about the role of the newly formed CIA. After the coup Marshall Plan funding was endorsed in the Senate by sixty-nine votes to seventeen, the US signed the Brussels Treaty, establishing mutual defence arrangements with western European countries (a seismic shift in US foreign policy in itself), and the role of the CIA was enormously extended.

President Truman had signalled these developments a year earlier. In Greece a civil war pitched left against right with autocratic Stalinists in one camp and corrupt royalists in the other. Truman wanted to support the royalists but the American population had no desire to get involved in obscure European squabbles. Speaking to a joint session of Congress on 12 March 1947, Truman chose to present the arguments in global terms: a conflict was being waged between good and evil, democracy and dictatorship, America and Russia. In what became known as the Truman Doctrine he announced a foreign policy that was at the same time a radical departure from anything that had gone before and the logical extension of the Monroe Doctrine to the whole world. In one sentence Truman declared the United States to be the world's policeman. 'It must be the policy of the United States', he said, 'to support free peoples who are resisting attempted subjugation by armed minorities or by outside pressures.' After more than half a century the principles of the Truman Doctrine have become such an integral part of US foreign policy that it is difficult to remember that they were once so revolutionary, or how they came into being. The Monroe Doctrine, which gave the US the right to intervene anywhere in the western hemisphere, was originally a response to the messianic musings of Tsar Alexander I and was intended explicitly to protect the hemisphere from invasion by European powers. Only over time did it become a charter for intervention in the internal affairs of countries in the region even when no prospect of foreign invasion was in sight. The Truman Doctrine was a response to the messianic musings of Joseph Stalin, but from the first it was aimed at suppressing internal enemies as well as external. Just as Lenin and Stalin had proclaimed their duty to support the communist cause everywhere in the world, the US was now proclaiming a similar duty. The Truman Doctrine signalled not just the end of pre-war isolationism but the beginning of an ideological empire, with its heart in Washington DC. This was not to be an empire in the traditional sense, in which occupying armies subjugated native populations (for such subjugation was entirely contrary to the ideology of democracy that the new empire professed), but rather was to be, in the phrase used by American presidents to describe military action in Afghanistan and Iraq, 'a coalition of the willing' – with one proviso; that where the willing were not willing enough the US would apply suitable persuasion to encourage their participation. The purpose of the new empire was not to enrich and glorify the United States, although that is what it did, but to enrich and glorify the ideology of corporatist democracy.

The policy discussions in Washington that culminated in the Truman Doctrine were uncannily mirrored in Moscow. Post-war Soviet archives record long discussions among Russian leaders on the need to intervene in western democracies to prevent the resurgence of fascism. Left and right arrived at the same place.

The ideological shorthands 'left' and 'right' had always disguised as much as they disclosed. The 'right' stretched from autocratic fascism to libertarian anarchism and the 'left' from autocratic communism to socialist anarchism. This swirling ideological complexity was quite alien to the American tradition, where since the earliest days in New England the world had divided into good and evil and in every debate God had taken sides. One of the most important ideological developments after the Second World War was to replace the multipolarity of European debate with the bipolarity of American. On one side was corporatist democracy conflating free elections and free markets; on the other was communism. Everything in between was a mistake; everyone who was not avowedly a wholehearted supporter of America or Russia was either a potential ally waiting to be shown the road to salvation or a crypto-communist with evil intent. It was this bipolarity that the CIA successfully hammered home in the Italian elections. Although the Christian Democrats were facing a broad left coalition, all their opponents were painted as the tools of Stalin and the harbingers of a return to dictatorship.

America's bipolar view of the world was to have a profound impact on its foreign policy. Time after time the assumption that anyone who was not a whole-hearted supporter of the American way of life must be a Soviet stooge led the United States to oppose 'radical' leaders and thereby push them into Moscow's arms. Fidel Castro was one example, but a more important one was to have a lasting influence on US policy in the Middle East. In 1956 Eisenhower had stunned Britain, France and Israel by siding with Egyptian president Gamel Abdul Nasser during the Suez canal crisis, but when Nasser later proclaimed himself to be 'non-aligned', courting Russia and America equally, the US became convinced that he must be a crypto-communist and shifted their support to his bitter enemy – Israel. (There were of course a host of other factors involved, but it is indicative that American leaders put ideological factors above their need to secure access to oil.)

Ideology was not enough, however. Money was the glue that would bind America's twentieth-century empire together: private funds used openly by corporations to buy market share overseas, thus enhancing economic power, and public funds used largely covertly to buy political power.

Covert operations and open democracy have always been uneasy bedfellows. The CIA's predecessor organisation had been abolished at the end of the war on the grounds that its activities were incompatible with the ideology of democracy, although at the founding conference of the UN in San Francisco in 1945 the US intercepted diplomatic traffic from forty-three of the forty-five delegations, Britain and perhaps Russia being the exceptions. The CIA was reformed under its new name in 1947 purely for intelligence gathering. That did not satisfy men like James Forrestal, who had just been made the nation's first secretary of defense; he started raising funds from his Wall Street friends to fund covert operations against the Red Menace. After the coup in Czechoslovakia such private enterprise became unnecessary, as the CIA's remit was extended to allow it to engage in covert and paramilitary activities anywhere in the world except within the United States. (Forrestal himself had a mental breakdown soon afterwards, and eventually committed suicide.)

In Italy the situation from Washington's point of view was clear cut. Stalin was funding the communists and the west needed to respond; a few million dollars to reinforce the ideology of democracy was no big deal. Nevertheless the CIA's actions represented something fundamentally new: covert empire building. American policy in Italy worked because it was secret – both from the public in Italy, whose free elections were being manipulated, and, most importantly, from the American public.

In the next major test of this new approach secrecy from the American public became an over-riding priority, as the American government moved from influencing free elections to overturning them.

Regime Change

The title of Stephen Kinzer's book, *Overthrow: America's Century of Regime Change From Hawaii to Iraq*, highlights an essential feature of American imperial policy and one that particularly came to the fore in the decade after the Second World War.

In March 1951 there were changes in the leadership of two nations on opposite sides of the world. By a majority of seventy-nine to twelve the Iranian parliament chose Dr Mohammed Mosaddeq as prime minister; at the same time Jacobo Arbenz Guzman gained 60 per cent of the vote in the first fully free presidential election in the history of Guatemala.

Mosaddeq was sixty-eight and had been part of Iran's established political elite since before the First World War. He had served as a provincial governor general, finance minister and foreign minister. Arbenz was a wealthy landowner and career army officer who had previously been Guatemala's minister of defence. Despite their different backgrounds and the very different conditions in their two nations, the two men had much in common. Both had reformist agendas and were determined to improve the lot of the poorest members of their societies; neither had any global aspirations or posed any threat to anyone beyond their borders; and both were overthrown in bloody coups. Half a century later, when US government records of the period were declassified, one final similarity was definitively proved: in both cases the coups against them were organised by the CIA.

The anti-imperialist rhetorics of America and Russia had a particular impact in the Middle East, where the rising tide of nationalism smashed against the rocks not just of traditional colonialism but also of the new corporatism. The region was the domain of the major oil companies, who had been among the first proponents of international corporatism. Iran became the first demonstration that the old European style of imperialism was giving way to something new: Britain handed over its imperial banner to the United States; Iranians were kept in their place despite the pious declarations at Yalta; and Russia sat watching, silent and inactive, on the sidelines.

Until 1951 the Iranian oilfields were controlled by a British corporation, the Anglo-Iranian Oil Company (AIOC), and the country was effectively run as the corporation's puppet – an oil-based equivalent of the United Fruit Company's banana republics in Central America. The ancient might of the Persian empire had long since disappeared to leave a nation proud but poor, unable to benefit from the one asset that remained – its oil. Popular discontent translated into increasing assertions of independence and, after negotiations for higher oil royalties failed, the Iranian parliament – with the assent of the new young shah – voted to nationalise the AIOC. A month later Islamic fundamentalists assassinated the Iranian prime minister and parliament voted Mohammed Mosaddeq into office.

The nationalisation of the AIOC was hugely popular in Iran, but the British government reacted in fury – a reaction of stunning hypocrisy given that Britain had only just nationalised a large part of its own economy, including its largest oil company, and AIOC's largest shareholder was now the British government. Churchill, recently back in power, announced that he would not allow Mosaddeq's government to export any oil produced in the formerly British-controlled facilities. The Royal Navy blockaded the Persian Gulf, and as Britain had long been the main market for Iran's oil the Iranian economy was thrown into crisis.

Despite the state of the economy Mosaddeq remained popular, and in 1952 was approved by parliament for a second term. However, the British boycott continued to bite and as the political and economic situation deteriorated further Mosaddeq resigned. His successor announced negotiations with Britain to end the oil dispute, but this sparked massive demonstrations throughout the country. The shah recalled Mosaddeq who, with the support of an uneasy coalition of socialists and militant Muslims, introduced a radical programme of social and agrarian reform.

What happened next was shrouded in controversy until 16 April 2000, when the *New York Times* carried a front page story headed 'What's New on the Iran 1953 Coup'. Using US government reports obtained under the Freedom of Information regulations, the article described Operation Ajax – the first US-organised 'regime change' outside the western hemisphere since the toppling of the Hawaiian monarchy six decades before. The chain of events leading up to armed soldiers surrounding the Iranian parliament building on 19 August 1953 is now a matter of record, as is the critical role played by the scion of one of America's greatest dynasties, Kermit Roosevelt, who continued the imperial traditions of his grandfather Theodore.

The impetus behind the coup came originally from Churchill, who refused all Mosaddeq's increasingly desperate attempts at compromise and asked for American assistance in countering what he claimed was a potential communist threat. British intelligence was already bribing potential conspirators, but the plot was quickly taken over by the chief of the CIA's near east and Africa division, Kermit Roosevelt. He was given a $1m budget to be used 'in any way that would bring about the fall of Mosaddeq'. The CIA's Tehran station launched a propaganda campaign, copying the successful Italian strategy, but it was clear that propaganda alone would be insufficient. In June American and British intelligence officials meeting in Beirut finalised a more robust strategy, and Roosevelt flew to Tehran to personally take charge.

The initial objective of Operation Ajax was to persuade the shah to dismiss his prime minister, but the shah refused to be persuaded. The CIA then determined on a coup and started 'black propaganda'. Iranian CIA operatives pretending to be Mosaddeq supporters threatened Muslim leaders, causing Islamic groups to turn against the government. Mosaddeq unwisely called a national referendum, which gave him emergency powers but turned many political factions, including the communists, against him. In August 1953 the shah finally bowed to

American blandishments and dismissed Mosaddeq, but the prime minister refused to go and the shah himself fled abroad. Roosevelt now sped around Tehran exhorting army leaders to rally to the shah's cause. Hundreds died as monarchists and pro-Mosaddeq nationalists clashed in the streets, and the CIA ensured that Mosaddeq loyalists were 'taken out'. The CIA and British MI6 distributed bribes on a massive scale among the military. Finally army tanks bombarded Mosaddeq's official residence and he surrendered. Many of his followers, including his foreign minister and numerous loyal army officers, were executed but Mosaddeq himself, after three years in prison, was sentenced to house arrest, where he remained until his death in 1967 at the age of eighty-four.

'Regime change' as an element of US foreign policy had arrived in the Middle East. And it had arrived in secret. Unlike earlier American interventions in, for example, Nicaragua and the Dominican Republic, the US government for long maintained that Mosaddeq had been ousted by a popular uprising – although everyone involved knew the truth and numerous participants had told their version of what happened. In 1979 Kermit Roosevelt himself published *Counter Coup: The Struggle for the Control of Iran*, but only when the *New York Times* published the official government documents in 2000 did the full truth emerge.

Secrecy has always been a feature of diplomacy, and America is not unique in that respect. Robert Kagan, in his authoritative study of American foreign policy in the eighteenth and nineteenth centuries, writes that 'Secrecy and deception were prominent features of American diplomacy from the start.' The group handling foreign relations for the independence plotters, which eventually became the state department, was initially called the committee of secret correspondence. The treaty negotiated by the American revolutionaries with France in 1778 contained a number of secret clauses, including the one by which America agreed not to negotiate a separate peace with Britain – a clause that America then secretly broke. At the conclusion of the war American diplomats negotiated a treaty with Spain, again in secret, but this time the secrecy was not to avoid assisting foreign powers but to prevent debate at home on the possible terms. The secrecy surrounding the Iranian coup was similarly designed to prevent debate within the United States.

Only with hindsight was Secretary of State Madeleine Albright able to admit nearly half a century later that 'the coup was clearly a setback for Iran's political development and it is easy to see now why many Iranians continue to resent this intervention by America'. At the time US policy-makers considered it a foreign policy triumph. The coup was not engineered solely, or even primarily, to help American corporate interests but to ensure that in the global struggle between the American and Russian empires Iran and its oil was in the American camp. It was the US equivalent of the coups that installed communist regimes in Poland and Czechoslovakia. And just as the US did not intervene in eastern Europe, Russia did not intervene in Iran. The official American line, put forward it would seem quite sincerely by Eisenhower and others, was that they acted to prevent Iran 'going communist'. The reality is that even though Russia had troops on the Iranian border they were never mobilised, the Iranian communist party was never wholeheartedly committed to Mosaddeq's cause and Mosaddeq himself never asked the Soviet Union for assistance. The Iran coup was an exercise in imperial policing by the new imperial superpower.

The coup was also one of the most naked examples of pure power-politics, denuded almost entirely from the cloaking ideology of democracy. There was no suggestion that the shah was in some way more 'democratic' than Mosaddeq. Just before the coup the *New York Times* reported that Mosaddeq was undoubtedly 'the most popular politician in the country' and *Time* magazine had made him one of their men of the year. A democratic neutral had been replaced by an autocratic pro-American. The fact that the means by which the regime change occurred were undemocratic is precisely why they had to be kept secret from the American people.

American military installations sprang up throughout the country. Electronic listening posts were set up on the Russian border; American spy planes used Iranian bases; espionage agents were smuggled across the frontier. Because the new regime had limited popular support the CIA had to help set up SAVAK, the Shah's notorious secret police. Twenty years later SAVAK's fearsome reputation would lead Amnesty International to claim that Iran had the world's worst human rights record.

The shah and the Iranian military realised that they owed their power to the United States, and Iran became a classic vassal state. The parallels with Stalin's vassal states in eastern Europe were inescapable.

The Iranian coup not only showed a new facet of American imperial strategy but demonstrated that global imperial power had passed definitively from Britain to America. Not only was Britain unable to protect its oil interests without US assistance, but once Mosaddeq had been removed American oil companies like Gulf Oil swiftly moved into the country, usurping what had once been a virtual British monopoly. In another sign of the times Kermit Roosevelt did not follow his grandfather Theodore and cousin Franklin into politics; when he left the CIA a few years later he joined Gulf Oil. The close relationship between American corporations and US covert operations that this exemplified was even more evident on the other side of the world, where events remarkably similar to those in Iran were unfolding with a cast of characters far more familiar to students of American history. America's next target was the government of Guatemala.

The coup in Iran could be presented as a legitimate move in the cold war between America and Russia. Soviet troops had not long before occupied parts of the country and still sat just over the border. Guatemala was nowhere near the Russian empire and had long been firmly entrenched in America's camp. The robber baron Minor Cooper Keith had died nearly a quarter of a century before but his creation, the United Fruit Company, still exercised quasi-feudal control over the country. It was this control that was threatened when, in the same month that Mohammed Mosaddeq became prime minister of Iran, Guatemala held its first ever democratic presidential elections.

Jacobo Arbenz Guzman, landowner, soldier and convinced capitalist, swept to power and announced plans for agrarian reform that were strikingly similar to those of the 1862 Homestead Act in the United States. Uncultivated land was to be compulsorily purchased and sold to smallholders. As the largest holder of such land was the United Fruit Company, this was bound to lead to conflict with the United States. Arbenz offered the company $3 an acre for its land, the value the company itself had declared when paying its property taxes, but United Fruit now declared the land to be worth $75 an acre. The scene was set for another imperial adventure, as United Fruit had far more powerful allies than the president of what one CIA document labelled a 'Banana Republic'.

CIA director Allen Dulles, his brother, US secretary of state John Foster Dulles, and the undersecretary of state Walter Bedell Smith were United Fruit shareholders. The Dulles's former law firm had long represented United Fruit, and Allen Dulles had served on the corporation's board of trustees. The company's top public relations officer (who produced an anti-Arbenz film called *Why the Kremlin Hates Bananas*) was the husband of President Eisenhower's private secretary. The corporation paid for American journalists to travel to Guatemala, where they were fed blood-curdling stories of supposed communist infamy, and in February 1954 the CIA launched Operation Washtub, a scheme to 'discover' phoney Soviet arms caches in Nicaragua to demonstrate Guatemalan ties to Moscow.

The campaign succeeded, and the CIA moved on to orchestrate a coup codenamed Operation PBSUCCESS. The agency set up a clandestine radio station to broadcast propaganda, jammed all Guatemalan stations and hired American pilots to bomb strategic points in Guatemala City. In this way the CIA's invasion force of just 150 men was able to convince the Guatemalan public and President Arbenz that a major invasion was underway. Guatemala's brief flirtation with democracy was snuffed out. Arbenz and his cabinet were allowed to flee the country, but hundreds of his supporters were rounded up and killed. Over the next forty years successive US-backed military regimes are said to have killed over 100,000 civilians as the repression that was necessary to maintain regime change continued. Arbenz himself spent the rest of his life in exile. In 1971 he was found dead in his bath in Mexico, prompting the same sort of rumours that had surrounded the death of a man whose fate he shared: Jan Masaryk in Prague.

While the CIA was spreading pro-corporatist subversion around the globe the KGB was spreading pro-communist subversion. Soviet records that have become available, such as those known as the Mitrokhin archives, show that the KGB operated in much the same way as the CIA. It too launched 'initiatives', especially in the third world, quite independent of the formal diplomatic policy-makers, confident, like the CIA, that its political contacts at the highest levels would protect it. It too had a vision of a bipolar world, which was a mirror image of the CIA's. Not only was the KGB convinced that American imperialism was constantly seeking Russia's destruction, but it retained an ideological vision every bit as strong as its opponent's. Readers of the Mitrokhin archives, knowing that communism was destined to collapse, may well find it bizarre that the bungling, brutality and bureaucracy of the KGB was not accompanied by unremitting cynicism but was leavened with an apparently genuine Marxist-Leninist world view: many of its leaders really believed that they were helping to act out the dramas Marx and Lenin had claimed to be historically inevitable, and that by encouraging anti-colonialist national liberation movements they would so weaken western capitalism that – as their ideology predicted – communism's onward march to world domination would become unstoppable.

The covert imperial adventures of both America and Russia after the Second World War were long shrouded in mystery. There still remains controversy about an aborted CIA project to depose the Iraqi president in 1959, a project now remembered mainly for the planned participation of a twenty-year-old CIA 'asset' named Saddam Hussein. With the end of the cold war Soviet archives began to be opened up, prompting America to do the same. In May 1997 the CIA released hundreds of documents relating to its 1954 coup in Guatemala, which demonstrated dramatically the moral equivalence of the two imperial powers. For example, the CIA documents included a list of fifty-eight people to be assassinated (although with the names of all fifty-eight carefully blanked out).

The success of covert operations in Italy, Iran and Guatemala have led many on the left to see the CIA as the sinister architect of America's global hegemony, just as their opponents have seen the KGB behind every American setback. Conspiracy theorists have found American spies under every rock. As secret archives are unlocked it has become obvious that the CIA has had amazingly long tentacles, which have encompassed enemies and allies alike. James Angleton, the CIA's director of counter-intelligence (who had previously represented the agency in Rome and been responsible for the manipulation of Italian elections after the Second World War), had a particular hatred for British prime minister Harold Wilson, and spent money to combat what he regarded as Wilson's subservience to the Kremlin. Similarly the agency seems to have worked actively against Gough Whitlam's government in Australia. But just because the United States tried to influence the course of events does not mean it succeeded. There is a danger of using the same faulty logic that pro-American observers used after the Second World War: the United States fought to bring down Hitler, Hitler was brought down, therefore the US brought down Hitler. The CIA wanted to push Wilson and Whitlam out; they were pushed out; therefore the CIA pushed them out. This is far too simplistic a reading of history. The CIA, like the KGB, has been just one of thousands of vectors carrying the influence of American and Russian rulers around the globe. It provides fertile soil to be tilled by thriller-writers, film makers and journalists, but the main tools of the new imperialism have been US financial institutions and corporations supported by old-fashioned military force.

The role of military force in American foreign policy is sometimes regarded as a modern development. The classic text on post-war US foreign policy is Ambrose and Brinkley's *Rise to Globalism*, first published in 1971 and regularly updated ever since. The book's very first sentence describes the glaringly different conditions today from those that existed in 1939 when 'no American troops were stationed in any foreign country'. Today, the argument goes, the United States has interests beyond its borders that were entirely absent before the Second World War. In fact what this sentence illustrates is not a change in underlying policies but in perceptions, because of course there were American troops stationed in what most of the world would have described as foreign countries; there were significant military forces in the Philippines and Cuba, not to mention the island of Guam – where the commandant of the naval station also acted as the island's governor. These were remnants of the old-style imperialism in which foreign territories from Florida to Hawaii had been annexed to become part of the United States. In 1939 the sailors at Subic Bay in the Philippines or Guantanamo Bay in Cuba were technically not in foreign countries; they were all part of the American empire (as indeed Guam remains, as does Guantanamo Bay – when it suits).

The scale of American military intervention overseas dipped dramatically between the two world wars, but it then increased dramatically. One academic study quoted by Ferguson identified 168 separate instances of American armed intervention overseas between 1946 and 1965, one intervention every six weeks. The transition away from using force as a last resort started in the Middle East, with troops sent to Lebanon to protect the pro-American government in 1958 and additional air force units to Saudi Arabia a few years later to stop incursions from Yemen. Initially these were exceptions, with the United States relying on dollar diplomacy to achieve its foreign policy objectives. Whereas in 1939 there were a handful of military outposts in the colonies, by 1967 US troops were stationed in sixty-four countries – nineteen in Latin America, thirteen in Europe, eleven in Africa, eleven in the Middle East and surrounding area and ten in the far east. The collapse of the Russian Empire, far from reducing the desire for overseas bases, provided new opportunities for expansion. By 2006 there were 702 bases in 130 countries.

The primacy of commercial over cold war objectives in driving military operations was clearly outlined in an unlikely source: Noam Chomsky quotes the *Marine Corps Gazette* of May 1990. General A.M. Gray, after noting that 'the majority of crises we have responded to since the end of the Second World War have not directly involved the Soviet Union', described the need for a 'credible military power projection capability' to ensure America's unimpeded access to overseas markets and to the resources needed by US industries. But for the first forty years after the Second World War America's objectives were usually expressed in terms not of selfish national interest but of the great ideological battle between the godly and the ungodly. American covert and overt interventions overseas were necessary for one reason only: to counter the evil ambitions of its former Soviet ally.

While America led a crusade to resist the Soviet devil, the driving force behind the startling post-war resurgence of Russian imperialism disappeared.

Russian Regime Change – The Death of the Ultimate Tsar

On 5 March 1953 Joseph Stalin died. One of history's most evil men, a man whose murderous reign had touched nearly every family in Russia, passed away and the nation collapsed into grief. It was said that flower shops across Russia sold out, and there were no flowers left for the funeral of the composer Prokofiev who died on the same day. The anguish that swept the country was spontaneous. At Stalin's funeral there was no need to bus in press-ganged factory workers for the carefully orchestrated demonstrations that had been such a feature of his reign. For millions of ordinary Russians Stalin was the man who had dragged their country into the twentieth century, and above all had saved them from barbarian invasion. He was the all-wise omnipotent autocrat in a nation that for centuries had been told to venerate its all-wise omnipotent tsar.

Stalin influenced every aspect of life in Russia and in its colonies. His secret police reached into every home, school, office, factory and field. More than any western president or prime minister of the twentieth century, more even than Churchill or De Gaulle, he stamped his mark on his country's character, history and even on its geography. He changed borders, relocated peoples, installed and replaced governments. He left an empire that stretched from the borders of Austria to the Pacific, an empire under his absolute personal control and an empire that – when that personal control was gone – would eventually collapse in on itself like a puppet whose strings had been cut.

Stalin had carved himself a place in history – but what place? Despite all the evidence of Stalin's atrocities that has emerged since his death, the veneration that was so evident when he died has not gone away.

The rewriting of historical events starts before they occur and continues long after they end. At the very moment that they happen actions are being perceived through ideological prisms built up over the preceding centuries. The ideology of autocracy conditioned the way Stalin was perceived. Russians looked to the tsars as the fathers of their nation; they might be flawed, they might be badly advised but they had the interests of all Russia in their hearts; they provided the strength of leadership that would safeguard their wellbeing, protect them from invasion and advance their glory. Stalin assumed the mantle of autocracy, and his subjects perceived all his actions in that light.

As time goes by these perceptions change: history is rewritten, but rarely overnight. History evolves and evolves selectively. Just as George Washington is remembered as a freedom fighter not a slave owner, so Stalin is remembered by many Russians for bringing electricity not suppressing elections. Just as the *Mayflower* is remembered and the Mystic Massacre forgotten, so the battle for Stalingrad is remembered and the Gulags obscured. A more balanced view may yet emerge in Russia but American experience provides no guarantee that it will. In 1988 a Russian presidential commission on the crimes of communism estimated that there were 30 million victims of Lenin and Stalin. The commission has been largely ignored. It is not just that Stalin is still venerated by a few of the old guard but that Russian society as a whole has never been forced to come to terms with its past. There has never been an educational programme of de-Stalinisation similar to the de-Nazification in Germany. 'Holocaust denial' in Germany is largely restricted to a lunatic fringe, but a recent poll showed that only 30 per cent of Russians thought that Stalin did more bad than good. And in another poll by the All-Russian Public Opinion Research Centre 20 per cent of respondents described Stalin's role in Russian history as 'very positive' and 30 per cent as 'somewhat positive'. Communist party leader Gennady Zyuganov was still proclaiming the 'great name of Stalin' more than half a century after his death, and calling for Volgograd to revert to the name Stalingrad.

Rayfield offers an illuminating example of modern Russia's attitude to its Stalinist past. In 2002 the Russian post office issued a series of stamps honouring the Russian Counter-Intelligence service; they featured some of the greatest mass murderers of modern times – men like Sergei Puzitsky, who organised the killing of half a million Cossacks, and Vladimir Styrne, who slaughtered thousands of Uzbeks on a whim of Stalin. The stamps excited virtually no comment inside Russia or outside.

Stalin's death fundamentally changed the course of Russian imperial history. By their very nature autocracies are more dependent on the character of individual autocrats than democracies are on the character of presidents or prime ministers. The Russian empire had sailed across the ocean of history for centuries, sometimes, when commanded by a Peter or Catherine, rushing forward, at other times appearing almost becalmed. Stalin took advantage of stormy seas to send the empire racing in new directions, and when he died it continued – still from a distance seeming to be under full sail, but actually drifting rudderless to its inevitable destruction on the rocks of nationalisms that only Stalin could suppress.

Just as the man Stalin most resembled, Ivan the Terrible, had surrounded himself with lesser mortals who proved incapable of following in his footsteps, so Stalin's entourage emerged blinking from his shadow and groped for a way forward. Cabinet posts were divided up among the most senior apparatchiks, who declared their commitment to collective leadership but were wracked with feuds and were devoid of anything that might be called vision. The one exception was the unlikely figure who immediately tried to seize the reins of power: the all-powerful interior ministry was taken by Lavrenti Beria, Stalin's last secret police chief, and a man who was if anything more manipulative, more sadistic and certainly more intelligent than Stalin himself. He rose up through the state apparatus on a tidal wave of blood. Unlike many who signed Stalin's death warrants, Beria personally tortured and murdered those in his way. For relaxation he was driven around Moscow in an American convertible, abducting women and, especially, young girls for his personal pleasure. He was simultaneously the fawning sycophant, brilliant administrator and cold-blooded killer. Too late it also transpired that he alone had a vision that might have preserved the empire he nearly inherited.

American presidents might boast of being born in a log cabin, but Beria was born in a three-walled hovel with a hole in the roof as a chimney – in what is now the hotly disputed territory of Abkhazia. Like Stalin, Beria was not a Russian but a Georgian (or more accurately in his case a Mingrelian, one of Georgia's ethnic minorities). Both men emerged from the vicious quasi-tribal politics of Russia's colonies in the Caucasus.

A photograph in Rayfield's classic work *Stalin and His Hangmen* shows Beria seated between the party secretaries of Abkhazia and Armenia at a conference in 1935. Within a year Beria had personally shot the Armenian and invited the Abkhaz, Nestor Lakoba, to dinner at his apartment, where he was poisoned. The fate of Lakoba perfectly illustrated the character of both Stalin and Beria. The Abkhaz leader had once been possibly the only close friend Stalin ever had. Year after year the men holidayed together with their families. Beria long conspired to undermine the influence Lakoba had on the Soviet dictator without success. Eventually Lakoba made the mistake of trying to persuade Stalin not to unleash the full force of his blood lust on Abkhazia, and Stalin turned on his supposed friend. Seizing his opportunity, Beria not only murdered Lakoba but also had his mother bludgeoned to death, his wife tortured for two years until she died, and his children held in prison until old enough to be tortured and executed.

Conspiracy theorists have held that Beria even murdered Stalin. The evidence is flimsy, although it is seems clear that Stalin had been planning yet another purge, with Beria marked as a potential victim, and when the Russian leader collapsed into a coma Beria delayed sending for medical support until it was too late.

Beria had an almost unique insight into the real working of the Russian empire. After decades in the secret police he knew better than anyone the strains that Stalin's terror and constant purges were creating on Russian society; through the immense network of prison industries he had his finger on the economic pulse of the nation, and his agents around the world provided massive amounts of sometimes fanciful data about the outside world. Beria saw what the rest of the communist oligarchs barely glimpsed: the Russian empire was overstretched and could not continue as it was; Stalin's legacy could not survive Stalin. The signs were already there. Red Army soldiers had returned from captured territory in Central Europe unsettled by the relative wealth they had encountered (and many had been shot or sent to the gulags to stop the contagion of their experience from spreading). Lend-Lease had demonstrated that the American economy was simply in another league. Unrest continued to simmer not just in the new colonies but also in many of the pre-war colonies in the Caucasus.

Within three days of Stalin's death Beria was starting to dismantle the gulag system and change the country's economic priorities. Massive civil engineering projects with little real benefit were stopped and 1.2 million prisoners were released. Half a million prosecutions that were in the pipeline were cancelled. The vast majority of political prisoners remained incarcerated, but some of the most famous were publicly rehabilitated; for example, Foreign Minister Molotov's wife was flown back from her camp, and remarried. Beria banned torture and had the notorious Leforotovo torture chambers in Moscow dismantled. More fundamentally, he started to dismantle the apparatus of empire. He rehabilitated nationalists in his native Georgia. Starting in Ukraine and Lithuania, and quickly spreading to Belarus and Latvia, he replaced Russian officials with locals. Official proceedings were once again to be conducted in the local language. It was an amazing turnaround. Beria had been responsible for ethnic and class cleansing in the occupied territories on a massive scale. He had arranged for hundreds of thousands of men, women and children to be deported from frontier regions before or during the war: Belarussians, Estonians, Finns, Germans, Iranians, Koreans, Kurds, Latvians, Lithuanians, Moldavians, Poles, Romanians, Western Ukrainians (Ruthenians) – and that ignores Caucasian tribes like the Chechens, which until recently few in the west had ever heard of. After the war hundreds of thousands more had been deported from the newly conquered territories. In the most famous case Beria recommended to Stalin in March 1940 the execution of 14,700 Polish prisoners of war and 11,000 other Polish prisoners: 4,143 were famously buried in the forest at Katyn – and the Katyn massacre of army officers and intellectuals became the most well known of hundreds of similar horrors organised by Beria.

The sudden storm of change unleashed by Beria on Stalin's death alarmed the rest of the cabinet, and their unease boiled over with Beria's next proposal: granting independence to the new colony of East Germany. Half a million East Germans, including 3,000 Communist party members, had fled to the west, and there were riots in the streets. Beria proposed reaching an agreement with the United States to create a unified and neutral Germany with a mixed economy. This was too much for the rest of the cabinet to stomach. After just a hundred days in power Beria was seized at a cabinet meeting, thrown into prison and six months later shot.

For the next forty years Soviet leaders persisted in their doomed attempt to keep Stalin's empire alive. Khrushchev, who became the next leader, really believed that the supposedly rational central planning of the Russian economic model would ultimately prove superior to the corporatist model in the west, but increasingly his successors came to realise that the economic gap between the two superpowers was continuing to widen. By the end of the century Russia produced around 1 per cent of world output, the US around 30 per cent. The Russian empire could only be held together with brute force, and without economic muscle and the manic spirit of Stalin himself brute force could not be sustained, although parts of the Soviet state machine tried to continue as if it could.

The KGB provided a route to the top for men like Yuri Andropov and Vladimir Putin, but it could not hold the empire together. The Red Army had the numbers to crush uprisings in eastern Europe, but when it came to colonial conflicts in Afghanistan or the Caucasus its numerical and nuclear superiority counted for nothing. Above all the economy could not keep pace with the rest of the world; in the age of the microchip the regimented armies of unskilled workers that had dragged Russia into the twentieth century stopped it entering the twenty-first.

It is obvious now that the Russian empire, which had seemed so threatening in the first decade after the Second World War, was destined to collapse – leaving America as the sole imperial power. It was not so obvious at the time. Two things seemed to stand in the way of the United States achieving global supremacy. The Soviet Union appeared to be proclaiming the dawning of its own new quasi-imperial era, and these pretensions had not yet been exposed for what they were. And while the Soviet dawn was breaking the banners of other empires still fluttered limply in the dusk. To establish and maintain its global supremacy the United States had to deal not only with Russia and recalcitrant banana republics but with its former allies in western Europe.

Ever since Thomas Paine urged the colonists to revolution, America's relationship with Britain had been ambivalent. Enemies as often as allies in the nineteenth century, the two nations joined together to fight two world wars in the twentieth, but there remained tensions. After the First World War the British ambassador in Washington had complained about being treated as a 'vassal', and there were times during the the Second World War when the patience of both governments wore thin.

There were fundamental differences between the way Britain and the other European imperial powers saw the world and the way it was seen from Washington. British wartime cabinet minutes show that disagreements between the allies were not restricted to political and military matters. The cabinet, for example, was much exercised by the racial policies of the US military. Churchill pleaded for understanding, but members of his cabinet – especially fellow Tory Viscount Cranbourne – were bitterly opposed to any 'colour bar' on British soil. (It was eventually decided that the US would be allowed to enforce racial segregation on its bases but British pubs and cinemas would be open to all.) Immediately after the war there were bitter disputes about the US assumption that the starving populations of liberated Europe should be fed from the carefully hoarded British reserves, without any rationing being imposed in the US; as Churchill said, the 'US soldier eats five times what ours does', and yet it was always British food stocks that were 'raided' when needed.

The root cause of tensions between the two nations was that psychologically Britain had not adjusted to the new global economic and military realities after 1918. The British empire had appeared to continue unchanged, but the Second World War made its fragility apparent to all and its dissolution inevitable. Exactly the same happened to the French empire. The batons of empire had passed across the Atlantic but the politicians in London and Paris failed to see how comprehensively the world had changed. Their illusions collapsed in 1956. The Egyptian dictator Gamel Abdul Nasser seized control of the Suez canal. Britain and France promptly invaded Egypt. President Eisenhower was furious. He was not concerned with the morality or legality of the invasion – indeed the United States used exactly the same arguments thirty-three years later when it invaded Panama – but with the fact that not only did the Anglo-French invasion, conducted in collusion with Israel, threaten America's strategy of buying Arab friendship to protect its oil supplies, but Britain and France had launched the attack without American knowledge, let alone permission. Eisenhower ordered the two European powers to withdraw immediately or face severe American sanctions. They had no choice but to obey; it was an ignominious end to three centuries of European imperial supremacy.

A new imperial age had arrived.

CHAPTER 14
WINNING THE WAR THAT WASN'T

Britain spent the twentieth century trying to deal with the consequences of what it had done in the nineteenth century. A vanishing legacy of imperial grandeur and industrial dominance caused a cultural angst summed up in Dean Acheson's remark that 'Great Britain had lost an empire but not yet found a role.' America, on the other hand, spent the twentieth century simply forgetting what it had done in the nineteenth. The aggressive imperial drive that drove a nation from the eastern seaboard across the continent, the ethnic cleansing of those who stood in its way, the enslavement of millions that made much of it possible, the irreconcilable ideological differences that culminated in a brutal civil war – all are entirely absent from the myth that an American dream, first envisaged by the Pilgrim Fathers, has inspired, and still inspires, the nation's every move.

Russia too turned its back on the past, not so much denying its imperial traditions as repudiating them. According to Edmund Burke, 'Those who don't know history are destined to repeat it.' The new communist autocrats prided themselves on knowing history but still repeated it. Stalin, the ultimate tsar, bequeathed an empire more extensive than any of his predecessors and controlled with the same tools of suppression and repression. His successors continued his posturing, especially towards the American arch-enemy. The decades following Stalin's death saw the

Russian empire, still preaching the inevitability of global revolution, pitched in a cold war against a rival that had long since forgotten its own revolutionary roots. In both cases histories were rewritten and ideologies adjusted. The lusts that had driven one nation to become the undisputed master of the western hemisphere and the other to become the dominant power on the Eurasian landmass remained – unacknowledged – and now focused on each other.

Hot War, Cold War, Phoney War

Thousands of books, acres of newsprint and uncountable hours of TV and radio time have been devoted to the origins, character and eventual conclusion of one of the most epic confrontations of all time: the cold war. From 5 March 1946, when Winston Churchill declared that an iron curtain had descended across Europe, until 9 November 1989, when its concrete manifestation in Berlin was torn down, the world was pitched into a titanic struggle between two superpower empires. For good or bad the life of everyone on the planet was touched in a global contest for supremacy that would determine the history of the foreseeable future; indeed it would determine whether the world would have a future. The cold war between America and Russia could so easily have turned into the ultimate hot war. Life on earth might have vanished in a nuclear Armageddon. But it didn't. In historical terms the cold war was a non-event. The terrorist attacks of 9/11 have been described by Niall Ferguson, in a phrase borrowed from A.J.P. Taylor, as 'the turning point at which history failed to turn'. Similarly the cold war was the war that wasn't.

Even the episode that came closest to realising the nuclear nightmare, the Cuban Missile Crisis, served only to illustrate that neither empire had the appetite for the ultimate confrontation. The United States positioned missiles in Turkey, threatening Russian cities across the border, and Russia retaliated by shipping missiles to Cuba within range of American cities. For a few tense days both sides thumped the table, but at the last minute President Kennedy agreed to remove his missiles from Turkey and the Russian ships turned back.

The historically important developments of the second half of the twentieth century had virtually nothing to do with the cold war. Advances in technology, the growing gap between poor and rich, the emergence of feminism, the re-emergence of religious fundamentalism, the revolution in communications, the continued growth and evolution of corporatism: none of these was triggered by the cold war. Only in the unravelling of the old European colonial empires did the conflict between the United States and Russia play a noticeable although essentially insignificant part. In geopolitical terms the outstanding feature of the period was the awesome global spread of American commercial and political control; Russia was as irrelevant to this process as Britain or France.

Russia pretended to be a superpower, a pretence endorsed by the United States, but the reality was very different. Soviet leaders gave opportunistic support to radical movements from Cuba to Angola, and the KGB scurried around the world to little effect funding a host of terrorist groups from Ireland to Iraq and arranging occasional assassinations, but apart from a miserable attempt to colonise Afghanistan – repeating the dramatic mistakes of the British a century before – the Red Army did no more than act as a police force in its new eastern European possessions. Unlike America, Russia had no overseas commercial interests to protect or resources it wanted to control. In the two most bloody 'confrontations' of the period, in Korea and Vietnam, the Red Army was noticeable for its absence. By the end of the century US corporations had penetrated almost every corner of the globe and American troops were sprinkled across the world, while the Russian empire hovered close to collapse.

With the benefit of hindsight it is clear that the outstanding feature of Russian history in the last half of the twentieth century was the doomed attempt first to consolidate the territories seized at the end of the Second World War into the Russian empire, and then more fundamentally to maintain the empire itself. By contrast the outstanding feature of American history was the success of American corporations, reinforced by the covert and overt might of the state, in expanding and deepening the commercial empire of the United States. It is now evident that in both cases the most crucial developments were *within* the two empires, and yet perceptions at the time were dominated by the cold war *between* them. It was not the weakening bonds that held the Soviet empire together or the massive capital flows within the American empire that captured the attention of contemporary observers but the bellicose pronouncements of politicians on both sides of the iron curtain and, above all, two full-scale wars in Asia – wars that seemed so very much more significant than history proved them to be.

The Korean and Vietnamese civil wars have been presented as America battling the Russo-Chinese communist empire, but of the 10 million people who died – half of them civilians – around 92,000, less than one in a hundred, were American. American bodies dominated the TV screens but not the graveyards. In both cases the conflicts were essentially civil wars between local dictators made horrifically worse by outside intervention.

The former Japanese colony of Korea was occupied by accident when the atomic bomb suddenly ended the Second World War. US troops diverted from invading Japan landed in the south and Russian troops diverted from invading Manchuria entered from the north. They met at the 38th parallel and partitioned the country, installing two dictators obsessed with toppling each other. At first Stalin simply told his protégé to shut up and America helped replace its first protégé with a more moderate version. Then in 1950 Stalin decided that action on the eastern front might distract attention from his antics in Europe and marginally increase his empire. North Korean forces rolled across the border, sweeping all before them. Having lost all but the south-eastern tip of the Korean peninsula, America and its allies responded with a flash of military genius when General MacArthur landed his forces at Inchon far to the north, cutting off the enemy advance and then pushing the North Koreans right back to the Chinese border. At this point Stalin apparently gave up and accepted that a pro-American Korea would sit on his frontier. However, Russia and America were not the only imperial powers in the region. Mao Tse-tung persuaded

Stalin to continue, and Chinese forces streamed across the border. Over three years 600,000 Chinese and countless Koreans died in a war that eventually changed nothing. In 1953 the two war-weary sides signed an armistice that left the country just as it had been when the war started.

The Korean War accelerated the division of the world into Russian and American camps. The Russian camp was an empire in all but name, albeit with China having a dominion-like status reminiscent of the role of Canada or Australia in the British empire. The American camp was not an empire in the traditional sense and the United States was anxious for it not to be seen as one, preferring to describe its realm as 'the free world'. The Orwellian nature of this term soon became apparent when, during the Korean War, the US established military bases in Morocco, Libya, Saudi Arabia and fascist Spain, none of whose regimes stood for 'freedom' as understood by Thomas Paine and the Founding Fathers. To show how far America's ideology had moved on since its own revolution against colonial authority, military aid was given to France to suppress the attempted revolution in its colony of Vietnam.

In Vietnam a scenario similar to Korea was played out with a different final act. Vietnamese partisans, the Vietminh, fought against the Japanese, who invaded their country during the Second World War, and then against the French, who tried to reassert control afterwards. Once the French were expelled the communist-controlled Vietminh took control of the north and – now rechristened Vietcong – fought to topple the regime the French had left in the south. Once again two dictatorships battled for control.

The first American to die in Vietnam was fighting not against the Vietcong but with them (or more correctly with the Vietminh). He was a military adviser working for the OSS (the Office of Strategic Services, the forerunner of the CIA), training the guerrillas to resist the Japanese occupiers. During the Korean Civil War America swapped sides in Vietnam and gave massive but ineffective aid to the French. Russia remained wholly committed to the Vietminh and encouraged their guerrilla war in the south. When US troops entered the war Russia redoubled its logistical support, but stopped short of committing its own forces. In the end the United States was defeated not by the military might of the communist empire but by the stubborn resistance of the North Vietnamese leadership and its supporters in the south. The Korean and Vietnamese wars are remarkable not as manifestations of the cold war but as examples of the futility of the traditional military model of imperial control. Ten million people died in Korea and Vietnam in wars that had no lasting global significance.

In 1968 the Tet or Lunar New Year was celebrated by a North Vietnamese offensive that heralded the beginning of the end for the US military occupation of South Vietnam. In 2002 Tet was celebrated in a very different way – by baking a gigantic 1,400 gram rice cake that garnered a place in the *Guinness Book of Records* for its fifty cooks and acres of positive publicity for the sponsor, Coca-Cola. The tentacles of American corporations and financial institutions have proved far more effective in changing the face of Vietnam than helicopter gunships and napalm.

Although the political rhetoric continued and even heated up after the Vietnam War, US corporations were acting far more pragmatically. Even as Reagan thundered against the 'Evil Empire', US business was doing its best to maintain that empire's economic well-being. The Soviet Union developed the world's largest iron and steel plant, constructed by the American McKee Corporation, and Europe's largest tube and pipe mill, again built largely with American equipment and technology. The period saw the full flowering of the commercial empire that had started to emerge after the Spanish-American War. The failure of military intervention in Vietnam seemed for a time to show the wisdom of moving away from the older, cruder imperial traditions that Russia continued to follow.

In 1956 Russia demonstrated that its commitment to traditional imperialism was as strong as ever when protests in Hungary turned into full-scale war: 6,000 Soviet tanks supported by artillery and air strikes smashed an attempt to stage a popular uprising. Possibly as many as 3,000 Hungarians died as well as over 700 Russians; 200,000 refugees fled to the west. American leaders had been vociferous in their support for Hungarian aspirations but in the face of Russian military force they hastily backed away. It was a pattern to be repeated in Georgia half a century later.

Left-wing historians have portrayed the Hungarian uprising as the workers trying to build genuine socialism to replace the travesty of Stalinism; American commentators saw it as a battle to replace socialism with democracy. The truth is that most Hungarians were simply fighting to achieve freedom from Russian rule; as in Czechoslovakia twelve years later the struggle was *against* imperialism, not *for* any particular political doctrine. It was a sign of the pressures forever bubbling across Russia's empire.

The Red Army was ready to crush colonial dissent, but heating up the cold war was not on the Kremlin's agenda. In both Korea and Vietnam America showed itself to be far more adventurous militarily than Russia, committing hundreds of thousands of troops. The Red Army stayed away even when in October 1950 two US Air Force planes 'accidentally' attacked a Russian airfield near Vladivostok, the first American attack on Russia since American troops had withdrawn from Vladivostok thirty years earlier after failing to hold the Trans-Siberian railway. (The two pilots were court-martialled but acquitted.)

Stalin's one direct intervention in the Korean War was to send Russian fighter pilots into combat. As he was insisting that the conflict was a spontaneous popular uprising in which the Soviet Union played no part, the pilots flew planes bearing North Korean markings and were told to speak to each other in Korean in case they were overheard by American eavesdroppers – a ludicrously impractical instruction that involved taping phrasebook pages inside the cockpits; it was usually forgotten in the heat of combat. Even more absurd were attempts by the United States to keep secret its blanket bombing of neutral Cambodia during the Vietnam War – as if the enemy might not have noticed the bombs raining down on them. Only the American electorate was kept in ignorance.

In some ways more surprising than such episodes is that both sides managed to hide so much from each other. In 1995 President Clinton ordered the release of thousands of documents relating to the cold war, including a CIA assessment dated 12 October 1950 that concluded Chinese intervention in the Korean War was 'not probable in 1950'. Just two weeks later 300,000 Chinese troops crossed into Korea. (Clinton's action caused immense dismay inside the CIA; despite the reports having been freely available for six years, the Bush administration had them reclassified and removed from the public archives in a deliberate attempt to rewrite history.) The KGB was no more successful in understanding the enemy. Just two weeks before America's final ignominious exodus from Vietnam the KGB leader Yuri Andropov warned that the US might win the war by launching an Inchon-style assault deep into North Vietnam.

The main reason for such intelligence failures was that both the CIA and KGB devoted most of their attention not to spying across the iron curtain but to policing their own empires. Much of their intelligence came from brutal secret police forces like the AVH in Hungary or SAVAK in Iran, who inevitably focused primarily on domestic dissent. Rhetoric might fly between the empires but action was centred within them. The CIA was more concerned with Central America than Central Europe.

Monroe Marches On

On the night of 16 April 1961 two men having a quiet cigarette on an island beach were gunned down. It is possible they never saw their killers or heard the order to fire given by the group's leader, CIA agent Grayson Lynch. They had become the first casualties to fall at the Bay of Pigs.

One of the foundation stones of American imperialism was the Monroe doctrine under which the United States gave itself the right to intervene in the affairs of other nations in the western hemisphere. Since the age of the filibusters before the civil war the US had regarded Central America and the Caribbean as part of its informal empire. US troops occupied or intervened openly in Cuba (1899 and 1961), the Dominican Republic (1916 and 1965), Grenada (1983), Guatemala (1954), Haiti (1915), Honduras (1912), Nicaragua (1927 and 1980s) and Panama (1989). As so often the US has imposed economic sanctions, and with the globalisation of the world economy such sanctions can have far-reaching effects: for example, the United States was recently able to stop Spain and Brazil selling military equipment to Venezuela as it contained US-made components.

The most famous case of military intervention in the region was, like Custer's last stand at the Little Bighorn eighty-five years earlier, an ignominious failure. In 1952 Fulgencio Batista staged a coup in Cuba that ended any chance of democratic government on the island. When six years later Fidel Castro, Che Guevara and eighty Cuban exiles landed to overthrow Batista their cause looked helpless; within days half of them had been captured or killed. But the people rose up against one of the most vicious and corrupt dictatorships in the region, and in January 1959 Castro marched triumphantly into Havana. Like the Hungarians the previous year the Cuban rebels were clearer on what they were fighting against than what they were fighting for. Castro himself was castigated as an 'adventurist' by the communists and set off for the US to garner support, but his revolution had disturbed too many powerful commercial interest groups (among them organised crime, which had controlled Cuba's lucrative casinos) for him to have any realistic prospect of success there. In a bipolar world Castro was clearly not a friend of America's corporatist empire.

The US response was to sponsor an invasion of the island, which started three days before the Bay of Pigs landing when American B-26 bombers attacked Cuban airfields. The population did not rise up as expected to welcome the invaders, mostly Cuban émigrés, and President Kennedy refused the CIA's pleas to commit overt US military forces. The invasion collapsed; most of the invaders were killed or captured. Castro turned to Moscow in earnest, eventually proclaiming himself a Marxist-Leninist, and becoming a Tony Blair to Russia's George Bush – providing rhetoric and troops to support imperial adventures around the world.

Most American interventions were more successful. As time went by the geographical limits of the Monroe Doctrine were swept away, and US actions in the Caribbean basin could be seen as exemplars of the imperial mindset that would later lead to military interventions in Asia and the Middle East. Nowhere was too small to be subject to US control when there was any deviation from the 'American Way'. The original Monroe Doctrine explicitly excepted existing European interests in the region, but in 1983 this caveat was ignored in the case of the tiny Caribbean island of Grenada.

Grenada's first post-Independence prime minister, Eric Gairy, was somewhat odd: he declared 1978 to be the Year of the UFO, and called for a UN Agency for Psychic Research into Unidentified Flying Objects and the Bermuda Triangle. More seriously, there were allegations of rigged elections and the Grenadan army and police received training in 'security' from the Chilean military regime of Augusto Pinochet. The opposition headed by Maurice Bishop seized power in a bloodless coup. For four years Bishop tried to find a middle way between competing ideologies – accepting aid from Cuba, increasing state spending in areas like health provision and allowing free rein to American corporations. The result was a reduction in unemployment, a significant improvement in per capita GDP and plaudits from the World Bank for his sound fiscal policies.

In the bipolar world of US foreign policy, however, consorting with Fidel Castro proved that Bishop was a crypto-communist. The US government refused to accept the credentials of the Grenadan ambassador in Washington, the US navy conducted an exercise, Operation Amber, designed to prepare itself for an invasion, and in July 1981 the CIA presented the Senate Intelligence Committee with plans for the island's economic destabilisation. At the same time Grenadan radicals were incensed by Bishop's attempts to mend fences with the US, and in 1983 seized control. Bishop was arrested, released after popular demonstrations on his behalf, and then rearrested and murdered along with many of his supporters.

The United States, whose policy of destabilising the Bishop regime had helped create the conditions for the latest coup, now sensed an opportunity. On the other side of the world the US marine barracks in Beirut was bombed, causing heavy loss of life, and President Reagan needed to be seen to act decisively somewhere. Two days after the

Beirut bombing 1,200 US troops invaded Grenada. The outnumbered Grenadans defended themselves and the invasion force eventually grew to 7,000, but the fighting was all over in three days. As one US soldier said, 'With the equipment we have, it's like Star Wars fighting cavemen.' The US lost eighteen men (only four of these killed by the enemy) and there are conflicting accounts of Grenadan military casualties, but it is known that twenty-four civilians were killed, including twenty-one patients in a psychiatric hospital accidentally bombed by US planes.

Just as with the Russian interventions in Hungary and Czechoslovakia, the US showed a total disregard for international opinion and international law: not only was the invasion condemned by the UN, but Mrs Thatcher was outraged at the invasion of a country whose head of state was still the British queen without Britain even being forewarned. It had, however, become politic to assert some element of international support. When Russian tanks crushed the Hungarian revolution in 1956 they did so alone; when they crushed the Prague Spring in 1968 they rolled as part of a Warsaw Pact mission that provided a fig leaf of legitimacy. Similarly the US enrolled small eastern Caribbean states in what was a pre-planned US operation.

The White House also successfully exercised a Soviet-style control of the media. No American media correspondents were allowed on the island until the fighting was over, and when they arrived they were shown the happy smiling faces of 'liberated' islanders. US authorities emphasised that independent polls conducted showed broad popular support for the invasion – without mentioning that polls also showed broad popular support for the Bishop government that they had conspired to bring down.

One bizarre aspect of the invasion was the reason the US gave for intervention: that the presence of up to 1,600 Cuban soldiers on the island created a threat to the United States. Leaving aside the fact that there proved to be only forty-three Cuban soldiers on the island, this justification was quite literally 'far fetched' – given that Cuban soldiers were further away from the US in Grenada than they would have been if they had stayed at home. But in offering this justification the US was merely continuing a tradition going back to the early settlers' attacks on poorly armed natives and Adams II's justification of the conquest of Florida on the grounds of protecting American 'security'. Similarly on May Day 1985 President Reagan issued 'Executive Order 12513 Prohibiting Trade and Certain Other Transactions Involving Nicaragua' in response to what he said was 'the threat to the security of the United States' posed by the tiny Central American republic. American history contains repeated examples of imperial actions being described as responses to fictional 'threats', the most recent being the toppling of Saddam Hussein. With good reason Russians often have an overwhelming fear of foreign attack and see enemies behind every boulder, but less understandably Americans have similar fears: one poll on the Iraq invasion showed that 60 per cent of Americans believed that the Iraqi dictator had been personally implicated in the 9/11 attack, despite the overwhelming evidence to the contrary.

One of the most infamous examples of US instigated regime change was the removal of the elected left-wing President of Chile, Salvador Allende, and his replacement by the military dictatorship of Augusto Pinochet. After CIA funding of his opponents failed to stop Allende's election, President Nixon vowed to make Chile's economy 'scream'. With the help of ITT (the American-owned International Telephone and Telegraph Corporation) the CIA devised a plan to destabilise the economy and eventually produce the Pinochet coup. Allende died in the ruins of the presidential palace, possibly by his own hand, and became another martyred hero. Although Pinochet had acted in the name of anti-communism, the leader of the Chilean Communist party was spared and, in an American brokered deal, exchanged with a Russian dissident. The two empires looked after their own.

The truth about Allende is more complex than his supporters sometimes admit. In previous elections he had failed dismally, and was finally elected by the narrowest of margins when his two opponents split the right-wing vote. The decisive factor may well have been that, as KGB files have since made clear, the Russians heavily outspent their American rivals. Although a socialist, not a communist, Allende was dependent on

Communist party support and received direct Russian financing himself. Russia had successfully copied America's post-war Italian strategy, but the United States then demonstrated that it had as little respect for elections as Stalin and proceeded to overturn an election that had produced the 'wrong' result. As a consequence the US government helped install and maintain a regime that brought one of Latin America's most civilised nations, with a 160 year democratic history, to the edge of barbarism.

The events of 9/11 1973 and 9/11 2001 warrant comparison: 3,000 people were murdered in 2001 and 3,200 in 1973, but in Chile a further 80,000 were imprisoned and perhaps 200,000 fled into exile. The most striking similarity is the ideological fanaticism behind the two events. Coups have been commonplace in much of Latin America, Chile excluded, but what was unusual this time was the orgy of political cleansing that followed. The bloodletting in Chile resembled the ethnic cleansing of the Mystic Massacre in its bestiality, but was driven by an ideology derived not from religious texts but from the texts of Chicago University economists. The messianic language of the coup leaders cast themselves as God's warriors battling the devil of international communism in order to lead their people to a promised land where all markets were free and all property was private. In the period before the Pinochet coup missionaries had arrived from Chicago preaching an extreme form of corporatist capitalism in which the state would be almost entirely dismantled and its roles, other than military, would be given to private corporations. Followers of these doctrines allied themselves with military leaders to plot the coup, and were installed in key government positions within twenty-four hours. Almost immediately they started handing over public assets to private corporations and dismantling the safeguards that had been erected to protect Chilean industry from foreign competitors.

The critical role of ITT in orchestrating the Chilean coup has led some to conclude that American imperial policy has been driven by and for the benefit of US corporations. The CIA and US marines, it is argued, act as a private army for the corporate oligarchs who pull the strings in Washington. This is to ignore the genuine ideological fervour of American leaders, who believe themselves to be engaged in a universal war of good against evil. President after president has worked with corporate leaders not out of selfish national interest but because they share the same values of corporatist democracy. Their aim was not to promote US commercial interests *per se* (although that of course was the result) but to defend the 'free world'. In 1960 the CIA happily worked with the Belgian corporation Union Minière to overthrow and assassinate the populist African leader Patrice Lumumba: in a bipolar world ideology was all important.

On achieving independence for the Congo, Lumumba had travelled to Washington seeking assistance, but was rebuffed. Like Fidel Castro a year earlier he then made the mistake of turning to Russia which, as KGB officials have since frankly admitted, regarded Africa as a hunting ground ripe for exploitation. As the Congo was America's only source of essential cobalt, President Eisenhower authorised Lumumba's assassination. The CIA station chief at the time, Larry Devlin, has described how he was sent poisoned toothpaste that he was supposed to smuggle into President Lumumba's bathroom. Devlin worked with the head of the Congolese army to mount a coup, which installed one of the most vicious and venal (and also long-lasting) dictatorships in the whole of Africa. Lumumba was murdered. American access to cobalt was maintained.

There is a view that the cold war was really a hot war fought by America and Russia using third world proxies. More people have died in conflicts since 1945 than during the Second World War itself. In most cases the two superpowers egged on the combatants, providing the money, weapons, training and moral support needed to make the conflicts as bloody as they have been. To depict these wars as primarily local manifestations of a global imperial struggle is, however, very wide of the mark. There were all sorts of factors driving people to war – historic, economic, ethnic, religious – which needed no outside encouragement. The guerrilla wars and tribal conflicts that erupted around the world from Cambodia to Nicaragua, from Kashmir to Nigeria, were not masterminded by imperial strategists in Moscow and Washington. The superpowers merely chose sides. What is surprising to many is the sides they chose. In the vast majority of cases the conflicts were between the poor and the powerful, between a ruling elite and those they ruled, and in the vast majority of cases the natural autocrats in Moscow sided with the underclass and the natural democrats in Washington sided with the oligarchs.

It is easy to see why Russia acted as it did. However imperial its practice in eastern Europe, its theory remained stuck in nineteenth-century Marxist dogma. The occupants of the Kremlin believed that the peasants and proletarians of the world were destined to throw off their chains. But why was America so keen to stop them? What had happened to the spirit of 1776? Why was a country created in revolution throwing its might into blocking the revolutions of others? Why was the world's greatest democracy committed to defending some of the most viciously anti-democratic regimes of the twentieth century?

Those who argue that the pursuit of corporate greed and national self-interest led to a cynical disregard for democracy point to the role of ITT in the bloody suppression of democracy in Chile or United Fruit in Central America. They emphasise the strategic value of the oil reserves conspicuously present in war zones from Angola to Iraq. But the US did not intervene in foreign conflicts just to grab oil or because corporate interests were at stake, or even because Russia was backing the other side. Support for dictators around the world was not confined to a few corporate oligarchs or state department apparatchiks. Polls showed that Americans believed overwhelmingly that their country was a power for good in the world and had convinced themselves that men like the Shah of Iran – whose despotic regime depended on a fearsome apparatus of torture and repression – were somehow defenders of 'western values'. Dictators from Vietnam to Venezuela were held up as standard bearers of a common ideology, the ideology of democracy.

To the Founding Fathers the idea that a Persian emperor could somehow symbolise the cause for which they had fought would have been incomprehensible, but their vision of democracy no longer survived; it had been replaced by the corporatist vision in which freedom and free markets had become synonymous. There developed a chain of logic as follows: Americans champion democracy, democracy includes free markets, free markets are those in which American corporations are free to operate, American corporations are encouraged by the regime in Country X (Iran, South Vietnam, Guatemala, Saudi Arabia, for example), therefore in supporting that regime the United States is fostering democracy.

US corporations are at the centre of America's informal empire, and the question of whether they aid or hinder development has been hotly debated. In terms of charting the history of the last century, however, the question is irrelevant. Foreign corporations, whatever their intent, are rich, powerful creatures who will almost inevitably be perceived as being aligned with the rich and powerful in any society. When conflict arises between the ruling elite and the masses (or those who claim to speak for the masses), American corporations will therefore automatically be viewed as part of the establishment and the US government will find itself on the side of the powerful against the powerless. In turn this pushed the United States down a track that Russia had followed since the Mongols: the path of terror.

The Use of Force

Terror had been a weapon in the American armoury since the Mystic Massacre, but one that until the cold war had become rusty with disuse. As the US moved to support assorted despots and dictators around the world it discovered what Russian autocrats from Ivan the Terrible to Joseph Stalin had instinctively understood: in order to survive, dictatorships need to be fortified by brute force.

Mass murder has been a feature of twentieth-century history. Even after the passing of Hitler and Stalin millions have died in such killing fields as Indonesia, Cambodia, Rwanda and especially China under the murderous regime of Chairman Mao. These were usually crazed, often genocidal, rampages that may have been sparked by the two superpowers but usually more by accident than design. One exception was the murder of between 500,000 and a million 'communists' in Indonesia between 1965 and 1969, which American dissidents like Noam Chomsky claim to have linked directly to the CIA. Even today the full death toll remains unknown. In his memoirs Barack Obama, who lived in Indonesia shortly after the coup, talks about a 'few hundred thousand, maybe; half a million'. Even the CIA, he says, lost count. In 1990 the *Washington Post* found confirmation that the CIA provided 'shooting lists' of three to four thousand 'leftists', who were then murdered by the Indonesian military. Journalist Kathy Kadane reported that one of the American Embassy officials who was involved admitted, 'I probably have a lot of blood on my hands,' before adding, 'there's a time when you have to strike hard at the decisive moment'. The spirit of the Mystic Massacre lived on.

In addition to such large-scale pogroms the post-war world also witnessed the systematic use of terror aimed at changing or maintaining the political status quo. Russia established terror schools in East Germany, Bulgaria and other parts of its empire, and many of the world's most infamous terrorists – men like Carlos the Jackal and assorted Middle Eastern murderers – were trained, equipped and to some extent managed by the KGB. Nevertheless it is now clear that statistically far more people were murdered or 'disappeared' at the hands of US-supported regimes than at those of Russia's proxies. Death squads, many led by graduates of the counter-insurgency school at Fort Bragg, North Carolina, operated in numerous countries with the full knowledge and sometimes active support of the CIA.

The study of recent history is always fraught. In theory records should be more complete and analysis therefore more robust, but the prisms of ideology are ever more refractive. Nowhere is this clearer than in the study of terrorism in the cold war period. Russia had an explicit commitment to the use of terror as a tool of revolution. America had no such commitment; indeed its official ideology could not be further away. Nevertheless, without the use of secret police, death squads and widespread torture it was impossible for US-sponsored regimes from Iran to Chile to maintain themselves in power.

American use of terror and torture peaked during the Vietnam War when, as openly disclosed much later, hundreds, perhaps thousands of civilians were killed in terror-raids or targeted assassinations. Terror raids on villages usually killed more women than men, often categorised in official statistics as 'Vietcong nurses' – leading one wag to crack that the Vietcong appeared to be the only army in history to have had more nurses than soldiers. A House of Representatives subcommittee heard how the Phoenix Program routinely included barbaric and fatal tortures. The lessons learnt in Vietnam were passed on elsewhere. Phoenix veteran John Kirkpatrick produced a manual that the CIA issued to the Contra terrorists in Nicaragua; one section, entitled 'Selective use of Violence for Propagandist Effects', explained the value of murdering 'carefully selected and planned targets such as court judges'.

One of America's most notorious torturers was Dan Mitrione, a CIA official who taught torture techniques in Brazil and then Uruguay. Using the slogan 'the right pain in the right place at the right time', Mitrione referred to his students as 'technicians'. A CIA colleague later recalled one lesson in which four homeless vagrants acted as subjects; all four were tortured to death. When Mitrione was eventually captured and executed by Uruguayan opposition forces, his body was flown back to the United States with great ceremony: Frank Sinatra performed at a benefit in his honour. Although Mitrione's true role was well known to the media in Latin America, it was hardly mentioned in America.

Having established the principle of conducting foreign policy interventions in secret in Italy, Iran and Guatemala, it was natural for America's support for death squads to be hidden from public scrutiny. The CIA agent responsible for the capture in Bolivia of Che Guevara has since described how he gave orders for Guevara to be murdered by a submachine gun blast to the chest so that it would appear that he had been killed in combat. As a consequence of such secrecy most Americans react in horror and disbelief when their opponents describe the United States as a terrorist state. And indeed such a description is a gross over-simplification. In countries like El Salvador CIA officials in one part of the US Embassy were working closely with paramilitaries, while in another part of the same embassy officials of AID (the US Agency for International Development) were handing out money to people like the Christian human rights worker Dr Rosa Cisneros, who was destined to become one of the paramilitaries' victims.

US public opinion and the American judiciary have developed a schizophrenic approach to terrorism. Instinctively Americans abhorred the use of terror even before 9/11; in many ways it represented the polar opposite to the democratic values on which the United States is assumed to have been built. But there have always been exceptions in practice. In 1976 a Cuban aircraft exploded after taking off from Barbados, killing all seventy-three on board. Luis Posada Carriles, a former CIA agent based in Venezuela, was accused of being the terrorist mastermind behind the bombing, but in 1985 he escaped from jail in Caracas and fled to the United States, where he successfully rebuffed attempts by Venezuela to extradite him for more than twenty years. Irish terrorists responsible for atrocities at home were allowed to live openly in the United States. Long after 9/11, and despite pleas from the families of those killed in the terrorist Omagh bombings, Bush II refused to shut down the websites run by the 'political wing' of those responsible, the 32 County Sovereignty Movement. The scandal over the use by the Reagan regime of funds from Iranian arms sales to fund Nicaraguan Contras focused on the legality of the scheme, not the fact that the Contras were one of the most sadistic terrorist organisations in the western hemisphere.

Since Mystic and the slave raids in Georgia, Americans – like Russians – have implicitly distinguished good terror (ours) from bad (yours). A clear demonstration of this came when John Negroponte was appointed by Bush II to head counter-terrorism activities after 9/11. Investigative reporters for the *Baltimore Sun* had previously established that the military commanders of one of Latin America's most vicious death squads, Battalion 3-16 in Honduras, had been on the CIA payroll during Negroponte's time as ambassador to Honduras. Negroponte has consistently denied knowledge of any wrongdoing by the Honduran military forces.

The most notorious twentieth-century example of America's use of terror occurred during the Vietnam War. The North Vietnamese started to transport troops and materials through neutral Cambodia, and President Johnson ordered the US Air Force to bomb the jungle tracks that were being used by the enemy. Initially the raids were restricted to a narrow band of territory within 30 miles of the frontier. Johnson's successor Richard Nixon went much further. According to transcripts published forty years later he ordered a 'massive bombing campaign' deep into Cambodia, with the incantation 'anything that flies on anything that moves'.

Just as Stalin's bureaucrats carefully documented the awful work of the Gulags, so the United States recorded the bombing raids on Cambodia. Documents declassified at the end of the century revealed that 2,756,941 tons of explosive had been dropped on to the villages and countryside of a nation with which the United States was nominally at peace – more explosives than the allies had dropped in the entire Second World War, including Hiroshima and Nagasaki. Cambodian prime minister Hun Sen later estimated that as many as 800,000 people died in US bombing. (Survivors were pushed into the arms of the one group that promised to protect them from the terror raining down on their homes – the Khmer Rouge, which in turn went on to murder an estimated 1.7 million in a further orgy of blood-letting.) After the initial raids on North Vietnamese supply lines there was no military rationale for the bombing, which served only to terrorise the rural population. The moral implications of Nixon's orders are open to argument. Noam Chomsky calls them genocide, just as others labelled Stalin's mass deportations in the Second World War genocide. To others both actions could be regarded as unfortunate consequences of modern war. The point is that the terror experienced by peasant families cowering as wave after wave of bombs descended on them (some villages were subject to raids lasting up to eight hours) can have been no less than that of families waking to the knock on the door that signalled the arrival of Stalin's secret police and the call of the Gulag.

Historians have pored over the psychology of mass murderers like Ivan the Terrible and Joseph Stalin, but have not usually put Richard

Nixon in the same category. Although the Cambodian men, women and children who died in their thousands may have considered him as evil as his Russian counterparts, the fact is he was no psychotic sadist. America's actions were not the result of one deranged individual. America's democratic values and the Constitution's checks and balances would constrain such overtly psychotic behaviour. Although the full scale of the raids was kept secret from the American people, thousands were in the know and actively supported the bombing, despite knowing full well what it implied for those innocent civilians on the ground. What was the psychology of these people? Was there a collective psychosis? The answer may be seen in the parallels with two more recent events: the invasion of the Caribbean island of Grenada immediately after the totally unrelated killing of US troops in Lebanon, and the second invasion of Iraq after the totally unrelated 9/11 attack. In all three cases the US, the most powerful empire in the world, found itself powerless against an enemy that in theory it should have been able to dispose of in an instant. The terrorist attacks in Lebanon and on 9/11 were bad enough – but that there was no immediate way to retaliate was unforgivable. Something had to be done; someone had to be hurt. Terror was unleashed not out of a lust for power like Stalin or a love of pain like Ivan the Terrible but out of simple frustration. Terror was made prosaic.

Terror remains a controversial weapon in the American imperial armoury; simple military might is a different matter. For most of their histories military force has been a key part of Russian and American foreign policy. Without it neither nation would have expanded its borders to anything like their current dimensions; neither would have gained an empire. Since US marines invaded Libya in 1805 American troops have on average intervened somewhere abroad more than once a year. War was also an inherent part of the ideology of autocracy; autocracy developed as warlords promised protection and glory to their followers. America was born in revolutionary struggle, and war was an inherent part of the young nation's ideology as it fought to impose democracy on a land populated by heathen 'savages' or inferior 'latinos'. As democracy evolved this militaristic emphasis diminished; in an age of human rights the crude application of military might became less acceptable.

Between the two world wars America rarely needed to flex its military muscle. The Second World War changed that, and a new philosophy emerged in which people could be killed in the name of human rights. The war had been necessary, it was argued, to stop the horrors of the concentration camps – although in fact nobody had declared war for that purpose. Wars could be justified to prevent greater evils.

War is always horrific, but in the twentieth century a mirage of sanitised atrocity-free conflict appeared in which 'the west' played by Geneva Convention rules. Such perceptions are once again distorted by the prisms of ideology. For example, on 8 November 2004 US forces attacked the city of Fallujah in Iraq. One of their main objectives was the town's main hospital, which they said had been used by insurgents. The hospital had been treating a stream of civilians injured in earlier US attacks, and thus was a powerful propaganda weapon for the rebels. US officials announced that the hospital had been successfully captured; they denied insurgent claims of casualties during the attack and reported that many of the staff and patients taken prisoner were later released. Article 19 of Geneva Convention I signed in 1949 is unambiguous. 'Fixed establishments and mobile medical units of the Medical Service may in no circumstances be attacked, but shall at all times be respected and protected by the Parties to the conflict. Should they fall into the hands of the adverse party, their personnel shall be free to pursue their duties.' Legally the US attack on Fallujah Hospital was a war crime. Few Americans would see it that way.

Today technology allows unseen men, women and children to be incinerated at the push of a button, and images of war on television screens segue into the banal world of video games. War a century ago seemed more horrific. In the First World War it was common for prisoners on both sides to be butchered, but by the Second World War Nazi Germany alone was the barbarian exception – utterly condemned by nations like France and the Netherlands, who then went on to commit appalling atrocities in vain attempts to keep their colonies. In the Korean and Vietnamese civil wars similar atrocities were repeatedly carried out by the troops of the rival dictators. US forces carried out a few of their own. The Korean War had only just started when US Air Force pilots strafed South Korean refugees escaping on foot near No Gun Ri south-east of Seoul, killing around a hundred. The survivors took cover under a nearby railway bridge, where they were subject to three days of machine gun attacks from soldiers of the First Cavalry Division; over 300 civilians – men, women and children – died. More than 500 Vietnamese civilians were similarly massacred in the village of My Lai in 1968. There was no systematic barbarism like that practised by Russian troops in their conquest of eastern Germany, although in Korea US troops were ordered to fire on refugee columns if they even suspected an enemy presence, but nor were American troops the possessor of some moral superiority that made them behave in a more 'democratic' manner: a message reinforced in Iraq.

Killing people in other countries – whether deliberate acts, accidental 'collateral damage' or unauthorised abuse – is the inevitable corollary of imperial ideologies. Any nation, be it Britain, Russia or America, that gives itself the right to intervene militarily overseas implicitly accepts that innocents will suffer.

Today the Monroe doctrine, which laid down that the United States had the unique right to intervene in the affairs of countries in the western hemisphere, has been extended to cover the whole world. In the so-called Carter Doctrine enunciated on 23 January 1980 America's self-declared policing role was explicitly extended to the Middle East. President Carter declared that the flow of Gulf oil was a 'vital interest' to the United States, and that as a consequence the US was empowered to use 'any means including military force' to keep the oil flowing. Objectively the Carter Doctrine was a classic statement of America's imperial right to intervene in the affairs of other nations, but seen through the prism of his own ideology it certainly did not appear so to Carter himself. Indeed, writing in the *Los Angeles Times* in November 2005 he attacked the regime of Bush II for what he called its 'revolutionary policies', under which 'There are determined efforts by US leaders to exert American imperial dominance throughout the world.'

The fracturing of the Russian empire coincided with increased tensions in the Middle East and stepped up oil exploration around the Caspian. The United States found that its access to Middle Eastern oil was increasingly jeopardised but that new opportunities were arising in former Russian colonies like Azerbaijan and especially Kazakhstan. Just as the Second World War provided Roosevelt II with an opportunity to develop an alliance with Saudi Arabia, so the 'war on terror' provided an opportunity to beef up US military presence in this area, a presence initiated in 1997, well before 9/11, with joint military exercises in Kazakhstan.

Possessing overwhelming military force remained a cornerstone of American foreign policy even after the collapse of the Soviet regime in Russia. The US navy currently has nearly 300 ships and half a million personnel, making it larger than the navies of the next seventeen nations put together. Its primary role is not to defend the homeland but to protect American imperial interests around the globe, a role that began with the attacks on Libya half a century after American Independence. American military forces are available to go where commercial priorities demand. For example, in 2003, despite tensions in the Middle East, it was announced that the aircraft carriers that had previously patrolled the Mediterranean would spend half their time off west Africa, reflecting increased US reliance on oil supplies from that region.

One of the clearest statements of current US policy was contained in a 1992 Defense Department draft entitled 'Defense Planning Guidance'. This laid down that the primary objective of US foreign and military policy was to stop the development of any regional power that might threaten the global supremacy of the United States, including any 'European-only security arrangements'. The United States must remain 'the predominant outside power' in those regions like the Middle East and south-west Asia, whose resources the United States needed to exploit. When this document was leaked US senator Joseph Biden attacked it as an attempt to impose 'Pax Americana' on the world. He was right, but rather than being a sudden change in America's relationship with the rest of the world it was the logical continuation of the centuries-long spread of Pax Americana from its birthplace on the eastern coastline of North America. The Carter doctrine merely recognised an imperial imperative that American corporations had long anticipated.

US oil companies had been interested in the Middle East since the 1920s, grabbing stakes in the British-discovered Iraqi fields and establishing themselves in Saudi Arabia. During the Second World War America moved to consolidate its position at Britain's expense by 'persuading' the beholden British government to share Iraq and Kuwait, while keeping Saudi Arabia to itself (and incidentally promising to leave Iran to Britain). The pressure to gain preferential access to oil pushed the US to intervene in ever more distant parts of the world. In 1992 Bush I intervened militarily in Somalia when the pro-American government was toppled and exclusive oil concessions held by four US oil corporations were threatened.

Military force and covert operations form one facet of the American way of empire-building. Far more important are other factors – economic, cultural and ideological. In the case of Russia, on the other hand, although ideology is what its proponents claimed was holding the Soviet empire together, the reality is that military force was by far the empire's most important glue. And it was the absence of other factors that ultimately signalled its collapse.

More Dissidents

Russian and American territorial aggrandisement in the nineteenth century was made possible by military might. Lots of other factors played their parts but Chechens and Apaches, Moldovans and Mexicans succumbed to overwhelming military force. The crushing superiority of the US navy in the Spanish-American War and the pathetic inferiority of the Russian navy in the Russo-Japanese War were litmus tests of the state of the two empires. Militarily enfeebled, the Romanov regime headed for oblivion; militarily omnipotent, the regimes of Roosevelt I and his successors walked softly along new paths confident that they were carrying a big stick.

The US stopped taking the land of others and embarked on a new form of corporate empire-building. In doing so it discovered that economic wealth created its own virtuous circle – the wealthier it became, the more its corporations could expand abroad and so the wealthier they became. Scale was as much an advantage to the nation as to the individual corporation. It seemed that the empire could thrive on dollars alone with no need for brute force. Russia never had that economic advantage. Its empire could only be held together by wielding a big stick. Stalin's Red Army provided that stick, but in the changing world – and changing metaphors – Stalin's successors discovered they needed guns *and* butter. Just as America was discovering that its economic interests in a post-war world needed the protection of secret police and US marines, so Russia discovered that secret police and military force alone could not sustain its empire.

From George Washington through Andrew Jackson and Dwight Eisenhower to Colin Powell American political life has been leavened with generals providing a different and purportedly action-orientated perspective from that of the political apparatchiks. In Russia since the death of Stalin this leavening has been added by secret policemen, culminating with Vladimir Putin. After Beria was arrested and shot, power in Russia passed to party men who through sycophancy and luck had survived Stalin's perpetual purges. In 1982 the crown passed to someone different. Yuri Andropov had headed the KGB and masterminded its continuing crackdown on dissidents. Where many in the FBI seemed to see reds under every bed, Andropov imagined Zionists under his. He was convinced there was an international Zionist conspiracy against the Soviet Union and devoted great effort to rooting it out. But like Beria he recognised that the Soviet economy had to change if the empire was to survive. Andropov moved power away from central planners to local managers, introduced incentive schemes for workers and attacked some of the corruption of the Brezhnev era that preceded him. His reign was another of those great might-have-beens of Russian history, but kidney disease did for him what bullets had done for Beria. The party gerontocracy then tried to stifle change by placing one of their own on the 'throne' but he soon died, and there came the final break with Stalinism.

It is said that corporate chief executives are best judged by the quality of the appointments they make. Andropov's most significant contribution to world history was his appointment to the inner circle of the man who arguably would produce the most massive change in Russian society since Peter the Great, greater even than the changes effected by Lenin – who had merely replaced one autocracy with another. In the summer of 1967 Yuri Andropov celebrated his promotion to head the KGB by holidaying at a spa near Stavrapol in the Caucasus. There he met a local party official who would become his protégé and who, thanks largely to Andropov's unstinting support, would eventually join him in the Kremlin: Mikhail Gorbachev.

When Gorbachev came to power in 1985 even he had no idea of how much the empire he was about to rule would be transformed. He recognised that wholesale economic modernisation was essential, but the far-reaching implications of his reforms were not at all apparent. Every aspect of Russian society needed restructuring (what he called *perestroika*), particularly its industrial base, but that could not be achieved without an unheard-of degree of honesty. For new economic policies to be developed and implemented there needed to be honest debate, for incentives to work there needed to be honest evaluation of performance, for corruption to be weeded out there needed to be honest admission of its existence. For *perestroika* to work there had to be openness: *glasnost*. Gorbachev understood that his reforms required objective reporting of what was happening in the country, but *glasnost* implied not just open reporting but open debate. For the first time political decisions, from top to bottom, were to be subject to scrutiny. It was then a small step from 'scrutiny' to 'critical scrutiny'. Intentionally or not Gorbachev was inviting open dissent.

A good way of understanding any society is to look at how it treats dissent. Under Lenin and Stalin dissent simply had no place, and dissidents of any sort were ruthlessly eradicated. After Stalin's death a few radical voices started to emerge. Intellectuals, writers and artists wrote open letters, circulated clandestine literature (samizdat) and occasionally staged demonstrations. They were joined by nationalists in various parts of the empire and by Christians, Jews and Muslims whose beliefs had survived nearly four decades of state atheism. Fundamentally, however, the repression inherent in autocracy continued, and the initial thaw of Khruschev's 'de-Stalinisation' did not last long – especially after the tanks rolled into Prague in the spring of 1968. The gulags continued, and thousands of dissidents were imprisoned there or in mental institutions. The names of most of these men and women have already been forgotten and their stories remain untold. Only a few of the more famous were able to make their voices heard. One such celebrity was Alexander Solzhenitsyn, who had seen active service in the Second World War and had twice been decorated. Towards the end of the war Solzhenitsyn was arrested for criticising Stalin to a friend. He was sentenced to eight years in the gulags after which he was permanently exiled to Kazakhstan, where he became a schoolteacher. He would have remained in Kazakh obscurity had he not written to a well-connected magazine editor, who approached Khrushchev with the manuscript of *One Day in the Life of Ivan Denisovich*, a searing indictment of the gulag system. Khrushchev approved publication, and the book caused a sensation inside the Soviet Union as much as outside. The hardliners in the Kremlin were horrified. Solzhenitsyn's subsequent efforts were banned, and after he won the Nobel Prize for Literature he was exiled from his own country.

The nuclear physicist Andrei Sakharov was another Nobel laureate who achieved fame in the west as a dissident. Sakharov had played a key role in developing Russia's nuclear arsenal but started to have qualms about the moral implications of his work. He tried to express his reservations within the system, but this only resulted in his being banned from military-related research. In 1970 he was one of the founders of the Moscow Human Rights Committee. Because of his distinguished scientific reputation he managed to escape reprisal, but when he denounced the Soviet invasion of Afghanistan he was banished to Nizhny Novgorod, out of bounds to foreigners. When Gorbachev came to power he was allowed to return and in 1989 was elected to Parliament, but he died a few months later.

To compare Stalin's extermination of dissent, or even his successors' more limited repression, with the treatment of dissent in the United States is problematic, but once again American history is Russian history writ small. From the earliest days of the republic dissidents, both religious and political, had on occasion been liable to retribution. In the middle of the nineteenth century a sixth of the US army was dedicated to destroying the Mormons, who were spared extermination only by the outbreak of the civil war. In the twentieth century the focus moved from religious dissent to political.

After the Second World War the Russian secret police were given formal guidelines on who they could seize. Among the crimes which warranted arrest was 'praising American democracy'. The FBI were given parallel guidelines in the form of the Smith Act. The suppression of dissent in modern America is primarily associated with the name of Joseph McCarthy, the Republican senator whose grotesque fantasies of communist conspiracies temporarily rescued his faltering political career and permanently destroyed the careers of many men and women of far greater integrity, but a more significant name was Howard Smith. A Virginia congressman, in 1940 he introduced the Alien Registration Act, the first statute since the Alien and Sedition Acts of 1798 to make the mere advocacy of ideas a federal crime. The Act was used to control dissent during the Second World War and had some surprising supporters, including the Communist party, which was happy to see it used against the Trotskyist Socialist Workers party.

In 1948 the Act was turned against the communists. Eleven defendants were charged in New York with conspiracy to 'organize as the Communist party and wilfully to advocate and teach the principles of Marxism-Leninism', and to 'publish and circulate . . . books, articles, magazines, and newspapers advocating the principles of Marxism-Leninism'. After a nine month trial all eleven were convicted and jailed. One of them, who had received a Distinguished Service Cross for bravery in the war, had his skull crushed by a group of Yugoslav fascists while in prison. For good measure each of the defence attorneys was imprisoned for contempt. The convicted communists appealed to the Supreme Court and, although they lost, the dissenting opinions of the two Supreme Court justices who supported their case are some of the most eloquent defences of free speech since Thomas Paine. Twenty-three more left-wingers, including Elizabeth Gurley Flynn, a founding member of the American Civil Liberties Union, were imprisoned in Chicago on similar charges. Eventually in 1957 the Supreme Court stopped the Smith Act trials, but by that time 140 Communist party leaders had been indicted and the party effectively crushed.

The voices being suppressed as 'un-American' in this period were not limited to those supporting the Soviet Union. The economist Paul Sweezy (described by Paul Samuelson, America's most famous economist, as 'among the most promising economists of his generation') was one of those sent to jail. At Harvard Sweezy had developed the theory of the 'kinked' demand curve in cases of oligopoly, and became a leading theoretician of monopolies, working closely with conservative guru Joseph Schumpeter. After serving with the OSS during the war Sweezy made the mistake of founding a left-wing (but decidedly non-communist) journal, the *Monthly Review*, which published articles from people like Albert Einstein and Jean-Paul Sartre.

As in Russia, America's dissidents were swelled by at least one Nobel laureate, Noam Chomsky. Chomsky's case is a better illustration of the American approach to dissent than the victims of the Palmer Raids after the First World War and the Smith Act after the Second World War. The legal persecution of dissent is a feature of American history, but the examples are startling in part because of their comparative rarity. More typical is informal censorship. In the late 1970s Chomsky and fellow-dissident Edward Herman contracted with a subsidiary of the Warner corporation to write a monograph describing the active support the US government was providing to some of the most bloodthirsty regimes in the third world. Twenty thousand copies were printed, and the book was advertised in the *New York Review of Books*. At this point Warner's senior management learnt of its existence and effectively stopped its distribution, so that, like Solzhenitsyn, Chomsky's work was more widely read abroad than at home. The French edition even had an introduction by Jean-Pierre Faye comparing the US treatment of the book with the Russian suppression of Solzhenitsyn's *Gulag Archipelago*.

In Russia the international fame of Solzhenitsyn and Sakharov afforded them a degree of protection that in America comes not from a Nobel prize but from Hollywood. The actress and activist Susan Sarandon commented that only celebrities are able to dissent in America. She was asked to appear on CNN to talk about first amendment issues and suggested that Noam Chomsky or Edward Said should go on with her; the network 'declined'.

In both Russia and America the issue of imperial wars abroad provoked particular dissent. Andrei Sakharov's opposition to the war in Afghanistan and Jane Fonda's opposition to the war in Vietnam gained international attention. William Buwalda, the American soldier imprisoned in 1909 for attending an anarchist rally, campaigned vociferously against American imperialism when he was released from prison. Drawing on his experiences as part of the American army of occupation in the Philippines, he wrote (in terms eerily similar to later Vietnam War protests) of 'men, women, and children hunted like wild beasts, and all this in the name of Liberty, Humanity, and Civilization'. The natives' only crime, he said, was to be 'fighting for their homes and loved ones', while the United States was inflicting 'legalized murder' on 'a weak and defenceless people. We have not even the excuse of self-defence.' Those attacking the dissidents also used the same language from one war to another. 'Mr President, reluctantly and only from a sense of duty am I forced to say that American opposition to the war has been the chief factor in prolonging it,' said one senator, who could have been talking about Vietnam or Iraq (or, had he been Russian, about Afghanistan or Chechnya). In fact Senator Beveridge was talking about dissidents like Buwalda, whom he claimed were prolonging the 'insurrection' in the Philippines.

Hollywood star Gregory Peck financed the film *The Trial of the Catsonville Nine* about the persecution of nine Jesuit priests, artists and intellectuals who burnt their draft cards to oppose Vietnam and CIA subversion in Latin America. The film was shown at the Cannes Film Festival in 1972, but even Peck could get only limited release in America. Nor did his celebrity status, or that of fellow dissident Jane Fonda, stop them being bugged by the Nixon administration. Chaplin's film *The Great Dictator* was banned in Russia; Peck's film was simply not shown in America.

Whereas tsarist and communist Russia had simply suppressed debate, over centuries the United States had evolved mechanisms for ensuring that open debate was managed in ways that ensured the continuity of the status quo. Contemporary dissidents like investigative journalist Greg Palast are permitted to openly express their views. Dissidents can gain fame, but not influence. Dissident composer Stephen Sondheim was awarded the National Medal of Arts, but his musical *Pacific Overtures*, with its damning depiction of US imperialism in Asia, might as well have remained unwritten. Perhaps the clearest example of the American celebrity dissident was John Kenneth Galbraith – heaped in honours and totally ignored. Galbraith penned the classic study of corporatism, *The New Industrial State*, in the mid-1960s and from then on was an outspoken critic of corporatist imperialism. In 2005 the ninety-six-year-old former Harvard University professor, US ambassador and adviser to presidents from Roosevelt II to Lyndon Johnson was still campaigning, insisting that without the power of the corporations America would never have invaded Iraq. Almost universally acknowledged as one of the greatest intellects of the twentieth century, there are hardly any aspects of American public life on which Galbraith did not wax eloquent to no effect.

The American approach to opposition is epitomised by the case of Juan Bosch. In 1963 the elected government of the Dominican Republic was overthrown in a US-approved military coup. Two years later supporters of the ousted president, Juan Bosch, tried to stage a counter coup and US marines, commanded by John S. McCain II, father of 2008 presidential candidate John S. McCain III, intervened. Government forces, protected by 20,000 US troops, butchered hundreds of rebel troops and civilians. In the Russian empire no more would have been heard of the deposed president, but Bosch sat down to write a book, published in New York, attacking what he called 'Pentagonism'. (He argued that for America old-style military conquests – designed to allow colonisation and economic exploitation – had been replaced by military adventures designed to reinforce the Pentagon's control of its own country.) As a dissident statesman Bosch could not be tolerated; as a dissident writer he could be safely ignored.

In the twenty-first century the new Russian leadership started to learn the more subtle methods of suppressing dissent that the United States had pioneered. Solzhenitsyn returned to Russia a national hero, although he found himself effectively sidelined politically. But in introducing *glasnost* in the 1980s Gorbachev had jumped from no debate to open debate with no such mechanisms. To him *glasnost* was just a way of oiling *perestroika*, but it turned out to be far more than this. He failed to anticipate its impact on the role of the Communist party, on the functioning of the economy, on the media, on almost every aspect of Soviet society. Above all, he did not understand the imperial implications of what he had unleashed.

The End of the Russian Empire?

At a very simplistic level, letting people speak out meant letting people speak out in their own language, and that in itself uncorked the genies of nationalism. The old Soviet Union had 149 distinct languages. Almost half the population had a language other than Russian as their native tongue, and a quarter did not speak Russian at all.

Glasnost would make visible the frailty of those bonds – military, economic and ideological – that the world believed were holding the empire together, and which *perestroika* was designed to re-invigorate. *Perestroika* could not work without *glasnost* but *glasnost* would destroy what *perestroika* was intended to save. Once it became plain that the Russian emperor had no clothes his capacity to instil fear evaporated.

The unravelling of the Russian empire happened with astonishing speed. In 1979 the Soviet Union launched its last imperial adventure when it occupied Afghanistan, and the mighty Red Army found itself bogged down in a fruitless war with American-armed Muslim tribesmen. At the same time the western colonies started to smoulder again. After Germany in 1953, Hungary in 1956 and Czechoslovakia in 1968 it was now the turn of Poland. Striking shipyard workers and their union Solidarity were suppressed in 1981, but by the time Gorbachev came to power it was clear that something had to give.

Russia was spending 18 per cent of its GDP on the military. Not only were its troops massed on the troubled frontier with China, policing its southern and western colonies and fighting a full-scale war in Afghanistan, but massive sums were being spent in an unwinnable arms race with America. Gorbachev tried to end this contest by offering to scrap all his nuclear weapons if the United States would do the same – an offer that the US, from its position of strength, contemptuously refused. In signing the Nuclear Non-Proliferation Treaty in 1968, the United States agreed under Article VI to work in 'good faith' towards the eventual elimination of nuclear weapons, but once US nuclear supremacy became overwhelming this article was ignored. (When in November 2004 the UN voted to ban the production of more fissile material – the essential ingredient of nuclear bombs – 147 nations voted for; only the US voted against.)

The openness of *glasnost* made ever more obvious the weakness not just of the economy but of the whole apparatus of the state. Under *perestroika* more and more power was being devolved, and for the first time since the civil war power centres began to emerge outside Moscow. Gorbachev pushed colonial leaders in eastern Europe into reform, replacing men like Gomulka in Poland who were unwilling to change, but this process was a double-edged sword – capable of both slashing bureaucracy and severing ties with Moscow. Nationalist pressures in the western colonies boiled over again, and with Gorbachev unwilling to intervene militarily East

Germany, Hungary, Czechoslovakia, Poland and Bulgaria gained their independence. Gorbachev was given a categorical assurance by the US that if he would agree to a reunited Germany remaining in NATO the US would not expand its empire eastward by admitting former Warsaw Pact nations to NATO, but as the American natives had long before, Russians learnt that US assurances were meaningless.

Yugoslavia and Romania had already achieved political independence, and they joined the others in throwing off the ideological chains of communist rule. Afghanistan was abandoned. The Baltic colonies incorporated into the Soviet Union after the Second World War took advantage of Gorbachev's political freedoms to demand independence. Despite brutal 'interventions' by interior ministry troops in Lithuania and Latvia in 1991, it was clear that the Union of Soviet Socialist Republics was coming apart at the seams.

The dismantling of empire was not smooth, and one reason is that Gorbachev was not trying to dismantle the empire. Troops were brought home from Afghanistan, where 50,000 of them had died, but attempts to hold the empire together by force continued in the Baltic colonies and especially in the south, where Azerbaijan and Armenia were almost at war with each other. In Georgia Soviet troops murdered twenty protesters, the majority women and girls, in a futile attempt to roll back the tides of nationalism. In the Caucasus and in the Asian republics ethnic tensions erupted into violence, and the Red Army brutally suppressed riots in Tajikistan and Uzbekistan. Nevertheless Belarus, Kirgizstan, Moldova, Tajikistan, Turkmenistan, Ukraine and Uzbekistan all proclaimed their sovereignty. Only a few of the smaller southern colonies, like Chechnya, remained, while the likes of Georgia and Armenia broke away, leaving a tangled mess of viciously feuding remnants. Not only did Russia's newest colonies in eastern Europe declare their independence, but so too did states that many in the west had long forgotten were imperial possessions, like Belarus and Ukraine.

In a 1954 press conference President Eisenhower had employed a metaphor that would become a linchpin of American foreign policy:

the nations of the world, he said, were like a 'row of dominos'; let the communists knock over one and they would all fall one after the other. The theory was right; he just got the wrong dominos.

At the beginning of 1991 Gorbachev turned to the tools of democracy to hold the empire together. He called a referendum in which more than three-quarters of those taking part voted to preserve the USSR. But the poll was boycotted in those regions where independence movements were strongest – the Baltic, Armenia, Georgia and Moldova. Increasingly isolated Gorbachev was caught between hard-line party bosses, reformers inside Russia and nationalists elsewhere. By the end of 1991 he had resigned and the USSR had been dissolved. The Russian empire, it seemed, was no more. It had disappeared so quickly because those on the fringes had retained their psychological independence, and as soon as the forces holding the empire together weakened they asserted their physical independence. The contrast with the way that America had grown was stark. The people in most of the territories conquered by the United States in the eighteenth and nineteenth centuries became psychologically committed to the American empire, usually because the original inhabitants were replaced by American settlers. But even where significant local populations survived, as in California, Hawaii, Puerto Rico and – in the twentieth century – the Danish West Indies, independence movements, although occasionally grabbing headlines, have been virtually irrelevant. (The two significant conquered territories that retained their psychological independence – Cuba and the Philippines – were granted their independence with little argument.) Neither tsars nor commissars ever achieved this degree of what might be called psychological imperialism.

Symbolically the most important development in the collapse of Russia's communist empire was the fracturing into three of the Slavic nations: Russia, Byelorussia and Ukraine. The shrunken Russian empire was left once again with the Kievan birthplace of the Rus sitting outside its borders. The 'Russian Federation' had been the largest of the republics in the USSR, but the new Russia was a shadow of what had been before.

It was an amazing series of events. In freeing the nations, Gorbachev had achieved, albeit by accident, far more than Alexander II had achieved by freeing the serfs or Lincoln had achieved by freeing the slaves. The failure of the old model of military imperialism had already been made plain by the collapse of the British empire half a century before. Now Russia demonstrated again that for an empire to survive economic power was all-important. Not only was a strong economy essential for military reasons, but more subtly it supported the ideological glue that might hold an empire together. The ideology of communism was rejected by Russia's colonies for two reasons. First was its inherent unreality: proclaiming equality, justice and international brotherhood while demonstrating inequality, injustice and international aggression was never going to convince for long. Second was the simple fact that communism did not work. Even if it was true that universal education, universal employment and universal healthcare provided the citizens of the Russian empire with real advantages, it became increasingly clear that life in the west was 'better'. Corporatist democracy delivered what communism didn't, but was it the corporatism or the democracy that produced the goods?

As Russia continued to evolve it seemed that corporatism might prove a stronger force than democracy and a new corporatist autocracy might emerge from the rubble of empire. The cold war warriors in Washington expected the collapse of communism to herald the arrival of free elections and free markets – an inversion of the historical determinism of Marxist dogma. They forgot that their vision of corporatist democracy did not spring fully formed from the ashes of Britain's North American empire but from the freebooting ways of the robber barons and party bosses. The Soviet state collapsed into a morass of corruption and chaos out of which seems to be emerging a new oligarchy imbued not with the spirit of modern America but with that of Tammany Hall and Standard Oil. Within fifteen years of the dissolution of the USSR – the supposed workers' paradise – there were reported to be 88,000 dollar millionaires in Russia; thirty-three Moscow residents were reportedly billionaires. Today the term 'oligarch' is associated with

Russia and with the kleptocracy of robber barons who seized control of the nation's economic infrastructure. It is worth remembering that a century earlier the term was being used to abuse the robber barons who had seized control of the American economic infrastructure. President Cleveland described the ringleaders of the Hawaiian coup as oligarchs and others applied it to the likes of J.D. Rockefeller and J.P. Morgan. With time the term faded from use in America as the oligarchs became part of the establishment. It is far too early to speculate on how history will deal with today's Russian oligarchs, but it seems that they too may be mutating into something with less pejorative connotations. Many of the 1990s oligarchs who made vast fortunes for themselves have been joined, or in some cases replaced, by a new breed who straddle the private and public sectors. Putin's finance minister, for example, chaired both Russia's second biggest bank and a company controlling 23 per cent of global diamond production. A 1997 law that made it compulsory for government ministers to declare their earnings from all sources dramatically illustrated the intertwining of politics and business. The minister of natural resources declared an income of £4.2m in 2005 from his extensive business interests, 2,000 times the national average. Many of these new oligarchs have close personal connections to Putin. The chairman of the company producing Lada cars and much of the arms industry served with Putin in the KGB in East Germany.

As in the United States, the oil industry provides the clearest examples of emerging trends. Russia now has the world's largest oil and gas reserves after Saudi Arabia and Iran, much of it in the hands of the Gazprom Corporation. In some ways Gazprom resembles American corporations, running schools, health services and even leisure centres, and its influence reaches deep into government. Its chairman was the first deputy prime minister and went on to succeed Putin as president. But it would be far too simplistic to suggest that Gazprom drives government policy; on the contrary, the government seems as likely to be determining corporate policy.

In the winter of 2005, for example, Gazprom provoked a diplomatic crisis by quadrupling the price of gas supplied to Ukraine, claiming that it was merely harmonising prices with global markets. It soon emerged that Gazprom was operating a very distinct pricing policy. Other former Soviet republics were being charged less, in some cases far less. It looked like the differential pricing once followed by Rockefeller's Standard Oil, designed to drive out competition, except that there was virtually no competition. The prices appeared to reflect the political priorities of the Kremlin, priorities determined by the new Russian leaders' determination to maintain an American-style 'sphere of influence' to replace the old-style empire. Belarus, a staunch Russian ally, got cheap gas; western-leaning Ukraine did not.

It is clear that in its corporatism Russia is developing along its own path. The same is true of its 'democracy'. Russia flirted with democracy and unbridled free markets under Gorbachev's successor, Boris Yeltsin, in the 1990s, and the result was the creation of a few fabulously rich oligarchs, an almost bankrupt government and most of the population being significantly worse off as inflation destroyed their savings. Russia has also become the first industrial society to experience a sustained fall in life expectancy; the average new-born Russian male has a life expectancy of fifty-nine, less than a Bangladeshi.

Even under Yeltsin elements of the old autocratic mindset remained, and these came to the forefront again with what has been called the 'managed democracy' of Putin, documented in works like Andrew Wilson's *Virtual Politics: Faking Democracy in the Post-Soviet World*. Despite his authoritarian tendencies – Putin effectively abolished free elections for the eighty-nine regional governors, for example – he achieved approval ratings undreamt of in western countries. Russia may have abandoned the formal ideology of autocracy but that does not imply the triumph of democracy in the American sense. In one survey 'strengthening democracy and freedom of speech' was ranked only eighth in a list of political priorities after such objectives as 'developing industry'. On 20 December 2006 President Putin celebrated 'Chekist Day' with a lavish televised party in the Kremlin. The day, officially Security Service Workers Day, commemorates the foundation in 1917 of the Bolshevik's notorious secret police, the Cheka, forerunner of the KGB.

Values that become embedded in ruling elites can continue even when leaders change. The casual assumptions implicit in American interventions in the Caribbean basin towards the end of the nineteenth century continued into the twentieth and twenty-first in Iran, Vietnam, Iraq and countless other places. The culture of violence inherent in communist autocracy has continued in the brave new world of managed democracy, with dissidents like television supremo Vladislav Listev and investigative journalist Anna Politkovskaya gunned down in what looked suspiciously like officially approved assassinations. Weeks before her murder, Politkovskaya warned that Putin had become a 'tsar' who believed he could do anything he liked with Russia and the Russian people.

Nor does the arrival of 'managed democracy' and the disappearance of most of the Russian empire imply that the imperial instinct has vanished. Putin called the break-up of the Soviet Union 'the greatest geopolitical catastrophe of the century'. Russia's vast gas reserves give it enormous power and this, coupled with the political stability that followed the Gorbachev and Yeltsin years, has renewed the nation's self-confidence. That in turn is reflected in the re-emerging imperial ideology, an ideology again presenting a mirror image of developments in the American empire. The attempts by the US to incorporate Georgia into its sphere of influence to 'protect' its oil supplies prompted the sort of military response from Russia that generations of tsars would have immediately recognised.

The Russian invasion of South Ossetia in 2008 is just one example of Russia's continuing imperial pretensions that continue to colour the Russian view of history. Sergei Yastrzhembsky, Vladimir Putin's European affairs adviser, was still insisting in May 2005 that there had been no Russian invasion of the Baltic states during the Second World War. 'There was no occupation,' he said; 'there were agreements at the time with the legitimately elected authorities in the Baltic countries.'

Russia has a thousand-year tradition of autocracy and imperialism. It is far too early to say that either has died. And yet there are those who asserted exactly that. Francis Fukuyama achieved celebrity status by proclaiming that the collapse of communism marked 'the end of history'. Rarely can a soundbite so absurd have achieved such fame. Fukuyama argued that at the time of the American Revolution democracy was just one among many competing theories of government, but as the twentieth century drew to a close it had become by far the most prevalent ideology in the world. All the alternatives had become discredited and democracy was accepted by the majority of governments. He asserted in effect that rather than Marx's proletariat destroying the bourgeoisie history had proved that by living peacefully together the two classes would maximise human welfare; only corporatist democracy made this possible. 'What we may be witnessing', he wrote, 'is not just the end of the cold war, or the passing of a particular period of post-war history, but the end of history as such: that is, the end point of mankind's ideological evolution and the universalisation of western liberal democracy as the final form of human government.'

To its advocates the triumph of corporatist democracy as an ideology and the triumph of America as the sole remaining superpower were merely two sides of the same coin. The world would be subject to Pax Americana not as the manifestation of Yankee imperialism but as the guarantee of prosperity, peace and justice. The United States was destined to be both the model for the rest of the world and the tool by which that model would be replicated. America had become a society of unprecedented prosperity, outstanding creativity and unabashed glory. Americans had personal freedoms undreamt of in much of the globe, and their nation – despite occasional alarms – was fundamentally secure within its borders. And this has all been achieved within the framework of democracy. Whether the abundance of easily exploitable resources – agricultural, mineral and human – made this democracy possible or whether democracy made possible the exploitation of those resources is a moot point, but what is certain is that most of its citizens believe that the nation's achievements are inescapably linked to its democratic values. This ideological certainty has spread far beyond America's borders.

Fukuyama was right to argue that in the court of public opinion liberal democracy had triumphed and communism dismally failed.

American-style democracy and communism both promised to create the most just and most productive society imaginable; the difference was that one delivered and one did not. The prophecy of de Tocqueville that Russia and America were each destined to hold in their hands 'the destinies of half the world' had seemed eerily prescient at the start of the twentieth century; but by the century's end it seemed that one pair of hands would hold the whole world.

CHAPTER 15
PAX AMERICANA

The road from Roanoke meandered through history to arrive in Baghdad. American troops approached Iraq with the same mixture of arrogance and ignorance that had characterised Englishmen sailing across the Atlantic in the opposite direction more than four hundred years before. Collective certainty eclipsed individual fears. They faced the unknown buttressed with the knowledge that God was on their side and that the natives would succumb to the justice of their cause and the power of their guns. The second Iraq War was not just an imperfect copy of the first but a copy of countless other wars down the years. Army reservists marching proudly off to invade Iraq mirrored the Kentucky militia marching off to invade Canada in 1812. 'Waist Deep in the Big Muddy', the despairing cry of the Vietnam War, became 'Waist Deep in the Big Sandy'.

America emerged the undisputed victor from the titanic struggle between the two great twentieth-century empires, but Fukuyama was wrong: history did not end. The fateful wartime meeting of US president and Arab monarch aboard the USS *Quincy* had triggered a series of events that would lead fifteen fanatics obsessed with the American 'occupation' of their Saudi homeland to murderous martyrdom on 9/11. The American response demonstrated the bipolarity that is fundamental to America's imperial world view: Bush II announced to the rest of the world that 'Either you are with us or you are with the terrorists.' Invading

Iraq became part of the 'war on terror' just as invading Grenada had been part of the 'war on communism'. The one demonstrated the power of the United States to those who dared to attack the World Trade Centre; the other responded similarly to the attack on the marine barracks in Beirut.

George Santayana, paraphrasing Edmund Burke, claimed that 'Those who do not learn from history are doomed to repeat it.' It is a maxim repeated so often that it has become conventional wisdom. And yet history never repeats itself exactly. There are parallels between the invasions of Canada, Grenada and Iraq, but there are far more differences. The early Puritans sending mercenaries to murder the natives of Mystic are not totally dissimilar from twentieth-century Americans sending their air force to 'bomb Vietnam back into the stone age' or wreak 'shock and awe' on the citizens of Baghdad – but they are not identical. More importantly there is no causal link. It is no more logical to say that the United States invaded Afghanistan 'because' it had previously invaded countries like Mexico or the Philippines than it would be to say that Afghanistan was invaded by America 'because' it had previously been invaded by Britain and Russia. Historical parallels are matters of subjective perception, not undisputed fact. The apparent repetitions in history say as much about how history comes to be written as about the events themselves. Santayana also said, more originally, 'History is a pack of lies about events that never happened told by people who weren't there.'

The history of the American empire is more subjective than most histories because it is not even an established fact that there is or ever has been an American empire. Nevertheless much of the twentieth century can be characterised as a Tale of Two Empires, and by the end of the century one stood alone. The Russian empire had disappeared from the map – but its ideology lingered on: President Putin publicly lamented the break-up of the USSR, his government continued to act as if it were an imperial power, a colonial war dragged on in Chechnya, and in everyday language the lost colonies were termed the 'near abroad' to differentiate them from the real abroad. In trying to re-establish Russian imperial authority in the Caucasus and elsewhere, Russia now seems to be following just that policy of 'determined opportunism' that America followed in establishing its own empire.

The ideologies that colour perceptions may arise from history, but they do not change in step with historical realities. The leaders of Britain and France continued to strut the world stage long after Suez punctured their imperial dreams, convinced that the trappings of yesteryear guaranteed them starring roles. In the United States, as in Russia, the ideology of empire continued to evolve while at its core remaining unchanged. It is this imperial ideology – unspoken because unconscious – that has guided the American nation from Roanoke to Baghdad.

American Democracy

Lenin and Stalin claimed to have a vision of a community of nations bound together not by force but by a common ideology: communism. They failed to achieve this vision. Many of America's Founding Fathers proclaimed a similar vision of a world united by a common ideology: democracy. At least within the American hegemon they succeeded. The American empire is bound together by economic ties and military alliances, but above all by this common ideology.

Right from its inception ideology was uniquely important to the American empire. The Russian people have a common Slavic ethnicity, a unique language, centuries of imperial history, and a territory whose borders may have been mobile but have always been relatively clear. The United States was born a melting pot with virtually no history and a borrowed language. Above all it had no sense of its territory. The Founding Fathers were agreed that their vision went far beyond the boundaries of the existing thirteen colonies – one of the reasons for the American Rebellion itself was the attempt by George III to limit colonial expansion – but how far beyond? The Ohio Valley? The Mississippi? The Canadian colonies? The Pacific? Or even further? With no instinctive patriotism linked to race or place, there evolved a patriotism linked to ideals. American greatness derived from American democracy. America deserved its empire not because Americans were superior to everyone else but because their form of government was superior. The global success of the United States rests in large part on its ability to convince itself and its followers around the world that Fukuyama was right to proclaim that democracy is 'the final form of human government'.

The success of the American vision of corporate democracy is thanks to its claim to have four great virtues: political, ethical, economic and practical. *Politically* American democracy ensures that the power of the state is used in accordance with the will of the majority: the American model of government is in principle fundamentally representative. *Ethically* the rule of law ensures that while the will of the majority prevails the rights of the minority are honoured: American democracy is in principle fundamentally just. *Economically* free markets and limited liability corporations ensure that the production and distribution of goods and services is optimised: American capitalism is in principle fundamentally efficient. *Practically* corporatist democracy works: whether the political, ethical and economic principles are accepted or disputed, the fundamental reality is that in practice they deliver. The American Dream above all rests on the assertion that life in America is 'better' than anywhere else, and that by following in its wake the rest of the world can achieve the same.

There are definitional problems with all four attributes, but in some ways what they mean or even whether they are true does not matter. What is important is that people believe that America's political processes will reflect their own desires, that its courts will bring justice, that its corporations will create wealth and that by being part of the American-defined 'free world' they will have a better life. The reality is that none of these assertions is entirely true. When similar claims were made (with far less justification) by Soviet Russian leaders the rest of the world rightly scoffed. US claims are widely accepted not just because they are constantly repeated but because there is a grain of truth in all of them.

When people talk of American democracy being 'representative' they are usually speaking philosophically not geographically, but the first obvious point to make is that America's institutions do not claim to represent the vast quasi-empire over which the United States exerts its influence. The term 'United States' when used in a geographical sense on official documents, acts and laws includes the fifty states plus Puerto Rico, the US Virgin Islands, Guam and American Samoa.[1] The hundreds of millions beyond its shores whose lives are directly influenced by the actions of its government have no claim to representation.

This is not the place to debate the 'representativeness' of contemporary political life, but history highlights two factors that are often overlooked: corporatism and corruption. In as much as corporatism has an ideology, it is firstly that corporations as much as human beings are citizens and secondly that wherever possible government should step aside and allow its corporate citizens to 'represent' the views and desires of the wider society. To say that unelected corporate executives have often usurped the role of elected governments is not to imply some dreadful right-wing conspiracy in which crazed corporate oligarchs set out to rule the world. Corporatism is not an ideology that sprung fully formed from the pen of a Thomas Paine or Karl Marx; it evolved gradually through the activities of men, and a few women, whose intentions were usually good and whose aspirations were often noble.

Consider for example Hurricane Katrina, which devastated New Orleans in 2005. Many corporations rushed to offer assistance, among them the Anglo-American corporation Pearson, owner of the Financial Times and Penguin Books. Pearson opened call centres to help direct the relief efforts, provided temporary classrooms and donated tens of thousands of schoolbooks and computers for schoolchildren in Louisiana and Mississippi. Of course Pearson's American chief executive realised the PR benefits, but it would be churlish to believe that this was her only motivation. Pearson's actions were universally welcomed because they were fundamentally decent. But considered in purely economic terms, what had happened is that private assets belonging to shareholders, in this

1 Even this is not straightforward. A series of Supreme Court rulings known as the Insular Cases determined that territories such as Puerto Rico belonged to, but were not part of, the United States and therefore, under Article IV, Section 3, paragraph 2 of the Constitution, Congress had the power to determine which parts of the Constitution applied there.

case including many British pension funds, had been devoted to activities that in earlier times would have been considered a public responsibility. The British pensioners might well have been happy to give some of their pension funds to charity (although as south-east Asia was struck by a tsunami and Kashmir by one of the world's worst ever earthquakes at roughly the same time, it is not obvious that they would have chosen to give their charitable donations to American schoolchildren), but they were not consulted; indeed there is no way they could have been consulted. British pensioners were effectively taxed to help American children not by their elected representatives but by one or two well-meaning oligarchs: precisely the taxation without representation that Americans believe their revolutionary war was about.

In millions of such tiny, innocent, day-to-day episodes corporations supplement, or supplant, democracy, not just within nations but internationally. Not only do corporations increasingly take on responsibilities formerly assumed by governments, but they themselves help to determine the actions of governments.

By accepting that corporations are 'citizens' in the same way that human beings are citizens, American democracy legitimises the role of corporations in influencing policy, including policy towards the rest of the world. Since the early days of Standard Oil corporations have sought to ensure that the US government represents their interests. There is a whole body of obscure academic analysis on the subject. For example, New York professor Benjamin Fordham conducted a detailed statistical study of the voting patterns of US senators in the 81st Congress (1949–50). He found that those supporting Truman's policy of alliance with western European countries through NATO were more likely to have come from states with powerful export industries and/or internationally focused banks. Conversely, Truman was opposed by senators from states where firms were likely to be hit by western European imports and by senators linked to the mining corporations, who favoured a more 'colonial' approach to foreign policy. Again this is not to suggest any secret conspiracy. America's government is 'representative' in that it represents the interests that are most salient in society, and corporations find it much easier to achieve such saliency than individuals.

The relationship between corporations and the state is not all one way. As with the emerging corporate autocracy in Russia, the US government makes use of corporations as an arm of foreign policy. For example, in 1991 the CIA hired a private sector company, the Rendon Group, to set up the Iraqi National Congress, bringing Iraqi exiles together in order to 'create the conditions' that would produce a coup against Saddam Hussein. Most US government use of its corporate levers is more subtle. In November 2005 a British newspaper, the *Financial Times*, sent $4,500 from London to Iran to pay the rent on its Tehran office. The money never arrived. One of the banking intermediaries had notified the US treasury, which seized the money.

Corporations in America have long provoked controversy. The first major scandal of the twenty-first century was Enron, where hundreds of millions of dollars of phoney profits were manufactured in a series of fraudulent accounting transactions, leading to lengthy prison sentences for a few corrupt oligarchs and penury for thousands of honest investors. What was remarkable about this scandal, apart from its sheer scale, was its insight into the tightening grip of corporatism on the levers of American democracy. No corporation in America's history had spent so much on political lobbying in so short a time: Bush II himself is on public record as having received $572,000. It was shocking for everyone, both inside and outside government, when Enron's leadership was ultimately revealed as corrupt. Governments around the world were 'encouraged' to privatise public utilities and sell them to Enron, both in America's traditional fiefdoms, for example Colombia, the Dominican Republic, Guatemala, Panama and the Philippines, and further abroad – in Argentina, India and Mozambique. Financing for these deals was provided directly by the US government (over $3bn) or indirectly by the World Bank. $23bn of overseas revenues flowed into Enron's coffers.

Scandals like Enron are the froth on the surface of the everyday world of corporatist politics in the United States. In the ten years before the

Enron scandal corporations legitimately donated $1.08bn in campaign contributions. (By way of comparison, the World Bank listed twenty-seven countries that had a GDP of less than this amount.)

At the same time that Putin was reining back the power of Russia's oligarchs the US Supreme Court was moving the other way. In 2006 it ruled as unconstitutional Vermont state legislation that attempted to limit the power of money to influence elections. The Constitution, it declared, prohibited any attempt to limit the amount of money candidates could spend on their election campaigns: an assertion that would undoubtedly have shocked many of the Founding Fathers, whose idea of democracy was formed in simpler times.

American corporations clothe oligarchy in the robes of democracy. Nowhere is this seen more clearly than in the Political Action Committees created by major corporations to fund political campaigns. Managers are instructed to persuade their staff to donate (after setting good examples themselves) in highly public gestures of apparent support for the political agenda of top management – for the other feature of this exercise in 'democracy' is the complete absence of any internal democracy. Although labelled committees, they are run entirely by senior management.

There is sometimes a fine line between corporate lobbying and corruption, but many countries have cases of corruption on a far larger scale than the United States. In Russia the Muscovite system of civil servants feeding off the rest of the population, kormlenie, which would now be regarded as blatant corruption, was for many years the bedrock on which effective government was built, and it has left its mark on Russian political culture to this day. Lying politicians are everywhere, and often the lies are blatant: the British general election of 1924 was determined in large part by the fears of Bolshevik revolution, stirred up by publication of an inflammatory letter from the Russian official Zinoviev, a letter later shown to be a forgery.

What has characterised American politics since the 1830s, and what differentiates it from politics in, for example, much of north-west Europe, is not that lies and corruption exist but the more or less resigned acceptance of their existence. The total corruption of political life in many large cities, starting with the control of New York's Tammany Hall by the Irish mafia, continued well into the twentieth century, with the election of John Kennedy in 1960 being aided by the manipulative skills of Richard Daley's Chicago political machine. Although there is no question of corruption or malpractice President Bush's opponents have alleged that his election in 2000 was similarly indebted to the Florida machine of his brother Jeb and that, as in Kennedy's case, partisan control of the judiciary made it impossible for the losers to successfully contest the result. His supporters would, of course, hotly deny this.

In Britain, campaigns based on deliberate fabrication by politicians are rare (the Zinoviev letter was a media scare almost certainly initiated by rogue officers in the security services, albeit soon exploited by politicians for their own ends). In the United States, on the other hand, since Andrew Jackson there has been a widespread assumption that politicians cannot be trusted (or perhaps more accurately a belief that whether politicians are honest or dishonest is not critically important), and a willingness of many in political circles to do far more than elaborate on the truth. Recent revelations that almost all the details of the Whitewater property scandal, in which President Clinton was supposedly implicated, had simply been made up by his opponents have gone almost unnoticed in the United States. It is unfair to push the argument too far; the morality of political life in the US today is not significantly better or worse than in, for example, Italy. The difference is that Italy does not purport to be leading a moral crusade to bring freedom and democracy to the rest of the globe.

Outright corruption is probably less prevalent in the United States than in many other parts of the western world, and where bribery is found it is usually rooted out. FBI director Robert Mueller reported in 2006 that around 500 government employees per year were convicted of corruption. Nevertheless the principles of the spoils system remain central to American political thinking. Leading supporters are often rewarded with ambassadorships and other public appointments. Legislators also reward themselves: congressional election results show that an amazing 97 per cent of those sitting members who stand for re-election are successful. This success rate is not because of the popularity of contemporary politicians but because of an eighteenth-century Massachusetts governor named Eldridge Gerry. Gerry was no friend of democracy. At the 1787 convention that drafted the US Constitution he opposed popular elections, declaring that 'the evils we experience flow from an excess of democracy'. (More wittily he opposed the creation of a large peacetime army by comparing a standing army to a man's standing member, 'an excellent assurance of domestic tranquillity but a dangerous temptation to foreign adventure'.) He soon found ways of avoiding the evils of excess democracy by skilfully drawing constituency boundaries to his own advantage, in one case producing a constituency that resembled nothing as much as a salamander or, as it was dubbed, a gerrymander. Gerrymandering is now a fundamental part of US politics. In 2003 the Republican-controlled legislature in Texas redrew constituency boundaries to give itself six extra seats in the US Congress. When Democrats took this gerrymandering to court the response of Texan Republicans, supported by the Bush administration, was not to deny gerrymandering but rather to argue that there was nothing unconstitutional about redrawing boundaries for pure partisan advantage. To the victor belongs the spoils. It is assumed to be natural that those with power will use it for their own benefit. This applies as much to the law as it does to politics.

American Justice

The assertion that American government is uniquely just rests on the impartiality of its judicial process. The US is famed for the way that nothing appears to be incapable of legal redress. Justice may sometimes seem absent but the law is omnipresent; legality is the benchmark against which all actions can be measured. The rule of law is fundamental to the way the United States functions as a nation. It is, however, largely irrelevant to the way it functions as an empire.

An example of this double standard emerged in investigations into the Iran Contra affair, in which the CIA funded the Contra terrorists in Nicaragua not only with funds from the Shah of Iran but with the proceeds of cocaine smuggling. Despite the near-universal illegality of drug smuggling, it emerged that the CIA had sought and received prior authority from the US attorney general: imperial adventures in Central America were deemed more important than obeying other people's laws, even when those laws were identical to America's own.

Throughout the nineteenth century the United States fought war after war to extend its frontiers, culminating in the Spanish American War of 1898 which brought with it 45 square miles of foreign soil that the US decided to hang on to: an enclave where, it is alleged, international law and human rights have no place – Guantanamo Bay.

Whether or not people were tortured at Guantanamo Bay is hotly debated, but the subject of torture itself gave rise to a particularly tortuous demonstrations of US legal reasoning. On 11 October 2002 the US army declared that the 1984 Convention on Torture, the International Covenant on Civil and Political Rights and the American Convention on Human Rights – all international conventions banning torture and signed up to by the United States – did not apply to the US military. US forces could carry on torturing people at Guantanamo because they were governed only by US domestic law. As leading international lawyer Philippe Sands puts it, 'Can you imagine how the US would react if another country tortured an American and defended it by saying "Oh, terribly sorry, but the international treaty we signed up to which prohibits torture isn't enforceable in our domestic law, so we don't have to apply it"?'

In 2006 the Associated Press news agency used the Freedom of Information Act to obtain 5,000 pages of transcript of military court hearings at the Guantanamo Bay prison. In one exchange a British prisoner quotes international law to demand the right to hear the evidence against him (a right that, incidentally, is normally present under American law); a US Air Force colonel angrily responds with the words, 'I do not care about international law. I do not want to hear the words international law. We are not concerned about international law.' The comments of one rogue officer do not constitute official policy, but they do illustrate an important strand of American imperial thought: international standards are for governing the rest of the world; they do not apply to the imperial power itself.

Sands catalogues a long list of international conventions and treaties that the United States has flouted or opted out of. Many examples are famous – the Kyoto Accord, the treaty to eliminate landmines, the Biological and Toxins Weapons Convention – but there are far more of interest only to specialists. A typical example concerns a protocol attached to the 1963 Vienna Convention on the arcane subject of consular access to foreign prisoners. The US was a leading advocate of the protocol and was one of the first to benefit when it successfully sued the Iranian government over access to the Americans held hostage in Tehran in 1979. In 2004, however, it was the United States that was successfully sued, by Mexico. To avoid the same thing happening again the US simply withdrew from the treaty.

The United States is not unique in this regard. Soviet Russia set a precedent in 1930 when an international arbitration tribunal awarded the British company Lena Goldfields £13m plus interest after the Soviet government revoked its concession to mine gold in the Urals and Siberia. Stalin simply abandoned the arbitration and refused to accept the award.

It is not merely that the US opts out of commitments when its interests are threatened but that it rejects the principle that it should ever be subject to enforceable internationally accepted standards. The 1989 Convention on the Rights of the Child is a statement of principle that in the fifteen years after its establishment was ratified by 192 countries. Only two refused to do so: Somalia and the US.

Dissident academic Noam Chomsky argues in *Failed States* that the US follows a principle of 'self-exemption' from international legal standards. He cites the Geneva Convention as an example of a standard that the US expects others to follow but from which it exempts itself, as its seizure of Fallujah General Hospital showed. He quotes Secretary of State Condoleezza Rice's assertion that international judicial processes have 'proven inappropriate for the United States' and that generally the

US is not to be subject to 'international laws and norms'. Some care needs to be taken not to pursue this argument too far. Polls have shown that a large majority of Americans favoured signing the Kyoto Accord and accepting the International Criminal Court; Chomsky argues that the refusal to accept international legal standards reflects political and business interests rather than the popular will. Nevertheless there is a popular assumption that Americans warrant a different legal standard.

In January 2006 American newspapers reported the trial of Lewis Welshofer Jr, who had killed a man by stuffing him head-first into a sleeping bag and then sitting on him. There were interviews with Welshofer's anguished wife pleading on behalf of their three children that he not be sent to prison. Her pleas were heard: Welshofer was merely fined $6,000. By American standards such a sentence was extraordinarily lenient, but this was no ordinary murder. Welshofer was an army officer serving in Iraq, and his victim was an Iraqi army general. There were no interviews with the victim's anguished family.

American law is intended primarily to protect Americans and their interests. Commercial law works to protect American commercial interests. This was perfectly illustrated in the case of the Vietnamese catfish, reported in the *Financial Times* in 2007. Lawyers acting for US fish farmers successfully argued that Vietnamese catfish, although genetically very close, were in fact a totally different fish to American catfish and therefore could not be sold in the US as catfish. The Vietnamese responded by adopting a new name (catfish in Vietnamese), and successfully resumed exports. US producers then used the same lawyers to successfully argue the exact reverse of what they had claimed before, namely that the two sorts of catfish were really just the same, and import tariffs should therefore be levied to avoid 'unfair' price competition.

'Fairness' is a difficult concept when it comes to international law. There was anger in the UK when the Blair government signed a treaty allowing the US to extradite suspects from Britain without first proving that there existed a *prima facie* case against them, but did not give the UK the same rights over extraditions from the US. Many newspapers and parliamentary opponents of the agreement attacked the inherent 'unfairness' of the American position, but this is to miss the point: the US negotiators were not trying to produce a fair accord; they were aiming to gain as much as possible for the United States while giving as little as possible away. That is how businesses negotiate. The US government is often negotiating on behalf of its corporate citizens, as when in 2007 it pressured the European Union to allow US airlines to operate routes within Europe, while European airlines continued to be banned from routes within the United States.

The 2008 financial crisis demonstrated once again the underlying America-first imperialist ideology that permeates American thinking. It is a basic tenet of financial regulation, in the European Union enshrined in law, that banking regulators must provide an equal degree of protection to all creditors worldwide. When Lehman Brothers went bankrupt the Financial Services Authority in the UK naïvely assumed that their American counterparts would live up to this obligation, and were stunned when the SEC and the Federal Reserve refused to hand back $8bn that had been moved from Lehman's London operations to its New York headquarters just days before the collapse. Effectively the US authorities allowed Lehman's British reserves, supposedly there to underpin its London trading, to be used to settle claims in New York, leaving British claimants in the lurch. The FSA have since announced they will change the rules to make US banks hold in Britain the reserves they need to support their British operations, but the surprise is that they ever imagined that in a crisis the US would do anything other than look after its own.

In terms of its relationships with the rest of the world American legal theory resembles less the British concept of equity than the traditional Russian belief that the law is not about achieving justice but about maintaining order, with the United States maintaining the privileged position once reserved for the Russian tsar. Nowhere is this seen more clearly than in the Monroe Doctrine and the Olney Corollary, which laid down that the United States had the right to supreme authority in the Americas. The Olney Corollary was formulated when Britain refused to agree to American arbitration in a dispute with Venezuela, the British prime minister pointing out not unreasonably that the Monroe Doctrine was a unilateral declaration with no standing in international law. President Cleveland's response was unambiguous: it may not have been added 'in so many words to the code of international law', but the US had the right to supremacy 'as certainly and securely as if it were specifically mentioned'.

US legal theory is predicated on the absolute certainty that its own actions are beyond reproach. As an example, when Admiral Doenitz, Hitler's U-Boat commander, was accused of war crimes, the American Admiral Nimitz testified that German submarines had done nothing that US submarines had not done. The American-led tribunal declared that by definition the US navy could not have committed war crimes, and so found Doenitz not guilty. A corollary to this belief is that American law is superior to foreign law. When two European charities providing aid to Palestine were investigated by the French and British governments they were completely cleared of any link with terrorism; on that basis National Westminster and Credit Lyonnais provided them with banking services. Despite the fact that the charities had absolutely no connection with the US, a New York judge allowed the banks to be sued there by lawyers claiming to act for victims of terrorism, declaring that the investigations by the British and French governments were irrelevant. This view underlies the US approach to the UN. The United Nations is to be supported only as long as it supports the United States. When it does not it is to be ignored, even to the extent of not paying the membership fees. (The USA's billion dollar arrears led British prime minister John Major to invert the famous slogan of the American Rebellion and quip that the United States sought 'representation without taxation'.)

The basic commitment to one law for Americans and another for foreigners is long established. Land ownership laws in the United States were for many years heavily biased against foreigners, who were often labelled as vile speculators at a time when American speculators were amassing vast riches in the frontier territories. In 1885 the *New York Times* thundered against 'an evil of considerable magnitude – the acquisition of vast tracts of land in the territories by English noblemen'. Two years later the federal Alien Property Act prohibited the ownership of land in the territories (that is in areas not yet incorporated into states) by aliens or by corporations in which aliens owned more than 20 per cent of the shares. A dozen states enacted similar legislation, the New Hampshire legislature declaring, for example, that 'American soil is for Americans, and should be exclusively owned and controlled by American citizens.' At the same time a number of states imposed punitive tax rates on foreign-owned corporations. When foreign governments complained, as for example when the state of Iowa levied special taxes on foreign fire insurers, the state department merely replied that it was nothing to do with the federal government. In 1887 the Indiana legislature even withdrew court protection from foreign companies.

New York owed its dominant position in global finance in part to laws enacted in the 1880s aimed at preventing foreign competition. The minimum paid-up capital of foreign insurance companies was set at 250 per cent of that required for American companies; foreign banks were prohibited from engaging in 'banking business' such as taking deposits and in 1914 foreign banks were banned from establishing branches in New York at all.

Such laws and values exist in many, probably most, countries. They certainly exist in Russia, and there is nothing particularly sinister or unexpected about them. What makes them significant is that the United States achieves its global dominance in large part by denying the validity of such values when expressed by others. When other nations restrict the 'right' of American corporations to operate they are condemned; when other nations ignore international law or UN resolutions they are attacked; when protective tariffs are erected against American exporters they are threatened with retaliation. Examples are numerous; here are just four.

America is the world's largest exporter of raw cotton, and yet a 2005 study found that although the world market price for cotton was

48 US cents per pound US cotton cost 78 cents per pound to produce. The explanation for the amazing success of high-cost American cotton farmers lay in the state aid they received from the US government: subsidies of $3.9bn per annum (more than three times the aid given by the US government to Africa). The direct result of these subsidies was to destroy the cotton industries in countries like Benin in west Africa, which depended on cotton for 60 per cent of its exports. In 2002 alone, when the US Farm Bill raised American subsidies to $250 per hectare, Benin's exports fell 9 per cent and its GDP was cut by 1.4 per cent as a direct result of the American policies.

Similarly the US is the world's third largest rice exporter, thanks to subsidies of well over $1bn a year, which allow US producers to sell their product in world markets at 30 per cent below what it costs to produce.

In 2007 the US imposed swingeing import tariffs on Chinese paper, alleging exactly the sort of government subsidy being given to American rice and cotton growers.

Despite its own high-tariff tradition, in the mid-1990s the US successfully appealed to the World Trade Organisation to force the European Union to end its tariff support for small-scale Caribbean banana producers in favour of US multinationals operating out of Central America, bringing enormous economic distress to islands like St Lucia.

The World Trade Organisation declared the American cotton subsidies illegal but the United States simply ignored the ruling. The casual disregard for international law appears to contrast strongly with the legalism at home, but throughout American history legal niceties have been readily abandoned when considered 'necessary'. During the civil war Lincoln even suspended the writ of habeas corpus, defying the Supreme Court in the process (and it is worth remembering that he did this not to control enemy infiltrators but to suppress the anti-war movement in the north).

International law is very often upheld or ignored depending on whether it provides economic benefits to the United States, and with the rise of corporatism this has come to mean benefits for US corporations.

The cotton subsidies that devastated poor producers in countries like Benin went overwhelmingly to large agribusinesses, some receiving tens of millions of dollars a year (and overwhelmingly to corporations in Texas, the home state of President Bush II); 60 per cent of US growers received no subsidy at all. (Interestingly the largest beneficiary of the rice subsidies was Riceland Foods, based in Arkansas, Bill Clinton's home state.)

The ideology of corporatism – the philosophy that abstract corporations have transcendent quasi-human rights – has as yet had limited appeal outside America, but an indication of how it might develop has been provided by an obscure legal case in Mexico. In 1987 the first treaty was signed that gave corporations the power to challenge the decisions of foreign governments and courts. Under the US-Canada Free Trade Act (extended seven years later to include Mexico) corporations were empowered to sue for non-compliance with the treaty. The implications of this legislation became apparent when a US waste disposal company was stopped from building a plant in Mexico after surveys found that it would pollute local water supplies: the corporation successfully sued the Mexican government for $16.7m compensation. Such environmental regulation, it argued, was tantamount to 'an indirect expropriation' and thus prohibited under the treaty. Protecting the property rights of US corporations was held to take priority over the right of the elected Mexican government to protect its environment in whatever way it thought fit.

Such arcane matters as trade agreements are important because of the way that the ideologies of democracy, imperialism and corporatism have been conflated. A notion has developed that what the United States does to maintain its commercial empire is not an expression of economic self-interest but an expression of some higher ideal. This idea can be traced at least as far back as the first Pan-American Congress, convened by the US in 1889. Billed as a conference to prevent the frequent wars that ravaged the hemisphere, the US lobbied vigorously, but unsuccessfully, for a customs union that would keep out European exporters. The argument was that free movement within and customs barriers without would create a prosperous Latin America, which would be less likely to engage in internecine wars. As the Latin Americans realised, it would also create a massive market for US business to exploit.Virtually identical arguments were put by Bush II 110 years later: 'The case for trade is not just monetary, but moral. Economic freedom creates habits of liberty. And habits of liberty create expectations of democracy.' America has not been expanding its commercial empire but acting as a beacon of liberty, demonstrating to the rest of the world that free markets are the very cornerstones of freedom. And yet the European and Asian press repeatedly report the limitations that in practice the United States places on free markets. 'British songwriters are losing millions of pounds in royalties', claimed *The Times*.'America will not pay European composers for music played in bars, clubs and restaurants despite World Trade Organisation obligations.' A reader who had booked a cruise from New York to Canada and then back to Florida complained to the travel pages of the *Observer* that he been made to leave the ship in Quebec City and travel overland to Montreal. The reason, it transpired, was that the US Jones Act (technically the Passenger Services Act) makes it illegal for passengers to travel from one US port to another on a non-US vessel. To avoid this protectionist legislation foreign cruise operators have to break their voyage into separate unconnected legs, each starting or terminating outside the US.

The theory of corporatist democracy might say that free trade and free elections are two sides of the same coin, but the imperial values underlying such sentiments ensure that their application is governed primarily by national self-interest. In 2006 an Arab-owned company tried to buy control of a number of US ports previously owned by a British company and the matter was referred to the presidential committee on foreign investments, which must approve any foreign takeover of a US company. A bitter dispute broke out, not about whether in a free market economy the state should be allowed to block foreign takeovers but whether, if the committee did allow the takeover, Congress would be able to overturn its ruling. The point that the United States had repeatedly argued for the right of its corporations to operate in Arab countries was hardly mentioned.

When it comes to the realm of international relations it is clear that the claim that America is somehow more just is false. The claim that America's business is more efficient than most of its competitors looks at first sight to be far more soundly based.

American Efficiency

Although the so-called Asian Tigers have come to dominate some key industries, American corporations remain overwhelmingly powerful. It seems obvious, therefore, that their competitive edge implies they are considerably more efficient than their foreign competitors. However, for every cogent argument in economics there is usually an equally cogent refutation. Even issues that non-economists might regard as matters of fact are endlessly disputed. The superiority of American over European business methods has long been widely accepted, but a number of respected authors have started to question whether this superiority has any basis in reality. Books like *The European Dream – how Europe's vision of the future is quietly eclipsing the American dream* by the American Jeremy Rifkin and *An UnAmerican Business – the rise of the new European enterprise model* by Dutch business school professor Donald Kalff suggest otherwise. Does the typical large American corporation, with its emphasis on hierarchy and short term results, massive salary differentials between top management and shop floor, use of simplistic 'key performance indicators' and more or less arbitrary target-setting really generate better economic performance?

One of the most respected economists of the twenty-first century, Professor John Kay, has commented on the powerful myths associated with the American economy. Writing in 2005 he said:

> One of the oddities about the last decade has been the belief – on no evidence – that the US is not just the world's most successful economy, but that it's so markedly more successful than any others. The truth is that the richest countries in the world are small western European states:

> Switzerland, Norway, Denmark and so on. . . . If you look at growth rates during the last twenty years, there is no marked difference between American economic performance and European economic performance. The bizarre thing is that not just Americans but a lot of Europeans seem to have brainwashed themselves into believing that Europe is doing much worse than the United States.

He goes on to draw an interesting conclusion from the economic statistics usually used to demonstrate American superiority: 'American GDP is 20 per cent above French; but French working hours are shorter. The only difference is the French have more holidays and longer lunches. There never has been a huge gap between European and American productivity.' In fact, OECD statistics show that productivity per hour worked is higher in France than the US, although productivity per head is lower. The difference is that the French not only work fewer hours per week but French workers average about seven weeks of paid vacation a year. In America that figure is less than four.

A study of corporate headquarters by a team from Ashridge Strategic Management Centre found that, after allowing for such factors as size of company, US firms typically employed 27 per cent more staff to do the same tasks as western European firms.

What US corporations have that many European corporations lack is scale. Economies of scale in classical economics are primarily about capital efficiencies: the theory is that the company producing a million widgets a day will do so more efficiently than the company producing a hundred widgets a day, because the larger company will be able to afford better widget-making machines. The reality, as the robber barons in America realised after the civil war, is that economies of scale are really nothing to do with capital efficiency but everything to do with naked power. Modern business textbooks no longer talk about achieving 'economies of scale' but simply about 'leveraging scale'. Scale gives corporations power: power against their suppliers; power against their smaller competitors (if you bought this book in an independent bookshop you can be sure the owner paid the publisher far more for it than the big bookselling chains would have done); power against their employees and their unions; and nowadays power against individual governments.

A classic illustration of the link between scale and American economic imperialism is the fate of the British institutions that once dominated the financial world. Margaret Thatcher, one of the most ideologically driven leaders of modern times, was an ardent advocate of the free market policies promoted by US corporations. One target of her ideological zeal was the collection of financial institutions known as the City, which had once formed the hub of the British commercial empire. The City was governed by a host of largely informal rules and demarcation lines that she swept away in a 'Big Bang' in October 1986. In his book *The Death of Gentlemanly Capitalism* Philip Augar describes what happened. Before Big Bang all the top ten British merchant banks were British owned; afterwards none of them were: three were European, five were American and the remaining two were characterised by Augur as international with a strong American influence. Firms that had been large by British standards were dwarves compared to the giants of Wall Street, and they were simply gobbled up. It is this scale rather than anything deriving from *laissez-faire* economic theory that has driven the ever-increasing power of US corporations. As J.K. Galbraith argued, corporations wield power by using the 'mystique of the market', but the reality is that they control the market rather than the other way round. Not only do corporations use the power derived from their scale to manipulate the markets, but US corporations often benefit from massive state support. Kevin Phillips presents a lengthy list of occasions between 1982 and 2005 when the American financial services industry received government subsidies; subsidies of $250bn were given to troubled building societies (known in the US as Savings and Loans) at the very same time that Thatcher was allowing American corporations to seize control of the City in the name of free markets.

The US takeover of the City is an example of commercial 'imperialism' not because the nationality of Britain's banking oligarchs happened to change but because of the consequent financial transfers. If companies wanted to raise money on the London Stock Exchange in the mid-1980s they would pay around 1.5 per cent to the various intermediaries. The equivalent cost in America was around 5 per cent, and after the Big Bang fees in Britain shot up to 'international levels'. The work being done was just the same, but British companies needing to raise new capital found themselves paying large dollops of extra commission that disappeared into the maws of Citibank, J.P. Morgan, Goldman Sachs and the like. A new stream of tribute was now passing across the Atlantic.

Whether in fact American corporations are more or less efficient than their global competitors is, in terms of history, largely irrelevant. As historical forces US corporations are simply more important than European corporations because they have shaped America and America is shaping the world.

Since its formation the United States of America has sought to reform the world in what it believes to be its own image, but it has always been an image distorted by the prism of ideology. A nation built very largely on slavery preached equality and justice for all; an empire built on conquest preached peace and respect. Nowadays the mantra is free markets, an ideology of corporatist democracy that is predicated on the supposed superior efficiency of US corporations, and on the assertion that this superiority derived from the free market nostrums that are now prescribed for the rest of the world. But the reality is that the US initially achieved its economic pre-eminence by avoiding the perils of free competition. Massive tariff barriers served to protect infant US industries from the chill winds of free markets.

One study of eleven industrial nations found that in 1875 by far the highest GDP growth rate was achieved by the United States, which also had by far the highest average tariff on imports (45 per cent: the next highest tariffs were in Denmark and Austria, each averaging 17.5 per cent; Britain averaged zero). Looking at the same countries in 1913 found almost identical results: the United States again had by far the highest tariffs (44 per cent) and a growth rate exceeded only by Sweden (which had increased tariffs from 4 per cent to 20 per cent in the intervening period). Such tariffs are now bitterly opposed by US corporations that are striving to leverage their scale in overseas markets.

It is hard to disagree with Cambridge professor Ha-Joon Chang's assertion (in his aptly titled book *Kicking Away The Ladder*) that the very methods used by America and other western countries to kick-start their own development are now being denied to developing countries. Not only was US development assisted by measures it now decries in others, but those economies it has pressured into following its ideological prescriptions rather than its example have suffered. Harvard economist Dani Rodrik compared the economic performance of Mexico and Vietnam – the former having 'benefited' from enormous US investment and a free trade agreement with its northern neighbour, the latter suffering from a full US trade embargo until 1994 and severe international trade restrictions for many years after that. His conclusion is that since 1992 (when Mexico signed the North American Free Trade Agreement) its per capita growth rate has barely been above 1 per cent; Vietnam's has been five times greater.

The claim that American-style corporatist democracy is the most economically efficient way to organise society is therefore no more robust than its claim to political and judicial superiority. But whatever may be the pros and cons of its political, legal and economic theories, the underlying reality is that America works. Hundreds of thousand of people clamour to get in because America quite simply offers a better life. The question is, better in what way?

America Delivers

It is easy for liberal Europeans to sneer at American society, to assert – in the snide phrase variously attributed to Oscar Wilde and George Clemenceau – that America is the only nation in history to go from barbarism to decadence without an intervening period of civilisation. But far more of the world's population wish they could live, if not in America, at least like Americans. They believe their lives would be better: richer, healthier and simply longer. Most of them are wrong.

Among the world's richest countries the United States ranks last or nearly last on almost every health indicator: infant mortality, average birth weight, life expectancy at birth, life expectancy for infants and so on. The average American male lives three and a half years less than the average Japanese. The American adolescent death rate is twice as high as England's. A recent survey of thirty-three industrialised nations found that only Latvia had a worse infant mortality rate than the US. Cubans, supposedly suffering under decades of dastardly dictatorship, can expect to live longer than the average American.

Of course Russians are worse off. They spend more of their lives sick than their counterparts in the United States, western Europe and Japan. Furthermore low birth-rates and high death-rates have created a demographic crisis; experts predict that by 2050 Russia's population will drop to 100 million from its current level of around 143 million. This in turn will cause catastrophic labour shortages, damning Russians' aspirations for a better life. One reason for the high death rate is that Russia now has the fourth highest per capita cigarette consumption in the world, encouraged by foreign tobacco corporations who have been among the largest investors in post-Soviet Russia. These corporations have focused their advertising on women, managing to more than double the rate of female smoking since the Soviet era.

America is a much wealthier society than Russia, but that wealth is concentrated at the top. At the end of the twentieth century the richest 1 per cent of the American population owned more of the nation's wealth than the bottom 90 per cent. The conspicuous consumption of the denizens of Wall Street may be beyond the comprehension of most of the world's population but, as one study put it, 'People die younger in Harlem than in Bangladesh.' Foreigners may snigger at obese Americans, but the US Department of Agriculture reports that 33 million Americans go hungry (or to use their jargon 33 million Americans live with 'food insecurity'). Twice as many have no health insurance.

One argument frequently cited to compensate for such statistics is that at least the poor in the US can 'haul themselves up by their bootstraps' and achieve the good life; America is not stuck with the rigid class structures that compel the poor elsewhere to stay poor. A Canadian study by Miles Corak looking at social mobility over four generations showed that the reality is quite different; not only do poor families in America have a smaller chance of rising up the social ladder than Canadians, but Americans were also less mobile than Scandinavians and even the French; indeed the only nation in the survey with marginally less social mobility was the United Kingdom.

In the last twenty years of the twentieth century US income differentials increased dramatically, the rich became a lot richer and the poor poorer: 145,000 people in the US, one in a thousand of the earning population, earned more than $1.6m each in 2002; this 0.1 per cent accounted for 7.4 per cent of the nation's income, more than double the share of the top 0.1 per cent in 1980. The average CEO in America earns 800 times the minimum wage – for a few hours at their desk they earn more than a worker on minimum wage earns in a year – although US research quoted by Richard Wachman has found no link between performance and high levels of executive pay. The American tax system ensured that the top 400 taxpayers, earning a minimum of $87m a year, paid virtually the same income, Medicare and social security taxes as people earning $50,000. (At the same time the power of corporatism was shown as the tax burden moved increasingly away from corporations to individuals. In 1960 corporations paid 23 per cent of US tax receipts; by 1990 this had fallen to 9 per cent.)

In the first five years of the twenty-first century average pay in the US actually declined in real terms. Massive inflows of cash from the expanding economies in Asia kept interest rates low and pumped up asset prices, which in turn led to big bonuses on Wall Street but did nothing for American wage-earners: by 2006 wages made up the lowest proportion of GDP since the Second World War. This cash inflow, which transferred wealth from the rest of the world to America, was remarkable in two ways: it failed to benefit large sections of American society, and it marked a significant change in the commercial dynamics of the American empire.

One of the characteristics of the British empire is that after the early days of naked exploitation the colonies became recipients of massive British capital investment. On the eve of the First World War the net outflow of capital from Britain was no less than 9 per cent of its GDP, a quite staggering figure. Not all of it went to the empire; the United States and (to a much lesser extent) Russia were significant beneficiaries.

The dynamics of this process are controversial. Ferguson sees Britain's investment in its empire as an act of unrecognised nobility for which former colonies should be grateful. Others – like the renowned Indian economist Amiya Kumar Bagchi – point out that the picture looks very different when other factors are considered. In the case of India taxes levied on locals to support the British occupation, pensions paid to imperial civil servants from Indian revenues, interest payments on government debt, profits made in Britain by 'adding value' to Indian exports and what has been called 'self-ransoming' all contributed to ensuring that the people of Britain gained far more economically than the people of the subcontinent. (The classic case of self-ransoming was the enormous debt incurred by the imperial Indian government to suppress the Indian mutiny.) Nevertheless, in terms of classical economics, which largely ignores such tribute-flows, investments were made on a very large scale by British firms in order to dominate economies across the globe.

The American empire developed in the same way but with one important difference: having become a net exporter of capital on the British model after the First World War, once it had achieved global domination it moved off in a new and different direction, but one that in many ways parallels Bagchi's interpretation of Britain's imperial tribute-gathering. By 1938 the value of US assets abroad had reached $11.5bn. After the Second World War private sector lending and investment continued to increase as US corporations strengthened their hold over foreign economies in just the same way that Britain had done in earlier times. Between 1960 and 1976 the US current account surplus reached nearly $70bn. Then something new happened: rather than pumping ever more money overseas the United States as a nation started sucking money back. Thirty years later the current account showed a deficit of nearly $900bn. (That is to say the US imported $900bn more than it exported. These numbers are usually expressed as a percentage of GDP, and the trend is startling: in 1997 the current account deficit was under 2 per cent; by 2007 it was nearly 7 per cent.) In part this was an inevitable consequence of American commercial success. As more of the world's business became American-owned it was natural that more of what Marx called surplus value – profit – ended up in the United States. It is worth emphasising again that this 'corporate imperialism' was not part of a giant conspiracy of megalomaniac oligarchs to rule the world; rather it was the accidental consequence of thousands of rational, routine activities buried in the interstices of corporate life. As an example, highly intelligent men and women of the utmost personal integrity toil away in corporate tax departments to find ways of maximising profits by minimising tax. These departments are benchmarked against each other on their ability to reduce their corporation's 'effective rate of tax'. The giant American corporation Procter & Gamble has sales of £2.6bn out of its Newcastle factories, filling British shopping baskets with everything from toothpaste to babies' nappies, but clever tax management ensures that it pays just £7m in British corporation tax. The British supermarket group Asda paid hundreds of millions of pounds in tax until it was taken over by the American Wal-Mart corporation, who promptly depressed its reported profits by loading it with debt. Such corporate creativeness is not only perfectly legal but is engaged in for sound business reasons that have nothing to do with 'imperialism', however defined. The incidental effect of Wal-Mart's tax management, however, is that funds that might have been building schools or hospitals in Britain have been diverted into the corporate coffers in Bentonville, Arkansas, and end up funding American consumption.

These international funds transfers are often lost sight of in political debate. In Britain the Private Finance Initiative (PFI), under which private corporations take over services previously run by government employees, is controversial, but one aspect is straightforward. Among the main PFI contractors are American corporations like the Texan behemoth EDS, which over four years obtained £11bn of PFI revenue on which it reportedly made £2.55bn profit. Whether this profit was justified or not is debatable, but what is not is that this enormous sum of taxpayers' money, instead of being injected into the UK economy, became available for US consumption. Tribute had passed across the ocean as surely as it had when the Britain's imperial civil servants retired to Bognor Regis with their Indian-funded pensions.

As important in driving international funds transfers as these corporate dynamics is what might be called America's PR success. Foreigners want to invest in America; they too believe the American dream. Individuals, corporations and even governments around the world have ploughed their savings into US government bonds and US corporate equities. In February 2005 the *New York Times* reported that the US was pulling in 80 per cent of total world savings 'largely to finance our consumption' It noted that '43 per cent of all US Treasury bills, notes and bonds are now held by foreigners.' As foreign savings flowed in, the funds available for American consumption increased. Not only did the US government and corporations rack up debt but so did individual Americans. In 1980 savings accounted for 7.4 per cent of the national income; a quarter of a century later the picture had reversed, with the average American spending $104 for every $100 of income. The dangers for the whole world of such an uncontrolled surge in US credit became all too apparent in 2008. Nevertheless the United States appears to have created a virtuous circle in which its commercial success draws in wealth from the rest of the world; this in turn allows American corporations to expand their influence overseas, which in turn draws in yet more wealth.

America's commercial empire is held together in large part by the primacy of the dollar. Two-thirds of world trade is dollar denominated and two-thirds of the foreign exchange reserves of the world's central banks are dollars. Crucially the world's oil markets operate in dollars. Oil importing countries must buy dollars and oil exporters are incentivised to invest in the US, thereby avoiding any foreign exchange risk. As the former US ambassador to Saudi Arabia explained to a congressional committee, the Saudis, in part out of friendship with the United States, insisted that everyone pay them in dollars: 'Therefore the US Treasury can print money and buy oil which is an advantage no other country has.' He worried that at some point they would ask themselves 'why they should be so kind to the United States'. One man tried to challenge the dollar's role: Saddam Hussein insisted that Iraqi oil sales be denominated in euros, a decision reversed after the American invasion of his country.

The primacy of the dollar and the capital transfers that go with it reinforce, and are reinforced by, the other imperial bonds that the United States has established around the world. The *Observer* quoted one prominent Harvard economist delicately warning that if the Euro ever weakened the status of the dollar it 'could complicate international military relationships'. As with most economic arguments it is possible to look at these monetary transfers through the other end of the economic telescope. Rather than arguing that America spends more than it earns, and therefore must be sucking in wealth from Asia and Europe, America's leading investment guru, the billionaire Warren Buffet, argues that the wealth transfers are in the opposite direction. In his words the trade imbalances are the 'force-feeding of American wealth to the rest of the world'. Buffet famously lives a modest life in a smallish home in Omaha, Nebraska. For him wealth is not what you spend but what you own. By buying US shares and bonds, says Buffet, foreigners are buying American assets. As these assets last for ever, while the money received by America in return is quickly spent, it is the foreigners who are becoming wealthy at America's expense, not the other way round.

As with so much in economics, Buffet's argument is advanced in a series of logical steps to arrive at a conclusion that defies common sense. Ask most people whether they would feel wealthier if they were given £10,000 to spend or £10,000 locked in a glass case to look at, and very few would choose the Warren Buffet option. His argument only makes sense if you believe that one day the foreigners will be able to open their glass cases, sell all their American bonds and shares and start spending the money themselves. But the sums are now so massive that nobody could afford to buy these supposed assets; if foreigners suddenly tried to unload them the markets would collapse. Collectively the foreign stockholders are locked in; America, almost entirely by accident, has created a virtuous circle for itself that mirrors a vicious circle for the rest of its empire. But that circle could unwind over time. Foreign central banks have enormous stockpiles of dollars – two-thirds held by just six countries: Japan, South Korea, Taiwan, Singapore and, more ominously for America, China and Russia. If the political environment changes, America's economy could be held to ransom.

From Invisible Empires to the Neo-Empire

America and Russia formed their empires in the same way at roughly the same time. Then in the twentieth century corporatism changed the face of American imperialism. For a time it seemed that, in the phrase of Alexis de Tocqueville, the two empires would hold in their hands 'the destinies of half the world', but as the century drew to a close America emerged as the sole superpower. The United States had won out not only because of its superior military might but because its ideology had triumphed. Throughout much of the world American values were perceived to be superior – politically, ethically, economically and practically. The Russian empire was deemed to match the American on none of these attributes. For most of their history the parallels between the two empires were remarkably strong, but the modern American empire seems to epitomise what the American sociologist Seymour Lipset called 'American exceptionalism': the United States is in fundamental ways different to every other society. But there remains one facet of Russian history that is a uniquely valuable comparator. The outstanding feature of the American empire is one that was shared perhaps only by the Soviet empire: the denial of its own existence.

Both empires hid from their own people. Russia installed an imperial puppet regime in Czechoslovakia in 1948 and America did the same in Iran a few years later. Both actions in any other age would not only have been regarded as 'imperial' by outsiders but would have been proudly proclaimed as such by the imperial power. In the twentieth century such proclamations were unthinkable, with the result that Russian soldiers sent to crush the 1968 uprising in Prague were genuinely taken aback by the popular hostility they encountered, and most Americans were similarly unprepared when Iranians stormed the US embassy in 1979 and held their diplomats hostage. The Soviet and American empires were unique in that their people stared uncomprehending at the realities of imperial power partly because they were shocked at the very idea of empire. Britons had been outraged by such imperial infamies as the Amritsar massacre, but they understood that theirs was an empire. For ideological reasons the new imperialists denied even that: the two sets of imperialists and their minions defined 'imperialism' so that it only covered the other side.

Algeria, hosting the 1973 Non-Aligned Conference, attacked both Russian and American imperialism, prompting Fidel Castro to launch into a spirited denial of Russian imperialism. 'How can the Soviet Union be labelled imperialist?' he asked. 'Where are its monopoly corporations? Where is its participation in multinational companies? What factories, what mines, what oilfields does it own in the underdeveloped world? What worker is exploited in any country of Asia, Africa or Latin America by Soviet capital?' Similarly apologists for US imperialism deny not just the crude military manifestations of the imperial dream but the whole commercial substructure on which the modern American empire is built.

During the second Iraq War an opinion poll found that a higher percentage of Americans than at any time since the end of the Vietnam War asserted that the United States 'should mind its own business'. The problem is that America's business is now global. Minding America's business no longer implies isolationism; it means making sure that foreign governments and citizens keep their 'surplus' assets rolling into America's coffers. America's human citizens can only carry on minding their own business in the narrow sense meant by the poll's respondents if the US government acts abroad to mind the business of its corporate citizens.

Protecting its corporate citizens may or may not mean invading Iraq, but it certainly means opting out of international treaties, protecting and subsidising domestic industries while stopping other governments doing the same, and where necessary directly intervening in the politics of nations around the globe. All these are activities that America's critics describe as 'imperialist', but they are only the superficial manifestations of a much deeper ideological 'empire' created by the relentless, and quite innocent, ideological indoctrination carried out as the values of American institutions and corporations are transferred to the rest of the world. The distinguishing characteristic of the more controversial and informal 'cultural' imperialism that some claim to see is that it is not imposed by evil foreign aggressors but has become embedded in the everyday lives of the new commercial colonies. Much of the world now accepts American values as their own.

On 1 September 2004 Chechen guerrillas seized a Russian school on the first day of the new school year. Hundreds of terrified children and adults were victims of one of the most barbaric hostage seizures in modern history. On the second night the sound of explosions sent fresh waves of anguish through the thousands of relatives and friends surrounding the school. The world's media descended on North Ossetia, and all over the world people were gripped by the unfolding horror of terrorism on the scale of 9/11. On the morning television in Britain, however, the school siege warranted only third place. Considered more important were a report that Hurricane Frances was expected to hit Florida later that day and the main story: a speech given by President Bush II in New York as part of his re-election campaign. To the British media a perfectly ordinary party political speech and a storm warning on the other side of the Atlantic were more newsworthy than a unique human tragedy on the other side of Europe. (Even later in the day, when the hostage crisis disintegrated into tragedy and pictures of the blood-soaked corpses of murdered children were being beamed on to the world's TV screens, British TV broke off to cross over to New York and report that former US president Bill Clinton had been admitted to hospital with chest pains and was being visited by his wife.) There are many ways to explain this apparently bizarre sense of priorities: the technical ease of getting comprehensive TV coverage from the US, an underlying sympathy with all things American, an instinctive lack of sympathy (going back to Châlons) with all things east European, a simple preference for TV interviews with people speaking the same language. The reasons for devoting so much more time to America than to Russia on that particular morning are unimportant; the fact is that it happened. Britons woke up to a diet of US news reinforcing US priorities and values. The images presented to them were Bush II claiming to be rescuing the world from terror, not Putin struggling to do the very same thing. In one very small way Britain was exhibiting its position as part of the American empire.

This was illustrated more dramatically in the American invasion of Iraq. Troops from client states like Britain, Spain, Italy and Australia joined America's war in much the same way as troops from Russia's client states joined the 1968 invasion of Czechoslovakia – because they saw the world through the same ideological prisms. Since its first attacks on the Barbary pirates the United States has been able to persuade other nations that its interests are the same as theirs. America's allies reimbursed $54bn of the $61bn cost of the first Gulf War. Although the US was unable to garner such financial support for the second war, British troops continued in their role as America's ghurkhas.

While most western leaders would deny that the invasion of Iraq was an act of 'imperialism' some Americans hailed it as what came to be called 'neo-imperialism'. Neo-imperialists argue that the fundamental objective of American foreign policy must be the security of the homeland and that this can only be achieved by possessing, and being willing to use, overwhelming military superiority. Such a doctrine is of course not at all 'neo'; it incorporates the conviction of the early Puritans that Americans are a specially chosen people, with the confidence in their own invulnerability that emerged after the Mystic Massacre, the ability to manufacture 'threats to security' like those used to justify the invasion of Florida and the doctrines of total war personified by Sherman in the Civil War.

Like America's traditional imperialism, its neo-imperialism is fundamentally military, but its proponents do not see it that way. They picture an empire that everyone would want to join, an alliance of democracies aspiring to the American way of life and over whom the United States would exercise a benign tutelage. In the words of William Seward, secretary of state after the Civil War, the American empire would 'expand not by force of arms but by attraction'.

The belief that US imperialism is qualitatively different from everybody else's goes right back to the Monroe Declaration and beyond, to the yearning for empire that contributed to the revolutionary fervour of America's Founding Fathers. America gained its liberty by force and Americans instinctively understand the yearning of other people for 'national liberation'. What they so often cannot understand is that for other nations liberty includes the right not to live as Americans live. Time after time the US has helped people struggle against oppression, only to find that those they have helped refuse to live by the rules America wants them to follow. That these guerrillas turn against the very forces that helped create them was astonishing to US strategists in Afghanistan as it had been to their predecessors in the Philippines a century earlier. Prestowitz comments that Americans 'are simply not good imperialists' because they are too eager to be liked.

From a historical perspective, what is odd is that Prestowitz sees today's American imperialism as new. He himself was a member of the Reagan administration that invaded Grenada. The US has always sought to impose its will on the world by military means if other means are unsuccessful; why this imperialism appears to be 'neo' is because for most of the twentieth century military force has not been necessary; corporate power has been sufficient. In the period between the end of the Spanish-American War and the end of the cold war it was easy to believe that American imperialism had died. It is with hindsight that the continuities between the classic imperialism of the eighteenth and nineteenth centuries and the 'new' imperialism of the twenty-first century can be seen. But hindsight requires accurate history, and that in turn requires the distortions of ideology to be stripped away.

It is a commonplace that communist ideologists saw only what they wanted to see, distorting reality to fit their preconceptions. What is less commonly accepted is that to some extent everyone does so. Even as informed an observer of Russian history as Robert Daniels could write: 'There is no American comparison with the way the Soviets enforce conformity to the official ideology, deny any discrepancy between theory and reality, and claim that the current interpretation of theory is the version that has always been valid.' And yet American leaders have repeatedly claimed that their vision of democracy has descended unchanged from the men who fought for independence from Britain, men who in fact were fighting to be allowed to continue to own slaves, to conquer the territory of their neighbours and to protect themselves against corporate power. The ideology of democracy in America has changed almost beyond recognition, and at each step those with alternative interpretations have been sidelined or even persecuted.

The Lessons of History

History is written from the moment it starts. Participants put an immediate spin on events and motives. Contemporary observers have their own agendas and each generation adds its own gloss. Historical balance tips one way or another as preoccupations change. Democracy is a fundamental part of the American ideology, so its history is taught in every school. On the other hand terrorising natives is no longer part of American life and memories of it have long disappeared. It is unsurprising, therefore, that American history texts devote much more attention to the town hall meetings in New England than to the Mystic Massacre. History may be consciously falsified, but more commonly unacceptable memories simply fade away.

Not only are ideologically unacceptable realities written out of history, but ideologically acceptable myths are written in. Kevin Phillips points out how the Confederate version of the civil war has become the accepted wisdom in large parts of the United States; for example, Kentucky is now regarded as a southern state and contains seventy-two Confederate monuments and just two Union monuments, but in reality Kentucky was overwhelmingly pro-northern: 90,000 men from the state fought to abolish slavery, against 35,000 fighting to defend it.

The impact of ideology on perceptions of history is illustrated by the impact of religion. Modern religious fundamentalists worry that society is becoming increasingly irreligious. American fundamentalists strive to return their nation to its original beliefs, to a time when all men were God-fearing and the only law was the Bible. While it is true that the original settlers in Massachusetts and Connecticut were often what today would be called fundamentalist, this was not true of most early colonists, whether in the south or in places like Maine, Rhode Island and New York. Religious observance has actually increased: 17 per cent of Americans stated some religious adherence in 1776, rising to 34 per cent in 1850, 45 per cent in 1890, 56 per cent in 1926, 62 per cent in 1980 and 63 per cent in 2000. Each morning American schoolchildren repeat a 'pledge of allegiance', which includes a commitment to 'one nation under God'. This sounds like a phrase redolent of history, but in fact the words 'under God' were only added in 1954. One modern poll found that three out of five Americans believe in the literal truth of the story of Noah's Ark; by contrast, seven of the nine Founding Fathers had doubts about the divinity of Jesus.

Professional historians seek to strip away the accretions of ages but add their own preconceptions and bias. They face an often overwhelming need to demonstrate that their efforts are 'relevant', that history has lessons to teach. Attempts are made to interpret history to justify contemporary actions or political programmes. Russian history provides numerous examples. In the mid-nineteenth century there were fierce arguments about the origins of peasant communes. Westernisers argued that Russian peasants like everyone else were inherently individualists, and that communes were a tsarist imposition to make tax collection easier. The nationalistic Slavophiles argued that the communes had always existed and that communal living demonstrated the superiority of Russian culture over the atomised culture of the west. Purportedly the debate was about historical fact, but the arguments were based on political prejudice rather than historical research.

There is an inevitable temptation for historians to use their expertise to smooth the road of progress. The most explicit western proponent of the view that history and historians exist to serve the purpose of the state was John Robert Seeley, the British historian whose religious views provoked the ire of Konstantin Pobedonostsev, Russian ideologue of autocracy. Seeley claimed that history should be seen as a science whose function was to solve political problems. In his case the solution that history produced to many of the world's problems was British imperialism. (Nowadays Seeley is remembered, if he is remembered at all, neither for his views on religion nor his views on the role of historians but for a single remark: that Britain had acquired its empire 'in a fit of absence of mind', a comment sometimes applied, wholly inappropriately, to the United States.)

The historian Richard Pipes did much to change the west's perception of tsarism (and in the process incurred the wrath of Alexander Solzhenitsyn, who angrily disputed the parallels Pipes drew between tsarism and Stalinism). In later life Pipes agreed to head a commission for President Reagan that investigated the Soviet Union's supposed ultra-secret and ultra-effective missile programme. The commission found no evidence for such a programme for the simple reason that it did not exist (as the Soviet specialists at the CIA told Pipes at the time, and as was to be proved definitively when the Soviet empire finally collapsed and its research secrets were revealed). Nevertheless Pipes, using his claimed expertise in understanding the Russian mind, developed the novel theory that as the Soviets wanted such a programme to exist it must indeed exist or be close to existing. On this basis Reagan commissioned the enormously expensive Star Wars programme to meet this non-existent threat. (The parallels with the imaginary weapons of mass destruction used to justify the invasion of Iraq are obvious.)

The real role of historians is not to explain the present or predict the future but delve below what people imagine happened in the past, to push away the prisms of transient ideologies and identify historical patterns with all their continuities and discontinuities. In doing so it is tempting to focus on the apparent discontinuities – the great, epic transformations like the American and Russian revolutions. But in reality the great paradigm shifts of history are rare, and many that seem to be such at the time prove with hindsight to have had remarkably little impact. In the 1920s and '30s many historians believed that the Bolshevik revolution had been one of the most momentous events in human history; it seems much less important now.

In Russia continuities in history are taken for granted; for centuries dynasties have passed political power from one generation to another, and the values of one era flow seamlessly into the next. In the United States the situation is different: as presidential power peacefully transfers every four or eight years, the reign of each new president looks like a new beginning. Whereas the last tsars fought a losing battle to preserve untouched the whole panoply of values inherited from their ancestors, modern American presidents can pick and choose the 'traditional values' they wish to claim as their own. The values that underlay the ethnic cleansing and slavery of the early colonies have disappeared, and new corporatist values that would have confounded the Founding Fathers have taken their place.

Despite a few examples like Adams I and II and Bush I and II (one of the Bushes stood as presidential or vice-presidential candidate in six of the seven elections between 1980 and 2004), family dynasties are not a fundamental part of American political life. Some powerful patrician families have provided an element of continuity within the political establishment, and this dynastic element has been particularly noticeable in the evolution of American foreign policy, but dynasties in America are incidental to the system of government, not inherent. The long-established political and business establishments of New England and New York have guided the nation's gradual transition from the crude imperialism of the early colonies to the corporate imperialism of today, but they do not form an inherited ruling class. Russian autocracy under the tsars was not only a dictatorship but a family dictatorship, and this bound the nation together. There is no real equivalence in America where the continuities are far less evident.

In Russia the continuities persisted even after the Romanov dynasty disappeared. Since before the Mongols Russian society has been controlled by a few powerful men who have put their own interests ahead of everyone else. They may have proclaimed different ideologies but the 'Great' tsars – Ivan, Peter, Catherine – would have recognised the soul of Stalin's Russia. And above all they would have recognised his imperial ambitions. In terms of both political ambition and personal character Stalin had compelling parallels with the likes of Ivan the Terrible or even Peter the Great. The political pygmies who followed Stalin, and under whom the communist dynasty decayed away, have their own parallels in a stream of forgotten tsars. Perhaps Russia is now undergoing a paradigm shift, but recent military adventures in the Caucasus would suggest that the yearning for empire continues undimmed.

In the case of America the continuities are also clear but largely ignored. The values that led Englishmen, and a few women, to risk their lives crossing the Atlantic in order to impose their dreams on a hostile new world are the values that led their successors on to the Pacific and led corporate America on to conquer much of the globe. Ideological certainty, technological superiority and sheer scale as much as military might have carried the Stars and Stripes to the four corners of the world.

But some things do change. The election of Barack Obama demonstrates that the soul of twenty-first-century America is radically different from the soul of the nation that stumbled into civil war in the nineteenth century. The election of a black man as president of the United States would have been unthinkable even to those struggling against segregation a generation ago. Obama has seen the reality of American imperialism first hand (in his memoirs he describes the crushing impact on his stepfather of the CIA-sponsored coup in Indonesia), but even for Obama overcoming racism may prove to be easier than abandoning imperialism. Obama is often likened to John F. Kennedy, who raised similar expectations when he hurdled a lower barrier to become the first Catholic president – but went on to authorise the failed invasion of Cuba and plunge into war in Vietnam. When President Medvedev asserted that Russia had the right to intervene in Georgia because in the nations on its borders Russia had a 'privileged interest', Obama, like most westerners, reacted angrily. And yet the Russian president was just applying to the Russian empire his own equivalent to the Monroe Doctrine, a doctrine Obama himself implicitly endorsed with his campaign attacks on the governments of Cuba and Venezuela. Obama's support for the expansion of Nato and stationing US missiles in Poland suggests that the vision of two competing empires is still as potent in Washington as in Moscow.

So what of the future? Unsurprisingly historians are divided. Former neo-conservative Francis Fukuyama has discovered that history has not ended, and in 2008 supported Barack Obama as the candidate most able to manage America's decline, only to be attacked by Robert Kagan, adviser to John McCain, who seems to have moved his analysis of American history from determined opportunism to determined optimism. The US, Kagan insists, is not in decline, not even relative decline; but as Paul Kennedy demonstrated in his magisterial 1987 study of European imperialism, all empires eventually suffer from 'imperial overstretch'. Kennedy claimed this was starting to happen to the United States. Kevin Phillips also looked at the Spanish, Dutch and British empires and noted one common characteristic: as they approached their end their richest and brightest citizens stopped exploring and conquering, trading and manufacturing, inventing and creating; instead they devoted themselves to something new: finance. They provided the investment and credit needed to ensure that the rest of the world would grow their food and produce their manufactured goods; they lived on interest, dividends and capital appreciation. In all three cases the financiers and bankers came up with ever more elaborate forms of financial wizardry – some that today would be recognised as options and derivatives – until eventually the whole imperial edifice imploded. The imperial centre could not live beyond its means for ever. When wealth could no longer be sucked in from abroad the empires collapsed. Phillips was writing in 2006; the financial crisis starting in 2008 may yet presage that a similar fate awaits the American empire.

America is a land of principles and privilege but, as President Eisenhower said, 'A people that values its privileges above its principles soon loses both.' When the nascent economic superpowers of Asia assert themselves will the world remain as deeply embedded in American culture, values and fads as it is now? What will happen when the rest of the world stops paying for America's consumption? Will China, flexing once again its imperial muscles, usurp America's pre-eminent position? Will America pollute itself and the world into oblivion? When will the road from Roanoke reach its final destination? As with Rurik's road, in the timescales of history it is far too soon to say.

BIBLIOGRAPHY

Suggestions for further reading and comments on some of the sources used are available on the website www.empiresapart.com.

Ambrose, Stephen E. and Brinkley, Douglas G., *Rise to Globalism, American Foreign Policy since 1938* (Penguin, 1997)

Andrew, Christopher and Mitrokhin, Vasili, *The Mitrokhin Archive II: The KGB and The World* (Allen Lane, 2005)

Applebaum, Anne, *Gulag, A History of the Soviet Camps* (Allen Lane, 2003)

Aslund, Anders, *Russia's Capitalist Revolution* (Peterson Institute for International Economics, 2007)

Augar, Philip, *The Death of Gentlemanly Capitalism* (Penguin, 2000)

Bacevich, Andrew, *The New American Militarism: How Americans Are Seduced by War* (Oxford University Press, 2005)

Bagchi, Amiya Kumar, 'The Other Side of Foreign Investment by Imperial Powers', *Economic & Political Weekly* (8 June 2002)

Bain, David Haward, *Empire Express. Building the First Transcontinental Railroad* (Penguin, 2000)

Bakan, Joel, *The Corporation: The Pathological Pursuit of Profit and Power* (Viking Canada, 2004)

Blum, William, *Killing Hope: US Military and CIA Interventions since the Second World War* (Common Courage Press, 2003)

Bosch, Juan, *Pentagonism: A Substitute for Imperialism* (Grove Press, 1969)

Brogan, Hugh, *Longman History of the United States of America* (Longman, 1985) (later editions renamed *Penguin History of the United States of America*)

Brown, Dee, *Bury My Heart at Wounded Knee: An Indian History of the American West* (Holt, Rinehart & Winston, 1970)

Burman, Stephen, *The State of the American Empire: How the USA Shapes the World* (Earthscan, 2007)

Carnegie, Andrew, 'Americanism versus Imperialism', *North American Review* (January 1899)

Cave, Alfred A., *The Pequot War* (The University of Massachusetts Press, 1996)

Chang, Ha-Joon, 'Foreign Investment Regulation in Historical Perspective – Lessons for the Proposed WTO Agreement on Investment' (Faculty of Economics and Politics, Cambridge University, March 2003)

Chang, Ha-Joon, *Kicking Away the Ladder – Development Strategy in Historical Perspective* (Anthem Press, 2002)
Chomsky, Noam and Herman, Edward S., *The Washington Connection and Third World Fascism* (Spokesman, 1979)
Chomsky, Noam, *Failed States* (Hamish Hamilton, 2006)
Chomsky, Noam, *Imperial Ambitions* (Hamish Hamilton, 2005)
Conquest, Robert, *Stalin: Breaker of Nations* (Penguin, 1991)
Conrad, Alfred and Meyer, John, 'The Economics of Slavery in the Ante-Bellum South,' *Journal of Political Economy* 66:1, pp. 95–130 (1958)
Corak, Miles (Statistics Canada), quoted in *New York Times* 'Class Matters' by Janny Scott and David Leonhardt (15 May 2005)
Daniels, R.V. (introduction by Edwin O. Reischauer), *Russia: The Roots of Confrontation* (Harvard University Press, 1985)
Elliott, Larry (quoting Dani Rodrik), 'Two countries, one booming, one struggling: which one followed the free-trade route?' *Guardian* (12 December 2005)
Ferguson, Niall, *Colossus. The Rise and Fall of the American Empire* (Allen Lane, 2004)
Ferguson, Niall, *Empire. How Britain Made the Modern World* (Allen Lane, 2003)
Ferguson, Niall, *The War of the World* (Allen Lane, 2006)
Figes, Orlando, *A People's Tragedy* (Jonathan Cape,1996),
Figes, Orlando, *Natasha's Dance* (Allen Lane, 2002)
Figes, Orlando, *The Whisperers* (Allen Lane, 2007)
Fordham, Benjamin O., 'Economic Interests, Party, and Ideology in Early Cold War Era US Foreign Policy', *International Organization*, vol. 52 (spring 1998)
Fukuyama, Francis, *The End of History and the Last Man* (Free Press, 1992)
Gaddis, John Lewis, *Cold War* (Allen Lane, 2006)
Galbraith, John Kenneth, *The New Industrial State* (updated edition, Princeton University Press, 2007)
Gosselin, Daniel P., 'Jus ad Bellum and the 1983 Grenada Invasion: the Limits of International Law' (Canadian Department of National Defence, 1998)
Gunns, Albert F., *Civil Liberties and Crisis: The Status of Civil Liberties in the Pacific Northwest, 1917–1940* (PhD dissertation, University of Washington, 1971), which quotes the 1927 annual report of the Washington Unit of the American Civil Liberties Union
Herbert, William, *Attila King of the Huns* (Henry Bohn, 1838)
Hutton, Will, *The World We're In* (Little, Brown, 2002)
Hutton, Will, *The Writing On The Wall* (Little, Brown, 2007)
Jacobs, Lawrence R. and Morone, James A., 'Health and Wealth', *The American Prospect* (June 2004)
Kagan, Robert, *Dangerous Nation: America and the World 1600–1898* (Atlantic Books, 2006)
Kagan, Robert, *The Return of History and the End of Dreams*, (Knopf, 2008)
Kalff, Donald, *An UnAmerican Business – the rise of the new European enterprise model* (Kogan Page, 2005)
Kay, John interviewed in *strategy + business*, Issue 32 (Booz Allen Hamilton, Fall 2003)
Kennedy, Paul *The Rise and Fall of the Great Powers* (Crown Publishing, 1987)
Kinzer, Stephen, *Overthrow: America's Century of Regime Change from Hawaii to Iraq* (Times Books, 2006)

Klare, Michael, *Blood and Oil* (Penguin, 2005)

Koblitz, Ann Hibner, *A Convergence of Lives: Sofia Kovalevskaia, Scientist, Writer, Revolutionary* (Rutgers University Press, 1993)

Le Blanc, Paul, *A Short History of the US Working Class* (Humanity Books, 1999)

Lenin, V.I., *Imperialism: The Highest Stage of Capitalism* (Pluto Press, 1996)

Lowe, Norman, *Mastering Twentieth Century Russian History* (Palgrave Macmillan, 2002)

Mackenzie, F.A., *American Invaders* (1902); full text available on http://www.archive.org/stream/americaninvaders00mackrich/americaninvaders00mackrich_djvu.txt

Maier, Charles, *Among Empires: American Ascendancy and Its Predecessors* (Harvard University Press, 2006)

Mazower, Mark, *Dark Continent* (Penguin, 1998)

McCoy, Alfred, *A Question of Torture: CIA Interrogations from the Cold War to the War on Terror* (Metropolitan Books, 2006)

Micklethwait, John and Wooldridge, Adrian, *The Company: a Short History of a Revolutionary Idea* (Modern Library, 2003)

Monbiot, George, *Captive State* (Macmillan, 2000)

Montefiore, Simon Sebag, *Stalin – The Court of the Red Tsar* (Weidenfeld & Nicolson, 2003)

Montefiore, Simon Sebag, *Young Stalin* (Weidenfeld & Nicolson, 2007)

Morison, Samuel Eliot, *The Oxford History of the American People* (Oxford University Press, 1965)

Nace, Ted, *Gangs of America* (Berrett-Koehler, 2003)

Neville, Peter, *Russia* (Windrush Press, 2003)

Newsinger, John, 'The CIA: A history of torture', *Lobster*, vol. 54 (2007)

Nye, Joseph, *The Paradox of American Power: Why the World's Only Superpower Can't Go It Alone* (Oxford University Press, 2003)

Obama, Barack *Dreams From My Father* (Crown Publishing, 1995)

Odom, William, *America's Inadvertent Empire* (Yale University Press, 2005)

Owen, Thomas C., *Russian Corporate Capitalism from Peter the Great to Perestroika* (Oxford University Press, 1995)

Phillips, Kevin, *American Theocracy* (Penguin, 2006)

Pipes, Richard, *Russia under the Old Regime* (Penguin, 1995)

Porter, Bernard, *Empire and Superempire* (Yale University Press, 2006)

Prestowitz, Clyde, *Rogue Nation: American Unilateralism and the Failure of Good Intentions* (Basic Books, 2003)

Pringle, Heather, *In search of ancient North America* (John Wiley & Sons, 1996)

Rayfield, Donald, *Stalin and His Hangmen* (Viking, 2004)

Reid, Anna, *The Shaman's Coat* (Weidenfeld & Nicholson, 2002)

Rieber, Alfred J., *Merchants and Entrepreneurs in Imperial Russia* (University of North Carolina Press, 1982)

Rifkin, Jeremy, *The European Dream – how Europe's vision of the future is quietly eclipsing the American dream* (Polity Press, 2004)

Roberts, J.M., *The Penguin History of the World* (Penguin, 1995)

Rosenbaum, R.A., *The Penguin Encyclopedia of American History* (Penguin, 2003)

Sampson, Anthony, *The Seven Sisters* (Coronet Books, 1975)

Sands, Philippe, *Lawless World – America and the Making and Breaking of Global Rules* (Allen Lane, 2005)

Sands, Philippe, *Torture Team: Deception, Cruelty and the Compromise of Law* (Allen Lane, 2008)

Schama, Simon, *The American Future: A History* (Bodley Head, 2008)
Seeley, John Robert, *The Expansion of England. Two Courses of Lectures* (Macmillan, 1883)
Service, Robert, *Comrades! A History of World Communism* (Harvard University Press, 2007)
Seton-Watson, Hugh, *The Russian Empire, 1801–1917* (Oxford University Press, 1967)
Shane, Scott, 'U.S. Reclassifies Many Documents in Secret Review', *New York Times* (21 February 2006)
Skidelsky, Robert, *John Maynard Keynes, Volume Three: Fighting for Freedom, 1937–1946* (Penguin, 2000)
Smith, Page, *America Enters the World* (Penguin Books, 1985)
Sobel, Robert, *The Age of Giant Corporations: a Microeconomic History of American Business* (Greenwood Press, 1984)
Stiglitz, Joseph E., *Globalization and Its Discontents* (Penguin, 2002)
Sturmer, Michael, *Putin and the Rise of Russia: The Country That Came in From the Cold* (Weidenfeld, 2008)
Taylor, Alan, *American Colonies* (Penguin, 2001)
Tremblay, Rodrigue, *The New American Empire* (Infinity Publishing, 2004)
Trenin, Dmitri, *Getting Russia Right* (Carnegie Endowment for International Peace, 2007)
Trotsky, Leon, 'If America Should Go Communist', *Liberty* (23 March 1935)
Trotsky, Leon (tr. B. Pearce), *How the Revolution Armed: Military Writings and Speeches of Leon Trotsky: 1920 vol. 3* (New Park Publications, 1981)
Wachman, Richard, 'Underachieved? Have a performance-related bonus!' *Observer* (23 April 2006)
Ward, Greg, *The Rough Guide History of the USA* (Rough Guides, 2003)
Warner, Jeremy, 'Lehman is a gravy train for lawyers', *Independent* (1 November 2008)
Weaver, Courtney, 'Kremlin is wary of Curbing Smoking', *New York Times* (28 September 2008)
Weiner, Tim, *Legacy of Ashes* (Doubleday, 2007)
Wheatcroft, Stephen G., editor, *Challenging Traditional Views Of Russian History* (Palgrave Macmillan, 2002)
Williams, Stephanie, *Olga's Story* (Viking, 2005)
Young, David et al, *Corporate Headquarters – An international analysis of their roles and staffing* (*Financial Times*/Prentice Hall, 2000)

INDEX